The Fair and Equitable Treatment Standard

The Fair and Equitable Treatment Standard

A Guide to NAFTA Case Law on Article 1105

Patrick Dumberry

Wolters Kluwer
Law & Business

Published by:
Kluwer Law International
PO Box 316
2400 AH Alphen aan den Rijn
The Netherlands
Website: www.kluwerlaw.com

Sold and distributed in North, Central and South America by:
Aspen Publishers, Inc.
7201 McKinney Circle
Frederick, MD 21704
United States of America
Email: customer.service@aspenpublishers.com

Sold and distributed in all other countries by:
Turpin Distribution Services Ltd
Stratton Business Park
Pegasus Drive, Biggleswade
Bedfordshire SG18 8TQ
United Kingdom
Email: kluwerlaw@turpin-distribution.com

Printed on acid-free paper.

ISBN 978-90-411-3288-8

FSC
MIX
FSC® C103993

À mes parents, à ma femme et à mes enfants

About the Author

Patrick Dumberry is an Associate Professor at the University of Ottawa (Civil Law Section), Canada. From 1998 to 2009, he practiced international law, international commercial arbitration and investor-State arbitration at law firms in Geneva (Lenz & Staehelin and Lalive), in Montreal (Ogilvy Renault, now Norton Rose Fulbright) as well as at Canada's Ministry of Foreign Affairs and International Trade (Trade Law Bureau). He completed his Ph.D. in international law at the Graduate Institute of International Studies in Geneva, Switzerland, in 2006. He also obtained a D.E.S. from the same institution in 2000 and an LL.B. from the Université de Montréal, Canada, in 1996. He is a member of the Quebec Bar. He is the author of more than thirty publications in the fields of international investment law and international law, including one book (*State Succession to International Responsibility*, Martinus Nijhoff, 2007) which received a Certificate of Merit ('High Technical Craftsmanship and Utility to Practicing Lawyers and Scholars') from the American Society of International Law in 2008.

Table of Contents

ix

Foreword

I first met Patrick in the most peculiar circumstances: the morning after the tragic events that took place on 11 September, 2001. We met in Geneva, Switzerland. I was chairing a three-member Panel of Commissioners appointed by the United Nations Compensation Commission (UNCC) to review claims filed by Kuwait against Iraq and Patrick was a young lawyer working with the Geneva-based law firm of Lalive which represented Iraq. A few years later, we worked together when he joined the law firm of Ogilvy Renault (now Norton Rose Fulbright). He assisted me in a number of investor-State arbitration disputes where I served as a member of ICSID or *ad hoc* Tribunals. I have since followed his career with great interest.

I was very flattered when Patrick asked me to write the foreword for his book.

This is a very important book for investment arbitration practitioners and academics. It is one of the very few books that have been published on the fair and equitable treatment ('FET') standard. The scope of the FET standard is one of the most controversial issues in modern international investment law. This book focuses on the FET standard in the specific context of NAFTA Article 1105. Its publication is very timely having regard to the number of NAFTA awards that have analyzed this provision in the last 20 years. Some of these awards have been contentious and have had a significant impact on the understanding and development of the concept of FET.

The first part of the book examines the framework of the FET standard protection under Article 1105. Patrick analyzes the origin and the development of the concepts of the 'minimum standard of treatment' and the FET standard as well as their interactions. He observes that the doctrinal debate as to whether the FET is an autonomous standard or linked to the minimum standard of treatment under international law simply does not arise in the context of NAFTA Article 1105. The provision contains an explicit reference to 'international law' which is not found in many BITs. Of course, the Free Trade Commission, in 2001, issued a binding interpretation regarding the proper meaning of the FET standard. Patrick also examines a number of other elements of State practice that further illustrate the specific parameters under which Article 1105 must be analyzed.

After his thorough analysis of NAFTA case law, Patrick concludes that these specific features of Article 1105 have had a direct consequence on the restrictive interpretation of this provision by NAFTA tribunals. These issues are addressed in the second part of the book. In my view, the chapter on the substantive content of the FET standard under Article 1105 is crucially important. Based on his thorough examination of case law, Patrick identifies those elements of protection which must be accorded to investors under Article 1105. I believe that counsel for parties to NAFTA proceedings as well as arbitrators will derive great benefit from Patrick's detailed analysis of the different concepts of legitimate expectations, transparency, arbitrary and discriminatory conduct, good faith, denial of justice and due process. He demonstrates very convincingly that only a limited number of these elements are in fact unequivocally part of the FET obligation under Article 1105. This result contrasts with the position taken by many tribunals that have interpreted FET clauses in BITs as encompassing notions such as legitimate expectations and transparency. Another specific feature highlighted by the author is the high threshold of severity and gravity that NAFTA tribunals have consistently required in order to conclude that the host State has breached any element of the FET standard under Article 1105. These findings confirm the truly unique nature of the FET standard under Article 1105.

This book is the most comprehensive study to date of NAFTA Article 1105. I have no doubt that it will become an invaluable treatise for practitioners and academics who research the nature, the scope and the content of the FET standard.

L. Yves Fortier CC, OQ, QC
Montréal
11 July 2013

Preface

Why write a book on NAFTA Article 1105? The idea emerged from my own experience as a lawyer. Before becoming professor at the University of Ottawa (Civil Law section) in 2009, I practiced law for about ten years in Geneva, Montreal and Ottawa, working primarily in the areas of international law and international arbitration. In 2008–2009, I worked for Canada's Ministry of Foreign Affairs and International Trade where I acted as counsel for Canada in NAFTA cases. At the Ministry's Trade Law Bureau, I was directly involved in the *Merrill & Ring* case and, more specifically, with the claimant's allegations of violation of the fair and equitable treatment standard (NAFTA Article 1105). In the context of these arbitration proceedings, I discovered the complexity of this standard of protection. Only a few years later would I finally have the opportunity (and the time ...) to put pen to paper and to write this book.

At the time, I felt that there was a need for the publication of a comprehensive book on Article 1105. Thus, since the entry into force of the NAFTA in 1994, several arbitral tribunals have rendered awards dealing with claims of breach of Article 1105. Some of these awards (*Pope & Talbot, Metalclad, Mondev, Loewen*, etc.) are amongst the most well-known decisions in investor-State arbitration. They have had a tremendous impact on the understanding and development of the concept of fair and equitable treatment. More generally, some of these awards, and the reaction by States that soon followed, have had a long-lasting influence on the evolution of international investment law. Yet, in spite of the fundamental importance of these awards, no comprehensive study had been undertaken to determine the meaning and the content of the fair and equitable treatment standard under NAFTA Article 1105. The objective of the present book is to fill this analytical gap.

It is true that in recent years, the fair and equitable treatment standard has been the object of a number of books.[1] The present book, however, differs from these monographs for at least two reasons.

---

1. Ioana Tudor, *The Fair and Equitable Treatment Standard in International Foreign Investment Law* (Oxford U. Press 2008); Gabriel Cavazos Villanueva, *The Fair and Equitable Treatment Standard: The Mexican Experience* (VDM Verlag 2008); Roland Kläger, *Fair and Equitable*

First, and contrary to the recently-published work on fair and equitable treatment, this book only examines the standard in the specific context of NAFTA Article 1105. No book (and very few articles) has focused solely on Article 1105. Books and articles on the standard typically analyze the concept more globally. They mainly canvass awards rendered by tribunals interpreting differently-worded fair and equitable treatment clauses contained within bilateral investment treaties for the promotion and protection of investments ('BITs'). While these publications also review NAFTA awards, they generally lack a systematical analysis of the origin, scope and content of the provision.

I believe that there are good reasons to undertake a distinct analysis of Article 1105 because this provision is in many ways different from typical fair and equitable treatment clauses contained within the majority of BITs. This book will examine the specific features of Article 1105 and the particular parameters under which it must be interpreted. I will also analyze how those specific features have influenced NAFTA tribunals' interpretation of that provision. The objective is to assess whether or not their analysis of the fair and equitable treatment standard differs from the awards rendered by other tribunals outside NAFTA.

The second reason why the present book is different from the ones recently published by scholars on the fair and equitable treatment is related to the scope of its theoretical analysis. It is not my intention to offer a grand all-encompassing and definitive theoretical thesis on what the fair and equitable treatment standard consists of. The purpose of this book is far more modest. The book focuses on how NAFTA tribunals, in light of the unique features of Article 1105, have defined the scope and content of the standard and applied it to disputes in practice. This contribution therefore truly aims to provide readers with a *practical guide* to NAFTA case law on Article 1105.

Treatment in International Investment Law, (Cambridge U. Press 2011); Alexandra Diehl, *The Core Standard of International Investment Protection: Fair and Equitable Treatment*, (Wolters Kluwer 2012); Martins Paparinskis, *The International Minimum Standard and Fair and Equitable Treatment*, (Oxford U. Press 2013); T. Weiler, *The Interpretation of International Investment Law: Equality, Discrimination and Minimum Standards of Treatment in Historical Context*, (Martinus Nijhoff, 2013); Andrea Schernbeck, *Der Fair and Equitable Treatment Standard in internationalen Investitionsschutzabkommen*, (Nomos 2012). *See also*: Abhijit P.G. Pandya, *Interpretations and Coherence of the Fair and Equitable Treatment Standard in Investment Treaty Arbitration* (Ph.D. thesis, London School of Economics and Political Science 2011).

Acknowledgements

This book is the result of more than three years of research. I would like to thank the Faculty of Law (Civil Law Section) of the University of Ottawa, my colleagues and members of the administrative staff (including Martine Saint-Louis and Lorraine DeVanthey) for their support throughout the years. Special thanks to Professor Céline Lévesque (as well as two anonymous readers) for having taken the time to review the general conclusion of this book and making comments and suggestions.

I am grateful to the University of Ottawa for having provided me with generous funding for the completion of this work through a variety of programs (Law Foundation of Ontario, Research Development Program, Work-Study Program, Undergraduate Research Opportunity Program). I am especially indebted to several bright and talented students from the University of Ottawa who have assisted me over the last three years with research and editing. Their assistance was invaluable to the completion of this book. I want to sincerely thank Christina Georgaklis, Isabel Valenta, Lila Amara, Ivana Nenadic, Jacob Stone, Kevin Mailloux, Francis Legault-Mayrand, Drew Tyler, Gabrielle Dumas-Aubin, Amélie B. Goudreau, Samantha McKenzie, Phil Chambers, Rébecca Longpré, Audrey-Anne Trudel, Noah Arshinoff and Vanessa Bensaid. All of them have done an amazing job.

Special thanks to Me L. Yves Fortier CC OQ QC for having written the foreword to this book. Me Fortier, who served as Canada's Ambassador and Permanent Representative to the United Nations in New York (1988–1992), is one of the world's leading arbitrators in the field of investor-State arbitration. I had the privilege of working with him in his capacity as an arbitrator in a number of cases during my time at the law firm of Ogilvy Renault (now Norton Rose Fulbright) in Montreal (2006–2007).

Many thanks to Eleanor Taylor of Kluwer Law International for her patience and support in the revision process for the publication of this book.

Most importantly, I would like to dedicate this book to my parents, my wife and my children. I would like to first express my gratitude to my parents for their unconditional support throughout my life. I also deeply wish to thank my wife, Ann-Julie, for her love and support in this adventure. Finally, I want to thank my children (Ophélie and Florent) for generously allowing me to work on the footnotes of this book during countless evenings and week-ends while we were watching (yet again!) *Dora the Explorer* and *Bob the Builder*! Your love and affection have given me the strength to write this book.

Patrick Dumberry
Montréal, Canada
July 2013

List of Abbreviations

A.d.V.	Archiv des Völkerrechts
ADF v. United States	*ADF Group Inc. v. United States*, ICSID No. ARB(AF)/00/1
AJIL	American Journal of International Law
Alberta L. Rev.	Alberta Law Review
Am.U.J.Int'l L.& Pol'y	American University Journal of International Law and Policy
Am. U. L. Rev.	American University Law Review
American Rev. Int'l Arb.	American Review of International Arbitration
Arb. Int'l	Arbitration International
Austrian Arb. Yb	Austrian Arbitration Yearbook
ASDI	Annuaire suisse de droit international
ASIL Proc.	American Society of International Law Proceedings
Azinian v. Mexico	*Robert Azinian, Kenneth Davitian, & Ellen Baca v. Mexico*, ICSID No. ARB (AF)/97/2
BITs	Bilateral investment treaties
British IICL	British Institute of International and Comparative Law
British YIL	British Yearbook of International Law
Bus. L. Int'l	Business Law International
CAD	Canadian dollar
Can. T.S.	Canada Treaty Series
Can. YIL	Canadian Yearbook of International Law
Canadian Cattlemen v. United States	*Canadian Cattlemen for Fair Trade v. United States*, UNCITRAL
Chemtura v. Canada	*Chemtura Corporation v. Canada*, UNCITRAL
Chicago JIL	Chicago Journal of International Law

xxi

Chinese JIL	Chinese Journal of International Law
Colum J. Transnat'l L.	Columbia Journal of Transnational Law
Cornell Int'l L.J.	Cornell International Law Journal
C.L.P.	Current Legal Problems
ECT	Energy Charter Treaty
Emory L.J.	Emory Law Journal
Emory Int'l L.Rev.	Emory International Law Review
EJIL	European Journal of International Law
ESIEL	European Society of International Economic Law
Feldman v. Mexico	*Marvin Roy Feldman Karpa v. Mexico*, ICSID No. ARB(AF)/99/1
FET	Fair and equitable treatment
Fordham Int'l LJ.	Fordham International Law Journal
FPS	Full Protection and Security
FTA	Free Trade Agreement
FTC	Free Trade Commission
FTC Note	Free Trade Commission Notes of Interpretation of 31 July 2001
Ga.J.Int'l. & Comp.L.	Georgia Journal of International and Comparative Law
Gami v. Mexico	*Gami Investments, Inc. v. Mexico*, UNCITRAL
G.A. Res.	General Assembly of the United Nations
Gaz.Pal.	Gazette du palais
Georgia L.R.	Georgia Law Review
Geo. Wash. Int'l L. Rev.	George Washington International Law Review
Glamis v. United States	*Glamis Gold, Ltd. v. United States*, UNCITRAL
Grand River v. United States	*Grand River Enterprises Six Nations, Ltd., et al. v. United States*, UNCITRAL
Harvard Int'l L.J.	Harvard International Law Journal
Harv.L.Rev.	Harvard Law Review
Hastings Int'l & Comp.L.Rev.	Hastings International and Comparative Law Review
Howard L.J.	Howard Law Journal
ICJ	International Court of Justice
ICJ Reports	International Court of Justice Reports of Judgments, Advisory Opinions and Orders
ICJ Statute	Statute of the International Court of Justice
ICLQ	International and Comparative Law Quarterly
ICSID	International Centre for Settlement of Investment Disputes

ICSID Rev.	ICSID Review – Foreign Investment Law Journal
ILA	International Law Association
ILC	International Law Commission
I.L.C. Articles on State Responsibility	Titles and Texts of the Draft Articles on Responsibility of States for Internationally Wrongful Acts Adopted by the Drafting Committee on Second Reading, 26 July 2001
I.L.C. Commentaries	Commentaries to the Draft Articles on Responsibility of States for Internationally Wrongful Acts Adopted by the International Law Commission at its Fifty-Third Session (2001), November 2001
ILM	International Legal Materials
IMS	International minimum standard
Indian JIL	Indian Journal of International Law
Int'l Law	International Lawyer
Int'l Bus. Law.	International Business Lawyer
Italian Y.I.L	Italian Yearbook of International Law
ITN	Investment Treaty News
JDI	Journal du droit international (Clunet)
JIDS	Journal of International Dispute Settlement
J. Int'l Arb.	Journal of International Arbitration
J.Int'l Econ.L.	Journal of International Economic Law
J.P.L.	Journal of Public Law
J. World Invest.	Journal of World Investment
J. World Invest. & Trade	Journal of World Investment & Trade
J. World Trade	Journal of World Trade
L. & Bus. Rev. Am.	Law and Business Review of the Americas
LPICT	Law and Practice of International Courts and Tribunals
Law & Pol'y Int'l Bus.	Law and Policy in International Business
Leiden JIL	Leiden Journal of International Law
Loewen v. United States	*Loewen Group, Inc. and Raymond L. Loewen v. United States*, ICSID No. ARB(AF)/98/3
LNTS	League of Nations Treaty Series
Max Planck Yrbk. UNL	Max Planck Yearbook of United Nations Law
McGill LJ	McGill Law Journal
Metalclad v. Mexico	*Metalclad Corporation v. Mexico*, ICSID No. ARB(AF)/97/1
Merrill & Ring v. Canada	*Merrill & Ring Forestry L.P. v. Canada*, UNCITRAL

Methanex v. United States	*Methanex Corporation v. United States*, UN-CITRAL
MFN	Most-Favored-Nation
Mobil v. Canada	*Mobil Investments Canada Inc. & Murphy Oil Corporation v. Canada*, ICSID Case No. ARB(AF)/07/4
Mondev v. United States	*Mondev International Ltd. v. United States*, ICSID No. ARB(AF)/99/2
Mich.J.Int'l L.	Michigan Journal of International Law
Mich. L. Rev.	Michigan Law Review
Minn.J.Global Trade	Minnesota Journal of Global Trade
MST	Minimum standard of treatment
NAFTA	North American Free Trade Agreement
Northwestern J. Int'l L.	Northwestern Journal of International Law
Nw. J. Int'l L. & Bus.	Northwestern Journal of International Law & Business
N.Y.Sch.J.Int'l. & Comp.L.	New York Law School Journal of International and Comparative Law
N.Y.U. J. Int'l L. & Pol.	New York University Journal of International Law & Politics
OECD	Organisation for Economic Co-operation and Development
P.C.I.J.	Permanent Court of International Justice
Penn State ILR	Penn State International Law Review
Pepp. L. Rev.	Pepperdine Law Review
RBDI	Revue belge de droit international
Rec des cours	Collected Courses of the Hague Academy of International Law
Rev. arb.	Revue de l'arbitrage
Rev Intern Dr Econ	Revue internationale de droit économique
RGDIP	Revue générale de droit international public
S. Tex. L Rev	South Texas Law Review
Suffolk Transnat'l L. Rev.	Suffolk Transnational Law Review
Sw. J.L. & Trade Am.	Southwestern Journal of Law and Trade in the Americas
Tex. Int'l L. J.	Texas International Law Journal
Thunderbird v. Mexico	*International Thunderbird Gaming Corporation v. Mexico*, UNCITRAL
Transnational Disp. Mgmt.	Transnational Dispute Management
Tul. L. Rev.	Tulane Law Review
U.N.	United Nations
UNCTAD	United Nations Conference on Trade and Development
UNTS	United Nations Treaty Series

UNRIAA	United Nations Reports of International Arbitral Awards
U. Miami Inter-Am. L. Rev.	University of Miami Inter-American Law Review
U. Pa. J. Int'l Econ. L.	University of Pennsylvania Journal of International Economic Law
UPS v. Canada	*United Parcel Service of America Inc. v. Canada*, UNCITRAL
US	United States
USD	United States Dollar
USTS	United States Treaty Series
Va.J.Int'l L	Virginia Journal of International Law
Vand. J. Transnat'l L.	Vanderbilt Journal of Transnational Law
Waste Management v. Mexico	*Waste Management, Inc. v. Mexico ('Number 2')*, ICSID No. ARB(AF)/00/3
Wm. & Mary L.Rev.	William & Mary Law Review
Yale J. Int'L L.	Yale Journal of International Law
Yearbook ILC	Yearbook of the International Law Commission
Yb Int'l Invest. L. & Pol.	Yearbook on International Investment of Law and Policy

Introduction

I   A PRIMER ON NAFTA CHAPTER 11

The North American Free Trade Agreement (hereinafter referred to as 'NAFTA', or the 'Agreement') was signed by Canada, Mexico and the United States on 17 December 1992 and came into force on 1 January 1994.[1] This multilateral treaty is based in part on the Free Trade Agreement ('FTA'), a bilateral treaty entered into by the United States and Canada in 1989.[2] NAFTA aims to eliminate most tariff and non-tariff barriers on the trade of goods and services between the three countries within a period of ten years. The Agreement is a complex legal framework consisting of twenty-two Chapters, several annexes, and two side agreements. Chapter 11 concerns investment. It is divided into three sections: Section A deals with the obligations of Canada, Mexico and the United States (hereinafter referred to as 'the Parties') with respect to treatment and protection of investments and investors, Section B concerns the mechanism to be used for the settlement of disputes, and finally, Section C defines the terms used in the Chapter.[3] This book analyzes one particular provision of NAFTA Chapter 11 that grants specific protections to foreign investors (and investments): Article 1105.

There is, of course, nothing specifically unique and revolutionary about the basic characteristics of investor-State arbitration proceedings existing under NAFTA Chapter 11.[4] On the one hand, the settlement of investment claims by arbitration has existed for years in the context of bilateral investment treaties ('BITs') as well as mixed claims commissions. On the other hand, the fact that NAFTA Chapter 11 allows investors to submit claims against States directly before an international arbitral

---

1. 32 ILM, 605 (1993).
2. The Free Trade Agreement was signed on 2 January 1988: 27 ILM, 281 (1988).
3. On the framework, *see*, P. Dumberry, *The NAFTA Investment Dispute Settlement Mechanism: A Review of the Latest Case Law*, 2(1) J. World Invest. 151-195 (2001).
4. Jack J. Coe, Jr., *Taking Stock of NAFTA Chapter 11 in Its Tenth Year: An Interim Sketch of Selected Themes, Issues and Methods*, 36 Vand. J. Transnat'l L. 1414 ff (2003).

1

tribunal is also not a novelty.[5] NAFTA Chapter 11 is nonetheless truly ground-breaking in three different respects.[6]

First, NAFTA is the first *multilateral* treaty to provide individuals and corporations direct access to a dispute settlement mechanism before a tribunal of an international nature.[7] Until NAFTA, foreign investors' access to arbitral tribunals was granted by BITs (as well as State contracts and some State's legislation). Since the coming into force of NAFTA, a number of multilateral investment treaties containing similar provisions have been adopted.

Second, NAFTA Chapter 11 is also a milestone since it is the first investment agreement between two developed countries: Canada and the United States.[8] Chapter 11 also marks the first time two OECD members agreed in an investment treaty on investor-State arbitration *between them*. Traditionally, BITs were concluded between a developed State and a developing State.[9] As explained by one writer, 'a BIT between a developed and a developing country is founded on a grand bargain: a *promise* of protection of capital in return for the *prospect* of more capital in the future'.[10] Although North-South BITs are in principle reciprocal, it is rare in practice that the developed State will ever face a claim by an investor of the developing State. In this context, it has been rightly argued that there is an asymmetry in BITs entered into between developing and developed States.[11] However, in the context of NAFTA, the treaty was not asymmetrical for both Canada and the United States. Thus, in 1994, Canada and the United States were each other's largest source of exports. Therefore, allowing direct arbitration claims by investors of the other Party necessarily led to an increased risk of litigation under Chapter 11 for *both States*.[12]

---

5. B. Legum, *The Innovation of Investor-State Arbitration Under NAFTA*, 43 Harvard Int'l L.J. 535 (2002).
6. *See*, P. Dumberry, *L'entreprise, sujet de droit international? Retour sur la question à la lumière des développements récents du droit international des investissements*, 108(1) RGDIP 103-122 (2004); Legum, *supra* n. 5, at 538.
7. A. Lemaire, *Le nouveau visage de l'arbitrage entre État et investisseur étranger: Le chapitre 11 de l'ALENA*, Rev. arb. 61-64 (2001).
8. R.J. Zedalis, *Claims by Individuals in International Economic Law: NAFTA Developments*, 7(2) American Rev. Int'l Arb. 266 (1996); Legum, *supra* n. 5, at 537-539; Guillermo Aguilar Alvarez & William W. Park, *The New Face of Investment Arbitration: NAFTA Chapter 11*, 28 Yale J. Int'L L. 365, 370 (2003).
9. It should be noted, however, that developing States are increasingly concluding treaties with each other. For instance, of the 44 new BITs signed in 2007, 13 were between developing countries. According to UNCTAD, *Recent Developments in International Investment Agreements* 3 (2007–June 2008) (IIA Monitor No. 2 2008), these 'South-South' BITs now represent 26% of the total number of BITs. The figure of almost 700 'South-South' BITs is impressive considering that only 47 such treaties existed in 1990.
10. J.W. Salacuse, *The Treatification of International Investment Law: a Victory of Form Over Life? A Crossroads Crossed?*' 3(3) Transnational Disp. Mgmt. 7 (2006) (emphasis in the original). *See also*: J.W. Salacuse & N.P. Sullivan, *Do BITs Really Work? An Evaluation of Bilateral Investment Treaties and Their Grand Bargain*, 46 Harvard Int'l L.J. 67 (2005).
11. J.W. Salacuse, *Towards a Global Treaty On Foreign Investment: The Search for a Grand Bargain*, in *Arbitrating Foreign Investment Disputes. Procedural and Substantive Legal Aspects* 70 (N. Horn & S. Kröll eds., 2004). *See also*: Gus van Harten, *Investment Treaty Arbitration and Public Law* 41 (Oxford U. Press 2007).
12. Legum, *supra* n. 5, at 537.

Another related unique feature of NAFTA is that it involves not only two developed States but also Mexico, a *developing* State. This aspect had a direct impact on the ultimate decision to include a chapter providing for the resolution of investor-State disputes.[13] The US-Canada FTA did not include any provision on investor-State arbitration. Throughout the negotiation of NAFTA's terms, the United States insisted on including an arbitration mechanism for such disputes essentially because it feared that Mexican courts would not be neutral and impartial[14] in the event of expropriations of American investments in Mexico.[15] It was ultimately decided that investor-State arbitration would apply to disputes involving all Parties.[16]

Third, NAFTA Chapter 11 is also Mexico's first international agreement to be subject to investor-State arbitration.[17] The implication of this engagement is far reaching since Mexico repudiated its long standing application of the 'Calvo Clause' to foreign investors for the first time. Since 1994, Mexico has entered into numerous BITs which include provisions pertaining to the resolution of investor-State disputes.[18]

These groundbreaking aspects of NAFTA would soon become very controversial. At the end of the 1990s, NAFTA Chapter 11 had thus come under attack by different segments of civil society as a result of several claims that had been filed by investors, some of them challenging measures and regulations protecting public health, safety, and the environment.[19] One important concern raised by the *New York Times* in a 2001 article was the lack of transparency of investor-State arbitration:

> Their meetings are secret. Their members are generally unknown. The decisions they reach need not be fully disclosed. Yet the way a small number of international tribunals handles disputes between investors and foreign governments has led to national laws being revoked, justice systems questioned and environmental regulations challenged.[20]

Another reason for the commotion that ensued in some circles about such arbitration proceedings was the fact that for the very *first time,* they involved Canada and the United States as *respondent* States. Thus, as noted by two writers, 'when claims for

---

13. Aguilar Alvarez & Park, *supra* n. 8, at 395.
14. *Ibid.,* at 395; Charles H. Brower II, *Investor-State Disputes Under NAFTA: A Tale of Fear and Equilibrium,* 29 Pepp. L. Rev. 47 (2002).
15. Gabriel Cavazos Villanueva, *The Fair and Equitable Treatment Standard: The Mexican Experience* 47 (VDM Verlag 2008); Gabriel Cavazos Villanueva & Luis F. Martinez Serna, *Private Parties in the NAFTA Dispute Settlement Mechanism: The Mexican Experience,* 77 Tul. L. Rev. 1029 (2003).
16. Aguilar Alvarez & Park, *supra* n. 8, at 395 ('Understandably, this investor protection scheme was based upon equality of treatment among the three countries. For Mexico to accept arbitration of investment disputes within its borders, Canada and the United States had to respect a similar dispute resolution process. It would have been unwise and unworkable for Chapter 11 to be applied by American and Canadian courts when claims were brought against the United States and Canada, but to have arbitrators appointed for claims against Mexico').
17. Villanueva, *supra* n. 15, at 28-39, 48, 64.
18. These BITs are examined in: *Ibid.,* at 138 ff.
19. *See,* Aguilar Alvarez & Park, *supra* n. 8; Brower, *supra* n. 14, at 43; Charles H. Brower II, *Structure, Legitimacy, and NAFTA's Investment Chapter,* 36 Vand. J. Transnat'l L. 36-37 (2003).
20. Anthony DePalma, *Nafta's Powerful Little Secret: Obscure Tribunals Settle Disputes, but Go Too Far, Critics Say,* New York Times, 11 March 2001.

unfair treatment were filed *against* the US government, arbitration looked different than when American companies were the investors' and, consequently, 'praise for arbitration's neutrality began to have competition in the form of complaints about infringement of national sovereignty and democracy'.[21] Thus, 'what was meant to be a shield to protect US investors ha[d] turned into a sword against the US government'.[22]

The reaction did not differ in Canada where Chapter 11 has been widely criticized since the government paid Ethyl Corp., a US company, USD 19.3 million in compensation in an out of court settlement in July 1998 and lifted its ban on the company's product (fuel additive MMT). In 1999, the International Trade Minister of Canada asked its U.S and Mexican counterpart to review and clarify Chapter 11 provisions.[23] In fact, the backlash against the investor-State arbitration mechanism was so strong that in the context of the then on-going negotiation to create the Free Trade Area of the Americas ('FTAA'), the International Trade Minister of Canada publicly stated at the end of 2000 that he would not sign any agreement that would include provisions akin to those contained within NAFTA Chapter 11.[24] In those early days, several authors also feared that Chapter 11 would open the floodgates to investor claims raising concerns about the future ability of governments to pass and implement policies on vital national areas of concerns, such as environmental protection, public health and safety issues.[25]

While, in retrospect, this concern would prove to be exaggerated, it remains that NAFTA Chapter 11 is the most widely-used investor-State dispute mechanism amongst investment treaties. According to one recent survey conducted by a Canadian NGO,[26] as of October 2010, sixty-six publicly known claims had been filed by investors under Chapter 11 since 1994. Twenty-eight claims had been filed against Canada, nineteen against the U.S. and another nineteen against Mexico.[27] The breakdown of these claims can be summarized as follows:

- Tribunals have held that Canada has breached NAFTA in three instances (*Pope & Talbot, S.D. Myers,* and *Mobil*). To date, tribunals have ordered Canada to

---

21. Aguilar Alvarez & Park, *supra* n. 8, at 393-394 (emphasis in the original).
22. Gilbert Gagné & Jean-Frédéric Morin, *The Evolving American Policy on Investment Protection: Evidence from Recent FTAs and the 2004 Model BIT,* 9 J. Int'l Econ. L. 363 (2006). M. Sornarajah, *The Fair and Equitable Standard of Treatment: Whose Fairness? Whose Equity?,* in *Investment Treaty Law: Current Issues II* 170 (Federico Ortino et al. eds., British IICL 2007), puts it more bluntly: 'The United States, being the largest investment receiving state is at the wrong end of the law it had sought to establish against developing states into which it exported capital. Now that the Investment picture is changing, it seeks to change the law. (...) Now that the birds are coming home to roost and the fear is that the standards will be used against it, the United States, quite logically is backtracking from its earlier stances'.
23. This is discussed in: Z.M. Eastman, *NAFTA's Chapter 11: For Whose Benefit?,* 16(3) J. Int'l Arb. 114-117 (1999); J.A. Soloway, *NAFTA's Chapter 11: The Challenge of Private Party Participation,* 16(2) J. Int'l Arb. 10-14 (1999).
24. Canadian Press, *Canada Seeks Review of NAFTA's Chapter 11,* 13 December 2000. This is discussed in: Eastman, *supra* n. 23, at 114-117.
25. *See,* Soloway, *supra* n. 23, at 10-11; Eastman, *supra* n. 23, at 105-118.
26. Canadian Center for Policy Alternatives, NAFTA Chapter 11 Investor-States Disputes (2010). The document can be found at this page: http://www.policyalternatives.ca/publications/ reports/nafta-chapter-11-investor-state-disputes-1.
27. *Ibid.,* at 23.

pay damages totaling USD 4.3 million.[28] Canada has also settled two claims filed by investors and agreed to pay them a total of USD 150 million in damages.[29]

- Tribunals have dismissed investors' claims filed against the United States in seven cases (*Loewen, Mondev, Methanex, ADF, Glamis, Canadian Cattlemen, Grand River*).
- Tribunals have awarded damages to investors in five cases filed against Mexico (*Metalclad, Feldman, Corn Products, ADM, Cargill*). Mexico has been compelled to pay damages of over USD 187 million.[30]

II   ARTICLE 1105: THE MOST CONTROVERSIAL NAFTA PROVISION

This book focuses on Article 1105, which provides as follows:

Article 1105: Minimum Standard of Treatment
1. Each Party shall accord to investments of investors of another Party treatment in accordance with international law, including fair and equitable treatment and full protection and security.
2. Without prejudice to paragraph 1 and notwithstanding Article 1108(7)(b), each Party shall accord to investors of another Party, and to investments of investors of another Party, non discriminatory treatment with respect to measures it adopts or maintains relating to losses suffered by investments in its territory owing to armed conflict or civil strife.
3. Paragraph 2 does not apply to existing measures relating to subsidies or grants that would be inconsistent with Article 1102 but for Article 1108(7)(b).

The analysis undertaken in this book is limited to the first paragraph of this provision (hereinafter simply referred to as 'Article 1105', instead of 'Article 1105 (al. 1)').

---

28. *Pope & Talbot Inc. v. Canada*, UNCITRAL, Award in Respect of Damages, (31 May 2002) (USD 461,566 + interest); *S.D. Myers Inc. v. Canada*, UNCITRAL, Second Partial Award, (21 October 2002), (CAD 6,050,000 + interest, i.e. around USD 3.8 million in 2002). The tribunal in *Mobil Investments Canada Inc. and Murphy Oil Corporation v. Canada*, ICSID No. ARB(AF)/07/4, Decision on Liability and on Principles of Quantum, (22 May 2012) concluded that claimants were entitled to recover damages incurred as a result of Canada's breach of Article 1106 and requested them to submit evidence of such damages. At the time of writing this book (June 2013), no award on damages had been rendered by the tribunal.
29. *Ethyl Corporation v. Canada*, UNCITRAL (USD 19.3 million); *AbitibiBowater Inc., v. Canada*, UNCITRAL, (CAD 130 million, i.e. approximately the same amount in USD). The terms of a third settlement with the claimant Trammel Crow are undisclosed.
30. *Metalclad Corporation v. Mexico*, ICSID No. ARB(AF)/97/1, Award, (30 August 2000) (USD 16.7 million, it should be noted that after the set aside decision of the B.C. Supreme Court the case was settled when Mexico paid an undisclosed amount of compensation to the investor); *Marvin Roy Feldman Karpa v. Mexico*, ICSID No. ARB(AF)/99/1, Award, (16 December 2002) (USD 1.5 million); *Corn Products International, Inc. v. Mexico*, ICSID Case No. ARB (AF)/04/1, Award, (18 August 2009) (USD 58.38 million); *Archer Daniels Midland Company and Tate & Lyle Ingredients Americas, Inc. v. Mexico*, ICSID Case No. ARB (AF)/04/5, Award, (21 November 2007) (USD 33.5 million); *Cargill, Inc. v. Mexico*, ICSID no. ARB(AF)/05/02, Award, (18 September 2009) (USD 77.329 million).

In the last two decades, Article 1105 has undoubtedly become the most controversial and contested provision of NAFTA Chapter 11.[31] In the words of one writer, 'Article 1105 has become the alpha and omega of investor-state arbitration under Chapter 11 of NAFTA'.[32] In fact, it is the heated debate that took place in the early 2000s' concerning NAFTA awards dealing with the scope and content of the fair and equitable treatment ('FET') standard that awakened this concept 'from its semi-hibernation'.[33]

The FET debate started in 2000 when three tribunals rendered awards that defined different aspects of the scope of Article 1105. On 30 August 2000, the *Metalclad* tribunal found that Mexico had failed to ensure a transparent and predictable framework for the investor's investment which constituted a breach of Article 1105. The tribunal awarded the investor USD 16.7 million, with interest, in compensation for breaches of Articles 1105 and 1110.[34] Soon after, the *S.D. Myers* tribunal rendered its Partial Award on 13 November 2000 which awarded the investor CAD 6 million (with interest) in compensation for the breach of both Articles 1102 and 1105. In the award, two of the three tribunal members came to the conclusion that a finding of a breach of the national treatment provision (Article 1102) established a breach of Article 1105.[35] Finally, and most importantly, on 10 April 2001, the *Pope & Talbot* tribunal released its Award on the Merits of Phase 2 and held, *inter alia*, that Article 1105 requires the application of the FET standard *independently* (and in *addition*) to the minimum standard of treatment under international law.[36]

All three NAFTA Parties expressly rejected the interpretation favored by these tribunals. The reaction to the *Pope & Talbot* award was particularly strong. Under the aegis of the Free Trade Commission ('FTC'), NAFTA Parties responded to these three awards by issuing the 'Notes of Interpretation of Certain Chapter 11 Provisions' (hereinafter referred to as 'the Note') on 31 July 2001. The Note clarified, *inter alia*, that 'Article 1105(1) prescribes the customary international law minimum standard of treatment of aliens as the minimum standard of treatment to be afforded to investments of investors of another Party' and that the concept of FET does 'not require treatment in addition to or beyond that which is required by the customary international law minimum standard of treatment of aliens'. In other words, the Note interpreted the FET standard restrictively by limiting the level of protection to be accorded to foreign investors to the one existing under custom. The Note itself rapidly became the center of an important controversy amongst parties to NAFTA arbitration proceedings, arbitrators and scholars.

---

31. M. Kinnear, A. Bjorklund & J.F.G. Hannaford, *Investment Disputes under NAFTA: An Annotated Guide to NAFTA Chapter 11* (Kluwer Law International, 2006), section on Article 1105, at 16; J.C. Thomas, *Reflections on Article 1105 of NAFTA: History, State Practice and the Influence of Commentators*, 17(1) ICSID Rev. 22 (2002).
32. Charles H. Brower, *Fair and Equitable Treatment under NAFTA's Investment Chapter; Remarks*, 96 ASIL Proc. 9 (2002).
33. Roland Kläger, *Fair and Equitable Treatment in International Investment Law*, 62 (Cambridge U. Press 2011).
34. *Metalclad Corporation v. Mexico*, Award, (30 August 2000), paras. 70, 76.
35. *S.D. Myers Inc. v. Canada*, First Partial Award, (13 November 2000), para. 266.
36. *Pope & Talbot Inc. v. Canada*, Award on the Merits of Phase II (10 April 2001).

More generally, it has been suggested that the issuance of the Note 'aimed at shifting power back from arbitral tribunals to the contracting parties in order to regain control over the interpretation of the obligations under NAFTA'.[37] This fundamental change of outlook is also reflected by the fact that both Canada and the United States soon adopted new Model BITs (as well as a number of BITs and FTAs) which were significantly more detailed with respect to the scope of substantive and procedural protections than previous investment treaties. The restrictive language contained within this new wave of treaties regarding the scope of the FET standard was clearly meant to address some of the controversial findings made by NAFTA tribunals. The objective was to prevent future tribunals from developing their own idiosyncratic interpretations of the FET standard. To put it bluntly, NAFTA Parties were ensuring that the rendering of awards similar to *Pope & Talbot* would no longer be possible.

In fact, NAFTA States' reaction to these awards arguably marked a turning point in the recent history of investor-State arbitration. It represents a switch of the pendulum which had been in favor of liberalization of trade and the proliferation of BITs in the 1990s.[38] The 1990s were indeed characterized as a new era of globalization where private foreign investments were (almost) universally deemed by States as an essential tool for their economic development.[39] During this decade, capital-exporting and developing States concluded BITs at a high frequency. In the next decade, however, the pendulum swung in the other direction as States have tried to regain control of investor-State arbitration.[40]

This controversy surrounding the FET is, of course, not limited to the NAFTA context. The NAFTA discussion on Article 1105 has had a great impact on other tribunals' interpretations of BITs containing FET clauses.[41] Outside NAFTA, both claimant investors and host States have consistently referred to NAFTA awards and the FTC Note to support their respective arguments in arbitration proceedings. In fact, the question of the scope and content of the FET standard is now one of the most contentious issues in investor-State arbitration. The FET standard has also become the most commonly alleged form of BIT breach.[42] The principle reason for this situation is the inherent vagueness of the terms 'fair' and 'equitable'.[43] Thus, the 'undefined and

---

37. S. Schill, *The Multilateralization of International Investment Law*, 271 (Cambridge U. Press 2009), for whom the Note is 'an attempt by the contracting parties to rebalance rule making and rule application under NAFTA and to manifest the power of the States as rule makers'.
38. Kläger, *supra* n. 33, at 62.
39. Thus, the 1992 *World Bank Guidelines on the Treatment of Foreign Direct Investment* explained in its preamble that it 'recognizes' that 'a greater flow of foreign direct investment brings substantial benefits to bear on the world economy and on the economies of developing countries in particular'.
40. *See*, Aguilar Alvarez & Park, *supra* n. 8, at 365.
41. Kläger, *supra* n. 33, at 76.
42. R. Dolzer, *Fair and Equitable Treatment: A Key Standard in Investment Treaties*, 39 Int'l Law 87 (2005) ('In current litigation practice, hardly any lawsuit based on an international investment treaty is filed these days without invocation of the relevant treaty clause requiring fair and equitable treatment').
43. Kläger, *supra* n. 33, at 3: 'This vagueness is both a blessing and a curse for international investment law. While it ensures the adaptability and flexibility of the investment protection standards, it also entails a certain degree of indeterminacy and even vacuity. Fair and equitable treatment appears as the most vaguely formulated investment protection standard'.

potentially elastic nature [of the FET standard in BITs] has made it a favorite of aggrieved investors and their lawyers when seeking compensation for the allegedly injurious acts of host country governments'.[44]

Claimant investors have thus claimed damages for breach of the FET standard in almost all NAFTA cases (some fifty-nine cases out of the sixty-six on which information was available as of October 2010).[45] The phenomenon is not limited to NAFTA. Thus, by October 2010, investment tribunals had addressed the merits of FET claims in no less than eight-four treaty-based disputes, including eighteen NAFTA Chapter 11 claims.[46] The sudden importance of the FET as a cause of action in the years 2000 is certainly due in great part to the far-reaching interpretation given by a few earlier NAFTA awards.[47] A number of arbitral tribunals outside the context of NAFTA would soon also start to render decisions favorable to claimant investors where the FET standard was given an extended meaning.

This book analyzes the origin, nature, meaning and content of the FET standard under Article 1105.

III   STRUCTURE OF THE ANALYSIS

This book is divided into the following two general parts and five chapters:

Part I The Framework of Article 1105
    Chapter 1 The Emergence of the Concepts of the Minimum Standard of Treatment and the Fair and Equitable Treatment Standard
    Chapter 2 The Meaning of Article 1105

Part II The Content of Article 1105
    Chapter 3 The Substantive Content of Article 1105
    Chapter 4 The Relationship between Article 1105 and other NAFTA Provisions
    Chapter 5 Assessment of Damages

Part I of this book examines the framework of the FET standard protection under Article 1105. Chapter 1 analyzes the origin and development of the concept of the 'minimum standard of treatment'. The present author will also determine what the content of this standard consists of and whether or not it can be considered as a norm of customary international law. The next section of this first chapter will focus on the

---

44. Jeswald. W. Salacuse, *The Law of Investment Treaties* 218 (Oxford U. Press 2010).
45. Canadian Center for Policy Alternatives, *supra* n. 26.
46. UNCTAD, *Fair and Equitable Treatment*, 61 (UNCTAD Series on Issues in International Investment Agreements II, United Nations, 2012). The report explains that these numbers exclude cases dismissed on jurisdictional grounds and awards where the merits of the FET claim were not addressed due to a finding of expropriation.
47. Kläger, *supra* n. 33, at 3.

emergence of the FET standard, and most importantly, on the reasons for its development in treaty practice after the Second World War. We will also undertake an examination of the controversial question of the interaction between the minimum standard of treatment and the FET. Specifically, this section addresses the question of whether the FET is an autonomous standard or whether it is linked to the minimum standard of treatment under international law. It will highlight the fact that the FET standard under Article 1105 must be analyzed under very specific parameters that do not exist under most FET clauses contained in BITs. The specificity of Article 1105 is first and foremost the result of the language contained in the provision. Under NAFTA Article 1105, the Parties must accord a 'fair and equitable treatment' under 'international law' to foreign investors. This explicit reference to 'international law' contrasts with the vast majority of BITs which contain FET clauses that do not make any reference to 'international law'.

Chapter 2 focuses on the meaning of the FET clause. The present author will begin with an analysis of the treaty practices of Canada and the United States with regards to FET clauses before 1994 and then discuss the evolution of the preliminary negotiation texts of Article 1105. The next section will survey the different rules of international law on treaty interpretation and attempt to uncover whether they can serve as guidance to determine the real meaning of Article 1105. Our attention will focus on the 'ordinary meaning' of the terms used in the provision as well as to a number of important contextual elements such as 'subsequent practice' and a 'subsequent agreement' between the Parties on the interpretation to be given to this provision.

Most importantly, this Chapter thoroughly analyzes the FTC Note. The present author will scrutinize how NAFTA tribunals have interpreted the Note and discuss a number of controversial questions examined by them, including whether arbitral awards are an element of State practice, whether non-NAFTA awards examining unqualified FET clauses are relevant to Article 1105, and whether tribunals are allowed to look at other sources of law than custom to interpret Article 1105. This section also examines the reasoning of some of the awards that have challenged the letter and the spirit of the FTC Note. The objective is to steer readers through the conflicting NAFTA awards on the question of the evolutionary character of the minimum standard of treatment under custom. Finally, the present author will critically assess the position of a number of tribunals that have come to the controversial conclusion that the FET standard has become a rule of customary international law in and of itself.

Part II of this book focuses on the content of Article 1105. Chapter 3 offers a road map for the analysis of the substantive content of the FET standard under Article 1105. Based on an analysis of case law, the present author will identify which specific elements of protection must be accorded to investors under Article 1105. We will address the issue as to whether or not NAFTA tribunals have considered the concepts of legitimate expectations, transparency, arbitrary conduct, discriminatory conduct, good faith, denial of justice and due process as part of the FET protection that Parties must accord to foreign investors. For each of these specific elements, we will also evaluate the threshold of severity that NAFTA tribunals have required in order to conclude that the host State has breached Article 1105. For example, the survey undertaken will not be limited to determining whether or not the prohibition of arbitrary conduct is an element contained within the FET obligation under Article 1105. Rather, the present author will concretely explain the contours of this prohibition of arbitrariness. As such, which facets of arbitrariness have been considered as illegal by tribunals, what type of measures or regulations have been deemed contrary to Article 1105 and what are the circumstances that tribunals have taken into account when making their decision on such matters are all questions to which answers will be provided. From this perspective, the present book is truly a guide for both investors and States insofar as it contains lists of do's and don'ts with respect to each element of the FET standard.

Chapter 4 examines the interaction between Article 1105 and Articles 1102 (national treatment), 1103 (the Most-Favored-Nation treatment clause), and 1110 (expropriation), as well as the element of full protection and security. Finally, Chapter 5 examines how NAFTA tribunals have assessed damages for breach of the FET standard.

The Framework of Article 1105

Part I of the book first examines the emergence of the concepts of the minimum standard of treatment ('MST') and the fair and equitable treatment ('FET') standard (Chapter 1). The second Chapter analyzes the meaning of Article 1105.

CHAPTER 1

The Emergence of the Concepts of the Minimum Standard of Treatment and the Fair and Equitable Treatment

This book is about the FET standard under NAFTA Article 1105. The law on this area has been subject to heavy debate and substantial case law. The first element under discussion will be the origin and development of the concept of the 'minimum standard of treatment', which provides protection for investors under international law (section §1.01). The next section will focus primarily on the emergence of the FET standard after the Second World War, and most importantly, the reasons for its development in treaty practice (section §1.02). The last section will then undertake an examination of the controversial question of the interaction between the minimum standard of treatment and the FET standard (section §1.03).

§1.01 THE MINIMUM STANDARD OF TREATMENT

The historical aspects of the emergence of the minimum standard of treatment have already been the subjects of substantial scholarship on international law.[1] Moreover, a

---

1. *See*, for instance, Edwin Borchard, *The "Minimum Standard" of the Treatment of Aliens*, 33 ASIL Proc. 51 (1939); Edwin Borchard, *The Diplomatic Protection of Citizen Abroad* (Bank Law Publishing Co. 1915); Edwin Borchard, *The "Minimum Standard" of the Treatment of Aliens*, 38 Mich. L. Rev. 445 (1940); Elihu Root, *The Basis of Protection to Citizens Residing Abroad*, 4 AJIL 521 (1919); Clyde Eagleton, *The Responsibility of States in International Law,* 103 (New York U. Press 1928); Andreas Hans Roth, *The Minimum Standard of International Law Applied to Aliens* (A.W. Sijthoff 1949).

number of recent articles[2] and books[3] have also made a significant contribution to the better understanding of the concept of the minimum standard of treatment. The purpose of this section however, will be to offer a *tour d'horizon* of the concept rather than a detailed analysis of its complex ramifications.

[A]   The Origin of the Concept

The origin of the minimum standard of treatment stems from the international law doctrine of State responsibility for injuries to aliens. It is rooted in a due diligence obligation for States to respect the rights of foreigners within their country. Before the twentieth century, the prevailing view was that individuals conducting business in another State should be subject to the law of that State.[4] One reason for the emphasis on local law was that, in many circumstances, Western States simply felt that there was no need for any international rules protecting their nationals abroad. Such was the case in the context of investments made in imperial State colonies (in Africa and parts of Asia for instance).[5] There was also no need for any 'international law' protection in the different context of the 'extraterritoriality' system that was imposed by powerful European States upon independent (yet weaker) States in Asia (the most well-known example being that of the legations in Chinese cities).[6] Thus, under these 'unequal treaties'[7] of capitulation, foreigners were not subject to local laws and representatives of their States adjudicated their disputes under their own laws.[8]

Another reason for the prevalence of the host State's laws was the strong opposition from many States, especially in Latin America, to any other solution. At the time, the Argentinian scholar Carlos Calvo developed a theory whereby foreigners should receive a treatment that was not more favorable than that accorded to nationals

---

2. *See, inter alia:* M.A. Orellana, *International Law on Investment: The Minimum Standard of Treatment (MST)*, 3 Transnational Disp. Mgmt. 1-2 (2004); Todd Weiler, *An Historical Analysis of the Function of the Minimum Standard of Treatment in International Investment Law*, in: *New Directions in International Economic Law: In Memoriam Thomas Wälde* (Todd Weiler & Freya Baetens eds., Martinus Nijhoff 2011); Alireza Falsafi, *The International Minimum Standard of Treatment of Foreign Investors' Property: A Contingent Standard*, 30 Suffolk Transnat'l L. Rev. 317 (2006-2007); Hussein Haeri, *A Tale of Two Standards: 'Fair and Equitable Treatment' and the Minimum Standard in International Law*, 27 Arb. Int'l 31-32 (2011).
3. Martins Paparinskis, *The International Minimum Standard and Fair and Equitable Treatment*, 39-83 (Oxford U. Press 2013); T. Weiler, *The Interpretation of International Investment Law: Equality, Discrimination and Minimum Standards of Treatment in Historical Context*, (Martinus Nijhoff, 2013).
4. C. Schreuer & R. Dolzer, *Principles of International Investment Law*, 11-12 (Oxford U. Press 2008); Ionna Tudor, *The Fair and Equitable Treatment Standard in International Foreign Investment Law*, 60 (Oxford U. Press 2008). This period is examined in detail in: Weiler, *supra* n. 2, at 337 ff.
5. M. Sornarajah, *The International Law on Foreign Investment*, 19-20 (2nd ed., Cambridge U. Press 2004).
6. *Ibid.*
7. Dong Wang, *China's Unequal Treaties: Narrating National History* (Rowman & Littlefield 2008).
8. Weiler, *supra* n. 2, at 346.

of the host State.[9] The Calvo doctrine also required foreigners to give up their right to receive diplomatic protection from their home State and prohibited access to international arbitration for dispute resolution. This view was based on the fundamental international law principle of the sovereign equality of States.[10] Latin American States adopted this position to counter so-called 'gunboat diplomacy' and other interferences in their internal affairs by Western States.[11] Such interferences by Western States had often been made under the pretext of protecting the interests of their nationals abroad.[12] In this context, many States rejected the idea that there existed any obligation under international law to accord a minimum protection to foreigners.[13]

Despite a strong opposition by many States, the early twentieth century nevertheless saw the gradual emergence of a minimum standard of treatment.[14] The development of this new standard of treatment grew out of a concern of capital-exporting States that governments of the territories receiving the investments lacked the most basic measures of protection for aliens and their property.[15] At the time, the minimum standard focused almost exclusively on the non-discriminatory aspects of the treatment of aliens and the prevention of denial of justice.[16] These concerns were legitimate and warranted due to the numerous acts of expropriation without compensation that took place in Russia in the context of the Revolution of 1917 and in Mexico in the turmoil of the 1930s.[17] Western States argued that all governments were bound under international law to treat foreigners with at least a minimum standard of protection.[18] Such minimum standard of treatment was required precisely because the existing standard of protection in many countries was considered too low.[19] As further explained by US Secretary of State, Mr. Elihu Root in an article published in 1910, States sought to establish a threshold below which certain treatments would be deemed unacceptable and contrary to international law:

> Each country is bound to give to the nationals of another country in its territory the benefit of the same laws, the same administration, the same protection, and the same redress for injury which it gives to its own citizens, and neither more nor less: *provided the protection which the country gives to its own citizens conforms to the established standard of civilization*. There is [however] a standard of justice

---

9. It is noteworthy that the 1933 *Montevideo Convention on the Rights and Duties of States* (Article 9, in AJIL, (1934) supp. 75) indicated that aliens and nationals were on the same footing and that 'foreigners may not claim rights other or more extensive than those of nationals'. These issues are discussed in: Falsafi, *supra* n. 2, at 326 ff.
10. Jeswald W. Salacuse, *The Law of Investment Treaties* 47 (Oxford U. Press 2010).
11. Orellana, *supra* n. 2, at 1-2.
12. Weiler, *supra* n. 2, at 345, providing a number of examples of such interventions and referring to 'no fewer than one hundred instances of "protection by force" between 1813 and 1927 by the United States alone, including two dozen in the 20th century'.
13. This issue is discussed in: Falsafi, *supra* n. 2, at 324 ff.
14. Weiler, *supra* n. 2, at 351.
15. Orellana, *supra* n. 2, at 1.
16. Paparinskis, *supra* n. 3, at 64.
17. Alexandra Diehl, *The Core Standard of International Investment Protection: Fair and Equitable Treatment*, 146-147 (Wolters Kluwer 2012).
18. Schreuer & Dolzer, *supra* n. 4, at 12-13.
19. Salacuse, *supra* n. 10, at 47; J.C. Thomas, *Reflections on Article 1105 of NAFTA: History, State Practice and the Influence of Commentators*, 17(1) ICSID Rev. 26 (2002).

very simple, very fundamental, and of such general acceptance by all civilized countries as to form a part of the international law of the world. The ... system of law and administration shall conform to this general standard. If any country's system of law and administration does not conform to that standard, although the people of the country may be content to live under it, no other country can be compelled to accept it as furnishing a satisfactory measure of treatment of its citizens.[20]

Several decades later, the NAFTA *S.D. Myers* tribunal would explain why such an 'absolute' (non-contingent)[21] standard of treatment is still necessary in modern investment treaty practice:

> The inclusion of a 'minimum standard' provision is necessary to avoid what might otherwise be a gap. A government might treat an investor in a harsh, injurious and unjust manner, but do so in a way that is no different than the treatment inflicted on its own nationals. The 'minimum standard' is a floor below which treatment of foreign investors must not fall, even if a government were not acting in a discriminatory manner.[22]

[B]   The *Neer* Case and Its Relevance Today

Notwithstanding early disagreements between States, international jurisprudence slowly developed the concept of a minimum standard of protection.[23] While a number of cases have had a significant impact on the emergence of that standard,[24] special attention should be given in the NAFTA context to the particularly important *Neer* case of 1926. The case was decided by the US-Mexico Claims Commission, which was established in the 1920s to adjudicate claims arising out of a widespread unrest in Mexico, which caused harm to U.S. nationals.[25] The case involved a claim for compensation for the death of an American citizen, Mr. Paul Neer, and alleged that 'the Mexican authorities showed an unwarrantable lack of diligence or an unwarrantable lack of intelligent investigation in prosecuting the culprits'.[26] While the Commission dismissed the claim, it nevertheless provided for an explanation of the minimum standard:

> The propriety of governmental acts should be put to the test of international standards, and ... the treatment of an alien, in order to constitute an international delinquency, should amounts to an outrage, to bad faith, to wilful neglect of duty,

---

20. Root, *supra* n. 1, at 521 (emphasis added). On this question, *see* Paparinskis, *supra* n. 3, at 39-46.
21. J. Roman Picherack, *The Expanding Scope of the Fair and Equitable Treatment Standard: Have Recent Tribunals Gone Too Far?* 9(4) J. World Invest. & Trade, 265 (2008). *Contra*: Falsafi, *supra* n. 2, at 354 (for whom the minimum standard of treatment is a contingent standard).
22. *S.D. Myers Inc. v. Canada,* UNCITRAL, First Partial Award, (13 November 2000), para. 259.
23. M. Kinnear, A. Bjorklund & J.F.G. Hannaford, *Investment Disputes under NAFTA: An Annotated Guide to NAFTA Chapter 11* (Kluwer Law International, 2006), section on Article 1105, at 11-12.
24. *See, inter alia*: Roberts v. Mexico, UNRIAA, Award, (2 November 1926), Vol. IV, at 77; *Chevreau v. United Kingdom,* UNRIAA, Award, (9 June 1931), Vol. II, at 1113; *George W. Hopkins v. Mexico,* UNRIAA, Award, (31 March 1926), Vol. IV, at 41, 50.
25. *USA (LF Neer) v. Mexico,* UNRIAA, Award, (15 October 1926), Vol. IV, at 60.
26. *Ibid.,* at 61.

or to an insufficiency of governmental action so far short of international standards that every reasonable and impartial man would readily recognize its insufficiency.[27]

As noted by one writer, 'the Commission attempted to define the international standard by means of analogy, deriving criteria of procedural outrage from the better-established rules of denial of justice and then applying these more generally'.[28] The *Neer* case has had considerable influence on the emergence of the concept of a minimum standard of treatment.[29] In fact, international law casebooks typically refer to *Neer* as evidence of the existence of such a standard.[30] This conclusion has recently been contested by several writers who have indicated that limited weight should be given to a three-page award which only makes a general statement not substantiated by State practice.[31] In the recent *Railroad Development Corporation* case, the tribunal also stated that the Commission 'did not formulate the minimum standard of treatment after an analysis of State practice' and further noted that it was 'ironic that the decision considered reflecting the expression of the minimum standard of treatment in customary international law is based on the opinions of commentators and, on its own admission, went further than their views without an analysis of State practice followed because of a sense of obligation'.[32] Others have rightly highlighted the fact that the case does not involve any issues related to the protection of investments per se,[33] therefore arguing that the award would only be relevant for 'cases of failure to arrest and punish private actors of crimes against aliens'.[34] The *Mondev* tribunal has persuasively explained this position as follows:

> The Tribunal would observe, however, that the *Neer* case, and other similar cases which were cited, concerned not the treatment of foreign investment as such but the physical security of the alien. Moreover the specific issue in *Neer* was that of Mexico's responsibility for failure to carry out an effective police investigation into the killing of a United States citizen by a number of armed men who were not even alleged to be acting under the control or at the instigation of Mexico. In general, the State is not responsible for the acts of private parties, and only in special

---

27. *Ibid.,* at 61-62.
28. Paparinskis, *supra* n. 3, at 64.
29. Roth, *supra* n. 1, at 95. The case is discussed in detail in: Thomas, *supra* n. 19, at 29 ff; Paparinskis, *supra* n. 3, at 48-54.
30. For instance, Ian Brownlie, *Principles of Public International Law,* 527-528 (Oxford U. Press 1998); J.L. Brierly, *The Law of Nations* 280 (6th ed. Clarendon Press 1963); G. Schwartzenberger, *International Law as Applied by International Courts and Tribunals,* 201 (Stevens & Sons 1949).
31. Stephen M. Schwebel, *Is Neer far from Fair and Equitable?* 27(4) Arb. Int'l (2011), at 555–561.
32. *Railroad Development Corporation v. Guatemala,* ICSID Case No. ARB/07/23, Award (29 June 2012), at para. 216. The tribunal also added that 'by the strict standards of proof of customary international law applied in *Glamis Gold, Neer* would fail to prove its famous statement (...) to be an expression of customary international law'.
33. R. Jennings, *General Course on Principles of International Law,* 121 Recueil des cours (1967-II), at 487; Jean-Pierre Laviec, *Protection et promotion des investissements, étude de droit international économique,* 88 (P.U.F. 1985).
34. Jan Paulsson, *Neer-ly Misled?,* Miami Law Research Paper, at 247 (*see also:* J. Paulsson & G. Petrochilos, *Neer-ly Misled?* 22(2) ICSID Rev. 242-257 (2007)). *See also:* Schwebel, *supra* n. 31.

circumstances will it become internationally responsible for a failure in the conduct of the subsequent investigation. Thus there is insufficient cause for assuming that provisions of bilateral investment treaties, and of NAFTA, while incorporating the *Neer* principle in respect of the duty of protection against acts of private parties affecting the physical security of aliens present on the territory of the State, are confined to the *Neer* standard of outrageous treatment where the issue is the treatment of foreign investment by the State itself.[35]

In spite of these sound criticisms, it remains that recent investment tribunals still refer to the *Neer* 'standard' as reflecting the 'traditional' definition of the minimum standard of treatment in international law.[36] Moreover, the *Neer* standard has been repeatedly invoked by parties in modern investor-State arbitration disputes. As observed by one writer, 'after languishing three-quarters of a century in relative obscurity, Neer was, it seems, resuscitated in Canada's pleadings in the *S.D. Myers* and *Pope & Talbot* cases'.[37] In its 2002 award, the *Pope* tribunal portrayed Canada's position as being one where 'the principles of customary international law were frozen in amber at the time of the *Neer* decision'.[38] In fact, in other subsequent arbitration proceedings of the same year, Canada refuted ever having taken such a position.[39]

As further discussed below,[40] there is a large consensus in the literature that the *Neer* case offers very little value in determining the actual content of the minimum standard of treatment in the context of contemporary international investment law.[41] This is essentially because the standard has evolved substantially since the 1920s. Thus, as explained by the *ADF* tribunal, 'there appears no logical necessity and no concordant state practice to support the view that the *Neer* formulation is automatically

---

35. *Mondev International Ltd. v. United States* [hereinafter *Mondev v. United States*], ICSID No. ARB(AF)/99/2, Award, (2 October 2002), para. 115. *See also*: *Merrill & Ring Forestry L.P. v. Canada* [hereinafter *Merrill & Ring v. Canada*], UNCITRAL, Award, (31 March 2010), para. 197 (noting that the *Neer* and others cases were 'dealing with situations concerning due process of law, denial of justice and physical mistreatment, and only marginally with matters relating to business, trade or investments'), 204 ('No general rule of customary international law can thus be found which applies the *Neer* standard, beyond the strict confines of personal safety, denial of justice and due process').
36. *Saluka v. Czech Republic*, UNCITRAL, Partial Award, (17 March 2006), para. 295; *LG&E Energy Corp., LG&E Capital Corp., and LG&E International, Inc. v. Argentina*, ICSID No. ARB/02/1, Decision on Liability, (3 October 2006), para. 123.
37. Paulsson, *supra* n. 34, at 247.
38. *Pope & Talbot Inc. v. Canada*, UNCITRAL, Award in Respect of Damages, (31 May 2002), para. 57.
39. *ADF Group Inc. v. United States* [hereinafter *ADF v. United States*], ICSID No. ARB(AF)/00/1, Second Submission of Canada Pursuant to NAFTA Article 1128, (19 July 2002), para. 33 ('Canada's position has never been that the customary international law regarding the treatment of aliens was "frozen in amber at the time of the *Neer* decision". Obviously, what is shocking or egregious in the year 2002 may differ from that which was considered shocking or egregious in 1926. Canada's position has always been that customary international law can evolve over time, but that the threshold for finding violation of the minimum standard of treatment is still high. The [*Pope*] Tribunal mischaracterized Canada's position').
40. *See*, the discussion at Chapter 2 section §2.03[B][2] below.
41. Andrew Newcombe & Luis Paradell, *Law and Practice of Investment Treaties: Standards of Treatment*, 237 (Kluwer 2009); Tudor, *supra* n. 4, at 64: Roland Kläger, *Fair and Equitable Treatment in International Investment Law*, 53 (Cambridge U. Press 2011); Paulsson, *supra* n. 34, at 257. For Paparinskis, *supra* n. 3, at 216, the *Neer* case 'operates as the default rule', to be 'replaced by more specific and detailed rules on the Issue when they exist or are developed' (at 53).

extendible to the contemporary context of treatment of foreign investors and their investments by a host or recipient State'.[42] This statement has also been endorsed by several other NAFTA tribunals.[43] However, in the specific context of NAFTA where Article 1105 refers expressly to the minimum standard of treatment (in its title), a number of recent tribunals have adopted a different position. Two recent NAFTA awards have thus held that the 'required severity of the conduct as held in *Neer* is maintained' (*Cargill*[44]) or that the 'fundamentals of the *Neer* standard thus still apply today' (*Glamis*[45]).[46] This conflicting NAFTA case law on this question will be examined below.[47]

[C]   **Challenges to the Existence of a Minimum Standard of Treatment and the Proliferation of BITs**

The evolution of the minimum standard until the 1940s has been summarized by Paparinskis as follows:

> The creation of the international minimum standard (...) passed through a number of stages. The first stage is reflected in the nineteenth-century state practice, (almost) exclusively focusing on the non-discriminatory aspects of the treatment of aliens and denial of justice. Elihu Root's speech of 1910 illustrates the second stage of development, simultaneously explicit about the non-exhaustive nature of the non-discriminatory aspect of the international standard, and uncertain and contradictory about the source and content of this exception that could go further and apply to outrageous cases. The third stage is exemplified by the 1926 award of the US-Mexico General Claims Commission in the LFH Neer and Pauline Neer (Neer) case. The Commission attempted to define the international standard by means of analogy, deriving criteria of procedural outrage from the better-established rules of denial of justice and then applying these more generally. Neer was a relative improvement, attempting to give some juridical certainty to the previously indefinable exception (...). However and simultaneously, the focus on procedural outrage made it more complicated to develop rules that fell outside this paradigm (...). Despite the implicit consensus of the nineteenth century and the first decades of the twentieth century on the existence of such a rule and the explicit confirmation by the PCIJ in the 1920s, State practice

---

42. *ADF v. United States*, Award, (9 January 2003), para. 181.
43. *Mondev v. United States*, Award, (2 October 2002), paras. 116, 117 ('it would be surprising if, this practice [of recent BITs] and the vast number of provisions it reflects, were to be interpreted as meaning no more than the *Neer* Tribunal (in a very different context) meant in 1927'); *Loewen Group, Inc. and Raymond L. Loewen v. United States* [hereinafter *Loewen v. United States*], ICSID No. ARB(AF)/98/3, Award on Merits, (26 June 2003), at para. 132.
44. *Cargill, Inc. v. Mexico*, Award, (18 September 2009), para. 284.
45. *Glamis Gold, Ltd. v. United States* [hereinafter *Glamis v. United States*], UNCITRAL, Award, (8 June 2009), para. 616.
46. In the context outside of NAFTA, the *Genin* tribunal (*Alex Genin, Eastern Credit Limited, Inc. and A.S. Baltoil v. Estonia*, ICSID Case No. ARB/99/2, Award, (25 June 2001), para. 93) also described the FET standard in words very similar to those used in the *Neer* ruling ('acts showing a wilful neglect of duty, an insufficiency of action falling far below international standards, or even subjective bad faith').
47. *See*, the discussion at Chapter 2 section §2.03[B][2] below.

in the 1930s Hague Conference during the 1930s raised questions about the continuing correctness of this view.[48]

In the context of large-scale expropriations that took place after the Second World War in Eastern Europe, the concepts of denial of justice and the minimum standard were considered unsatisfactory in addressing such wrongs; arbitration practice focuses instead on the issue of compensation.[49] In the 1960s and 1970s, a group of States revived the opposition towards the concept of the minimum standard of treatment. This era was fundamentally marked by the arrival of a growing number of newly independent States in Asia and Africa that openly contested the *legitimacy* of existing customary international law. These States demanded a revision of these 'outdated' rules that did not respond to the fundamental changes that had prevailed in the international community since the end of the colonization period.[50] According to one prominent scholar, these States '[did] not easily forget that the same body of international law that they [were] now asked to abide by, sanctioned their previous subjugation and exploitation and stood as a bar to their emancipation'.[51] Developing States thus rejected having to provide any minimum standard of protection to foreign investors under customary international law.[52] The conflicting ideologies of the time are summarized as follows by Judge Schwebel:

> Capital-exporting States generally maintained that host States were bound under international law to treat foreign investment at least in accordance with the 'minimum standard of international law'; and where the host State expropriated foreign property, it could lawfully do so only for a public purpose, without discrimination against foreign interests, and upon payment of prompt, adequate and effective compensation. Capital importing States maintained that host States were not in matters of the treatment and taking of foreign property bound under international law at all; that the minimum standard did not exist; and that States were bound to accord the foreign investor only national treatment, only what their

---

48. Paparinskis, *supra* n. 3, at 64.
49. *Ibid.*, at 67-73, 83.
50. Georges Abi-Saab, *The Newly Independent States and the Rules of International Law: An Outline*, 8 Howard L.J., 118 (1962).
51. *Ibid.*, at 100. Accordingly, a revision of the existing rules of customary international law was needed in order 'to redress the balance of centuries of domination and exploitation by these big power of the newly independent states' (at 119). *See also*: Guha-Roy, *Is the Law of Responsibility of States for Injuries to Aliens A Part of Universal International Law?*, 55 AJIL 863, 866 (1961): 'The history of the establishment and consolidation of empires overseas by some of the members of the old international community and of the acquisition therein of vast economic interests by their nationals teems with instances of a total disregard of all ethical considerations. A strange irony of fate now compels those very members of the community of nations on the ebb tide of their imperial power to hold up principles of morality as shields against the liquidation of interests acquired and held by an abuse of international intercourse. Rights and interests acquired and consolidated during periods of such abuse cannot for obvious reasons carry with them in the mind of the victims of that abuse anything like the sanctity the holders of those rights and interests may and do attach to them. To the extent to which the law of responsibility of states for injuries to aliens favours such rights and interests, it protects an unjustified status quo or, to put it more bluntly, makes itself a handmaid of power in the preservation of its spoils'.
52. Sornarajah, *supra* n. 5, at 140 ff; OECD, *International Investment Law: A Changing Landscape: A Companion Volume to International Investment Perspectives*, 82 (2005).

domestic law provided or was revised to provide. The foreign investor whose property was taken was entitled to no more than the taking State's law afforded.[53]

A compromise between these different approaches was eventually reached in 1962 with the adoption by the United Nations General Assembly of the *Resolution on Permanent Sovereignty over Natural Resources* affirming the right for host States to nationalize foreign-owned property, but nevertheless requiring 'appropriate compensation' in accordance with international law.[54] The so-called 'Hull formula' which provided for 'prompt, adequate and effective' compensation in the event of expropriation was, however, rejected by developing States in 1974 with the General Assembly's adoption of the *Charter of Economic Rights and Duties of States*.[55] Under this 'New International Economic Order' the requirement to provide 'appropriate compensation' for expropriation still existed, but any related disputes (or 'controversy') had to be 'settled under the domestic law of the nationalizing State and by its tribunals' and not by an international tribunal under international law. The debate on this issue of compensation for expropriation illustrates a lack of any broad international consensus on the existing protection for foreign investors. In the famous *Barcelona Traction* case of 1970, the International Court of Justice ('ICJ') explained that such a lack of consensus prevented the development and crystallization of rules of customary international law in the field of international investment law:

> Considering the important developments of the last half-century, the growth of foreign investments and the expansion of international activities of corporations, in particular of holding companies, which are often multinational, and considering the way in which the economic interests of states have proliferated, it may at first sight appear surprising that the evolution of the law has not gone further and that no generally accepted rules in the matter have crystallized on the international plane.[56]

It is in this historical context that bilateral investment treaties emerged. As explained by two scholars, it is precisely because 'customary law was deemed be too amorphous and not be able to provide sufficient guidance and protection' to foreign investors that capital-exporting and developing States started to frenetically conclude *ad hoc* BITs.[57] The 1990s were marked by a new era of globalization. As explained by Schreuer and

---

53. S.M. Schwebel, *The United States 2004 Model Bilateral Investment Treaty: An Exercise in the Regressive Development of International Law*, 3(2) Transnational Disp. Mgmt. 3 (2006).
54. G.A. Res. 1803 (XVII), 14 December 1962.
55. G.A. Res. 3281 (XXIX), 12 December 1974. The 'Hull formula' was first articulated by the US Secretary of State, Mr. Cordell Hull, in a letter to his Mexican counterpart in response to Mexico's nationalization of U.S. companies in 1936. Mr. Hull argued that international law required 'prompt, adequate and effective' compensation for the expropriation of foreign investments (in: Green H. Hackworth, 3 *Digest of International Law*, 228 (1942).
56. *Barcelona Traction, Light and Power Co., Ltd. (Belgium v. Spain)*, ICJ Reports 1970, 3, at 46-47.
57. R. Dolzer & A. von Walter, *Fair and Equitable Treatment - Lines of Jurisprudence on Customary Law*, in *Investment Treaty Law, Current Issues II* 99 (F. Ortino ed., 2007). *See also*: Kläger, *supra* n. 41, at 264; Orellana, *supra* n. 2, at 3; Laviec, *supra* n. 33, at 87-88; Jean d'Aspremont, *International Customary Investment Law: Story of a Paradox*, in *International Investment Law: The Sources of Rights and Obligations* 15-17 (E. de Brabandere & T. Gazzini eds., Martinus Nijhoff 2012).

Dolzer, as a result of the new climate of international economic relations of the 1990s, 'the fight of previous decades against customary rules protecting foreign investment had abruptly become anachronistic and obsolete'.[58] Consequently, by the 1990s, 'the tide had turned' and developing States were no longer opposed to the application of a minimum standard of protection under custom, and instead granted 'more protection to foreign investment than traditional customary law did, now on the basis of treaties negotiated to attract additional foreign investment'.[59] One fundamental element of such enhanced protection that was now being offered by States under BITs is the FET standard (a point further discussed below[60]).

Finally, reference should be made to the position of several writers arguing in favor of the 'return' of custom *precisely because* of the proliferation of BITs. One controversial issue currently being debated in academia and amongst arbitrators is whether BITs represent the 'new' custom in this field.[61] For instance, Schwebel believes that 'customary international law governing the treatment of foreign invest-ment has been *reshaped* to embody the principles of law found in more than two thousand concordant bilateral investment treaties'.[62] The *CME* tribunal reached the same conclusion in its ruling.[63] The *Mondev* tribunal also held that the 'content' of 'current international law' was '*shaped* by the conclusion of more than two thousand bilateral investment treaties and many treaties of friendship and commerce'.[64] Accord-ing to the writers advocating for the return of custom, the content of custom would now simply be the *same* as that of thousands of BITs.[65] As pointed out by one writer, it is quite a paradox that the process of 'treatification' that emerged *because* of the lack of customary rules in international investment law, could somehow have led to the creation of custom.[66] In any event, the present author has explained elsewhere the

---

58. Schreuer & Dolzer, *supra* n. 4, at 16.
59. *Ibid.*
60. *See*, at sections §1.02[B] and §1.02[C] below.
61. *See*, Stephen M. Schwebel, *Investor-State Disputes and the Development of International Law: The Influence of Bilateral Investment Treaties on Customary International Law*, 98 ASIL Proc. 27-30 (2004); Steffen Hindelang, *Bilateral Investment Treaties, Custom and a Healthy Investment Climate: The Question of Whether BITs Influence Customary International Law Revisited*, 5 J. World Invest. & Trade 789-809 (2004); Andreas F. Lowenfeld, *Investment Agreements and International Law*, 42 Colum. J. Transnat'l L. 123-130 (2003); Bernard Kishoiyian, *The Utility of Bilateral Investment Treaties in the Formulation of Customary International Law*, 14(2) Northwestern J. Int'l L. 327-375; A. Andrew T. Guzman, *Why LDCs Sign Treaties That Hurt Them: Explaining the Popularity of Bilateral Investment Treaties*, 38(4) Va.J.Int'l L. 639-688 (1998); Abdullah Al Faruque, *Creating Customary International Law Through Bilateral Invest-ment Treaties: A Critical Appraisal*, 44 Indian JIL 292 (2004); T. Gazzini, *The Role of Customary International Law in the Protection of Foreign Investment*, 8(5) J. World Invest. & Trade 691 (2007); C. McLachlan, *Investment Treaties and General International Law*, 57(2) ICLQ 361-401 (2008); Cai Congyan, *International Investment Treaties and the Formation, Application and Transformation of Customary International Law Rules*, 7(3) Chinese JIL, 659–679 (1998).
62. Schwebel, *supra* n. 61, at 27 (emphasis added).
63. *CME Czech Republic B.V. v. Czech Republic*, UNCITRAL, Award, (14 March 2003), para. 498.
64. *Mondev v. United States*, Award, (2 October 2002), para. 125 (emphasis added).
65. Ian A. Laird, *A Community of Destiny - The Barcelona Traction Case and the Development of Shareholder Rights to Bring Investment Claims*, in *International Investment Law and Arbitration: Leading Cases from the ICSID, NAFTA, Bilateral Treaties and Customary International Law* 95-96 (T. Weiler ed., Cameron May 2005).
66. D'Aspremont, *supra* n. 57, at 20.

reasons for which the preferable view is that custom in the field of international investment law *does not* correspond to the *total sum* of 2,500 BITs.[67]

[D] The Minimum Standard of Treatment Is a Norm of Customary International Law

Despite some disagreement between States on the existence of the minimum standard of treatment in the last few decades, the concept is nowadays predominantly recognized as a rule of customary international law. This means in practical terms that this obligation applies to *all States*, including those that have not entered into any BITs. It also means that the standard of protection can be invoked by *any foreign investor* regardless of whether its State of origin has entered into a BIT with the country where it makes its investment.[68]

A number of States have explicitly stated that the minimum standard of treatment was part of customary international law. This is, for instance, the position taken by the Member States of the Organization for Economic Co-operation and Development (OECD) in the context of the 1967 OECD Draft Convention,[69] and as stated in a more recent 2005 report as well.[70] This (now) undisputed fact has also been recognized by several NAFTA awards, including *Mondev*,[71] *Waste Management*,[72] and *Glamis*.[73]

---

67. P. Dumberry, *Are BITs Representing the "New" Customary International Law in International Investment Law?*, 28(4) Penn State ILR 675-701 (2010).
68. A different question is whether or not a tribunal has jurisdiction to enforce the minimum standard of treatment. On this point, *see*: UNCTAD, *Fair and Equitable Treatment*, (UNCTAD Series on Issues in International Investment Agreements II, United Nations 2012), at 19: 'The question is whether an investor would be able to enforce the minimum standard of treatment of aliens through an IIA's investor-State dispute settlement (ISDS) mechanism. This will depend on the breadth of the treaty's ISDS clause. For instance, the ISDS clause in the India Singapore Comprehensive Economic Cooperation Agreement applies only to disputes "concerning an alleged breach of an obligation of the former under this Chapter" (Article 6.21); therefore, given the absence of the FET clause in the treaty, claims alleging breaches of the minimum standard of treatment of aliens will fall outside the tribunal's jurisdiction. In contrast, the New Zealand-Thailand Closer Economic Partnership Agreement's arbitration clause encompasses all disputes "with respect to a covered investment" (Article 9.16) – there is no requirement that relevant claims arise from a violation of the Agreement itself. Such a clause is broad enough to include, among others, claims of violation of the minimum standard of treatment of aliens under customary international law'.
69. OECD, *1967 Draft Convention on the Protection of Foreign Property*, in 7 ILM, 117, 120 (1968), commentary on Article 1 of the Draft Convention indicating that the FET standard 'conforms in effect to the "minimum standard" which forms part of customary international law'.
70. OECD, *supra* n. 52, at 82 ('The international minimum standard is a norm of customary international law which governs the treatment of aliens, by providing for a minimum set of principles which States, regardless of their domestic legislation and practices, must respect when dealing with foreign nationals and their property').
71. *Mondev v. United States*, Award, (2 October 2002), para. 121 ('the phrase "minimum standard of treatment" has historically been understood as a reference to a minimum standard under customary international law').
72. *Waste Management, Inc. v. Mexico ("Number 2")* [hereinafter *Waste Management v. Mexico*], ICSID No. ARB(AF)/00/3, Award, (30 April 2004), para. 91, where the tribunal endorsed the position taken by the *Mondev* tribunal: 'the *Mondev* tribunal found that the FTC interpretation … resolves any dispute about whether there was such a thing as a minimum standard of treatment of investment in international law in the affirmative'.
73. *Glamis v. United States*, Award, (8 June 2009), para. 627, referring to 'the customary international law minimum standard of treatment, as codified in Article 1105 of the NAFTA'.

This position has also been adopted by a majority of writers.[74] In fact, only a few scholars have rejected the customary status of the minimum standard of treatment. Porterfield, for instance, believes that the assumption that customary international law includes a minimum standard of treatment has 'never been supported by any comprehensive empirical study of the actual practice of nations with regard to foreign investment'.[75] He is also critical of the role played by tribunals' decisions as 'guiding the evolution of the minimum standard'.[76] Another prominent writer taking this position is Sornarajah who denies the existence of any rule of customary law since 'it would be difficult to show that there was free consent on the part of all the developing states to the creation of any customary international law' in international investment law.[77] For Sornarajah, any such rules of custom would have been imposed on developing States which have always rejected them:

> The formation of customary principles has been associated with power. The role of power in this area is evident. Powerful States sought to construct rules of investment protection largely aimed at developing States by espousing them in their practice and passing them off as customary principles. They were always resisted ...Nevertheless, the norms that were supported by the developed states were maintained on the basis that they were accepted as custom though that was never the case. The significance of the General Assembly resolutions associated with the New International Economic Order is that they demonstrated that there were a large number, indeed a majority, of states of the world, which did not subscribe to the norms maintained by the developed world. After that, it was no longer credible to maintain that there was in fact an international law on foreign investment, though the claim continues to be made simply because of the need to conserve the gains made for investment protection by developed States.[78]

Sornarajah also believes that even 'if there was such customary international law, many developing States would regard themselves as persistent objectors who were not bound by the customary law'.[79] The present author has argued elsewhere that tribunals

---

74. J.C. Thomas, *Fair and Equitable Treatment under NAFTA's Investment Chapter; Remarks*, 96 ASIL Proc. 9, 14 (2002); Rudolf Dolzer & Margrete Stevens, *Bilateral Investment Treaties*, 58 (Martinus Nijhoff Publ. 1995); Sir Robert Jenning & Sir Arthur Watts, *Oppenheim's International Law*, vol. I (Peace: Introduction and Part 1), 931 (9th ed., Longman 1996); L. Reed, J. Paulsson & N. Blackaby, *A Guide to ICSID Arbitration*, 48 (Kluwer Law 2004); Tudor, *supra* n. 4, at 61-62, 67; Newcombe & Paradell, *supra* n. 41, at 234; Diehl, *supra* n. 17, at 145; Gabriel Cavazos Villanueva, *The Fair and Equitable Treatment Standard: The Mexican Experience* 63-64 (VDM Verlag 2008); D. Carreau, *Investissements*, in: *Répertoire de droit international*, para. 135 (Dalloz 1998); Marcela Klein Bronfman, *Fair and Equitable Treatment: An Evolving Standard*, 10 Max Planck Yrbk. UNL, 624 (2006); Picherack, *supra* n. 21, at 265; Graham Mayeda, *Playing Fair: The Meaning of Fair and Equitable Treatment in Bilateral Investment Treaties*, 41(2) J. World Trade, 273-291, 280 (2007).
75. M.C. Porterfield, *An International Common Law of Investor Rights?*, 27 U. Pa. J. Int'l Econ. L., 81-82 (2006).
76. *Ibid.*, at 98. *See also* at 103, 113.
77. Sornarajah, *supra* n. 5, at 213.
78. *Ibid.*, at 92–93.
79. *Ibid.* The author admits (at 89) that there are 'few' rules of custom in the field of international investment law. He also argues elsewhere (at 151) that 'it is difficult to establish that state responsibility for economic injuries to alien investors was recognized as a principle of customary international law. Latin American states as well as African and Asian States must be taken to be

should not apply the controversial concept of persistent objector in the context of international investment law.[80] In subsequent writing, Sornarajah admits that a minimum standard may have emerged, but *only* amongst NAFTA Parties in the context of a regional custom.[81]

In any event, this theoretical controversy is of limited importance in the specific context of NAFTA. Thus, the title of Article 1105 refers to the minimum standard of treatment. As pointed out by the *ADF* tribunal, in the context of NAFTA 'the long-standing debate as to whether there exists such a thing as a minimum standard of treatment of non-nationals and their property prescribed in customary international law, is closed'.[82] The *Mondev* tribunal also mentioned:

> [I]t is clear that Article 1105 was intended to put at rest for NAFTA purposes a long-standing and divisive debate about whether any such thing as a minimum standard of treatment of investment in international law actually exists. Article 1105 resolves this issue in the affirmative for NAFTA Parties.[83]

[E]   The Content of the Minimum Standard of Treatment

If there is no doubt as to the existence of a minimum standard of treatment that must be respected by States and the fact that this is a customary norm of international law, what remains controversial is to determine the actual *content* of that standard.

The minimum standard of treatment is an *umbrella concept*, which in *itself*, incorporates different elements. As pointed out by Roth in 1949, 'the international standard is nothing else but a set of rules, correlated to each other and deriving from one particular norm of general international law, namely that the treatment of an alien is regulated by the law of nations'.[84] Similarly, for Newcombe, the minimum standard of treatment 'consists of a series of interconnecting and overlapping elements or standards that apply to both the treatment of foreigners and their property'.[85] The United States has consistently interpreted the minimum standard of treatment as an umbrella concept in NAFTA proceedings. The submission by the United States in *ADF* stands as a noteworthy exemplification of this position:

---

persistent objectors to the formation of such customary international law'. *See also*: M. Sornarajah, *Power and Justice in Foreign Investment Arbitration*, 14(3) J. Int'l Arb., 103-140, 118 (1997); Stephen Vasciannie, *The Fair and Equitable Treatment Standard in International Investment Law and Practice*, 70 British YIL, 99 (1999), at footnote 305.

80. P. Dumberry, *The Last Citadel! Can a State Claim the Status of 'Persistent Objector' to Prevent the Application of a Rule of Customary International Law in Investor-State Arbitration?*, 23(2) Leiden JIL 379-400 (2010). *See also*, more generally: P. Dumberry, *Incoherent and Ineffective: The Concept of Persistent Objector Revisited*, 59 ICLQ 779-802 (2010).

81. M. Sornarajah, *The Fair and Equitable Standard of Treatment: Whose Fairness? Whose Equity?* in *Investment Treaty Law: Current Issues II* 177 (Federico Ortino et al. eds., British IICL 2007); Sornarajah, *supra* n. 5, at 328. This position is also presented in: J. Fouret, *The Notion of Fair and Equitable Treatment of Foreign Direct Investment*, McGill University, LL.M. Thesis (2003), at 133 ff.

82. *ADF v. United States*, Award, (9 January 2003), para. 178.

83. *Mondev v. United States*, Award, (2 October 2002), para. 120.

84. Roth, *supra* n. 1, at 127.

85. Newcombe & Paradell, *supra* n. 41, at 236.

The 'international minimum standard' embraced by Article 1105(1) is an umbrella concept incorporating a set of rules that over the centuries have crystallized into customary international law in specific contexts. The treaty term 'fair and equitable treatment' refers to the customary international law minimum standard of treatment. The rules grouped under the heading of the international minimum standard include those for denial of justice, expropriation and other acts subject to an absolute, minimum standard of treatment under customary international law. The treaty term 'full protection and security' refers to the minimum level of police protection against criminal conduct that is required as a matter of customary international law.

The rules encompassed within the customary international law minimum standard of treatment are specific ones that address particular contexts. There is no single standard applicable to all contexts. The customary international law minimum standard is in this sense analogous to the common-law approach of distinguishing among a number of distinct torts potentially applicable to particular conduct, as contrasted with the civil-law approach of prescribing a single delict applicable to all conduct. As with common-law torts, the burden under Article 1105(1) is on the claimant to identify the applicable rule and to articulate and prove that the respondent engaged in conduct that violated that rule.[86]

In *Glamis*, the tribunal agreed with the United States' description of the minimum standard of treatment as an umbrella concept.[87] It also explained that Mexico had adopted the same position.[88] The *Cargill* and *Mobil* tribunals also endorsed this umbrella concept description.[89]

A number of writers have emphasized the vagueness of the concept of the minimum standard of treatment and its lack of precise content.[90] In a recent 2012 report, UNCTAD also stated that the minimum standard is 'highly indeterminate, lacks a clearly defined content and requires interpretation'.[91] The report suggests that '[t]he MST is a concept that does not offer ready-made solutions for deciding modern

---

86. *ADF v. United States*, US Post Hearing Submission, (27 June 2002), at 2-4. *See also: Glamis v. United States*, US Counter-Memorial, (9 September 2006), at 223; *Loewen v. United States*, US Counter-Memorial, (30 March 2001), at 124; *Methanex Corporation v. United States* [hereinafter *Methanex v. United States*], UNCITRAL; US Memorial on Jurisdiction and Admissibility, (13 November 2000), at 43-44.
87. *Glamis v. United States*, Award, (8 June 2009), para. 618: 'As the United States explained in its 1128 submission in *Pope & Talbot*, and as Mexico adopted in its [Article] 1128 submission to the *ADF* tribunal: "fair and equitable treatment" and "full protection and security" are provided as examples of the customary international law standards incorporated into Article 1105(1). ... The international law minimum standard [of treatment] is an umbrella concept incorporating a set of rules that has crystallized over the centuries into customary international law in specific contexts'. (Citing and quoting the following documents: *Pope & Talbot Inc. v. Canada*, US Fourth Article 1128 Submission, (1 November 2000), paras. 3, 8; *ADF v. United States*, Mexico's Second Article 1128 Submission, (22 July 2002), at 8).
88. *Glamis v. United States*, Award, (8 June 2009), para. 618, citing *ADF v. United States*, Mexico's Second Article 1128 Submission, (22 July 2002), at 8.
89. *Cargill Inc. v. Mexico*, Award, (18 September 2009), para. 268 (citing the position of Mexico in *ADF v. United States*, Mexico's Second Article 1128 Submission, (22 July 2002), at 8). In its award, the *Mobil* tribunal endorsed the position taken by *Cargill* (*Mobil Investments Canada Inc. & Murphy Oil Corporation v. Canada* [hereinafter *Mobil v. Canada*], ICSID Case No. ARB(AF)/07/4, Decision on Liability and on Principles of Quantum (22 May 2012), para. 135).
90. Sornarajah, *supra* n. 81, at 172; Sornarajah, *supra* n. 5, at 328; Porterfield, *supra* n. 75, at 80.
91. UNCTAD, *supra* n. 68, at 28. *See also* at 44.

investment disputes; at best, it gives a rough idea of a high threshold that the challenged governmental conduct has to meet for a breach to be established'.[92]

Roth's identification of eight rules on the treatment of aliens in 1949 (not dealing specifically with foreign investment) constitutes an earlier attempt to define the *actual content* of the minimum standard of treatment.[93] A recent OECD report states that 'case law points to a number of areas across which the notion of an international minimum standard applies' including 'the administration of justice in cases involving foreign nationals, usually linked to the notion of denial of justice', 'the treatment of aliens under detention', full protection and security, and finally, the 'general right of expulsion by the host State' which 'should be the least injurious to the person affected'.[94] The 2012 UNCTAD report merely indicates that '[t]he MST is often understood as a broad concept intended to encompass the doctrine of denial of justice along with other aspects of the law of State responsibility for injuries to aliens'.[95] The report refers in turn, to an earlier 2004 OECD report[96] concluding that 'the international minimum standard applies in the following areas: (a) the administration of justice,

---

92. *Ibid.*, at 46-47.
93. Roth *supra* n. 1, at 185-186, identifying the following eight rules that general international law imposes on States with regards to the treatment of aliens: '(1) An alien, whether a natural person or a corporation, is entitled by international law to have his juridical personality and legal capacity recognized by the receiving state. (2) The alien can demand respect for his life and protection for his body. (3) International law protects the alien's personal and spiritual liberty within socially bearable limits. (4) According to general international law, aliens enjoy no political rights in their State of residence, but have to fulfil such public duties as are not incompatible with allegiance to their home state. (5) General international law gives aliens no right to be economically active in foreign States. In cases where national economic policies of foreign States allows aliens to undertake economic activities, however, general international law assures aliens equality of commercial treatment among themselves. (6) According to general international law, the alien's privilege of participation does not go so far as to allow him to acquire private property. The State of residence is free to bar him from ownership of all certain property, whether movables or realty. (7) Where an alien enjoys the privilege of ownership of property, international law protects his rights in so far as his property may not be expropriated under any pretext, except for moral or penal reasons, without adequate compensation. Property rights are to be understood as rights to tangible property which have come into concrete existence according to the municipal law of the alien's State of residence. (8) International law grants the alien procedural rights in his State of residence as primary protection against violation of his substantive rights. These procedural rights amount to freedom of access to court, the right to a fair, non-discriminatory and unbiased hearing, the right to full participation in any form in the procedure, the right to a just decision rendered in full compliance with the laws of the State within a reasonable time'.
94. OECD, *supra* n. 52, at 82. This definition is endorsed by Tudor, *supra* n. 4, at 62.
95. UNCTAD, *supra* n. 68, at 44. A very similar approach is adopted by Sornarajah, *supra* n. 81, at 172: '[t]he precise extent of the content of an international minimum standard has yet to be worked out. ... Yet, the international minimum standard, the existence of which is denied collectively by the developing states, has not been fleshed out. Outside the standards applicable to expropriation and to state responsibility for denying protection and security to aliens which are separately provided for in investment treaties, international minimum standard captures the category which involves a denial of justice'. *See also*: Sornarajah, *supra* n. 5, at 329 ('There are three instances in which the old cases on state responsibility may provide guidance as to the international minimum standard. These relate to compensation for expropriation, responsibility for destruction or violence by non-state actors and denial of justice').
96. OECD, *Fair and Equitable Treatment Standard in International Investment Law*, Working Papers on International Investment Law, No. 2004/3 (2004).

usually linked to the notion of the denial of justice; (b) the treatment of aliens under detention; and (c) full protection and security'.[97] The UNCTAD report concluded that 'there are no other aspects of the MST that have become apparent to date in customary international law'.[98] Other writers have defined the content of the minimum standard more broadly.[99]

In sum, there is a large consensus to the effect that the minimum standard of treatment encompasses (at the very least):

– An obligation for host States to prevent denial of justice in the administration of justice.
– An obligation not to expropriate a foreign investor's investment unless the taking is for a public purpose, as provided by law, conducted in a non-discriminatory manner and with compensation in return.
– An obligation to prevent arbitrary conduct.
– An obligation to provide investors with 'full protection and security'.

One of the most controversial questions in the field of investor-State arbitration (further examined below[100]) is whether or not the FET standard is one of the elements *encompassed* within the larger umbrella concept of the minimum standard of treatment or whether the FET is an autonomous standard.

§1.02   THE FAIR AND EQUITABLE TREATMENT STANDARD

Just like the minimum standard of treatment, the FET is an 'absolute' (non-contingent) standard of treatment.[101] It is quite different from the national treatment (a 'relative' standard), which is defined by reference to the treatment accorded to *other specific*

---

97. UNCTAD, *supra* n. 68, at 44.
98. *Ibid.*, at 45. *See also*, Kläger, *supra* n. 41, at 53 ('the concept of the international minimum standard, in its classic sense, may have produced rules for the compensation for expropriation, the physical protection of aliens and the enforcement of the pertinent laws. Beyond that, however, it is highly questionable whether it entails any further guidelines relating to the protection of economic interests of foreign corporations or individuals').
99. Based on the list mentioned by the tribunal in *Waste Management v. Mexico*, Award, (30 April 2004), para. 98, Newcombe & Paradell, *supra* n. 41, at 238, indicate that a 'number of specific elements of the minimum standard of treatment where state responsibility may arise for mistreatment of foreign investors and investment, including, but not exhaustively: denial of justice, lack of due process, lack of due diligence, and instances of arbitrariness and discrimination'. Paparinskis, *supra* n. 3, at 182, 239, 246–247, 256, argues that denial of justice, arbitrariness and non-discrimination are elements of the minimum standard of treatment.
100. *See*, at section §1.03[A].
101. S. Schill, *The Multilateralization of International Investment Law* 78 (Cambridge U. Press 2009); Meg Kinnear, *The Continuing Development of the FET Standard*, in *Investment Treaty Law: Current Issues III* (Andrea K. Bjorklund, Ian A. Laird & Sergey Ripinsky eds., British IICL 2009), 18 (paper version); Dolzer & Stevens, *supra* n. 74, at 58; A.A. Fatouros, *Government Guarantees to Foreign Investors* 135–41 (Columbia U. Press 1962); U.N. Centre on Transnational Corporations, *Key Concepts in International Investment Arrangements and Their Relevance to Negotiations on International Transactions in Services* 12 (1990); Katia Yannaca-Small, *Fair and Equitable Treatment Standard: Recent Developments*, in *Standards of Investment Protection* 111 (A. Reinisch ed., Oxford U. Press 2008); Vasciannie, *supra* n. 79, at 105–106.

investments (i.e., the treatment accorded by the host State to its own investors).[102] On the contrary, the FET standard 'applies to investments in a given situation without a reference to how other investments or entities are treated by the host State'.[103]

The history of the emergence of the FET clause has previously been examined in detail by several authors.[104] For the purposes of this book, it suffices to simply highlight some of the most salient features of these important historical developments (section §1.02[A]). One important question that will be addressed below is why States began to include such a standard in their BITs in the 1960s and 1970s, a period where the very existence of the minimum standard of treatment under international law was a highly contentious issue (section §1.02[B]). Finally, we will examine the widespread use of the FET standard in modern BITs (section §1.02[C]).

[A]   Early Appearances of the Standard in Multilateral Instruments

The first reference to 'equitable treatment' can be found at Article 23(e) of the League of Nations Covenant, which commits its Member States 'to secure and maintain ... equitable treatment for the commerce of all Members of the League'.[105] The League convened an International Conference on the Treatment of Foreigners to develop an applicable standard of treatment under Article 23(e) and later adopted a Draft Convention on the matter, which did not, however, refer to any FET obligation.[106]

The 1948 *Havana Charter for an International Trade Organization* (hereinafter 'Havana Charter') is generally considered as the first legal instrument that makes reference to the FET standard.[107] Although the Havana Charter focused on trade issues, it also contained a number of provisions related to investments including a reference that a future organization would be authorized to 'make recommendations for and promote bilateral or multilateral agreements on measure designed ... to assure just and equitable treatment for the enterprise ...'.[108] It is noteworthy that the Havana Charter

---

102. This question is further discussed at Chapter 4 section §4.05 below. *See,* however, the critical analysis of Kläger, *supra* n. 41, at 305 ('the differentiation between absolute and relative standards is based on a fundamental misconception related to the myth of the intrinsic content of vague general clauses like fair and equitable treatment (...). Moreover, the gateway character of fair and equitable treatment and the associated process of balancing display the inherently flexible nature of this norm, resembling by no means the misguided image of an absolute standard of protection'). He believes that the 'common distinction between relative (or contingent) and absolute (or non-contingent) obligations should be abandoned'.
103. UNCTAD, *supra* n. 68, at 6.
104. *See inter alia*: Vasciannie, *supra* n. 79, at 99; Thomas, *supra* n. 19; Kinnear et al., *supra* n. 23; UNCTAD, *Fair and Equitable Treatment* (UNCTAD Series on Issues in International Investment Agreements 1999); UNCTAD, *supra* n. 68, at 5 ff.; Haeri, *supra* n. 2, at 83 ff.
105. *See* the analysis of Theodore Kill, *Don't Cross the Streams: Past and Present Overstatement of Customary International Law in Connection with Conventional Fair and Equitable Treatment Obligations,* 106 Mich. L. Rev, 869 ff (2008).
106. *Ibid.,* at 870-871.
107. *See*: Thomas, *supra* n. 19, at 40 ff.; Kill, *supra* n. 105, at 871-873. A number of other initiatives are discussed in: Weiler, *supra* n. 2, at 358 ff.
108. Havana Charter for an International Trade Organization, 24 March 1948, Article II(2), in: U.N. Conference on Trade & Employment, Final Act and Related Documents 8-9, U.N. Doc. E/Conf. 2/78, U.N. Sales No. 1948.II.D.4 (1948).

did not, in itself, provide a guarantee, but rather that 'it merely authorized the International Trade Organization to recommend that this standard be included in future agreements'.[109] The Havana Charter never came into force. At the same time, the Organization of American States adopted the *Economic Agreement of Bogotá* (hereinafter 'Bogotá Agreement') in 1948, which mentioned at Article 22 that 'foreign capital shall receive equitable treatment'.[110] The document was, however, never ratified.[111] It has been argued that the drafters of both the Bogotá Agreement and the Havana Charter 'understood the requirement to provide equitable treatment as additive to a state's duties toward aliens under customary international law'.[112]

Ten years later in 1959, a group of European businesspersons and lawyers under the leadership of Mr. Hermann Abs and Lord Shawcross drafted the Abs-Shawcross *Draft Convention on Investments Abroad*. The document specifically offered protection in terms of 'fair and equitable treatment' to foreigner's property.[113] The clause offered wide protection and covered 'the most constant protection and security' and forbade discrimination against a foreigner's property.

In 1967, the OECD developed a convention to protect private property: the *Draft Convention on the Protection of Foreign Property* (hereinafter 'Draft Convention').[114] It provides that 'each party shall at all times ensure FET to the property of the nationals of the other parties'.[115] One of the reasons why the Draft Convention included such a reference to FET may be because several OECD members had, at the time, already started to adopt the FET clause in their respective BITs (a point discussed below[116]).[117] Although the Draft Convention was never opened for signature, its importance should not be underestimated since it 'represented the collective view and dominant trend of OECD countries on investment issues'.[118] The Draft Convention also provided OECD Member States with guidelines that were subsequently used by them as a model to draft their own BITs.[119] In fact, it has been rightly observed that the many textual similarities between the different treaty models used by developed OECD Member States as a basis for treaty negotiation with developing countries, has led to a greater

---

109. Vasciannie, *supra* n. 79, at 108.
110. Organization of American States, Economic Agreement of Bogotá, Art. 22, May 1948, L. Treaty Ser. No. 25, OAS Doc. No. OEA/Ser.A/4 (SEPF). The full provision reads as follows: '[f]oreign capital shall receive equitable treatment. The States therefore agree not to take unjustified, unreasonable or discriminatory measures that would impair the legally acquired rights or interests of nationals of other countries in the enterprises, capital, skills, arts or technology they have supplied'.
111. Kill, *supra* n. 105, at 873.
112. *Ibid.*
113. Article 1. Hermann Abs & Hartley Shawcross, *The Proposed Convention to Protect Private Foreign Investment: A Round Table: Comment on the Draft Convention by its Authors*, 9 J.P.L., 115-132 (1960).
114. OECD, *Draft Convention on the Protection of Foreign Property*, Article 1 cmt., adopted 12 October 1967, 7 ILM 117 (1967).
115. Article 1(a).
116. *See*, at section §1.02[B].
117. K.J. Vandevelde, *Bilateral Investment Treaties: History, Policy and Interpretation*, 199 (Oxford U. Press 2010).
118. OECD, *supra* n. 96, at 2 ff.
119. *Ibid.*; Tudor, *supra* n. 4, at 19; Bronfman, *supra* n. 74, at 161.

uniformity in BIT language.[120] Thus, the origin of the FET clause that is now commonly found in modern BITs can (at least in part) be traced to this 1967 OECD Draft Convention.[121]

Finally, it is worth mentioning that a number of non-binding instruments have also included protective measures for FET,[122] including the *Draft United Nations Code of Conduct on Transnational Corporations*,[123] and the 1992 World Bank *Guidelines on the Treatment of Foreign Direct Investment*.[124]

[B]   Reasons for the Emergence of the Standard in BITs in the 1960s and 1970s

The failure to negotiate multilateral accords eventually led States to enter into bilateral agreements instead.[125] The common feature of the FET standard in the above-mentioned multilateral instruments certainly influenced States to incorporate such a standard at the bilateral level.[126] The late 1960s saw a substantial growth in the number of BITs between developed and developing countries. The first groups of BITs that mentioned the FET were those concluded by European States (including Germany and Switzerland) in the early 1960s.[127] By the 1970s, FET was specifically mentioned in most BITs between capital-exporting and capital-importing countries.[128] According to some estimates, the standard was mentioned in over 300 BITs between the 1960s and 1990s.[129]

One of the most controversial questions discussed in scholarship in recent years is why States began to include the term 'fair and equitable treatment' in their BITs throughout the 1960s and 1970s.

According to one view, Western States incorporated the concept of FET in their BITs to simply reflect the minimum standard of treatment that existed under international law.[130] This approach has been endorsed by a number of writers.[131] They

---

120. K.J. Vandevelde, *The Political Economy of a Bilateral Investment Treaty,* 92 AJIL, 621, 628 (1998); Vasciannie, *supra* n. 79, at 113.
121. Vasciannie, *supra* n. 79, at 113.
122. These instruments are examined in detail by Vasciannie, *supra* n. 79, at 114-119; Bronfman, *supra* n. 74, at 616; OECD, *supra* n. 52, at 78; Weiler, *supra* n. 2, at 358 ff.
123. Article 48, U.N. Centre on Transnational Corporation, *The United Nations Code of Conduct on Transnational Corporations,* Current Studies, Series A (United Nations 1986) UN Doc. ST/CTC/ SER. A/4, Annex 1.
124. Article III (2)(3), World Bank, *Guidelines on the Treatment of Foreign Direct Investment* (1992), 'each State will extend to investments established in its territory by nationals of any other State fair and equitable treatment according to the standards recommended in the Guidelines'.
125. Thomas, *supra* n. 19, at 43.
126. Salacuse, *supra* n. 10, at 219; Paparinskis, *supra* n. 3, at 90–92.
127. Vandeveld, *supra* n. 117, at 196.
128. UNCTAD, *supra* n. 104, at 8-9; OECD, *supra* n. 52, at 78.
129. M. Khalil, *Treatment of Foreign Investment in BITs,* 8 ICSID Rev, 355 (1992).
130. *See* the analysis of Newcombe & Paradell, *supra* n. 41, at 268; Thomas, *supra* n. 19, at 44, 47; Dominique Carreau & Patrick Julliard, *Droit international économique,* 454 (4th ed., L.G.D.J. 1998).
131. *See,* for instance: Picherack, *supra* n. 21, at 264 ('When the language of fair and equitable treatment first began to emerge in draft multilateral instruments and investment agreements in the 1950s and 1960s, it was likely then intended to serve as a reference to the minimum

typically refer to the above-mentioned 1967 OECD Draft Convention as representing the position of developed States at the time on matters of protection of foreign investments.[132] This is because the OECD's Commentary to the 1967 Draft Convention indicated that the concept of FET flowed from the 'well established general principle of international law that a State is bound to respect and protect the property of nationals of other States'.[133] The Drafting Committee also added that the phrase FET refers to 'the standard set by international law for the treatment due by each State with regard to the property of foreign nationals' and that 'the standard required conforms in effect to the minimum standard which forms part of customary international law'.[134] The same position was also taken by OECD Member States in 1984.[135] This position is also confirmed by the practice of some Western States.[136] This narrative has, however, been subject to dissent by many scholars.[137] While it is possible that the OECD commentary reflected what their Member States (all developed States) *themselves* viewed as what

---

standard of treatment existing in international law. ... The desire to set down a fair and equitable treatment provision in the text of multilateral instruments and investment agreements could be seen as an attempt at the time to solidify the minimum international standard in the face of the Calvo doctrine and many developing countries' assertions which denied the existence of a minimum standard of treatment in customary international law separate from a national treatment standard'); Paparinskis, *supra* n. 3, at 160-163 ('If one takes together the pre- and post-Second World War materials pre-dating investment arbitrations, it seems permissible to conclude that the ordinary meaning of fair and equitable treatment was a reference to customary minimum standard, in particular regarding administration of justice'); S. Montt, *State Liability in Investment Treaty Arbitration* (Hart Publ. 2009), at 69 ('If the historical background is to be taken seriously, then the FET standard, when first used, could not have meant anything higher than IMS. At a time when the opposing North-South legal camps were, respectively, IMS and national treatment, the FET standard could not have referred to either an autonomous standard or to a higher standard than those minima').

132. Vasciannie, *supra* n. 79, at 112-113; UNCTAD, *supra* n. 104, at 8; OECD, *supra* n. 96, at 4.
133. OECD, *supra* n. 114, at 119.
134. *Ibid.*
135. Thomas, *supra* n. 19, at 48 referring to: OECD Committee on International Investment and Multinational Enterprise, Inter-Governmental Agreements Relating to Investment in Developing Countries, Doc. No. 84/14, 27 May 1984, at 12, para. 36 ('[a]ccording to all Member countries which have commented on this point, fair and equitable treatment introduced a substantive legal standard referring to general principles of international law even if this is not explicitly stated').
136. *See* the examples examined by Newcombe & Paradell, *supra* n. 41, at 268 (referring to US, UK, Swiss and Canadian treaty practice); Thomas, *supra* n. 19, at 48-51; Paparinskis, *supra* n. 3, at 162 ('pleadings in the ICJ (...) show that such States as Belgium, Spain, the UK, and the US used the language of fair and equitable treatment to refer to the customary of law administration of justice'). On Swiss practice, *see*: Statement of the Swiss Department of External Affairs (Mémoire, JAAC 1979, fasc. 43/IV, no. 113) in: L. Caflisch, *La pratique suisse en matière de droit international public,* 36 ASDI 178 (1980) ('On se réfère ainsi au principe classique du droit des gens selon lequel les États doivent mettre les étrangers se trouvant sur leur territoire et leurs biens au bénéfice du "standard minimum" international, c'est-à-dire leur accorder un minimum de droits personnels, procéduraux et économiques"'). This position is examined in: Matthias-Charles Kraft, *Les accords bilatéraux sur la protection des investissements conclus par la Suisse,* in *Foreign Investment in the Present and New International Economic Order* (D.C. Dicke ed., Univ. Press, Fribourg, 1987) at 79; Huu-Tru Nguyen, *Le réseau suisse d'accords bilatéraux d'encouragement et de protection des investissements,* 92 RGDIP 605 (1988); Jean-Christophe Liebeskind, *The Legal Framework of Swiss International Trade and Investments,* 7(3) J. World Invest. & Trade 368 (2006).
137. Kill, *supra* n. 105, at 876-877; Bronfman, *supra* n. 74, at 615.

was customary international law at the time, they were certainly not representative of what developing States believed was their legal obligations in the 1960s.[138]

As explained by two scholars, the use of a 'different and more politically neutral term [FET] might be explained by the historical political sensitivities regarding the minimum standard of treatment', which was 'historically viewed with suspicion because of the legacy of gun-boat diplomacy and imperialism'.[139] For these writers, '[f]air and equitable treatment may simply have been viewed as a convenient, neutral and acceptable reference to the minimum standard of treatment'.[140] It has also been argued that developing States have long-refused to incorporate the FET clause in their BITs *precisely* because Western States have viewed it as the equivalent of the minimum standard of treatment existing under international law.[141]

A more convincing approach has been adopted by a number of writers, wherein the growing use of the term 'fair and equitable treatment' by Western States in BITs was intended to counter the assertion made by developing States about the inexistence of any minimum standard of treatment under international law.[142] Thus, Western States started including such a reference in their BITs in the 1960s precisely *because* of the ambiguities surrounding the concept of the minimum standard of treatment.

The actual drafting language used by States in their BITs supports this approach. As pointed out by two authors, 'if the parties to a treaty want to refer to customary international law, one would assume that they will refer to it as such rather than using

---

138. Kill, *supra* n. 105, at 879.
139. Newcombe & Paradell, *supra* n. 41, at 263-264. *See also*: *AWG Group v. Argentina*, UNCITRAL, Decision on Liability, (30 July 2010), Judge Nikken's separate opinion, paras. 14–15 ('Therefore, it is not so easy to say that the concept of international minimum standard was a *well-established* concept. It certainly was for the capital-exporting countries, but not for the rest of the world (...) Clauses on the treatment of foreign investment referring to the "international minimum standard" could hardly be agreed upon, as some of the Parties to those treaties were not willing to accept it *expressis verbi*. "International minimum standard" was a "forbidden phrase" in a treaty for the very many countries that had rejected that standard, because it was associated with unjust international relations, as has been recognized by scholars who have addressed the issue. The explanation suggested by the NAFTA Free Trade Commission interpretation, which reveals the intention of the NAFTA Parties to consider fair and equitable treatment and international minimum standard as identical, was that a formula had to be found for saying the same thing but with different words, neutral words, which were not historically demonized. The phrase "fair and equitable treatment" is a neutral expression in relation to which there was no controversy and it had been used in another context in the Havana Charter signed in 1948 and in the Economic Agreement of Bogota, also signed in 1948').
140. Newcombe & Paradell, *supra* n. 41, at 263-264. *See also*: Montt, *supra* n. 131, at 69-70.
141. Vasciannie, *supra* n. 79, at 162 ('In practice, however, such [developing] States have historically been reluctant to incorporate the fair and equitable standard in their investment relations, mainly because, on one interpretation, the fair and equitable standard is synonymous with the international minimum standard consistently supported by capital-exporting countries'). On China's practice, *see* Norah Gallagher & Wenhua Shan, *Chinese Investment Treaties* (Oxford U. Press 2009), noting that 'most principles of general/customary international law had emerged and been developed in the context of Europe and among developed states, and China has not participated in this process' (at 128) and that 'China has been cautious, particularly in her earlier years, in accepting "principles of international law". Mainly this was due to fears that it would lead to the application of customary international law or the IMS standard' (at 130).
142. *See*, the analysis of Thomas, *supra* n. 19, at 48. *Contra*: Paparinskis, *supra* n. 3, at 163.

33

a different expression'.[143] Incidentally, most BITs do *not* make such an explicit link to the minimum standard of treatment under custom.[144] The present author's own survey of some 365 BITs has shown that only 19% of the treaties examined do make such an explicit reference to 'international law' and that a mere 1% refer to 'customary international law'.[145] For the vast majority of BITs containing an FET clause that does not make reference at all to international law, the standard should *not* be considered as an implicit reference to the minimum standard of treatment.[146] Thus, '[a]s a matter of textual interpretation, it seems implausible that a treaty would refer to a well-known concept like the "minimum standard of treatment in customary international law" by using the expression "fair and equitable treatment"'.[147] This is especially the case considering the (above-mentioned) contentious debates between developed and developing States as to the very existence of a minimum standard of treatment.[148] As pointed out by Vasciannie:

> bearing in mind that the international minimum standard has itself been an issue of controversy between developed and developing states for a considerable period, it is unlikely that a majority of states would have accepted the idea that this standard is fully reflected in the fair and equitable standard without clear discussion.[149]

In sum, there are good reasons to interpret the increased use of the term 'fair and equitable treatment' by States in their BITs as a reference to something *other* than the minimum standard of treatment under customary international law. This seems to be the most compelling approach considering the origin and the historical development of the FET standard. Yet, as logical and sound as it may be, this interpretation is *not* convincing in cases where a BIT *does* in fact *explicitly* link the FET standard to 'international law'. Moreover, this interpretation is *simply not* sustainable in situations where parties to a treaty have expressly stated that their intention was in fact for the

---

143. Schreuer & Dolzer, *supra* n. 4, at 124. *See also*: Bronfman, *supra* n. 74, at 621; Laviec, *supra* n. 33, at 94; Salacuse, *supra* n. 10, at 226; Vasciannie, *supra* n. 79, at 105; UNCTAD, *supra* n. 104, at 13.
144. This issue is further discussed below at section §1.02[C].
145. In 2011, the present author received funding from the Canadian federal government ('SSHRC') to investigate the existing rules of customary international law in the field of international investment law. As part of the project, 365 BITs from 28 countries were examined. The findings with respect to the FET clause will be published in 2014-2015. This project is hereinafter referred to as 'P. Dumberry, *Rules of Customary International Law in the Field of International Investment Law*, SSHRC Research Project, (2012-2014)'.
146. UNCTAD, *supra* n. 104, at 13.
147. Schreuer & Dolzer, *supra* n. 4, at 124.
148. Diehl, *supra* n. 17, at 151.
149. Vasciannie, *supra* n. 79, at 131. *See also*: UNCTAD, *supra* n. 104, at 13 ('Attempts to equate the two standards may be perceived as paying insufficient regard to the substantial debate in international law concerning the international minimum standard. More specifically, while the international minimum standard has strong support among developed countries, a number of developing countries have traditionally held reservations as to whether this standard is a part of customary international law. Against this background of uncertainty, it is difficult to assume that most countries have accepted that the international minimum standard should be applied to their investment treaties in instances in which they have not opted to incorporate that standard *expressis verbis*'); Salacuse, *supra* n. 10, at 226-7; Diehl, *supra* n. 17, at 152.

FET standard to make reference to the minimum standard of treatment under custom. These vexing questions are further discussed below.[150]

[C] The Widespread Use of the Standard in Modern BITs

A detailed analysis conducted in the early 1990s of 335 BITs shows that only 28 BITs did not include a reference to FET.[151] From the 1990s onwards, the standard has been included in the vast majority of BITs. Thus, the model BITs adopted by most capital-exporting countries such as Canada, the United States, Germany, the United Kingdom and France, all incorporate an FET clause.[152] It was estimated at the time that by the year 2000, 'bilateral investment treaties which omit reference to fair and equitable treatment constitute the exception rather than the rule'.[153] This is confirmed by Tudor's recent book published in 2008 examining 365 BITs with only 19 of them not containing a reference to fair and equitable treatment.[154] The present author has conducted its own analysis in 2012 of some 365 treaties (not the same treaties as those examined by Tudor) and concluded that only 28 of them did not contain a reference to FET.[155]

The FET standard is now also found in several multilateral investment treaties,[156] in a number of recent FTAs (containing investment chapters),[157] as well as in a number of other multilateral economic instruments.[158] Another remarkable feature of recent State practice is the fact that the FET clause has been embraced not only by developed States, but also by developing States.[159] The standard has thus been included in regional multilateral instruments relative to the protection of foreign investments in Europe,[160] Latin America,[161] Asia,[162] and Africa.[163] The standard has also been included in BITs entered into *between* developing countries;[164] and in Model BITs of developing States (including Chile and China).[165]

---

150. *See*, at section §1.03 below.
151. Khalil, *supra*, n. 129, at 351-355.
152. Vasciannie, *supra* n. 79, at 129.
153. *Ibid.*, at 114.
154. Tudor, *supra* n. 4, at 23.
155. Dumberry, *supra* n. 145.
156. *See*, the analysis in: Tudor, *supra* n. 4, at 45 ff.
157. These treaties are listed in: OECD, *supra* n. 52, at 78.
158. *See*, for instance, Article 12(d), *Convention Establishing the Multilateral Investment Guarantee Agency*, in ILM 24 (1985) 1605: *Fourth Convention of the African, Caribbean and Pacific Group of States (ACP) and the European Economic Community (EEC) ("Lomé IV").*
159. OECD, *supra* n. 52, at 78; Vasciannie, *supra* n. 79, at 119, 122; UNCTAD, *supra* n. 68, at 4; OECD, *supra* n. 96, at 5.
160. *Energy Charter Treaty* (1995), Article 10(1), in: 34 ILM 373 (1995).
161. *Colonia Protocol on Reciprocal Promotion and Protection of Investments*, Article 3, signed by the MERCOSUR States in 1994, in: UNCTAD, *International Investment Instruments: A Compendium*, Vol. 2 (United Nations 1996) at 513.
162. *ASEAN Treaty for the Promotion and Protection of Investments*, Article IV, in: 27 ILM 612 (1987).
163. *Common Market for Eastern and Southern Africa* (COMESA), Article 159(1)a).
164. Vasciannie, *supra* n. 79, at 129-130; OECD, *supra* n. 96, at 5.
165. Vasciannie, *supra* n. 79, at 129.

While the vast majority of BITs include an FET clause, there nevertheless remains a considerable degree of variation in the actual content of the clause.[166] These variations can be summarized as follows:[167]

- Reference to the FET solely in a treaty preamble which therefore does not impose any binding obligations on the host State.
- Autonomous and unqualified reference to the FET.
- Reference to the FET in combination with other standards of protection (such as national treatment and the Most-Favored-Nations clause).
- Reference to the FET with an additional specification that this treatment prohibits arbitrary and discretionary measures.
- Reference to the FET combined with a reference to international law.
- Reference to the FET combined with a reference to customary international law.

The present author's own analysis of some 365 BITs has shown that a large number of FET clauses (197) contain some additional specifications that this treatment prohibits arbitrary and/or discriminatory measures.[168] It also indicates that while a number of BITs (65) contain an 'unqualified' stand-alone FET clause, an equally significant number of other treaties make explicit reference to international law (70) or to customary international law (5).[169] This book focuses on Article 1105 of the NAFTA, which makes explicit reference to 'international law'.

§1.03 THE INTERACTION BETWEEN THE MINIMUM STANDARD OF TREATMENT AND THE FAIR AND EQUITABLE TREATMENT STANDARD

The question of the interaction between the minimum standard of treatment and the FET standard has been amply debated in the field of investor-State arbitration. This section first briefly examines this controversial issue (section §1.03[A]). We will then examine the practice of tribunals (section §1.03[B]). Finally, a third section will discuss the specific situation under NAFTA Article 1105 (section §1.03[C]).

---

166. Kläger, *supra* n. 41, at 22.
167. The present typology is based on the work of Tudor, *supra* n. 4, at 22 ff; Kläger, *supra* n. 41, at 9 ff.; Diehl, *supra* n. 17, at 129 ff. UNCTAD, *supra* n. 68, at xiii, identifies four different approaches: '(a) Unqualified obligation to accord fair and equitable treatment; (b) FET obligation linked to international law; (c) FET obligation linked to the minimum standard of treatment of aliens under customary international law; (d) FET obligation with additional substantive content such as denial of justice'.
168. Dumberry, *supra* n. 145.
169. *See also*: Jack Coe, *Fair And Equitable Treatment Under NAFTA's Investment Chapter*, 96 ASIL Proc. 9, 18 (2002), examining some 500 BITs and finding only 12% of them containing a reference to international law.

[A] Is the Fair and Equitable Treatment an Autonomous Standard or Is It Linked to the Minimum Standard of Treatment Under International Law?

On this issue, the following two distinct approaches have been adopted by writers:[170]

- First, FET can be viewed as an *independent* treaty standard that has a distinct and separate meaning from the minimum standard of treatment. In this context, the standard would provide treatment protections *above and beyond* the minimum standard of treatment. From this perspective, the level of treatment required by the host State would be *more extensive* than that existing under custom and foreign investors would be given *more rights*. This approach is generally referred to as the 'additive' or the 'plain meaning' theory (because the terms 'fair and equitable' are given their ordinary meaning under such an interpretation).[171] As further discussed below,[172] it has even been argued by some supporters of this approach that the FET has now, in fact, emerged as a rule of customary international law *of its own*.[173] For one author, the minimum standard of treatment and the FET standard should be considered as two distinct customary standards with only the latter operating in the field of international investment law.[174]

- Second, FET can be viewed as a reflection of the minimum standard of treatment under customary international law. From this perspective (sometimes referred to as the 'equalizing' approach), the standard would *not* provide treatment protections above and beyond the minimum standard of treatment.[175] Under this interpretation, the FET standard is *one* of the elements encompassed under the umbrella concept of the minimum standard of treatment.[176]

---

170. These approaches are examined in: Newcombe & Paradell, *supra* n. 41, at 263; Tudor, *supra* n. 4, at 53 ff.
171. UNCTAD, *International Investment Agreements: Key Issues,* 212 (2004); Newcombe & Paradell, *supra* n. 41, at 264.
172. *See,* at Chapter 2 section §2.03[B][3] below.
173. *See,* Tudor, *supra* n. 4, at 65-68; Diehl, *supra* n. 17, at 10-11, 125-153, 175-179; Todd Weiler, *NAFTA Investment Arbitration and the Growth of International Economic Law,* 2 Bus. L. Int'l, 188 (2002); I. Laird, *Betrayal, Shock and Outrage - Recent Developments in NAFTA Article 1105,* in *NAFTA Investment Law and Arbitration: The Early Years* 70, 74 (T. Weiler ed., Transnational Publ. 2004); Jan Schokkaert & Yvon Heckscher, *International Investments Protection: Comparative Law Analysis of Bilateral and Multilateral Interstate Conventions, Doctrinal Texts and Arbitral Jurisprudence Concerning Foreign Investments* 331 (Bruylant 2009).
174. Tudor, *supra* n. 4 at 62, 65, for whom the minimum standard 'remains a customary international law standard to be respected by the State, independently from the FET' (at 67), but adding that 'each one of the two standards is designed however to operate in a specific field of international law, has a distinctive function, and is enforceable under different circumstances and in different types of fora' (at 66).
175. UNCTAD, *supra,* n. 41, at xv; Bronfman, *supra* n. 74, at 623.
176. Newcombe & Paradell, *supra* n. 41, at 264.

37

As mentioned above,[177] Western States started to include references to the FET standard in their BITs throughout the 1960s and 1970s not only *because* of the ambiguities surrounding the concept of the minimum standard of treatment, but also due to the fact that at the time, developing States were rejecting the concept. Thus, in the context of BITs between developed and developing States, the introduction of the FET standard must have had a distinct meaning in relation to the minimum standard of treatment. These historical developments support the theory that the FET is an *independent* treaty standard with an autonomous meaning from the minimum standard of treatment. This is the position adopted by the majority of writers.[178] It should be noted, however, that a number of scholars have rejected this interpretation.[179]

---

177. *See*, at section §1.02[B] above.

178. F.A. Mann, *British Treaties for the Promotion and Protection of Investments*, 52 British YBIL, 241, 244 (1981) ('The terms "fair and equitable treatment" envisage conduct which goes far beyond the minimum standard and afford protection to a greater extent and according to a much more objective standard than any previously employed form of words. A tribunal would not be concerned with a minimum, maximum or average standard. It will have to decide whether in all the circumstances the conduct in issue is fair and equitable or unfair and inequitable. No standard defined by other words is likely to be material. The terms are to be understood and applied independently and autonomously'); Newcombe & Paradell, *supra* n. 41, at 263; Dolzer & Stevens, *supra* n. 74, at 60; Vasciannie, *supra* n. 79, at 144 ('These considerations point ultimately towards the conclusion that the two standards in question are not identical: both standards may overlap significantly with respect to issues such as arbitrary treatment, discrimination and unreasonableness, but the presence of a provision assuring fair and equitable treatment in an investment instrument does not automatically incorporate the international minimum standard for foreign investors'); P. Muchlinski, *Multinational Enterprises and the Law*, 635-647 (2nd ed. Oxford U. Press 2007); C. McLachlan, L. Shore & M. Weiniger, *International Investment Arbitration: Substantive Principles*, 226-247 (Oxford U. Press 2007); Dolzer & Schreuer, *supra* n. 4, at 124-128; Tudor, *supra* n. 4, at 53-104; Diehl, *supra* n. 17, at 151-152; C. Schreuer, *Fair and Equitable Standard (FET): Interaction with Other Standards*, 4(5) Transnational Disp. Mgmt. 17 (2007); R. Dolzer, *Fair and Equitable Treatment: A Key Standard in Investment Treaties*, 39(1) Int'l Law, 360 (2005); Haeri, *supra* n. 2, at 34 (2011); Kinnear, *supra* n. 101, at 7; Margaret Clare Ryan, *Glamis Gold, Ltd. v. The United States and the Fair and Equitable Treatment Standard*, 56(4) McGill LJ 932-934 (2011); Salacuse, *supra* n. 10, at 226-227; Roy Preiswerk, *New Developments in Bilateral Investment Protection - With Special Reference to Belgian Practice*, 3 RBDI 173, 186 (1967); Nigel Blackaby, Constantine Partasides, Alan Redfern & J. Martin H. Hunter, *Redfern and Hunter on International Arbitration*, 494 (Oxford U. Press 2009).

179. Picherack, *supra* n. 21, at 260-262, 265, 291 ('there is good evidence that States intended for the fair and equitable treatment standard in their investment agreements to be a reference to the minimum standard of treatment. The minimum standard of treatment in customary international law has traditionally been construed narrowly, though it has evolved according to the evolution in State practice and international law. The fair and equitable treatment standard should be understood and applied in accordance with this narrow scope, as outlined in many NAFTA and other non-NAFTA decisions'); Thomas, *supra* n. 19, at 50 ('While the precise wording varied, it is evident that states propounding the negotiation of investment protection treaties saw a clear and intended link between constant (or full) protection and security, fair and equitable treatment, and the international minimum standard at general international law. The former were considered to be expressions of the latter'); Mayeda, *supra* n. 74, at 273-291; Orellana, *supra* n. 2, at 7; Barnali Choudhury, *Evolution or Devolution? Defining Fair and Equitable Treatment in International Investment Law*, 6(2) J. World Invest. & Trade 317-320 (2005); Sornarajah, *supra* n. 81, at 170 ff.; Charles Leben, *L'évolution du Droit International des Investissements*, in: Société Française pour le Droit International, *Un accord multilatéral sur l'investissement: d'un forum de négociation à l'autre?* 7-28 (1999); Maximo Romero Jiménez,

Apart from the historical origin of the FET standard from the 1960s and 1970s,[180] scholars have put forward a number of other arguments supporting the autonomous approach. One such argument frequently invoked is that the minimum standard is not appropriate to address the complexities of modern trade and investment.[181] Another argument often cited is that equalizing the FET standard to the minimum standard would limit the rights offered to investors to 'extreme cases' only.[182] The autonomous approach, on the contrary, 'offers the foreign Investor a type of guarantee which is much more generous and designed to be operational'.[183] In practical terms, it is often argued that to equate the FET standard to the minimum standard would result in providing investors with a lower level of protection that would otherwise be provided under the FET conceived as an autonomous standard.[184] It has also been argued that it could not have been the intention of States to lower the standard of protection when in fact they signed treaties to grant the best protection to investors.[185] For all these reasons, some writers believe that 'neither investors nor host States would benefit from equating the FET standard with the IMS'.[186]

Another often cited argument is that the application of the plain-meaning approach would have the considerable advantage of improving 'the uniformity of the interpretation of the standard issued by Arbitral Tribunals'.[187] However, the reality is that the adoption of the plain-meaning approach does not provide much guidance to tribunals as to how to actually interpret what is 'fair' and 'equitable'. These are somewhat subjective and vague terms that lack precision.[188] In fact, the plain-meaning approach may have the opposite effect by increasing uncertainty with 'the potential proliferation of multiple interpretations and applications of the standard, raising the potential for inconsistent and conflicting decisions and reasoning'.[189]

A further difficulty raised by the adoption of the plain-meaning approach is that it does not 'refer to an established body of law or to existing legal precedents' but instead 'presumes that, in each case, the question will be whether the foreign investor has been treated fairly and equitably, without reference to any technical understanding

---

Considerations of NAFTA Chapter 11, 2 Chicago JIL 243, 244 (2001); Paparinskis, *supra* n. 3, at 163; Montt, *supra* n. 131, at 302-310.
180. Tudor, *supra* n. 4, at 65-66; Haeri, *supra* n. 2, at 34.
181. Tudor, *supra* n. 4, at 65-68. *Contra*: Paparinskis, *supra* n. 3, at 164.
182. Tudor, *supra* n. 4, at 67. *See also*: Diehl, *supra* n. 17, at 151.
183. Tudor, *supra* n. 4, at 67. *See also*: Diehl, *supra* n. 17, at 151.
184. Bronfman, *supra* n. 74, at 666.
185. *Ibid.*, at 666, 678.
186. Diehl, *supra* n. 17, at 152.
187. Bronfman, *supra* n. 74, at 673. *See also*: Kläger, *supra* n. 41, at 87 ('fair and equitable treatment should construed as representing only one single concept. Any division into distinct constructions of the standard - such as a presumably lower customary minimum standard and a presumably higher self-contained standard - would threaten consistency in international investment law. It would furthermore cause remarkable uncertainties for states and investors in relation to the implications of slightly differing formulations in investment treaties. Additionally, it would encourage forum shopping of investors, in order to receive the highest possible level of protection').
188. Salacuse, *supra* n. 10, at 228; Vasciannie, *supra* n. 79, at 103.
189. Picherack, *supra* n. 21, at 261.

of the meaning of fair and equitable treatment'.[190] The fact that arbitral tribunals are invited to apply their own view of what is 'fair,' or 'equitable' has been considered by one author as 'extremely dangerous to good governance'.[191] To be fair, linking FET with the MST does not eliminate the difficulties associated with interpretation. For UNCTAD, 'it presupposes the existence of a general consensus as to what constitutes the minimum standard of treatment of aliens under customary international law' when in fact 'the minimum standard itself is highly indeterminate, lacks a clearly defined content and requires interpretation'.[192]

Finally, some writers have argued that the whole controversy is misguided and that the dichotomy is based on false assumptions.[193] And while there is some truth to that, this debate cannot be solved in purely abstract terms. In fact, the practice of tribunals shows that the solution will essentially depend on the specific drafting of each FET clause. This question will be discussed in the next section.

[B]   The Practice of Tribunals: The Solution Depends on the Drafting of the Fair and Equitable Treatment Clause

As mentioned above, while the vast majority of BITs do include an FET clause, there exist several different formulations of these clauses.[194] The most important drafting distinction lies between the following two groups of provisions:[195]

- Clauses explicitly linking the FET standard to the standard existing under international law.
- Clauses containing an unqualified formulation of the FET obligation (i.e., a stand-alone obligation to provide FET without any reference to international law).

The approach developed by tribunals shows that these different formulations are pivotal elements in the determination of the actual scope of the FET obligation. Thus, arbitral tribunals have adopted either the plain-meaning or the equalizing approach

---

190. Vasciannie, *supra* n. 79, at 103.
191. Orellana, *supra* n. 2, at 7, adding that such 'kind of second-guessing of governmental action ... invited by this type of standard is antithetical to democracy and is indefensible'.
192. UNCTAD, *supra* n. 68, at 28. *See also*: Kläger, *supra* n. 41, at 264.
193. McLachlan et al., *supra* n. 178, at 203. *See also*: Kläger, *supra* n. 41, at 86 ('it seems that the "controversy" is misguided, and [that] the dichotomy presented by the opposing views is a false one on a number of levels. Arguably, these misconceptions are based on simplistic premises and a false perspective in addressing fair and equitable treatment. In particular, the dichotomy is presented as a struggle between a presumably restrictive and clear-cut minimum standard and a far reaching fair and equitable treatment obligation that is at the disposal of arbitrators'). For him, both approaches are 'ultimately incapable of explaining comprehensively the role of international law in the construction of fair and equitable treatment' (at 111). He insists that tribunals should take 'arguments from any source of international law' so that they have 'the opportunity to provide comprehensive reasoning and thereby to manage all social and legal developments influencing a particular investment dispute' without 'being based on the wrong premise of pegging a high or low level of protection for foreign investors' (at 111).
194. *See*, at section §1.02[C].
195. UNCTAD, *supra* n. 68, at 17.

depending on the actual drafting of the FET clause.[196] This is the conclusion reached by a 2004 OECD paper:

> Because of the differences in its formulation, the proper interpretation of the 'fair and equitable treatment' standard depends on the specific wording of the particular treaty, its context, the object and purpose of the treaty, as well as on negotiating history or other indications of the parties' intent. For example, some treaties include explicit language linking or, in some cases limiting, fair and equitable treatment to the minimum standard of international customary law. Other treaties which either link the standard to international law without specifying custom, or lack any reference to international law, could, depending on the context of the parties' intent, for example, be read as giving the standard a scope of application that is broader than the minimum standard as defined by international customary law.[197]

A 2012 UNCTAD report further suggests that the drafting variations in FET clauses have in fact been interpreted as meaning *different content* as well as *different thresholds*:

> [The] identification of the correct source of the FET standard – whether it is grounded in customary international law or is a self-standing obligation – can have important consequences in terms of the standard's content and, more precisely, of the types of State measures that can be challenged as well as the required threshold for finding a violation, that is, the required degree of seriousness of the breach.[198]

Many arbitral tribunals have therefore interpreted an unqualified FET standard as 'delinked from customary international law' and have therefore 'focused on the plain-meaning of the terms "fair" and "equitable,"' which 'may result in a low liability threshold and brings with it a risk for State regulatory action to be found in breach of it'.[199] This phenomenon has been recognized by many scholars.[200] The vast majority of tribunals have interpreted an unqualified FET standard as having an autonomous

---

196. UNCTAD, *supra* n. 68, at xiv; Newcombe & Paradell, *supra* n. 41, at 263-264; Paparinskis, *supra* n. 3, at 94.
197. OECD, *supra* n. 96, at 40. *See also*: Yannaca-Small, *supra* n. 101, at 113-114.
198. UNCTAD, *supra* n. 68, at 8.
199. *Ibid.*, at 22.
200. Haeri, *supra* n. 2, at 26 ('the fair and equitable treatment standard has emerged in investment arbitration jurisprudence as a distinct and relatively broad standard where it is not expressly linked with the international minimum standard. By contrast, the development of the international minimum standard, in accordance with customary international law, has been more cautious: the threshold for violating the standard remains high'); R. Dolzer, *Fair And Equitable Treatment International Law, Remarks*, 100 ASIL Proc. 69 (2006); Yannaca-Small, *supra* n. 101, at 115; Christopher F. Dugan, Don Wallace, Jr., Noah Rubins & Borzu Sabahi, *Investor-State Arbitration* 496 (Oxford U. Press 2008); Dolzer & Schreuer, *supra* n. 4, at 126; Kläger, *supra* n. 41, at 85. On the contrary, *see* the position adopted by the following writers: Stephan Schill, *Fair and Equitable Treatment as an Embodiment of the Rule of Law*, in *The International Convention on the Settlement of Investment Disputes (ICSID): Taking Stock after 40 Years* 33 (R. Hofmann & C. Tams eds., Nomos 2007) (stating that it is 'questionable whether substantial differences result from the different framing of the standard with a view to the actual practice of investment tribunals'); Kenneth J. Vandevelde, *A Unified Theory of Fair and Equitable Treatment*, 43 N.Y.U. J. Int'l L. & Pol. 47 (2010) ('Differences in the contexts in which the standard appears have made little difference to tribunals interpreting the standard. Rather, the awards have yielded a single coherent theory of the standard, although perhaps not consciously so').

character, which hence provides a level of treatment higher than under the minimum standard.[201] In fact, only a limited number of tribunals have interpreted an unqualified FET standard as an implicit reference to international law.[202]

A good illustration is the tribunal's reasoning in *Saluka*, which held that the FET standard had an autonomous character in the specific context of the BIT at hand precisely because it was not linked to international law.[203] The tribunal added that in the context of such an autonomous FET clause, 'in order to violate the standard, it may be sufficient that States' conduct displays a relatively lower degree of inappropriateness'[204] while in contrast, under the minimum standard, 'in order to violate that standard, States' conduct may have to display a relatively higher degree of inappropriateness'.[205]

This situation contrasts with the approach adopted by tribunals faced with an FET clause containing an explicit reference to 'international law'.[206] Tribunals have overall been divided on the proper interpretation and use of these words. While some tribunals have held that the term 'international law' found in an FET clause was a reference to the minimum standard under custom,[207] others have interpreted such an express reference in much the same way as an unqualified FET standard.[208]

The same assessment can be made with regards to FET clauses containing a slightly different reference to international law: 'investment shall at all times be

---

201. See Newcombe & Paradell, *supra* n. 41, at 263–264, referring to the following cases: *MTD Equity Sdn. Bhd. & MTD Chile S.A. v. Chile.*, ICSID Case No. ARB/01/7, Award, (25 May 2004), paras. 110–112; *Occidental Exploration and Production Company v. Ecuador*, LCIA Case No. UN3467, Final Award, (1 July 2004), paras. 188–190; *CMS Gas Transmission Company v. Argentina*, ICSID Case No. ARB/01/8, Award, (12 May 2005), paras. 282–284; *Saluka v. Czech Republic*, Partial Award, (17 March 2006), paras. 286–295; *LG&E Energy Corp., LG&E Capital Corp., and LG&E International, Inc v. Argentina*, Decision on Liability, (3 October 2006), para. 125-131; *PSEG Global Inc. and Konya Ilgin Elektrik Üretim ve Ticaret Limited Şirketi v. Turkey*, ICSID Case No. ARB/02/5, Award, (19 January 2007), para. 239.
202. See, for instance, *Siemens AG v. Argentina*, ICSID No. ARB/02/8, Award, (17 January 2007), para. 291.
203. *Saluka v. Czech Republic*, Partial Award, (17 March 2006), para. 294. '[Article 3.1 of the Treaty] omits any express reference to the customary minimum standard. The interpretation of Article 3.1 does not therefore share the difficulties that may arise under treaties (such as the NAFTA) which expressly tie the "fair and equitable treatment" standard to the customary minimum standard. Avoidance of these difficulties may even be regarded as the very purpose of the lack of a reference to an international standard in the Treaty. This clearly points to the autonomous character of a "fair and equitable treatment" standard such as the one laid down in Article 3.1 of the Treaty'.
204. *Ibid.*, para. 293. See also: *Enron Corporation and Ponderosa Assets, L.P. v. Argentina*, ICSID No. ARB/01/3, Award, (22 May 2007), para. 258.
205. *Saluka v. Czech Republic*, Partial Award, (17 March 2006), para. 292.
206. UNCTAD, *supra* n. 68, at 22.
207. See, in particular, *M.C.I. Power Group L.C. and New Turbine, Inc. v. Ecuador*, ICSID No. ARB/03/6, Award, (31 July 2007), para. 369 ('The Tribunal notes that fair and equitable treatment conventionally obliges States parties to the BIT to respect the standards of treatment required by international law. The international law mentioned in Article II of the BIT refers to customary international law …').
208. See, for instance, *Compañía de Aguas del Aconquija S.A. and Vivendi Universal S.A. v. Argentina*, ICSID No. ARB/97/3, Award, (20 August 2007), paras. 7.4.5 ff.; *Técnicas Medioambientales Tecmed, S.A. v. Mexico*, ICSID No. ARB(AF)/00/2, Award, (29 May 2003), para. 155.

accorded fair and equitable treatment ... and shall in no case be accorded treatment less than that required by international law'. Under this clause, the FET standard is *not* directly linked or attached to the level of treatment existing under international law; international law only sets a floor below which State actions are considered illegal.[209] A number of tribunals have interpreted such a clause in much the same way as an autonomous FET clause, thus requiring a treatment 'additional to, or beyond that of, customary law'.[210] Other tribunals have, on the contrary, held that such a clause provides for a standard of protection no different than that of the MST under custom.[211]

The fact that variances in FET clause drafting translates to variances in content and levels of liability is further evidenced by the reactions of several States in recent years. Many of them have started to explicitly specify in their most recent BITs that FET is not only linked to international law, but that it is a reference to the MST under custom.[212] As further discussed below,[213] this is clearly the path that has been followed by NAFTA Parties. This recent phenomenon however, is not limited to NAFTA States.[214] As further discussed below,[215] a number of recent treaties *not only* explicitly state that 'international law' is an allusion to custom, but *also* provide an express and precise definition of customary international law. States have also started to conclude treaties that contain language that provides additional clarification on the meaning of the FET obligation.[216] The UNCTAD report speaks of an 'emerging trend' where BITs are adding 'substantive content to FET clauses,' such as the prohibition of denial of justice or the prohibition of arbitrary, unreasonable or discriminatory measures.[217] The goal of such clauses is to clarify the content of the FET obligation and provide additional predictability with regards to its implementation by States and potential subsequent interpretation by tribunals.[218] The language of such a clause may, for instance, be intended to *limit* the scope of the content of the FET standard to the denial

---

209. Laird, *supra* n. 173, at 51; Picherack, *supra* n. 21, at 260; L. Paradell, *The BIT Experience of The Fair And Equitable Treatment Standard*, in *Investment Treaty Law, Current Issues II* 123 (Federico Ortino et al. eds., British IICL 2007); Vandevelde, *supra* n. 200, at 47.
210. *Enron v. Argentina*, Award, (22 May 2007), para. 258. *See also: Sempra Energy International v. Argentina*, ICSID Case No. ARB/02/16, Award, (28 September 2007), para. 302; *Azurix Corp. v. Argentina*, ICSID No. ARB/01/12, Award, (14 July 2006), para. 361; *Lemire v. Ukraine*, ICSID No. ARB/06/18, Decision on Jurisdiction and Liability, (21 January 2010), paras. 253–254.
211. *Occidental Exploration and Production Co v. Ecuador*, Award, (1 July 2004), paras. 188–190; *Lauder v. Czech Republic*, UNCITRAL, Final Award, (3 September 2001), para. 292; *Alex Genin, Eastern Credit Limited, Inc. and A.S. Baltoil Genin v. Estonia*, Award, (25 June 2001), para. 367.
212. UNCTAD, *supra* n. 68, at 29, explaining the reasons why States may want to make such changes: 'from the host country perspective, linking the FET standard to the minimum standard of treatment of aliens may be seen as a progressive step, given that this will likely lead tribunals to apply a higher threshold for finding a breach of the standard, as compared with unqualified FET clauses'.
213. *See*, at Chapter 2 section §2.02[C][5] below.
214. Many treaties are mentioned in: UNCTAD, *supra* n. 68, at 25.
215. *See*, at Chapter 2 section §2.02[C][5] below.
216. UNCTAD, *supra* n. 68, at 13; Haeri, *supra* n. 2, at 43, 45; Tudor, *supra* n. 4, at 33; David A. Gantz, *The Evolution of FTA Investment Provisions: From NAFTA to the United States - Chile Free Trade Agreement*, 19(4) Am. U. L. Rev., 724-731 (2003).
217. UNCTAD, *supra* n. 68, at 30.
218. *Ibid.*, at 29–30.

of justice. This approach has been adopted by NAFTA Parties[219] and also by other States.[220]

[C]   The Specific Features of NAFTA Article 1105

As mentioned above,[221] the present author believes that there are *in general*, good reasons to interpret the term 'fair and equitable treatment' found in most BITs, as a reference to something *other than* the minimum standard of treatment under custom. This is certainly the case when an FET clause is unqualified and contains no reference whatsoever to international law.[222] One notable difficulty is the interpretation of those other FET clauses that *do* refer to international law. Case law seems to be divided on how to properly interpret such clauses. What was the actual intention of the parties when they made reference to those terms?[223] In the present author's view, any possible ambiguities disappear when there is clear and undeniable evidence that the intention of the State parties was in fact that the FET standard be considered as a reference to the minimum standard of treatment under custom.[224] This is clearly the case under NAFTA Article 1105.

---

219. *See*, for instance, the specification that the FET standard 'includes the obligation not to deny justice in criminal, civil, or administrative adjudicatory proceedings in accordance with the principle of due process embodied in the principal legal systems of the world' which is found in the following two BITs entered by the United States: Treaty between the United States and Uruguay Concerning the Encouragement and Reciprocal Protection of Investment, with Annexes and Protocol, signed on 4 November 2005, entered into force on 1 November 2006, Article 5(1)(2); Treaty between the United States and Rwanda Concerning the Encouragement and Reciprocal Protection of Investment, signed on 19 February 2008, entered into force on 1 January 2012, Article 5(1)(2). A similar clause indicating that 'For greater certainty, "fair and equitable treatment" includes the obligation not to deny justice in criminal, civil or administrative adjudicatory proceedings in accordance with the customary international law minimum standard of treatment of aliens' is also found in one BIT entered into by Canada: Agreement between Canada and Romania for the Promotion and Reciprocal Protection of Investments, signed on 8 May 2009, entered into force on 23 November 2011, Article II(2).
220. *See*, for instance, ASEAN *Comprehensive Investment Agreement* (2009), Article 11; *Investment Agreement for COMESA* (2007) Article 14.
221. *See*, at section §1.02[B] below
222. Kläger, *supra* n. 41, at 61; Haeri, *supra* n. 2, 33 ('Thus, absent specific treaty wording linking the fair and equitable treatment standard with the international minimum standard in customary international law, the better view is that the fair and equitable treatment standard is an autonomous standard. In such circumstances, the fair and equitable treatment standard cannot be construed as a reference to the international minimum standard in customary international law'); C. Schreuer, *Fair and Equitable Treatment in Arbitral Practice*, 6 J. World Invest. & Trade, 363-366, 365, 385 (2005) ('in the context of the NAFTA, it is now established that the term as used in Article 1105(1) therein is no more than a reference to established principles of international law. In other contexts, notably that of BITs' the answer depends on the wording of the particular clause. In the absence of indications to the contrary, the better view is to give it an autonomous meaning').
223. Paparinskis, *supra* n. 3, at 160 ('in abstract terms, differences in treaty practice may, as always, be read in two ways. They may signify that when States wish to refer to customary law they do so in express terms, and the absence of such a reference *a contrario* suggests that the analysis should be limited to treaty law. Alternatively, the uncontroversial practice of making the references to customary law could suggest that some States make *ex abundanti cautela* express an arrangement that would have been otherwise valid').
224. The technique of reference (*renvoi*) is often used in treaties: Paparinskis, *supra* n. 3, at 160.

It follows that the above-mentioned debate as to whether the FET is an autonomous standard or linked to the minimum standard of treatment under international law is simply *not relevant* in the context of NAFTA Article 1105. Schreuer, for instance, argues that as a result of the FTC Note (further discussed below[225]), 'it may now be regarded as established that, in the context of Article 1105(1), the concept of fair and equitable treatment is equivalent to the minimum standard of treatment under customary international law'.[226]

Under Article 1105, the FET standard must be considered as *one of the elements* included in the umbrella concept of the minimum standard of treatment.[227] In fact, this is evident because the provision requires NAFTA Parties to provide foreign investors treatment in accordance with 'international law' (a reference to the minimum standard of treatment as reaffirmed by the FTC Note of Interpretation[228]), *including* fair and equitable treatment. As further discussed below, several NAFTA tribunals have endorsed this approach.[229] The *Waste Management* tribunal made the first ever attempt by a NAFTA tribunal to provide a comprehensive definition of the FET standard. The tribunal refers to the 'minimum standard of treatment of fair and equitable treatment'.[230] This formulation suggests that the FET standard is part of the larger concept of the 'minimum standard of treatment'. The same conclusion was reached in the *Cargill* ruling:

> In summation, the Tribunal finds that the obligations in Article 1105(1) of the NAFTA are to be understood by reference to the customary international law minimum standard of treatment of aliens. The requirement of fair and equitable treatment *is one aspect of this minimum standard.*[231]

Clearly, Article 1105 must be analyzed under very specific parameters that do not exist under most other FET clauses. This book examines what those specific features are and how they have influenced NAFTA tribunals' interpretation of that provision. The specific features of Article 1105 also mean, in turn, that many of the findings related to this provision are not easily transferable and applicable to tribunals operating outside of NAFTA. In other words, a great deal of the controversies examined in this book will have no impact outside the NAFTA context. This is certainly the case for the vast

---

225. *See*, at Chapter 2 section §2.02[C][3] below.
226. Schreuer, *supra* n. 222, at 363.
227. Diehl, *supra* n. 17, at 150 ('the wording of Article 1105(l)- especially the reference to the "Minimum standard of Treatment" in the heading - suggests that under the NAFTA provision FET is part of general international law, more specifically IMS').
228. *See*, at Chapter 2 section §2.02[C][3] below.
229. *See*, for instance, *United Parcel Service of America Inc. v. Canada* [hereinafter *UPS v. Canada*], UNCITRAL, Award (Jurisdiction), (22 November 2002), para. 97 ('the obligation to accord fair and equitable treatment is not in addition to or beyond the minimum standard. Our reasons in brief are, first, that that reading accords with the ordinary meaning of article 1105. That obligation is "included" within the minimum standard').
230. *Waste Management v. Mexico*, Award, (30 April 2004), para. 98.
231. *Cargill, Inc. v. Mexico*, Award, (18 September 2009), para. 296 (emphasis added). It should be noted that the tribunal in *Glamis v. United States*, Award, (8 June 2009), para. 627, speaks of 'the customary international law minimum standard of treatment, as codified in Article 1105 of the NAFTA'. This formulation suggests that FET and full protection and security are in fact the *only two* elements comprised in the umbrella concept of the minimum standard of treatment.

majority of BITs that contain an *unqualified* FET clause *not* linked in any way to international law.[232] Yet, the conclusion the present author intends to draw from NAFTA case law will, to a large extent, apply to FET clauses containing language similar to that of Article 1105 for which the standard is expressly linked to international law (or to the minimum standard of treatment under customary international law). Schreuer summarizes the fundamental reasons why findings of tribunals reached in the context of NAFTA are irrelevant in the context of FET clauses that are worded differently:

- Article 1105 refers to the 'Minimum Standard of Treatment' in its heading.
- Article 1105 refers to 'international law, including fair and equitable treatment,' suggesting that the fair and equitable treatment standard is part of customary international law.
- Article 1105 was the object of a binding interpretation by an authorized treaty body.[233]

---

232. Schreuer, *supra* n. 222, at 363-365; Dolzer & Schreuer, *supra* n. 4, at 126; Salacuse, *supra* n. 10, at 227-228; Emmanuel Gaillard, *C.I.R.D.I., Chronique des sentences arbitrales*, 130 JDI 164 (2003).
233. Schreuer, *supra* n. 222, at 364. *See also*: Salacuse, *supra* n. 10, at 226.

CHAPTER 2

The Meaning of Article 1105

This chapter focuses on the meaning of the FET clause in Article 1105. We will begin with an analysis of the history of Article 1105 (section §2.01). This section examines earlier treaty practices by Canada and the United States with regards to FET clauses before 1994. We will then discuss the evolution of the preliminary negotiation texts of Article 1105. The next section (section §2.02) will survey the different rules of international law on treaty interpretation and attempt to discover whether they can serve as guidance to determine the real meaning of Article 1105. The final section will look at how NAFTA tribunals have interpreted the meaning and scope of this provision (section §2.03).

§2.01 HISTORY OF ARTICLE 1105

[A] Earlier Treaty Practice of the Parties before NAFTA

This section examines State practice of Canada and the United States regarding the inclusion of FET clauses in investment treaties before the entry into force of the NAFTA in 1994.[1] As mentioned above, Mexico had never entered into a treaty that made reference to the concept of FET before NAFTA.

Before the Second World War, the United States entered into several bilateral treaties on Friendship, Commerce and Navigation ('FCN') that contained a provision to the effect that nationals of the other party should be accorded 'the most constant protection and security for their persons and property, and shall enjoy in this respect that degree of protection that is required by international law'.[2] After the war, several

---

1. These developments are examined in detail in: Kenneth J. Vandevelde, *United States Investment Treaties: Policy and Practice* (Kluwer Law 1992); M. Kinnear, A. Bjurklund & J.F.G. Hannaford, *Investment Disputes under NAFTA: An Annotated Guide to NAFTA Chapter 11* (Kluwer Law International 2006), section on Article 1105, at 8.
2. These treaties are examined in: J.C. Thomas, *Reflections on Article 1105 of NAFTA: History, State Practice and the Influence of Commentators*, 17(1) ICSID Rev. 39 (2002); Stephen

FCN treaties also contained an express assurance that nationals of the other party would receive an 'equitable' treatment in addition to protection under international law.[3] In a number of other FCN treaties, reference was also made to 'fair and equitable' treatment.[4] It is generally recognized that these slightly different formulations had no bearing in terms of the scope of protection offered under the treaty.[5]

It was only during the 1980s that the United States began to actively sign BITs.[6] It is noteworthy that at the time, the 1982 US Model BIT required Parties to provide protection under international law, but did not contain a reference to 'fair and equitable' treatment.[7] Such reference was found for the first time in the 1982 US-Panama BIT, which specified that the FET 'shall be in accordance with applicable national laws and international law'.[8] While only a few of the BITs ratified in the 1980s used the same language,[9] others referred to the FET standard 'in accordance with applicable national laws', but added that such treatment should be no 'less than that required by international law' (this type of clause will be referred to hereinafter as a 'no less' FET clause).[10]

Vasciannie, *The Fair and Equitable Treatment Standard in International Investment Law and Practice,* 70 British YIL 110 (1999); Kinnear et al., *supra* n. 1, at 8; Todd Weiler, *An Historical Analysis of the Function of the Minimum Standard of Treatment in International Investment Law,* in *New Directions in International Economic Law: In Memoriam Thomas Wälde* 346 (Todd Weiler & Freya Baetens eds., Martinus Nijhoff 2011).

3.   A typical clause reads as follow: 'Each party shall at all time accord equitable treatment to the capital of nationals and companies of the other party (...)'. OECD, *International Investment Law: A Changing Landscape: A Companion Volume to International Investment Perspectives* 77 (2005), indicates that US FCN treaties with Ireland (1950), Greece (1954), Israel (1954), France (1960), Pakistan (1961), Belgium (1963) and Luxembourg (1963) contained such reference to 'equitable treatment'.

4.   *Ibid.*, referring to treaties entered into with the Federal Republic of Germany (1956), Ethiopia (1953) and the Netherlands (1957).

5.   A.A. Fatouros, *Government Guarantees to Foreign Investors* 167 (Columbia U. Press 1962); Kenneth J. Vandevelde, *The Bilateral Treaty Program of the United States,* 21 Cornell Int'l L.J. 220 (1988).

6.   Vandevelde, *supra* n. 1, at 217-218. *See also* Patricia M. Robin, *The BIT Won't Bite: The American Bilateral Investment Treaty Program,* 33 Am. U. L. Rev. 931 (1984).

7.   Draft Treaty Between the United States and ____ Concerning the Reciprocal Encouragement and Protection of Investments, 11 January 1982, (hereinafter the '1982 Model BIT'), in: Vandevelde, *supra* n. 1, at Appendix A-1 ('[t]he treatment, protection and security of investments shall never be less than that required by international law').

8.   Treaty between the United States and Panama Concerning the Treatment and Protection of Investments, 1982, signed on 27 October 1982, entered into force on 30 May 1991, Article II(2). *See also*: K.J. Vandevelde, *Bilateral Investment Treaties: History, Policy and Interpretation* 201 (Oxford U. Press 2010).

9.   Treaty between the United States and Cameroon Concerning the Reciprocal Encouragement and Protection of Investment, signed on 26 February 1986, entered into force on 6 April 1989, Article II(4). *See also*: Treaty between the United States and Egypt Concerning the Reciprocal Encouragement and Protection of Investments, signed on 29 September 1982, entered into force on 27 June 1992, Article II(4) (containing in essence the same clause: 'The treatment, protection and security of investments shall never be less than that required by international law and national legislation').

10. Treaty between the United States and Bangladesh Concerning the Reciprocal Encouragement and Protection of Investment, signed on 12 March 1986, entered into force on 25 July 1989, Article II(3); Treaty between the United States and Senegal Concerning the Reciprocal Encouragement and Protection of Investment, with Protocol, signed on 6 December 1983, entered into force on 25 October 1990, Art. II(4); Treaty between the United States and Zaire

The reference to 'applicable national law' was later abandoned in subsequent BITs containing a 'no less' clause.[11]

These changes were reflected in the 1987 US Model BIT, which also contained a 'no less' type of clause.[12] The exact same FET clause was adopted in thirteen of the BITs signed by the United States in the 1990s.[13] The 1994 US Model BIT also included a 'no less' type of clause (with a slight variation of language).[14] It should also be noted

---

Concerning the Reciprocal Encouragement and Protection of Investment, with Protocol, signed on 3 August 3, 1984, entered into force on 28 July 1989, Art. II(4).

11. Treaty Between the United States and Grenada Concerning the Reciprocal Encouragement and Protection of Investment, signed on 2 May 1986, entered into force on 3 March 1989, Art. II(2).

12. The 1987 Draft Treaty Between the United States and ____ Concerning the Reciprocal Encouragement and Protection of Investments (hereinafter the '1987 Model BIT'), available in: Vandevelde, *supra* n. 1, at Appendix A-4: '[i]nvestment shall at all times be accorded fair and equitable treatment, shall enjoy full protection and security and shall in no case be accorded treatment less than that required by international law'. *See also*: Vandevelde, *supra* n. 1, at 77 referring to the 1983, 1984 and 1987 draft versions of the US Model BIT and to other BITs.

13. Treaty between the United States and the People's Republic of the Congo [Brazzaville] Concerning the Reciprocal Encouragement and Protection of Investment, signed on 12 February 1990, entered into force on 13 August 1994, Art. II(2); Treaty between the United States and Tunisia Concerning the Reciprocal Encouragement and Protection of Investment, with Protocol, signed on 15 May 1990, entered into force on 7 February 1993, Art. II(3); Treaty between the United States and Sri Lanka Concerning the Encouragement and Reciprocal Protection of Investment, with Protocol and Related Exchange of Letters, signed on 20 September 1991, entered into force on 1 May 1993, Art. II(2); Treaty between the United States and Argentina Concerning the Reciprocal Encouragement and Protection of Investment, with Protocol, signed on 14 November 1991; and an Amendment to the Protocol Effected by Exchange of Notes signed on 24 August and 6 November 1992, entered into force on 20 October 1994, Art. II(2); Treaty between the United States and Kazakhstan Concerning the Reciprocal Encouragement and Protection of Investment, Signed on 19 May 1992, entered into force on 12 January 1994, Art. II(2); Treaty between the United States and Romania Concerning the Reciprocal Encouragement and Protection of Investment, with Protocol and Related Exchange of Letters, signed on 28 May 1992, entered into force on 15 January 1994, Art. II(2); Treaty between the United States and Bulgaria Concerning the Encouragement and Reciprocal Protection of Investment, with Protocol and Related Exchange of Letters, signed on 23 September 1992, entered into force on 2 June 1994, Art. II(2); Treaty between the United States and Kyrgyzstan Concerning the Encouragement and Reciprocal Protection of Investment, signed on 19 January 1993, entered into force on 12 January 1994, Art. II(2); Treaty between the United States and Moldova Concerning the Encouragement and Reciprocal Protection of Investment, with Protocol and Related Exchange of Letters, signed on 21 April 1993, entered into force on 25 November 1994, Art. II(3); Treaty between the United States and Poland Concerning Business and Economic Relations, with Protocol and Four Related Exchanges of Letters, signed on 21 March 1990, entered into force on 6 August 1994 (amended on 1 May 2004), Art. II(6); Treaty between the United States and the Czech and Slovak Federal Republic Concerning the Reciprocal Encouragement and Protection of Investments, with Protocol and Three Related Exchange of Letters, signed on 22 October 1991, entered into force on 19 December 1992 (amended on 1 May 2004), Art. II(2); Treaty between the United States and Armenia Concerning the Reciprocal Encouragement and Protection of Investment, signed on 23 September 1992, entered into force on 29 March 1996, Art. II(2); Treaty between the United States and Ecuador Concerning the Encouragement and Reciprocal Protection of Investment, with Protocol and a Related Exchange of Letters, signed on 27 August 1993, entered into force on 11 May 1997, Art. II(3).

14. The 1994 Draft Treaty Between the United States and ____ Concerning the Reciprocal Encouragement and Protection of Investments (hereinafter the '1994 Model BIT'), Article II(3)(a): 'Each Party shall at all times accord to covered investments fair and equitable treatment and full protection and security, and shall in no case accord treatment less favourable than that required by international law'.

that two BITs from the same period refer to FET 'in a manner consistent with international law' instead of the 'no less' formulation.[15] In both cases however, the 'Letter of Submittal' sent by the US State Department to the US President requesting approval of the BIT by the US Senate, described the protection under that provision as according FET 'in no case less than that required by international law'.[16] This suggests that for the US government, these two different formulations basically meant the same thing and provided for the same scope of protection.

In fact, all BITs at the time explicitly linked the FET standard to 'international law'. The exact meaning of that term would later become one of the most contentious issues in NAFTA case law. In his 1992 book on US investment treaty practice, Vandevelde indicates that the reference to international law in 'no less' FET clauses found in most BITs at the time 'serve[d] simply to incorporate customary international law by reference into a BIT'.[17] This last affirmation is supported by the statement made by the US State Department to the Senate about the 'no less' FET clause contained in the 1992 US Model BIT (the same clause as in the 1987 Model BIT) which is described as setting 'a minimum standard of treatment based on customary international law'.[18] This position is also supported by five 'Letters of Submittal' sent by the US State Department to the US President in 1993, requesting approval of the BITs by the US Senate. These 'Letters of Submittal' describe the 'no less' FET clause contained in the treaties as a guarantee that investments shall be granted FET 'in accordance with international law' and adding that 'this paragraph sets out a minimum standard of treatment based on customary international law'.[19] After 1994, all 'Letters of Submittal' sent by the U.S. State Department would systematically contain the same phrase explicitly stating that the term international law constitutes a reference to the minimum standard of treatment under custom.[20]

At this juncture, it is noteworthy to highlight the important fact that the language finally adopted under NAFTA Article 1105 in 1994 is slightly different from the one that until then had been typically used by the United States in its BITs. Thus, at the time, no

---

15. Treaty between the United States and Morocco Concerning the Encouragement and Reciprocal Protection of Investments, with Protocol, signed on 22 July 1985, entered into force on 29 May 1991, Art. II(3); Treaty between the United States and Turkey Concerning the Reciprocal Encouragement and Protection of Investments, with Protocol, signed on 3 December 1985, entered into force on 18 May 1990, Art. II(3).
16. US-Turkey BIT, *ibid.*, 'Letter of Submittal', 19 February 1986; US-Morocco BIT, *ibid.*, 'Letter of Submittal', 20 February 1986.
17. Vandevelde, *supra* n. 1, at 77-78.
18. Description of the United States Model Bilateral Investment Treaty (BIT) – February 1992, Submitted by the State Department, 30 July 1992, in: Hearing before the Committee on the Foreign Relations, United States Senate, 102nd Congress, Second Session, 4 August 1992, S. HRG. 102-795, at 62, quoted in: Andrew Newcombe & Luis Paradell, *Law and Practice of Investment Treaties: Standards of Treatment* 269 (Kluwer 2009).
19. US-Kazakhstan BIT, *supra* n. 13, Letter of Submittal, 4 September 1993; US-Armenia BIT, *supra* n. 13, Letter of Submittal, 27 August 1993; US-Kyrgyzstan BIT, *supra* n. 13, Letter of Submittal, 7 September 1993; US-Moldova BIT, *supra* n. 13, Letter of Submittal, 25 August 1993; US-Ecuador BIT, *supra* n. 13, Letter of Submittal, 7 September 1993.
20. The letters can be found at this page of the website of the Office of the United States Trade Representative: http://tcc.export.gov/Trade_Agreements/Bilateral_Investment_Treaties/index.asp.

US BIT made reference to treatment 'in accordance with international law' *before* the mention of FET. All BITs referred to the two concepts, but in reverse order.

The same is certainly true for Canada's investment treaties. Since 1989, Canada has been entering into Foreign Investment Protection and Promotion Agreements ('FIPAs') largely based on the 1967 OECD Draft Convention.[21] Canada entered into five such agreements between 1990 and 1993. One of them (the Canada-Hungary FIPA) referred to FET without any mention of 'international law'.[22] The other four contained the following clause:

> Investments or returns of investors of either Contracting Party shall at all times be accorded fair and equitable treatment in accordance with principles of international law and shall enjoy full protection and security in the territory of the other Contracting Party.[23]

[B]   The Evolution of the Negotiation Texts

The history of the preliminary negotiation texts that led to the adoption of Article 1105 has been described in detail by Kinnear et al.[24] They explain that in the context of the negotiation of NAFTA, the drafters did not leave any formal set of *travaux préparatoires* but rather only a series of successive negotiation documents, with no explanation regarding the changes between one version and another.[25] This section provides a number of observations on the evolution of the text.[26]

In earlier drafts, the text of the provision had been placed under a general heading and it was only later on that it became a free-standing article under the heading 'Minimum Standard of Treatment'.[27] In any event, all draft versions contained the three basic elements of Article 1105: full protection and security; fair and equitable

---

21. *See*, Kinnear et al., *supra* n. 1, at 9 ff.
22. Agreement between Canada and Hungary for the Promotion and Reciprocal Protection of Investments, signed on 3 October 1991, entered into force on 21 November 1993, Can.-Hung., E101513-CTS 1993 No. 14, Article III(1): 'Investments or returns of investors of either Contracting Party shall at all times be accorded fair and equitable treatment and shall enjoy full protection and security in the territory of the other Contracting Party'.
23. Agreement between Canada and Poland for the Promotion and Reciprocal Protection of Investments, signed on 6 April 1990, entered into force on 22 November 1990, Can.-Pol., E101511-CTS 1990 No. 43, Article III(1); Agreement between Canada and the Union of Soviet Socialist Republics for the Promotion and Reciprocal Protection of Investments, signed on 20 November 1989, entered into force on 27 June 1991, E101516 – CTS 1991 No. 31, Article III(1); Agreement between Canada and Argentina for the Promotion and Reciprocal Protection of Investments, signed on 5 November 1991, entered into force on 29 April 1993, E101514 – CTS 1993 No. 11, Article II(4); Agreement between Canada and the Czech and Slovak Federal Republic for the Promotion and Protection of Investments, signed on 15 November 1990, entered into force on 22 January 2012, E101515 – CTS 1992 No. 10, Article III(1).
24. Kinnear et al., *supra* n. 1, at 1.
25. *Ibid.*, (section on Article 1131), at 14.
26. On 16 July 2004, the NAFTA FTC issued a Joint Statement determining that the document related to the negotiation history of the NAFTA would be released to the public. These documents are available for consultation at this page of the website of the Ministry of Foreign Affairs of Canada: http://www.international.gc.ca/trade-agreements-accords-commerciaux/disp-diff/trilateral_neg.aspx?lang=en&view=d.
27. Kinnear et al., *supra* n. 1, at 3.

treatment; and a reference to international law. It is only the *order* in which these different features were placed that changed over time. The evolution of the text can be divided into three distinct phases:[28]

- The first draft versions contained a 'no less' clause clearly based on the US 1987 Model BIT.[29]
- The 'no less' clause was subsequently replaced by a clause referring instead to FET treatment 'in accordance with international law'.[30] The same type of clause had been found in a limited number of earlier US BITs and was similar to the four FIPAs concluded by Canada in the 1990s. No explanation was given for this change. In any event, there is evidence (at least from the US government) suggesting that such variations in language had no impact on the actual scope of protection.[31]
- Later, the text was rearranged and the order of the reference to international law and FET was reversed.[32] Thus, as explained by Kinnear, 'the Parties moved the reference to international law forward in the text, and coupled it with the other two elements (fair and equitable treatment and full protection and security) through the use of the word "including"'.[33] Again, the available negotiation documents do not provide any explanation as to why the Parties ultimately decided to do this. As mentioned above, no US or Canadian BITs at the time referred to treatment 'in accordance with international law' *before* mentioning FET.

The final text of Article 1105 establishes a clear hierarchy between a *generic* concept ('treatment in accordance with international law') and *two examples* of that concept ('fair and equitable treatment' and 'full protection and security'):

> The final formulation, however, addressed such ambiguities by subsuming fair and equitable treatment, along with full protection and security, into the broader concept of 'treatment in accordance with international law'. The first phrase sets out this general obligation (to accord 'treatment in accordance with international law'), with the subsidiary clause prefaced by the word 'including'. 'Fair and equitable treatment' and 'full protection and security' are thus provided as

---

28. For a comprehensive analysis, *see*: *Ibid.*, at 1.
29. *See*, for instance, draft of 19 December 1991, Article 402: 'Investments of nationals and companies of a Party in the territory of another Party shall at all times be accorded fair and equitable treatment, shall enjoy full protection and security and shall in no case be accorded treatment less than that required by international law'.
30. *See*, for instance, INVESTMT.06M, Washington Composite (6 March 1992) at 5. Slightly different variations of this type of clause were subsequently put forward indicating, for instance, that 'in all other respects' or 'in all other respects as well' the treatment must be in accordance with international law. *See*: INVEST.501, Chapultepec Composite (1 May 1992) at 3; INVEST.513, Toronto Composite (13 May 1992) at 3; INVEST.522, Washington Composite (22 May 1992) at 4.
31. *See*, the analysis above: text attached to footnotes 17 to 20.
32. INVEST.826, Lawyers' Revision (26 August 1992) at 3, Article 2106: 'Each Party shall accord to investments of investors of another Party treatment in accordance with international law, including fair and equitable treatment and full protection and security'.
33. Kinnear et al., *supra* n. 1, at 4.

non-exclusive examples of the minimum standard of treatment provided at international law. There is, in other words, a hierarchy established by the plain text of Article 1105(1). International law is the generic concept, with the subsidiary clause containing examples of the generic.[34]

One particularly important point is that the phrase 'customary international law' is not mentioned in any of the different drafts. In the *Methanex* case, the claimant filed a witness statement by Mr. Guillermo Aguillar Alvarez, who had acted as Mexico's lead negotiator of the NAFTA, to the effect that the concept of 'customary international law' had been discussed at length by the Parties during negotiation and it was ultimately decided not to include such reference with full knowledge that this would result in expanding the coverage of Article 1105.[35] Not surprisingly, Mexico filed an Article 1128 submission that strongly rejected Mr. Alvarez's personal recollection of events.[36] Canada also concluded that the declaration was 'neither credible nor relevant'.[37] The United States took the same view.[38]

---

34. *Ibid.*, at 20. *See also*: Jeswald W. Salacuse, *The Law of Investment Treaties* 224 (Oxford U. Press 2010).
35. *Methanex Corporation v. United States* [hereinafter *Methanex v. United States*], UNCITRAL, Investor's First Submission on FTC Notes of Interpretation, (18 September 2001), at 6, summarizing Mr. Alvarez's statement as follows: 'In fact, the word "customary" was actually *deleted* from one of the negotiating texts of NAFTA. Mr. Guillermo Aguilar Alvarez, one of the principal Chapter 11 negotiators for Mexico, recalls that one of the proposed versions of what became Article 1105 or its equivalent used the phrase "customary international law." (The United States almost certainly has a copy of this text; however, it has chosen to withhold it from this Tribunal). When Mexico resisted the use of the term "customary," the United States negotiators pointed out that deleting the word would expand the coverage of Article 1105 by bringing in other legal obligations, including independent treaty obligations between or among the NAFTA Parties. Mexico had no objection to incorporating such obligations into Article 1105, and the three countries eventually agreed to the present text of NAFTA Article 1105'.
36. *Methanex v. United States*, Mexico's Third Article 1128 Submission, (11 February 2002), at 3-4: 'The Commission, the NAFTA's most authoritative interpreter, has issued a binding interpretation regarding Article 1105. That, alone, is dispositive. It would be inappropriate in such circumstances for a Tribunal bound by Article 1131(2) to interpret Article 1105 in a manner contrary to the Commission as Mr. Aguilar Álvarez suggests. (...) Mr. Aguilar Álvarez's statement proffered by the Claimant is based solely on his personal recollection of events that transpired approximately ten years ago, and, therefore, does not meet the generally accepted criteria for *travaux preparatoires*. It does not even reach the status of an unagreed record produced by a participating state because Mexico does not agree with Mr. Aguilar Álvarez's statement or the conclusions that he sets out. (...) [A]s a purely factual matter, as the United States previously advised the Tribunal, Mexico has conducted a search of its records of the negotiations. Mexico has found no negotiating proposal by any of the three Parties that included the word "customary" in relation to "international law" and therefore no evidence that the word was deleted after discussion by the Parties. The Government of Mexico does not agree with Mr. Aguilar Álvarez's analysis of the negotiations or of the legal effect of the text that ultimately emerged from them'.
37. *Methanex v. United States*, Canada's Third Article 1128 Submission, (8 February 2002), para. 20, arguing that the declaration 'should not be considered' by the tribunal since it 'is not appropriate or necessary for the application of Article 1105 and that such consideration would violate the proper approach to treaty interpretation' (at para. 15). Canada added that the declaration was 'not preparatory work as described in Article 32 of the *Vienna Convention*' but 'an *ex post facto* declaration outlining the recollection of one negotiator and falls far short of careful recordings of conference proceedings which may be considered, if indeed supplementary materials were necessary' (at para. 20). *See also* at para. 21.
38. *Methanex v. United States*, US Rejoinder to Methanex's Reply Submission Concerning the NAFTA FTC's July 31, 2001 Interpretation, (17 December 2001), at 4 ('the Declaration of

In its award of May 2002 (rendered *after* the FTC Note[39]), the *Pope & Talbot* tribunal examined the drafting documents submitted by Canada during the proceedings and concluded that they did not support Canada's position that the words 'international law' at Article 1105 referred to the minimum standard of treatment existing under *customary* international law.[40] For the tribunal, the absence of the term 'customary' in any one of these documents was meaningful since the negotiators of NAFTA stood 'as sophisticated representatives' of their government, and were necessarily aware that the concept of 'international law' was actually 'a broader concept than customary international law, which is only one of its components'.[41] In other words, had the Parties intended to refer to custom, they would have simply used the the term at Article 1105. This interpretation is controversial in the NAFTA context. As mentioned above[42] (and further discussed below[43]), evidence suggests that at the time (i.e., 1994), the use of the term 'international law' in an FET clause was meant, for both Canada and the United States, to be a reference to the minimum standard of treatment under custom.

In sum, the earlier practices of Canada (except for one treaty) and the United States regarding FET clauses show that all BITs signed by them before 1994 explicitly linked the FET standard to 'international law'. Yet, none of the BITs contained the same language as Article 1105. Contrary to this provision's final text, reference to treatment 'in accordance with international law' in these BITs appeared *after* the mention of FET. The same language was also found in the first drafts of Article 1105. The available negotiation documents do not provide any explanation as to why the Parties ultimately changed the order of the wording when adopting the final version of the text. In other words, the history of Article 1105 does not provide much guidance as to the meaning of FET under this clause. The next section turns to the general rules of treaty interpretation to examine whether they can serve as guidance to determine the meaning of this provision.

§2.02   ARTICLE 1105 IN LIGHT OF THE GENERAL RULES OF TREATY INTERPRETATION

This section examines whether the rules of treaty interpretation under international law can provide any guidance as to the meaning of Article 1105. It has been suggested

---

Guillermo Aguilar Alvarez is not *travaux préparatoires* but a statement by a paid fact witness as to his recollection of what transpired in discussions that occurred over nine years ago – a recollection unsupported by any of the *travaux* that Mexico or counsel for the United States could locate after a diligent search').

39. The FTC Note is further discussed below at section §2.02[C][3].
40. *Pope & Talbot Inc. v. Canada*, UNCITRAL, Award in Respect of Damages, (31 May 2002), para. 25.
41. *Ibid.*, para. 46. The tribunal had already noted (at para. 20) that it is 'well accepted' that the content of 'international law' is 'a good deal broader' than the notion of 'customary' international law since the latter is only one of the sources of international law.
42. *See*, the analysis above: text attached to footnotes 17 to 20.
43. *See*, at section §2.02[C][2] below.

that the classic rules of interpretation may be of limited help in the context of the interpretation of the FET standard.[44] It is undoubtedly true that in general:

> any approach relying exclusively on the general rules of interpretation necessarily suffers from undetermination, since it is impossible to grasp a presumably existing meaning that is intrinsic to fair and equitable treatment with the coarse tools provided by Article 31 of the VCLT.[45]

However, tribunals should examine Article 1105 based on these rules of interpretation.[46] According to NAFTA Article 1131(1), a tribunal set up to resolve a dispute between an investor and a NAFTA Party under Chapter 11 must 'decide the issues in dispute in accordance with this Agreement and applicable rules of international law'.[47] NAFTA Article 102 provides that NAFTA's provisions are to be interpreted and applied 'in accordance with applicable rules of international law'. One source that has consistently been applied by NAFTA tribunals[48] to interpret NAFTA provisions are the rules of interpretation codified in Articles 31 and 32 of the *Vienna Convention on the Law of Treaties* (hereinafter '*Vienna Convention*').[49] In fact, for NAFTA tribunals, these interpretive rules are part of customary international law and must therefore apply to disputes under the NAFTA.[50]

Article 31(1) of the *Vienna Convention* requires a tribunal to interpret the NAFTA 'in good faith in accordance with the ordinary meaning to be given to the terms of the treaty in their context and in the light of its object and purpose'. Article 32 provides that:

> [R]ecourse may be had to supplementary means of interpretation, including the preparatory work of the treaty and the circumstances of its conclusion, in order to confirm the meaning resulting from the application of article 31, or to determine

---

44. Alexandra Diehl, *The Core Standard of International Investment Protection: Fair and Equitable Treatment* 327 (Wolters Kluwer 2012); Roland Kläger, *Fair and Equitable Treatment in International Investment Law* 45-46 (Cambridge U. Press 2011); Stephan Schill, *Fair and Equitable Treatment as an Embodiment of the Rule of Law*, in *The International Convention on the Settlement of Investment Disputes (ICSID): Taking Stock after 40 Years* 37 (R. Hofmann & C. Tams eds., Nomos 2007).
45. Kläger, *supra* n. 44, at 46.
46. Diehl, *supra* n. 44, at 313, 327; Martins Paparinskis, *The International Minimum Standard and Fair and Equitable Treatment* 111 (Oxford U. Press 2013).
47. Article 1131(2) also requires a tribunal to apply any interpretation of the NAFTA issued by the FTC. This question is further discussed below at Section §2.02[C][3].
48. *See, inter alia*: *International Thunderbird Gaming Corporation v. Mexico* [hereinafter *Thunderbird v. Mexico*], UNCITRAL, Award, (26 January 2006), para. 91; *Ethyl Corporation v. Canada*, UNCITRAL, Decision on Jurisdiction, (24 June 1998), para. 55; *Methanex v. United States*, Award, (3 August 2005), Part II, Ch. B, para. 15; *Fireman's Fund Insurance Company v. Mexico*, ICSID No. ARB(AF)/02/1, Award, (14 July 2006), para. 136.
49. *Vienna Convention on the Law of Treaties*, (23 May 1969), Can. T.S. 1980 No. 37 (also published in: 1155 UNTS 331, (1969); 8 ILM 679).
50. *See*, for instance: *Methanex v. United States*, Award, (3 August 2005), Part IV, Ch. B, para. 29; *Terminal Forest Products Ltd. v. United States*, UNCITRAL, Decision on Preliminary Question, (6 June 2006), para. 177; *S.D. Myers Inc. v. Canada*, UNCITRAL, First Partial Award, (13 November 2000), paras. 200-202; *Pope & Talbot, Inc v. Canada*, Interim Award, (26 June 2000), paras. 64-69; *ADF Group Inc. v. United States* [hereinafter *ADF v. United States*], ICSID No. ARB(AF)/00/1, Award, (9 January 2003), para. 147.

the meaning when the interpretation according to article 31: (a) leaves the meaning ambiguous or obscure; or (b) leads to a result which is manifestly absurd or unreasonable.

The next four sections of this book will examine Article 1105 in light of the following different rules of interpretation:

- Ordinary meaning (section §2.02[A]).
- Object and purpose (section §2.02[B]).
- Context (section §2.02[C]).
- Supplementary means of interpretation (section §2.02[D]).

[A]   Ordinary Meaning

Under Article 31 of the *Vienna Convention*, Article 1105 must be interpreted in accordance with the 'ordinary meaning to be given to the terms' of the provision. The task of any tribunal is therefore to 'focus first on the actual language of the provision being construed' before examining the objective and purpose of a treaty.[51] This is because 'the text of the treaty is deemed to be the authentic expression of the intentions of the parties; and its elucidation, rather than wide-ranging searches for the supposed intentions of the parties, is the proper object of interpretation'.[52]

NAFTA Article 1105(1) reads as follows: 'Each Party shall accord to investments of investors of another Party treatment in accordance with international law, including fair and equitable treatment and full protection and security'. As mentioned above,[53] the FET is an 'absolute' (non-contingent) standard of treatment. It is therefore different from a 'relative' standard of treatment (like the national treatment clause) which is defined by reference to the treatment accorded to the host State's own investors.

The first notable feature of Article 1105 is that it offers protection to '*investments* of investors' and *not* to *investors* themselves.[54] This nuance was implicitly recognized by the *Grand River* tribunal.[55] The language of Article 1105 contrasts with the one

---

51. *ADF v. United States*, Award, (9 January 2003), para. 147.
52. *Methanex v. United States*, Award, (3 August 2005), Part II, Ch. B, para. 22.
53. *See*, Chapter 1 section §1.02 above.
54. Kinnear et al., *supra* n. 1, at 19; Newcombe & Paradell, *supra* n. 18, at 261-262. *Contra*: T. Weiler, *Good Faith and Regulatory Transparency: The Story of Metalclad v. Mexico*, in *International Investment Law and Arbitration: Leading Cases from the ICSID, NAFTA, Bilateral Treaties and Customary International Law* 726 (T. Weiler ed., Cameron May 2005) (arguing that as a result of the FTC Note making explicit reference to the standard of protection offered under custom to 'aliens' the coverage of Article 1105 has in fact expanded to now include protection to *investors themselves*, and not just their investments); Ioana Tudor, *The Fair and Equitable Treatment Standard in International Foreign Investment Law* 236 (Oxford U. Press 2008) ('the treatment in question, fair and equitable, is aimed at the Investor not at the State; it is the Investor who has to be treated fairly and equitably; it is not the obligation of the Investor to treat the State in a fair and equitable manner').
55. *Grand River Enterprises Six Nations, Ltd., et al. v. United States* [hereinafter *Grand River v. United States*], UNCITRAL, Award, (12 January 2011), para. 177 ('The required treatment must be accorded to "investments of investors of another Party". Article 1105 provides no scope for individual investors' claims that they have received treatment contrary to international law,

adopted elsewhere in Chapter 11 (for instance, Articles 1105(2), 1102 and 1103) where protection is accorded to both investments *and* investors.[56]

A more complicated question is to determine the actual meaning of 'fair' and 'equitable'. When faced with the difficult task of interpreting an FET clause, tribunals have often turned to dictionaries.[57] The *Concise Oxford Dictionary* defines the word 'fair' as 'just, unbiased, and equitable, in accordance with rules'.[58] The concept of 'equitable' must clearly be distinguished from the different notion of 'equity' under international law.[59] Article 1105 clearly does not allow a tribunal to decide *ex aequo et bono*.[60] For another writer, FET refers to the concept of 'equitableness', defined as 'a general principle that commands an equitable application of the law in order to avoid, in practice, absurd or unreasonable results'.[61]

Yet, as noted by another writer, any 'enquiry into the ordinary meaning of the words "fair" and "equitable" usually yields very little'.[62] This is because, as pointed out by the *Saluka* tribunal, '[t]he "ordinary meaning" of the "fair and equitable treatment" standard can only be defined by terms of almost equal vagueness'.[63] Consider for instance, the *MDT* tribunal's conclusion that in their ordinary meaning, the terms 'fair' and 'equitable' mean 'just', 'evenhanded', 'unbiased', 'legitimate'.[64] As noted by many writers, these findings are often more circular than anything else.[65]

In any event, while the origin of the concept of 'fair and equitable treatment' was certainly grounded in these two ideas (i.e., 'fair' and 'equitable'), it is now recognized

---

except as that treatment affects a covered investment'). *See also*, at paras. 206, 220 (the 'narrowly framed language of Article 1105' is 'assuring the minimum standard of protection for investors' investment, not for the investors themselves'). The point is developed in: *Ibid.*, US Counter-Memorial, (22 December 2008), at 126.

56. Thomas, *supra* n. 2, at 67.
57. *See*, for instance: *MTD Equity Sdn. Bhd. and MTD Chile S.A. v. Chile*, ICSID No. ARB/01/7, Award, (25 May 2004), para. 113.
58. *The Concise Oxford Dictionary of Current English* 420 (8th ed., Clarendon Press 1990) (quoted in: UNCTAD, *Fair and Equitable Treatment* 7 (UNCTAD Series on Issues in International Investment Agreements II, United Nations, 2012). For the UNCTAD report, *ibid.*, at 7, 'fairness connotes, among other things, equity'. *See also*: Tudor, *supra* n. 54, at 126, referring to the ideas of justice and of reasonableness.
59. Equity is an independent source of law available to a judge (when the parties agree) to decide a dispute based on considerations of fairness and not on existing law. This is allowed under Article 38(2) of the ICJ Statute and Article 42 of the ICSID Convention. *See*: Christoph Schreuer, *Fair and Equitable Treatment in Arbitral Practice*, 6(3) J. World Invest. & Trade, (2005); Christoph Schreuer, *Decisions Ex Aequo et Bono Under the ICSID Convention*, 11 ICSID Rev. 37 (1996).
60. Newcombe & Paradell, *supra* n. 18, at 274; Meg Kinnear, *The Continuing Development of the FET Standard*, in *Investment Treaty Law: Current Issues III* 20 (Andrea K. Bjurklund, Ian A. Laird & Sergey Ripinsky eds., British IICL 2009) (paper version); Ioana Knoll-Tudor, *The Fair and Equitable Treatment Standard and Human Rights Norms*, in *Human Rights in International Investment Law and Arbitration* 319 (P.M. Dupuy, F. Francioni & E.U. Petersmann eds., Oxford U. Press 2009); Schreuer, *supra* n. 59, at 365.
61. Tudor, *supra* n. 54, at 128.
62. Salacuse, *supra* n. 34, at 229. *See also*: Schill, *supra* n. 44, at 37.
63. *Saluka Investments B.V. v. Czech Republic*, UNCITRAL, Partial Award, (17 March 2006), para. 297.
64. *MTD Equity Sdn. Bhd. and MTD Chile S.A. v. Chile*, Award, (25 May 2004), para. 113, where the tribunal referred to the *Concise Oxford Dictionary of Current English* (5th ed.).
65. Kläger, *supra* n. 44, at 41, 45-46; Diehl, *supra* n. 44, at 313; Stephen Schill, *The Multilateralization of International Investment Law* 264 (Cambridge U. Press 2009).

that the concept has a 'technical legal content of its own and the two notions composing it have only a limited direct effect on its meaning'.[66] In other words, the FET obligation has a *specific content* of its own.[67] This has been recognized by a number of tribunals,[68] including the *Mondev* tribunal.[69] In fact, it is generally recognized that the FET standard consists of a *single* obligation rather than *two* distinct obligations.[70] Finally, the use of the term is interchangeable.[71] For instance, 'fair and equitable' does not have a different meaning than 'equitable and reasonable'.[72]

Under Article 1105, 'international law' is the 'controlling element' in applying the concept of 'fair and equitable treatment' and determining its content.[73] While there is no doubt that the words 'in accordance with international law' at Article 1105 make it clear that this is an 'absolute' and 'objective' standard of treatment,[74] one of the most contentious issues debated in case law and academia has been to determine exactly what 'international law' actually means. The ordinary meaning of 'international law' simply refers to the body of rules that have historically been developed by States in their international relations. According to several NAFTA tribunals, this is a reference to Article 38(1) of the *Statute of the International Court of Justice* (hereinafter the 'ICJ Statute'), which sets out the sources of international law.[75] Article 38 of the ICJ Statute defines international law to include: (a) international conventions, (b) international

---

66. Tudor, *supra* n. 54, at 129.
67. UNCTAD, *supra* n. 58, at 61; Schreuer, *supra* n. 59, at 365; Kinnear, *supra* n. 60, at 20.
68. *See*, for instance, *Saluka v. Czech Republic*, Partial Award, (17 March 2006), para. 284.
69. *Mondev International Ltd. v. United States* [hereinafter *Mondev v. United States*], ICSID No. ARB(AF)/99/2, Award, (2 October 2002), para. 119 ('[the tribunal] may not simply adopt its own idiosyncratic standard of what is "fair" or "equitable", without reference to established sources of law'). The statement was subsequently approved by the tribunal in *ADF v. United States*, Award, (9 January 2003), para. 184.
70. Kläger, *supra* n. 44, at 41; Rudolf Dolzer, *Fair and Equitable Treatment, A Key Standard in Investment Treaties*, 39 Int'l Law 87, 91 (2005); Newcombe & Paradell, *supra* n. 18, at 275-276; José E. Alvarez, *The Public International Law Regime Governing International Investment* 206 (Hague Academy of International Law 2011); Salacuse, *supra* n. 34, at 221-222 ('Two considerations support this view. First, the consistency with which states have linked the two terms in the verbal formula of "fair and equitable treatment" supports the view that states believe there is a single standard … Second, if states intended "fair and equitable" to refer to two separate standards, they would have made that meaning explicit in the treaty texts. No state has chosen to do so. They could, for example, set out the fairness standard in one treaty provision, and the equity standard in another. The fact that they have not done so indicates that the contracting states intended the phrase "fair and equitable treatment" to connote a single standard').
71. UNCTAD, *supra* n. 58, at 7; Dolzer, *supra* n. 70, at 93-94; Salacuse, *supra* n. 34, at 222.
72. *Parkerings-Compagniet AS v. Lithuania*, ICSID No. ARB/05/8, Award, (7 September 2011), paras. 271–278.
73. *Grand River v. United States*, Award, (12 January 2011), para. 174 ('The text makes clear that the controlling element in applying Article 1105 is international law. "Fair and equitable treatment" and "full protection and security" do not exist as independent, free-standing concepts drawing content from sources such as equity or the policy preferences of individual arbitrators. Their content is determined by international law').
74. Kinnear et al., *supra* n. 1, at 19.
75. *Methanex v. United States*, Award, (3 August 2005), Part II, Ch. B, para. 3; *Thunderbird v. Mexico*, Award, (26 January 2006), paras. 89–90; *Merrill & Ring Forestry L.P. v. Canada* [hereinafter *Merrill & Ring v. Canada*], UNCITRAL, Award, (31 March 2010), paras. 183–184.

custom, and (c) 'the general principles of law recognized by civilized nations'.[76] Article 38 also refers to two other subsidiary sources: 'judicial decisions and the teachings of the most highly qualified publicists of the various nations'. In the context of Article 1105, the debate has opposed those for whom international law refers only to the minimum standard of treatment under custom, and others supporting an interpretation based on *all sources* of international law. This controversial question will be examined in a separate section below.[77]

In sum, looking at the 'ordinary meaning' of the terms used at Article 1105 ('fair', 'equitable' and 'international law') does not provide much guidance as to the proper interpretation to be given to this provision. The next sections will examine other elements of treaty interpretation (i.e., object and purpose, context, etc.).

[B] Object and Purpose

Under Article 31 of the *Vienna Convention*, Article 1105 must be interpreted in light of the *object and purpose* of the Agreement. NAFTA Article 102(2) also specifically indicates that the Parties shall interpret and apply NAFTA provisions 'in the light of [NAFTA's] objectives set out in [Article 201(1)] and in accordance with applicable rules of international law'. Right from the outset, Article 201(1) indicates that the 'objectives of this Agreement' are 'elaborated more specifically through its principles and rules, including national treatment, most-favored-nation treatment and transparency'. Article 201(1) further states the following objectives:

a) eliminate barriers to trade in, and facilitate the cross-border movement of, goods and services between the territories of the Parties;
b) promote conditions of fair competition in the free trade area;
c) increase substantially investment opportunities in the territories of the Parties;
d) provide adequate and effective protection and enforcement of intellectual property rights in each Party's territory;
e) create effective procedures for the implementation and application of this Agreement, for its joint administration and for the resolution of disputes; and
f) establish a framework for further trilateral, regional and multilateral cooperation to expand and enhance the benefits of this Agreement.

A brief discussion of two NAFTA awards (*Metalclad* and *ADF*) that have examined the object and purpose of the NAFTA in their findings will be sufficient in light of the objective of this book.[78]

---

76. Article 38, Statute of the ICJ, reprinted in *International Court of Justice, Charter of the United Nations, Statute and Rules of Court and other Documents* 61 (No. 4 1978).
77. *See*, at section §2.03[A][3] below.
78. *See also*, for instance, *Canadian Cattlemen for Fair Trade v. United States* [hereinafter *Canadian Cattlemen v. United States*], UNCITRAL, Award on Jurisdiction, (28 January 2008), paras. 160–170. Non-NAFTA case law is examined by Tudor, *supra* n. 54, at 146 ff.

The *Metalclad* award is one example of a NAFTA tribunal's reliance on the object and purpose of the treaty to discover the meaning of the FET. After having noted that NAFTA Article 102(2) provides that the Agreement 'must be interpreted and applied in the light of its stated objectives and in accordance with applicable rules of international law', the tribunal stated that these 'objectives specifically include transparency and the substantial increase in investment opportunities in the territories of the Parties'.[79] Later, the tribunal reiterated that '[p]rominent in the statement of principles and rules that introduces the Agreement is the reference to "transparency"'.[80] Based on these findings, the tribunal concluded that when interpreted in light of the preamble to the NAFTA, Article 1105 includes obligations of transparency and predictability (this controversial finding is further discussed below[81]).

This reasoning by the tribunal is certainly open to criticism. The plain reading of Article 102(2) makes it clear that transparency is *not* one of the 'objectives' of the treaty; rather, it is one of the 'principles and rules' (others include national treatment and Most-Favored-Nation treatment) through which the objectives are 'elaborated more specifically'.[82] The *Metalclad* award's section on Article 1105 was later set-aside by Justice Tysoe of the Supreme Court of British Columbia, who made the following observation on this point:

> [T]he Tribunal incorrectly stated that transparency was one of the objectives of the NAFTA. In that regard, the Tribunal was referring to Article 102(1), which sets out the objectives of the NAFTA in clauses (a) through (f). Transparency is mentioned in Article 102(1) but it is listed as one of the principles and rules contained in the NAFTA through which the objectives are elaborated. The other two principles and rules mentioned in Article 102, national treatment and most-favored nation treatment, are contained in Chapter 11. The principle of transparency is implemented through the provisions of Chapter 18, not Chapter 11. Article 102(2) provides that the NAFTA is to be interpreted and applied in light of the objectives set out in Article 102(1), but it does not require that all of the provisions of the NAFTA are to be interpreted in light of the principles and rules mentioned in Article 102(1).[83]

Some writers have criticized Justice Tysoe's reasoning as being a misinterpretation of Article 102.[84] In any event, while transparency was *not* one of the 'objectives' of the

---

79. *Metalclad Corporation v. Mexico* [hereinafter *Metalclad v. Mexico*], ICSID No. ARB(AF)/97/1, Award, (30 August 2000), para. 70.
80. *Ibid.*, para. 76.
81. *See*, at Chapter 3 section §3.02[C] below.
82. Akira Kotera, *Regulatory Transparency*, in *The Oxford Handbook of International Investment Law* 625 (Peter Muchlinski, Federico Ortino & Christoph Schreuer eds., Oxford U. Press 2008).
83. *Mexico v. Metalclad*, 2001 BCSC 664, Supreme Court of British Columbia, Judgment and Reasons for Decision (2 May 2001), para. 71.
84. Carl-Sebastian Zoellner, *Transparency: An Analysis of an Evolving Fundamental Principle in International Economic Law*, 27 Mich. J. Int'l L. (2006), at 613-614 ('Given both the clear command to interpret the provisions in light of NAFTA's objectives and the fact that the transparency principle "elaborates" those objectives, it is hard to see how Justice Tysoe could deny the relevance of transparency in the interpretation of article 1105(1). His claim that chapter 18 of NAFTA exclusively codified the transparency principle does not logically follow from the wording, nor is it true; In fact, NAFTA is "positively riddled with transparency enhancing norms", many of which are not found in chapter 18'). *See also*, other grounds of criticism

Treaty, it remains that the *Metalclad* tribunal was right to refer to it since the concept is mentioned in, *inter alia,* NAFTA Chapter 18, and was therefore undoubtedly part of the 'context' of NAFTA, which includes its entire text.[85]

Many authors have argued that reliance on the object and purpose of the treaty provides limited guidance as to the actual meaning of Article 1105. This is because the purpose of an international investment treaty typically refers to the protection and promotion of foreign investments and the deepening of mutual economic relations between the contracting States.[86] These are very general objectives that are not particularly helpful in determining the meaning of FET. In fact, they can also be interpreted differently: either as providing extensive protection to investors or as leaving regulatory flexibility for the host State.[87] In other words, it is not clear whether these objectives result in extending or limiting the scope of the FET that host States must accord to foreign investments. Consider, for instance, the reasoning of the *Siemens* tribunal, which after having examined the object and purpose of the applicable Argentina-US BIT, came to the following conclusion:

> [i]t follows from the ordinary meaning of "fair" and "equitable" and the purpose and object of the Treaty that these terms denote treatment in an even-handed and just manner, conducive to fostering the promotion and protection of foreign investment and stimulating private initiative.[88]

It is not entirely clear in this case, whether reference to the object and purpose of the BIT was helpful in determining the meaning of the FET.

These concerns were echoed in the *ADF* ruling wherein the tribunal minimized the importance of the object and purpose of an agreement in the assessment of the meaning of a provision.[89] The tribunal rightly observed at the outset that an analysis of the object and purpose should only be undertaken after having first examined the actual language used in the provision. This is because '[t]he object and purpose of the parties to a treaty in agreeing upon any particular paragraph of that treaty are to be found, in the first instance, in the words in fact used by the parties in that paragraph'.[90] This is especially true when the object and purpose refers to vague and general objectives. The tribunal then explained that it was not 'suggest[ing] that the general objectives of NAFTA are not useful or relevant'.[91] Thus, '[t]hose general objectives may be conceived of as partaking of the nature of *lex generalis* while a particular detailed provision set in a particular context in the rest of a Chapter or Part of NAFTA

---

mentioned by these writers: Todd Weiler, *Metalclad v. Mexico: A Play in Three Parts*, 2 J. World Invest. 701 (2001); Weiler, *supra* n. 54, at 718; Gabriel Cavazos Villanueva, *The Fair and Equitable Treatment Standard: The Mexican Experience* 103 (VDM Verlag 2008); Kotera, *supra* n. 82, at 630. *Contra*: J.C. Thomas, *A Reply to Professor Brower*, 40 Colum. J. Transnat'l L. 438-439 (2001-2002).

85. C. Schreuer & R. Dolzer, *Principles of International Investment Law* 136 (Oxford U. Press 2008).
86. Schill, *supra* n. 44, at 262.
87. Kläger, *supra* n. 44, at 45.
88. *Siemens AG v. Argentina*, ICSID No. ARB/02/8, Award, (17 January 2007), para. 290.
89. The tribunal made these findings in the context of its analysis of Articles 1102, 1106 and 1108 (not Article 1105).
90. *ADF v. United States*, Award, (9 January 2003), para. 147.
91. *Ibid*.

functions as *lex specialis*.[92] For the tribunal, while the object and purpose 'may frequently cast light on a specific interpretive issue', it remains that ultimately they cannot 'be regarded as overriding and superseding' the actual text of a provision.[93]

In sum, looking at the object and purpose of Article 1105 provides limited guidance as to its actual meaning.

[C]   Context

As mentioned above, Article 31(1) of the *Vienna Convention* requires that any provision must be interpreted not only according to its ordinary meaning, but also in its *context* and in light of its object and purpose. For the *ADF* tribunal, the context consists mainly of NAFTA's other provisions.[94] Article 31(2) of the *Vienna Convention* further indicates that the context also includes the preamble and annexes to the agreement.[95] Under Article 31(3), the context includes the following two other elements:

(a) any *subsequent agreement* between the parties regarding the interpretation of the treaty or the application of its provisions;
(b) any *subsequent practice* in the application of the treaty which establishes the agreement of the parties regarding its interpretation …

As rightly noted by Roberts, this provision 'requires, rather than permits, recourse to subsequent agreements and practice, treating them as a primary, rather than a secondary, source of interpretation'.[96] The following sections will examine five distinct contextual elements:

- The provision's title (section §2.02[C][1]).
- Official statements made by Canada and the United States for the implementation of the Agreement (section §2.02[C][2]).
- The FTC's Note of Interpretation (section §2.02[C][3]).
- Article 1128 submissions made by non-disputing Parties (section §2.02[C][4]).
- Model BITs adopted by the United States and Canada (section §2.02[C][5]).

---

92. *Ibid.* This position was later endorsed by the tribunal in *Canadian Cattlemen v. United States*, Award on Jurisdiction, (28 January 2008), para. 166.
93. *ADF v. United States*, Award, (9 January 2003), para. 147.
94. *Ibid. See also: Canadian Cattlemen v. United States*, Award on Jurisdiction, (28 January 2008), para. 166, indicating that NAFTA Chapter 11 must be considered in the larger context of the Agreement as a whole.
95. *See*, case law examined in: Tudor, *supra* n. 54, at 146-148.
96. A. Roberts, *Power and Persuasion in Investment Treaty Interpretation: The Dual Role of States*, 104 AJIL 200 (2010) (referring to the work of Richard K. Gardiner, *Treaty Interpretation* 32 (Oxford U. Press 2008); Mark Villiger, *Commentary on the 1969 Vienna Convention on The Law of Treaties* 429 (Martinus Nijhoff Publ. 2009)). *See also:* Georg Nolte (ed.), *Treaties and Subsequent Practice* (Oxford Univ. Press 2013).

[1]   The Provision's Title

The title of a provision is undoubtedly part of its context; it 'indicates the drafters' intention to describe in a summary was the contents of the substantive obligations that follow'.[97] Article 1105 is titled 'Minimum Standard of Treatment'. This is undoubtedly a reference to the minimum standard of treatment to aliens existing under customary international law.[98] Thus, the heading of Article 1105 clearly suggests that the words 'international law' contained in that provision simply mean the minimum standard of treatment.

[2]   Official Statements Made by Canada and the United States for the Implementation of the Agreement

Canada's 'Statement on Implementation' of 1994 explained that the FET obligation under Article 1105 constitutes a reference to the minimum standard of treatment under customary international law.[99] In its 1993 Statement of Administrative Action submitted to Congress, the United States simply paraphrased Article 1105.[100] As mentioned above,[101] in the context of BITs containing language similar to that of NAFTA Article 1105, the US State Department has made numerous statements in 1993–1994 and onward to the effect that the guarantee of FET under international law 'sets out a minimum standard of treatment based on customary international law'.[102]

What is the formal interpretative value of these unilateral official statements made by Canada and the United States around the time of the implementation of NAFTA?[103] As accurately concluded by the *Canadian Cattlemen* tribunal, these statements cannot be considered as a 'subsequent agreement' between the Parties on the

---

97. Thomas, *supra* n. 2, at 29, *see also* at 55-56. *See also*: Dolzer & Schreuer, *supra* n. 85, at 126.
98. Diehl, *supra* n. 44, at 150; Schreuer, *supra* n. 59, at 362; Salacuse, *supra* n. 34, at 224. *See also*: Christopher Greenwood, retained as expert by the United States in the case *Loewen Group, Inc. and Raymond L. Loewen v. United States* [hereinafter *Loewen v. United States*], ICSID No. ARB(AF)/98/3, Second Opinion, (16 August 2001), para. 75.
99. Department of External Affairs, NAFTA, Canadian Statement on Implementation, *Canada Gazette*, 1 January 1994, 68, at 149 ('Article 1105, which provides for treatment in accordance with international law, is intended to assure a minimum standard of treatment of investments of NAFTA investors. National treatment provides a relative standard of treatment while this article provides for a minimum absolute standard of treatment, based on long-standing principles of customary international law').
100. United States Statement on Administrative Action, November 1993, at 141.
101. *See*, the analysis above, text attached to footnotes 17 to 20.
102. Thomas, *supra* n. 2, at 49-50.
103. It should be noted that these statements differ from pleadings made by a State respondent in ongoing arbitration proceedings. Tribunals have refused to rely on such pleadings because they are of limited value to the interpretation of a treaty provision. *See*, for instance: *Gas Natural SDG S.A. v. Argentina*, ICSID No. ARB/03/10, Decision on Preliminary Questions on Jurisdiction, (17 June 2005), para. 47 (fn no. 12) ('We do not believe, however, that an argument made by a party in the context of an arbitration reflects practice establishing agreement between the parties to a treaty within the meaning of Article 31(3)(b) of the Vienna Convention on the Law of Treaties'). *See also*: Dolzer & Schreuer, *supra* n. 85, at 34; Roberts, *supra* n. 96, at 217-219.

interpretation of Article 1105 pursuant to Article 31(3)(a) of the *Vienna Convention*.[104] Thus, nothing in these statements suggests that 'parties intended their understanding to constitute an agreed basis for interpretation'.[105]

Furthermore, can these official statements be deemed as 'subsequent practice' under Article 31(3)(b) of the *Vienna Convention*? A *single* unilateral statement made by *one* State party to a treaty should normally not be considered as 'subsequent practice' since there is simply *no accord between the parties* on any interpretation.[106] However, it is generally considered that different statements made by *more than one State* that all support the same interpretation, could *together* be considered as 'subsequent practice' pursuant to Article 31(3)(b) of the *Vienna Convention*.[107] As summarized by two writers, subsequent practice needs to be 'concordant, common, and consistent'.[108]

The issue was addressed by the *Canadian Cattlemen* tribunal wherein the United States submitted that several elements of 'subsequent practice', including its own 1993 Statement of Administrative Action and Canada's Statement on Implementation of the NAFTA, confirmed its interpretation of Article 1101(1)(a).[109] The tribunal first noted that:

> [t]he value and significance of subsequent practice will naturally depend on the extent to which it is concordant, common, and consistent. A practice is a sequence

---

104. *Canadian Cattlemen v. United States*, Award on Jurisdiction, (28 January 2008), paras. 186–187.
105. Roberts, *supra* n. 96, at 199.
106. Newcombe & Paradell, *supra* n. 18, at 268, *see also* at 117-118; Roberts, *supra* n. 96, at 221.
107. Roberts, *supra* n. 96, at 220-221 ('subsequent practice is not limited to pleadings or interventions in investment disputes but can include other public statements by the treaty parties. Such statements have the advantage of being general in their application and not tied to the facts of specific disputes. A state could include a place for such statements on its Website, perhaps where it lists its investment treaties, or appropriate statements could be recorded in the state's yearbook of international law. (...) While the statements of one state alone will not create an agreement on interpretation, they may be persuasive when the other treaty parties agree with, or acquiesce in, these interpretations'); C. McLachlan, L. Shore & M. Weiniger, *International Investment Arbitration: Substantive Principles* 224 (Oxford U. Press 2007) (stating that such statements 'will inevitably carry less weigh, if they are simply unilateral statements, uncorroborated by the other party').
108. M. Fitzmaurice & P. Merkouris, *Canons of Treaty Interpretation: Selected Case Studies from the World Trade Organization and the North American Free Trade Agreement*, in: *Treaty Interpretation and the Vienna Convention on the Law of Treaties: 30 Years On* 233 (M. Fitzmaurice, O. Elias & P. Merkouris eds., Martinus Nijhoff Publishers 2010), (quoting from: Ian Sinclair, *The Vienna Convention on the Law of Treaties* 137 (Manchester U. Press 1984)). *See also*: Villiger, *supra* n. 96, at 431 (for whom practice 'must be consistent rather than haphazard' and 'should have occurred with a certain frequency'); Julian Arato, *Subsequent Practice and Evolutive Interpretation: Techniques of Treaty Interpretation over Time and Their Diverse Consequences*, 9 LPICT 461 (2010) ('for a party's conduct to qualify as subsequent practice it must *at least* be describable as consisting of non-isolated actions, committed consistently in the application of the treaty, reflecting a position on interpretation, and engaged in or legitimately acquiesced in by all of the parties').
109. The United States argued that the proper interpretation to be given to this provision was that NAFTA Chapter 11's scope only covered investors of a party which invested in *another* NAFTA Party.

of facts or acts and cannot in general be established by one isolated fact or act or even by several individual applications.[110]

The tribunal then concluded that the material referred to by the United States should be considered as subsequent practice because it was 'evidence of a sequence of facts and acts that amounts to a practice that is concordant, common, and consistent' which 'confirmed the Tribunal's interpretation of the ordinary meaning of Article 1101(1)(a) of the NAFTA'.[111] In the present author's view, the reasoning of the tribunal in *Canadian Cattlemen* is applicable in the context of Article 1105 insofar as it deals with the same type of practice.

In the context of Article 1105, the *Mondev* tribunal specifically examined the above-mentioned Canadian Statement on Implementation of the NAFTA and two submittal letters sent by the US State Department to the President for the ratification of BITs.[112] The tribunal concluded that such 'explanations given by a signatory government to its own legislature in the course of ratification or implementation of a treaty' could 'certainly shed light on the purposes and approaches taken to the treaty, and thus can evidence *opinio juris*'.[113] The *Mondev* tribunal did not go so far as to explicitly consider these official statements as 'subsequent practice'.

In the present author's view, the *Mondev* tribunal was probably correct in not qualifying these statements as 'subsequent practice' per se. The 1994 Canadian Statement on Implementation is evidently not *subsequent* to the entry into force of the NAFTA, but *simultaneous* to it. Similarly, those letters sent from the US State Department to the President for the ratification of BITs *before 1994* do not qualify as 'subsequent' practice for the purposes of Article 31(3)(b) of the *Vienna Convention*. Yet, significant weight should be given to these statements precisely because they were issued before or simultaneously to the entry into force of the NAFTA. The importance to be given to these statements is further confirmed by the fact that they are 'concordant, common, and consistent' with respect to the proper meaning to be given to Article 1105; they all state that the 'fair and equitable treatment' to be accorded under 'international law' constitutes a reference to the minimum standard of treatment under custom.

[3] The FTC Note of Interpretation

On 31 July 2001, under the aegis of the Free Trade Commission ('FTC'),[114] the trade ministers for the three NAFTA Parties, issued the 'Notes of Interpretation of Certain Chapter 11 Provisions' regarding two issues: access to documents and the minimum standard of treatment (since this book is only concerned with the latter we will refer to

---

110. *Canadian Cattlemen v. United States,* Award on Jurisdiction, (28 January 2008), para. 182 (citing Sinclair, *supra* n. 108, at 137).
111. *Ibid.,* paras. 188–189.
112. *Mondev v. United States,* Award, (2 October 2002), para. 111 (referring to the US-Ecuador BIT, 1993 and the US-Albania BIT, 1995).
113. *Ibid.*
114. The Commission is composed of one representative from each NAFTA Party (Article 2001).

it as the 'Note' instead of the 'Notes'). The Note indicates that it was adopted by the FTC after 'having reviewed the operation of proceedings conducted' by Chapter 11 arbitral tribunals, and 'in order to clarify and reaffirm the meaning of certain of its provisions'. The relevant part of the Note on Article 1105 reads as follows:

1. Article 1105(1) prescribes the customary international law minimum standard of treatment of aliens as the minimum standard of treatment to be afforded to investments of investors of another Party.
2. The concepts of 'fair and equitable treatment' and 'full protection and security' do not require treatment in addition to or beyond that which is required by the customary international law minimum standard of treatment of aliens.
3. A determination that there has been a breach of another provision of the NAFTA, or of a separate international agreement, does not establish that there has been a breach of Article 1105(1).

[a]   The Context in Which the Note Was Adopted

There exists no official documents and very limited governmental information about the actual *reasons* as to why NAFTA Parties decided to issue the Note in July 2001.[115] However, the *context* in which the Note was issued is well known. The Note was clearly a reaction by the Parties to the controversial rulings rendered by three tribunals in 2000–2001: *Metalclad, S.D. Myers* and *Pope & Talbot*.[116] As noted by one author, the awards 'created both the opportunity and the motive' for the FTC interpretation.[117] For another writer, Canada sought such changes as early as 1998 because 'NAFTA tribunals were not agreeing with the arguments that each NAFTA Party was making about NAFTA Article 1105'.[118] These events – which eventually led Parties to issue the Note in July 2001 – can be chronologically summarized as follows:

– On 30 August 2000, the *Metalclad* tribunal concluded that when interpreted in light of the preamble to the NAFTA, Article 1105 included obligations of transparency and predictability.[119] The tribunal found that Mexico had failed to ensure a transparent and predictable framework for the investor's investment and that this constituted a failure to provide FET as required under Article 1105. The tribunal awarded the investor USD 16.7 million in compensation for Mexico's breach of Articles 1105 and 1110. As further

---

115. In the context of the (then) on-going proceedings in the *Pope & Talbot* case, Canada simply sent a letter on 10 August 2001 to the tribunal attaching the Note and stating: 'We respectfully draw the Tribunal's attention to NAFTA Article 1131(2) which states that interpretations by the Commission of a provision of the NAFTA is binding on Tribunals established under Section B of Chapter Eleven of NAFTA'.
116. Gabrielle Kaufmann-Kohler, *Interpretive Powers of the NAFTA Free Trade Commission – Necessary Safety Valve or Infringement of the Rule of Law?*, in *Fifteen Years of NAFTA Chapter 11 Arbitration* 181 (Frédéric Bachand ed., JurisNet 2011).
117. Charles H. Brower II, *Why the FTC Notes of Interpretation Constitute a Partial Amendment of NAFTA Article 1105*, 46 Va. J. Int'l L. 347, 352-353 (2006).
118. Weiler, *supra* n. 84, at 703. *See also*: Todd Weiler, *NAFTA Investment Arbitration and the Growth of International Economic Law*, 2 Bus. L. Int'l 158, 180 (2002), vigorously criticizing the role played by Canada's governmental lawyers working on these arbitration cases.
119. *Metalclad v. Mexico*, Award, (30 August 2000), paras. 70, 76.

discussed below,[120] the tribunal's finding was criticized on the ground that the so-called obligation of transparency was not explicitly referred to in NAFTA Chapter 11, and could only be found in other chapters of the treaty. In other words, for many, the tribunal had misstated the applicable law.

–   Soon after, the *S.D. Myers* tribunal rendered its Partial Award on 13 November 2000, which awarded the investor CAD 6 million[121] in compensation for the breach of both Articles 1102 and 1105. In the award, two of the three tribunal members came to the conclusion that a finding of a breach of the national treatment provision (Article 1102) supported a claim for a breach of Article 1105.[122] This conclusion was rejected by the Parties.[123] Another controversial finding was the tribunal's interpretation of the FET clause as an 'overriding' provision that covers other standards of protection, including the national treatment.[124]

–   On 8 February 2001, Canada commenced set-aside proceedings before the Federal Court of Canada against the *S.D. Myers* Award and contested the tribunal's conclusion on the articulation between Articles 1102 and 1105. The case was still pending at the time the Note was issued by the Parties (some six months later).

–   On 10 April 2001, the *Pope & Talbot* tribunal released its Award on the Merits of Phase 2 concluding, *inter alia*, that Article 1105 requires the application of the 'fair and equitable treatment' *independently* (and *in addition*) to the minimum standard of treatment under international law.[125] One important aspect of the case is that during the proceedings, all three NAFTA Parties had expressly rejected that interpretation. The tribunal finally came to the conclusion that Canada had breached its obligations under Article 1105 regarding one aspect of the implementation of the 1996 bilateral Canada–United States *Softwood Lumber Agreement* (i.e., the 'verification review' process). The tribunal's assessment of damages was left for the next phase of the proceedings. In other on-going NAFTA arbitration cases at the time, NAFTA Parties strongly rejected the reasoning of the *Pope & Talbot* tribunal; the United States affirmed (only *two days* after the award was rendered) that it was 'poorly reasoned and unpersuasive';[126] Canada stated that the tribunal had 'arrived at an incorrect interpretation of fair and equitable';[127] and Mexico indicated that the tribunal's 'refusal to adopt the

---

120. *See*, at Chapter 3 section §3.02[C][1] below.
121. Around USD 4 million in 2000.
122. *S.D. Myers v. Canada*, First Partial Award, (13 November 2000), para. 266. Arbitrator Chiasson dissented and considered that a breach of another provision cannot be the foundation for a violation of Article 1105.
123. Kinnear et al., *supra* n. 1, at 23.
124. *See* the analysis in: Kläger, *supra* n. 44, at 66. The proposition that the FET is an 'overriding' provision is further discussed below at Chapter 4 section §4.01.
125. *Pope & Talbot Inc. v. Canada*, UNCITRAL, Award on the Merits of Phase II (10 April 2001).
126. *Methanex v. United States*, US Reply Memorial on Jurisdiction, Admissibility and the Proposed Amendment, (12 April 2001), at 26.
127. *Ibid.*, Canada's Second Article 1128 Submission, (30 April 2001).

Parties' shared view [on this point] can only be viewed as perverse'.[128] Government officials also voiced their concern in several noteworthy articles on the issue.[129]

– In the meantime, Mexico had commenced set-aside proceedings of the *Metalclad* award before the Supreme Court of British Columbia (the seat of the arbitration proceedings) to challenge, *inter alia*, the tribunal's broad interpretation of Article 1105. Justice Tysoe issued his decision on 22 May 2001, a little over a month after the controversial *Pope & Talbot* award.[130] In his decision, Justice Tysoe rejected in rather strong terms, the reasoning behind the *Pope & Talbot* ruling on Article 1105 and concluded that the protection under this provision was limited to the minimum standard of protection afforded by *customary* international law. His conclusion reflected the position that had been advanced by NAFTA Parties in the proceedings.[131] Justice Tysoe rejected the *Metalclad* tribunal's findings on the so-called obligation of transparency and set-aside the part of the award related to Article 1105.

The state of the case law in the spring of 2001 has been described as follows by Kinnear:

> By the spring of 2001, the case law concerning Article 1105 was in a rather unusual state. The conclusions in the *Metalclad* Award concerning Article 1105 had been set aside (although one allegation concerning expropriation had been upheld). The *S.D. Myers* award, which included reasoning similar to that of the *Metalclad* award, was subject to set-aside proceedings but had not yet been heard by the court. And the *Pope & Talbot* tribunal, which had been specifically questioned by Mr. Justice Tysoe, was proceeding to an assessment of damages for a breach of Article 1105.[132]

The issuance of the Note in July 2001 was made in great part due to timing. At the time, the *Pope & Talbot* tribunal had just started the next phase of its proceedings for the assessment of damages resulting from Canada's breach of Article 1105. If any 'mistakes' had been made by the tribunal, now was the perfect time to 'correct' them. Also, set-aside proceedings of the *S.D. Myers* award were pending before the Federal Court of Canada. Canada wanted to provide further guidance to the Court in view of the rather confusing state of affairs prevailing at the time concerning the proper interpretation to be given to Article 1105.

There is another clear reason why the Note was issued precisely at that time. NAFTA Parties were concerned that the controversial findings of these three awards which gave a broad interpretation to Article 1105 would somehow set a trend that

---

128. *Ibid.*, Mexico's Article 1128 Submission, (30 April 2001).
129. *See*, for instance, the position of U.S. State Department lawyer, Mark Clodfelter, *U.S. State Department Participation in International Economic Dispute Resolution*, 42 S. Tex. L Rev 1273 (2001).
130. *Mexico v. Metalclad*, 2001 BCSC 664, Supreme Court of British Columbia, Judgment and Reasons for Decision (2 May 2001).
131. Kinnear et al., *supra* n. 1, at 27.
132. *Ibid.*

would be followed by future tribunals.[133] Thus, several other high profile NAFTA arbitration cases were then pending (*UPS, Loewen, Mondev, Methanex, ADF, Waste Management*) wherein the scope of Article 1105 had already been hotly debated between the parties. For one writer, the NAFTA Parties have used the FTC interpretation 'as the vehicle to pre-empt further losses'.[134]

The Note has thus been considered by some writers as an opportunistic method that was put in place in order to avoid liability in on-going arbitration cases where they were acting as respondents.[135] NAFTA Parties were accused by investors,[136] and scholars, of acting as both party and judge 'in an attempt to change the ground rules in mid-game'.[137] This appears to be the position taken by the *Pope & Talbot* tribunal in a letter sent to the parties:

> Without pre-empting at this time the implications properly to be drawn it appears to the Tribunal that if the Commission viewed its Interpretation to have a retroactive effect on this case, its actions could be viewed as seeking to overturn a treaty interpretation already made by a NAFTA Chapter 11 Tribunal, Canada acting both as disputing party and as member of a reviewing body.[138]

Critics of the Note have not limited themselves to the fact that Parties were acting as both party and judge in the proceedings.[139] Some writers have also noted the Parties' 'failure to adopt procedures that serve the fundamental values of accountability, transparency, and democratic participation' since they were issued 'out of the blue', 'without any prior public consultation', and without giving 'any warning to investors party to ongoing Chapter Eleven arbitrations'.[140] In fact, the Note has even been described as 'the most recent, and perhaps the most serious development in the legitimacy crisis of NAFTA's investment chapter'.[141] In a legal opinion, one prominent British scholar 'protested' against 'the impropriety of the three governments making such an intervention well into the process of arbitration' contrary to the 'most

---

133. Weiler, *supra* n. 84, at 703-704; Weiler, *supra* n. 118, at 405, 422; Thomas, *supra* n. 84, at 462.
134. Brower, *supra* n. 117, at 347, 352-353, 356. *See also*: I. Laird, *Betrayal, Shock and Outrage – Recent Developments in NAFTA Article 1105*, in *NAFTA Investment Law and Arbitration: The Early Years* 53 (T. Weiler ed., Transnational Publ. 2004).
135. Charles H. Brower II, *Structure, Legitimacy, and NAFTA's Investment Chapter*, 36 Vand. J. Transnat'l L. 81 (2003).
136. *See*: *ADF v. United States*, Investor's Reply to the US Counter-Memorial on Competence and Liability, (28 January 2002), para. 215; *Methanex v. United States*, Claimant's Reply to U.S Amended Statement of Defense, (19 February 2004), para. 203.
137. Charles N. Brower, *NAFTA's Investment Chapter: Dynamic Laboratory, Failed Experiments and Lessons for the FTAA: Concerns of the NAFTA Parties and Civil Society*, 97 ASIL Proc. 251, 253 (2003).
138. *Pope & Talbot Inc. v. Canada*, Award in Respect of Damages, (31 May 2002), para. 12, letter of 17 September 2001. *See also*, the following comment made by the tribunal in a letter dated 23 October 2001 (quoted in: *Ibid.*, para. 13): 'it may be taken as a rule of international law that no-one shall be judge in his own cause, and that the purpose of this arbitral mechanism is under Article 1105 to assure due process before an impartial tribunal'.
139. For an overview, *see*: Kaufmann-Kohler, *supra* n. 116, at 188.
140. Brower, *supra* n. 135, at 93, 79-81.
141. *Ibid.*, at 82. *See also*: Guillermo Aguilar Alvarez & William W. Park, *The New Face of Investment Arbitration: NAFTA Chapter 11*, 28 Yale JIL 397 (2003).

elementary rules of the due process of justice'.[142] Similarly, for Schreuer '[i]t is obvious that a mechanism whereby a party to a dispute is able to influence the outcome of judicial proceedings, by issuing official interpretation to the detriment of the other party, is incompatible with principles of a fair procedure and is hence undesirable'.[143] These are sound criticisms. Kaufmann-Kohler has recently well-explained why some aspects of the Note may be considered as contrary to due process:

> The difficulty here lies in the two hats worn by the respondent State. That State is at the same time a litigant and a member of the FTC. As a member of the FTC, it contributes to the content of the interpretation. As a litigant, it will benefit from the interpretation if the latter influences the outcome in its favor. This appears to be contrary to due process, specifically contrary to the principle of independence and impartiality of justice, which includes the principle that no one can be the judge of its own cause. It can also be argued that such an interpretation breaches the principle of equal treatment of the parties and the opportunity to be heard of the other party.[144]

For all of these reasons, a number of writers have argued that the Note should only be binding on *future* tribunals, not on-going arbitration disputes.[145] While there are good reasons to believe that this is indeed how the Note should have been applied at the time,[146] the issue is now moot more than ten years after the event.

Not surprisingly, NAFTA Parties have refuted these different arguments put forward by investors and scholars. For instance, in *Loewen*, the United States explained that the FTC interpretation was perfectly legal under NAFTA and that there was nothing surprising about the fact that it would apply to on-going arbitration proceedings.[147]

In any event, as properly summarized by Weiler, the ultimate goal of the NAFTA Parties in issuing the Note was to 'correct' three 'mistakes' that had been made by previous NAFTA tribunals.[148] In fact, NAFTA Parties have publicly acknowledged such

---

142. *Methanex v. United States*, Second Opinion, filed by Sir Robert Jennings on behalf of the Investor, (18 September 2001), at 6-7 (quoted in: *Methanex v. United States*, Investor's Reply to US Amended Statement of Defence, (19 February 2004), para. 203).
143. C. Schreuer, *Diversity and Harmonization of Treaty Interpretation in Investment Arbitration*, in: Fitzmaurice et al., *supra* n. 108, at 148.
144. Kaufmann-Kohler, *supra* n. 116, at 192.
145. Charles Brower II, *Investor-State Disputes Under NAFTA: The Empire Strikes Back*, 40 Colum J. Transnat'l L. 43, 56 (2001-2002). *See also*: Weiler, *supra* n. 84, at 705. *Contra*: Thomas, *supra* n. 84, at 454-455.
146. Kaufmann-Kohler, *supra* n. 116, at 193.
147. *Loewen v. United States*, US Rejoinder, (27 August 2001), at 146, 147 ('Finally, there is no merit to claimants' assertion that the Commission's interpretation represents an impermissible "intrusion" into an ongoing arbitration. In submitting their claims to arbitration, claimants expressly consented to arbitration "in accordance with the procedures set out in this Agreement" NAFTA Art. 1121(1)(a). Those procedures have always included Article 1131(2)'s provision for the Commission to issue interpretations binding on Chapter Eleven tribunals. Nor is it any surprise that neither Article 1131(2) nor the July 31 interpretation suggests that ongoing arbitrations should be unaffected by a Commission interpretation; the general rule in international law is that agreements as to the interpretation of a treaty provision are retroactive in effect, since an interpretation does not change the content of a provision, it merely clarifies what the provision always meant').
148. Weiler, *supra* n. 118, at 183. *See also*: Weiler, *supra* n. 84, at 703-704.

'correctional' dimension in their proceedings.[149] The Note basically 'overruled' the extensive interpretation of Article 1105 put forward by these three awards.[150]

The *first two* paragraphs of the Note overruled *Pope & Talbot*'s holding that the FET standard of protection should be considered *in addition* to the minimum standard of treatment existing under international law.[151] It was now clear that the FET clause was a reference to the minimum standard of treatment existing under customary international law. This clarification effort has been criticized by many. It was characterized as an 'attempt to create ambiguity where none exists' since international law has a 'clearly established meaning'.[152] Also, as a result of the Note, it was argued that the debate on the proper meaning of 'international law' had simply moved to the equally vague expression of 'international minimum standard' under custom.[153] In other words, the Note did not clarify the actual scope of Article 1105 to any substantial degree.[154] This is indeed the position adopted by many investors in NAFTA proceedings.[155]

The first two paragraphs of the Note were also meant to address (and correct) the *Metalclad* award. Thus, the tribunal recognized the existence of an obligation of transparency under Article 1105 solely based on treaty provisions found in NAFTA chapters *other* than Chapter 11. In doing so, the tribunal effectively applied a standard of protection *in addition* to the minimum standard of treatment under custom (where

---

149. *ADF v. United States*, US Post-Hearing Submission on Article 1105(1) and Pope & Talbot, (27 June 2002), at 18 (indicating that the Note was issued 'largely to address the Pope tribunal's failure to heed the NAFTA Parties' proper statements regarding the interpretation of Article 1105(1)').

150. Brower, *supra* n. 117, at 354.

151. Laird, *supra* n. 134, at 65; J.C. Thomas, *Fair and Equitable Treatment under NAFTA's Investment Chapter; Remarks*, 96 ASIL Proc. 9, 15 (2002); Weiler, *supra* n. 84, at 703-704.

152. Brower *supra* n. 145, at 56; *See also*: Brower, *supra* n. 135, at 78-79; *Methanex*, Second Opinion of Sir Robert Jennings, 5 November 2002, at 6; Alvarez, *supra* n. 70, at 189-193.

153. Courtney C. Kirkman, *Fair and Equitable Treatment: Methanex v. United States and the Narrowing Scope of NAFTA Article 1105*, 34 Law & Pol'y Int'l Bus. 343, 390 (2002-2003); D.A. Gantz, *International Decision: Pope & Talbot*, 97 AJIL 949 (2003); Todd Weiler, *NAFTA Chapter 11 Jurisprudence: Coming Along Nicely*, 9 Sw. J.L. & Trade Am. 245, 264 (2002-2003); Marcela Klein Bronfman, *Fair and Equitable Treatment: An Evolving Standard*, 10 Max Planck Yrbk. UNL 669 (2006); L. Paradell, *The BIT Experience of the Fair and Equitable Treatment Standard*, in *Investment Treaty Law: Current Issues II* 123 (F. Ortino et al. eds., British IICL 2007); Newcombe & Paradell, *supra* n. 18, at 273; Stefan Matiation, *Arbitration with Two Twists: Loewen v. United States and Free Trade Commission Intervention in NAFTA Chapter 11 Disputes*, 24 U. Pa. J. Int'l Econ. L. 451, 470, 490, 501-502 (2003); M.C. Porterfield, *An International Common Law of Investor Rights?*, 27 U. Pa. J. Int'l Econ. L. 92 (2006).

154. Newcombe & Paradell, *supra* n. 18, at 273; Matiation, *supra* n. 153, at 470, 490, 501-502; Porterfield, *supra* n. 153, at 92.

155. *See*, for instance: *United Parcel Service of America Inc. v. Canada* [hereinafter *UPS v. Canada*], UNCITRAL, Investor's Reply to Article 1128 Submissions, (21 May 2002), para. 19; *ibid.*, Investor's Counter Memorial, (26 March 2002), para. 70; *ADF v. United States*, Investor's Post-Hearing Submissions on Article 1105 and Pope & Talbot, (11 July 2002), para. 30; *Chemtura Corporation v. Canada* [hereinafter *Chemtura v. Canada*], UNCITRAL, Investor's Memorial, (2 June 2008), para. 343.

no such obligation of transparency is said to exist[156]).[157] This is the conclusion reached, for instance, by the *Merrill & Ring* tribunal.[158]

It is not entirely clear, however, whether or not these first two paragraphs were also aimed at correcting *S.D. Myers*'s succinct analysis of Article 1105.[159] Thus, on the one hand, the tribunal mentioned that the words 'fair and equitable treatment' could not be read 'in isolation', but instead 'in conjunction' with the introductory phrase 'treatment in accordance with international law'.[160] In fact, the *Pope & Talbot* tribunal rejected the award precisely because it interpreted it as an endorsement of the view that the FET clause was indeed a reference to the minimum standard of treatment.[161] On the other hand, some passages of the *S.D. Myers* award suggest that the tribunal viewed the concept of FET as *distinct* from that of the minimum standard.[162] This is, for instance, how the *Merrill & Ring* tribunal interpreted the award.[163]

The *third* paragraph of the Note overruled the *S.D. Myers* award's reasoning that a breach of one *provision* of Chapter 11 could establish a breach of another.[164] This 'correction' has been portrayed as an 'over-reaction' to the actual finding of the *S.D. Myers* tribunal.[165] The third paragraph of the Note was also aimed at correcting the mistake made by the *S.D. Myers* tribunal for whom a breach of the national treatment clause at Article 1102 (which is considered as a *treaty obligation* and *not* a customary international law obligation) could establish a violation of the minimum standard under custom.[166] The Note makes it clear that the finding of a breach of a separate international agreement does not establish a breach of Article 1105. Yet, as noted by one writer, 'even if the breach of separate treaty obligations does not "establish" a

---

156. This controversial question is further discussed at Chapter 3 section §3.02[C] below.
157. Laird, *supra* n. 134, at 59; C. Tollefson, *Metalclad vs. United Mexican States Revisited: Judicial Oversight of Nafta's Chapter Eleven Investor-State Claim Process*, 11 Minn. J. Global Trade 183 (2001-2002).
158. *Merrill & Ring v. Canada*, Award, (31 March 2010), para. 189 ('In linking fair and equitable treatment with the requirement of transparency under international law, but not identifying a specific source of this requirement, the *Metalclad* tribunal appears to have relied on some kind of autonomous role of fair and equitable treatment').
159. Laird, *supra* n. 134, at 63.
160. *S.D. Myers v. Canada*, First Partial Award, (13 November 2000), para. 262.
161. *Pope & Talbot Inc. v. Canada*, Award on the Merits (Phase 2), (10 April 2001), para. 113, fn. 108: '[the *S.D. Myers* tribunal] apparently interpreted the BITs as simply establishing a minimum standard of conduct. (...) By not appreciating the plain language of the BITs, the *Myers* tribunal did not address the implications of that language on the proper interpretation of Article 1105. For that reason, this Tribunal does not consider the *Myers* Partial Award to be a persuasive precedent on this matter and will not be bound by it'.
162. *See*, the analysis of Todd Weiler, *NAFTA Article 1105 and the Free Trade Commission; Just Sour Grapes, or Something more Serious?*, 29(11) Int'l Bus. Law. 493 (2001).
163. *Merrill & Ring v. Canada*, Award, (31 March 2010), para. 189.
164. *S.D. Myers v. Canada*, First Partial Award, (13 November 2000). The same position was also taken by arbitrator Bryan Schwartz in his Separate Opinion, at para. 237.
165. Laird, *supra* n. 134, at 62 ('A close reading of the award makes it clear that majority of the tribunal sought merely to confirm the fairly obvious conclusion that the facts that support a breach of another investment obligation "will tend to weigh heavily in favour of finding a breach of Article 1105." (...) it is not the national treatment breach itself that establishes the breach of Article 1105, but the facts leading to the national treatment breach that support both breaches').
166. *See, Pope & Talbot Inc. v. Canada*, US Fifth Submission, (1 December 2000), paras. 3–9.

violation of Article 1105 per se, tribunals might still characterize treaty violations as relevant, perhaps even strong, evidence of unfair and inequitable treatment'.[167]

In a more abstract sense, Schill argues that the Note is an 'attempt to relink the content of investment treaties to customary international law' and 'cannot be viewed only as an effort to establish the meaning of fair and equitable treatment', but also as 'part of the struggle to determine whether tribunals or States have the ultimate power of interpreting investment treaties and the principles they contain'.[168]

[b]   The Note Is a Binding Subsequent Agreement Representing the
        Definitive Meaning of Article 1105

NAFTA Article 1131(2) makes it clear that any Note of Interpretation issued by the FTC is binding on NAFTA tribunals. The plain and ordinary meaning of the word 'binding' leaves no room for any other interpretation. All NAFTA Parties (Canada,[169] the United States[170] and Mexico[171]) have consistently adopted this obvious position in their pleadings when acting as respondents (as well as in their respective Article 1128 submissions[172]). Moreover, most claimants have explicitly recognized the binding nature of the Note;[173]

---

167. Brower, *supra* n. 135, at 78-79; Barnali Choudhury, *Evolution or Devolution? Defining Fair and Equitable Treatment in International Investment Law*, 6(2) J. World Invest. & Trade 314 (2005) ('the [*S.D. Myers*] Decision is still good law in establishing that discriminatory conduct, particularly with respect to a State's better treatment of its domestic investors than its foreign investors, can establish a breach of the fair and equitable treatment standard').

168. Schill, *supra* n. 65, at 269-270.

169. See, for instance: *Merrill & Ring v. Canada*, Canada's Rejoinder, (27 March 2009), para. 145; *ibid.*, Canada's Counter-Memorial, (13 May 2008), para. 446; *Chemtura v. Canada*, Canada's Rejoinder, (10 July 2009) at para. 126; *ibid.*, Canada's Counter-Memorial, (20 October 2008), paras. 668–669; *Pope & Talbot Inc. v. Canada*, Canada's Submission, (10 August 2001); *UPS v. Canada*, Memorial of Canada on Preliminary Jurisdictional Objections, (14 February 2002), paras. 89, 95; *ibid.*, Canada's Reply Memorial on Preliminary Jurisdictional Objections, (12 April 2002), paras. 93, 94.

170. See, for instance: *ADF v. United States*, US Counter-Memorial on Competence and Liability, (1 June 2001), at 48, 49; *ibid.*, US Rejoinder on Competence and Liability, (29 March 2002), at 34; *Glamis Gold, Ltd. v. United States* [hereinafter *Glamis v. United States*], UNCITRAL, US Counter-Memorial, (19 September 2006), at 219; *Grand River v. United States*, US Counter-Memorial, (22 December 2008), at 88, 89; *Loewen v. United States*, US Rejoinder, (27 August 2001), at 56, 111, 112, 144; *Methanex v. United States*, US Amended Statement of Defence, (19 February 2004), para. 352; *ibid.*, US Post-Hearing Submission, (20 July 2001), at 3; *Mondev v. United States*, US Rejoinder on Competence and Liability, (1 October 2001), at 15; *ibid.*, Award, (11 October 2002), para. 106 (describing the position of the United States).

171. See, for instance: *Cargill, Inc. v. Mexico*, ICSID no. ARB(AF)/05/02, Award, (18 September 2009), para. 240.

172. See, for instance: *UPS v. Canada*, US Second Submission, (13 May 2002), para. 11; *Grand River v. United States*, Canada's Article 1128 Submission, (19 January 2009), para. 4; *Methanex Corporation v. United States*, Mexico's Article 1128 Submission, (11 February 2002), at 3; *ibid.*, Canada's Third Article 1128 Submission, (8 February 2002), para. 18.

173. See, for instance: *Chemtura v. Canada*, Claimant's Redacted Memorial, (2 June 2008), para. 343; *ibid.*, Claimant's Redacted Reply, (15 May 2009), para. 320; *ADF v. United States*, Claimant's Post-Hearing Submission on NAFTA Article 1105(1) and the Damages Award in Pope & Talbot, (11 July 2002), para. 9; *Thunderbird v. Mexico*, Investor's Particularized Statement of Claim, (15 August 2003), para. 59.

and only a few investors have openly argued otherwise.[174] There is also consensus amongst writers on this point.[175]

All NAFTA tribunals have concluded that the Note is binding.[176] This is even the case with the *Pope & Talbot* tribunal. It ruled that the Note was in fact an amendment, but nevertheless acknowledged that pursuant to Article 1131(2), it was binding.[177]

In any event, the Note must be considered as a 'subsequent agreement between the parties' regarding the interpretation of Article 1105 pursuant to Article 31(3)a of the *Vienna Convention*.[178] This position was clearly endorsed by the *Methanex* tribunal when it concluded that it had 'no difficulty in deciding' that the Note 'is properly characterized as a "subsequent agreement" on interpretation falling within the scope of Article 31(3)(a) of the Vienna Convention'.[179] The same position was adopted by the *ADF* tribunal stating that '[n]o more authentic and authoritative source of instruction on what the Parties intended to convey in a particular provision of NAFTA, is possible'.[180] In practical terms, this means for any tribunal that examines Article 1105 that it 'should look to the ordinary meaning of the provision in accordance with Article 31(1) of the Vienna Convention, and also take into account the interpretation of 31st July 2001 pursuant to Article 31(3)(a) of the Vienna Convention'.[181]

As put by Canada in *Merrill & Ring*, 'whatever ambiguities may have previously existed have been definitively resolved by the 2001 Note'.[182] Thus, the Note represents

---

174. *UPS v. Canada*, Investor's Memorial (Merits Phase), (23 March 2005), paras. 697–699; *ibid.*, Investor's Rejoinder (Jurisdictional Phase), (19 April 2002), para. 36; *Pope & Talbot Inc. v. Canada*, Investor's Post-Hearing Submissions (Damages Phase), (14 December 2001), para. 35.
175. It should be noted, however, that a number of authors believe that the Notes is an 'amendment' and, therefore, that it is *not* binding on tribunals: Brower *supra* n. 145, at 56, ft. 71; Kirkman, *supra* n. 153, at 382; Weiler, *supra* n. 84, at 705.
176. *See*, for instance, *Merrill & Ring v. Canada*, Award, (31 March 2010), paras. 190–192; *UPS v. Canada*, Award (Jurisdiction), (22 November 2002), para. 96; *ADF v. United States*, Award, (9 January 2003), para. 176; *Glamis v. United States*, Award, (8 June 2009), para. 599; *Grand River v. United States*, Award, (12 January 2011), para. 175; *Methanex v. United States*, Award, (3 August 2005), Part IV, Ch. C, para. 20; *Loewen v. United States*, Award, (26 June 2003), para. 126; *Cargill, Inc. v. Mexico*, Award, (18 September 2009), paras. 135, 268. Other tribunals have also come to the same conclusion by applying the Note without discussing its binding nature: *Chemtura v. Canada*, Award, (2 August 2010), para. 120; *Mondev v. United States*, Award, (11 October 2002), paras. 120–122; *Waste Management, Inc. v. Mexico ("Number 2")* [hereinafter *Waste Management v. Mexico*], ICSID No. ARB(AF)/00/3, Award, (30 April 2004), paras. 90, 91; *Thunderbird v. Mexico*, Award, (26 January 2006), para. 192; *Mobil Investments Canada Inc. and Murphy Oil Corporation v. Canada* [hereinafter *Mobil v. Canada*], ICSID No. ARB(AF)/07/4, Decision on Liability and on Principles of Quantum, (22 May 2012), para. 135.
177. *Pope & Talbot Inc. v. Canada*, Award in Respect of Damages, (31 May 2002), para. 51.
178. Schill, *supra* n. 65, at 268; Newcombe & Paradell, *supra* n. 18, at 117; Roberts, *supra* n. 96, at 215; J. Romesh Weeramantry, *Treaty Interpretation in Investment Arbitration* 83 (Oxford U. Press 2012).
179. *Methanex v. United States*, Award, (3 August 2005), Part II, Ch. B, paras. 21, 23. *See also*, at Part IV, Ch. C, para. 20.
180. *ADF v. United States*, Award, (9 January 2003), para. 177. *See also: Canadian Cattlemen v. United States*, Award on Jurisdiction, (28 January 2008), paras. 184, 185.
181. *Methanex v. United States*, Award, (3 August 2005), Part II, Ch. H, para. 23.
182. *Merrill & Ring v. Canada*, Canada's Rejoinder (27 March 2009), paras. 145, 151. *See also: Ibid.*, Canada's Counter-Memorial, (13 May 2008), para. 446; *Chemtura v. Canada*, Canada's Counter-Memorial, (20 October 2008), para. 669.

the *definitive meaning* of Article 1105,[183] which is 'no longer open to debate'.[184] For all NAFTA Parties, the FTC interpretation 'does not change the meaning of Article 1105(1) – it merely clarifies the meaning that the Article has always had'.[185]

A number of claimants have rejected this line of arguments.[186] One claimant went so far as to even suggest that it was simply 'impossible' that the Note could in fact reflect the Parties' 'true intention' when they drafted the NAFTA.[187] Canada responded that 'as one of the Parties to the NAFTA', it was 'well-positioned to speak to the issue of the "true intention" of the Parties when drafting Article 1105'.[188]

[c] *The Note Is Not an Amendment*

One contentious issue in case law has been the allegation that the FTC Note is not at all an 'interpretation' under Article 1131, but an attempt to 'amend' NAFTA. The issue first arose in the context of the *Pope & Talbot* case. In its third award of 2002, the

---

183. *See, Mondev v. United States,* Award, (11 October 2002), para. 103, describing the position of the United States (indicating that the Notes constitute 'the definitive statement of what the Parties intended from the source designated by the Treaty as the ultimate and most authoritative source of its meaning, the Parties themselves').

184. *ADF v. United States,* US Rejoinder on Competence and Liability, (29 March 2002), at 34. *See also: ibid.,* US Counter-Memorial on Competence and Liability, (1 June 2001), para. 50.

185. *ADF v. United States,* US Final Post-Hearing Submission on Article 1105(1) and *Pope & Talbot,* (1 August 2002), at 3. *See also: Pope & Talbot Inc. v. Canada,* US Sixth Submission (Corrected), (2 October 2001); *Loewen v. United States,* Canada's Article 1128 Submission, (19 November 2001), para. 12; *Chemtura v. Canada,* Canada's Counter-Memorial, (20 October 2008), paras. 667, 895; *ibid.,* Canada's Rejoinder, (10 July 2009), para. 247; *Pope & Talbot Inc. v. Canada,* Canada's First Submission Re: The NAFTA FTC Statement, (10 September 2001), at 2; *ibid.,* Canada's Second Submission Re: The NAFTA FTC Statement, (1 October 2001), at 3; *ibid.,* Mexico's Letter, (5 October 2001); *UPS v. Canada,* Canada's Memorial on Preliminary Jurisdictional Objections, (14 February 2002), paras. 93, 95; *ibid.,* Canada's Reply Memorial on Preliminary Jurisdictional Objections, (12 April 2002), para. 92; *Methanex v. United States,* Canada's Third Article 1128 Submission, (8 February 2002), paras. 5, 18; *ibid.,* Mexico's Article 1128 Submission, (11 February 2002).

186. *See,* for instance: *Pope & Talbot Inc. v. Canada,* Investor's First Submission Re: The NAFTA FTC Statement, (10 September 2001), at 3-5; *ibid.,* Investor's Post-Hearing Submissions (Damages Phase), (14 December 2001), para. 37; *Methanex v. United States,* Reply of Claimant to U.S. Amended Statement of Defense, (19 February 2004), para. 204; *ibid.,* Post-Hearing Submission of Claimant, (20 July 2001), at 2.

187. *Merrill & Ring v. Canada,* Investor's Reply, (15 December 2008), paras. 292–295, 297 ('The second reason why Canada's position on the Notes is not correct is that they run counter to the plain and ordinary meaning of NAFTA Article 1105(1). (…) NAFTA Article 1105(1) clearly states that Canada must "accord investments of investors of another Party treatment in accordance with *international law*" not *customary* international law. The ordinary meaning of "international law" refers to all sources of international law enumerated in Article 38(1) of the *ICJ Statute* not only customary international law. The drafters of the NAFTA were fluent in the language of international law, and were surely alert to the distinction. (…) In the end, carrying the Notes through to their logical conclusion would deprive the words "fair and equitable treatment" in NAFTA Article 1105(1) of any meaning, thereby leading to an absurd or unreasonable result. This runs counter to one of the most basic tenets of treaty interpretation (…). In short, it is simply impossible that the Notes accurately reflect the Parties' true intention at the time they drafted the NAFTA. Accordingly, this Tribunal should interpret NAFTA Article 1105(1) in accordance with its original wording. This means interpreting the words "fair and equitable treatment" according to their ordinary meaning' (emphasis in the original).

188. *Merrill & Ring v. Canada,* Canada's Rejoinder, (27 March 2009), paras. 149, 151.

tribunal had to determine whether its previous 2001 award (where it adopted a controversially broad interpretation of Article 1105 and held that Canada had breached this provision) was at all compatible with the FTC's Note, which had been issued in the meantime. The investor argued that the Note was an amendment of Article 1105 since the word 'customary' was inserted before the expression 'international law' in order to limit its scope.[189] The *Pope & Talbot* tribunal took the same view.[190] Since the NAFTA Parties did not enact this 'amendment' in accordance with the procedure set out at Article 2202,[191] the investor argued that the Note should be considered an *ultra vires* amendment not binding on tribunals.[192]

Since then, several claimants have put forward the same argument.[193] They have, for instance, complained that such a 'retroactive amendment' was in breach of the 'most elementary notions of due process' and 'utterly incompatible with the regime of independent, impartial arbitration' under NAFTA Chapter 11.[194] They have also argued that the Note was contrary to basic principles of treaty interpretation.[195] It should be noted that in more recent cases, claimant investors have seldom raised that argument; with the notable exception of *Merrill & Ring*.[196] In all NAFTA cases, Canada,[197] the United States[198] and Mexico[199] have consistently maintained in their proceedings (as

189. *Pope & Talbot Inc. v. Canada,* Letter of the Investor, (10 September 2001).
190. *Ibid.,* Award in Respect of Damages, (31 May 2002), para. 47.
191. Article 2202 provides that in order for 'any modification of or addition to this Agreement' to 'constitute an integral part' of NAFTA, they must be 'approved in accordance with the applicable legal procedures of each Party'.
192. *Pope & Talbot Inc. v. Canada,* Letter of the Investor, (10 September 2001).
193. *See,* for instance: *Merrill & Ring v. Canada,* Investor's Reply, (15 December 2008), paras. 300, 301; *UPS v. Canada,* Investor's Reply to Article 1128 Submissions, (21 May 2002), paras. 21, 22; *ADF v. United States,* Investor's Reply, (22 January 2002), paras. 216–217. *See also: Mondev v. United States,* Award, (11 October 2002), para. 102, describing the position of the investor.
194. *Methanex v. United States,* Investor's First Submission on the FTC Notes, (18 September 2001), at 19, 20.
195. *UPS v. Canada,* Investor's Memorial (Merits Phase), (23 March 2005), paras. 687, 697.
196. *Merrill & Ring v. Canada,* Investor's Reply, (15 December 2008), paras. 300, 301 ('In the case of the Notes, the Parties did not follow the proper procedures; rather, they sought to amend the NAFTA through a less cumbersome and more politically expedient channel. This was an improper attempt to circumvent the requirements of the NAFTA, and disguise an "amendment" in the garb of an "interpretation". This amendment is therefore *ultra vires* the powers of the Free Trade Commission, and of no legal force or effect').
197. *Merrill & Ring v. Canada,* Canada's Rejoinder, (27 March 2009), paras. 151, 155-157; *ibid.,* Canada's Counter-Memorial, (13 May 2008), paras. 445, 446; *Chemtura v. Canada,* Canada's Counter-Memorial, (20 October 2008), para. 891; *Pope & Talbot Inc. v. Canada,* Canada's Letter, (10 September 2001), at 2; *UPS v. Canada,* Canada's Counter-Memorial (Merits Phase), (22 June 2005), para. 45.
198. *ADF v. United States,* US Post-Hearing Submission on Article 1105(1) and Pope & Talbot, (27 June 2002), at 3; *Loewen v. United States,* US Rejoinder, (27 August 2001), at 146; *Methanex v. United States,* US Amended Statement of Defense, (5 December 2003), para. 352; *ibid.,* US Response Concerning the FTC Notes, (26 October 2001), at 3-5; *ibid.,* US Rejoinder Concerning the FTC Notes, (17 December 2001), at 3.
199. *Thunderbird v. Mexico,* Mexico's Statement of Defense, (18 December 2003), para. 57, footnote 190.

well as in their respective Article 1128 submissions[200]) that the Note was not an amendment, but rather, an interpretation.

A number of writers have also argued that the Note is an amendment to NAFTA,[201] and that NAFTA tribunals should therefore reject it.[202] A comprehensive argument was put forward by Brower II.[203] He subsequently argued that the FTC Note can, to some extent, be considered as a reasonable interpretation since it effectively prohibits the incorporation of free-standing treaty rights into Article 1105. Yet, he maintains that it should be considered as an amendment if it was meant to exclude 'general principles of international law' from that provision.[204] A number of writers have indeed found it questionable that the Note limits the meaning of international law solely to custom and excludes all other sources mentioned at Article 38 of the ICJ Statute.[205] For others, the Note is *not* an amendment since the Parties always meant for the reference to 'international law' in Article 1105 to refer to 'customary international law'.[206]

---

200. *Grand River v. United States*, Canada's Article 1128 Submission, (19 January 2009), para. 5; *Loewen v. United States*, Canada's Article 1128 Submission, (19 November 2001), paras. 8–10; *Methanex v. United States*, Mexico's Third Article 1128 Submission, (11 February 2002), at 1; *ibid.*, Canada's Third Article 1128 Submission, (8 February 2002), para. 5; *Mondev v. United States*, Award, (11 October 2002), para. 103 (describing the US position); *ADF v. United States*, Canada's Second Article 1128 Submission, (19 July 2002), para. 18.

201. Alvarez & Park, *supra* n. 141, at 397-398 (speaking of a de facto amendment); Brower, *supra* n. 137, at 255-256; Weiler, *supra* n. 84, at 706-707; Weiler, *supra* n. 118, at 180-181; Todd Weiler, *NAFTA Investment Law in 2001: As the Legal Order Starts to Settle, the Bureaucrats Strike Back*, 36 Int'l Law 345, 347 (2002).

202. Weiler, *supra* n. 118, at 185.

203. Brower *supra* n. 145, at 56: 'The Notes of Interpretation, however, resolve few (if any) debates about the meaning of Article 1105(1). [...] First, it is not clear that the Notes of Interpretation have any binding force. While Article 1131(2) authorizes cabinet-level representatives to adopt binding "interpretations" of NAFTA's provisions, Article 2202 governs "amendments" of NAFTA's provisions. According to Article 2202, the NAFTA Parties may agree on any "modification of or addition to" NAFTA, but such amendments become "an integral part" of NAFTA only upon approval by the NAFTA Parties "in accordance with the applicable legal procedures of each Party". In other words, NAFTA draws a fundamental distinction between interpretation and modification: cabinet-level officials have the authority to resolve ambiguities, but not the power to modify obligations without submitting the proposed text for domestic political approval. If, as the author believes, the Free Trade Commission's purported "interpretation" of Article 1105 actually constitutes a "modification", it represents an *ultra vires*, attempted amendment that has no binding force'. The same volume of the Columbia Journal of Transnational Law contained a reply by Thomas to the arguments put forward by Brower: Thomas, *supra* n. 84, at 454-456.

204. Brower, *supra* n. 117, at 347, 349, 363. See also: Charles H. Brower II, *Fair and Equitable Treatment under NAFTA's Investment Chapter; Remarks*, 96 ASIL Proc. 11 (2002).

205. Anthony Vanduzer, *NAFTA Chapter 11 to Date: The Progress of a Work in Progress*, at 13, NAFTA Chapter 11 Conference (Carleton University, 18 January 2002); David Williams, *Challenging Investment Treaty Arbitration Awards: Issues Concerning the Forum Arising from the Metatclad Case*, Bus. L. Int'l 156 (2003).

206. Thomas, *supra* n. 84, at 454-456; Matiation, *supra* n. 153, at 483, 487; Zachary Douglas, *The International Law of Investment Claims* 87 (Cambridge U. Press 2009); Kirkman, *supra* n. 153, at 383, 391; Alexander Orakhelashvili, *The Normative Basis of "Fair and Equitable Treatment": General International Law on Foreign Investment?* A.d.V. 94 (2008).

In *Pope & Talbot*, Canada argued (just like all other NAFTA Parties in subsequent proceedings[207]) that the tribunal did not have the power to challenge an 'interpretation' rendered by the FTC because of its binding nature. The *Pope* tribunal rejected this argument. It held, on the contrary, that it had 'a duty to consider and decide that question and not simply to accept that whatever the Commission has stated to be an interpretation is one for the purposes of Article 1131(2)'.[208] The issue was not addressed by NAFTA tribunals[209] until the *ADF* award. In this case, the tribunal held that it did *not* have the power (implied or otherwise) to determine for itself whether the FTC Interpretation was truly an 'interpretation' or rather an 'amendment' since the document is expressly qualified by the Parties as an interpretation:

> We have noted that the Investor does not dispute the binding character of the FTC Interpretation of 31 July 2001. At the same time, however, the Investor urges that the Tribunal, in the course of determining the governing law of a particular dispute, is authorized to determine whether an FTC interpretation is a 'true interpretation' or an 'amendment'. We observe in this connection that the FTC Interpretation of 31 July 2001 expressly purports to be an interpretation of several NAFTA provisions, including Article 1105(1), and not an 'amendment', or anything else. No document purporting to be an amendment has been submitted by either the Respondent or the other NAFTA Parties. There is, therefore, no need to embark upon an inquiry into the distinction between an 'interpretation' and an 'amendment' of Article 1105(1). But whether a document submitted to a Chapter 11 tribunal purports to be an amendatory agreement in respect of which the Parties' respective internal constitutional procedures necessary for the entry into force of the amending agreement have been taken, or an interpretation rendered by the FTC under Article 1131(2), we have the Parties themselves – all the Parties – speaking to the Tribunal. No more authentic and authoritative source of instruction on what the Parties intended to convey in a particular provision of NAFTA, is possible. Nothing in NAFTA suggests that a Chapter 11 tribunal may determine for itself whether a document submitted to it as an interpretation by the Parties acting through the FTC is in fact an 'amendment' which presumably may be disregarded until ratified by all the Parties under their respective internal law. We do not find persuasive the Investor's submission that a tribunal is impliedly authorized to do that as part of its duty to determine the governing law of a dispute. A principal difficulty with the Investor's submission is that such a theory of implied or incidental authority, fairly promptly, will tend to degrade and set at naught the binding and overriding character of FTC interpretations. Such a theory also overlooks the systemic need not only for a mechanism for correcting what the Parties themselves become convinced are interpretive errors but also for consistency and continuity of interpretation, which multiple ad hoc arbitral tribunals are not well suited to achieve and maintain.[210]

---

207. *See*, for instance, *ADF v. United States*, US Post-Hearing Submission on Article 1105 (1) and Pope & Talbot, (27 June 2002), at 8; *ibid.*, Canada's Second Article 1128 Submission, (19 July 2002), paras. 8–13; *Methanex v. United States*, US Response Concerning the FTC Notes, (26 October 2001), at 4; *ibid.*, US Rejoinder Concerning the FTC Notes, (17 December 2001), at 2.
208. *Pope & Talbot Inc. v. Canada*, Award in Respect of Damages, (31 May 2002), paras. 23, 24.
209. For instance, the tribunal in *UPS v. Canada*, Award (Jurisdiction), (22 November 2002), paras. 97–98, expressly deciding *not* to address the issue.
210. *ADF v. United States*, Award, (9 January 2003), para. 177.

The reasoning of the *ADF* tribunal is persuasive. In fact, there is nothing in NAFTA that allows a tribunal to second-guess the nature of the work of the FTC. The unambiguous determination by the FTC itself that this is an interpretation is sufficient proof for any tribunal that this is indeed a proper interpretation. There is simply no ground for a tribunal to qualify an interpretation as anything else than precisely that.[211] It has been suggested by writers that a tribunal would be exceeding its jurisdiction if it were to simply disregard a binding FTC interpretation.[212] The *ADF* tribunal rightly concluded that the Note was an interpretation, rather than an amendment.[213] The *Methanex*[214] and *Mondev* tribunals[215] have also reached the same conclusions.

In fact, the question of whether or not the Note is an interpretation or an amendment produces limited practical consequences. *All* tribunals (even those who may believe that the FTC Note is not an interpretation) *must* apply the Note for the simple reason that it is binding under NAFTA Article 1131(2). It has also been argued that even if the Note was considered as an amendment, it would in any event be binding on tribunals since under Articles 39 and 11 of the *Vienna Convention* parties can amend a treaty by 'any means if agreed' (and the Note provides for such an agreement).[216]

Tribunals have indeed recognized the binding nature of the Note. For instance, the *Pope & Talbot* tribunal, at least implicitly and in the form of an obiter dictum, concluded that the Commission's exercise was not within its power since it went beyond the simple 'interpretation' it was empowered to give. The *Pope* tribunal thus explained that 'were [it] required to make a determination whether the Commission's action is an interpretation or an amendment, it would choose the latter'.[217] The *Mondev* tribunal rightly summarized this passage from the *Pope & Talbot* award as an expression of the 'view that the FTC's decision probably amounted to an amendment rather than an interpretation'.[218] In any event, the *Pope* tribunal decided that it was *not*

---

211. Thomas, *supra* n. 84, at 454-456: 'Brower then says that the Note of Interpretation is actually a modification, not an interpretation. To succeed, he must overcome the fact that under the Agreement, the Free Trade Commission is the highest and most authoritative interpreter of the Treaty. All three Ministers are advised by counsel and all three Executives are aware of the difference between modification and amendment. The legislatures of all three Parties approved all of NAFTA, including this power vested in the ministers to interpret the Agreement. As the Commission is the three NAFTA Parties acting by consensus, it will be an unusual tribunal (and one that invites judicial review) that characterizes the Commission's interpretations as anything other than *bona fide*. When all of this is taken together and considered in light of the presumption of good faith that the three Parties are assumed to enjoy, a tribunal would be ill advised to second-guess the Commission'.
212. Thomas, *supra* n. 2, at 99; Thomas, *supra* n. 84, at 454-456.
213. *ADF v. United States*, Award, (9 January 2003), para. 177.
214. *Methanex v. United States*, Award, (3 August 2005), Part IV, Ch. C, para. 20 ('Even assuming that the FTC interpretation was a far-reaching substantive change (which the Tribunal believes not to be so with respect to the issue relating to this case), Methanex cites no authority for its argument that far-reaching changes in a treaty must be accomplished only by formal amendment rather than by some form of agreement between all of the parties').
215. *Mondev v. United States*, Award, (11 October 2002), para. 121 ('There is no difficulty in accepting this as an interpretation of the phrase "in accordance with international law"').
216. Kaufmann-Kohler, *supra* n. 116, at 191.
217. *Pope & Talbot Inc. v. Canada*, Award in Respect of Damages, (31 May 2002), para. 47.
218. *Mondev v. United States*, Award, (11 October 2002), para. 105.

required to make such a determination. It recognized that it was, regardless, obliged under NAFTA Article 1131(2) to apply the binding FTC Note. The rest of the tribunal's reasoning was therefore made on the basis of the assumption that the Commission's exercise was a proper 'interpretation'.[219] The *Merrill & Ring* tribunal adopted the same position and stated that the Note 'seems in some respect to be closer to an amendment of the treaty, than a strict interpretation',[220] but nevertheless applied the Note because of its binding nature.[221]

[4]   *Article 1128 Submissions Made by Non-Disputing Parties*

NAFTA Article 1128 allows non-disputing Parties (i.e., those not acting as respondents) to intervene in arbitration proceedings by filing written submissions concerning questions pertaining to treaty interpretation with a tribunal (hereinafter referred to as 'Article 1128 submissions').

   Methanex was the first case where the NAFTA Parties addressed the legal effects of Article 1128 submissions.[222] The United States argued that Article 1128 submissions of non-disputing States, that supported its own position in these proceedings (with regards to the proper interpretation of two NAFTA provisions: Articles 1101 and 1105), constituted a 'subsequent practice' pursuant to Article 31(3)(b) of the *Vienna Convention*.[223] Both Canada and Mexico agreed with this position.[224] Later in the proceedings, the United States changed its position and argued that Article 1128 submissions in fact,

---

219. The *Pope* tribunal's timid approach on this point starkly contrasts with its earlier position taken in the above mentioned (*supra* n. 138) letter of 17 September 2001 sent to the parties to the proceedings where it explicitly complained that Canada was acting as both judge and party contrary to 'a rule of international law that no-one shall be judge in his own cause'. *See also,* the tribunal's letter of 23 October 2001.
220. *Merrill & Ring v. Canada,* Award, (31 March 2010), para. 192.
221. The binding nature of the FTC Note is referred to in the award at paras. 190, 192. The tribunal is nevertheless critical about the Note suggesting that it does not 'necessarily reflects the present state of customary and international law' (para. 192).
222. Brief mention should be made here to three other cases where the issue of Article 1128 submissions was raised. In *Pope & Talbot Inc. v. Canada,* Award on the Merits Phase II, (10 April 2001), para. 79, the tribunal noted that both Mexico and the United States had agreed in their respective Article 1128 submissions with Canada's position on Article 1102. The tribunal rejected that position without, however, examining the weight to be given to such submissions. In *ADF v. United States,* Award, (9 January 2003), para. 179, the tribunal stated that it was 'equally important to note that' both Canada and Mexico (in their respective Article 1928 submissions) had accepted the United States' position on the evolution of the concept of customary international law. The tribunal did not, however, further address the question. In *Cargill, Inc. v. Mexico,* Award, (18 September 2009), para. 275, the tribunal mentioned that statements by States, including Article 1128 submissions, 'can – with care – serve as evidence of the content of custom'. The tribunal noted, however, that 'the weight of these [Article 1128 submissions] statements needs to be assessed in light of their position as respondents at the time of the statement'.
223. *Methanex v. United States,* US Memorial on Jurisdiction and Admissibility, (13 November 2000), at 13.
224. *Ibid.,* Canada's Second Article 1128 Submission, (30 April 2001), paras. 8, 37; *ibid.,* Mexico's Article 1128 Submission, (30 April 2001), paras. 1, 3.

constituted a subsequent *agreement*.[225] For the United States, such an agreement under Article 31(3)(a) of the *Vienna Convention* does not require any 'formal instrument of agreement', such as a treaty, but instead 'applies to any condition in which the parties are in a state of agreement, as may be evidenced by concordant statements of position'.[226] More specifically, the United States argued that the Parties' submissions on the interpretation of Article 1105 constituted such a subsequent agreement.[227]

In its final award, the *Methanex* tribunal only went so far as to agree with the United States that 'no particular formality is required for there to be an "agreement" under Article 31(3)(a) of the Vienna Convention'.[228] Having concluded that the FTC Note was a subsequent agreement, it held that it was therefore 'unnecessary' to decide whether or not the 'express consensus formed by the three NAFTA Parties' (in US pleadings and in Canada and Mexico's respective Article 1128 submissions) was 'also capable of qualifying as such an "agreement"'.[229]

The *Canadian Cattleman* tribunal was the first to take a firm stand on the issue. It held that Article 1128 submissions can be considered as 'subsequent practice' for the purposes of Article 31(3)(b) of the *Vienna Convention* to the extent that they are 'concordant, common, and consistent' in supporting the same interpretation.[230] It is noteworthy that the 'practice' invoked by the United States was Mexico's Article 1128 submission in *that* case, but also US Article 1128 submissions in *other cases*.[231]

The position adopted by the *Canadian Cattleman* tribunal is correct. It is generally recognized that interventions by non-disputing Parties such as Article 1128 submissions, are a form of 'subsequent practice' under Article 31(3)(b) of the *Vienna Convention*.[232] Thus, as noted by one scholar, 'where interventions by all of the other treaty parties support interpretations by the respondent state, this subsequent practice

---

225. This position was adopted at the hearing (*Methanex v. United States*, Arbitration hearing. volume 1, 12 July 2001, at 233 and 238) and subsequently in written submissions: US Post-Hearing Submission, (20 July 2001). This is discussed in: Céline Lévesque, *The Risk of Inconsistency Inherent to International Investment Law: The Example of the Mexican Sweetener Trio of Cases under NAFTA*, ESIEL Conference (July 2010).
226. *Methanex v. United States*, US Post-Hearing Submission, (20 July 2001), at 3.
227. *Ibid.*, at 2.
228. *Ibid.*, Award, (3 August 2005), Part II, Ch. B, para. 20.
229. *Ibid.*, para. 21.
230. *Canadian Cattlemen v. United States*, Award on Jurisdiction, (28 January 2008), paras. 188, 189.
231. *Ibid.*, paras. 184, 185.
232. Roberts, *supra* n. 96, at 219 ('Interventions by non-disputing treaty parties form another obvious kind of subsequent practice. Tribunals and commentators generally appear more comfortable relying on interventions than respondent pleadings, probably because intervening states are not attempting to avoid liability in that case and are more likely to limit their observations to general interpretive points'). *Contra*: Margaret Clare Ryan, *Glamis Gold, Ltd. v. The United States and the Fair and Equitable Treatment Standard*, 56(4) McGill LJ 951 (2011) ('the [Glamis] tribunal attributed to these [Article 1128] statements more than their due weight. (...) [T]hese parties' submissions are not binding in the same way as the FTC interpretive powers. Considering non-party submissions as such is unjust to claimants, given that the NAFTA parties share an interest in successfully defending chapter 11 claims and invariably assert the narrowest possible construction of its provisions. (...) Because these interventions are submitted in the course of a dispute, to ascribe such weight to them approaches an abuse of process, as it enables NAFTA parties to change the rules of the game in the middle of a pending arbitration').

constitutes good evidence of an agreement on interpretation and thus should be given considerable weight'.[233]

Moreover, all Article 1128 submissions (made *before* the FTC issued its Note of Interpretation of July 2001) were 'concordant, common, and consistent' in their support of the same interpretation of Article 1105. Thus, the Article 1128 submissions filed by Mexico in *S.D. Myers*,[234] *Methanex*,[235] and *Pope & Talbot* have all stated that the FET was one example of the 'customary international law standards incorporated into Article 1105(1)'.[236] The United States made two Article 1128 submissions in the context of the *Pope & Talbot* case (*before* the FTC's Note was issued) and also came to the conclusion that NAFTA drafters 'chose a formulation that expressly tied fair and equitable treatment to the customary international minimum standard rather than to some subjective, undefined standard'.[237] Finally, in the *Methanex* case, Canada made an Article 1128 submission which stated that all three NAFTA Parties agreed that FET 'is explicitly subsumed under the minimum standard of treatment at customary international law' and that 'Article 31(3)(b) of the *Vienna Convention* instructs that such agreement of the Parties regarding the interpretation of this provision shall be taken into account'.[238]

The *Canadian Cattleman* tribunal however, denied that Article 1128 submissions constituted a subsequent 'agreement' between NAFTA Parties:

> All of this [the evidence submitted by the United States] is certainly suggestive of something approaching an agreement, but, to the Tribunal, all of this does not rise to the level of a 'subsequent agreement' by the NAFTA Parties. Although there is no evidence on the record that any of the NAFTA Parties has voiced a discordant view on this issue, the Tribunal is mindful that there is limited experience thus far with many of the subtleties and implications of Chapter Eleven of the NAFTA. Too, the Tribunal notes the absence of any Article 1128 submission by Canada before this Tribunal. This cannot be seen as evidence of Canadian support for the Claimants' position on this issue, but it also cannot be seen as evidence of Canadian opposition. The Tribunal concludes that there is no subsequent agreement on this issues within the meaning of Article 31(3)(a) of the Vienna Convention.[239]

Writers and scholars have praised this award to a substantial level.[240] While NAFTA Parties have continued to argue in recent cases that Article 1128 submissions by

---

233. Roberts, *supra* n. 96, at 219.
234. *S.D. Myers v. Canada*, Mexico's Article 1128 Submission, (14 January 2000), para. 28.
235. *Methanex v. United States*, Mexico's Article 1128 Submission, (30 April 2001), paras. 9, 11.
236. *Pope & Talbot Inc. v. Canada*, Mexico's Post-Hearing Submission (Phase Two), (1 December 2000), at 3; *ibid.*, Mexico's Article 1128 Submission, (5 November 2000), at 2.
237. *Pope & Talbot Inc. v. Canada*, US Fourth Submission, (1 November 2000), paras. 2-8; *ibid.*, US Fifth Submission, (1 December 2000), para. 4.
238. *Methanex v. United States*, Canada's Second Article 1128 Submission, (30 April 2001), paras. 26, 27, 33, 34, 37.
239. *Canadian Cattlemen v. United States*, Award on Jurisdiction, (28 January 2008), para. 187.
240. Orakhelashvili, *supra* n. 206, at 167; Fitzmaurice et al., *supra* n. 108, at 219, 225, 234.

non-disputing Parties in support of the respondent's own position constitute a 'subsequent agreement',[241] such a claim has not been endorsed by any NAFTA tribunal thus far.

[5] Model BITs Adopted by the United States and Canada

The Model BITs adopted by the Unites States and Canada (both in 2004) make it clear that treatment in accordance with 'international law' refers to the minimum standard of treatment under customary international law.[242] These changes were adopted to refute the expanding interpretation applied by some NAFTA tribunals, most notably the *Pope & Talbot* tribunal, and to incorporate the clarification made in the FTC Note of July 2001.[243] Schwebel is very critical about the changes adopted in the 2004 US Model BIT, calling them 'regressive development' and adding that 'what was the floor has become the ceiling'.[244]

Article 5(1) of the 2004 US Model BIT provides that '[e]ach Party shall accord to covered investments treatment in accordance with *customary* international law, including fair and equitable treatment and full protection and security'.[245] The one important difference between NAFTA Article 1105 and the US Model BIT is, of course, the addition of the word 'customary' before 'international law'. This specification is further reiterated at Article 5(2) which states the following:

---

241. *See*, for instance: *Mobil v. Canada*, Canada's Reply to US and Mexico's Article 1128 Submissions, (1 September 2010), para. 7.
242. Kenneth Vandevelde, *A Comparison of the 2004 and 1994 US Model BITs*, 1 Yb Int'l Invest. L. & Pol. 291 (2008-2009).
243. Céline Lévesque, *Influences on the Canadian Model FIPA and US Model BIT: NAFTA Chapter 11 and Beyond*, 44 Can. YIL 255 ff (2006); Vandevelde, *supra* n. 242, at 291. *See also*: C. Lévesque & A. Newcombe, *Commentary on the Canadian Model Foreign Promotion and Protection Agreement*, in *Commentaries on Selected Model International Investment Agreements* 78-80 (Chester Brown, ed., Oxford U. Press 2013).
244. Stephen Schwebel, *The United States 2004 Model Bilateral Investment Treaty: An Exercise in the Regressive Development of International Law*, in: *Global Reflections on International Law, Commerce and Dispute Resolution, Liber Amicorum in honour of Robert Briner* 647 (ICC Pub. No. 693, 2005): 'the profound, and startling, deficiency of the 2004 provision is that there is no agreement within the international community on the content of 'customary international law' on which the 2004 Model BIT relies. There was, and is, no agreement within the international community on the content of 'the customary international law minimum standard of treatment of aliens', or even on whether such a minimum standard existed or exists. (…) Rather than concluding treaties that invite controversy over the content of a customary international law that concordant provisions of some 2200 bilateral investment treaties have been in the process of reshaping, why not adhere to provisions that have been accepted more than two thousand times by the vast majority of States throughout the world, including, until 2004, the United States? Why jettison the characteristic protections of BITs against unfair and inequitable treatment, protections widely viewed as a fundamental advance on the prior confined if not confused state of customary international law, in favor of invocation of a minimum standard that is hardly accepted as such?'.
245. Treaty between the Government of the United States of America and the Government of [Country] Concerning the Encouragement and Reciprocal Protection of Investment, (emphasis added). *See*, Gilbert Gagné & Jean-Frédéric Morin, *The Evolving American Policy on Investment Protection: Evidence from Recent FTAs and the 2004 Model BIT*, 9 J. Int'l Econ. L. 357 (2006).

2. For greater certainty, paragraph 1 prescribes the customary international law minimum standard of treatment of aliens as the minimum standard of treatment to be afforded to covered investments. The concepts of 'fair and equitable treatment' and 'full protection and security' do not require treatment in addition to or beyond that which is required by that standard, and do not create additional substantive rights...

The two BITs entered into by the United States after 2004 with Uruguay and Rwanda contain the same clause referring specifically to the minimum standard of treatment under custom.[246] Recent FTAs entered into by the United States also contain the same FET clause.[247] It is noteworthy that both the 2004 and 2012 US Model BITs *also* explicitly add what customary international law actually means; i.e., 'a general and consistent practice of States that they follow from a sense of legal obligation'.[248] This addition is also featured in the United States' most recent BITs[249] and FTAs. Finally, the 2004 and 2012 Model BITs also clarify that the obligation to provide FET under Article 5(1) 'includes the obligation not to deny justice in criminal, civil, or administrative adjudicatory proceedings in accordance with the principle of due process embodied in the principal legal systems of the world'.[250]

The 2004 Model FIPA adopted by Canada contains the following FET clause:

1. Each Party shall accord to covered investments treatment in accordance with the customary international law minimum standard of treatment of aliens, including fair and equitable treatment and full protection and security.
2. The concepts of 'fair and equitable treatment' and 'full protection and security' in paragraph 1 do not require treatment in addition to or beyond that which is required by the customary international law minimum standard of treatment of aliens.

Recent BITs (and FTAs) entered into by Canada also contain such language.[251]

---

246. Treaty between the United States and Uruguay Concerning the Encouragement and Reciprocal Protection of Investment, with Annexes and Protocol, signed on 4 November 2005, entered into force on 1 November 2006, Article 5(1)(2); Treaty between the United States and Rwanda Concerning the Encouragement and Reciprocal Protection of Investment, signed on 19 February 2008, entered into force on 1 January 2012, Article 5(1)(2).
247. *See*, Andrew P. Tuck, *The "Fair And Equitable Treatment" Standard Pursuant to the Investment Provisions of the U.S. Free Trade Agreements with Peru, Colombia and Panama*, 16 L. & Bus. Rev. Am. 385 (2010).
248. Thus, a footnote to Article 5 indicates that this provision 'shall be interpreted in accordance with Annex A', which contains the following paragraph: 'The Parties confirm their shared understanding that "customary international law" generally and as specifically referenced in Article 5 [Minimum Standard of Treatment] (. ...) results from a general and consistent practice of States that they follow from a sense of legal obligation. With regard to Article 5 [Minimum Standard of Treatment], the customary international law minimum standard of treatment of aliens refers to all customary international law principles that protect the economic rights and interests of aliens'.
249. *See*, *supra* n. 246.
250. This addition is also featured in the United States' most recent BITs (*see*, *supra* n. 246) and FTAs.
251. It should be added that there is some degree of variation in language in some of the recent BITs entered into by Canada. For instance, the Agreement between Canada and Romania for the Promotion and Reciprocal Protection of Investments, signed at Bucharest on 8 May 2009,

Legal scholarship has generally recognized that Model BITs adopted by States can be considered as 'subsequent practice' for the purposes of Article 31(3)(b) of the *Vienna Convention* to the extent that an agreement on interpretation can be inferred therein.[252] As highlighted by the *Canadian Cattleman* tribunal, such 'subsequent practice' must be 'concordant, common, and consistent' in its support of the same interpretation.[253] Yet, it should be recalled that under Article 31(3)(b) of the *Vienna Convention*, for an instrument to be considered as a subsequent practice of the NAFTA, it must made 'in the application of the treaty'. The Model BITs were *not* drafted by the United States and Canada 'in the application' of the NAFTA. These treaties were conceived as models for the drafting of *future* BITs. Therefore, the Model BITs cannot be considered as a 'subsequent practice' for the purposes of interpreting Article 1105 under Article 31(3)(b) of the *Vienna Convention*.

No NAFTA tribunal has examined the issue of whether or not these Model BITs can be considered as subsequent practice. The *Cargill* tribunal only went so far as to suggest that some weight should be given to them in interpreting Article 1105.[254] In the

---

entered into force on 23 November 2011, E105170, Annex D, contains an explanatory note which adds that: 'For greater certainty, "fair and equitable treatment" includes the obligation not to deny justice in criminal, civil or administrative adjudicatory proceedings in accordance with the customary international law minimum standard of treatment of aliens; and "full protection and security" requires the level of police protection required under the customary international law minimum standard ot treatment ot aliens'. A mention similar to this explanatory note is also found in the Canada-Colombia FTA, signed on 21 November 2008, entered into force on 15 August 2011. Another example is the Agreement between Canada and China for the Promotion and Reciprocal Protection of Investments, signed on 9 September 2012 (not yet entered into force), where Article 4 uses this language: '1. Each Contracting Party shall accord to covered investments fair and equitable treatment and full protection and security, in accordance with international law. 2. The concepts of "fair and equitable treatment" and "full protection and security" in paragraph 1 do not require treatment in addition to or beyond that which is required by the international law minimum standard of treatment of aliens as evidenced by general State practice accepted as law'. The clause thus uses the term 'international law' instead of the phrase 'customary international law minimum standard of treatment of aliens' commonly used in other BITs. Also, the first and second paragraph avoid using the term 'custom' (most probably for political reasons) but at the same time expressly refer to the two elements of the definition of custom ('evidenced by general State practice accepted as law').

252. Roberts, *supra* n. 96, at 221 ('Clarifications and explanations in the treaty parties' model BITs are another example of subsequent practice from which an agreement on interpretation may be inferred. As a model BIT represents the "set of norms that the relevant state holds out to be both reasonable and acceptable as a legal basis for the protection of foreign investment in its own economy" [quoting from Z. Douglas, *The Hybrid Foundations of Investment Treaty Arbitration*, 74(1) British YIL 159 (2003)] these clarifications and explanations fairly evidence a state's general understanding of treaty terms and cannot be dismissed as opportunistic attempts to avoid liability in a particular case'). Another different question is whether or not *other* BITs entered into by a State can be considered as examples of subsequent practice. This issue is discussed in: *Aguas del Tunari SA v. Bolivia*, ICSID No. ARB/02/3, Decision on Respondent's Objections to Jurisdiction, (21 October 2005), paras. 291, 292.
253. *Canadian Cattlemen v. United States*, Award on Jurisdiction, (28 January 2008), paras. 188-189.
254. *Cargill, Inc. v. Mexico*, Award, (18 September 2009), para. 275: 'The Tribunal acknowledges that the weight of [Article 1128 submissions] statements needs to be assessed in light of their position as respondents at the time of the statement. However, the Tribunal also observes that, for example, the United States maintains a similar position as to the customary international law standard of fair and equitable treatment in its model bilateral investment treaty, a situation

present author's view, the position taken by the *Cargill* tribunal is correct. The fact that both Model BITs were adopted ten years after the entry into force of NAFTA is not significant. As pointed out by one writer, 'an updated model BIT may also be relevant to the interpretation of investment treaties based on previous model BITs or ones with slightly different language'.[255] Both Canada and the United States have modified their Model BITs in order to clarify the scope of the FET clause found in earlier treaties.[256] Moreover, it has been argued that 'the influence of model BITs in shaping investment treaty jurisprudence will be enhanced' whenever a State 'takes a proactive approach to updating and explaining its model, including by adopting revisions to endorse or reject important developments in case law'.[257] Both Model BITs were adopted to expressly incorporate the clarification made by the FTC Note, which was itself issued to counter case law that had given an extensive interpretation to Article 1105.[258] In sum, although the Model BITs should not be considered as a 'subsequent practice' for the purpose of interpreting Article 1105, it remains that significant weight should be accorded to these instruments with regards to the interpretation of this provision.

[D]   Supplementary Means of Interpretation

Article 32 of the *Vienna Convention* makes reference to 'supplementary means of interpretation', which includes the treaty's preparatory work (*travaux préparatoires*) and the circumstances of its conclusion. The *Canadian Cattleman* tribunal explained that the 'supplementary means of interpretation' were not limited to those two elements and held that it also included judicial decisions.[259] Under Article 32 of the *Vienna Convention*, a tribunal may have recourse to those 'supplementary means of interpretation' to *confirm* the meaning resulting from the application of Article 31 (i.e., the application of the ordinary meaning of the terms in their context and in light of the treaty's object and purpose). A tribunal may also have recourse to these supplementary means of interpretation to *determine* the meaning whenever the interpretation under Article 31 leads to a result that is 'ambiguous or obscure', or leads to a 'manifestly absurd or unreasonable' conclusion.

NAFTA tribunals have adopted startlingly different approaches on the use of *travaux préparatoires* for the interpretation of Article 1105; one tribunal (*Pope &*

---

in which it is at least equally possible that the United States would be in the position of either respondent or the state of nationality of the claiming investor'.
255. Roberts, *supra* n. 96, at 221.
256. Lévesque, *supra* n. 243, at 255 ff. The use in the 2004 US Model BIT of phrases such as 'for greater certainty' (Article 5(2)) and 'the Parties confirm their shared understanding' (Annex A) confirms this clarification aim.
257. Roberts, *supra* n. 96, at 222.
258. *Ibid.* ('The United States, for example, besides arguing for certain interpretations before tribunals as a respondent or an intervener, modifies its model BIT to confirm or reject specific jurisprudence, which helps to crystallize certain *de facto* precedents and stall or prevent the formation of others').
259. *Canadian Cattlemen v. United States*, Award on Jurisdiction, (28 January 2008), para. 50.

Talbot) examined these documents, while another (*Methanex*) categorically refused to make use of them.[260]

In its 'Award in Respect of Damages' of 31 May 2002, the *Pope & Talbot* tribunal stated that it was 'beyond argument' that Article 1105 contained 'ambiguities that had to be resolved by those charged with interpreting' the text and that 'in such cases, it is common and proper to turn to the negotiation history of an agreements to see if that might shed some light on the intentions of the signatories'.[261] This proposition is, of course, controversial in itself (a point further discussed below[262]). In the context of other proceedings, NAFTA Parties argued that the *Pope* tribunal should not have resorted to the *travaux préparatoires* since there were no existing ambiguities in the first place.[263] For the *Pope* tribunal, since Canada had failed to provide a 'full negotiating history' of Chapter 11 and submitted only 'a series of negotiating drafts', it could not 'reach a fully informed conclusion based upon a complete history'.[264] In any event, the tribunal concluded that these documents did not support Canada's position that the words 'international law' at Article 1105 referred to the standard of treatment existing under *customary* international law.[265]

The *Methanex* tribunal took a completely different approach when faced with a request from the claimant for a disclosure of the negotiation history of several provisions, including Article 1105.[266] The tribunal first noted the limited usefulness of the *travaux* since 'the text of the treaty is deemed to be the authentic expression of the intentions of the parties; and its elucidation, rather than wide-ranging searches for the supposed intentions of the parties, is the proper object of interpretation'.[267] The tribunal refused to examine these documents on the grounds that the claimant had failed to specify:

> why interpretation in accordance with Article 31 of the Vienna Convention leads to a result that is ambiguous or obscure, or that is manifestly absurd or unreasonable, or that its interpretation in accordance with Article 31 would be confirmed by the travaux under Article 32.[268]

In any event, the usefulness of supplementary means of interpretation would be limited in the specific context of Article 1105 due to the existence of a 'subsequent agreement' between the Parties with regards to its proper interpretation (i.e., the FTC Note of Interpretation).[269]

---

260. The *Mobil* tribunal also refused to resort to supplemental means of interpretation in the context of Article 1106. *See Mobil v. Canada*, Decision on Liability and on Principles of Quantum, (22 May 2012), para. 226.
261. *Pope & Talbot Inc. v. Canada,* Award in Respect of Damages, (31 May 2002), para. 26.
262. *See,* the discussion at section §2.03[B][1].
263. *ADF v. United States,* US Post-Hearing Submission on Article 1105(1) and Pope & Talbot, (27 June 2002), at 18, 19.
264. *Pope & Talbot Inc. v. Canada,* Award in Respect of Damages, (31 May 2002), para. 43.
265. *Ibid.,* paras. 44, 46.
266. *Methanex v. United States,* Award, (3 August 2005), Part II, Ch. B, para. 22.
267. *Ibid.*
268. *Ibid.,* Part II, Ch. H, para. 19. The tribunal also rejected claimant's request because it had been made too late in the proceedings (para. 16).
269. *Ibid.,* Part II, Ch. H, para. 24.

The *Methanex* tribunal is correct – the usefulness of referring to the *travaux* in the context of NAFTA Article 1105 is significantly minimal for three reasons. First, there exists a 'subsequent *agreement*' between the Parties (the FTC Note of Interpretation). As a result, whatever 'ambiguities' may have existed as to the proper interpretation to be given to Article 1105 simply no longer existed after 31 July 2001. Second, the proper interpretation of the FET obligations under this provision has also been determined by substantial 'subsequent *practice*' between the Parties (such as Article 1128 submissions made by non-disputing Parties). Third, as already mentioned,[270] in the context of the negotiation of NAFTA, the drafters did not leave any formal set of *travaux preparatoires*, but only a series of successive negotiating texts with no explanation about changes from one version to another.[271]

[E]   Conclusion

This section sought to examine whether the rules of treaty interpretation under international law could provide any guidance as to the meaning of Article 1105. Under Article 31(1) of the *Vienna Convention,* Article 1105 must be interpreted according to the ordinary meaning given to the terms used in the provision taking into account the context and the object and purpose of the NAFTA.

An enquiry into the ordinary meaning of the words 'fair' and 'equitable' does not provide much guidance as to the scope of Article 1105. Similarly, the term 'international law' is central to this provision and has proven to be a very contentious notion. The proper interpretation of this term simply cannot be resolved by only looking at its ordinary meaning. In fact, looking at the 'ordinary meaning' of the terms used at Article 1105 does not provide much guidance as to the proper interpretation to be given to this provision. Similarly, looking at the object and purpose of Article 1105 also provides only limited insight as to its actual meaning.

An examination of the context of Article 1105 has proven to be a more enlightening endeavor. For one thing, the heading of Article 1105 clearly suggests that the words 'international law' simply mean the minimum standard of treatment under custom. The present author has also found that Article 1128 submissions made by non-disputing Parties are a 'subsequent practice' by the Parties which establishes an agreement between them regarding the proper interpretation to be given to Article 1105. This 'subsequent practice' supports the conclusion that the FET that NAFTA Parties must accord to foreign investors under 'international law' is a reference to the minimum standard of treatment under customary international law.

Unilateral official statements were made by both Canada and the United States when NAFTA was being implemented (Canada's 1994 'Statement on Implementation' as well as numerous US State Department's statements made in 1993–1994 onward). These statements do not qualify as 'subsequent' practice for the purposes of Article 31(3)(b) of the *Vienna Convention* because they were issued *before* or *simultaneously*

---

270. *See*, at section §2.01[B] above.
271. Kinnear et al., *supra* n. 1 (section on Article 1131) at 14.

with the entry into force of the NAFTA. Yet, this timing is precisely the reason why significant weight should be given to these statements. The importance of these statements is further confirmed by the fact that they are 'concordant, common, and consistent' in unanimously stating that the FET to be accorded under 'international law' constitutes a reference to the minimum standard of treatment under custom. Finally, although the Model BITs adopted by the United States and Canada should not be considered as a 'subsequent practice', it remains that significant weight should be given to these instruments for the purposes of interpreting Article 1105.

Most importantly, this interpretation of Article 1105 is also confirmed by a subsequent *agreement* between the Parties regarding its meaning: namely, the FTC Note of Interpretation. The Note is a binding subsequent agreement representing the definitive meaning to be given to Article 1105. It states that under Article 1105, foreign investors must be accorded 'the customary international law minimum standard of treatment of aliens'.

Finally, because of the overwhelming evidence in support of the view that 'international law' constitutes a reference to the minimum standard of treatment under customary international law, the use of supplementary means of interpretation is unnecessary.

§2.03   NAFTA CASE LAW

As previously mentioned,[272] a number of elements of subsequent practice by the NAFTA Parties in their application of Article 1105 establish an agreement between them on its interpretation. This interpretation is also confirmed by a subsequent *agreement* between the Parties regarding the meaning of Article 1105: namely, the FTC Note of Interpretation.[273] This section examines how NAFTA tribunals have applied the Note.

The fact that the Note is a binding subsequent agreement that provides a definitive meaning of Article 1105 should have, as a matter of principle, solved any controversy related to the meaning of this provision. At section §2.03[A], it will be explained that this is generally what happened. Thus, all NAFTA tribunals have concluded that Article 1105 provides for FET protection in accordance with the minimum standard of treatment under custom. While there is a general consensus on these core issues, a limited number of controversial questions remain at the margin. We will examine some of these questions.

A troubling issue that surrounds this discussion is the fact that some tribunals have challenged the letter and the spirit of the FTC Note. Section §2.03[B] will examine the *Pope & Talbot*'s awards that have started this trend. Also subject to discussion are two basic arguments that have been put forward by investors and endorsed by some NAFTA tribunals. One controversial question examined in this section is the evolutionary character of the minimum standard of treatment under custom. Another one is

---

272. *See*, at sections §2.02[C][2], §2.02[C][4] and §2.02[C][5].
273. *See*, at section §2.02[C][3].

the customary nature of the FET obligation. As further discussed below, in the present author's view the position taken by these tribunals undermines the effectiveness of the Note.

[A]   General Consensus on the Core Issues and the Remaining Peripheral Controversies

Not a single NAFTA tribunal has ever contested the obvious fact that in accordance with the Note, the term 'fair and equitable treatment' under 'international law' at Article 1105 constitutes a reference to the minimum standard of treatment under customary international law.[274] The *Mondev* tribunal added that this is a reference to custom 'as it stood no earlier than the time at which NAFTA came into force'.[275] All tribunals have also concluded, as mandated by the Note, that the FET obligation under Article 1105 does not require treatment in addition to or beyond that existing under custom.[276] While tribunals have all agreed on these fundamental issues, a limited number of peripheral questions have been controversial. All of these questions are related to the concrete application of the concept of customary international law in the context of Article 1105. The following three controversial questions will be examined:

- Are arbitral awards an element of State practice? (section §2.03[A][1]).
- Are non-NAFTA awards that examine unqualified FET clauses relevant to Article 1105? (section §2.03[A][2]).
- Can tribunals look at other sources of law than custom to interpret Article 1105? (section §2.03[A][3]).

[1]   *Are Arbitral Awards an Element of State Practice?*

Before examining this first controversial question, a few brief observations should be made at the outset on the concept of customary international law. Custom is one of the sources of international law. Under Article 38(1)b of the ICJ Statute, 'international

---

274. *See*, for instance, *Pope & Talbot Inc. v. Canada*, Award in Respect of Damages, (31 May 2002), paras. 178, 183; *Chemtura v. Canada*, Award, (2 August 2010), para. 121; *Merrill & Ring v. Canada*, Award, (31 March 2010), paras. 211, 213; *Glamis v. United States*, Award, (9 June 2009), paras. 599, 608; *Loewen v. United States*, Award, (26 June 2003), para. 128; *Thunderbird v. Mexico*, Award, (26 January 2006), para. 193; *Mobil v. Canada*, Decision on Liability and on Principles of Quantum, (22 May 2012), paras. 135, 152; *Cargill, Inc. v. Mexico*, Award, (18 September 2009), paras. 267, 268.
275. *Mondev v. United States*, Award, (11 October 2002), para. 125, later approved by *Waste Management v. Mexico*, Award, (30 April 2004), para. 91 (the Note 'incorporates current international customary law, at least as it stood at the time that NAFTA came into force in 1994, rather than any earlier version of the standard of treatment').
276. *UPS v. Canada*, Award (Jurisdiction), (22 November 2002), para. 97; *Loewen v. United States*, Award, (26 June 2003), para. 128; *Mondev v. United States*, Award, (11 October 2002), para. 122; *Grand River v. United States*, Award, (12 January 2011), para. 176; *Waste Management v. Mexico*, Award, (30 April 2004), para. 91.

custom' requires a 'general practice' that is 'accepted as law'.[277] Custom has therefore two constitutive elements: a 'constant and uniform' (but not necessarily unanimous) State practice in international relations and the belief by States that such practice is required by law (opinio juris).[278] This double requirement has been recognized by several ICJ decisions[279] and consistently applied by tribunals in the context of investor-State arbitration. For instance, the *UPS* tribunal stated that 'to establish a rule of customary international law, two requirements must be met: consistent state practice and an understanding that the practice is required by law'.[280] It should be added that a number of recent treaties entered into by the Unites States[281] and Canada[282] expressly refer to this double requirement of custom.

NAFTA tribunals have also repeatedly affirmed that the burden of proving the existence of a rule of customary international law rests on the party that alleges it.[283] The *ADF* tribunal rejected the argument put forward by the United States that a claimant 'must show a violation of a *specific rule* of customary international law relating to foreign investors and their investments'.[284] Thus, the tribunal indicated that there is no need to prove that 'current customary international law concerning standards of treatment consists only of discrete, specific rules applicable to limited contexts'.[285] The *ADF* tribunal refers instead to 'a *general* customary international law standard of treatment'.[286]

The question of whether or not arbitral awards are an element of State practice was addressed in *Merrill & Ring*. The investor argued that arbitral awards can 'contribute to the actual "formation" of customary international law'.[287] Moreover, the investor added that a tribunal 'is not only *permissible* to inform the meaning of the

---

277. Article 38, ICJ Statute, *supra* n. 76.
278. International Law Association (ILA), *Statement of Principles Applicable to the Formation of General Customary International Law*, Final Report of the Committee, London Conference (2000), at 8.
279. *Continental Shelf (Libya v. Malta)*, ICJ Reports 1985, 13, (13 June 1985), paras. 27, 29, 30 ('It is of course axiomatic that the material of customary international law is to be looked for primarily in the actual practice and *opinio juris* of States'). *See* also: *Lotus Case (France v. Turkey)* 1927 PCIJ Series A No. 9, (7 September 1927), paras. 18, 28; *Asylum Case (Colombia v. Peru)*, ICJ Reports 1950, 265, (13 June 1950), at 276-277; *Right of Passage Case (Portugal v. India)*, ICJ Reports 1960, 6, (12 April 1960), at 42, 43; *North Sea Continental Shelf Cases (Federal Republic of Germany v. Denmark / Federal Republic of Germany v. Netherlands)*, ICJ Reports 1969, 3, (20 February 1969), at 44.
280. *UPS v. Canada*, Award (Jurisdiction), (22 November 2002), para. 84. *See also: Glamis v. United States*, Award, (9 June 2009), para. 602; *Cargill, Inc. v. Mexico*, Award, (18 September 2009), paras. 271, 274.
281. *See*, for instance, the 2004 and 2012 US Model BITs (*supra* n. 248) and BITs entered into with Uruguay and Rwanda (*supra* n. 246).
282. *See*, Canada-China BIT, *supra* n. 251. While the BIT does not refer explicitly to 'custom', it speaks of 'the international law minimum standard of treatment of aliens as evidenced by general State practice accepted as law'.
283. *UPS v. Canada*, Award (Jurisdiction), (22 November 2002), paras. 84–86; *ADF v. United States*, Award, (9 January 2003), paras. 183–185; *Cargill, Inc. v. Mexico*, Award, (18 September 2009), paras. 271, 273; *Glamis v. United States*, Award, (9 June 2009), paras. 601–603.
284. *ADF v. United States*, Award, (9 January 2003), para. 182, emphasis added.
285. *Ibid.*, para. 185.
286. *Ibid.*, para. 186, emphasis in the original.
287. *Merrill & Ring v. Canada*, Investor's Reply, (15 December 2008), para. 308.

customary "fair and equitable treatment" in NAFTA Article 1105 with reference to international jurisprudence, but it is in fact *required*.[288] The investor based its reasoning on this ambiguous passage taken from the *ADF* award:

> We understand *Mondev* to be saying – and we would respectfully agree with it – that any general requirement to accord 'fair and equitable treatment' and 'full protection and security' must be disciplined by being based upon State practice and judicial or arbitral caselaw or other sources of customary or general international law...[289]

This passage seems to suggest that 'judicial or arbitral case law' is an element of customary international law along with State practice. Such interpretation would, of course, be contrary to the traditional definition of customary international law being comprised of State practice and opinio juris.[290] In any event, the investor's argument in *Merrill & Ring* was rejected by Canada, which explained that 'custom can only be established by the actual practice of States, and not by the practice of international tribunals' and that 'the relevant *opinio juris* is that of States, and not that of judges or arbitrators'.[291] Canada nevertheless added that these 'awards can play an important evidentiary role in elucidating the content of international law' insofar as they 'sometimes contain valuable analysis of State practice and *opinio juris* in relation to a specific area of law, and future tribunals may choose to be guided by this analysis'.[292] The *Merrill & Ring* tribunal agreed with Canada on this point and concluded that 'judicial decisions, while not a source of the law in themselves, are a fundamental tool for the interpretation of the law and have contributed to its clarification and development'.[293]

Other tribunals have concurred with this reasoning. In *Glamis*, the United States made it clear that 'international tribunals do not create customary international law. Only nations create customary international law'.[294] The *Glamis* tribunal agreed and concluded that awards 'do not constitute State practice and thus cannot create or prove customary international law'.[295] The tribunal added that arbitral awards can also 'serve as illustrations of customary international law if they involve an examination of

---

288. *Ibid.*, para. 309, emphasis in the original.
289. *ADF v. United States*, Award, (9 January 2003), para. 184.
290. *Merrill & Ring v. Canada*, Canada's Counter-Memorial, (13 May 2008), para. 470 ('The *ADF* Tribunal only suggests (wrongly, in Canada's view) that "judicial or arbitral caselaw" is a source of customary international law along with State practice. Canada submits that the *ADF* Tribunal's assessment is contrary to Article 38 of the I.C.J. Statute, which states that "judicial decisions" (along with doctrine) are only a subsidiary source of law, and not an element of customary international law *per se*').
291. *Ibid.*, Canada's Rejoinder, (27 March 2009), paras. 160, 161.
292. *Ibid. See also, Chemtura v. Canada*, Canada's Counter-Memorial, (20 October 2008), para. 744.
293. *Merrill & Ring v. Canada*, Award, (31 March 2010), para. 188.
294. *Glamis v. United States*, Award, (9 June 2009), para. 543 (quoting from Counsel for Respondent, Tr. 105:17–19). *See also*, at para. 554 ('Customary international law cannot be proven, alleges Respondent, by decisions of international tribunals, as they do not constitute State practice').
295. *Glamis v. United States*, Award, (9 June 2009), para. 605.

customary international law'.[296] Similarly, the *Cargill* tribunal stated that awards 'do not create customary international law but rather, at most, reflect customary international law'.[297] In fact, the only support for the proposition that arbitral awards can be considered as an element of State practice is found in Wälde's separate opinion in *Thunderbird* where he mentions that an 'authoritative jurisprudence' (i.e., 'a consistent line of reasoning [by arbitral tribunals] developing a principle and a particular interpretation of specific treaty obligations'[298]) may 'acquire the character of customary international law and must be respected'.[299]

In sum, the question of the relevance of awards in the development of custom now seems to be settled. The position taken by all NAFTA tribunals (except perhaps for *ADF*) is in line with recent case law outside NAFTA where a tribunal rightly concluded that 'as such, arbitral awards do not constitute State practice'.[300]

[2] Are Non-NAFTA Awards that Examine Unqualified Fair and Equitable Treatment Clauses Relevant to Article 1105?

A controversial question that has been raised by investors is whether the analysis of *non-NAFTA* awards that examine BITs containing *unqualified FET* clauses is at all relevant to NAFTA tribunals having to interpret Article 1105 (where the FET is linked to the minimum standard of treatment under custom). NAFTA tribunals have responded to this question in the negative.[301] The *Glamis* tribunal thus distinguished Article 1105-type clauses from other unqualified FET clauses contained in BITs because they refer to *different sources* of international law:

> The Tribunal notes that it finds two categories of arbitral awards that examine a fair and equitable treatment standard: those that look to define customary international law and those that examine the autonomous language and nuances of the underlying treaty language. Fundamental to this divide is the treaty underlying the dispute: those treaties and free trade agreements, like the NAFTA, that are to be understood by reference to the customary international law minimum standard of treatment necessarily lead their tribunals to analyze custom; while those treaties with fair and equitable treatment clauses that expand upon, or move beyond, customary international law, lead their reviewing tribunals into an

---

296. *Ibid. See also*, at para. 603 where the tribunal does not list 'arbitral decisions' amongst the potential 'authoritative sources' of State practice which can demonstrate the existence of a rule of custom.
297. *Cargill, Inc. v. Mexico*, Award, (18 September 2009), para. 277. The tribunal added that 'the evidentiary weight to be afforded [to awards] is greater if the conclusions therein are supported by evidence and analysis of custom'.
298. *Thunderbird v. Mexico*, Separate Opinion of Thomas Wälde, (1 December 2005), para. 16.
299. *Ibid.*
300. *Railroad Development Corporation (RDC) v. Guatemala*, Award, ICSID No. ARB/07/23, (29 June 2012), para. 217.
301. It should be noted, however, that in *S.D. Myers v. Canada*, First Partial Award, (13 November 2000), para. 259, the tribunal mentioned, rather ambiguously, that '[t]he minimum standard of treatment provision of the NAFTA is similar to clauses contained in BITs'. The tribunal did not further examine the question.

analysis of the treaty language and its meaning, as guided by Article 31(1) of the Vienna Convention.[302]

The *Glamis* tribunal concluded that awards rendered by tribunals interpreting unqualified FET clauses were not relevant to the analysis of Article 1105:

> [t]he Tribunal finds that arbitral decisions that apply an autonomous standard provide no guidance inasmuch as the entire method of reasoning does not bear on an inquiry into custom. The various BITs cited by Claimant may or may not illuminate customary international law; they will prove helpful to this Tribunal's analysis when they seek to provide the same base floor of conduct as the minimum standard of treatment under customary international law; but they will not be of assistance if they include different protections than those provided for in customary international law.[303]

More specifically, the tribunal held that 'the language or analysis of the *Tecmed* award' (which had interpreted an FET clause in the Spain-Mexico BIT as an autonomous standard of protection) was 'not relevant to the Tribunal's consideration'.[304] It added that 'it may look solely to arbitral awards – including BIT awards – that seek to be understood by reference to the customary international law minimum standard of treatment, as opposed to any autonomous standard'.[305] The *Cargill*[306] and *Grand River* tribunals[307] reached the same conclusions.

In sum, it appears to be well-settled now that awards rendered by tribunals outside NAFTA that interpret *unqualified* FET clauses are simply not relevant for the analysis of Article 1105 which belong to a different species of FET clauses. *A contrario*, NAFTA tribunals can be guided by non-NAFTA arbitral decisions where tribunals have interpreted FET clauses similar to Article 1105 (where the standard is expressly linked to international law).

---

302. *Glamis v. United States*, Award, (9 June 2009), para. 606. *See also*, at para. 607: 'Ascertaining custom is necessarily a factual inquiry, looking to the actions of States and the motives for and consistency of these actions. By applying an autonomous standard, on the other hand, a tribunal may focus solely on the language and nuances of the treaty language itself and, applying the rules of treaty interpretation, require no party proof of State action or *opinio juris*. This latter practice fails to assist in the ascertainment of custom'.
303. *Glamis v. United States*, Award, (9 June 2009), para. 608.
304. *Ibid.*, para. 610.
305. *Ibid.*, para. 611.
306. *Cargill, Inc. v. Mexico*, Award, (18 September 2009), para. 278 ('A substantial number of arbitral decisions have been rendered over the last decade in proceedings based on such BITs. In the Tribunal's view, these decisions are relevant to the issue presented in Article 1105(1) only if the fair and equitable treatment clause of the BIT in question was viewed by the Tribunal as involving, like Article 1105, an incorporation of the customary international law standard rather than autonomous treaty language'). *See also* at para. 280 where the tribunal held that 'the holding in *Tecmed* is not instructive in this arbitration as to the scope and bounds of the fair and equitable treatment required by Article 1105 of the NAFTA' because the award did not 'bear on the customary international law minimum standard of treatment, but rather reflect an autonomous standard based on an interpretation of the text'. *See also*, at para. 279.
307. *Grand River v. United States*, Award, (12 January 2011), para. 176 ('the content of the obligation imposed by Article 1105 must be determined by reference to customary international law, not to standards contained in other treaties (...)'.

[3]   Can Tribunals Look at Other Sources of Law than Custom to Interpret Article 1105?

Despite the clear language of the Note which explicitly refers to 'customary international law', investors have repeatedly argued that the term 'international law' at Article 1105 should be given a much broader meaning. They have thus argued that the Note 'does not by its own terms preclude the Tribunal from considering and applying rules of international law other than those that have the status of custom'.[308] For one investor, Article 1105 'explicitly requires' treatment in accordance with 'international law' not 'customary international law' and 'until such protections are actually deleted from the text of NAFTA through the formal amendment process required under Article 2202, they must be the controlling legal principles in this case'.[309] The investor in *Merrill & Ring* argued that there was a conflict between NAFTA Article 1131(1) (which requires a tribunal to consider 'all applicable rules of international law') and the Note (which restricts it 'to applying only rules of customary international law'[310]). Because of this conflict, the investor argued that the tribunal should therefore simply disregard the Note and 'interpret NAFTA Article 1105(1) in accordance with its original wording', i.e., a reference to all sources of international law, not only custom.[311] In fact, the investor in *Merrill & Ring* went so far as to affirm that 'the practice of deciding international legal disputes with reference to all the sources of international law is in-and-of-itself customary international legal practice'.[312] Not surprisingly, respondent States have consistently argued that the treatment accorded to investors under Article 1105 was limited to the one existing under customary international law, and not any other sources of law.[313]

The reasoning of some tribunals seems to suggest that when interpreting Article 1105, they are permitted to look *beyond* customary international law at other sources of international law. This is indeed the case of a passage from the *Mondev* award where the tribunal mentioned that the standard of treatment under Article 1105 'is to be found by reference to international law, i.e., by reference to the normal sources of international law determining the minimum standard of treatment of foreign investors'.[314] However, the tribunal later went on to conclude that the Note now 'makes it clear that Article 1105(1) refers to a standard existing under customary international law, and not

---

308. *UPS v. Canada*, Investor's Reply to Article 1128 Submissions, (21 May 2002), para. 20. *See also*: *Ibid.*, Investor's Rejoinder (Jurisdiction), (26 August 2004), para. 36; *Glamis v. United States*, Investor's Reply, (15 December 2006), paras. 207, 213; *Pope & Talbot Inc. v. Canada*, Investor's Letter, (10 September 2001), at 4, 5.
309. *Methanex v. United States*, Investor's First Submissions on FTC Notes, (18 September 2001), at 2.
310. *Ibid.*, at 2, 5.
311. *Merrill & Ring v. Canada*, Investor's Reply, (15 December 2008), paras. 297, 291, 292, 295, 296.
312. *Ibid.*, paras. 303, 304-306. This argument was strongly rejected by Canada in its Rejoinder, (27 March 2009), paras. 159–161.
313. *See*, for instance, *Merrill & Ring v. Canada*, Canada's Counter-Memorial, (13 May 2008), paras. 453–454; *UPS v. Canada*, Canada's Reply (Jurisdiction) (12 April 2002), para. 97; *Methanex v. United States*, US Post-Hearing Submissions on FTC Note, (17 December 2001), at 7.
314. *Mondev v. United States*, Award, (11 October 2002), para. 120.

to standards established by other treaties of the three NAFTA Parties'.[315] The *Mondev* award therefore clearly states that under Article 1105, 'international law' refers *only* to custom. It is therefore perplexing that the *ADF* tribunal subsequently interpreted the *Mondev* award differently:[316]

> We understand *Mondev* to be saying – and we would respectfully agree with it – that any general requirement to accord 'fair and equitable treatment' and 'full protection and security' must be disciplined by being based upon State practice and judicial or arbitral caselaw or other sources of customary or general international law…
>
> It does not appear inappropriate, however, to note that it is not necessary to assume that the customary international law on the treatment of aliens and their property, including investments, is bereft of more general principles or requirements, with normative consequences, in respect of investments, derived from - in the language of Mondev - 'established sources of [international] law'.[317]

Both paragraphs suggest that sources of international law other than custom are relevant under Article 1105.[318] This is clear when reading the footnotes of these two paragraphs where the tribunal refers to authors concluding that 'general principles of law' are one of the sources of international law.[319]

The position adopted by the *ADF* award was later followed to some extent by the tribunal in *Merrill & Ring*. The tribunal first noted that according to its ordinary meaning, the term 'international law' refers to *all sources* mentioned in the ICJ Statute and is *not* limited to custom:

> The meaning of international law can only be understood today with reference to Article 38(1) of the Statute of the International Court of Justice, where the sources of international law are identified as international conventions, international custom, general principles of law, and judicial decisions and the teachings of the most highly qualified publicists as a subsidiary means for the determination of the rules of law. The Investor's understanding of the role of Article 38(1) of such Statute in the context of this particular discussion is correct. In fact, the reference that Articles 1105(1) and 1131(1) make to 'international law' must be understood as a reference to the sources of this legal order as a whole, not just one of them.[320]

---

315. *Ibid.*, para. 121. This position was later endorsed by the tribunal in: *Cargill, Inc. v. Mexico*, Award, (18 September 2009), para. 268.
316. Based on *ADF's* interpretation of the *Mondev* award, some writers have argued that the *Mondev* award actually supports the view that custom is not the only relevant source of international law under Article 1105. *See*: Brower, *supra* n. 117, at 362; Ryan, *supra* n. 232, at 943.
317. *ADF v. United States*, Award, (9 January 2003), paras. 184, 185.
318. Brower, *supra* n. 117, at 362, citing the *ADF* award as one example of a tribunal having 'quietly revolted against the elimination of general principles as a source of "international law" for purposes of Article 1105(1)'.
319. *ADF v. United States*, Award, (9 January 2003), para. 185, footnote 176: 'Schwarzenberger [*International Law* (vol. 1, 3rd ed. Stevens & Sons 1957] at p. 231 makes the comment that "[i]t is arguable that the law-creating process on which [the minimum] standard [of treatment of aliens] now rests is either international customary law or the general principles of law recognized by civilized nations."; Bin Cheng, *General Principles of Law* (1953) stresses the organic nature of general principles of law as one of the sources of international law'.
320. *Merrill & Ring v. Canada*, Award, (31 March 2010), para. 184.

The *Merrill & Ring* tribunal added that 'had a more limited meaning been intended [by the Parties] it would have had to be specifically identified in the terms of the Agreement, which was not the case'.[321] The reasoning of the tribunal completely disregards the fact that in 2001, the Parties had expressly stated in the Note that it was their intention (to paraphrase the tribunal) to give a 'more limited meaning' to the term 'international law'. Another example of the tribunal's disregard for the Note is the following comment: 'to the extent relevant, it is thus possible for the Tribunal to examine various sources of international law in the effort to identify the precise content of this standard'.[322] However, the FTC Note expressly provides for this standard to be examined *only* in light of *one source* of international law (custom), and *not* all of them. Having said so, the *Merrill & Ring* tribunal then explained that treaties (such as BITs) were 'not of great help' to determine the content of Article 1105 since 'as for the most part, they also contain rather general references to fair and equitable treatment ... without further elaboration'.[323] For this reason, the tribunal concluded that all of this 'leaves customary international law as the other principal source to be applied'.[324] In the end, the tribunal seems to have solely applied custom for *practical reasons,* rather than because it was simply required to do so under the binding FTC Note.

There is some support amongst writers for the proposition advanced by the *ADF* and *Merrill & Ring* tribunals that international law includes custom as well as other sources of law.[325] Brower argues that while the reference to 'international law' at Article 1105 excludes independent treaty obligations,[326] it remains that 'given their role in developing the law of state responsibility and the minimum standard of treatment for aliens,' general principles of law are necessarily part of the scope of international law to be applied by a tribunal under this provision.[327] The preferable view however, is

---

321. *Ibid.,* para. 185.
322. *Ibid.,* para. 186.
323. *Ibid.*
324. *Ibid.* The tribunal nevertheless added that 'general principles of law also have a role to play in this discussion' (para. 187). Thus, it mentioned that concepts such as 'good faith, the prohibition of arbitrariness, discrimination' were 'to a large extent the expression of general principles of law and hence also a part of international law'.
325. Weiler, *supra* n. 153, at 263-264 ('It is the *existence* of the *minimum standard* which has achieved the status of custom. To understand the *content* of this *minimum standard,* evidence must be provided, which can be drawn from any of the sources of international law set out in Article 38(1) of the *Statute of the Court of International Justice',* emphasis in the original); Weiler, *supra* n. 162, at 492; Weiler, *supra* n. 54, at 724. *See also,* the reasoning of Kläger, *supra* n. 44, at 111, for whom tribunals should take 'arguments from any source of international law' so that they have 'the opportunity to provide comprehensive reasoning and thereby to manage all social and legal developments influencing a particular investment dispute'. He believes that FET 'mainly serves as a gateway for the systemic integration other sources of international law' (at 111).
326. Brower, *supra* n. 117, at 358. *See also*: Ari Afilalo, *Meaning, Ambiguity and Legitimacy: Judicial (Re)Construction of NAFTA Chapter 11,* 25 Nw. J. Int'l L. & Bus. 279, 298 (2004-2005); Kirkman, *supra* n. 153, at 343, 383.
327. Brower, *supra* n. 117, at 363. *See also* at 361 ('In short, when used to describe the minimum standard of treatment for aliens, the ordinary and historically accepted meaning of "international law" includes general principles of law. None of the relevant context qualifies that meaning for purposes of Article 1105(1). Nor does drafting history disclose the intent to exclude

certainly that of all other NAFTA tribunals that have rejected this interpretation.[328] This is, for instance, the clear position adopted by the *Grand River* tribunal:

> the content of the obligation imposed by Article 1105 must be determined by reference to customary international law, not to standards contained in other treaties or other NAFTA provisions, or in other sources, unless those sources reflect relevant customary international law.[329]

In sum, it is apparent that based on the clear guidance provided by the binding FTC Note, NAFTA tribunals should look solely to custom as a source of international law in their interpretation of Article 1105.

[B]   Challenging the Note

Some tribunals have challenged the letter and the spirit of the FTC Note and thereby undermined its real effectiveness. These tribunals have basically used two distinct (yet closely related) sets of arguments.[330]

First, some tribunals have interpreted customary international law as an evolving and flexible concept (section §2.03[B][2]).[331] In other words, faced with the binding FTC Note that *restricts* the extent of investors' rights, these tribunals have simply 'moved the goal post'. They have interpreted customary international law broadly by emphasizing its evolutionary character. Under this interpretation, the level of protection offered to foreign investors under Article 1105 is (at least theoretically) *superior* to the treatment under the minimum standard. This is precisely the reasoning adopted by the *Pope & Talbot* tribunal in its 2002 ruling. This approach is even clearer in two subsequent NAFTA awards (*Mondev* and *ADF*). As further discussed below, the present author believes that in doing so these two awards have (at least implicitly) challenged the FTC Note. The *Merrill & Ring* tribunal later took the approach that supports the evolutionary interpretation of customary international law to the extreme. The *Merrill & Ring* tribunal's interpretation is a direct challenge to the FTC Note.

Second, a number of tribunals have come to the controversial conclusion that the FET standard has become a rule of customary international law in and of itself (section

---

general principles from the scope of Article 1105(1)') at 349 ('To the extent that the Notes exclude general principles of law from the minimum standard, they constitute an *ultra vires* amendment (...)').

328. *Waste Management v. Mexico*, Award, (30 April 2004), para. 91 (The FTC Notes 'clarifies that Article 1105 refers to a standard existing under customary law, not standards under other treaties of the NAFTA Parties or other provisions within NAFTA'). *See also*: *Chemtura v. Canada*, Award, (2 August 2010), para. 121.

329. *Grand River v. United States*, Award, (12 January 2011), para. 219 ('As the basis of the fair and equitable treatment standard of Article 1105, the customary standard of protection of alien investors' investments does not incorporate other legal protections that may be provided investors or classes of investors under other sources of law. To hold otherwise would make Article 1105 a vehicle for generally litigating claims based on alleged infractions of domestic and international law and thereby unduly circumvent the limited reach of Article 1105 as determined by the Free Trade Commission in its binding directive'). *See also*, at paras. 176, 181.

330. Schill, *supra* n. 65, at 272. *See also*: Kläger, *supra* n. 44, at 75.

331. Kaufmann-Kohler, *supra* n. 116, at 186.

§2.03[B][3]). As further explained below, their reasoning openly contradicts the clear intention of NAFTA Parties when the Note was issued in 2001.

Before examining these two lines of arguments in detail, we will first analyze the two *Pope & Talbot* awards (section §2.03[B][1]). As mentioned above,[332] the first award was one of the principal reasons why the NAFTA Parties issued the FTC Note in the first place. The second award offered a blueprint for future tribunals on how to by-pass the Note.[333]

[1]   The Pope & Talbot Saga

In its April 2001 award, the *Pope & Talbot* tribunal indicated that the language of Article 1105 was 'suggesting' that FET was *included* in the minimum standard of treatment under international law.[334] However, even though the language of Article 1105 'suggest[ed] otherwise', the tribunal favored 'another possible interpretation' whereby FET was considered as '*additive*' to the requirement of international law'.[335] In other words, investors under NAFTA would be entitled to the protection of the minimum standard of treatment, *plus* the FET.[336] In support of its alternative interpretation, the tribunal pointed out that the 'language of Article 1105 grew out' of similar FET provisions included in BITs entered into by the United States and other industrialized countries.[337] The tribunal referred specifically to the 'no less' clause found in the 1987 US Model BIT and held that such formulation was 'expressly adopting the additive character' of the FET.[338] This conclusion was also said to be supported by the 'language and the intention of the BITs'.[339] In fact, for the tribunal 'a contrary reading would do violence to the BIT language'.[340] In doing so, the tribunal rejected the reasoning of the *S.D. Myers* tribunal, which had, in its view, interpreted Article 1105 as a reference to the minimum standard of treatment.[341]

---

332. *See*, at section §2.02[C][3][a].
333. Schill, *supra* n. 65, at 272.
334. *Pope & Talbot Inc. v. Canada*, Award on the Merits Phase II, (10 April 2001), para. 109. The tribunal also acknowledged that both Canada *and the investors* subscribed to this interpretation.
335. *Ibid.*, para. 110 (emphasis in the original).
336. *Ibid.*
337. *Ibid.*
338. *Ibid.*, para. 111. The tribunal added (at para. 111): 'Investors are entitled to those elements, no matter what else their entitlement under international law. A logical corollary to this language is that compliance with the fairness elements must be ascertained free of any threshold that might be applicable to the evaluation of measures under the minimum standard of international law'. In its subsequent award of 2002 (*Pope & Talbot Inc. v. Canada*, Award in Respect of Damages, (31 May 2002), para. 44), the tribunal made the same observation: 'It will be recalled that the Tribunal, and most other observers, concluded that, in that formulation [i.e., that of the 1987 US Model BIT), the international law standard of treatment is "additive" to the requirements for fair and equitable treatment'.
339. *Pope & Talbot Inc. v. Canada*, Award on the Merits Phase II, (10 April 2001), para. 113.
340. *Ibid.*
341. *Ibid.*, the tribunal explained that 'by not appreciating the plain language' of the BITs, the *S.D. Myers* tribunal 'did not address the implications of that language on the proper interpretation of Article 1105'.

The conclusion reached by the tribunal on this point is, in itself, controversial. The evidence overwhelmingly suggests that at the time (i.e., prior to the entry into force of the NAFTA in 1994), the United States viewed the 'no less' clause found in most US BITs simply as a reference to the minimum standard of treatment under customary international law.[342] As mentioned above,[343] this position was taken, for instance, by the US State Department in official letters describing the 1992 US Model BIT, and also in other letters sent to the US President explaining the content of 5 BITs signed in 1993 (and numerous other BITs signed in 1994 onward). More troubling, however, is the fact that in its submission to the tribunal in these proceedings, the United States had specifically refuted the *Pope* tribunal's own interpretation of the 1987 U.S. Model BIT. In its Article 1928 submission, the United States made it clear that it had always used the terms 'fair and equitable treatment' in its BITs as 'no more than a shorthand reference to elements of the developed body of customary international law governing the responsibility of a State for its treatment of the nationals of another State'.[344] At the time of the award, the tribunal was therefore fully aware that its own interpretation of the US 1987 Model BIT had been rejected by that same country.

The award can also be criticized on this point for its very selective use of doctrinal authority to support its 'additive character' interpretation of Article 1105. In the 2001 award, the tribunal referred to three authorities in support of its interpretation of Article 1105.[345] It is noteworthy that the tribunal failed to refer to the later work of Mann who seems to have changed his mind by adopting the view that the FET was essentially the same as the minimum standard of protection under custom.[346] Another important point not mentioned at all by the tribunal, but which had been explained during the proceedings by both the United States[347] and Canada,[348] is the fact that Mann was examining provisions contained in British BITs (and more specifically, a recently concluded UK-Philippines BIT) which, contrary to NAFTA Article 1105, did not refer at all to 'international law'.[349] Especially troubling is the tribunal's misrepresentation of Dolzer and Stevens' opinion by only referring to a part of their work while

---

342. Vandevelde, *supra* n. 1, at 77-78.
343. *See*, the analysis above: text attached to footnotes 17 to 20.
344. *Pope & Talbot Inc. v. Canada*, US Fourth Submission, (1 November 2000), paras. 2, 3, 5, 7.
345. *Ibid.*, Award on the Merits Phase II, (10 April 2001), para. 111, footnote 105, referring to the work of F.A. Mann, *British Treaties for the Promotion and Protection of Investments*, 52 British YBIL, 241, 244 (1981); Rudolf Dolzer & Margrete Stevens, *Bilateral Investment Treaties* 65 (Martinus Nijhoff Publ. 1995); UNCTAD, *Fair and Equitable Treatment*, 39-40 (UNCTAD Series on Issues in International Investment Agreements 1999).
346. F.A. Mann, *The Legal Aspect of Money: with Special Reference to Comparative Private and Public International Law* 510 (Clarendon Press, 1992): 'In some cases, it is true, treaties merely repeat, perhaps in slightly different language, what in essence is a duty imposed by customary international law; the foremost example is the familiar provision whereby states undertake to accord fair and equitable treatment to each other's nationals and which in law is unlikely to amount to more than a confirmation of the obligation to act in good faith, or to refrain from abuse or arbitrariness'. The argument is developed in: Thomas, *supra* n. 2, at 57-58; Thomas, *supra* n. 151, at 15.
347. *Pope & Talbot Inc. v. Canada*, US Fifth Submission, (1 December 2000), paras. 6, 7.
348. *Ibid.*, Canada's Response to Phase Two Post-Hearing Submissions of Mexico and the United States, (15 December 2000), para. 14.
349. Thomas, *supra* n. 2, at 55-56.

omitting the most important caveat made by the authors concerning Article 1105. The award thus mentions the passage where the authors explain that *in general*, FET clauses are 'probably evidence of a self–contained standard', but completely omits the rest of the paragraph indicating '*[h]owever*, in the North American Free Trade Agreement (NAFTA), the fair and equitable standard is *explicitly subsumed* under the minimum standard of customary international law'.[350] This omission is worrisome considering that Canada had made an express reference to this passage in its pleadings.[351]

In any event, the tribunal flatly rejected the United States' interpretation of Article 1105 on the (very peculiar) ground that it was 'only' based on the plain meaning of the provision:

> The United States asserts that, whatever the meaning of the BITs, the drafters of NAFTA Chapter 11 'excluded any possible conclusion that the parties were diverging from the customary international law concept of fair and equitable treatment'. The United States supports [its] contention solely by pointing to the language of Article 1105; it offered no other evidence to the Tribunal that the NAFTA parties intended to reject the additive character of the BITs. Consequently, the suggestions of the United States on this matter do not enjoy the kind of deference that might otherwise be accorded to representations by the parties to an international agreement as to the intentions of the drafters with respect to particular provisions in that agreement.[352]

This passage has been criticized by scholars on the ground that the tribunal required the United States to prove a negative (i.e., that it did not intend to adopt the interpretation that *the tribunal* attributed to the BIT's text).[353] Similarly, it has been rightly observed that the tribunal 'dismissed the plain language of Article 1105 in favor of an interpretation founded on the perceived intention of the Parties'.[354] The tribunal's dismissal of the plain and ordinary meaning of Article 1105 is clear from this passage in its subsequent award of 2002, which summarizes its previous findings:

> The Tribunal determined that, *notwithstanding the language of Article 1105, which admittedly suggests otherwise*, the requirement to accord NAFTA investor fair and

---

350. Dolzer & Stevens, *supra* n. 345, at 60 (emphasis added).
351. *Pope & Talbot Inc. v. Canada*, Canada's Response to Phase Two Post-Hearing Submissions of Mexico and the United States, (15 December 2000), para. 20.
352. *Pope & Talbot Inc. v. Canada*, Award on the Merits Phase II, (10 April 2001), para. 114.
353. Thomas, *supra* n. 2, at 77: 'It might have been thought that pointing to the treaty's text was good evidence of the Parties' intent. Not to this Tribunal which required the United States to prove a negative. The United States was criticized for failing to adduce proof that the NAFTA Parties had not intended to adopt the interpretation that the Tribunal, not the United States, attributed to the BITs text. It is difficult to conceive how a state is to provide evidence that it intended to depart from an interpretation of a treaty that it did not hold. The evidence of state practice was to the contrary of the meaning attributed to the BITs provision by the Tribunal. Equally troubling is the Tribunal's refusal to follow the express language of the NAFTA and to insist on other evidence to prove that the text meant what it said'.
354. Kinnear et al., *supra* n. 1, at 11. *See also*: Kläger, *supra* n. 44, at 69-70; Thomas, *supra* n. 2, at 77-80, Gantz, *supra* n. 153, at 943; Patrick G. Foy, *Effectiveness of NAFTA's Chapter 11 Investor-State Arbitration Procedures*, 18 ICSID Rev. 101 (2003).

equitable treatment was independent of, not subsumed by, the requirement to accord them treatment required by international law.[355]

This part of the award was also widely criticized by various authors[356] as well as by NAFTA Parties in other subsequent arbitration proceedings as being a clear departure from basic canons of interpretation under the *Vienna Convention*. Thus, in *Methanex*, the United States (respondent in the proceedings) qualified the 'additive' interpretation adopted by the *Pope & Talbot* tribunal as 'poorly reasoned and unpersuasive',[357] while Canada stated that the tribunal 'arrived at an incorrect interpretation' by 'ignor[ing] the first general rule of interpretation in the *Vienna Convention*'[358] and Mexico stated that the tribunal's 'refusal to adopt the Parties' shared view [on Article 1105] can only be regarded as perverse'.[359] The award was also strongly condemned by Justice Tysoe of the Supreme Court of British Columbia in his judicial review of the *Metalclad* award rendered *before* the FTC Note was issued.[360]

Another questionable statement made by the *Pope* tribunal is its assertion that '[n]either Mexico nor Canada has subscribed to the version of the intent of the drafters put forward by the United States with respect to Article 1105.[361] This is, quite simply, incorrect. Thus, at the time when the tribunal rendered its award in April 2001, *all* NAFTA Parties had expressly indicated in several pleadings that they *unanimously* considered that Article 1105 incorporates the minimum standard of treatment under

355. *Pope & Talbot Inc. v. Canada*, Award in Respect of Damages, (31 May 2002), para. 9 (emphasis added).
356. Fitzmaurice et al., *supra* n. 108, at 214: 'The Tribunal further departed from the 1969 [Vienna Convention] canons of interpretation, (the interpretation based on a textual analysis), and focused on the intention of the parties that went beyond the text of the Article. To this end, it expressed the view that the US did not furnish evidence that Parties to the NAFTA intended to reject the additive character of the BITs and that the US relied only on the language of Article 1105 in order to prove the intention of the Parties. In order to prove that the elements of fairness were additive to the requirements of Article 1105, the Tribunal took into account treaties concluded between the US and other Parties. This interpretative approach did not comply with Article 31 of the VCLT that includes for the purpose of the interpretation of a treaty any agreements or instruments concluded between parties to a treaty, not with other states outside the treaty framework'.
357. *Methanex v. United States*, US Reply Memorial on Jurisdiction, Admissibility and the Proposed Amendment, (12 April 2001), at 29. *See also*: *Mondev v. United States*, Award, (11 October 2001), at 15; *ADF v. United States*, US Final Post-Hearing Submissions, (1 August 2002), at 3, 13.
358. *Methanex v. United States*, Canada's Second Article 1128 Submission, (30 April 2001), para. 38.
359. *Ibid.*, Mexico's Article 1128 Submission, (30 April 2001), para. 11.
360. *Mexico v. Metalclad*, Supreme Court of British Columbia, Judgment and Reasons for Decision (2 May 2001), paras. 62, 65: 'With respect, I am unable to agree with the reasoning of the Pope & Talbot tribunal. It has interpreted the word "including" in Article 1105 to mean "plus", which has a virtually opposite meaning. Its interpretation is contrary to Article 31(1) of the Vienna Convention, which requires that terms of treaties be given their ordinary meaning. The evidence that the NAFTA Parties intended to reject the "additive" character of bilateral investment treaties is found in the fact that they chose not to adopt the language used is such treaties and I find it surprising that the tribunal considered that other evidence was required. The NAFTA Parties chose to use different language in Article 1105 and the natural inference is that the NAFTA Parties did not want Article 1105 to be given the same interpretation as the wording of the provision in the Model Bilateral Treaty of 1987'.
361. *Pope & Talbot Inc. v. Canada*, Award on the Merits Phase II, (10 April 2001), para. 114, footnote 109.

custom. Both Mexico's Article 1128 submission[362] and Canada's pleading made this point very clearly.[363]

For the tribunal, 'notwithstanding the position espoused by the United States', there were 'very strong reasons for interpreting the language of Article 1105 consistently with the language in the BITs'.[364] Thus, the tribunal mentioned the 'basic unlikelihood' that NAFTA Parties intended for Article 1105 to provide each other's investors (and investments) with a more *limited* protection than the one actually granted in BITs to foreign investors of *other countries*, with whom they do not share a relationship as close as that amongst NAFTA members.[365] This argument will be further discussed below when examining the MFN clause.[366] The tribunal concluded that it was 'unwilling to attribute to the NAFTA parties an intention that would lead to such a patently absurd result'.[367] This part of the reasoning of the tribunal has also been described as contrary to basic rules of treaty interpretation.[368]

Ultimately, the tribunal held that Canada had breached Article 1105 and that the investor was therefore entitled to compensation, which was to be awarded in a subsequent decision. In the mean time, the FTC had issued its Note of Interpretation in July 2001. As mentioned above,[369] the Note clearly overruled the *Pope* tribunal's 'additive character' interpretation of Article 1105 by stating that the FET 'did not require treatment in addition to or beyond that which is required by the customary international law minimum standard of treatment of aliens'. In its subsequent Award in Respect of Damages of May 2002, the tribunal had no choice but to address the

362. *Ibid.*, Mexico's Article 1128 Submission, (1 December 2000), at 4.
363. *Ibid.*, Canada's Response to Phase Two Post-Hearing Submissions of Mexico and United States, (15 December 2000), paras. 12–13 ('The submissions of the three NAFTA Parties with respect to the proper construction and scope of Article 1105 are consistent. Mexico expressly adopts the portions of the United States' Third Submission that address the key parameters of the Article 1105 obligation. Canada also concurs with the interpretation of the provision offered in the U.S. submission. In particular, the Parties agree that Article 1105 incorporates the customary international law concept of the minimum standard of treatment and that the phrase "fair and equitable treatment" does not expand the scope of the provision beyond this standard (…)'). *See also* at para. 20 ('[I]n Article 1105 the terms "fair and equitable treatment" cannot be understood and applied independently and autonomously. The phrase "fair and equitable treatment" is included within the ambit of "treatment in accordance with international law", and the obligation is entitled "Minimum Standard of Treatment"').
364. *Pope & Talbot Inc. v. Canada*, Award on the Merits Phase II, (10 April 2001), para. 115.
365. *Ibid.*
366. *See*, at Chapter 4 section §4.04[B][1].
367. *Pope & Talbot Inc. v. Canada*, Award on the Merits Phase II, (10 April 2001), para. 118.
368. Thomas, *supra* n. 2, at 79-80 ('There is no evidence of which this writer is aware that the United States thought that it was obtaining better treatment from other states than from its NAFTA Partners. The "absurdity" that the Tribunal thought it had established resulted from an incorrect application of the Vienna Convention Article 32. That Article is applied only when the interpretation according to Article 31 (which in this case is applied to Article 1105) leads "to a result which is manifestly absurd or unreasonable". Here, the absurdity was found not from a good faith interpretation of the ordinary meaning of the terms of Article 1105 in their context and in light of the NAFTA's objective and purpose, but rather from referring to treaties between a NAFTA Party and other states').
369. *See*, at section §2.02[C][3][a].

delicate question of the impact of the Note on its own interpretation of Article 1105 in its previous award.[370]

In its 2002 award, the tribunal asked the following rhetorical question: '[w]as the decision made by the Tribunal based on an interpretation different from that made by the Commission?'[371] It gave the following answer:

> At one level this might appear to be so since the Tribunal expressly referred to the fairness elements as being additions to the requirements of the international law minimum and interpreted Article 1105 to require that covered investors and investments receive the benefits of the fairness elements under ordinary standards applied in the NAFTA countries without any threshold limitation.[372]

However, in the next paragraph, the tribunal stated that this 'conclusion alone does not mean that the Tribunal's award was incompatible with the [FTC's] interpretation'.[373] The question of their inconsistencies would depend on 'whether the concept behind the fairness elements under customary international law is different from those elements under ordinary standards applied in NAFTA countries'.[374] In other words, faced with the Note's unambiguous clarification, the tribunal had no other option but to abandon its own 'additive character' interpretation of Article 1105. The tribunal then decided to simply shift its attention to the other question of the *actual content* of the treatment required under custom.

The *Pope* tribunal explained that it rejected Canada's 'static conception' according to which the principles of customary international law applicable to the treatment of foreign investors were 'frozen in amber' at the time of the *Neer* decision.[375] The tribunal indicated that in the proceedings, Canada had 'urged the Tribunal to award damages only if its conduct was found to be an "egregious" act or failure to meet internationally required standards'.[376] On the contrary, the tribunal noted that 'there has been evolution in customary international law concepts since the 1920s'[377] and that since then, 'the range of actions subject to international concern has broadened beyond the international delinquencies considered in *Neer* to include the concept of fair and equitable treatment'.[378] The tribunal added that 'many' BITs 'require state conduct to be evaluated under the fairness elements apart from the standards of customary international law'.[379] In one passage (further discussed below), the tribunal clearly suggests that since the FET standard was now found in so many BITs, it had *itself*

---

370. *Pope & Talbot Inc. v. Canada*, Award in Respect of Damages, (31 May 2002). *See*, P. Dumberry, *The Quest to Define 'Fair and Equitable Treatment' for Investors under International Law: The Case of the NAFTA Chapter 11 Pope & Talbot Awards*, 3(4) J. World Invest. 657-691 (2002).
371. *Pope & Talbot Inc. v. Canada*, Award in Respect of Damages, (31 May 2002), para. 55.
372. *Ibid.* At the outset of the award (at para. 46), the tribunal also mentioned that the drafting documents did not support Canada's position that the words 'international law' at Article 1105 referred to the minimum standard of treatment existing under *customary* international law.
373. *Ibid.*, para. 56.
374. *Ibid.*
375. *Ibid.*, paras. 57–58.
376. *Ibid.*, para. 57.
377. *Ibid.*, para. 59.
378. *Ibid.*, para. 60.
379. *Ibid.*, para. 61.

become a rule of customary international law.[380] In sum, the tribunal rejected 'Canada's contention on the present content of customary international law'.[381]

In the present author's view, the reasoning of the tribunal on this point clearly undermines the effectiveness of the Note.[382] The tribunal was understandably uncomfortable in having no choice but to apply the Note which, for all purposes, had overruled its previous award. The 'problem' with the Note was that it expressly required tribunals to apply the minimum standard under custom thus *restricting* the extent of investors' rights under Article 1105. Faced with such a 'problem', the tribunal simply 'moved the goal post'. On the one hand, the tribunal respected the Note by applying customary international law; but on the other hand, it emphasized its evolutionary character which was no longer that of the 1920s. The adoption of this interpretation necessarily led to an increase of the level of protection offered to foreign investors under Article 1105. In sum, by adopting such an evolutionary interpretation, the tribunal had found a way to by-pass the Note. As pointed out by Schill:

> the notion of evolutionary customary international law ingeniously allowed the [*Pope*] tribunal to reintroduce the content of an autonomous interpretation of fair and equitable treatment under the label of customary international law without effectively imposing the limits on its judicial freedom that would have resulted from a strict application of the FTC Note.[383]

Ultimately, the tribunal did not have to use this evolutionary interpretation to conclude that its previous award was *not* incompatible with the Note. It held that applying Canada's so-called 'restrictive' interpretation of custom to the facts of the case would lead to the exact same conclusion it had reached in its previous award. Thus, for the tribunal, even under Canada's so-called 'static conception' of custom, the 'verification review' process implemented by Canada constituted a breach of Article 1105. The conduct of Canada's Softwood Lumber Division (SLD) during the 'verification review' process was described by the tribunal as 'egregious'[384] which caused it 'shock and outrage'.[385] The tribunal awarded the investor the total amount of USD 461,566 with interest.

By qualifying the events as 'egregious', the tribunal opportunistically avoided having to publicly retract from its (now moot) interpretation of Article 1105. It should be recalled that in its previous award of 2001, the tribunal had interpreted Article 1105 'without any threshold limitation that the conduct complained of be "egregious", "outrageous" or "shocking", or otherwise extraordinary' and consequently decided to 'test Canadian implementation of the SLD against the fairness elements without applying that kind of threshold'.[386] In the first 2001 award, the tribunal held that the 'verification review process [was] nothing less than a denial of the fair treatment

---

380. *Ibid.,* para. 62. This question is further discussed below at section §2.03[B][3].
381. *Ibid.,* para. 65.
382. *See also,* Schill, *supra* n. 65, at 270-273.
383. *Ibid.,* at 273.
384. *Pope & Talbot Inc. v. Canada,* Award in Respect of Damages, (31 May 2002), para. 67.
385. *Ibid.,* para. 68.
386. *Pope & Talbot Inc. v. Canada,* Award on the Merits Phase II, (10 April 2001), para. 118.

required by NAFTA Article 1105'.[387] In that award, the tribunal did not refer at all to the conduct of SLD as being 'egregious'. This is probably because it used a different test where such qualification was unnecessary. A careful reading of both awards' description of the facts on the breach of Article 1105 shows a slight change of tone.[388] It seems that the exact same events had suddenly become somewhat more egregious in the second award of 2002. This is clear from the dramatic conclusion reached by the tribunal in the second award where it stated that it would 'hope that these actions by the SLD would shock and outrage every reasonable citizen of Canada; they did shock and outrage the Tribunal'.[389]

For all of these reasons, the two *Pope & Talbot* awards have been strongly criticized by most scholars. In fact, it seems that support for the award can only be found from writers who argue that the FET standard is an autonomous standard detached from the minimum standard of treatment under custom.[390]

[2]   The Controversial Question of the Evolutionary Character of the Minimum Standard of Treatment under Custom

Nowadays, there is a general agreement between NAFTA Parties that, as a matter of principle, customary international law is not static and can evolve over time.[391] While the question of the *potential* evolution of custom is not disputed, one of the most

---

387. *Ibid.,* para. 181.
388. Thus, compare the following two descriptions: *Ibid.,* para. 181 ('the end result for the Investment was being subjected to threats, denied its reasonable requests for pertinent information, required to incur unnecessary expense and disruption in meeting SLD's requests for information, forced to expend legal fees and probably suffer a loss of reputation in government circles. While administration, like legislation, can be likened to sausage making, this episode goes well beyond the glitches and innocent mistakes that may typify the process'); *Pope & Talbot Inc. v. Canada,* Award in Respect of Damages, (31 May 2002), para. 68 ('Briefly, the Tribunal found that when the Investor instituted the claim, in these proceedings, Canada's Softwood Lumber Division ("SLD") changed its previous relationship with the Investor and the Investment from one of cooperation in running the Softwood Lumber Regime to one of threats and misrepresentation. Figuring in this new attitude were assertions of non-existent policy reasons for forcing them to comply with very burdensome demands for documents, refusals to provide them with promised information, threats of reductions and even termination of the Investment's export quotas, serious misrepresentations of fact in memoranda to the Minister concerning the Investor's and the Investment's actions and even suggestions of criminal investigation of the Investment's conduct. The Tribunal also concluded that these actions were not caused by any behaviour of the Investor or the Investment, which remained cooperative until the overreaching of the SLD became too burdensome and confrontational. One would hope that these actions by the SLD would shock and outrage every reasonable citizen of Canada; they did shock and outrage the Tribunal').
389. *Pope & Talbot Inc. v. Canada,* Award in Respect of Damages, (31 May 2002), para. 68.
390. Bronfman, *supra* n. 153, at 651; Tudor, *supra* n. 54, at 59-60 ('The contribution of the Pope & Talbot case to the discussion on the relationship between the IMS [international minimum standard] and FET is double: first because it separated FET from the IMS and second because it insisted on the evolutionary character of FET, ruling that it has to be interpreted upon the circumstances of the case. It is mainly the second point, the evolutionary character of FET, that will be reconfirmed in the majority of the arbitral awards that followed the pioneering Pope & Talbot award').
391. The position of the NAFTA Parties is discussed in: *Cargill, Inc. v. Mexico,* Award, (18 September 2009), paras. 272, 281, 282.

contentious issues has been whether or not any such evolution *has actually taken place* in the context of international investment law. In other words, has the minimum standard of treatment under custom evolved since the famous *Neer* case? On this question, some tribunals (*Mondev, ADF*) have come to the conclusion that custom has evolved since the 1920s (section §2.03[B[[2][a]]). On the contrary, other more recent tribunals (*Glamis, Cargill*) have concluded that the standard of treatment was the same as the one in *Neer* (section §2.03[B[[2][b]]). Finally, one tribunal (*Merrill & Ring*) adopted the so-called theory of 'convergence' and affirmed that custom had evolved so rapidly that it now had the same content as an autonomous FET clause (section §2.03[B[[2][c]]).

[a]   *Tribunals Endorsing the Proposition that Custom Has Evolved*

The *Mondev* and *ADF* tribunals were the first ones to address the controversial issue of custom's evolutionary character. The *Mondev* tribunal rejected the relevance of the *Neer* case on the ground that it 'concerned not the treatment of foreign investment as such but the physical security of the alien'.[392] Thus, for the tribunal, there was 'insufficient cause for assuming' that BITs were 'confined to the *Neer* standard of outrageous treatment where the issue is the treatment of foreign investment by the State itself'.[393] The *Mondev* tribunal also invoked a second reason:

> Secondly, *Neer* and like arbitral awards were decided in the 1920s, when the status of the individual in international law, and the international protection of foreign investments, were far less developed than they have since come to be. In particular, both the substantive and procedural rights of the individual in international law have undergone considerable development. In the light of these developments it is unconvincing to confine the meaning of 'fair and equitable treatment' and 'full protection and security' of foreign investments to what those terms – had they been current at the time – might have meant in the 1920s when applied to the physical security of an alien. To the modern eye, what is unfair or inequitable need not equate with the outrageous or the egregious. In particular, a State may treat foreign investment unfairly and inequitably without necessarily acting in bad faith.[394]

The *ADF* tribunal also rejected the relevance of the *Neer* case in the context of modern investment treaties:

> There appears no logical necessity and no concordant state practice to support the view that the Neer formulation is automatically extendible to the contemporary context of treatment of foreign investors and their investments by a host or recipient State. For both customary international law and the minimum standard of treatment of aliens it incorporates, are constantly in a process of development.[395]

---

392. *Mondev v. United States*, Award, (11 October 2002), para. 115.
393. *Ibid.*
394. *Ibid.*, para. 116.
395. *ADF v. United States*, Award, (9 January 2003), para. 181.

On the question of the evolution of custom, the *Mondev* tribunal came to the conclusion that 'the content of the minimum standard today cannot be limited to the content of customary international law as recognized in arbitral decisions in the 1920s'.[396] The *ADF* tribunal essentially agreed with that conclusion:

> What customary international law projects is not a static photograph of the minimum standard of treatment of aliens as it stood in 1927 when the Award in the *Neer* case was rendered. For both customary international law and the minimum standard of treatment of aliens it incorporates, are constantly in a process of development.[397]

For both tribunals, the FET standard was therefore no longer limited to instances of egregious and outrageous acts as was the case in the 1920s. Their position is well-summarized (and endorsed) by the *Waste Management II* tribunal as follows:

> Both the *Mondev* and *ADF* tribunals rejected any suggestion that the standard of treatment of a foreign investment set by NAFTA is confined to the kind of outrageous treatment referred to in the *Neer* case, i.e. to treatment amounting to an 'outrage, to bad faith, to wilful neglect of duty, or to an in insufficiency of governmental action so far short of international standards that every reasonable and impartial man would readily recognize its insufficiency'.[398]

The reasoning of the *Mondev* and *ADF* tribunals was also endorsed by the *Gami* tribunal.[399] The *Thunderbird* tribunal also noted 'the evolution of customary law since the decisions such as the *Neer* claim in 1926', but added that the 'threshold for finding a violation of the minimum standard of treatment still remains high'.[400] Recently, the *Chemtura* tribunal also concluded that the interpretation of NAFTA Article 1105 'cannot overlook the evolution of customary international law, nor the impact of BITs on this evolution'.[401]

In the present author's view, there is no doubt that, as a matter of principle, custom can evolve over time. The statements made by the *Mondev* and *ADF* tribunals to that effect are non controversial. Yet, as pointed out by one writer, 'it appears quite remarkable that almost no tribunal has made an effort to explain in more detail how far the minimum standard might have evolved and what shape it is deemed to have today'.[402] For him, 'it remains relatively unclear as to what extent this body of customary rules has evolved and how this process of evolution has taken place'.[403] The *Mondev* and *ADF* tribunals have, indeed, not demonstrated that an evolution of the

396. *Mondev v. United States*, Award, (11 October 2002), para. 123.
397. *ADF v. United States*, Award, (9 January 2003), para. 179.
398. *Waste Management v. Mexico*, Award, (30 April 2004), para. 93 (quoting from the *Neer* award).
399. *Gami Investments, Inc. v. Mexico*, UNCITRAL, Award, (15 November 2004), para. 95.
400. *Thunderbird v. Mexico*, Award, (26 January 2006), para. 194.
401. *Chemtura v. Canada*, Award, (2 August 2010), para. 121. *See also*, at para. 122, where the tribunal states that 'in line with *Mondev*' it 'will take account of the evolution of international customary law in ascertaining the content of the international minimum standard'.
402. Kläger, *supra* n. 44, at 76. *See also*: Matthew C. Porterfield, *A Distinction Without a Difference? The Interpretation of Fair and Equitable Treatment Under Customary International Law by Investment Tribunals*, 3(3) ITN 3 (2013).
403. Kläger, *supra* n. 44, at 264.

minimum standard has actually taken place. They have not undertaken any specific analysis of State practice and opinio juris to show such an evolution.

In this context, the adoption by these tribunals of the evolutionary approach can certainly be considered as an implicit challenge of the FTC Note.[404] By adopting the evolutionary approach, these tribunals have simply 'moved the goal post'. Thus, having no other option but to apply the FET in accordance with the minimum standard of treatment under custom, these tribunals have simply circumvented this apparent limitation by giving a broader interpretation to that standard. Under this interpretation, the level of protection offered to foreign investors under Article 1105 is (at least theoretically) *superior* to the treatment under the minimum standard. For Schill, the adoption of this interpretation by these tribunals have allowed them to 'comply with the institutional infrastructure of NAFTA, and the apparent will of the contracting parties, while at the same time allowing them to continuously expend their own power as decision makers'.[405]

Finally, it should be emphasized that the adoption of this evolutionary approach by these tribunals has had no practical impact on the outcome of these cases in terms of liability. In other words, these tribunals did not find the respondent States responsible for any breaches of Article 1105 even under this approach.

[b]   *Tribunals Affirming that the Standard of Treatment Has Not Changed*

Most likely in reaction to the approach taken by the *Mondev* and *ADF* tribunals, two recent NAFTA tribunals (*Glamis* and *Cargill*) have seemingly adopted a different view on the question of the evolution of the minimum standard of treatment under custom.

The *Glamis* tribunal first noted that the claimant had the burden to prove that custom had evolved quite substantially since the *Neer* case.[406] It added that it was 'difficult to establish a change in customary international law'.[407] The tribunal concluded that the claimant had not established that current customary international law had moved beyond the minimum standard of treatment of aliens, which existed at the time of the *Neer* case in the 1920s:

> As regards the second form of evolution – the proposition that customary international law has moved beyond the minimum standard of treatment of aliens

---

404. Schill, *supra* n. 65, at 273-274; Laird, *supra* n. 134, at 71; Kläger, *supra* n. 44, at 75-76.
405. Schill, *supra* n. 65, at 275.
406. *Glamis v. United States*, Award, (9 June 2009), para. 601 ('As a threshold issue, the Tribunal notes that it is Claimant's burden to sufficiently answer each of these questions. The State Parties to the NAFTA (at least Canada and Mexico) agree that "the test in *Neer* does continue to apply," though Mexico "also agrees that the standard is relative and that conduct which may not have violated international law [in] the 1920's might very well be seen to offend internationally accepted principles today." If, as Claimant argues, the customary international law minimum standard of treatment has indeed moved to require something less than the "egregious," "outrageous," or "shocking" standard as elucidated in *Neer*, then the burden of establishing what the standard now requires is upon Claimant'). *See also*, at para. 603.
407. *Ibid.*, para. 602. The tribunal also mentioned that 'the difficulty in proving a change in custom' results in 'effectively freez[ing] the protections provided for in this provision at the 1926 conception of egregiousness'.

as defined in *Neer* – the Tribunal finds that the evidence provided by Claimant does not establish such evolution. This is evident in the abundant and continued use of adjective modifiers throughout arbitral awards, evidencing a strict standard. *International Thunderbird* used the terms *'gross* denial of justice' and *'manifest* arbitrariness' to describe the acts that it viewed would breach the minimum standard of treatment. *S.D. Myers* would find a breach of Article 1105 when an investor was treated 'in *such an unjust or arbitrary* manner'. The *Mondev* tribunal held: '[t]he test is not whether a particular result is surprising, but whether the *shock or surprise* occasioned to an impartial tribunal leads, on reflection, to justified concerns as to the judicial propriety of the outcome ...'[408]

It therefore appears that, although situations may be more varied and complicated today than in the 1920s, the level of scrutiny is the same. The fundamentals of the *Neer* standard thus still apply today: to violate the customary international law minimum standard of treatment codified in Article 1105 of the NAFTA, an act must be sufficiently egregious and shocking – a gross denial of justice, manifest arbitrariness, blatant unfairness, a complete lack of due process, evident discrimination, or a manifest lack of reasons – so as to fall below accepted international standards and constitute a breach of Article 1105(1). The Tribunal notes that one aspect of evolution from *Neer* that is generally agreed upon is that bad faith is not required to find a violation of the fair and equitable treatment standard, but its presence is conclusive evidence of such. Thus, an act that is egregious or shocking may also evidence bad faith, but such bad faith is not necessary for the finding of a violation. The standard for finding a breach of the customary international law minimum standard of treatment therefore remains as stringent as it was under *Neer*; it is entirely possible, however that, as an international community, we may be shocked by State actions now that did not offend us previously.[409]

The *Glamis* award has been criticized by some because of its 'reassertion of the *Neer* standard as the applicable threshold test for finding a violation of Article 1105' which 'represents a major deviation, which the tribunal did not fully justify, from NAFTA awards rendered after the FTC interpretation'.[410] It should be reiterated however, that the *Glamis* tribunal essentially makes two complementary propositions:

–   On the one hand, the 'fundamentals' of the *Neer* standard still apply today. Thus, to prove a violation of the minimum standard of treatment under custom, an investor must show that the conduct was 'egregious' and 'shocking'.
–   On the other hand, what is considered today as 'egregious' and 'shocking' has changed over time since the 1920s.[411]

---

408. *Ibid.*, para. 614 (emphasis in the original).
409. *Ibid.*, para. 616.
410. Ryan, *supra* n. 232, at 949. *See also*, at 950 (stating that the tribunal did not explain why the *Neer* case 'should be accepted as the definitive pronouncement on the content of customary international law, either in 1926 or in 2009'). *See also*: Charles H. Brower II, *Hard Reset vs Soft Reset: Recalibration of Investment Disciplines Under Free Trade Agreements*, Kluwer Arbitration Blog (16 December 2009) (blog), online: < http://kluwerarbitrationblog.com/blog > .
411. *Glamis v. United States*, Award, (9 June 2009), paras. 613, 616. This is indeed how Canada summarized the *Glamis* finding on this point: 'customary international law standard "has not evolved from the 'shocking and egregious' standard described in *Neer*" but that "what is

In other words, while the '*test*' may not have changed ('egregious' and 'shocking'), it nevertheless remains that the *meaning* of these words has evolved overtime. Consider, for instance, the events described above[412] (as well as further discussed below[413]) in the *Pope & Talbot* awards about the shortcomings of the so-called 'verification review' process. These events would have not been considered as contrary to the minimum standard back in the 1920s. Yet, the *Pope* tribunal nevertheless held that they should be considered as 'egregious' and 'shocking' when judged by modern sensibilities. In other words, the type of State conduct that would have certainly not been considered a breach of the minimum standard of treatment at the time, may (depending on each tribunal) be deemed a violation of the standard today. Put differently, while the standard of treatment may have remained the same, there has been a change in how it is perceived.

In the present author's view, this is a sign in and of itself of an *evolution*. Thus, the *Glamis* reasoning allows a tribunal to, on the one hand, reject the proposition that custom has fundamentally changed since the *Neer* case, but, on the other hand, to endorse a liberal interpretation of what it considers to be 'egregious' and 'shocking' State conduct.[414] Therefore, the practical differences between the reasoning adopted by the *Glamis* tribunal and that of the *Mondev* and *ADF* tribunals may be more apparent than real.[415] The veracity of this premise will ultimately depend on how each tribunal evaluates changes in mentality towards what it considers to be 'egregious' and 'shocking'.

The reasoning of the *Cargill* tribunal is similar to that of *Glamis*. The tribunal first stated that 'the customary international law minimum standard of treatment may evolve in accordance with changing State practice manifesting to some degree expectations within the international community'.[416] The tribunal then noted that 'the Parties disagree, however, as to how that customary standard has in fact, if at all, evolved since that time'.[417] For the tribunal, 'the burden of establishing any new elements of this custom is on Claimant'.[418]

The tribunal noted that the situation of foreign investment today is different from that in the *Neer* award.[419] It also:

'egregious and shocking' has developed since 1926'" (*Mobil v. Canada*, Decision on Liability and on Principles of Quantum (22 May 2012), para. 126, describing Canada's position).

412. *See, supra* n. 388.

413. *See,* at Chapter 3 section §3.02[G][6].

414. *See,* C. Lévesque, *Chronique de Droit international économique en 2010-2011 – Investissement,* 48 Can YIL 311-313 (2010).

415. This is precisely the reason why the award was criticized by some writers: Jordan C. Kahn, *Striking NAFTA Gold: Glamis Advances Investor-State Arbitration,* 33 Fordham Int'l LJ. 101, 153-154 (2009-2010) ('despite its sophistry, the tribunal's article 1105 is a positive development that will promote foreign direct investment. Its artificial construct of Neer enables the tribunal to avoid finding that customary international law has evolved while holding that article 1105 affords protection against government conduct that is now universally understood to be unfair').

416. *Cargill, Inc. v. Mexico,* Award, (18 September 2009), para. 282.

417. *Ibid.,* para. 273.

418. *Ibid.*

419. *Ibid.,* para. 282 ('As the world and, in particular, the international business community become ever more intertwined and interdependent with global trade, foreign investment, BITs and free

111

observe[d] a trend in previous NAFTA awards, not so much to make the holding of the *Neer* arbitration more exacting, but rather to adapt the principle underlying the holding of the *Neer* arbitration to the more complicated and varied economic positions held by foreign nationals today.[420]

However, it held that 'even as more situations are addressed, the required severity of the conduct as held in *Neer* is maintained' today.[421] The tribunal noted the use of words such as 'gross' and 'misconduct' by other NAFTA tribunals to establish a high threshold of liability:

> As outlined in the *Waste Management II* award quote above, the violation may arise in many forms. It may relate to a lack of due process, discrimination, a lack of transparency, a denial of justice, or an unfair outcome. But in all of these various forms, the 'lack' or 'denial' of a quality or right is sufficiently at the margin of acceptable conduct and thus we find – in the words of the 1128 submissions and previous NAFTA awards – that the lack or denial must be 'gross', 'manifest', 'complete', or such as to 'offend judicial propriety.' The Tribunal grants that these words are imprecise and thus leave a measure of discretion to tribunals. But this is not unusual. The Tribunal simultaneously emphasizes, however, that this standard is significantly narrower than that present in the *Tecmed* award where the same requirement of severity is not present.[422]

The tribunal summarized its findings by concluding that the present standard of treatment under custom was essentially that of the *Neer* award adapted to contemporary international investment law:

> The Tribunal holds that the current customary international law standard of 'fair and equitable treatment' at least reflects the adaptation of the agreed *Neer* standard to current conditions, as outlined in the Article 1128 submissions of Mexico and Canada. If the conduct of the government toward the investment amounts to gross misconduct, manifest injustice or, in the classic words of the *Neer* claim, bad faith or the wilful neglect of duty, whatever the particular context the actions take in regard to the investment, then such conduct will be a violation of the customary obligation of fair and equitable treatment.[423]

In sum, the *Cargill* award fully endorsed the *Neer* 'fundamentals', without, however, following the proposition made by *Glamis* regarding the evolution of the perception of what is considered today as 'egregious' and 'shocking'. It should be added that the *Cargill* tribunal also referred to the need to 'adapt' the *Neer* standard 'to the more complicated and varied economic positions held by foreign nationals today'.[424] It also stated that 'the idea of what is the minimum treatment a country must afford to aliens is arising in new situations simply not present at the time' of *Neer*.[425] It remains to be

---

trade agreements, the idea of what is the minimum treatment a country must afford to aliens is arising in new situations simply not present at the time of the *Neer* award which dealt with the alleged failure to properly investigate the murder of a foreigner').

420. *Ibid.*, para. 284.
421. *Ibid.*
422. *Ibid.*, para. 285.
423. *Ibid.*, para. 286.
424. *Ibid.*, para. 284.
425. *Ibid.*, para. 282.

determined whether or not this 'new situation' could include State conduct that would be considered today as 'egregious' and 'shocking', but which would have certainly not be deemed as such to an arbitral tribunal fifty years ago. Could the events described above[426] by the *Pope & Talbot* tribunal in its two awards about the shortcomings of the 'verification review process' be considered as such a 'new situation'? In any event, while the reasoning of the *Cargill* tribunal formally endorsed the strict standard in *Neer*, it leaves a great margin of appreciation for future tribunals to determine exactly how the *Neer* fundamentals should be 'adapted' to take these new situations into consideration.

[c]   *Tribunals Supporting the Theory of Convergence*

One tribunal (*Merrill & Ring*) has recently endorsed the controversial position that custom has evolved so rapidly in recent years that it now has the same content as an unqualified FET clause. This is the so-called theory of 'convergence'. Before examining the *Merrill & Ring* award, a few observations should be made about this theory.

In BIT arbitration *outside* the NAFTA context, a number of tribunals have recently concluded that the long-standing debate on the differences between the protection offered to investors under the minimum standard of treatment and an unqualified FET clause, had only minimal practical relevance.[427] The *Saluka* tribunal noted that 'it appears that the difference between the Treaty standard laid down in Article 3.1 [of the BIT] and the customary minimum standard, when applied to the specific facts of a case, may well be more apparent than real'.[428] This situation results from the fact that the level of treatment to be accorded to foreign investors under the minimum standard of treatment under custom has apparently evolved in recent years. As a result of this rapid evolution, this level of protection is said to now be the same as that existing under BITs containing an unqualified FET clause.[429] A number of (non-NAFTA) tribunals have come to this conclusion.[430]

---

426. See, *supra* n. 388.
427. UNCTAD, *supra* n. 58, at 8, noting that 'There are some considerations that, with time, can lead to the convergence of the international minimum standard and the unqualified FET standard as far as the actual content of the obligation is concerned'. *See also*: Newcombe & Paradell, *supra* n. 18, at 274 ('even if it were accepted that in principle the standards are different, the trend appears to be towards convergence, not divergence'); Kläger, *supra* n. 44, at 86 ('by emphasising the evolutionary character of the customary minimum standard, the tribunals have usually declared that there was no necessity to decide whether fair and equitable treatment diverges from an evolved minimum standard. To this extent, irrespective of the pertinent investment treaty formulation, a real difference as regards the practical outcome between the two approaches when considering the facts of a specific case seems to be non-existent').
428. *Saluka Investments B.V. v. Czech Republic*, Partial Award, (17 March 2006), para. 291.
429. *Azurix Corp. v. Argentina*, ICSID No. ARB/01/12, Award, (14 July 2006), para. 361.
430. *CMS Gas Transmission Company v. Argentina*, ICSID No. ARB/01/8, Award, (12 May 2005), paras. 282–284 ('While the choice between requiring a higher treaty standard and that of equating it with the international minimum standard might have relevance in the context of some disputes, the Tribunal is not persuaded that it is relevant in this case. In fact, the Treaty standard of fair and equitable treatment and its connection with the required stability and

There are good reasons to believe that the minimum standard of treatment under custom has in fact *not* converged with the free-standing FET standard contained in many BITs.[431] Thus, tribunals that have adopted this approach do not make any attempt to actually *demonstrate* the rapid evolution of the minimum standard under customary international law.[432] They simply state in passing that this is the case without further examining the issue.[433]

The theory of 'convergence' has been put forward by a number of claimants in NAFTA proceedings. All NAFTA Parties have strongly rejected this line of argumentation.[434] The *Glamis* tribunal summarily rejected the convergence theory as 'an

---

predictability of the business environment, founded on solemn legal and contractual commitments, is not different from the international law minimum standard and its evolution under customary law'); *Occidental Exploration and Production Co v. Ecuador*, LCIA No. 3467, Award, (1 July 2004), para. 190; *Biwater Gauff (Tanzania) Ltd v. Tanzania*, ICSID No. ARB/05/22, Award and Concurring and Dissenting Opinion, (24 July 2008), para. 592 ('the Arbitral Tribunal also accepts, as found by a number of previous arbitral tribunals and commentators, that the actual content of the treaty standard of fair and equitable treatment is not materially different from the content of the minimum standard of treatment in customary international law'); *Duke Energy Electroquil Partners and Electroquil SA v. Ecuador*, ICSID No. ARB/04/19, Award, (18 August 2008), para. 333 ('the Tribunal is of the opinion that the discussion about the autonomous character of the standard is irrelevant given the circumstances of the case. It also appears overtaken by the evolution in the latest ICSID decisions'), para. 337 ('The Tribunal concurs with this statement [made by the *Azurix* tribunal] and with the conclusion that the standards are essentially the same'); *Rumeli Telekom AS and Telsim Mobil Telekomikasyon Hizmetleri AS v. Kazakhstan*, ICSID No. ARB/05/16, Award, (29 July 2008), para. 611 ('[this tribunal] shares the view of several ICSID tribunals that the treaty standard of fair and equitable treatment is not materially different from the minimum standard of treatment in customary international law').

431. UNCTAD, *Investor–State Dispute Settlement and Impact on Investment Rulemaking* 75 (United Nations 2007) ('some arbitral decisions had the effect of equating the minimum standard under customary international law with the plain meaning approach to the text. However, it is not self-evident that customary international law has evolved to such a degree'). *See also*: Theodore Kill, *Don't Cross the Streams: Past and Present Overstatement of Customary International Law in Connection with Conventional Fair and Equitable Treatment Obligations*, 106 Mich. L. Rev. 853 (2008), arguing that these tribunals have relied on the reasoning of other tribunals (such as *Tecmed*) that had adopted an *additive* interpretation of the standard in a *different context* of an 'autonomous' FET clause not linked to the MST. For him (at 864-865), 'the *Tecmed* tribunal went out of its way to clarify that the standard it was enunciating was *not* customary international law but rather a conventional standard based on a reading of the specific terms of the treaty that applied only as between the two parties. *Tecmed* tried to warn future tribunals not to cross the streams'. He further argues (at 857-858) that 'having defined the applicable standard with reference to the jurisprudence of the tribunals adopting an additive approach, the convergence tribunals then simply announce that the standard articulated is in fact equal to the minimum standard required under customary international law'.

432. Kill, *supra* n. 431, at 865; Porterfield, *supra* n. 153, at 81-82; J. Roman Picherack, *The Expanding Scope of the Fair and Equitable Treatment Standard: Have Recent Tribunals Gone Too Far?* 9(4) J. World Invest. & Trade, 271, 287, 285 (2008); Gus Van Harten, *International Treaty Arbitration and Public Law* 89 (Oxford U. Press 2007).

433. Kill, *supra* n. 431, at 866.

434. *See*, for instance, the position of Mexico described by the tribunal in *Cargill, Inc. v. Mexico*, Award, (18 September 2009), para. 244; *Methanex v. United States*, Response Concerning the FTC Notes, (26 October 2001), at 5, 6; *Chemtura v. Canada*, Canada's Rejoinder, (10 July 2009), para. 155; *Merrill & Ring v. Canada*, Canada's Rejoinder, (27 March 2009), para. 168.

overstatement'.[435] The tribunal ultimately decided to 'look solely to arbitral awards – including BIT awards – that seek to be understood by reference to the customary international law minimum standard of treatment, as opposed to any autonomous standard'.[436]

The *Merrill & Ring* ruling is the only case where a NAFTA tribunal has adopted the convergence theory. The tribunal first stated that the FTC Note had the 'effect of linking fair and equitable treatment with customary law'.[437] Yet, while the tribunal indicated that it was 'mindful' of the FTC Interpretation 'which understood Article 1105 as a minimum standard of treatment under customary law',[438] it nevertheless added that the Note may not 'necessarily reflect[] the present state of customary and international law'.[439] This comment suggests that custom had somehow evolved in the last ten years since the Note was issued. Thus, as a result of custom's alleged rapid evolution, the Note's linkage of Article 1105 to the minimum standard of treatment under custom would now (in 2010) be outdated. On this point, the tribunal observed that 'Canada has maintained that, to the extent that an evolution might have taken place, it must be proven that it has occurred since 2001, when the FTC Interpretation was issued, and this almost certainly has not happened'.[440] In response to this argument, the tribunal simply stated that 'such a view is unconvincing'[441] without providing any further explanation. The tribunal held that 'the evolutionary nature' of custom 'provides scope for the interpretation of Article 1105, *even in the light of the Free Trade Commission's 2001 interpretation*'.[442] The tribunal's objective was clearly to evaluate how custom had evolved in recent years *in spite* of what the Parties had enunciated in the 2001 FTC Note.

The tribunal characterized the *Neer* and *ELSI* cases, 'dealing with situations concerning due process of law, denial of justice and physical mistreatment',[443] as 'the first track of the evolution of the so-called minimum standard of treatment'.[444] By the 1960s, State practice was apparently 'increasingly seen as being inconsistent' with the first track concept of the minimum standard as set out in these older cases.[445] In this context, the tribunal explained that a 'second track' of the evolution of the minimum standard of treatment had emerged which dealt specifically with the 'treatment of aliens in relations to business, trade and investments'.[446] This 'new' standard was 'more liberal', as it did not require the demonstration of 'outrageous' treatment in order

---

435. *Glamis v. United States*, Award, (9 June 2009), para. 609 ('Claimant has agreed with this distinction between customary international law and autonomous treaty standards but argues that, with respect to this particular standard, BIT jurisprudence has "converged with customary international law in this area". The Tribunal finds this to be an over-statement').
436. *Ibid.*, para. 611.
437. *Merrill & Ring v. Canada*, Award, (31 March 2010), para. 189.
438. *Ibid.*, para. 191.
439. *Ibid.*, para. 192.
440. *Ibid.*, para. 194.
441. *Ibid.*
442. *Ibid.*, para. 192 (emphasis added).
443. *Ibid.*, para. 197.
444. *Ibid.*, para. 201.
445. *Ibid.*, para. 204.
446. *Ibid.*, para. 205. *See also*: para. 201.

to establish a breach of the standard.[447] Yet, and surprisingly so, all of the cases referred
to by the tribunal in support of this so-called 'new' standard actually date back to the
1920s.[448]

The tribunal observed that custom had evolved since the 1920s: 'today's minimum standard is broader than that defined in the *Neer* case and its progeny'.[449] Earlier
in the award, the tribunal stated that 'in spite of arguments to the contrary, there
appears to be a shared view that customary international law has not been frozen in
time and that it continues to evolve in accordance with the realities of the international
community'.[450] For the tribunal, the minimum standard of treatment 'provides for the
fair and equitable treatment of alien investors within the confines of *reasonableness*'.[451] In other words, the minimum standard has evolved to the point where it
protects all foreigners against State conduct that is 'unreasonable'. Thus, any 'unreasonable' act would now be considered as a violation of international law. The *Merrill
& Ring* tribunal also noted that 'in the end, the name assigned to the standard does not
really matter'.[452] Thus, the minimum standard under custom and an unqualified FET
clause offer the *same* level of protection to foreign investors. For the tribunal, '[w]hat
matters is that the standard protects against all such acts or behavior that might
infringe a sense of fairness, equity and reasonableness'.[453]

These are very controversial findings. As rightly pointed out by UNCTAD, 'the
Merrill & Ring tribunal failed to give cogent reasons for its conclusion that the MST
made such a leap in its evolution'.[454] Earlier in the award, the *Merrill & Ring* tribunal
mentioned that the important issue consisted of 'establish[ing] in which direction
customary law has evolved' and added that 'State practice and *opinio juris* will be the
guiding beacons of this evolution'.[455] Yet, the tribunal omitted to cite *a single* example
of State practice in support of its convergence thesis. No arbitral decision is mentioned
to illustrate its position that custom had evolved so rapidly in recent years. The old
arbitration cases from the 1920s that the tribunal refers to[456] in support of its claim of
the existence of a so-called 'second track' of the evolution of the minimum standard of
treatment do not demonstrate such an evolution. In any event, it should be noted that
these controversial findings have had no *practical effect* on the host State's liability. The
tribunal ruled that Canada did not breach Article 1105.

---

447. *Ibid.*, para. 205.
448. *Ibid.*, para. 206, referring to the following cases: *Case Concerning Certain German Interests in
Polish Upper Silesia* (Merits), PCIJ, Series A. No. 7, at 19 (1926); *German Settlers in Poland*,
PCIJ, Series B., No. 6, 19-20, 35-38 (1923); *Aboilard Case*, (Haiti, France), 9 UNRIAA, 71, at
79-81 (1925); *Robert E. Brown Case*, (United Kingdom, United States), 6 UNRIAA, 120, at
129-130 (1923); *George W. Cook Case*, (Mexico, United States), 4 UNRIAA, 213, at 214-215
(1927); *Hopkins Case*, (Mexico, United States), 4 UNRIAA, 41, at 46–47 (1926); *Lalanne and
Ledoux Case*, (France, Venezuela), 10 UNRIAA, 17, at 18 (1902).
449. *Merrill & Ring v. Canada*, Award, (31 March 2010), para. 213.
450. *Ibid.*, para. 193.
451. *Ibid.*, para. 213 (emphasis added).
452. *Ibid.*, para. 210.
453. *Ibid.*
454. UNCTAD, *supra* n. 58, at 57.
455. *Merrill & Ring v. Canada*, Award, (31 March 2010), para. 193.
456. *See, supra* n. 448.

While it affirmed in its award that 'convergence is not really the issue',[457] the fact remains that the *Merrill & Ring* tribunal has clearly endorsed the theory of convergence put forward by the investor. The claimant had argued that 'such has been the development of the "fair and equitable treatment" standard in recent years that the plain meaning approach, on the one hand, and, on the other, the minimum standard approach, have largely converged'[458] and that the 'difference between the autonomous standard and customary law standard' was 'fast disappearing'.[459] For the investor, as a result of this convergence, 'the question about the impact of the FTC's Notes is largely academic' since 'the end result appears to be the same: NAFTA Article 1105(1) requires Canada to accord foreign investors "fair and equitable treatment" in accordance with the plain and ordinary meaning of the term'.[460]

The investor is right on this point. The endorsement of the 'convergence' theory by the *Merrill & Ring* tribunal completely 'deprived the 2001 NAFTA Interpretative Statement of any practical effect'.[461] That reasoning refutes the clear intention of the NAFTA Parties when they issued the Note to limit the level of protection to the one existing under custom. If one now considers that the level of treatment under the MST under custom has increased to reach that of an unqualified FET clause, this means that in practical terms, the FTC Note no longer plays a role. Moreover, what the NAFTA Parties had in mind in 2001 when issuing the Note was certainly not that the FET obligation under Article 1105 should protect foreign investors 'against all such acts or behavior that might infringe a sense of fairness, equity and reasonableness'.[462] In other words, back in 2001, the Parties could certainly not have expected that merely ten years later, the minimum standard of treatment under custom would be considered to be 'within the confines of *reasonableness*'.[463] The FTC Note had been issued precisely to prevent tribunals from giving an excessively broad interpretation of the FET standard under Article 1105. For all these reasons, the reasoning of the *Merrill & Ring* tribunal completely undermines the effectiveness of the FTC Note.

[3] The Controversial Question of the Customary Nature of the Fair and Equitable Treatment Obligation

The second line of argumentation used by some tribunals to undermine the effectiveness of the Note is also very controversial.[464] Some tribunals have taken the position that the FET standard has become a rule of customary international law in and of itself.

---

457. *Merrill & Ring v. Canada*, Award, (31 March 2010), para. 209 ('The parties have extensively discussed whether the customary law standard might have converged with the fair and equitable treatment standard, but convergence is not really the issue. The situation is rather one in which the customary law standard has led to and resulted in establishing the fair and equitable treatment standard as different stages of the same evolutionary process').
458. *Ibid.*, Investor's Reply, (15 December 2008), para. 315.
459. *Ibid.*, para. 316.
460. *Ibid.*, para. 320.
461. UNCTAD, *supra* n. 58, at 57.
462. *Merrill & Ring v. Canada*, Award, (31 March 2010), para. 210.
463. *Ibid.*, para. 213 (emphasis added).
464. Schill, *supra* n. 65, at 272.

Whether or not this is the case is outside the scope of this book. Suffice it to say that there are solid reasons to believe that the FET standard has *not* become a rule of custom. Thus, and contrary to the position taken by some writers,[465] the practice of States is not at all 'constant and uniform'. As mentioned above,[466] there are many different types of FET clauses. Moreover, as noted earlier,[467] the different language contained in FET clauses does matter a great deal; tribunals have concluded that they provide for *different levels of treatment* for investors.[468] There is also no support for the view taken by some writers that the practice of States with regards to FET clauses 'may be understood as the confirmation of *opinio juris*'.[469] There is certainly no evidence of any opinio juris by States as they become parties to BITs.[470] As the *UPS* tribunal stated: '[w]hile BITs are large in number, their coverage is limited ... and in terms of *opinio juris* there is no indication that they reflect a general sense of obligation'.[471]

In any event, it is clear that the affirmation that the FET standard has become a rule of customary international law in and of itself is not of practical relevance in the NAFTA context. Thus, according to the Note, tribunals are required to apply the treatment under the minimum standard of treatment. That standard is considered as a norm of customary international law. As mentioned above,[472] the better view is that the FET standard under Article 1105 is *one of many elements* that are *included* in the customary norm that is the minimum standard of treatment. As a result, in the *specific context* of Article 1105, it is *clearly unnecessary* to examine the question whether or not the FET standard is *itself* a rule of custom.[473] This is because custom is applicable anyways.

This discussion raises the question as to why investors (and writers) argue that the FET standard has become a rule of custom *independent* from the minimum

---

465. Tudor, *supra* n. 54, at 77; Tudor, *supra* n. 60, at 316; Diehl, *supra* n. 44, at 135-136.
466. *See*, at Chapter 1 section §1.02[C].
467. *See*, at Chapter 1 section §1.03[B].
468. UNCTAD, *supra* n. 58, at 8, 22; OECD, *Fair and Equitable Treatment Standard in International Investment Law* 40 (Working Papers on International Investment, Paper No. 2004/3, 2004); Hussein Haeri, *A Tale of Two Standards: 'Fair and Equitable Treatment' and the Minimum Standard in International Law*, 27 Arb. Int'l 26 (2011); Christopher F. Dugan, Don Wallace, Jr., Noah Rubins & Borzu Sabahi, *Investor-State Arbitration* 496 (Oxford U. Press 2008).
469. Tudor, *supra* n. 54, at 80-84. *See also*: Diehl, *supra* n. 44, at 138, 145, 178, for whom the existence of *opinio juris* is found in the concept of the 'general interests' of States.
470. Abdullah Al Faruque, *Creating Customary International Law Through Bilateral Investment Treaties: A Critical Appraisal*, 44 Indian JIL 310 (2004); C. McLachlan, *Investment Treaties and General International Law*, 57(2) ICLQ 393 (2008); Cai Congyan, *International Investment Treaties and the Formation, Application and Transformation of Customary International Law Rules*, 7(3) Chinese JIL, para. 14 (1998); Andrew T. Guzman, *Why LDCs Sign Treaties That Hurt Them: Explaining the Popularity of Bilateral Investment Treaties*, 38(4) Va. J. Int'l L. 687 (1998).
471. *UPS v. Canada*, Award (Jurisdiction), (22 November 2002), paras. 84, 97.
472. *See*, at Chapter 1 section §1.03[C].
473. This theoretical question is, however, relevant in the different context of BITs containing an autonomous FET standard (i.e., detached from international law) and in situations where no BIT exists.

standard of treatment.[474] This argument is simply used to *increase* the standard of protection offered to investors in comparison to the lower level existing under the minimum standard. This is clear from this passage from Tudor, a supporter of this theory:

> The main problem with equalizing FET with IMS is that it limits the scope of FET. The IMS provides for action only in extreme cases. In other words, the rights of the foreign Investor have to be violated in a serious manner in order for the Investor to obtain reparation from the host State. In contrast, it appears that FET offers the foreign Investor a type of guarantee which is much more generous and designed to be operational.[475]

This willingness to *increase* the level of protection stands in the face of the clear aim of the FTC Note to *limit the scope* of the FET standard to that existing under custom. In other words, interpreting the FET standard as a customary norm in the NAFTA context completely disregards the undeniable intention of the Parties when they issued the Note in 2001.

The first tribunal to have openly adopted this view was the *Pope & Talbot* tribunal in its second award of 2002:

> Canada's views on the appropriate standard of customary international law for today were perhaps shaped by its erroneous belief that only some 70 bilateral investment treaties have been negotiated, however, the true number, now acknowledged by Canada, is in excess of 1800. Therefore, applying the ordinary rules for determining the content of custom in international law, one must conclude that the practice of states is now represented by those treaties.[476]

For the tribunal, the fact that the FET standard was found in so many BITs basically established the element of State practice necessary to prove the existence of a rule of customary international law. The tribunal's reasoning is controversial and questionable on many grounds. First, the tribunal completely disregarded the requirement to show opinio juris as proof of custom. Second, the tribunal did not at all discuss the actual content of these BITs – which is a requirement in international law to prove that State practice is actually consistent.

These grounds of criticism were echoed in the subsequent *ADF* case where the tribunal made reference to the United States' view that '[t]he *Pope and Talbot* Tribunal

---

474. Tudor, *supra* n. 54, at 65-68. *See also*: Diehl, *supra* n. 44, at 125-153, 175-179, 10-11 ('it is submitted here that FET is an independent standard which has developed into a rule of customary law'). She however admits (at 150) that her findings do not apply to NAFTA Article 1105.
475. Tudor, *supra* n. 54, at 67. *See also*: Diehl, *supra* n. 44, at 178 ('the FET standard has passed into the corpus of customary international law according to the two-elements-theory'), 179 ('the FET standard is independent from the IMS [international minimum standard] and prescribes for a higher and more flexible standard than granted by the IMS. Equating FET with IMS would limit the scope of FET in an unacceptable way due to the fact that the IMS only grants remedies under limited circumstances and was created in a State-State setting, that is, in diplomatic protection cases. The FET standard when viewed as an autonomous standard – allows for more flexibility in a State-investor context. For example, the individual expectations of the investor may (and should be) taken into consideration').
476. *Pope & Talbot Inc. v. Canada,* Award in Respect of Damages, (31 May 2002), para. 62.

119

did not examine the mass of existing BITs to determine whether those treaties represent concordant state practice and whether they constitute evidence of the *opinio juris* constituent of customary international law' and that the tribunal was therefore 'not in a position to state whether any particular BIT obligation has crystallized into a rule of customary international law'.[477] In the *Mondev* ruling, the tribunal also referred to the NAFTA Parties' strong disapproval of the reasoning of the *Pope & Talbot* award on this issue. This is the relevant passage of the *Mondev* award:

> In their post-hearing submissions, all three NAFTA Parties challenged holdings of the Tribunal in *Pope & Talbot* which find that the content of contemporary international law reflects the concordant provisions of many hundreds of bilateral investment treaties. In particular, attention was drawn to what those three States saw as a failure of the *Pope & Talbot* Tribunal to consider a necessary element of the establishment of a rule of customary international law, namely *opinio juris*. These States appear to question whether the parties to the very large numbers of bilateral investment treaties have acted out of a sense of legal obligation when they include provisions in those treaties such as that for 'fair and equitable' treatment of foreign investment.[478]

The *Mondev* tribunal mentioned that the question was 'entirely legitimate'.[479] The tribunal added also that '[i]t is often difficult in international practice to establish at what point obligations accepted in treaties, multilateral or bilateral, come to condition the content of a rule of customary international law binding on States not party to those treaties'.[480] For the tribunal, the answer was quite simple: the respondent (United States) had apparently contended that 'when adopting provisions for fair and equitable treatment and full protection and security in NAFTA (as well as in other BITs), the intention was to incorporate principles of customary international law'.[481] In other words, these statements represented opinio juris. The tribunal concluded, in the NAFTA context, as follows:

> Thus the question is not that of a failure to show *opinio juris* or to amass sufficient evidence demonstrating it. The question rather is: what is the content of customary international law providing for fair and equitable treatment and full protection and security in investment treaties?[482]

This passage is ambiguous. It is not entirely clear whether the tribunal endorsed the position adopted by the *Pope & Talbot* tribunal wherein the FET standard had become a rule of customary international law. However, there are a few passages in the award that seem to suggest that this is indeed the case. Thus, the tribunal mentions that the

---

477. *ADF v. United States*, Award, (9 January 2003), para. 112, quoting from *Pope & Talbot Inc. v. Canada*, US Post-Hearing Submission on Article 1105(1) and Pope & Talbot, (27 June 2002), at 21. *See also*, the *ADF* tribunal's reference to Mexico's position (at para. 125) to the effect that 'given the absence of "a careful analysis of state practice and opinion juris", the sheer number of extant BITs today does not suffice to show that conventional international law has become customary international law'.
478. *Mondev v. United States*, Award, (11 October 2002), para. 110.
479. *Ibid.*, para. 111.
480. *Ibid.*
481. *Ibid.*
482. *Ibid.*, para. 113. *See also*, at para. 122.

2,000 existing BITs 'almost uniformly' contain an FET clause adding that 'such a body of concordant practice will necessarily have influenced the content of rules governing the treatment of foreign investment in current international law'.[483] It also added that the content of 'current international law', 'is shaped by the conclusion of more than two thousand bilateral investment treaties and many treaties of friendship and commerce' and that 'those treaties largely and concordantly' include an FET clause.[484] This position was later endorsed by the *Chemtura* tribunal, which stated that the determination of NAFTA Article 1105 'cannot overlook the evolution of customary international law, nor the impact of BITs on this evolution'.[485] In sum, the different statements made by the *Mondev* tribunal suggest that this 'uniform' practice of States incorporating FET clauses in their BITs led to the formation of a rule of custom.[486]

A few months later in 2003, the *ADF* tribunal stated that while the *Mondev* tribunal was 'implying that the process was in motion', it had in fact *not* endorsed the position that the FET obligation was a customary rule.[487] In any event, the *ADF* tribunal expressly *rejected* the contention (made by the investor in the proceedings) that the FET standard had become part of custom:

> We are not convinced that the Investor has shown the existence, in current customary international law, of a general and autonomous requirement (autonomous, that is, from specific rules addressing particular, limited, contexts) to accord fair and equitable treatment and full protection and security to foreign investments. The Investor, for instance, has not shown that such a requirement has been brought into the corpus of present day customary international law by the many hundreds of bilateral investment treaties now extant. It may be that, in their current state, neither concordant state practice nor judicial or arbitral caselaw provides convincing substantiation (or, for that matter, refutation) of the Investor's position.[488]

The *Merrill & Ring* tribunal took a different view. It held that 'against the backdrop of the evolution of the minimum standard of treatment' it was 'satisfied that fair and equitable treatment has *become a part of customary law*'.[489] It is unclear what the tribunal meant by that. It seems to suggest that the FET standard had become a customary norm *as a result* of the evolution of the minimum standard of treatment. Such proposition would, of course, be contrary to the double requirement of custom (State practice and opinio juris) recognized at Article 38(1)b) of the ICJ Statute.[490] In any event, the *Merrill & Ring* tribunal did not embark on a concrete analysis of State practice and opinio juris. This is so even if, as the tribunal itself acknowledged in the same paragraph, 'Canada has argued that the existence of [a rule of customary international law] must be proven'.[491] The tribunal also made another controversial

---

483. *Ibid.*, para. 117.
484. *Ibid.*, para. 125.
485. *Chemtura v. Canada*, Award, (2 August 2010), para. 121.
486. Orakhelashvili, *supra* n. 206, at 78; Laird, *supra* n. 134, at 67, 69, 70.
487. *ADF v. United States*, Award, (9 January 2003), para. 183.
488. *Ibid.*, paras. 183, 185.
489. *Merrill & Ring v. Canada*, Award, (31 March 2010), para. 211 (emphasis added).
490. *See*, at section §2.03[A][1].
491. *Merrill & Ring v. Canada*, Award, (31 March 2010), para. 211.

statement suggesting that consistent and uniform State practice can be considered as representing the opinio juris of States:

> A requirement that aliens be treated fairly and equitably in relation to business, trade and investment is the outcome of this changing reality and as such it has become sufficiently part of widespread and consistent [State] practice so as to demonstrate that it is reflected today in customary international law as *opinio juris*.[492]

As demonstrated previously,[493] State practice on FET clauses is not at all consistent. In any event, such State practice does not establish opinio juris. The *Cargill* tribunal adopted a much more cautious approach. First, it stated that it is 'widely accepted that extensive adoption of identical treaty language by many States may in and of itself serve - again with care - as evidence of customary international law'.[494] The tribunal mentioned the fact that FET clauses were widespread in BITs, but also noted that their actual language varies. For this reason, it held that 'significant evidentiary weight should not be afforded to autonomous clauses inasmuch as it could be assumed that such clauses were adopted precisely because they set a standard other than that required by custom'.[495] The tribunal concluded that it did not 'believe it prudent to accord significant weight to even widespread adoption of such [FET] clauses'.[496]

In sum, the affirmation by the *Pope & Talbot* and *Merrill & Ring* tribunals that the FET standard has become a rule of customary international law is baseless and not supported by actual State practice and opinio juris. Moreover, this proposition completely undermines the clear intention of the NAFTA Parties to limit the scope of the FET standard to that existing under custom.

[C]   Conclusion

All NAFTA tribunals have concluded that Article 1105 provides for FET protection in accordance with the minimum standard of treatment under custom and that the clause does not require treatment in addition to or beyond that which exists under custom. While tribunals have all agreed on these fundamental issues, a limited number of peripheral questions related to the concrete application of the concept of customary international law have been controversial. All tribunals (except perhaps for *ADF*) have concluded that arbitral awards do not constitute State practice and thus cannot create customary international law, but can serve (in some circumstances) as illustrations of such custom. There is also now a consensus amongst tribunals to the effect that awards rendered outside NAFTA that interpret 'unqualified' FET clauses are irrelevant in the context of an analysis of Article 1105 which belong to a different species of FET clauses. While some tribunals' reasoning suggests that when interpreting Article 1105, they are permitted to look beyond customary international law at other sources of international

---

492. *Ibid.*, para. 210.
493. *See*, at Chapter 1 section §1.02[C].
494. *Cargill, Inc. v. Mexico*, Award, (18 September 2009), para. 276.
495. *Ibid.*
496. *Ibid.*

law, it remains that the predominant view (held by the majority of tribunals) is that they should turn solely to custom.

Some tribunals have challenged the letter and spirit of the FTC Note, and have thereby undermined its real effectiveness. These tribunals have basically used two distinct (yet closely related) sets of arguments.

While there is a general agreement between NAFTA Parties that, as a matter of principle, customary international law is not static and can evolve over time, one of the most contentious issues remains that of whether or not any such evolution *has actually taken place*. NAFTA tribunals have so far provided conflicting answers.

Faced with the binding FTC Note that *restricts* the extent of investors' rights, a number of tribunals (*Pope & Talbot*, *Mondev*, *ADF* and others) have interpreted customary international law broadly by emphasizing its evolutionary character. Under this interpretation, the level of protection offered to foreign investors under Article 1105 is (at least theoretically) *superior* to the treatment under the minimum standard. However, these tribunals have *not demonstrated* that an evolution of the minimum standard has actually taken place. In doing so, these awards have (at least implicitly) challenged the FTC Note. Yet, it should be noted that the adoption of this 'evolutionary' approach by tribunals has had no practical impact on the outcome of these cases in terms of liability; these tribunals (except for *Pope & Talbot*) did not find the respondent States responsible for any breaches of Article 1105, even under this approach.

The *Merrill & Ring* tribunal later took this 'evolutionary' approach to the extreme by adopting the so-called theory of 'convergence'. The *Merrill & Ring* tribunal held that the minimum standard has evolved to the point where it now protects all foreigners 'against all such acts or behaviour that might infringe on a sense of fairness, equity and reasonableness'.[497] This approach is flawed for many reasons, including the failure to actually *demonstrate* the alleged rapid evolution of the minimum standard under custom. In any event, the adoption of this theory by the *Merrill & Ring* tribunal is a direct challenge to the FTC Note. It refutes the clear intention of the NAFTA Parties when they issued the Note to limit the level of protection to the one existing under custom. If one now considers that the level of treatment under the minimum standard has increased to the level under an unqualified FET clause, this means that, in practical terms, the FTC Note no longer has any purpose.

On the contrary, other tribunals (*Glamis, Cargill*) have concluded that no evidence had been presented to establish that current customary international law had moved beyond the minimum standard of treatment of aliens. Thus, to prove a violation of the minimum standard, an investor must show that the conduct was 'egregious' and 'shocking'. Yet, the *Glamis* tribunal added that what is considered today as 'egregious' and 'shocking' has changed since the 1920s. Thus, the type of State conduct that would have certainly not been considered a breach of the minimum standard of treatment at the time, may (depending on each tribunal) be deemed a violation of the standard today. At the end of the day, the practical differences between the reasoning adopted by the *Glamis* tribunal and that of others may be more apparent than real.

---

497. *Merrill & Ring v. Canada*, Award, (31 March 2010), para. 210.

A second line of argumentation has also been used by some tribunals (*Pope & Talbot, Merrill & Ring*) to undermine the effectiveness of the Note. They have taken the position that the FET standard has become a rule of customary international law in and of itself. There are solid reasons to support the contrary. Moreover, investors (and writers) who advocate this approach do so in order to *increase* the standard of protection offered to investors in comparison to the lower level existing under the minimum standard. This approach disregards the undeniable intention of the NAFTA Parties when they issued the Note in 2001 to *limit the scope* of the FET standard.

The Content of Article 1105

Part II of the book first examines the substantive content of Article 1105 (Chapter 3). The next chapter focuses on the relationship between Article 1105 and other NAFTA provisions (Chapter 4). Finally, we will look at the issue of the assessment of damages arising from a breach of Article 1105 (Chapter 5).

CHAPTER 3

The Substantive Content of Article 1105

This chapter examines the content of the FET standard under Article 1105. Before specifically reviewing how NAFTA tribunals have defined the actual scope of the standard (at section §3.02), we will first make a few observations on the important role played by arbitral tribunals in that respect (section §3.01[A]). We will also briefly examine the manner in which different scholars have determined the various 'elements' that comprise the FET standard (section §3.01[B]).

§3.01   GENERAL REMARKS

[A]   The Critical Role Played by Tribunals in Determining the Content of the Fair and Equitable Treatment Standard

As mentioned above,[1] the obligation for NAFTA Parties to provide foreign investors with an FET does not simply mean that they must be treated 'fairly' and 'equitably'. The concept of FET has a distinct meaning *of its own*. At the same time, the standard is flexible and depends on the circumstances of each case.[2] Its inherent flexibility results from the fact that it is a '*standard*'.[3] The concept of a 'standard' in international investment law has recently been examined by scholars.[4] As stated by the *Waste*

---

1. *See*, at Chapter 2 section §2.02[A].
2. Christoph Schreuer, *Fair and Equitable Treatment in Arbitral Practice*, 6(3) J. World Invest. & Trade 364 (2005).
3. Alexandra Diehl, *The Core Standard of International Investment Protection: Fair and Equitable Treatment* 329 (Wolters Kluwer 2012); Ionna Tudor, *The Fair and Equitable Treatment Standard in International Foreign Investment Law* 155 (Oxford U. Press 2008).
4. Tudor, *supra* n. 3, at 123, distinguishes between two distinct elements of a legal standard: the 'normative, element (the actual source of the standard, i.e., the text of the provision) and the 'descriptive' (or 'subjective') elements (the circumstances and the facts that are relevant for the application of the standard by a judge, or arbitrator, to a specific case). For Tudor, 'the subjective element is the flesh that covers the carcass of the standard, giving it life. It is only when the FET standard is applied to a specific case that it becomes alive' (at 117, *see also*, at

Management tribunal, the FET standard 'is to some extent a flexible one which must be adapted to the circumstances of each case'.[5] The *Mondev* tribunal also came to the conclusion that '[a] judgment of what is fair and equitable cannot be reached in the abstract; it must depend on the facts of the particular case. It is part of the essential business of courts and tribunals to make judgments such as these'.[6]

Although the inherent flexibility of the FET standard leaves tribunals with a certain margin of discretion, it is not an *unlimited* one.[7] This important nuance has been recognized by NAFTA tribunals. The *Mondev* tribunal, for instance, referred to the position of the United States in its pleadings to the effect that 'Article 1105(1) did not give a NAFTA tribunal an unfettered discretion to decide for itself, on a subjective basis, what was "fair" or "equitable" in the circumstances of each particular case'.[8] For the United States, 'while possessing a power of appreciation', it remains that a NAFTA tribunal was 'bound by the minimum standard as established in State practice and in the jurisprudence of arbitral tribunals' and therefore 'could not simply adopt its own idiosyncratic standard of what is "fair" or "equitable", without reference to established sources of law'.[9] The *Mondev* tribunal fully endorsed the following proposition: '[t]he Tribunal has no difficulty in accepting that an arbitral tribunal may not apply its own idiosyncratic standard in lieu of the standard laid down in Article 1105 (1)'.[10] In other words, NAFTA tribunals' discretion is limited by the requirement to apply the minimum standard of treatment existing under custom.

It may be argued that some NAFTA tribunals have in fact applied their very own idiosyncratic version of the FET standard, detached from the requirements found in the text of the provision and the FTC Note. This is certainly the case with both the *Merrill & Ring* and *Pope & Talbot* tribunals.

Tribunals play a critical role in determining the substantive content of the FET standard precisely because of the flexible nature of the standard.[11] Some scholars have

---

123: 'The vague and abstract notion of FET becomes concrete and it is the arbitrator who—in the case of FET—breathes life into the standard'). Diehl, *supra* n. 3, at 29, 33, gives the following definition of a standard in international investment law: 'a binding and enforceable legal category of considerable broadness and evolutionary character that leaves a large margin of discretion to the judge/arbitrator, the reference point of which is a level of treatment deemed acceptable by international law, taking into consideration the local laws and regulations in place at the time of the investment'.

5. *Waste Management, Inc. v. Mexico ("Number 2")* [hereinafter *Waste Management v. Mexico*], ICSID No. ARB(AF)/00/3, Award, (30 April 2004), para. 99.
6. *Mondev International Ltd. v. United States* [hereinafter *Mondev v. United States*], ICSID No. ARB(AF)/99/2, Award, (2 October 2002), para. 118.
7. A. Newcombe, *The Boundaries of Regulatory Expropriation in International Law*, 4 Transnat'l Disp. Mgmt 274 (2007).
8. *Mondev v. United States*, Award, (2 October 2002), para. 119.
9. *Ibid.*
10. *Ibid.*
11. Diehl, *supra* n. 3, at 28 ('The role of the judge/arbitrator differs in the case of the standard and the rule. When applying a rule, a judge has to verify whether all the elements contained therein are fulfilled. If that is the case, the judge has to apply the corresponding sanction. The task of the judge is consequently a mechanical one. (...) In the case of the standard, however, the role of the judge includes a much higher level of personal assessment and creativity. The judge has to weigh and balance the circumstances of the case before him before applying the standard and its sanction. The judge thus becomes the vehicle through which social, economic or

argued that when an arbitral tribunal has to interpret a broad provision, to fill gaps, and to clarify ambiguities in a provision such as the FET standard, its role is not limited to the *interpretation* and *application* of the law created by others (the States).[12] In fact, in these circumstances, tribunals have a *creative* role in determining the very content of international law.[13] For Schill, FET clauses are an example of a 'fundamental shift in power from States to arbitral tribunals' whereby 'substantial rule making power' has, in effect, been transferred to tribunals whose 'function is not restricted to applying pre-existing rules and principles to the facts of a case, but extends to developing the existing principles into more precise rules and standards of conduct'.[14] Brower speaks of the FET clause as an 'intentionally vague term, designed to give adjudicators a quasi-legislative authority to articulate a variety of rules necessary to achieve the treaty's object and purpose in particular disputes'.[15] This important function has also been recognized by tribunals themselves. In this light, the *Saluka* tribunal has explained that the standard was 'susceptible of specification through judicial practice' by other tribunals.[16] The *Enron* tribunal also stated that the evolution of the FET standard that had taken place in recent years 'is for the most part the outcome of a case by case determination by courts and tribunals'.[17] Yet, as mentioned above, NAFTA tribunals have a much narrower margin of discretion on these matters as a result of the contextual elements examined in the previous chapter.

But how have tribunals actually used their 'creative' role in the context of the FET clause? For the most part, they have simply looked at what *other* tribunals have done in the past.[18] One prominent example is the *Waste Management II* decision where the

---

political factors acquire a normative character. The content of the standard is mutable, depending on elements like actors involved, time, duration or location'); Tudor, *supra* n. 3, at 155, 207, 233; UNCTAD, *Fair and Equitable Treatment* 7 (UNCTAD Series on Issues in International Investment Agreements II, United Nations, 2012), at xv, 61; V. Lowe, *Fair and Equitable Treatment under NAFTA's Investment Chapter; Remarks*, 100 ASIL Proc. 69, 73 (2006). For a critical analysis of this role, *see*: M. Sornarajah, *The Fair and Equitable Standard of Treatment: Whose Fairness? Whose Equity?* in *Investment Treaty Law: Current Issues II* 173 (Federico Ortino et al. eds., British IICL 2007); Jeswald W. Salacuse, *The Law of Investment Treaties* 228 (Oxford U. Press 2010).

12. A. Roberts, *Power and Persuasion in Investment Treaty Interpretation: The Dual Role of States*, 104 AJIL, 179, 188 (2010).

13. *Ibid. See also*: Roland Kläger, *Fair and Equitable Treatment in International Investment Law*, 36-37 (Cambridge U. Press 2011) ('Rather than providing a ready and fixed concept that is hidden somewhere behind the text, the parties to international investment agreements by stipulating fair and equitable treatment have only "set the scene and open[ed] the game". Therefore, the text of investment agreements and the fair and equitable treatment only provide a starting point, but can hardly be said to entail already a unique correct answer to every legal question. As a result, it can hardly be denied that one important function of arbitrators in applying the norms of international investment law is to concretise and to develop norms and, thus, to construct a particular normative conception that is applied to specific facts').

14. S. Schill, *The Multilateralization of International Investment Law* 275 (Cambridge U. Press 2009). *See also*, at 332.

15. Charles H. Brower II, *Structure, Legitimacy, and NAFTA's Investment Chapter*, 36 Vand. J. Transnat'l L. 66 (2003).

16. *Saluka v. Czech Republic*, UNCITRAL, Partial Award, (17 March 2006), para. 284.

17. *Enron Corporation and Ponderosa Assets, L.P. v. Argentina*, ICSID No. ARB/01/3, Award, (22 May 2007), para. 257.

18. Martins Paparinskis, *The International Minimum Standard and Fair and Equitable Treatment*, at 99-100 (Oxford U. Press 2013) (referring to numerous cases). *See also*, his analysis at 120-167

tribunal defined the content of Article 1105 based on four earlier NAFTA cases.[19] A recent UNCTAD report notes that the 'practice of tribunals to refer to, and discuss, earlier awards' in order to determine the substantive content of the FET standard has resulted in a 'considerable convergence in terms of the elements that the FET standard incorporates, regardless of how it is expressed in the treaty'.[20] As noted by one author, tribunals do not 'obtain the normative content by interpreting Article 1105, NAFTA or by using the earlier arbitral decisions as a subsidiary means of interpretation' but instead treat them 'as if they constituted an authoritative interpretation by the contracting parties and were binding upon the Tribunal'.[21] The same writer therefore speaks of a process of self-institutionalization through the use of precedents[22] whereby 'investment jurisprudence thus assumes and fulfills a law-making function in concretizing the normative content of the core investor rights for the entire system of investment protection'.[23]

Many authors have criticized the constant reliance on precedents by tribunals and have noted their failure to provide any comprehensive assessment of the normative content of the FET treatment.[24] These shortcomings have led some scholars to develop different theories on the nature and the content of the FET standard. The next section will briefly examine these different approaches.

---

where he considers (based on the rules of treaty interpretation of the *Vienna Convention*) the question of 'how can the arbitral interpretations of different rules of international law be taken into account as admissible materials for the interpretation of the particular treaty rule?' (at 120).

19. *Waste Management v. Mexico*, Award, (30 April 2004), para. 98. *See*, the critical analysis in: Matthew C. Porterfield, *A Distinction Without a Difference? The Interpretation of Fair and Equitable Treatment Under Customary International Law by Investment Tribunals*, 3(3) ITN, 2013, at 4.
20. UNCTAD, *supra* n. 11, at xv.
21. Schill, *supra* n. 14, at 333.
22. *Ibid.*, at 338.
23. *Ibid.*, at 339. *See also*, at 367-368.
24. One example is Stephan Schill, *Fair and Equitable Treatment as an Embodiment of the Rule of Law*, (New York Univ. IILJ Working Paper 2006/6) at 32 ('the frequency with which [the FET standard] is invoked by foreign investors and applied as a basis for state responsibility by arbitral tribunals contrasts with an astonishingly fundamental lack of conceptual understanding about the principle's normative content'). *See also*, at 70 ('While the arbitral jurisprudence continuously develops a more precise meaning of fair and equitable treatment, it nevertheless meanders around without any clear conceptual vision of the principle's function. The reasoning in arbitral awards is therefore often weak or even unconvincing in its legal analysis. It regularly restricts itself to invoking equally weakly reasoned precedent or refers in an inconclusive manner to the object and purpose of BITs without any deeper justification of how the specific construction contributes to the treaties' objective. Ultimately, these shortcomings endanger the suitability of fair and equitable treatment as a concept against which the conduct of host states can be measured. The main concern in this context is that the jurisprudence does not produce predictable results that are accepted by states but endorse an approach that allows for a broad *ex post facto* control of host state conduct. Predictability in its application is, however, essential for host states and foreign investors alike who need to know beforehand what kind of measures entail the international responsibility of the state and, accordingly, against which kind of political risk fair and equitable treatment protects').

[B]   Brief Overview of Different Theoretical Approaches Adopted by Scholars and Tribunals

As mentioned above,[25] this book focuses on how NAFTA tribunals have *in practice* defined the scope and content of the FET standard and applied it to disputes (see section §3.02 below). The present author does not intend to conduct a theoretical analysis of the nature of the FET standard; this exercise has already been undertaken by several authors in a number of recent books[26] and articles.[27] This section will therefore only briefly examine some of the approaches that have been adopted by various scholars to define the nature and the content of the FET standard.[28] This excercise is necessary to determine whether or not NAFTA tribunals have in fact endorsed any of these theories.

On one end of the spectrum, a number of writers have emphasized that the FET standard does *not* have a *fixed* content. For instance, Tudor argues that 'since the FET is a standard, it is natural that it has a variable content that depends on the circumstances of the case as well as more objective elements like the wording of the clause or the various exceptions found in the annexes of the treaties'.[29] For Tudor, 'the lack of fixed content' of the FET standard 'is not a weakness; on the contrary, it constitutes its strength'.[30] In fact, 'only such a flexible concept can be adapted to such diversity of factual situations arising in the context of the international law of foreign investment'.[31] Tudor's affirmation that FET 'has no stable or fixed content'[32] has been contested by many writers for whom this results in the standard having no normative content whatsoever.[33] Moreover, as pointed out by one writer, 'how [can] a norm without fixed content … become a norm of customary international law?'[34]

---

25. *See*, section on Introduction.
26. Tudor, *supra* n. 3; Kläger, *supra* n. 13; Diehl, *supra* n. 3; Paparinskis, *supra* n. 18.
27. *See*, *inter alia*: Schill, *supra* n. 24, at 70; Kenneth J. Vandevelde, *A Unified Theory of Fair and Equitable Treatment*, 43(1) N.Y.U. J. Int'l L. & Pol. 43 (2010).
28. Rudolf Dolzer, *Fair and Equitable Treatment: A Key Standard in Investment Treaties*, 39 Int'l Law 93-94 (2005), describing three different approaches taken by tribunals: 'one line of reasoning derives a definition from the essential elements: the standard on the basis of abstract reasoning. A second approach resists an attempt of a broader definition and will decide ad hoc whether certain conduct satisfies the requirements of the standard. Yet a third approach will attempt to primarily base its decision on previous decisions or will build upon relevant precedents by way of analogy or by drawing ill the same principle'.
29. Tudor, *supra* n. 3, at 155. *See also*: Peter Muchlinski, *Multinational Enterprises and the Law* 625 (Oxford U. Press 1995): 'The concept of fair and equitable treatment is not precisely defined. (…) It is, therefore, a concept that depends on the interpretation of specific facts for its content. At most, it can be said that the concept connotes the principle of non-discrimination and proportionality in the treatment of foreign investors'.
30. Tudor, *supra* n. 3, at 155. *See also*: Salacuse, *supra* n. 11, at 228.
31. Tudor, *supra* n. 3, at 237.
32. *Ibid.*, at 133.
33. Stephan W. Schill, book review of Tudor, in: 20 EJIL 229, 238 (2009); *See also*: Kläger, *supra* n. 13, at 122-125.
34. Schill, *ibid.*, at 237. Tudor, *supra* n. 3, supports the position that the FET standard has become a norm of customary international law. This question was examined above at Chapter 2 section §2.03[B][3].

Similarly, other writers believe that the purpose of an FET clause is only to 'fill gaps which may be left by the more specific standards, in order to obtain the level of investor protection intended by the treaties'.[35] Thus, the standard would function 'to guide the interpretation of other treaty provisions and assure that the general standard of fair and equitable treatment of foreign investment, a fundamental treaty goal, is attained'.[36]

Another notable feature of the literature on the FET is the tendency of scholars to offer (based on their reviews of relevant case law) a list of the different 'elements' of which the standard is said to be comprised. Some writers have described the FET standard as a multitude of 'fact patterns',[37] while others have referred to a list of 'factual situations',[38] of 'elements' encompassing this standard,[39] or even 'lines of jurisprudence'.[40] A prominent example of this approach is found in Tudor's book wherein she lists nine 'factual situations' covered by the FET standard.[41] Similarly, both the 2004 OECD report[42] and the 2012 UNCTAD report[43] have identified a list of five (different) 'elements' contained within the FET standard. A number of writers have also adopted similar lists of elements.[44]

---

35. Dolzer, *supra* n. 28, at 90. *See also*: P. Juillard, *L'évolution des sources du droit des investissements*, 250 Rec. Cours 83 (1994); Meg Kinnear, *The Continuing Development of the FET Standard*, in *Investment Treaty Law: Current Issues III* 35 (paper version) (Andrea K. Bjorklund, Ian A. Laird & Sergey Ripinsky eds., British IICL 2009); Kenneth J. Vandevelde, *United States Investment Treaties: Policy and Practice* 76 (Kluwer Law 1992); Salacuse, *supra* n. 11, at 227.
36. Salacuse, *supra* n. 11, at 227; Vandevelde, *ibid.*, at 76.
37. Diehl, *supra* n. 3, at 328; C. McLachlan, L. Shore & M. Weiniger, *International Investment Arbitration: Substantive Principles* 239 (Oxford U. Press 2007).
38. Tudor, *supra* n. 3, at 155, 180.
39. OECD, *Fair and Equitable Treatment Standard in International Investment Law* 26 (Working Papers on International Investment, Paper No. 2004/3, 2004); UNCTAD, *supra* n. 11, at xv.
40. Kläger, *supra* n. 13, at 117-118.
41. Tudor, *supra* n. 3, at 155, 180-181. The 'factual situations' are the following: lack of respect for the obligation of vigilance and protection; denial of due process and/or procedural fairness; non-observance of the investor's legitimate expectations; coercion and harassment by organs of the host State; failure to offer a stable and predictable legal framework; unjustified enrichment; evidence of bad faith; absence of transparency; and arbitrary and discriminatory treatment.
42. OECD, *supra* n. 39, at 26: 'a) Obligation of vigilance and protection, b) Due process including nondenial of justice and lack of arbitrariness, c) Transparency, d) Good faith – which could include transparency and lack of arbitrariness and e) Autonomous fairness elements'.
43. UNCTAD, *supra* n. 11, at xv: '(a) Prohibition of manifest arbitrariness in decision-making, that is, measures taken purely on the basis of prejudice or bias without a legitimate purpose or rational explanation; (b) Prohibition of the denial of justice and disregard of the fundamental principles of due process; (c) Prohibition of targeted discrimination on manifestly wrongful grounds, such as gender, race or religious belief; (d) Prohibition of abusive treatment of investors, including coercion, duress and harassment; (e) Protection of the legitimate expectations of investors arising from a government's specific representations or investment inducing measures, although balanced with the host State's right to regulate in the public interest'.
44. *See*, for instance, the following authors: Schreuer, *supra* n. 2, at 357 (referring to the principles of transparency, the protection of the investor's legitimate expectations, freedom from coercion and harassment, procedural propriety and due process, and good faith); Barnali Choudhury, *Evolution or Devolution? Defining Fair and Equitable Treatment in International Investment Law*, 6(2) J. World Invest. & Trade 297 (2005) (concluding that the FET standard requires transparency, due process, good faith and prohibites breach of legitimate expectations, arbitrary or discriminatory conduct, and acts beyond the scope of legal authority); Katia Yannaca-Small, *Fair and Equitable Treatment Standard: Recent Developments*, in *Standards of Investment*

A number of tribunals have endorsed this 'shopping list' approach.[45] For instance, the *Bywater* tribunal refers to the FET standard as being comprised of a number of different 'components' that have been elaborated in case law in response to 'specific fact situations':

> The general standard of 'fair and equitable treatment' as set out above comprises a number of different components, which have been elaborated and developed in previous arbitrations in response to specific fact situations. ... In so far as they are relevant to the dispute here, these separate components may be distilled as follows:
>
> — *Protection of legitimate expectations:* the purpose of the fair and equitable treatment standard is to provide to international investments treatment that does not affect the basic expectations that were taken into account by the foreign investor to make the investment as long as these expectations are reasonable and legitimate and have been relied upon by the investor to make the investment.
> — *Good faith:* the standard includes the general principle recognised in international law that the contracting parties must act in good faith, although bad faith on the part of the State is not required for its violation.
> — *Transparency, consistency, non-discrimination:* the standard also implies that the conduct of the State must be transparent, consistent and non-discriminatory, that is, not based on unjustifiable distinctions or arbitrary.[46]

Another attempt by the *Rumeli* tribunal refers to the following five 'principles' of the FET standard:

> The parties rightly agree that the fair and equitable treatment standard encompasses *inter alia* the following concrete principles:
>
> — the State must act in a transparent manner;
> — the State is obliged to act in good faith;
> — the State's conduct cannot be arbitrary, grossly unfair, unjust, idiosyncratic, discriminatory, or lacking in due process;
> — the State must respect procedural propriety and due process.

Protection 111, 129 (A. Reinisch ed., Oxford U. Press 2008) (referring to '(a) the obligation of vigilance and security which usually interacts with the standard of full protection and security; (b) denial of justice and due diligence; (c) protection against arbitrariness and discrimination, which often tends to override specific treaty provisions on arbitrariness and non-discrimination; and (d) transparency, stability, and the investor's legitimate expectations'); Salacuse, *supra* n. 11, at 230 ('Among the principles most often relied upon by tribunals when applying the fair and equitable standard is whether the host state has: (1) failed to protect the investor's legitimate expectations; (2) failed to act transparently; (3) acted arbitrarily or subjected the investor to discriminatory treatment; (4) denied the Investor access to justice or procedural due process; or (5) acted in bad faith'), at 244 ('a state treats an investor fairly and equitably when its actions respect the investor's legitimate expectations, are transparent, are not arbitrary or discriminatory, respect due process and access to justice and are done in good faith').

45. On this question, *see*: Paparinskis, *supra* n. 18, at 99-100.
46. *Biwater Gauff (Tanzania) Ltd v. Tanzania*, ICSID No. ARB/05/22, Award and Concurring and Dissenting Opinion, (24 July 2008), para. 602.

The case law also confirms that to comply with the standard, the State must respect the investor's reasonable and legitimate expectations.[47]

The 'shopping list' approach has been criticized by several writers who have emphasized the need to establish a more elaborate theoretical framework to properly understand the FET standard.[48]

One such comprehensive theory has been developed by Schill. He attributes to the FET standard, a 'quasiconstitutional function that serves as a yardstick for the exercise of the host states' administrative, judicial or legislative activity vis-à-vis foreign investors'[49] where the standard is 'functionally equivalent to the understanding of the requirements deduced from the rule of law under domestic legal systems'.[50] He argues that even though the 'exact content and the requirements of the rule of law are often debated, it nevertheless seems to constitute a viable approach to explain the normative content of fair and equitable treatment'.[51] Based on his analysis of the relevant case law, he identifies 'seven specific normative principles' which are

---

47. *Rumeli Telekom A.S. and Telsim Mobil Telekomunikasyon Hizmetleri A.S. v. Kazakhstan*, ICSID No. ARB/05/16, Award, (29 July 2008), para. 609. *See also*: *Bayindir Insaat Turizm Ticaret Ve Sanayi A.S. v. Pakistan*, ICSID No. ARB/03/29, Award, (27 August 2009), para. 178 ('The Tribunal agrees with Bayindir when it identifies the different factors which emerge from decisions of investment tribunals as forming part of the FET standard. These comprise the obligation to act transparently and grant due process, to refrain from taking arbitrary or discriminatory measures, from exercising coercion or from frustrating the investor's reasonable expectations with respect to the legal framework affecting the investment'); *Siag and Vecchi v. Egypt*, ICSID No. ARB/05/15, Award, (1 June 2009), para. 450 ('While its precise ambit is not easily articulated, a number of categories of frequent application may be observed from past cases. These include such notions as transparency, protection of legitimate expectations, due process, freedom from discrimination and freedom from coercion and harassment').
48. Diehl, *supra* n. 3, at 329; Stephan Schill, *Fair and Equitable Treatment as an Embodiment of the Rule of Law*, in *The International Convention on the Settlement of Investment Disputes (ICSID): Taking Stock after 40 Years* 33 (R. Hofmann & C. Tams eds., Nomos 2007). *See also*: Kläger, *supra* n. 13, at 117-120, 125, identifying five 'lines of jurisprudence' that have emerged from case law (legitimate expectations, non-discrimination, fair procedure, transparency and proportionality). He is nevertheless critical of the approach adopted by writers consisting in identifying the content of the FET standard as factual situations. He argues (at 121) for the need to elaborate a 'comprehensive doctrinal concept': 'A doctrinal approach that amounts to nothing more than the categorisation of lines of jurisprudence, in order to simplify fair and equitable treatment by the specification of factors and fact situations possibly indicating a breach of the standard, is unable to guide arbitrators in difficult cases. This is because such a lowering of complexity will never lead to a scheme that is detailed enough so as to cover all difficult cases. Therefore, a comprehensive doctrinal concept needs to go beyond a mere analysis of case law and be capable of indicating in difficult cases as well, what justificatory arguments are admissible'.
49. Schill, *supra* n. 48, at 34. *See also*: Schill, *supra* n. 14, at 79.
50. Schill, *supra* n. 24, at 37.
51. Schill, *supra* n. 48, at 41. For him (at 40-41), the rule of law 'translates into procedural requirements for the deployment of legal processes' including 'the right to a hearing before a decision is made, the right to have the decision made in an unbiased and impartial fashion, the right to know the basis of the decision so that it can be contested, the right to reasons for the official's decision, and the right to a decision that is reasonably justified by all relevant legal and factual considerations'. He also indicates (at 40-41) that 'the rule of law is often also at the origin of the idea of proportionality, referring to the proper balance that has to be struck between the interests of the individual and competing public interests'. Finally, he mentions that the rule of law 'mandates a basic separation of powers and the possibility to seek review of public acts by an independent judiciary'.

considered by tribunals 'as elements' of the FET standard and which all 'figure prominently as sub-elements or expressions of the broader concept of the rule of law in domestic legal systems'.[52] In other words, the FET standard contained in BITs is the equivalent of the rule of law found in the domestic law of many countries.

In a recent publication, Diehl has similarly argued that the FET standard 'is an embodiment of the rule of law',[53] in which she identifies four pillars (certainty, equality, generality and proportionality).[54] Similarly, in a recent article, Vandevelde argues that 'international arbitral awards interpreting the fair and equitable treatment standard have incorporated the substantive and procedural principles of the rule of law into that standard' and that 'these principles explain virtually all of the awards applying the fair and equitable treatment standard'.[55] A notable feature of this theory is the suggestion that 'tribunals should use a comparative method that draws on domestic and international law regarding the concept of the rule of law'.[56]

Kläger has criticized this burdensome requirement arguing that the 'concept of the rule of law, at least at the international level, is still relatively indeterminate in itself and is therefore incapable of alleviating the burden of arbitral tribunals to provide a comprehensively reasoned justification for their decisions'.[57] For Kläger, the concept of the FET standard 'expresses ideas of justice and moral ethics' and therefore the 'application of the norm aims to establish a just relationship between the host state and

---

52. Schill, *supra* n. 48, at 79-80, the principles are the following: (1) the requirement of stability, predictability and consistency of the legal framework, (2) the principle of legality, (3) the protection of investor confidence or legitimate expectations, (4) procedural due process and denial of justice, (5) substantive due process or protection against discrimination and arbitrariness, (6) the requirement of transparency and (7) the requirement of reasonableness and proportionality.
53. Diehl, *supra* n. 3, at 330.
54. *Ibid.*, at 336.
55. Vandevelde, *supra* n. 27, at 52. He identifies (at 52) the procedural dimension of the rule of law as the principle of due process and states that 'four principles—reasonableness, consistency (or security), nondiscrimination, and transparency—are the core of the substantive dimension of the rule of law'. For him (at 106), '[i]n short, the existing awards describe fair and equitable treatment in accordance with a broad understanding of the rule of law—an understanding that demands reasonableness, consistency, nondiscrimination, transparency, and due process. The results in the awards, however, can be explained more parsimoniously by a narrower understanding of the rule of law—an understanding that demands open and principled conduct—that demands, in short, that states act with integrity'.
56. Schill, *supra* n. 48, at 61. *See also*: Benedict Kingsbury & Stephan Schill, *Investor-State Arbitration as Governance: Fair and Equitable Treatment, Proportionality and the Emerging Global Administrative Law* 19 (New York Univ. Public Law & Legal Theory Research Paper Series Working Paper No. 09-46).
57. Kläger, *supra* n. 13, at 128. *See also*, at 126-127: 'there are also some difficulties in the application of a comparative rule of law approach. (...) [T]he existence of a whole range of different concepts of the rule of law, influenced by the particular domestic law background, involves a laborious search for common elements among the various perceptions. (...) Further problems result from the practice that a comparative approach draws primarily from legal systems having a strong rule of law tradition - thus mainly ideas originating from European or American legal thinking'.

135

the foreign investor'.[58] To that effect, he identifies ten 'principles of FET' that must be balanced together by tribunals.[59]

In recent years, a number of writers have emphasized the need for tribunals to apply a proportionality test when assessing allegations of breach of the FET standard.[60] Schill explains that the use of such a test 'allows for the balancing of the interests of host states and foreign investors' and 'helps to counter fears about the dominance of investors' rights over the interests of host states'.[61] Diehl has identified the following composing elements of the proportionality test: suitability (i.e., 'does the measure adopted by the State or government serve a legitimate governmental purpose and is it generally suitable to achieve this purpose?'), necessity (i.e., 'are there other less intrusive means with regard to the right or interest affected that are equally able to achieve the stated goal?') and proportionality *stricu sensu* (i.e., 'is the measure excessive with regard to the objective pursued, taking into count all available factors such as cost-benefit analysis, the importance of the rights effected, the degree of interference, the length of interference and the availability of alternative measures?').[62] It has been argued that tribunals are increasingly using this test in deciding FET claims[63] and, more specifically, in determining whether *some elements* of the standard (such as denial of justice) have been breached.[64]

The next section examines how NAFTA tribunals have concretely defined the substantive content of the FET standard under Article 1105. As will be explained in further detail below, tribunals have generally adopted the 'shopping list' approach supported by a number of writers. NAFTA tribunals have not endorsed any of the comprehensive theories previously mentioned that equate, for instance, the FET standard with the rule of law under domestic law.

---

58. Kläger, *supra* n. 13, at 129 ff.
59. *Ibid.*, at 154 ff. These principles are: sovereignty; legitimate expectations; *pacta sunt servanda*; non-discrimination; sustainable development; fair procedure; due process; denial of justice; transparency, and proportionality. While admitting (at 245) that 'case law reveals little consistency' in the application of the principle of proportionality and that 'it is not yet fully established in arbitral jurisprudence', he nevertheless argues (at 119) that tribunals should use a proportionality test requiring that 'any state measure affecting the investment is built upon a reasonable and traceable rationale; the measure strains the investment not more than necessary; and the interests of the state and the foreign investor should be weighed against each other'.
60. Diehl, *supra* n. 3, at 330 ff; Kläger, *supra* n. 13, at 235 ff, 278 (indicating that proportionality is one of six 'sub-principles of fair and equitable treatment'); Kingsbury & Schill, *supra* n. 56, at 9 ('the requirement of reasonableness and proportionality' is one of the five 'clusters of normative principles [that] recur in the more detailed specification by arbitral tribunals of elements of fair and equitable treatment'); Drew Tyler, *Fair, Equitable and Reasonable Treatment: The Concept of Reasonableness within the Fair and Equitable Treatment Standard* (LL.M. Research Paper, University of Ottawa 2011).
61. Schill, *supra* n. 48, at 54-55. *See also*: Stephan Schill & Benedict Kingsbury, *Public Law Concepts to Balance Investors' Rights with State Regulatory Actions in the Public Interest - The Concept of Proportionality*, in: *International Investment Law and Comparative Public Law* 75-140 (Stephan Schill ed., Oxford U. Press 2010).
62. Diehl, *supra* n. 3, at 334.
63. Kläger, *supra* n. 13, at 245.
64. Schill & Kingsbury, *supra* n. 61, at 96.

§3.02 ANALYSIS OF NAFTA AWARDS

[A] Introduction

As previously mentioned, NAFTA tribunals have generally adopted the 'shopping list' approach. In the next sections, we will conduct a detailed examination of the different 'elements' that have been recognized by NAFTA tribunals to be encompassed within the FET standard under Article 1105. The following six elements will be analyzed:

- Legitimate expectations (section §3.02[B]).
- Transparency (section §3.02[C]).
- Arbitrary conduct (section §3.02[D]).
- Discriminatory conduct (section §3.02[E]).
- Good faith (section §3.02[F]).
- Denial of justice and due process (section §3.02[G]).

This list of elements is generally consistent with the classification used by other writers.[65]

Before examining each of these elements, it should be briefly explained why the issue of *contract* violations is not going to be analyzed specifically in this section. It is generally agreed that while 'a failure to perform a contract may amount to a violation of the FET standard', at the same time, 'it is doubtful whether any violation of a contractual obligation by a host State or one of its entities automatically amounts to a violation of the FET standard'.[66] Thus, if this were the case, the FET clause would become the equivalent of an 'umbrella clause' by elevating simple contract breaches into BIT violations.[67] In the context of NAFTA, the following passage taken from the *Mondev* award does suggest that contractual breaches amount to a FET violation per se:

---

65. *See, inter alia*, Tudor, *supra* n. 3, at 155; Diehl, *supra* n. 3, at 338; Kläger, *supra* n. 13, at 154; OECD, *supra* n. 39, at 26; UNCTAD, *supra* n. 11, at xv. *See also*, the list of writers mentioned at *supra* n. 44.
66. C. Schreuer, *Fair and Equitable Standard (FET): Interaction with Other Standards*, 4(5) Transnational Disp. Mgmt. 18 (2007); J. Roman Picherack, *The Expanding Scope of the Fair and Equitable Treatment Standard: Have Recent Tribunals Gone Too Far?* 9(4) J. World Invest. & Trade 274 (2008); Graham Mayeda, *Playing Fair: The Meaning of Fair and Equitable Treatment in Bilateral Investment Treaties*, 41(2) J. World Trade 278 (2007). *Contra*: Tudor, *supra* n. 3, at 196 for whom 'a State that would fail to comply with its contractual obligations, would violate the FET standard'); Vandevelde, *supra* n. 27, at 69 ('The clearest case of a [FET] violation is where the host state enters into a contract with the investment or investor and then repudiates the contract').
67. Schreuer, *supra* n. 66, at 18 ('Taken to its logical conclusion this argument would put all agreements between the investor and the host State under the protection of the FET standard. If this position were to be accepted, the FET standard would be nothing less than a broadly interpreted umbrella clause'). *See also*: Schreuer, *supra* n. 2, at 379; Salacuse, *supra* n. 11, at 236. *Contra*: Tudor, *supra* n. 3, at 196 ('the effect of the FET clause is to elevate a contractual claim to the level of a treaty claim, in the same manner as the umbrella clause allows the elevation of a contractual claim to the level of a treaty breach').

> A governmental prerogative to violate investment contracts would appear to be inconsistent with the principles embodied in Article 1105 and with contemporary standards of national and international law concerning governmental liability for contractual performance.[68]

On the contrary, the *Waste Management* tribunal (later upheld by the *Gami* tribunal[69]) concluded that a *simple* breach of contract by a State would *not* trigger a violation of the FET unless one can show an 'outright repudiation of the contract' by the host State:

> [e]ven the persistent non-payment of debts by a municipality is not to be equated with a violation of Article 1105, provided that it does not amount to an outright and unjustified repudiation of the transaction and provided that some remedy is open to the creditor to address the problem.[70]

It should be noted that overall, case law is divided on this controversial issue.[71] In any event, it makes sense (and it is much more practical) to examine alleged contract violations in the specific context of the different elements of the FET standard. For this reason, the question of whether or not a breach of contract violates an investor's legitimate expectations or should be considered as an 'arbitrary conduct' by the host State will be examined in the sections below that specifically discuss these different elements.

[B]   Legitimate Expectations

It should be emphasized from the outset that this section examines the issue of legitimate expectations only in the context of the host State's obligation to provide FET to investors, and *not* in the different context of *expropriation*.[72] The reasons why an investor's expectations are an important factor in its decision to invest is explained by one writer as follows:

> Investor expectations are fundamental to the investment process. It is the inves-
> tor's expectations with respect to the risks and rewards of the contemplated
> investment that have a crucial influence on the investor's decision to invest. States
> seek to influence these investment decisions through their actions, laws, regula-
> tions, and policies. Indeed, the very idea of investment promotion, which is a
> fundamental goal of virtually all investment treaties, is to create an expectation of
> profit in the minds of potential investors that will lead them to commit their capital

---

68. *Mondev v. United States*, Award, (2 October 2002), para. 134. A number of other tribunals (outside the NAFTA context) have also adopted this approach: *SGS Société Générale de Surveillance S.A. v. Philippines*, ICSID No. ARB/02/6, Decision on Jurisdiction, (29 January 2004), para. 163; *Noble Ventures, Inc. v. Romania*, ICSID No. ARB/01/11, Award, (12 October 2005), para. 182.
69. *Gami Investments, Inc. v. Mexico* [hereinafter *Gami v. Mexico*], UNCITRAL, Award, (15 November 2004), para. 101.
70. *Waste Management v. Mexico*, Award, (30 April 2004), para. 115.
71. C. Schreuer & R. Dolzer, *Principles of International Investment Law*, 140-142 (Oxford U. Press 2008). *See*, several cases examined in: Vandevelde, *supra* n. 27, at 69; Diehl, *supra* n. 3, at 381.
72. On that issue, *see*: Stephen Fietta, *Expropriation and the 'Fair and Equitable' Standard: The Developing Role of Investor 'Expectations' in International Investment Arbitration*, 23(5) J. Int. Arb. 375-399 (2006).

and technology to the country in question. Thus, when a state has created certain expectations through its laws and acts that have led the investor to invest, it is generally considered unfair for the state to take subsequent actions that fundamentally deny or frustrate those expectations.[73]

The concept of legitimate expectations is narrowly linked to the phenomenon of regulatory changes made by governments that may potentially affect foreign investors.[74] This concept has increasingly gained attention from scholars.[75] The aim of this section is *not* to examine the legal foundation of the concept of legitimate expectations.[76] The objective is more modest and is comprised of three facets. First, to determine, *based on NAFTA case law*, whether or not the protection of the legitimate expectations of investors should be considered as one of the elements encompassed within the FET standard under Article 1105. Second, to identify the actual scope of the expectations protected under this provision. Finally, the aim is to concretely determine whether or not the reasoning of NAFTA tribunals regarding legitimate expectations has been any different from that of *non-NAFTA* tribunals.[77]

This section examines two NAFTA awards (*Thunderbird* and *Glamis*) that provide a thorough analysis of the concept of legitimate expectations in the context of Article 1105 (sections §3.02[B][2] and §3.02[B][3]). But first, we will briefly examine two precursor awards (section §3.02[B][1]). *Metalclad* was the first NAFTA tribunal to examine the issue and the *ADF* tribunal the first one to actually use the expression 'legitimate expectations'. We will then conclude with a discussion of a number of other awards (*Merrill & Ring, Grand River, Cargill, Mobil*) that also touch on the concept and include several pertinent observations by the tribunals.

The present author has decided however, not to analyze awards (including *Methanex*) that have examined the concept *exclusively* in the *different context* of expropriation claims. This is because a different threshold of liability applies in cases of expropriation.[78] The next sections will discuss the reasoning of some tribunals (such

---

73. Salacuse, *supra* n. 11, at 231.
74. UNCTAD, *supra* n. 11, at 64 ('Claims relating to breach of legitimate expectations arise in situations when an investor is suffering losses due to the changes brought about by certain State measures. In other words, when a host State's conduct causes adverse effects to an investment, that is, it reduces its economic value, an investor may allege that the State violates legitimate expectations that the investor had when making the investment. The question is thus whether, and to what degree, the FET standard includes protection of such legitimate expectations. A particularly important subquestion concerns the kind of expectations that can be considered legitimate').
75. A number of writers have published papers specifically on the concept: Julien Cazala, *La protection des attentes légitimes de l'investisseur dans l'arbitrage international*, 23 Rev Intern Dr Econ. 5-32 (2009); E. Snodgrass, *Protecting Investors' Legitimate Expectations and Recognizing and Delimiting a General Principle*, 21 ICSID Rev. 53 (2006); Felipe Mutis Téllez, *Conditions and Criteria for the Protection of Legitimate Expectations Under International Investment Law*, 27(2) ICSID Rev. 432 (2012); Trevor Zeyl, *Charting the Wrong Course: The Doctrine of Legitimate Expectations in Investment Treaty Law*, 49(1) Alberta L. Rev. 203 (2011).
76. For such an analysis, *see, inter alia*: Diehl, *supra* n. 3, at 339.
77. This question is addressed in the concluding section at §3.02[B][5].
78. Diehl, *supra* n. 3, at 427, 428 ('reflections of tribunals concerning the scope of legitimate expectations made in the context of indirect expropriation may be a useful guideline for tribunals dealing with an alleged violation of the FET standard. Tribunals should, however, be aware of the fact that the threshold and focus may be slightly different'). For her, 'Investment tribunals

as *Thunderbird* and *Grand River*) that have examined the concept more generally and applied it to *both claims* under Articles 1105 and 1110. We will, however, forego a discussion on cases where tribunals did not address claimants' allegations of breaches of investors' legitimate expectations.[79]

[1]   Metalclad and ADF

The first case where a NAFTA tribunal cited a claimant's reliance on governmental assurances as a basis of claim under Article 1105 was the *Metalclad* case. While the tribunal did not use the term 'legitimate expectation' (it only referred to the investor's 'expectation'[80]), the case is nonetheless considered as relevant to the analysis of the concept of legitimate expectations.[81]

In 1990, the claimant's Mexican subsidiary was authorized by the federal government of Mexico to build a hazardous waste landfill facility near the city of Gualdalcazar in the State of San Luis Potosí, Mexico.[82] One of the key issues of the case was whether in addition to other permits, a *municipal* permit for the construction of a hazardous waste landfill was also required.[83] The tribunal explained that when the claimant enquired on the matter, the 'federal officials assured it that it had all that was needed to undertake the landfill project'.[84] As a result of these specific representations made by the authorities, 'Metalclad was led to believe, and did believe, that the federal and state permits allowed for the construction and operation of the landfill'.[85] Thus, since it was 'relying on the representations of the federal government', Metalclad 'started constructing the landfill, and did this openly and continuously, and with the full knowledge of the federal, state, and municipal government'.[86] For the tribunal, since the investor had based its actions on such representations, it was therefore *legitimate* to expect that had the missing municipal permit been a problem, it would have been told so promptly by the authorities.[87] The authorities did nothing for some five months.

---

have also appeared to use a higher threshold concerning investor expectations for purposes of expropriation claims. Where investors are not specifically made to believe in certain State assurances, as in the Metalclad case, or where they are entering a high-risk market, their expectations appear to be regarded as less legitimate for property protection purposes'.

79. *See*, for instance, the award in *Chemtura Corporation v. Canada* [hereinafter *Chemtura v. Canada*], UNCITRAL, Award, (2 August 2010), referring to the claimant's arguments on legitimate expectations (*see*, at paras. 112, 114, 164, 167, 194-199) without, however, specifically examining the question. It was also decided to examine the case of *Gami v. Mexico*, Award, (15 November 2004), in the section on arbitrary conduct (*see*, at section §3.02[D][3]).
80. *Metalclad Corporation v. Mexico* [hereinafter *Metalclad v. Mexico*], ICSID No. ARB(AF)/97/1, Award, (30 August 2000), para. 89.
81. Fietta, *supra* n. 72, at 386.
82. The claimant acquired its Mexican subsidiary in 1993 after that company had obtained its first federal permit to operate the hazardous waste facility.
83. *Metalclad v. Mexico*, Award, (30 August 2000), para. 79.
84. *Ibid.*, para. 80.
85. *Ibid.*, para. 85.
86. *Ibid.*, para. 87.
87. Tudor, *supra* n. 3, at 166 ('The authorities usually have numerous occasions to cooperate with the Investor and to rectify his eventual misinterpretations or misrepresentations of the national

In October 1994, the municipality ordered that construction of the facility cease due to the absence of a municipal construction permit. Other specific representations were made by the Mexican authorities at that point. According to the tribunal, Metalclad had, at the time, 'asserted that federal officials told it that if it submitted an application for a municipal construction permit, the Municipality would have no legal basis for denying the permit and that it would be issued as a matter of course'.[88] For the tribunal, the investor had legitimate expectations that were 'reasonable' in light of the circumstances: 'Metalclad was *entitled to rely on the representations* of federal officials and to believe that it was entitled to continue its construction of the landfill'.[89]

Having received this information, the claimant submitted an application for the municipal permit and without waiting any further resumed the construction of the facility, which was completed in March 1995. However, the claimant was prevented from opening the landfill due to demonstrations organized in part by the local authorities that opposed the landfill opening because of environmental concerns. On 25 November 1995, the claimant and the federal government of Mexico entered into an agreement providing for, and allowing the operation of the landfill.[90] The response by the municipality finally came some thirteen months after the claimant applied for the permit. In December 1995, the municipality denied Metalclad's application for a construction permit.[91]

The tribunal held that the '[m]unicipality's insistence upon and denial of the construction permit in this instance was improper'[92] and in violation of due process and the so-called obligation of transparency (two points further discussed below[93]).[94] It did not address the question of whether such conduct breached any obligation to protect legitimate expectations.[95] While it has been argued by some writers that the

---

law. For instance, if the authorities repeatedly act in a way which leads the Investor to believe he is acting in a lawful way, the same authorities may not suddenly decide to treat this behaviour as unlawful, without violating the legitimate expectations of the Investor').

88. *Metalclad v. Mexico*, Award, (30 August 2000), para. 88. For the tribunal, 'the absence of a clear rule as to the requirement or not of a municipal construction permit, as well as the absence of any established practice or procedure as to the manner of handling applications for a municipal construction permit, amounts to a failure on the part of Mexico to ensure the transparency required by NAFTA'.

89. *Ibid.*, para. 89 (emphasis added).

90. The five-year agreement stated that an environmental audit had been conducted on site to verify the project's compliance with Mexico's laws and regulations. The agreement also mentioned a number of environmental protection requirements that were already fulfilled by the claimant such as the submission of an action plan to correct certain deficiencies and the creation of different supervision committees.

91. *Metalclad v. Mexico*, Award, (30 August 2000), paras. 90, 97. Shortly after denying the permit, the local authorities instituted court proceedings regarding the recently concluded 1995 agreement between the claimant and the federal government.

92. *Ibid.*, para. 97.

93. *See*, at sections §3.02[G][5] and §3.02[C][1], respectively.

94. *Metalclad v. Mexico*, Award, (30 August 2000), para. 99.

95. It should be noted that the tribunal does mention (*Ibid.*, para. 99) that 'the totality of these circumstances demonstrates a lack of orderly process and timely disposition in relation to an investor of a Party acting in the *expectation* that it would be treated fairly and justly in accordance with the NAFTA' (emphasis added). This passage is, however, unrelated to the concept of legitimate expectations.

tribunal also found that Mexico had breached the investor's legitimate expectations,[96] there is no clear indication that this is the case.

Nonetheless, the *Metalclad* award is still noteworthy because of its emphasis on three key points: (1) an investor's expectations must be based on *specific representations*; (2) such representations must be made by governmental *officials*, and finally, (3) the expectations must be *reasonable* in the circumstances.[97] These three essential points will be reiterated in all subsequent NAFTA awards dealing with the concept of legitimate expectations.

In 2003, the *ADF* award was the first to actually use the term legitimate expectations.[98] ADF had entered into a contract to supply steel for a highway construction project in the State of Virginia. Virginia contractually required ADF to use only American-made steel. It prohibited ADF from cutting and processing American-made steel in Canada, which greatly increased ADF's costs. The claimant argued that the 'Buy America' provision in section 165 of the Surface Transportation Assistance Act (STAA) of 1982 was, *inter alia*, in breach of Article 1105.[99] More specifically, the claimant argued that the Federal Highway Administration (FHWA) of the U.S. Department of Transportation 'refused to follow and apply pre-existing case law in respect of ADF International in the Springfield Interchange Project, thus ignoring the Investor's legitimate expectations generated by that case law'.[100] The tribunal stated that it did 'not believe that the refusal of the FHWA to follow prior rulings, judicial or administrative is, in itself, in the circumstances of this case, grossly unfair or unreasonable'.[101] In any event, not only was the case law which the claimant referred to *not relevant* to the application of the present statute,[102] but 'any expectations that the Investor had with respect to the relevancy or applicability of the case law it cited were not created by any misleading representations made by authorized officials of the U.S. federal Government but rather, it appears probable, by legal advice received by the Investor from private U.S. counsel'.[103] In other words, for the tribunal, no legitimate expectations existed since governmental authorities had not made any representations in the first place.

The *ADF* award does not examine the concept of legitimate expectations in great detail. Yet, the tribunal's reference to *misleading* representations made by *authorized officials* seems to confirm *Metalclad's* finding to the effect that only *specific* representations can be the basis for any legitimate expectations.

---

96. I. Laird, *Betrayal, Shock and Outrage - Recent Developments in NAFTA Article 1105*, in *NAFTA Investment Law and Arbitration: The Early Years* 58 (T. Weiler ed., Transnational Publ. 2004); T. Weiler, *Metalclad v. Mexico: A Play in Three Parts*, 2 J. World Invest. 685, 692 (2001).
97. *See*, Fietta, *supra* n. 72, at 386.
98. *ADF Group Inc. v. United States* [hereinafter *ADF v. United States*], ICSID No. ARB (AF)/00/1, Award, (9 January 2003), para. 189.
99. *Ibid.*, para. 72.
100. *Ibid.*, para. 189. *See also*, at para. 72: 'the application of the Buy America provision to the Investor arbitrarily dissolves the legitimate expectations created by previous decisions of U.S. courts and administrative agencies "with respect to "buy national" "policies"'.
101. *Ibid.*, para. 189.
102. *Ibid.*
103. *Ibid.* This issue is discussed in: Cazala, *supra* n. 75, at 21.

Finally, it should be mentioned that a few years later, the *Methanex* tribunal would examine the question of legitimate expectations in a different context – that of *expropriation*. In that context, the tribunal mentioned the following:

> [A]s a matter of general international law, a non-discriminatory regulation for a public purpose, which is enacted in accordance with due process and, which affects, inter alios, a foreign investor or investment is not deemed expropriatory and compensable unless *specific commitments* had been given by the regulating government to the then putative foreign investor contemplating investment that the government *would refrain from such regulation*.[104]

Again, the award is relevant for its emphasis on the requirement of *specific* commitments.

[2]   Thunderbird

Until the *Thunderbird* award, three NAFTA tribunals (*Metaclad*, *ADF* and *Methanex*) had already set the table by identifying the basic contours of the concept of legitimate expectations under Article 1105. The *Thunderbird* award however, was the first one to thoroughly examine the concept.

In *Thunderbird*, the claimant had used a Mexican company (EDM) to investigate with the government the legality and propriety of its intended operations in Mexico. In August 2000, EDM solicited an official opinion in the form of a letter (hereinafter the '*Solicitud*') from the Mexican authorities in charge of gambling regulation (SEGOB). It is important to note that gambling is illegal in Mexico. SEGOB's response to the letter (hereinafter the '*Oficio*') explained that based on the information provided in the letter, the machines would be legal under Mexican law because they did not involve luck or gambling. Thus, the *Oficio* letter explained that:

> according to your statement, the machines that your representative operates are recreational video game devices for purposes of enjoyment and entertainment of its users, with the possibility of obtaining a prize, without the intervention of luck or gambling, but rather the user's ability and skilfulness.[105]

The letter added that 'if the machines that your representative exploits operate in the form and conditions stated by you, this governmental entity is not able to prohibit its

---

104. *Methanex Corporation v. United States* [hereinafter *Methanex v. United States*], UNCITRAL, Award, (3 August 2005), Part IV, Ch. D, para. 7 (emphasis added). Fietta, *supra* n. 72, at 391-392, argues that the language used by the tribunal is 'reminiscent more of a "fair and equitable" analysis than an "expropriation" one' and that the tribunal's analysis 'would have been far more relevant to its analysis of the Article 1105 claim than to questions of expropriation under Article 1110'. He concludes (at 393) that the award 'cannot be treated as setting out an authoritative analysis of the role to be played by claimants' disappointed expectations in the context of arguments of expropriation or failure to accord fair and equitable treatment'.

105. *International Thunderbird Gaming Corporation v. Mexico* [hereinafter *Thunderbird v. Mexico*], UNCITRAL, Award, (26 January 2006), para. 55.

use'.[106] The investor made its investment and a few months later SEGOB discovered the true nature of the machines and closed down the already operational facilities.

In its award, the tribunal addressed the question whether or not any legitimate expectations had been created by SEGOB's response letter (the *Oficio*).[107] While the *Thunderbird* award is the first one to comprehensively analyze the concept of legitimate expectations, it is noteworthy that its analysis is *not* specifically made with respect to Article 1105, but is generally applicable to other provisions as well.[108]

The investor argued that the *Oficio* had created a legitimate expectation upon which it was reasonable to rely.[109] Thus, it was led to believe that its gambling activities were lawful and would be protected. Mexico denied this. The letter was an advisory opinion, not an approval or a permit, and could therefore not create any such expectation.[110] In any event, Mexico argued that the letter was based on the information provided by EDM in the *Solicitud*, which turned out to be incorrect. Mexico also denied that Thunderbird had relied on the *Oficio* as the basis for its investments in the country.[111]

The tribunal started its analysis by providing a definition of the concept of legitimate expectations:

> The concept of 'legitimate expectations' relates, within the context of the NAFTA framework, to a situation where a Contracting Party's conduct creates reasonable and justifiable expectations on the part of an investor (or investment) to act in reliance on said conduct, such that a failure by the NAFTA Party to honor those expectations could cause the investor (or investment) to suffer damages.[112]

The award therefore reiterated the three basic points which had already been made in *Metalclad*, and added a fourth one (the requirement that damages be caused to the investor).

The tribunal concluded that the letter (*Solicitud*) had not 'generated a legitimate expectation upon which EDM could reasonably rely in operating its machines in Mexico'.[113] The tribunal rightly noted that in order to assess whether Thunderbird could 'reasonably rely to its detriment on SEGOB's response to the Solicitud', the first

---

106. *Ibid.*
107. The award is examined by these writers: S. Fietta, *International Thunderbird Gaming Corporation v. Mexico: An Indication of the Limits of "Legitimate Expectation" Basis of Claim under Article 1105 of NAFTA*, 3(2) Transnat. Disp. Mgmt. (2006); S. Fietta, *The Legitimate Expectations Principle under Article 1105 NAFTA-International Thunderbird Gaming Corporation v. Mexico*, 7 J.World Invest. & Trade 423 (2006).
108. *Thunderbird v. Mexico*, Award, (26 January 2006). Thus, the tribunal deliberately addressed this question *before* examining the investor's claims under Articles 1105, 1110, and 1102 (paras. 168 ff.). It did so because the claimant contended that the issue was relevant to the application of all these provisions (para. 137). A number of writers believe that the award is not a solid precedent in the context of Article 1105 because of this specific feature: Fietta, *supra* n. 72, at 393, 395, 397; C. Lévesque, *Chronique de Droit international économique en 2010-2011 – Investissement*, 45 Can YIL 395-396 (2007).
109. *Thunderbird v. Mexico*, Award, (26 January 2006), para. 139.
110. *Ibid.*, para. 141.
111. *Ibid.*, para. 144.
112. *Ibid.*, para. 147.
113. *Ibid.*, para. 148.

enquiry should be to 'ascertain what was requested by Thunderbird in the Solicitud'.[114] The tribunal explained that the information presented by EDM in the *Solicitud* was 'incomplete and, in particular, inaccurate in two regards'.[115] First, the letter wrongly stated that the machines operated by EDM did not involve 'luck or betting'.[116] Second, it wrongly stated that players did not have to pay to use the machine.[117] On this point, the tribunal concluded that 'the *Solicitud* is not a proper disclosure and that it puts the reader on the wrong track' since it 'creates the appearance that the machines described are video arcade games, designed solely for entertainment purposes'.[118]

For the tribunal, SEGOB's response to the *Solicitud* indicates that 'if the machines operate in accordance with EDM's representations in the *Solicitud* [i.e., that the machines operate 'without the intervention of luck of gambling'] SEGOB does not have jurisdiction over said machines'.[119] However, EDM's representations were clearly misleading. The machines were betting (i.e., 'slot') machines, not machines involving any skills or ability.[120] Thunderbird was fully aware when it chose to invest in Mexico that gambling was an illegal activity under Mexican law.[121] Furthermore:

> at the time EDM requested an official opinion from SEGOB on the legality of its machines, EDM must also be deemed to have been aware that its machines involved some degree of luck, and that dollar bill acceptors coupled with winning tickets redeemable for cash could be reasonably viewed as elements of betting.[122]

For the tribunal, based on these misleading representations, the investor 'could not have reasonably relied to its detriment upon the *Oficio* to operate its gaming facilities in Mexico'.[123] The tribunal therefore concluded that the *Oficio* did not create any legitimate expectations.[124] The reasoning of the tribunal implies that, as a matter of

---

114. *Ibid.*, para. 149.
115. *Ibid.*, para. 151.
116. *Ibid.*, para. 152.
117. *Ibid.*, para. 153.
118. *Ibid.*, para. 154. The tribunal also rejected the investor's allegation that SEGOB was well aware of the nature of the EDM machines (paras. 156–158) or that SEGOB should have made a request for additional information regarding the operation of the machines (para. 159). Thus, for the tribunal, 'the *Solicitud* did not give the full picture, even for an informed reader' (para. 159).
119. *Ibid.*, para. 161.
120. For a critical assessment of the reasoning of the tribunal on this point, *see* Santiago Montt, *The Award in Thunderbird v. Mexico*, in *The Reasons Requirement in International Investment Arbitration: Critical Case Studies* 272-280 (Guillermo Aguilar Alvarez & W. Michael Reisman eds., Nijhoff 2008).
121. *Thunderbird v. Mexico*, Award, (26 January 2006), para. 164. The tribunal added (at para. 164) that the investor 'must be deemed to have been aware of the potential risk of closure of its own gaming facilities and it should have exercised particular caution in pursuing its business venture in Mexico'. On this point, *see*: Montt, *supra* n. 120, at 287-289. The award was criticized by Gabriel Cavazos Villanueva, *The Fair and Equitable Treatment Standard: The Mexican Experience* 134 (VDM Verlag 2008), for whom Mexico's legislation was in fact not clear at all on which forms on gambling was considered illegal, adding that 'gaming facilities in Mexico are in most cases opened and maintained based solely on the discretion of the authorities and their capacity to litigate with the owners of the facilities'.
122. *Thunderbird v. Mexico*, Award, (26 January 2006), para. 164.
123. *Ibid.*, para. 163.
124. *Ibid.*, para. 166.

principle, expectations could be based on representations made by an administrative agency. In any event, the tribunal expressed doubt over the fact that Thunderbird had actually invested in Mexico based solely on the *Oficio*.[125]

The tribunal rejected the claimant's allegation of a breach of its legitimate expectations. This award is important not only because it clearly defines the concept of legitimate expectations, but also because it provides a concrete example of a situation where expectations are 'unreasonable' and can therefore not be relied upon by the investor when making its investment. Thus, representations made by the host State in response to 'incomplete, inaccurate and misleading' information given by an investor cannot be the basis for any 'reasonable' expectations.[126] In other words, in order for an investor to rely on a governmental response as a basis for claiming any legitimate expectations, it must disclose all relevant information to the government.[127] In any event, ambiguous assurances given by the government cannot be relied upon by an investor when the legality of the investment is doubtful in the first place.[128]

A disappointing feature of the award however, is the fact that it does not explain how the concept of legitimate expectations should apply in the specific context of a breach of Article 1105.[129] Right after having defined the concept of legitimate expectations, the tribunal added that '[t]he threshold for legitimate expectations may vary depending on the nature of the violation alleged under the NAFTA and the circumstances of the case'.[130] In other words, the threshold for breaching the obligation to protect an investor's legitimate expectations may depend on whether the allegations are related to Article 1105 or Article 1110. Unfortunately, the tribunal does not explain what the threshold is for a breach of Article 1105.[131] Yet, later in the award, the tribunal determined that a breach of Article 1105 requires that the act 'amount to a gross denial of justice or manifest arbitrariness falling below acceptable international standards'.[132] It has been suggested by one writer that this is in fact the threshold for a breach of legitimate expectations under that provision.[133] In the present author's view, this is

---

125. *Ibid.,* para. 167.
126. Fietta, *supra* n. 107, at 432; Picherack, *supra* n. 66, at 276.
127. Fietta, *supra* n. 107, at 431, for whom a request made by an investor to the responsible State authorities 'must include as complete and accurate a disclosure as possible of all of the pertinent facts-particularly those that are in the exclusive knowledge of the investor. Representations or assurances that are made by host State authorities on the basis of incomplete or inaccurate disclosures by an investor, as was the case in Thunderbird, will not generally be capable of providing the essential ingredients for a legitimate expectations-based claim'.
128. Diehl, *supra* n. 3, at 390 ('if illegality or "quasi-illegality" of an investment existed from the beginning, ambiguous governmental representations must be interpreted in accordance with domestic law, rejecting possible illegal interpretations. Put differently: Ambiguous assurances do not confer legitimate expectations if those would run *contra legem* or *contra* established interpretations').
129. Thus, as mentioned above, the tribunal analyzed the concept *before* examining the investor's claims of breach of Articles 1105, 1110, and 1102.
130. *Thunderbird v. Mexico,* Award, (26 January 2006), para. 148.
131. Fietta, *supra* n. 107, at 431.
132. *Thunderbird v. Mexico,* Award, (26 January 2006), para. 194.
133. Picherack, *supra* n. 66, at 276, for whom as a result, 'it is possible that a State may breach an investor's legitimate expectations but that in the circumstances the State's conduct does not amount to a "gross denial of justice or manifest arbitrariness" and so does not breach the fair and equitable treatment standard'.

simply a reference to the threshold that exists for *other elements* of the FET standard under Article 1105 (i.e., denial of justice, arbitrary conduct, etc.).

[3] Wälde's Separate Opinion in Thunderbird

In his separate opinion, Professor Wälde adopts a much broader approach towards the issue. For him, NAFTA includes an obligation of transparency for the host State, which is intertwined with the obligation to respect an investor's legitimate expectations:

> The main principles underlying the NAFTA (preamble, Art. 102) as developed in the most recent and authoritative jurisprudence by arbitral tribunals require that in case of doubt, the risk of ambiguity of a governmental assurance is allocated rather to the government than to a foreign investor and that the government is held to high standards of transparency and responsibility for the clarity and consistency in its interaction with foreign investors. If official communications cause, visibly and clearly, confusion or misunderstanding with the foreign investor, then the government is responsible for pro-actively clarifying its position. The government can not rely on its own ambiguous communications, which the foreign investor could and did justifiably rely on, in order to later retract and reverse them– in particular in change of government situations.[134]

Wälde clearly identifies legitimate expectations as one of the elements encompassed within the FET standard under Article 1105.[135] He describes the 'general conditions' of a legitimate expectations claim to be as follows:

> An expectation of the investor to be caused by and attributed to the government, backed-up by investment relying on such expectation, requiring the legitimacy of the expectation in terms of the competency of the officials responsible for it and the procedure for issuing it and the reasonableness of the investor in relying on the expectation.[136]

---

134. *Thunderbird v. Mexico*, Separate Opinion of Thomas Wälde (1 December 2005), para. 4. The link between this so-called obligation of transparency and the requirement to respect an investor's legitimate expectations is even clearer in this passage (at para. 36): 'These objectives of the NAFTA – both the general objective of enhancing the attractiveness of the host state for foreign investors and the instrumental tool of using greater transparency, clarity and predictability to enable better investment planning– have therefore to guide the process of both defining the conditions of the "legitimate expectations" principle under Art. 1105 and of applying it to the particular facts of a specific situation'.

135. *Ibid.*, para. 30: 'The wide acceptance of the "legitimate expectations" principle therefore supports the concept that it is indeed part of "fair and equitable treatment" as owed by governments to foreign investors under modern investment treaties and under Art. 1105 of the NAFTA. It is before this international and comparative law background that one needs to make sense out of several recent investment treaty awards which have applied the legitimate expectations principle, both under Art. 1105 of the NAFTA and the equivalent provisions of applicable bilateral investment treaties. These awards – Metalclad v. Mexico, Tecmed v. Mexico, Occidental v. Ecuador, Waste Management v. Mexico II and MTD v. Chile – may not have explained the doctrinal background of the principle, its scope and contours specifically, but these authoritative precedents have contributed towards establishing the "legitimate expectation" as a sub-category of "fair and equitable treatment" in the for this [sic] dispute here most pertinent investment treaties (including NAFTA Chapter XI's Art. 1105)'.

136. *Ibid.*, para. 1.

He also emphasizes the requirement that the expectations be 'legitimate' which he describes as those 'created by government officials in an official way (i.e., attributable to the government of Mexico)' who 'must have been competent (or at least appeared, credibly, to be competent) for the trust-inspiring action'.[137] He describes the kind of conduct or representation necessary for legitimate expectations to exist to be as follows:

> A review of these cases suggests that conduct, informal, oral or general assurances can give rise to or support the existence of a legitimate expectation. But the threshold for such informal and general representations is quite high. On the other hand, a legitimate expectation is assumed more readily if an individual investor receives specifically formal assurances that display visibly an official character and if the official(s) perceive or should perceive that the investor intends, reasonably, to rely on such representation (the element of 'investment-backed expectation'). The strongest way to build a legitimate expectation is if both formal and official elements are followed and reinforced by conduct that carries the same message as the investor reads – and can reasonably read – into an interpretative assurance or 'comfort letter'.[138]

Concerning the *Solicitud*, Wälde indicates that Thunderbird had, in effect, requested from SEGOB a 'comfort letter', which was 'desired to provide legal certainty for the investment envisaged'.[139] Unlike the majority of the tribunal, Wälde saw 'no lack of required disclosure'[140] by the investor on the type of machines to be operated.[141] Thus, for him somebody of experience would have known with the information provided that Thunderbird's investment was in fact video gaming devices. Moreover, had SEGOB found the information insufficient, it should have requested additional information or conducted an inspection of the machines.[142] Wälde also considered that SEGOB's *Oficio* did not clearly and unequivocally forbid Thunderbird from operating its machines.[143] Moreover, since the letter came from competent officials, Thunderbird's expectations of getting the green light for its exploitation should be qualified as being 'legitimate'.

Wälde also gave a lot of importance to factors other than the *Solicitud* and the *Oficio*. He referred to the six months of inactivity by the Mexican government following the reception of the *Oficio* and held that a 'consistent and prolonged treatment of a person in a particular way, can create a reasonable expectation that the treatment will be continued until further notice'.[144] Thus, the combination of the *Oficio* with this

---

137. *Ibid.*, para. 21.
138. *Ibid.*, para. 32.
139. *Ibid.*, para. 64.
140. *Ibid.*, para. 65.
141. *Ibid.*, para. 73.
142. *Ibid.*, para. 76. The reasoning of Wälde on this point has been criticized by writers: Fietta, *supra* n. 107, at 430.
143. *Ibid.*, para. 88: 'if SEGOB did not want to accept Thunderbird's type of operation, it should have said so, clearly, and if it saw that Thunderbird did not get the message properly, it should have repeated the message and ensured it was clearly conveyed and understood'.
144. *Ibid.*, para. 96.

inactive behavior creates a 'much stronger case for a protected legitimate expectation'.[145] Finally, for Wälde, it is important not only to consider how the legitimate expectations 'were created but also how they were breached'.[146] The absence of favoritism is thus an important factor in examining a potential breach of legitimate expectations.[147] Wälde believes that the investor had received discriminatory treatment since SEGOB had not targeted its Mexican competitor, Mr. Guardia, 'who had pioneered the "skill" machine operation since 1999 and openly defied SEGOB'.[148] In sum, it is this combination of factors that led Wälde to conclude that Thunderbird had legitimate expectations that it would be able to legally carry out its gaming business in Mexico without government intervention.[149]

[4]   Glamis

The *Glamis Gold* case involves a Canadian company's proposal to develop the 'Imperial Project', a gold mining operation located on US federal lands within the California Desert Conservation Area (CDCA) — an area of land protected under the 1976 Federal Land Policy and Management Act (FLMPA).[150] The project had raised some concerns about the potential impact of open-pit metallic mines on the environment and on Native American cultural resources. The Imperial Project was first approved by the US Department of the Interior's Bureau of Land Management (BLM). But approval for the project was later withdrawn by the Department of the Interior based on a legal opinion (the 'M-Opinion'). At the same time, California's State Mining and Geology Board also passed regulations in December 2000 requiring all future open-pit metallic mines to be backfilled. These regulations came into effect with the passage of Senate Bill (SB 22) in April 2003, which also provided for the backfilling of open-pit metallic mines that were located near Native American sacred sites. The effect of this legislation was, in the words of the tribunal, to 'permanently prevent the approval of the Glamis Gold Mine project and any other metallic mineral projects that presented an immediate threat to [Native] sacred sites located in areas of special concern'.[151]

The claimant argued, *inter alia*, that the actions taken by the State of California and the U.S. federal government were arbitrary and discriminatory since they were designed to block the Imperial Project and constituted a breach of Article 1105 (these two grounds of complaint will be further examined below[152]). The claimant also argued that these two governments had violated its legitimate expectations that the project would be approved based on the prevailing mining regime which existed at the time the

---

145. *Ibid.*
146. *Ibid.*, para. 102.
147. *Ibid.*
148. *Ibid.*, para. 104. *See also*, at para. 102.
149. *Ibid.*, para. 23.
150. *See*, Jordan C. Kahn, *Striking NAFTA Gold: Glamis Advances Investor-State Arbitration*, 33 Fordham Int'l LJ. 148 ff (2009-2010); Margaret Clare Ryan, *Glamis Gold, Ltd. v. The United States and the Fair and Equitable Treatment Standard*, 56(4) McGill LJ 951 (2011).
151. *Glamis Gold, Ltd. v. United States* [hereinafter *Glamis v. United States*], UNCITRAL, Award, (8 June 2009), para. 177.
152. *See*, at sections §3.02[D][4] and §3.02[E][4], respectively.

plan was submitted and based on the fact that the project had been approved earlier on in the review process. The claimant was of the view that the principle of legitimate expectations was 'part of the fair and equitable treatment standard as an expression and part of the "good faith" principle recognized in international law'.[153] More specifically, as summarized by the tribunal, the claimant referred to 'two particular duties that it argues are current requirements of a host State under its obligations to provide fair and equitable treatment' including 'an obligation to protect legitimate expectations *through establishment of a transparent and predictable business and legal framework*'.[154] The United States argued, on the contrary, that the 'frustration of an investor's expectations cannot form the basis of a stand-alone claim under NAFTA Chapter 11' since it had 'not became a part of the minimum standard of treatment under customary international law'.[155] In any event, for the US, 'if States were prohibited from regulating in any manner that frustrated expectations—or had to compensate for any diminution in profit—they would lose the power to regulate'.[156]

For the tribunal, the element of legitimate expectations was clearly a part of the FET standard under Article 1105 (a point further discussed below[157]). The tribunal also made three theoretical findings of great importance.

First, the tribunal addressed the question of the natural 'expectations' of each party that the other party would respect the terms of the contract. The United States had argued that 'even those expectations that manifest in a contract are insufficient to provide a basis for a breach of the minimum standard of treatment'.[158] The tribunal essentially agreed with the United States: '[t]he mere contract breach, without something further such as denial of justice or discrimination, normally will not suffice to establish a breach of Article 1105'.[159] In other words, the legitimate expectations of one party to a contract is not violated by the mere fact that the other party has breached the terms of the contract. Something more is required. The tribunal indicates that 'something more' could be a denial of justice or discrimination committed by the wrongdoer. The tribunal added that 'merely not living up to expectations' (i.e., that the other party will respect the contract) 'cannot be sufficient to find a breach of Article

---

153. *Glamis v. United States,* Award, (8 June 2009), para. 568.
154. *Ibid.,* para. 561 (emphasis added). The other 'duty' referred to by the investor is an obligation to provide protection from arbitrary measures. This question is examined below at section §3.02[D][4].
155. *Ibid.,* paras. 575–576 (citing US Counter-Memorial, (19 September 2006), paras. 230, 233).
156. *Ibid.,* para. 576 (citing US Counter-Memorial, (19 September 2006), para. 233).
157. *See,* at section §3.02[B][5].
158. *Glamis v. United States,* Award, (8 June 2009), para. 620. The tribunal summarized (at para. 577) the respondent's position as follows: 'Respondent cites to the fact that a breach of contract does not rise to the level of a Chapter 11 claim without something beyond mere breach as the best example of why the duty to protect legitimate investor expectations is not a component of the customary international law minimum standard of treatment. Respondent asserts that a claimant must demonstrate something more than a contract breach, such as denial of justice or repudiation in a discriminatory way, or in a manner motivated by non-commercial considerations. According to Respondent, if "the expectations [that] manifest in a contract cannot provide a basis for a breach of the minimum standard of treatment, no lesser basis for such expectation can do so"'.
159. *Ibid.,* para. 620.

1105 of the NAFTA'.[160] This is an important finding that will have a long-lasting influence on NAFTA case law.

Second, the tribunal reiterated the statement of the *Thunderbird* tribunal to the effect that any legitimate expectation must be based on 'specific assurance or commitment to the investor so as to induce its expectations'.[161] Third, the tribunal made another important finding on the type of 'expectations' required under Article 1105. It held (quoting the *Thunderbird* tribunal) that the expectations of the investor must be 'reasonable and justifiable'.[162] For the tribunal, what matters is the *objectively* based expectations of the investor: 'a State may be tied to the objective expectations that it creates *in order to induce* investment'.[163] As further discussed below, according to the tribunal, these objective (not subjective) expectations must be based on *specific assurances* given by the host State.

After having made these three important statements, the tribunal first examined the measures taken by the federal government. At the outset, the tribunal acknowledged that:

> it appears indisputable that, under the decades-long rule of the 'unnecessary or undue degradation' standard, mining operators *developed expectations* that the discovery of Native American artifacts at a mining site could necessitate mitigation, but would not lead to denial of the project's [Plan of Operation].[164]

Moreover, the tribunal also recognized that 'the shift in the 1999 M-Opinion to a definition of "undue impairment" that allowed for the denial of a [Plan of Operation] represented a significant change from settled practice'.[165] In fact, according to the tribunal, that legal opinion (the '1999 M-Opinion') 'changed a decades-old rule and century-old regime upon which Claimant had based *reasonable expectation*'.[166] The tribunal then defined the legal question to be examined under Article 1105 as being the following:

> The issue presented to the Tribunal therefore is whether a lengthy, reasoned legal opinion violates customary international law because it changes, in an arguably dramatic way, a previous law or prior legal interpretation upon which an investor has based its reasonable, investment-backed expectations.[167]

Having concluded in the meantime that the M-Opinion was not 'arbitrary',[168] that it did not exhibit 'a manifest lack of reasons', and did not demonstrate 'blatant unfairness or

---

160. *Ibid.*
161. *Ibid.* To support this assertion, the *Glamis* tribunal refers to *Methanex v. United States*, Award, (3 August 2005), Part IV, Ch. D, para. 7, which dealt with the investor's expectations under Article 1110. *See*: Kahn, *supra* n. 150, at 148.
162. *Glamis v. United States*, Award, (8 June 2009), para. 621.
163. *Ibid.* (emphasis in the original). *See also*, at para. 627, where the tribunal refers to the 'creation by the State of objective expectations'.
164. *Ibid.*, para. 758 (emphasis added).
165. *Ibid.*, para. 759.
166. *Ibid.*, para. 761 (emphasis added).
167. *Ibid.*
168. This aspect of the claim is examined at section §3.02[D][4] below.

evident discrimination',[169] the tribunal started its analysis of the issue by making this important statement:

> A violation of Article 1105 based on the unsettling of reasonable, investment-backed expectation requires, as a threshold circumstance, at least a quasi-contractual relationship between the State and the investor, whereby the State has purposely and specifically induced the investment.[170]

For the tribunal, *as a matter of principle*, there is no violation of an investor's legitimate expectations as a result of a change in the host State's regulations. This is so *even* in cases where the expectations of the investor were 'reasonable' when it made its investment based on the prevailing legal framework at that time. For the tribunal, there is a need for a 'quasi-contractual' relationship between the State and the investor. Thus, an investor's expectations can only be considered legitimate when based on some *specific representations* made by the host State and when specific *commitments* or *assurances* ('purposely and specifically induced') have been given to *encourage* the investment.[171] Thus, vague and general representations made by the host State to an investor about some elements of the existing legal framework under which its investment would be governed would *not pass* the required threshold of a 'quasi-contractual' relationship. The tribunal came to the conclusion that no such commitment had been made by the federal government in this case:

> The Tribunal does not find these circumstances in the facts of this case. First, Claimant was operating in a climate that was becoming more and more sensitive to the environmental consequences of open-pit mining. Second, although the M-Opinion and ROD came to a different result than a reasonable investor might expect under the mining regulatory regime as it stood, the federal government did not make specific commitments to induce Claimant to persevere with its mining claims. It did not guarantee Claimant approval of its claims, nor did it offer Claimant any benefits to pursuing such claims beyond the customary chance to exploit federal land for possible profit. There did not exist, therefore, the quasi-contractual inducement that the Tribunal has found is a prerequisite for consideration of a breach of Article 1105(1) based upon repudiated investor expectations.[172]

The tribunal then examined the question of whether or not the acts of the State of California violated the investor's legitimate expectations. The investor argued that Senate Bill 22 had 'an illegal impact' since the 'fundamental shift in the legal framework surrounding open pit metallic mining in the State of California' had marked a significant change from the previous legal context in which Glamis operated, which therefore denies it a 'transparent and predictable framework'.[173] The claimant's allegation was that the '*effect* of the bill illegally deprived [it] of a transparent and predictable framework that upset its reasonable, investment-backed expectations'.[174]

---

169. *Glamis v. United States*, Award, (8 June 2009), paras. 762–765.
170. *Ibid.*, para. 766.
171. *Ibid.*
172. *Ibid.*, para. 767.
173. *Ibid.*, para. 798.
174. *Ibid.*, (emphasis in the original).

The claimant therefore linked its expectations to an alleged obligation of transparency for the host State.

The tribunal rejected the existence of such a link and reasserted that a 'State Party's duty under Article 1105 arises only when the State has induced these expectations in a quasi-contractual manner'.[175] The tribunal added:

> In this way, a State may be tied to the objective expectations that it creates *in order to induce* investment. Such an upset of expectations thus requires something greater than mere disappointment; it requires, as a threshold condition, the active inducement of a quasi-contractual expectation.[176]

The tribunal concluded that the State of California did not give 'specific assurances' to the investor.[177] Regardless, the 'assurances' which the claimant mentioned during the proceedings were not sufficient to meet the required threshold under Article 1105.[178] According to the tribunal, such assurances would have to be 'definitive, unambiguous and repeated'.[179] While the tribunal did not specifically address Glamis' other allegation that it received specific *oral* assurances from the government,[180] it has been suggested that such assurances would have not, in all likelihood, passed the high threshold imposed by the tribunal.[181]

Lastly, the tribunal examined the SMGB Regulations passed by the State of California which imposed mandatory backfilling and which the claimant argued upset its reasonable expectations.[182] The tribunal acknowledged that 'this imposition of mandatory backfilling surprised Claimant and upset its expectations',[183] but added that whether the investor's expectations 'were reasonable or not is not an inquiry that the Tribunal need make'.[184] For the tribunal, the relevant inquiry was 'solely whether California, or the federal government, made specific assurances to Claimant that such a requirement would not be instituted in order to induce Claimant's investment in the Imperial Project'.[185] The tribunal concluded that no specific assurances had been given to the claimant.[186] It also came to the conclusion that 'there were no specific assurances to Claimant with respect to the emergency regulations that induced quasi-contractual

---

175. *Ibid.*, para. 799.
176. *Ibid.* (emphasis in the original).
177. *Ibid.*, para. 801.
178. *Ibid.*, para. 802.
179. *Ibid.*, citing from *Marvin Roy Feldman Karpa v. Mexico* [hereinafter *Feldman v. Mexico*], ICSID No. ARB(AF)/99/1, Award, (16 December 2002), para. 148, which, however, dealt with a claim of expropriation, not Article 1105. This feature has been criticized by writers: *see*, Kahn, *supra* n. 150, at 151.
180. *Glamis v. United States*, Award, (8 June 2009), para. 637.
181. Kahn, *supra* n. 150, at 151.
182. *Glamis v. United States*, Award, (8 June 2009), para. 809.
183. *Ibid.*, para. 810.
184. *Ibid.*, para. 811.
185. *Ibid.*
186. *Ibid.* In this context, the tribunal added that 'as no duty of the State was thus created ensuring maintenance of Claimant's reasonable expectations, the Tribunal also need not address what level of repudiation of this duty would be required to find such an act a violation of State obligations under Article 1105'.

investment'.[187] Finally, the tribunal made this important statement: 'a claimant cannot have a legitimate expectation that the host country will not pass legislation that will affect it'.[188] The tribunal therefore rejected all of the claimant's allegations of legitimate expectations breaches.

In sum, the *Glamis* award is the most comprehensive analysis of the concept of legitimate expectations under Article 1105. For the first time, the award addressed the issue whether an investor's expectations arising from a *contract* can be the basis of a *legal* claim of breach of legitimate expectations under Article 1105. Also, while the award reiterated *Thunderbird's* finding that an investor's expectations must be 'reasonable and justifiable', it further clarified that such *objective* expectations must be based on *specific* 'definitive, unambiguous and repeated' *assurances* or *commitments* made by the host State to the investor 'purposely and specifically' to 'induce' its investment. The full implication of these important findings will be discussed in the next section.

[5]   Conclusion

To date, no NAFTA tribunal has come to the conclusion that a host State stood in violation of an investor's legitimate expectations under Article 1105. Tribunals have nonetheless made a number of important findings on the scope of this concept. In the following paragraphs, nine observations will be made on NAFTA case law.

First, the reasoning of some of the earlier awards suggests that these tribunals did *not* view the concept of legitimate expectations as a *stand-alone* element of the FET standard. For instance, the *Waste Management* tribunal (which did not, however, deal with any specific allegations of breach of legitimate expectations) stated that 'the minimum standard of treatment of fair and equitable treatment' was infringed when State conduct was 'arbitrary, grossly unfair, unjust or idiosyncratic, is discriminatory ... or involves a lack of due process ...'.[189] The tribunal added that '*in applying this standard* it is *relevant* that the treatment is in breach of representations made by the host State which were reasonably relied on by the claimant'.[190] Thus, for the tribunal the concept of legitimate expectations is only relevant in the context of its assessment of whether or not State conduct is arbitrary, grossly unfair, etc. Meanwhile, the *Merrill & Ring* ruling is silent on the question,[191] and the *Grand River* tribunal does not seem to take a position.[192]

---

187. *Ibid.*, para. 812.
188. *Ibid.*, para. 813.
189. *Waste Management v. Mexico*, Award, (30 April 2004), para. 98.
190. *Ibid.* (emphasis added).
191. *Merrill & Ring Forestry L.P. v. Canada* [hereinafter *Merrill & Ring v. Canada*], UNCITRAL, Award, (31 March 2010), para. 233.
192. *Grand River Enterprises Six Nations, Ltd., et al. v. United States* [hereinafter *Grand River v. United States*], UNCITRAL, Award, (12 January 2011), para. 140 ('The Tribunal understands the concept of reasonable or legitimate expectations in the NAFTA context to correspond with those expectations upon which an investor is entitled to rely as a result of representations or conduct by a state party').

Some writers have argued that the *Thunderbird* award marked a milestone in that it was the first one to recognize the concept of legitimate expectations as part of the FET standard.[193] A statement made by Wälde in his separate opinion suggests that this is the case. He indicated that he concurred with his colleagues on 'the general view that the principle of legitimate expectation forms part, i.e., a subcategory, of the duty to afford fair and equitable treatment under Article 1105 of the NAFTA'.[194] In any event, Wälde's separate opinion explicitly endorsed this position:

> One can observe over the last years a significant growth in the role and scope of the legitimate expectation principle, from an earlier function as a subsidiary interpretative principle to reinforce a particular interpretative approach chosen, to its current role as a self standing subcategory and independent basis for a claim under the 'fair and equitable standard' as under Art. 1105 of the NAFTA.[195]

Yet, the issue is not entirely clear. The *Thunderbird* award only goes so far as to say that the concept of 'legitimate expectations' relates, *within the context of the NAFTA framework*, to a situation where ...'.[196] The tribunal simply does not go on to discuss whether the concept is one element of the FET standard under Article 1105.

The *Glamis* tribunal's reasoning *does* suggest that the concept of legitimate expectations is an element of the FET standard. However, it is open to criticism. On the question of the evolution of custom, the tribunal first came to the following conclusion:

> It therefore appears that, although situations may be more varied and complicated today than in the 1920s, the level of scrutiny is the same. The fundamentals of the *Neer* standard thus still apply today: to violate the customary international law minimum standard of treatment codified in Article 1105 of the NAFTA, an act must be sufficiently egregious and shocking—a gross denial of justice, manifest arbitrariness, blatant unfairness, a complete lack of due process, evident discrimination, or a manifest lack of reasons—so as to fall below accepted international standards and constitute a breach of Article 1105(1) (...). The standard for finding a breach of the customary international law minimum standard of treatment therefore remains as stringent as it was under *Neer* ... .[197]

It is noteworthy that, in this passage, the tribunal does not make any reference to legitimate expectations in its listing of acts susceptible of breaching the FET standard under Article 1105. Earlier in the award, the tribunal thoroughly explained the U.S. position that an investor's expectations cannot form the basis of a stand-alone claim under NAFTA Chapter 11 and that there exists no customary international law rule requiring a State to protect such expectations.[198] The tribunal never expressly responded to these arguments. In the award's section where the tribunal found it 'appropriate to address, in turn, each of the State obligations Claimant asserts are potential parts of the protection afforded by fair and equitable treatment',[199] the

---

193. Fietta, *supra* n. 107, at 425.
194. *Thunderbird v. Mexico*, Separate Opinion of Thomas Wälde, (1 December 2005), para. 1.
195. *Ibid.*, para. 37.
196. *Thunderbird v. Mexico*, Award, (26 January 2006), para. 147 (emphasis added).
197. *Glamis v. United States*, Award, (8 June 2009), para. 616.
198. *Ibid.*, paras. 575–576.
199. *Ibid.*, para. 618.

tribunal simply refrained from analyzing whether or not legitimate expectations constitute an element of the FET standard under Article 1105. One explanation for this omission may be the fact that the tribunal had already concluded at this stage that the United States had not breached Article 1105 on this ground. Thus, the tribunal explained that since 'no specific assurances were made to induce Claimant's "reasonable and justifiable expectations"' it 'need not determine the level, or characteristics, of state action in contradiction of those expectations that would be necessary to constitute a violation of Article 1105'.[200] The concept of legitimate expectations is in fact only introduced at the very end of the tribunal's reasoning on this issue. In the one-paragraph section of the award entitled 'Final Disposition of the Tribunal with respect to the Scope of the Fair and Equitable Legal Standard', the tribunal made this final theoretical remark regarding Article 1105:

> The Tribunal holds that Claimant has not met its burden of proving that something other than the fundamentals of the *Neer* standard apply today. The Tribunal therefore holds that a violation of the customary international law minimum standard of treatment, as codified in Article 1105 of the NAFTA, requires an act that is sufficiently egregious and shocking—a gross denial of justice, manifest arbitrariness, blatant unfairness, a complete lack of due process, evident discrimination, or a manifest lack of reasons—so as to fall below accepted international standards and constitute a breach of Article 1105. *Such a breach may be exhibited by* a 'gross denial of justice or manifest arbitrariness falling below acceptable international standards;' *or the creation by the State of objective expectations in order to induce investment and the subsequent repudiation of those expectations.*[201]

The last sentence of this quote makes it clear that the tribunal considers legitimate expectations as an element of the FET standard. Thus, the concept is mentioned along with *other elements* of the FET standard under Article 1105.[202] Yet, this reference to the obligation to respect an investor's legitimate expectations seems contradictory to the first sentence of the quote stating that 'the fundamentals of the *Neer* standard apply today'. Clearly, the concept of legitimate expectations goes far beyond the traditional definition of the MST.[203] The tribunal, on the one hand, seems to restrict the scope of the FET standard by referring to the *Neer* fundamentals, while, on the other hand, extending it by including this new obligation. These different approaches are difficult

---

200. *Ibid.*, para. 622.
201. *Ibid.*, para. 627 (emphasis added).
202. This conclusion is also supported by this other passage (at para. 828): 'Thus addressing the record as a whole, the Tribunal holds that Claimant has not established that the acts complained of fall short of the customary international law minimum standard of treatment. The complained-of acts were not egregious and shocking—a gross denial of justice, manifest arbitrariness, blatant unfairness, a complete lack of due process, evident discrimination, or a manifest lack of reasons. *There was no specific inducement of Claimant's expectations'* (emphasis added).
203. *See*, Kahn, *supra* n. 150, at 148, 153-154: 'the tribunal's expectations-based article 1105 standard is especially removed from Neer (...). It is disingenuous to equate this standard with "shocking" or "outrageous" behavior, whether the conduct is judged by 1926 or modern sensibilities. While Glamis commendably recognizes expectation protection as a feature of article 1105, its view that the combination of language from U.S. and NAFTA takings jurisprudence equates with Neer is preposterous'.

to reconcile. For all of these reasons, the *Glamis* award does not seem to be the most solid precedent in favor of recognizing the concept of legitimate expectations as an element of the FET standard.

In sum, the *Glamis* award is the only award that supports (to some extent) the view that legitimate expectations constitute a stand-alone element of the FET standard under Article 1105. This situation is in sharp contrast with the position adopted by the majority of *non-NAFTA* awards which have recognized that the FET standard encompass an obligation to protect an investor's legitimate expectation.[204] For instance, the *Saluka* tribunal stated that the FET standard was 'closely tied to the notion of legitimate expectations which is the dominant element of the standard'.[205] The vast majority of writers also believe that the concept of legitimate expectations is one of the elements of the FET standard.[206]

In the present author's view, the *Mobil* tribunal adopted a more convincing approach. It did not include legitimate expectations in its definition of the FET standard under Article 1105,[207] but added that the concept 'will be a relevant factor' in assessing whether or not any breach of the FET standard has occurred:

> On the basis of the NAFTA case-law and the parties' arguments, the Tribunal summarizes the applicable standard in relation to Article 1105 as follows:
> (1) the minimum standard of treatment guaranteed by Article 1105 is that which is reflected in customary international law on the treatment of aliens;
> (2) the fair and equitable treatment standard in customary international law will be infringed by conduct attributable to a NAFTA Party and harmful to a claimant that is arbitrary, grossly unfair, unjust or idiosyncratic, or is discriminatory and exposes a claimant to sectional or racial prejudice, or involves a lack of due process leading to an outcome which offends judicial propriety.
> (3) in determining whether that standard has been violated it will be a relevant factor if the treatment is made against the background of
> (i) clear and explicit representations made by or attributable to the NAFTA host State in order to induce the investment, and

---

204. *See*, case law examined in: Vandevelde, *supra* n. 27, at 66 ff. A number of tribunals have, however, taken a different position (*see*, cases referred to at *infra* n. 212).
205. *Saluka v. Czech Republic*, Partial Award, (17 March 2006), para. 302.
206. Tudor, *supra* n. 3, at 155, 163-168, 154; Choudhury, *supra* n. 44, at 316-317; Kläger, *supra* n. 13, at 117-118, 154, 164; R. Kreindler, *Fair and Equitable Treatment – A Comparative International Law Approach*, 3(3) Transnational Disp. Mgmt. 9 (2006); Fietta, *supra* n. 107, at 432; Fietta, *supra* n. 72, at 397-398; Thomas J. Westcott, *Recent Practice on Fair and Equitable Treatment*, 8(3) J. World Invest. & Trade 425 (2007); Schreuer & Dolzer, *supra* n. 71, at 134-135; Andrew Newcombe & Luis Paradell, *Law and Practice of Investment Treaties: Standards of Treatment*, 279-280, 282-283 (Kluwer 2009); Yannaca-Small, *supra* n. 44, at 129; UNCTAD, *supra* n. 11, at 62, 63.
207. *Mobil Investments Canada Inc. and Murphy Oil Corporation v. Canada* [hereinafter *Mobil v. Canada*], ICSID No. ARB(AF)/07/4, Decision on Liability and on Principles of Quantum, (22 May 2012), para. 152 ('the fair and equitable treatment standard in customary international law will be infringed by conduct attributable to a NAFTA Party and harmful to a claimant that is arbitrary, grossly unfair, unjust or idiosyncratic, or is discriminatory and exposes a claimant to sectional or racial prejudice, or involves a lack of due process leading to an outcome which offends judicial propriety').

    (ii) were, by reference to an objective standard, reasonably relied on by the investor, and

    (iii) were subsequently repudiated by the NAFTA host State.[208]

Thus, for the *Mobil* tribunal, while the host State's failure to respect an investor's legitimate expectations would *not in itself* constitute a breach of the FET standard, it remains that such a 'factor' may be taken into account when assessing whether or not *other* elements of the standard have been breached (i.e., whether State conduct was arbitrary, grossly unfair, involved a lack of due process, etc.). It should be added that another recent award (*Cargill*) also gave a general definition of what constitutes a violation of the FET standard under Article 1105 without specifically referring to the concept of legitimate expectations.[209] In fact, the *Cargill* tribunal concluded that 'no evidence' had been put forward by the claimant to sustain its argument that NAFTA Parties are bound to 'provide a stable and predictable environment in which reasonable expectations are upheld'.[210] It added that no such requirement exists 'in the NAFTA or in customary international law, at least where such expectations do not arise from a contract or quasi-contractual basis'.[211]

    In the context outside of NAFTA, a limited number of tribunals have also concluded that there is *no* legal obligation for the host State to protect an investor's legitimate expectations. They have held that such expectations are only one relevant factor amongst others to determine a breach of the FET standard.[212] The reasons why this approach is sound are examined in the next paragraph (our second observation).

    Second, NAFTA Parties have consistently objected to the view that the concept of legitimate expectations imposes any legal obligation, *solely on its own,* under Article

---

208. *Ibid.,* para. 152.
209. *Cargill Inc. v. Mexico*, ICSID Case no. ARB(AF)/05/2, Award, (18 September 2009), para. 296.
210. *Ibid.,* para. 289.
211. *Ibid.,* para. 290.
212. *See,* for instance, *CMS Gas Transmission Company v. Argentina*, ICSID Case No. ARB/01/8, Decision on Annulment, (25 September 2007), para. 89 ('[a]lthough legitimate expectations might arise by reason of a course of dealing between the investor and the host State, these are not, as such, legal obligations, though they may be relevant to the application of the fair and equitable treatment clause contained in the BIT'); *MTD Equity Sdn Bhd and MTD Chile SA v. Chile*, ICSID No. ARB/01/7, Decision on Annulment, (16 February 2007), paras. 67–69 ('The Committee can appreciate some aspects of these criticisms. For example the TECMED Tribunal's apparent reliance on the foreign investor's expectations as the source of the host State's obligations (such as the obligation to compensate for expropriation) is questionable. The obligations of the host State towards foreign investors derive from the terms of the applicable investment treaty and not from any set of expectations investors may have or claim to have. A tribunal which sought to generate from such expectations a set of rights different from those contained in or enforceable under the BIT might well exceed its powers, and if the difference were material might do so manifestly'. But the tribunal added that 'legitimate expectations generated as a result of the investor's dealings with the competent authorities of the host State may be relevant to the application of the guarantees contained in an investment treaty'); *AWG Group v. Argentina*, UNCITRAL, Decision on Liability, (30 July 2010), Judge Nikken's Separate Opinion, para. 3 ('The assertion that fair and equitable treatment includes an obligation to satisfy or not to frustrate the legitimate expectations of the investor at the time of his/her investment does not correspond, in any language, to the ordinary meaning to be given to the terms "fair and equitable". Therefore, prima facie, such a conception of fair and equitable treatment is at odds with the rule of interpretation of international customary law expressed in Article 31.1 of the Vienna Convention on the Law of Treaties'). *See also*: Picherack, *supra* n. 66, at 277-278.

1105.[213] Thus, both the United States[214] and Canada[215] have insisted that the so-called 'obligation' to protect an investor's legitimate expectations is *not* part of the customary international law minimum standard of treatment of aliens. This is because claimants have not put forward any evidence of State practice and opinio juris to support such a claim. Thus, for Canada:

> [W]hile NAFTA tribunals have considered as a relevant element the repudiation of the legitimate expectations of foreign investors, assuming they reasonably existed at the time of the investment and are based on specific representations ... they have not found that the failure to fulfill legitimate expectations constituted in and of itself a breach of a rule of customary international law part of the minimum standard of treatment under Article 1105.[216]

NAFTA Parties are right on this point. No tribunal has gone through the exercise of determining the customary nature of the concept of legitimate expectations. No attempt has been made to comprehensively examine State practice and opinio juris. In the

---

213. It should be noted, however, that all NAFTA Parties agree that the issue is relevant to a claim of regulatory expropriation *under NAFTA Article 1110. See,* for instance, the position of the United States described in: *Grand River v. United States,* Award, (12 January 2011), para. 127.

214. *See,* for instance, *Grand River v. United States,* US Counter-Memorial, (22 December 2008), at 96, 97 ('As a matter of international law, although an investor may develop its own expectations about the legal regime that governs its investment, those expectations do not impose a legal obligation on the State') and at 99 ('Claimants submit no evidence of State practice establishing a legal obligation not to frustrate an investor's expectations formed at the time the investor made its investment. State practice, in fact, tends to support the opposite view. As Claimants acknowledge, under customary international law, States may regulate to achieve legitimate objectives to benefit the public welfare and will not incur liability solely because the change interferes with an investor's "expectations" about the state of the business environment. The protection of public health falls squarely within that regulatory authority under international law').

215. For instance, *United Parcel Service of America Inc. v. Government of Canada* [hereinafter *UPS v. Canada*], UNCITRAL, Canada's Counter-Memorial, (22 June 2005), paras. 941–945; *ibid.,* Canada's Rejoinder, (6 October 2005), para. 296 ('The Claimant argues that fair and equitable treatment includes the obligation to protect legitimate expectations (...). The Claimant cites no *opinio juris* or state practice for the assertion that legitimate expectations, transparency or general fairness constitute customary rules of international law. In any event, the Claimant would be unable to prove that a customary obligation to protect legitimate expectations exists. The concept of legitimate expectations can only be relevant where a legal obligation exists'); *Merrill & Ring v. Canada,* Canada's Counter-Memorial, (13 May 2008), paras. 508, 509 ('The "obligation" to protect the legitimate expectations of an investor is not part of the customary international law minimum standard of treatment of aliens. There is no such "obligation" under Article 1105'); *Vito G. Gallo v. Canada,* UNCITRAL, Canada's Statement of Defence, (15 September 2008), para. 196; *ibid.,* Canada's Counter-Memorial, (29 June 2010), para. 272; *Mobil v. Canada,* Canada's Counter-Memorial (1 December 2009), paras. 242, 252–253, 268, 270; *ibid.,* Decision on Liability and on Principles of Quantum, (22 May 2012), paras. 123, 124 (describing Canada's position).

216. *Mobil v. Canada,* Decision on Liability and on Principles of Quantum, (22 May 2012), para. 124 (quoting from Canada's Counter-Memorial, (1 December 2009), para. 270). It should be noted that in its pleadings Canada offers an alternative position (*Ibid.,* para. 125) whereby there are four 'prerequisites necessary for the expectations of a foreign investor to be entitled to protection' i.e. 'First, the Claimants' legitimate expectations must be based on objective expectations; second, the investor must have relied on a specific assurance by the state to induce the investment; third, the legitimate expectations must be those which existed at the time the investment was made and; fourth, to assess the legitimacy of the expectations, all circumstances must be taken into account'.

present author's view, there is little support for the assertion that there exists under customary international law any obligation for host States to protect investors' legitimate expectations.[217]

Third, supporters of the inclusion of the concept of legitimate expectations as one of the elements of the FET standard have never carried out the exercise of establishing that the concept has been recognized as a rule of customary international law. They instead rely on the fact that the concept is said to be widely accepted *under municipal law*.[218] The separate opinion of Wälde in *Thunderbird* accurately illustrates such an argument:

> The 'fair and equitable standard' can not be derived from subjective personal or cultural sentiments; it must be anchored in objective rules and principles reflecting, in an authoritative and universal or at least widespread way, the contemporary attitude of modern national and international economic law. The wide acceptance of the 'legitimate expectations' principle therefore supports the concept that it is indeed part of 'fair and equitable treatment' as owed by governments to foreign investors under modern investment treaties and under Article 1105 of the NAFTA.[219]

A number of writers (and tribunals[220]) have thus argued that the concept of legitimate expectations is a general principle of law because it is a recognized rule in many domestic legal systems.[221] For this reason, they consider that arbitral tribunals should apply this principle of law in resolving disputes as a source of international law pursuant to Article 38(1)(c) of the ICJ Statute. One variation of this argument is to view the concept of legitimate expectations as based on the requirement of good faith, which is itself one of the general principles referred to at Article 38(1)(c) of the ICJ Statute.[222]

---

217. Yannaca-Small, *supra* n. 44, at 130. *Contra*: Dolzer & Schreuer, *supra* n. 71, at 135 ('there is authority to the effect that transparency and the investor's legitimate expectations are protected even without a treaty guarantee of FET').
218. Diehl, *supra* n. 3, at 360, provides another reason: 'the normative justification for the legal protection of legitimate expectations is very strong. The protection of such expectations is to be derived from the fairness element of the FET standard. Fairness requires protection of legitimate expectations for one main reason: Expectations are central to autonomy and planning of one's life or in a business context of one's business development (rule of law/certainty theory'.
219. *Thunderbird v. Mexico*, Separate Opinion of Thomas Wälde, (1 December 2005), para. 30.
220. *Total S.A. v. Argentina*, ICSID Case No. ARB/04/01, Decision on Liability (27 December 2010), para. 128; *Thunderbird v. Mexico*, Separate Opinion of Thomas Wälde, (1 December 2005), paras. 27–28.
221. Snodgrass, *supra* n. 75, at 53; Diehl, *supra* n. 3, at 170-174, 551; Kingsbury & Schill, *supra* n. 56, at 11-12; Kläger, *supra* n. 13, at 278 ('All principles and sub-principales of fair et equitable treatment – sovereignty, the protection of legitimate expectations, pacta sunt servanda, non-discrimination, sustainable development, fair procedure, due process, denial of justice, transparency and proportionality – are accepted principal of international law deeply rooted within one or several of the sources of international law'). *Contra*: Paparinskis, *supra* n. 18, at 255-256 ('even among the unrepresentative sample of legal systems of the traditional claimant States considered, there are significant differences in the way in which legitimate expectations are addressed, in particular regarding the distinction between substantive expectations and expectations relating to due process'). *See*, more generally: S. Schønberg, *Legitimate Expectations in Administrative Law* (Oxford U. Press 2000).
222. *Total S.A. v. Argentina*, Decision on Liability (27 December 27, 2010), para. 128; *Thunderbird v. Mexico*, Separate Opinion of Thomas Wälde, (1 December 2005), para. 25.

In the present author's view, interpreting legitimate expectations as a general principle of law is of limited relevance in the specific context of Article 1105. As mentioned above,[223] the reasoning of some NAFTA tribunals (*ADF*[224] and *Merrill & Ring*[225]) seems to suggest that when interpreting Article 1105, they are allowed to look *beyond* customary international law at other sources of international law, including general principles of law. Yet, the position of the majority of NAFTA tribunals is that 'the content of the obligation imposed by Article 1105 must be determined by reference to customary international law, not to standards contained (…) [within] other sources, unless those sources reflect relevant customary international law'.[226] In other words, based on the clear guidance provided by the binding FTC Note, NAFTA tribunals should look *solely* to custom as a source of international law in their interpretation of Article 1105, not at general principles of law.

In any event, it is not at all clear to what extent relying on the concept of legitimate expectations as a general principle of law would be helpful to a NAFTA tribunal. It is generally recognized that the concept of general principles of law 'was inserted into Article 38 [of the ICJ Statute] as a source of law, to close the gap that might be uncovered in international law and solve this problem which is known legally as *non liquet*'.[227] In other words, such principles were 'intended to offer judges an additional source of law in the event of absence or unclearness in the relevant treaties and custom'.[228] It has been argued that the minimum standard of treatment is sufficiently developed with respect to the scope of protection that States must accord to foreign investors (and their investments) without the need for tribunals to resort to any general principle, including legitimate expectations.[229]

Fourth, all tribunals have defined the obligation to protect the legitimate expectations of an investor quite *narrowly*. Tribunals have thus repeatedly *qualified* the concept in several ways in order to significantly *reduce its scope*. The narrow approach that has been consistently adopted by NAFTA tribunals remains in sharp contrast with the stance taken by a number of non-NAFTA tribunals.

Some of these non-NAFTA awards have read into the FET standard an obligation for the host State to maintain a stable legal and business environment.[230] One

---

223. *See*, at Chapter 2 section §2.03[A][3].
224. *ADF v. United States*, Award, (9 January 2003), paras. 184, 185.
225. *Merrill & Ring v. Canada*, Award, (31 March 2010), para. 184.
226. *Grand River v. United States*, Award, (12 January 2011), paras. 176, 181, 219.
227. M.N. Shaw, *International Law* 98 (6th ed., Cambridge U. Press 2008).
228. Tudor, *supra* n. 3, at 94.
229. Paparinskis, *supra* n. 18, at 256 ('is not the case that, in the absence of a hypothetical rule on expectations, the international standard would be entirely lacking in criteria to apply to evaluating the international lawfulness of changes in the domestic legal system: (…) the considerations of non-arbitrariness, transparency, and due process, and most likely also non-discrimination, would still discipline the host State').
230. *CMS Gas Transmission Company v. Argentina*, Award, (12 May 2005), para. 274 ('there can be no doubt, therefore, that a stable legal and business environment is an essential element of fair and equitable treatment'), para. 284 ('In fact, the Treaty standard of fair and equitable treatment and its connection with the required stability and predictability of the business environment, founded on solemn legal and contractual commitments, is not different from the international law minimum standard and its evolution under customary law'); *Enron Corporation and Ponderosa Assets, L.P. v. Argentina*, Award, (22 May 2007), para. 260 ('Thus, the

161

prominent illustration of that trend is the ruling by the *Tecmed* tribunal, which interpreted an FET clause as requiring the host State to 'provide to international investments treatment that does not affect the *basic expectations* that were taken into account by the foreign investor to make the investment'.[231] The tribunal then explained that a foreign investor should expect the host State to act:

> free from ambiguity and totally transparently in its relations with the foreign investor, so that it may know beforehand any and all rules and regulations that will govern its investments, as well as the goals of the relevant policies and adminis- trative practices or directives, to be able to plan its investment and comply with such regulations.[232]

A foreign investor should also expect the host State to act *consistently*, i.e., to act 'without arbitrarily revoking any pre-existing decisions or permits issued by the State that were relied upon by the investor to assume its commitments as well as to plan and launch its commercial and business activities'.[233] The extensive interpretation given by the *Tecmed* tribunal and others has been rightly criticized by many for being too demanding of host States and 'nearly impossible to achieve'.[234] Worse, this approach 'would potentially prevent the host State from introducing any legitimate regulatory change, let alone from undertaking a regulatory reform that may be called for'.[235] Some writers believe, on the contrary, that the so-called requirement of a stable legal and business framework is in fact *itself* one autonomous element contained within the FET standard.[236] This proposition has been contested by a number of other scholars.[237]

Tribunal concludes that a key element of fair and equitable treatment is the requirement of a 'stable framework for the investment', which has been prescribed by a number of decisions. Indeed, this interpretation has been considered 'an emerging standard of fair and equitable treatment in international law'); *Duke Energy Electroquil Partners and Electroquil SA v. Ecuador*, ICSID No. ARB/04/19, Award, (18 August 2008), para. 339; *LG&E Energy Corp v. Argentina*, Decision on Liability, (3 October 2006), paras. 124, 125, 131; *PSEG Global et al. v. Turkey*, ICSID No. ARB/02/5, Award, (19 January 2007), paras. 246–256; *Occidental Explora- tion and Production Co v. Ecuador*, LCIA No. UN 3467, Award, (1 July 2004), paras. 183, 190, 196, 252, 253.

231. *Técnicas Medioambientales Tecmed, S.A. v. Mexico*, ICSID No. ARB (AF)/00/2, Award, (29 May 2003), para. 154 (emphasis added).
232. *Ibid.*
233. *Ibid.*
234. UNCTAD, *supra* n. 11, at 65.
235. *Ibid.*, at 67.
236. Tudor, *supra* n. 3, at 169; T. Weiler & I. Laird, *Standards of Treatment*, in *The Oxford Handbook of International Investment Law*, 276-277 (Peter Muchlinski, Federico Ortino & Christoph Schreuer eds., Oxford U. Press 2008); Westcott, *supra* n. 206, at 425; Christina Knahr, *Fair and Equitable Treatment and its Relationship with other Treatment Standards*, in *Austrian Arb. Yb 2009*, 504 (Christian Klausegger et al. eds., C.H. Beck, Stämpfli & Manz 2009).
237. Newcombe & Paradell, *supra* n. 206, at 286 ('While some awards to date might suggest that the requirement for a stable and predictable framework for investment is an independent element of fair and equitable treatment, caution should be exercised in referring to freestanding obligations of stability and predictability. The majority of cases where tribunals have invoked the element of stability and predictability have arisen in contexts where there was reliance on specific representations or undertakings and the investors in question had acquired invest- ments with those legitimate expectations. In these cases, tribunals have found that the legal framework cannot "be dispensed with altogether when specific commitments to the contrary have been made". When the host state has made no specific assurances or guarantees linked

In contrast, not a single NAFTA tribunal (with the possible exception of *Merrill &
Ring*, discussed in the next paragraph) has pinpointed an obligation to maintain a
stable legal and business framework as a constitutive element of the concept of
legitimate expectations. In fact, only Wälde's separate opinion in *Thunderbird* supports the view that 'greater transparency, clarity and predictability' must 'guide the
process of both defining the conditions of the legitimate expectations principle under
Article 1105 and of applying it to the particular facts of a specific situation'.[238]

As mentioned above, the one possible exception to this line of consistent case law
is the *Merrill & Ring* award. The tribunal first acknowledged that in the case at hand,
Canada had not made any representations to the investor.[239] Because of such a lack of
representation, the tribunal stated that 'if it were necessary to reach a decision on the
question, the Tribunal would be likely to conclude ... that Canada had not contravened
the provisions of Article 1105(1)'.[240] In spite of this conclusion, the tribunal nevertheless made the following controversial statement obiter dictum:

> The Investor raises the violation of its legitimate expectations as another issue.
> While it is clear that no representations have been made by Canada to induce the
> Investor to make a particular decision or to engage in conduct that is later
> frustrated, any investor will have an expectation that its business may be con-
> ducted in a normal framework free of interference from government regulations
> which are not underpinned by appropriate public policy objectives. Emergency
> measures or regulations addressed to social well-being are evidently within the
> normal functions of a government and it is not legitimate for an investor to expect
> to be exempt from them. Yet, regulations which end-up creating benefits for a
> certain industry, to the detriment of an investor, might be incompatible with what
> that investor might reasonably expect from a government.[241]

This passage is very similar to other broad interpretations that have been given by
non-NAFTA tribunals on the stability of the legal environment.[242] In any event, it is not
at all clear what the tribunal means when it states that the 'investor will have an
expectation' that the government will refrain from any interference whatsoever. Is this
a reference to any general expectation that an investor may have when doing business

---

to specific acquired rights, such as in a license or permit, tribunals are less likely to find there
is a legitimate expectation that the legal framework will not change'). *See also*: Picherack, *supra*
n. 66, at 271, 278-282.

238. *Thunderbird v. Mexico*, Separate Opinion of Thomas Wälde, (1 December 2005), para. 36.
239. *Merrill & Ring v. Canada*, Award, (31 March 2010), para. 233. Later in the award (at para. 242),
the tribunal reiterated that there was a 'complete absence of evidence of any representation by
Canada to the Investor which might be said to have induced or even encouraged its
investment'.
240. *Ibid.*, para. 242. But the tribunal explained (at para. 243) that it was not 'necessary' to reach a
decision on the matter since it decided to examine instead whether the investor had proven any
damages for the alleged breaches. It ultimately concluded that no damage was proven (para.
266).
241. *Ibid.*, para. 233.
242. This is clear from other passages of the award (*Ibid.*, at para. 232) where the tribunal noted that
'the stability of the legal environment is also an issue to be considered in respect of fair and
equitable treatment', adding that 'State practice and jurisprudence have consistently supported
such a requirement in order to avoid sudden and arbitrary alterations of the legal framework
governing the investment'.

abroad? The first sentence of the quoted passage suggests that this is in fact a reference to the *legal* concept of legitimate expectations. This would mean, in turn, that mere 'interference' by a government regulation that is 'not underpinned by appropriate public policy objectives' could breach an investor's expectation. The existence of such a broad obligation would require a tribunal to determine each time whether or not a regulation is in fact in line with the host State's 'public policy objectives' and, moreover, to verify the 'appropriateness' of such objectives. Earlier in the award, the tribunal stated that '[c]ustomary international law has for long recognized that the minimum standard of treatment may be curtailed for reasons of public policy, which necessarily has to pursue a genuine public policy'.[243] The tribunal does not provide any reasons for the adoption of such a broadly defined obligation. It is submitted that future tribunals should not follow this approach.

Fifth, all NAFTA tribunals that have examined the concept have endorsed the four-elements definition of legitimate expectations adopted by the *Thunderbird* tribunal. As mentioned above, the tribunal defined the concept as follows:

> Having considered recent investment case law and the good faith principle of international customary law, the concept of 'legitimate expectations' relates, within the context of the NAFTA framework, to a situation where a Contracting Party's conduct creates reasonable and justifiable expectations on the part of an investor (or investment) to act in reliance on said conduct, such that a failure by the NAFTA party to honour those expectations could cause the investor (or investment) to suffer damages.[244]

In fact, this definition reflects an earlier statement made by the *Metalclad* tribunal to the effect that legitimate expectations must be reasonable in the circumstances and be based on specific representations made by governmental officials.[245] As mentioned above, the *Waste Management* tribunal also referred to the same three basic points ('breach of representations made by the host State which were reasonably relied on by the claimant').[246] As subsequently pointed out by the *Mobil* tribunal,[247] these different statements suggest that a legitimate expectations claim requires the following *four elements*:

-   Conduct or representations have been made by the host State.
-   The claimant has relied on such conduct or representations to make its investment.
-   Such reliance by the claimant on these representations was 'reasonable'.

243. *Ibid.*, para. 224.
244. *Thunderbird v. Mexico,* Award, (26 January 2006), para. 147.
245. *Metalclad v. Mexico*, Award, (30 August 2000), para. 89.
246. *Waste Management v. Mexico*, Award, (30 April 2004), para. 98.
247. *Mobil v. Canada*, Decision on Liability and on Principles of Quantum, (22 May 2012), para. 152 ('In determining whether that standard has been violated it will be a relevant factor if the treatment is made against the background of (i) clear and explicit representations made by or attributable to the NAFTA host State in order to induce the investment, and (ii) were, by reference to an objective standard, reasonably relied on by the investor, and (iii) were subsequently repudiated by the NAFTA host State'). *See also*, at para. 154.

– The host State subsequently repudiated these representations therefore causing damages to the investor.[248]

Sixth, subsequent NAFTA tribunals have all followed these four requirements. They
have also continued to further *qualify* and *narrowly* define these requirements. The
most significant development came three years later in 2009 when the *Glamis* tribunal
rendered its award. This award is important for having greatly clarified the scope of an
investor's legitimate expectations as protected under Article 1105. In its ruling, the
tribunal reiterated *Thunderbird's* proposition that an investor's expectations must be
'reasonable and justifiable'. The requirement is also recognized by other non-NAFTA
awards.[249] What is 'reasonable' of course will depend on the circumstances of the
case.[250]

The *Glamis* award also clarified three fundamental aspects of the concept of
legitimate expectations. First, the expectations must be *objective*. Other tribunals have
come to the same conclusion.[251] As pointed out by one writer, the investor's expectations 'must be objective and reasonable, rather than subjective or held by one party
alone'.[252] This means that an investor 'takes the law of the host State as it finds it and
cannot subsequently complain about the application of that law to its investment'.[253]
The reasonableness of an investor's expectations is therefore a function of its actual
knowledge of the general regulatory framework and political and economical environment of the country in which it plans to invest.[254] The *Duke* tribunal speaks of a
requirement to take into account 'all circumstances, including not only the facts
surrounding the investment, but also the political, socioeconomic cultural and historical conditions prevailing in the host State'.[255] In other words, an investor must assess

---

248. *See*, Fietta, *supra* n. 107, at 430; Picherack, *supra* n. 66, at 276.
249. *Duke Energy Electroquil Partners and Electroquil SA v. Ecuador*, Award, (18 August 2008), para.
340.
250. Newcombe & Paradell, *supra* n. 206, at 277: 'Whether reliance by a foreign investor upon host
state conduct is "reasonable" is a highly contextual inquiry. Tribunals and commentators have
identified a number of factors that are potentially relevant in assessing an investor's reasonable
reliance. These include: (i) the timing and specificity of the representation; (ii) whether there
were any disclaimers by the state; (iii) the position of the person making the representation
within the government hierarchy; (iv) the relative skills and expertise of the parties; (v) the
foresee-ability of reliance; (vii) changes in circumstances or conditions upon which the
representations were based; (viii) the extent to which there were mistaken assumptions; (ix)
the extent to which the investor sought to protect itself for a specific risk; (x) the conduct of the
investor'.
251. *See*, for instance, *LG&E Energy Corp v. Argentina*, Decision on Liability, (3 October 2006), para.
131 (speaking of 'justified expectations of the foreign investor').
252. Kinnear, *supra* n. 35, at 26; Salacuse, *supra* n. 11, at 232.
253. Kinnear, *supra* n. 35, at 22; Dolzer, *supra* n. 28, at 103; *see*: *LG&E Energy Corp v. Argentina*,
Decision on Liability, (3 October 2006), para. 130; Salacuse, *supra* n. 11, at 232; Dolzer &
Schreuer, *supra* n. 71, at 134.
254. UNCTAD, *supra* n. 11, at 71 (referring to several cases); Tudor, *supra* n. 3, at 164-165.
255. *Duke Energy Electroquil Partners and Electroquil SA v. Ecuador*, Award, (18 August 2008), para.
340.

and bear the risk associated to the business it intends to conduct.[256] Case law requires a high degree of due diligence from investors.[257]

The second clarification made by the *Glamis* award is that expectations must be based on *specific* 'definitive, unambiguous and repeated' *assurances* or *commitments* made by the host State to the investor. Non-NAFTA tribunals have also highlighted the requirement of specific representations.[258] As pointed out by Fietta, 'the more specific the assurances that are given, the more likely they are to give rise to some basis for a legitimate expectations-based claim'.[259] The additional qualification mentioned by the *Glamis* tribunal that representations be not only specific, but also 'definitive, unambiguous and repeated' suggests the adoption of an even narrower interpretation of the concept of legitimate expectations. A third qualification made by the *Glamis* award is the fact that any assurances given by the host State to the investor must have been made 'purposely and specifically' to have 'induced' its investment. This qualification has the effect of further narrowing down the scope of application of the concept of legitimate expectations under Article 1105.

Seventh, under Article 1105, legitimate expectations *cannot* be based simply on the host State's existing domestic legislation on foreign investments at the time when the investor makes its investment. This is clear from the *Glamis* award's emphasis on a *threshold* requirement of a *quasi-contractual* relationship between the investor and the host State. Other NAFTA tribunals have also adopted the same position.

Thus, the *Grand River* tribunal held that *general legislation* could not be the source of legitimate expectations, which requires *specific* assurances by the government.[260] The tribunal noted that the 'conduct' of the United States said to be giving rise to some expectations were in fact an international treaty (the Jay Treaty) and its own domestic legislation (U.S. federal Indian law).[261] The tribunal was reluctant to admit that these instruments could 'serve as sources of reasonable or legitimate expectations for the purposes of a NAFTA claim'.[262] Thus, it explained that '[o]rdinarily, reasonable

---

256. Peter Muchlinski, *Caveat Investor'? The Relevance of the Conduct of the Investor Under the Fair and Equitable Treatment Standard*, 55 ICLQ 527, 530 (2006); UNCTAD, *supra* n. 11, at 78 ('Investors have a due diligence obligation to determine the extent of the risk to which they are subjected, including country and regulatory risks, and to have expectations that are reasonable in all the circumstances. In particular, when planning their investments, investors should take account of the conditions in the particular host State, including the standards of governance and regulatory development prevailing in that State').

257. Diehl, *supra* n. 3, at 415, 429.

258. *See*, Vandevelde, *supra* n. 27, at 75 (referring and discussing a number of cases).

259. Fietta, *supra* n. 107, at 431; Yannaca-Small, *supra* n. 44, at 126; Diehl, *supra* n. 3, at 386 ('the cases decided so far suggest that the less formal public communications are, the less likely is the emergence of a legitimate expectation'). *See also*: Newcombe & Paradell, *supra* n. 206, at 279; UNCTAD, *supra* n. 11, at 68.

260. *Grand River v. United States*, Award, (12 January 2011), para. 127. The tribunal decided to examine this question in the award's section dealing with the expropriation claim, but added that its reasoning would also apply to the Article 1105 claim. In this case, the claimant argued that 'as a member of one of the First Nations in North America and the nature of his business activities, which he described as involving trade among sovereign indigenous peoples', he had a 'legitimate expectation not to be subjected to MSA-related regulatory actions by the states of the United States in respect of his tobacco-related activities' (para. 128).

261. *Ibid.*, para. 141.

262. *Ibid.*

or legitimate expectations of the kind protected by NAFTA are those that arise through *targeted representations or assurances* made explicitly or implicitly by a state party'.[263] The tribunal concluded that these instruments could not 'serve as sources of reasonable or legitimate expectations for the purposes of a NAFTA claim'.[264] This is because the investor could not have reasonably relied on the unsettled legal framework of the U.S. federal Indian law to create any expectations.[265] Similarly, the reasoning of the *ADF* tribunal suggests that an investor's legitimate expectations cannot be generated by its sole reliance on domestic *case law* when it decides to make its investment.[266] Thus, the tribunal emphasized upon the requirement of *misleading* representations made by *authorized officials* about such case law. In other words, 'mere silence or evasive statements do not suffice and will not generate legitimate expectations with regard to the status of the law'.[267]

The consistent position adopted by these NAFTA tribunals contrasts with that of other non-NAFTA tribunals that have held that legitimate expectations could even be protected *without any specific* representations made by the host State.[268] For these non-NAFTA tribunals, an investor's expectation could be based merely on the existing domestic legislation of the host State concerning foreign investments (which was later changed) if it can be shown that the investor actually *relied* upon such legislation when deciding to make its investment.[269] Amidst the literature on this issue, this remains a contentious approach.[270]

---

263. *Ibid.*, (emphasis added).

264. *Ibid.*

265. *Ibid.*, para. 142 ('As to U.S. domestic law, given its unsettled nature in relevant respects, it is implausible to find that Mr. Montour could have reasonably expected, and reasonably relied on such an expectation as a prudent investor, that states would refrain from applying the MSA measures to him as they have done'). *See*, C. Lévesque, *Chronique de Droit international économique en 2010-2011 – Investissement*, 49 Can YIL 360 (2011).

266. Diehl, *supra* n. 3, at 400; Yannaca-Small, *supra* n. 44, at 125.

267. Diehl, *supra* n. 3, at 422. *See also*: Choudhury, *supra* n. 44, at 309.

268. *Parkerings-Compagniet AS v. Lithuania*, ICSID No. ARB/05/8, Award, (11 September 2007), para. 131 ('The expectation is legitimate if the investor received an explicit promise or guarantee from the host state, or if implicitly, the host state made assurances or representation that the investor took into account in making the investment. Finally, in the situation where the host state made no assurance or representation, the circumstances surrounding the conclusion of the agreement are decisive to determine if the expectations of the investor are legitimate').

269. *See*, for instance, *Suez, Sociedad General de Aguas de Barcelona S.A., and Vivendi Universal S.A. v. Argentina*, ICSID No. ARB/03/19, Decision on Liability, (30 July 2010), para. 226. *See also*: UNCTAD, *supra* n. 11, at 77.

270. Diehl, *supra* n. 3, at 402 ('Although protection of legitimate expectations based on governmental conduct that does not reach the level of a contract or formal promise may be desirable from a policy point of view, a requirement that an expectation be based on some individualized act of government seems an appropriate limitation. This is especially true in the context of the FET standard - a standard whose wide scope needs to be limited in order to achieve legal certainty and predictability. It is submitted that legitimate expectations should more readily be identified on the basis of individualized administrative conduct or communication than on the basis of general legislation or quasi-legislative administrative rule-making'), at 429 ('legitimate expectations can arise as a result of overt governmental conduct that, while it may take various forms, has to be specific, unambiguous and beneficial to the individual or company towards which it is directed. Legitimate expectations will generally not be based upon legislation or legislative-type regulations, but will derive from targeted and individualized governmental

Eighth, the *Mobil* tribunal has clearly held that an investor's expectations are *not* violated by the simple fact that the host State *changed* the regulation (even drastically) upon which the investor may have based its decision to make its investment. The tribunal added that Article 1105 only protects investors against changes of legislation that are 'arbitrary or grossly unfair or discriminatory':

> This [FET] applicable standard does not require a State to maintain a stable legal and business environment for investments, if this is intended to suggest that the rules governing an investment are not permitted to change, whether to a significant or modest extent. Article 1105 may protect an investor from changes that give rise to an unstable legal and business environment, but only if those changes may be characterized as arbitrary or grossly unfair or discriminatory, or otherwise inconsistent with the customary international law standard. In a complex international and domestic environment, there is nothing in Article 1105 to prevent a public authority from changing the regulatory environment to take account of new policies and needs, even if some of those changes may have far-reaching consequences and effects, and even if they impose significant additional burdens on an investor. Article 1105 is not, and was never intended to amount to, a guarantee against regulatory change, or to reflect a requirement that an investor is entitled to expect no material changes to the regulatory framework within which an investment is made. Governments change, policies changes and rules change. These are facts of life with which investors and all legal and natural persons have to live with. What the foreign investor is entitled to under Article 1105 is that any changes are consistent with the requirements of customary international law on fair and equitable treatment.[271]

It is generally recognized that the requirement for a State to respect an investor's expectations does not mean that it is consequently prevented from regulating.[272] Consequently, many tribunals have held that an investor certainly cannot expect 'that the circumstances prevailing at the time the investment is made remain totally unchanged'.[273] An investor's reasonable expectations must be balanced against the 'host State's legitimate right subsequently to regulate domestic matters in the public interest'.[274] This is the case even if such changes negatively affect a foreign investor.[275] Such conduct would not be considered as breaching the investor's legitimate expectations.[276] As pointed out by some tribunals, States have the right to change their laws:

> It is each State's undeniable right and privilege to exercise its sovereign legislative power. A State has the right to enact, modify or cancel a law at its own discretion. Save for the existence of an agreement, in the form of a stabilisation clause or otherwise, there is nothing objectionable about the amendment brought to the

---

conduct'). The issue is discussed by these authors: Kinnear, *supra* n. 35, at 24; Vandevelde, *supra* n. 27, at 134; Fietta, *supra* n. 72, at 397.

271. *Mobil v. Canada*, Decision on Liability and on Principles of Quantum, (22 May 2012), para. 153.
272. Picherack, *supra* n. 66, at 277.
273. *Saluka v. Czech Republic*, Partial Award, (17 March 2006), para. 305. *See also: Parkerings-Compagniet AS v. Lithuania*, Award, (11 September 2007), para. 333.
274. *Saluka v. Czech Republic*, Partial Award, (17 March 2006), paras. 304–308.
275. UNCTAD, *supra* n. 11, at 74; Diehl, *supra* n. 3, at 429.
276. UNCTAD, *supra* n. 11, at 74.

regulatory framework existing at the time an investor made its investment. As a matter of fact, any businessman or investor knows that laws will evolve over time. What is prohibited however is for a State to act unfairly, unreasonably or inequitably in the exercise of its legislative power.[277]

While investors must therefore anticipate that laws will change over time, they can also expect that 'such changes will be implemented in good faith and in a non-abusive manner and that public-interest arguments will not be used as a disguise for arbitrary and discriminatory measures'.[278] This was the conclusion reached by the *Mobil* tribunal as well.

A ninth point is that representations can be made in the context of a State contract (via a stabilization clause). The existence of a contract *does not* mean however, that *any* violation of that contract by the host State necessarily amounts to a violation of the FET obligation. In other words, the investor may 'expect' that a contract will be executed, but a breach of the contract does not necessarily violate *its legitimate expectations* under the FET standard. This is, in fact, the position taken by several non-NAFTA tribunals.[279] The *Glamis* award confirmed that under Article 1105, an investor's expectation is not violated by the mere fact that the host State (party to a contract with the investor) has breached the contract.

In sum, under Article 1105, an investor's legitimate expectations is *not* a stand alone *element* of the FET standard, but rather a 'factor' that should be taken into account by a tribunal when assessing whether or not *other* elements of the standard have been breached. The different NAFTA cases examined above suggest that a tribunal should consider an investor's expectations when the following criteria are fulfilled:

(1) An investor's expectations must be 'reasonable' and 'justifiable' (*Waste Management*,[280] *Thunderbird*,[281] *Glamis*,[282] *Mobil*[283]).
(2) Such 'objective' expectations must be, at the very least, based on the conduct of the host State (*Thunderbird*,[284] *Grand River*[285]) or on 'representations'

---

277. *Parkerings-Compagniet AS v. Lithuania*, Award, (11 September 2007), para. 332. *See also*: *Continental Casualty v. Argentina*, ICSID No. ARB/03/9, Award, (5 September 2008), para. 258; *EDF (Services) Limited v. Romania*, ICSID No. ARB/05/13, Award, (8 October 2009), para. 217.
278. UNCTAD, *supra* n. 11, at 77.
279. *Parkerings-Compagniet AS v. Lithuania*, Award, (11 September 2007), para. 344; *Gustav FW Hamester GmbH & Co KG v. Ghana*, ICSID No. ARB/07/24, Award, (18 June 2010), para. 337; *Impregilo S.p.A. v. Argentina*, ICSID Case No. ARB/07/17, Final Award, (21 June 2011), para. 292. *See also*: UNCTAD, *supra* n. 11, at 70; Salacuse, *supra* n. 11, at 236; Paparinskis, *supra* n. 18, at 255.
280. *Waste Management v. Mexico*, Award, (30 April 2004), para. 98.
281. *Thunderbird v. Mexico*, Award, (26 January 2006), para. 147.
282. *Glamis v. United States*, Award, (8 June 2009), para. 621.
283. *Mobil v. Canada*, Decision on Liability and on Principles of Quantum, (22 May 2012), para. 152.
284. *Thunderbird v. Mexico*, Award, (26 January 2006), para. 147.
285. *Grand River v. United States*, Award, (12 January 2011), para. 140.

made by the host State (*Metlaclad*,[286] *Waste Management*,[287] *ADF*,[288] *Merrill*,[289] *Mobil*[290]).[291]

(3) Moreover, the *Glamis* tribunal has suggested that an investor's expectations must be based on 'definitive, unambiguous and repeated'[292] specific 'commitments'[293] (or 'assurances'[294]) made by the host State to have 'purposely and specifically induced the investment'[295] by the investor. These findings have been endorsed by subsequent tribunals (implicitly[296] or explicitly[297]) with occasional slight differences in the use of terminology.[298]

---

286. *Metalclad v. Mexico*, Award, (30 August 2000), para. 87.
287. *Waste Management v. Mexico*, Award, (30 April 2004), para. 98.
288. *ADF v. United States*, Award, (9 January 2003), para. 189.
289. *Merrill & Ring v. Canada*, Award, (31 March 2010), para. 150. In the award's section on *expropriation*, the tribunal reiterated the *Thunderbird* and *Glamis* tribunals' statements to the effect that for legitimate expectations 'to give rise to actionable rights requires there to have been some form of representation by the state and reliance by an investor on that representation in making a business decision'.
290. *Mobil v. Canada*, Decision on Liability and on Principles of Quantum, (22 May 2012), para. 156, where the tribunal refers to 'promises' 'made, either expressly or by any pattern of behavior over a ten year period, such as to give rise to a representation that there would not be changes to the regulatory regime'.
291. *Thunderbird v. Mexico*, Award, (26 January 2006), suggesting that representations by the host State would include the opinion of administrative agencies.
292. *Glamis v. United States*, Award, (8 June 2009), para. 802.
293. *Ibid.*, para. 767.
294. *Ibid.*, paras. 800–801.
295. *Ibid.*, para. 766. *See also, ibid.*, para. 767.
296. *Cargill Inc. v. Mexico*, Award, (18 September 2009), para. 290: 'No evidence, however, has been placed before the Tribunal that there is such a requirement in the NAFTA or in customary international law, at least where such expectations do not arise from a *contract or quasi-contractual basis*' (emphasis added).
297. *Mobil v. Canada*, Decision on Liability and on Principles of Quantum, (22 May 2012), para. 170 ('In the absence of evidence indicating that the Claimants were induced to make their investments by clear and explicit representations in relation to any future change to the regulatory framework, or the Benefits Plans, whether by or attributable to the Respondent, the Tribunal concludes that there can be no violation of Article 1105 of the NAFTA on the ground alleged by the Claimants').
298. *See*, for instance, *Grand River v. United States*, Award, (12 January 2011), para. 141, referring to 'targeted representations or assurances' made by the host State. *See also*: *Mobil v. Canada*, Decision on Liability and on Principles of Quantum, (22 May 2012), para. 152 (referring to 'clear and explicit representations' made by the host State), para. 156 ('For the reasons set out below, having carefully studied the record and all the evidence the Tribunal is unable to conclude that any such *'promises' were made, either expressly or by any pattern of behavior over a ten year period, such as to give rise to a representation* that there would not be changes to the regulatory regime. In order to be able to rely upon an expectation that is said to exist, evidence would need to be tendered to show *clear and explicit representations* together with an indication as to reliance being placed upon such representations. The record in this case shows no such evidence, including of any subjectively held expectation that might be claimed to have existed', emphasis added).

(4) An investor must have relied on those representations, commitments or assurances when it decided to make its investment (*Waste Management*,[299] *Thunderbird*,[300] *Grand River*,[301] *Merrill*,[302] *Mobil*[303]).

(5) The host State must have subsequently failed to respect the reasonable and justifiable expectations created by its conduct, which resulted in damages for the investor (*Thunderbird*,[304] *Mobil*[305]).

[C] Transparency

The question of whether or not there exists any obligation of transparency for host States under international investment law is currently amongst the most controversial issues. While a number of writers have concluded that the FET standard includes an obligation of transparency,[306] others have come to the opposite conclusion.[307] Similarly, a 2004 OECD working paper provided that transparency was 'a relatively new

---

299. *Waste Management v. Mexico*, Award, (30 April 2004), para. 98.
300. *Thunderbird v. Mexico*, Award, (26 January 2006), para. 147.
301. *Grand River v. United States*, Award, (12 January 2011), para. 141.
302. *Merrill & Ring v. Canada*, Award, (31 March 2010), para. 150 ('reliance by an investor on that representation in making a business decision').
303. *Mobil v. Canada*, Decision on Liability and on Principles of Quantum, (22 May 2012), para. 156.
304. *Thunderbird v. Mexico*, Award, (26 January 2006), para. 147.
305. *Mobil v. Canada*, Decision on Liability and on Principles of Quantum, (22 May 2012), para. 152.
306. Carl-Sebastian Zoellner, *Transparency: An Analysis of an Evolving Fundamental Principle in International Economic Law*, 27 Mich.J.Int'l L. 579, 616 (2006) ('It could argue that due to the transparency enhancing provisions found in countless BITs, other multilateral investment treaties: and NAFTA itself, as well as with to the due process component of transparency, the principle has indeed gained relevance in interpreting the customary international law minimum standard guaranteed by fair and equitable treatment or expropriation provisions'), at 627 ('tribunals have recognized transparency as the underlying rationale of international economic provisions and a vital component of the success and functioning of le WTO and NAFTA legal orders (...) Hence, it does not seem premature to refer to it as an interpretative principle of international economic law'); Diehl, *supra* n. 3, at 454 ('Serious violations of the requirement to act in a transparent manner will, however, lead to a violation of the FET standard irrespective of whether individual expectations based on identifiable State conduct have been formed - and should be protected'); Villanueva, *supra* n. 121, at 103, 186-7; Charles H. Brower II, *Investor-State Disputes Under NAFTA: A Tale of Fear and Equilibrium*, 29 Pepp. L. Rev. 43, 83 (2002); John Hanna, Jr, *Is Transparency of Governmental Administration Customary International Law in Investor-Sovereign Arbitrations? Courts and Arbitrators May Differ*, 21(2) Arb. Int'l 187 (2005); Kinnear, *supra* n. 35, at 20; Kreindler, *supra* n. 206, at 9; A. Lemaire, *Traitement juste et équitable*, 124 Gaz.Pal., Cahiers de l'arbitrage 43 (2004); Salacuse, *supra* n. 11, at 237 ('even where an investment treaty does not specifically provide for transparency a fair and equitable treatment clause implicitly requires transparency by the host government'); Weiler, *supra* n. 96, at 738; Knahr, *supra* n. 236, at 500; Laird & Weiler, *supra* n. 236, at 277, 278 ('there is certainly support for the proposition that regulatory transparency is now a requirement of customary international law'); Kläger, *supra* n. 13, at 234-235 (who nevertheless points out to the lack of uniformity in tribunal's understanding of transparency which gives only relative weight to the concept as autonomous); UNCTAD, *Fair and Equitable Treatment*, 51 (UNCTAD Series on Issues in International Investment Agreements 1999) ('where an investment treaty does not expressly provide for transparency, but does for fair and equitable treatment, then transparency is implicitly included in the treaty').
307. Vandevelde, *supra* n. 27, at 83-84 ('The transparency principle may be the most conceptually troubled element of the fair and equitable treatment standard. Several tribunals have regarded

concept not generally considered a customary international law standard'.[308] This position seems to be consistent with that adopted by UNCTAD in 2012.[309]

In any event, it is not entirely clear what such an obligation of 'transparency' would entail for the host State. Some scholars have put forward a broad definition of such an obligation.[310] One illustration of a tribunal imposing extensive obligations upon States is the *Tecmed* award where it was stated that in order to plan for an investment adequately, an investor should expect to:

> know beforehand any and all rules and regulations that will govern its investments, as well as the goals of the relevant policies and administrative practices or directives, to be able to plan its investment and comply with such regulations. Any and all State actions conforming to such criteria should relate not only to the guidelines, directives or requirements issued, or the resolutions approved there under, but also to the goals underlying such regulations.[311]

---

the fair and equitable treatment standard as requiring transparency, but no rule that describes the extent of transparency required has emerged (...). Awards in favor of the claimant, however, generally have been issued only where one, and usually both, of the following factors is present: (1) the host state failed to make material disclosures during discussions with the claimant; or (2) the host state's conduct also violated other principles, and thus the lack of transparency was not the sole basis for finding a violation of the fair and equitable treatment standard'); Akira Kotera, *Regulatory Transparency*, in: *The Oxford Handbook of International Investment Law* 632 (Peter Muchlinski, Federico Ortino & Christoph Schreuer eds., Oxford U. Press 2008) ('Taking into account the current situation of developing states, and the prevailing view that each country is required to provide treatment for foreign investors that is equivalent to that for nationals, it is difficult to say that transparency, even the public availability of information of relevant laws, should be a minimum standard towards foreign investors under customary international law'); Yannaca-Small, *supra* n. 44, at 130 ('Transparency, stability, and legitimate expectations are, among the interpretative elements of fair and equitable treatment, the only ones not "well grounded" in customary international law but which emerge from general principles and the recurrent opinion of arbitral tribunals in the last few years. It is too early to say whether we are witnessing a sign of evolution of the international custom as it is also too early to establish a definitive list of elements for the interpretation of the "fair and equitable treatment" standard since the jurisprudence is still constantly evolving'); Patrick G. Foy & Robert J.C. Deane, *Foreign Investment Protection under Investment Treaties: Recent Developments under Chapter 11 of the North American Free Trade Agreement*, 16 ICSID Rev. 319-320 (2001): Hussein Haeri, *A Tale of Two Standards: 'Fair and Equitable Treatment' and the Minimum Standard in International Law*, 27(1) Arb. Int'l 38 (2011); Marcela Klein Bronfman, *Fair and Equitable Treatment: An Evolving Standard*, 10 Max Planck Yrbk. UNL, 640 (2006); Picherack, *supra* n. 66, at 271.

308. OECD, *supra* n. 39, at 37.
309. UNCTAD, *supra* n. 11, at 72 ('While there is no doubt that transparency in the conduct towards, and consultation with, the investor is a good practice, not all countries have the regulatory and institutional framework in place to allow for full transparency and participation. Very few countries can claim to be fully transparent in their regulatory decision-making and implementation process. An inflexible and unrealistic approach to these issues would in effect transfer the risk of operating in a developing country environment from an investor to the host State').
310. Diehl, *supra* n. 3, at 454 ('The term transparency covers the following items: to establish contact points for facilitation of communications; to publish, in advance, any relevant measure that a contracting party proposes to adopt and to provide the opportunity to comment on proposed measures; to respond to question pertaining to any actual proposed measure; to institute administrative proceedings and to establish or maintain administrative tribunals or procedures for the purpose of prompt review').
311. *Técnicas Medioambientales Tecmed, S.A. v. Mexico*, ICSID No. ARB (AF)/00/2, Award, (29 May 2003), para. 154.

Many writers have concluded that the FET standard obliges the host State to publish its laws, regulations and policies that are applicable to foreign investments and investors.[312] However, according to most scholars, there is no obligation to notify investors of any amendments to laws and regulations before a decision is made or to give them the opportunity to comment on such changes.[313] More generally, according to Schill, transparency is closely related to the concept of the rule of law whereby it refers to 'procedural aspects of administrative law, such as the requirement to give sufficient reasons and the obligation to act in a comprehensible and predictable way'.[314]

Metalclad was the first NAFTA tribunal to discuss whether or not an obligation of transparency exists under Article 1105. The award is examined in the next section. This section does not examine cases where allegations of a breach of the obligation of transparency were raised by claimants, but not addressed by tribunals.[315] In *Glamis*, the claimant argued, *inter alia,* that the different measures adopted by the federal and Californian governments were non-transparent. It considered transparency as a stand-alone obligation under Article 1105.[316] The United States rejected this position.[317] Nevertheless, the tribunal decided to examine the issue of transparency as part of the larger concept of legitimate expectations.[318] For this reason, this case will not be

---

312. Tudor, *supra* n. 3, at 176; Newcombe & Paradell, *supra* n. 206, at 291; Vandevelde, *supra* n. 27, at 84 ('With respect to policy disclosures, the transparency principle does not seem to require disclosure of internal deliberations, but has been violated where a government refused to disclose its policy once the policy had been adopted').
313. Newcombe & Paradell, *supra* n. 206, at 291 ('There is little state practice to suggest that states have a general duty to specifically notify foreign investors of laws or changes to laws that might affect them. A fortiori, there is even less authority for the proposition that governments have an obligation to provide foreign investors with an opportunity to comment on changes to state regulation before changes are implemented. That said, a failure by a government to notify foreign investors of changes to laws, regulations and policies and to allow comments may well be one factor in determining whether there has been a breach of fair and equitable treatment'); Picherack, *supra* n. 66, at 284 ('an absolute transparency requirements subsumed under the fair and equitable treatment provision should not be employed to create a broad requirement to consult and cooperate with foreign investors in the formation of government regulations and legislation, or in administrative decision-making'). *Contra*: UNCTAD, *supra* n. 306, at 51.
314. Schill, *supra* n. 48, at 52-53.
315. *See,* for instance, *Chemtura v. Canada*, Investor's Memorial, (2 June 2008), paras. 434–435, 437, 439, 364), rejected by Canada (Canada's Counter-Memorial, (20 October 2008), paras. 837, 838), acknowledged by the tribunal in its award (Award, (2 August 2010), para. 112) but not specifically addressed. *See also*: *Grand River v. United States*, Award, (12 January 2011), where the question was raised by the claimants (paras. 182, 189), but not examined by the tribunal since it declined jurisdiction over that part of their Article 1105 claim (para. 204).
316. This is clear from several passages of the award: *Glamis v. United States*, Award, (8 June 2009), paras. 542, 572, 573 ('Claimant argues that numerous tribunals—interpreting BITs and other instruments around the world—have concluded that measures which lack transparency, fail to provide predictability or are otherwise arbitrary violate the customary international law obligation to provide fair and equitable treatment'). *See also*: Claimant's Reply Memorial, (15 December 2006), paras. 222, 224, 229.
317. *Ibid.*, Award, (8 June 2009), paras. 578–580.
318. *Ibid.*, para. 561, where the tribunal refers to one of two 'particular duties' that the claimant argued exist under Article 1105: 'an obligation to protect legitimate expectations through establishment of a transparent and predictable business and legal framework'. This is confirmed by the title of the award's section dealing with this issue: 'Asserted Obligation to

---

examined here. Similar arguments were also raised by the claimant in *Merrill & Ring*,[319] and rejected by Canada.[320] In two passages (which will be examined in the conclusion section below[321]), the *Merrill & Ring* tribunal rejected the assertion that the obligation of transparency was a part of customary international law.[322] Finally, in the *Cargill* case, where the investor had raised the issue,[323] the tribunal came to the same conclusion in one single passage (examined below).[324] In this instance, Mexico had argued that no breach of the obligation of transparency had occurred.[325]

[1]   Metalclad

The facts of this case have already been examined above.[326] In their pleadings, the parties specifically addressed the question of the existence of an obligation of transparency. The claimant argued that one of the elements comprising the FET standard was 'transparency and stability of investment conditions',[327] while Mexico rejected that the FET obligation 'extend[ed] to transparency and predictability requirements'.[328] In any event, Mexico argued that in the present case there had been no lack of transparency.[329]

As mentioned above,[330] the tribunal stated that one of the NAFTA's 'objectives' specifically include transparency.[331] The tribunal later reiterated that '[p]rominent in the statement of principles and rules that introduces the Agreement is the reference to transparency'.[332] On this point, the present author has already noted that this conclusion is contrary to the plain reading of NAFTA Article 102(2).[333] These grounds of criticism were echoed by Justice Tysoe in his decision to set aside the award.[334]

The *Metalclad* tribunal defined the principle of 'transparency' as follows:

> The Tribunal understands this to include the idea that all relevant legal requirements for the purpose of initiating, completing and successfully operating investments made, or intended to be made, under the Agreement should be capable of

---

Protect Legitimate Expectations Through Establishment of a Transparent and Predictable Legal and Business Framework' (paras. 619 ff).

319. *Merrill & Ring v. Canada*, Claimant's Memorial, (13 February 2008), para. 228.
320. *Ibid.*, Canada's Rejoinder, (27 March 2009), paras. 190, 191.
321. *See*, section §3.02[C][2].
322. *Merrill & Ring v. Canada*, Award, (31 March 2010), paras. 187, 231.
323. *Cargill, Inc. v. Mexico*, Award, (18 September 2009), paras. 262–263.
324. *Ibid.*, para. 294. *See*, at section §3.02[B][1].
325. *Ibid.*, para. 264.
326. *See*, at section §3.02[B][1].
327. *Metalclad v. Mexico*, Claimant's Memorial, (8 October 1997), paras. 162–164, 177.
328. *Ibid.*, Mexico's Counter-Memorial, (17 February 1998), para. 860.
329. *Ibid.*, paras. 861, 862.
330. *See*, at Chapter 2 section §2.02[B].
331. *Metalclad v. Mexico*, Award, (30 August 2000), para. 70.
332. *Ibid.*, para. 76.
333. *See*, at Chapter 2 section §2.02[B]. Thus, that provision makes it clear that transparently is not one of the 'objectives' of the treaty; it is rather one of the 'principles and rules' (others include national treatment and Most-Favoured-Nation treatment) through which the objectives are 'elaborated more specifically'. *See*: Kotera, *supra* n. 307, at 625.
334. *Mexico v. Metalclad*, 2001 BCSC 664, Supreme Court of British Columbia, Judgment and Reasons for Decision (2 May 2001), para. 71.

being readily known to all affected investors of another Party. There should be no room for doubt or uncertainty on such matters. Once the authorities of the central government of any Party (whose international responsibility in such matters has been identified in the preceding section) become aware of any scope for misunderstanding or confusion in this connection, it is their duty to ensure that the correct position is promptly determined and clearly stated so that investors can proceed with all appropriate expedition in the confident belief that they are acting in accordance with all relevant laws.[335]

One of the central issues of the case examined by the tribunal was whether or not a municipal permit was required for the construction of a hazardous waste landfill. The tribunal referred to a number of specific representations that had been made by the federal government regarding this issue both before and after the municipality ordered that the construction of the facility be stopped because of the absence of such a permit.[336] The tribunal found that:

the absence of a clear rule as to the requirement or not of a municipal construction permit, as well as the absence of any established practice or procedure as to the manner of handling applications for a municipal construction permit, amounts to a failure on the part of Mexico to ensure the transparency required by NAFTA.[337]

The tribunal then referred to a number of due process irregularities (to be examined below[338]). As such, the tribunal came to the conclusion that 'Mexico failed to ensure a transparent and predictable framework for Metalclad's business planning and investment'[339] in violation of Article 1105.

The award's section on Article 1105 was later set aside precisely with respect to this point in a decision rendered in 2001 by Justice Tysoe of the Supreme Court of British Columbia (B.C.).[340] Justice Tysoe applied the BC International Commercial Arbitration Act which only allow a court to set aside an award based on limited grounds for review (i.e., those set out at Article 34 of the UNCITRAL Model Law).[341] With regards to Article 1105, Justice Tysoe stated that '[n]o authority was cited or evidence introduced to establish that transparency has become part of customary international law'.[342] He concluded that the tribunal had exceeded its authority since it misstated the applicable law to the dispute. The tribunal had thus made its decision on the basis of

---

335. *Metalclad v. Mexico*, Award, (30 August 2000), para. 76.
336. *Ibid.*, paras. 85, 87–89.
337. *Ibid.*, para. 88.
338. *See*, at section §3.02[G][5].
339. *Metalclad v. Mexico*, Award, (30 August 2000), para. 99.
340. *Mexico v. Metalclad*, Supreme Court of British Columbia, Judgment and Reasons for Decision (2 May 2001).
341. These issues are examined in detail in: Charles H. Brower II, *Investor-State Disputes Under NAFTA: The Empire Strikes Back*, 40 Colum J. Transnat'l L. 61-66, 69 (2001-2002); Charles H. Brower II, *Beware the Jabberwock: A Reply to Mr. Thomas*, 40 Colum. J. Transnat'l L. 465, 471-479 (2002); H.C. Alvarez, *Setting Aside Additional Facility Awards: The Metalclad Case*, in *Annulment of ICSID Awards* 108-117, 153-154, (E. Gaillard & Y. Banifatemi eds., Juris Publ. 2004); J.C. Thomas, *A Reply to Professor Brower*, 40 Colum. J. Transnat'l L. 444 (2001-2002).
342. *Mexico v. Metalclad*, Supreme Court of British Columbia, Judgment and Reasons for Decision (2 May 2001), para. 68.

a breach of the obligation of transparency when no such obligation exists under NAFTA Chapter 11:

> In its reasoning, the Tribunal discussed the concept of transparency after quoting Article 1105 and making reference to Article 102. It set out its understanding of transparency and it then reviewed the relevant facts. After discussing the facts and concluding that the Municipality's denial of the construction permit was improper, the Tribunal stated its conclusion which formed the basis of its finding of a breach of Article 1105; namely, Mexico had failed to ensure a transparent and predictable framework for Metalclad's business planning and investment. Hence, *the Tribunal made its decision on the basis of transparency.* This was a matter beyond the scope of the submission to arbitration because there are no transparency obligations contained in Chapter 11.[343]

In the present author's view, Justice Tysoe's affirmation that 'the Tribunal made its decision on the basis of transparency' is open for debate. The lack of transparency was arguably *not* the only grounds for finding a breach of Article 1105.[344] Thus, the tribunal also found that Mexico had breached its obligation of due process (a point further discussed below).[345] There was therefore no apparent reason for setting aside the tribunal's *entire* reasoning supporting Article 1105 solely based on its flawed analysis on transparency.[346]

Other elements of Justice Tysoe's reasoning have also come under attack by several scholars. Some have argued that while the Judge emphasized that a high level of deference should be shown toward arbitral tribunals in the context of commercial arbitration in order to minimize judicial intervention, he did not rule accordingly.[347] Thus, under the pretence of an examination as to whether or not the tribunal had applied the 'proper law', the Judge rather set aside an award because it was inconsistent with *his own view* on what the applicable law should be.[348] There is indeed a difference between a tribunal setting the incorrect standard of law (where a court should intervene) and a tribunal making an 'error' in applying a correct standard (where a court should not intervene).[349] In the present case, it seems as though Justice Tysoe believed that the tribunal only erred with respect to the *application* of the legal standard. As such, both the tribunal and the Court agreed that the applicable legal standard was 'international law'; they only disagreed upon the proper *application* of that legal standard, i.e., whether or not any obligation of transparency existed pursuant

---

343. *Ibid.*, para. 72 (emphasis added).
344. Laird, *supra* n. 96, at 58; Weiler, *supra* n. 96, at 692; T. Weiler, *Good Faith and Regulatory Transparency: The Story of Metalclad v. Mexico*, in *International Investment Law and Arbitration: Leading Cases from the ICSID, NAFTA, Bilateral Treaties and Customary International Law* 716 (T. Weiler ed., Cameron May 2005); Dolzer & Schreuer, *supra* n. 71 at 143; Kingsbury & Schill, *supra* n. 56, at 17.
345. *See*, at section §3.02[G][5].
346. Weiler, *supra* n. 344, at 718.
347. Brower, *supra* n. 341, at 68, 75; Zoellner, *supra* n. 306, at 612-613.
348. Zoellner, *supra* n. 306, at 612; Weiler, *supra* n. 96, at 699-700; Brower, *supra* n. 341, at 68; W.S. Dodge, *International Decisions: Metalclad Corporation v. Mexico; Mexico v. Metalclad Corporation*, 95 AJIL 916-918 (2001).
349. David Williams, *Challenging Investment Treaty Arbitration Awards: Issues Concerning the Forum Arising from the Metatclad Case*, Bus. L. Int'l 169 (2003).

176

to international law. Arguably, this last question was a matter that should have been left to the tribunal to decide on.[350] According to Brower, the 'heightened judicial review of the Metalclad award [by the B.C. Court] represents an independent violation of Chapter 11' for which Canada could be held accountable.[351]

At any rate, whether or not Justice Tysoe's findings were beyond the Court's jurisdiction is outside the scope of this book. The important issue is whether or not he was indeed correct in concluding that the principle of transparency is not amongst the obligations imposed upon States as per Article 1105. There are good reasons to believe that his reasoning was accurate.[352] This question will be discussed in the next section.

[2] Conclusion

The *Metalclad* award is the first and only case where a tribunal concluded that the FET standard under Article 1105 includes an obligation of transparency. As just mentioned, that component of the award was set aside in judicial review before a B.C. Court.[353] It is therefore somewhat surprising that in subsequent proceedings, investors have often argued that the *Metalclad* tribunal's reasoning on the notion of transparency was still perfectly valid despite having been overruled by the B.C. Court.[354] Contrary to the position held by some investors, the B.C. Court's decision cannot simply be dismissed as irrelevant on the grounds that a provincial court cannot overrule an international tribunal's decision.[355] NAFTA Article 1136(3) specifically authorizes the review of final awards by local courts at the seat of the arbitration proceedings under the applicable domestic legislation in cases applying the UNCITRAL Arbitration Rules or the ICSID

---

350. Weiler, *supra* n. 96, at 700 ('it is precisely because this particular judge decided that he knew better than an expert tribunal what the "usual and ordinary meaning" of "international law" must be that he stepped beyond the bounds of his legislative mandate'). *Contra*: Patrick G. Foy, *Effectiveness of NAFTA's Chapter 11 Investor-State Arbitration Procedures*, 18 ICSID Rev. 104 (2003).
351. Brower, *supra* n. 341, at 81, noting however (at 81-85) that the claimant in this case lacked standing under Chapter 11 to challenge excessive judicial review by the B.C. Supreme Court since it had not made an investment in Canada (but in Mexico). He examined two other possibilities for challenging the Court's decision. His position has been strongly contested by other writers: Thomas, *supra* n. 341, at 455. This issue is further discussed in: Brower, *supra* n. 341, at 483-484.
352. A different view is adopted by Zoellner, *supra* n. 306, at 614.
353. *Mobil v. Canada*, Decision on Liability and on Principles of Quantum, (22 May 2012), para. 140 (where the tribunal mentioned that it was 'not aware of any subsequent decisions that have followed the approach taken by the Metalclad tribunal').
354. *See*, for instance: *Waste Management v. Mexico*, Claimant's Reply, (22 January 2003), para. 4.35, footnote 214; *Glamis v. United States*, Claimant's Reply Memorial, (15 December 2006), para. 227; *Merrill & Ring v. Canada*, Investor's Memorial, (13 February 2008), paras. 232–234.
355. *Merrill & Ring v. Canada*, Investor's Memorial, (13 February 2008), paras. 232–234 ('A domestic court decision does not affect the weight given to a NAFTA tribunal's decision under international law. The Metalclad Tribunal's conclusion that NAFTA Article 1105 obliges Parties to act transparently remains a correct expression of the law').

Additional Facility Rules.[356] Thus, while many features of the B.C. Court's decision can be rightfully criticized, it remains that it constitutes a precedent.[357]

In fact, all NAFTA tribunals have subsequently expressly rejected the proposition that the principle of transparency is part of customary international law precisely based on the conclusion reached by the B.C. Court in its judicial review of the *Metalclad* award. The *Glamis*,[358] *Merrill & Ring*[359] and *Cargill*[360] tribunals have all ruled that transparency is not a stand-alone element of the FET standard and that it does not impose any obligation on host States under Article 1105.[361] Professor Schwartz also made the same determination in his concurring opinion in the *S.D. Myers* case.[362] In his separate opinion in *Thunderbird*, Wälde also opined that transparency is only relevant to evaluate whether a breach of legitimate expectations has occurred.[363] This consensus was effectively summarized by the recent *Cargill* tribunal:

---

356. The argument is developed in: *Ibid.*, Canada's Counter-Memorial, (13 May 2008), paras. 532, 533.
357. Other writers have taken a different position: Zoellner, *supra* n. 306, at 616-617 ('In contrast to the [*Metalclad*] tribunal's interpretation, the judgment by the British Columbia Supreme Court is flawed for several reasons and consequently should have minimal impact. Moreover, because national courts cannot bind international tribunals and their conclusions on matters of international law are therefore of limited value, the reasoning of the appeal should not function as a powerful precedent outside of British Columbia'); Courtney N. Seymour, *The NAFTA Metalclad Appeal- Subsequent Impact or Inconsequential Error? Only Time Will Tell*, 34 U. Miami Inter-Am. L. Rev. 220 (2002); Weiler, *supra* n. 344, at 719.
358. *Glamis v. United States*, Award, (8 June 2009), para. 561. By examining transparency in the award's section dealing with the obligation to protect the investor's legitimate expectations, the tribunal implicitly rejected the investor's argument that transparency was a stand-alone element of the FET standard.
359. *Merrill & Ring v. Canada*, Award, (31 March 2010), para. 231.
360. *Cargill Inc. v. Mexico*, Award, (18 September 2009), para. 294.
361. To this list could be added: *Feldman v. Mexico*, Award, (16 December 2002), para. 133), where the tribunal briefly discussed the question of transparency in the different context of allegations of breach of Article 1110 (expropriation). It considered the reasoning of the B.C. Court as 'instructive' and added that 'it is doubtful that lack of transparency alone rises to the level of violation of NAFTA and international law, particularly given the complexities not only of Mexican but most other tax laws'.
362. *S.D. Myers Inc. v. Canada*, Separate Opinion by B. Schwartz, (13 November 2000), para. 255 ('S.D. Myers has not provided evidence that procedural fairness and transparency in the making of regulations is part of general international law and, as such, applicable worldwide. Rather, S.D. Myers has appealed to the letter or spirit of a provision of the 1947 GATT, and case law associated with it, to argue that procedural fairness and transparency is part of the minimum international standard. But the GATT agreement, while widely accepted, has by no means been adopted by all states. It is far from obvious, in the absence of evidence, that basic GATT norms like transparency and procedural fairness have been accepted by states throughout the world and so have passed into the body of general (or "customary") international law'). Other writers have given a different interpretation of his reasoning: Weiler, *supra* n. 96, at 701; Diehl, *supra* n. 3, at 443.
363. *Thunderbird v. Mexico*, Award, (26 January 2006), Separate Opinion of Thomas Wälde, (1 December 2005), para. 36 ('These objectives of the NAFTA – both the general objective of enhancing the attractiveness of the host state for foreign investors and the instrumental tool of using greater transparency, clarity and predictability to enable better investment planning– have therefore to guide the process of both defining the conditions of the "legitimate expectations" principle under Art. 1105 and of applying it to the particular facts of a specific situation').

The Tribunal holds that Claimant has not established that a general duty of transparency is included in the customary international law minimum standard of treatment owed to foreign investors per Article 1105's requirement to afford fair and equitable treatment. The principal authority relied on by the Claimant—Tecmed—involved the interpretation of a treaty-based autonomous standard for fair and equitable treatment and treated transparency as an element of the 'basic expectations' of an investor rather than as an independent duty under customary international law.[364]

Finally, it should be noted that while the *Merrill & Ring* tribunal also concluded that 'a requirement for transparency may not at present be proven to be part of the customary law standard, as the judicial review of *Metalclad* rightly concluded', it added that such a requirement was 'nonetheless approaching that stage'.[365]

The fact that transparency is *not* a stand-alone obligation under Article 1105 does not mean that the concept is altogether irrelevant. In *Glamis*, the United States explained that there are some aspects of transparency within the minimum standard of treatment in the context of denial of justice.[366] As such, the concept of transparency may be relevant to aid tribunals in assessing whether or not other firmly established elements of the FET standard (such as arbitrary conduct, due process, etc.) have been breached by a State.[367] This conclusion seems to be consistent with that reached by the *Waste Management* tribunal through its referral to 'a complete lack of transparency and candour in an administrative process', not as a stand-alone element of the FET standard, but as one illustration of State conduct that 'involves a lack of due process leading to an outcome which offends judicial propriety'.[368] In other words, the *Waste Management* tribunal considered that lack of transparency is relevant in order to determine whether a State has breached its due process obligation.

The position adopted by all post-*Metalclad* tribunals is fitting with that of all of the NAFTA Parties which have repeatedly rejected the view that the FET standard

---

364. *Cargill Inc. v. Mexico*, Award, (18 September 2009), para. 294.
365. *Merrill & Ring v. Canada*, Award, (31 March 2010), para. 231. *See also*, the other passage (at para. 187) where the tribunal suggests that the principle of transparency was 'fast approaching' being considered as a 'general principle of law'.
366. *Glamis v. United States*, Award, (8 June 2009), para. 578, quoting from Counsel for Respondent, Tr. 1444:10-18: '[O]bviously in established sets of rules recognized as being part of the minimum standard of treatment, there are some transparency aspects. For example, in a judicial denial of justice, the accessibility of the foreign national to the courts and the availability of records, for example, is obviously a part of the protection. You might call that transparency, but no stand-alone rule of transparency [exists] for all State conduct'.
367. Haeri, *supra* n. 307, at 38; Choudhury, *supra* n. 44, at 305; Picherack, *supra* n. 66, at 285; UNCTAD, *supra* n. 306, at 51 ('the degree of transparency in the regulatory environment will therefore affect the ability of the investor to assess whether or not fair and equitable treatment has been made available in any given case').
368. *Waste Management v. Mexico*, Award, (30 April 2004), para. 98 (the relevant part of the passage reads as follows: 'Taken together, the S.D. Myers, Mondev, ADF and Loewen cases suggest that the minimum standard of treatment of fair and equitable treatment is infringed by conduct attributable to the State and harmful to the claimant if the conduct (...) *involves a lack of due process leading to an outcome which offends judicial propriety* –as might be the case with a manifest failure of natural justice in judicial proceedings or a *complete lack of transparency and candour in an administrative process*', emphasis added).

under Article 1105 includes any obligation of transparency.[369] Mexico,[370] Canada,[371] and the United States all made such a submission when acting as respondents in proceedings.[372] It is noteworthy in this context that BITs recently entered into by Canada include a transparency obligation in a distinct provision (i.e., separate from the FET clause).[373] The 2004 US Model BIT also includes two transparency-related provisions.[374] However, these instruments expressly exclude any recourse to investor-State arbitration for matters arising from a breach of such transparency obligations.[375]

The conclusion reached by NAFTA tribunals that Article 1105 does not include any obligation of transparency is in sharp contrast with that prevailing under BITs outside of the NAFTA context where tribunals have recognized that transparency is an element of the FET standard.[376] As mentioned above, a number of non-NAFTA tribunals have also found that the stability and predictability of the legal framework is an essential element of the FET standard.[377] Some of these tribunals have mentioned that this stability requirement also includes an obligation of transparency.[378] On the contrary, in the context of NAFTA, the *Mobil* tribunal concluded that it had 'not been

---

369. *Glamis v. United States,* Award, (8 June 2009), para. 580 ('all three States Parties to the NAFTA have agreed that there is no general transparency requirement in Article 1105 and have expressly rejected the notion that transparency forms part of customary international law').
370. *Metalclad v. Mexico,* Mexico's Counter-Memorial, (17 February 1998), para. 860.
371. *See,* for instance: *UPS v. Canada,* Canada's Statement of Defence, (7 February 2003), para. 120; *ibid.,* Canada's Counter-Memorial, (22 June 2005), paras. 943, 944; *ibid.,* Canada's Rejoinder, (6 October 2005), para. 323; *Vito G. Gallo v. Canada,* Canada's Statement of Defence, (15 September 2008), at 102; *Chemtura v. Canada,* Canada's Counter-Memorial, (20 October 2008), paras. 837, 838.
372. *Grand River v. United States,* US Counter-Memorial, (22 December 2008), at 100, 101; *Methanex v. United States,* US Rejoinder on Jurisdiction, Admissibility and the Proposed Amendment, (27 June 2001), para. 33; *Glamis v. United States,* US Counter-Memorial, (19 September 2006), at 226, 227; *ibid.,* US Rejoinder, (15 March 2007), at 154.
373. Canada's Model FIPA, Article 19 entitled 'Transparency' reads as follows: '1. Each Party shall, to the extent possible, ensure that its laws, regulations, procedures, and administrative rulings of general application respecting any matter covered by this Agreement are promptly published or otherwise made available in such a manner as to enable interested persons and the other Party to become acquainted with them. 2. To the extent possible, each Party shall: (a) publish in advance any such measure that it proposes to adopt; and (b) provide interested persons and the other Party a reasonable opportunity to comment on such proposed measures. 3. Upon request by a Party, information shall be exchanged on the measures of the other Party that may have an impact on covered investments'. The same (or very similar) wording is also found in recent BITs entered into by Canada.
374. US Model BIT 2004 (Articles 10-11). *See also,* the same clause found in recent BITs entered into with Uruguay (2006) and Rwanda (2012). *See,* Kotera, *supra* n. 307, at 625-626.
375. Canada Model BIT, Article 19, footnote 7; US Model BIT, Article 24 (where an investor is nevertheless allowed to file a claim for breach of Article 10 dealing with 'publication of laws and decisions respecting investment').
376. *See,* for instance: *Emilio Augustin Maffezini v. Spain,* ICSID No. ARB/9717, Award, (13 November 2000), para. 83 ('the lack of transparency with which this loan transaction was conducted is incompatible with Spain's commitment to ensure the investor a fair and equitable treatment in accordance with Article 4(1) of the same treaty').
377. *See,* the discussion above at section §3.02[B][5].
378. *LG&E Energy Corp v. Argentina,* Decision on Liability, (3 October 2006), para. 131 (where the tribunal stated that the FET standard 'consists of the host State's consistent and transparent behaviour, free of ambiguity that involves the obligation to grant and maintain a stable and predictable legal framework').

provided with any material to support the conclusion that the rules of customary international law require a legal and business environment to be maintained or set in concrete'.[379]

[D] Arbitrary Conduct

[1] Defining Arbitrariness

The objective of the present section is not to examine the origin and development of the concept of arbitrariness under international law in exhaustive detail. This exercise has already been undertaken by a number of scholars.[380] Arbitrariness is a multifaceted term that has different meanings depending on the context surrounding it. In legal terms, *Black's Law Dictionary* defines 'arbitrary' as a conduct 'founded on prejudice or preference rather than on reason or fact'.[381] This definition has been adopted by several investor-State arbitration tribunals.[382] In its 2012 study,[383] UNCTAD put forward the following definition in the context of international investment law:

> In its ordinary meaning, 'arbitrary' means 'derived from mere opinion', 'capricious', unrestrained', 'despotic'. Arbitral conduct has been described as 'founded on prejudice or preference rather than on reason or fact'. Arbitrariness in decision-making has to do with the motivations and objectives behind the conduct concerned. A measure that inflicts damage on the investor without serving any legitimate purpose and without a rational explanation, but that instead rests on prejudice or bias, would be considered arbitrary.[384]

The classic definition of arbitrary conduct in international law was enunciated by the ICJ in its 1989 *ELSI* case.[385] It involved allegations of mistreatment in the context of a requisition by an Italian mayor of a factory owned in part by American investors, which was contrary to the 1948 U.S.-Italy Treaty of Friendship, Commerce and Navigation specifically prohibiting arbitrary measures. In deciding the issue in favor of Italy, the Court addressed the notion of arbitrariness in two oft-cited passages:

---

379. *Mobil v. Canada*, Decision on Liability and on Principles of Quantum, (22 May 2012), para. 153.
380. Jacob Stone, *Arbitrariness, The Fair and Equitable Treatment Standard and the International Law of Investment*, 25(1) Leiden JIL (2012); C. Schreuer, *Protection against Arbitrary or Discriminatory Measures*, in *The Future of Investment Arbitration* 183 (R.P. Alford & C.A. Rogers eds., Oxford U. Press 2009); K.J. Hamrock, *The ELSI Case: Toward an International Definition of "Arbitrary Conduct"*, 27(3) Tex. Int'l L.J. 837-864 (1992); A. Kiss, *L'abus de droit en droit international* (L.G.D.J. 1952).
381. *Black's Law Dictionary* (8th ed., West Group 2004), *see*, under 'arbitrary'.
382. Stone, *supra* n. 380, at 94, referring to a number of cases.
383. UNCTAD, *supra* n. 11, at 78.
384. *Ibid.* The report refers to: *Oxford English Dictionary* 464 (2nd ed., Clarendon Press 1989); *Lauder v. Czech Republic*, UNCITRAL, Award, (3 September 2001), para. 221; *Plama Consortium Limited v. Bulgaria*, ICSID No. ARB/03/24, Award, (27 August 2008), para. 184; *Joseph C. Lemire v. Ukraine*, ICSID No. ARB/06/18, Decision on Jurisdiction and Liability, (21 January 2010), para. 385.
385. *Sicula S.p.A. (ELSI) (US v. Italy)* [hereinafter *ELSI*], ICJ Rep. 1989, Judgment (20 July 1989). *See*: Sean D. Murphy, *The ELSI Case: An Investment Dispute at the International Court of Justice*, 16 Yale JIL 391-452 (1991); Hamrock, *supra* n. 380.

by itself, and without more, unlawfulness cannot be said to amount to arbitrariness...To identify arbitrariness with mere unlawfulness would be to deprive it of any useful meaning in its own right. Nor does it follow from a finding by a municipal court that an act was unjustified, or unreasonable, or arbitrary, that that act is necessarily to be classed as arbitrary in international law, though the qualification given to the impugned act by a municipal authority may be a valuable indication (...).[386]

Arbitrariness is not so much something opposed to a rule of law, as something opposed to the rule of law. This idea was expressed by the Court in the Asylum case, when it spoke of 'arbitrary action' being 'substituted for the rule of law' (Asylum, Judgment, I.C.J. Reports 1950, p. 284). It is a wilful disregard of due process of law, an act which shocks, or at least surprises, a sense of juridical propriety.[387]

The Court therefore applied a high threshold of liability for finding a breach of arbitrary conduct (i.e., 'wilful disregard of due process of law, an act which shocks, or at least surprises, a sense of juridical propriety'). The decision has been criticized by some writers not only for the vagueness of the standard it enunciates,[388] but also for its lack of relevance as a precedent in the context of the FET standard.[389] Yet, it remains that this definition has been endorsed by numerous investor-State tribunals.[390]

Case law suggests that there is 'substantive'[391] arbitrariness when no rational relationship exists between a measure adopted by the government and the alleged purpose or goal of that measure.[392] In this analysis, whether the measure is unwise, insufficient or inconsistent with domestic law is not pertinent.[393] Writers have also

---

386. *ELSI, ibid.*, at para. 124.
387. *Ibid.*, para. 128. In his dissenting opinion, Judge Stephen Schwebel (paras. 108–121) disagreed with the Court's conceptualization of arbitrariness, finding instead that, when contained in an FCN treaty, a prohibition of arbitrary measures is an obligation of result.
388. Hamrock, *supra* n. 380, at 849, 863, referring to a 'nebulous test' and proposing instead its own four-stage test.
389. Stephen Vasciannie, *The Fair and Equitable Treatment Standard in International Investment Law and Practice,* 70 British YIL 137 (1999): 'Generally, therefore, the ELSI decision, though possibly providing guidance on the meaning of the fair and equitable standard in practice, is ambivalent in important respects. If the majority approach is read as concluding that the treatment of the shareholders of ELSI was consistent with the fair and equitable standard, then the case serves as a precedent for the proposition that judicial bodies, considering matters ex post facto, should be disinclined to overrule the assessment of administrators or other decision-makers as to what constitutes fair and equitable treatment in particular circum-stances. On the other hand, having regard to the majority judgment, it is doubtful that ELSI should be perceived as an instance of the application of the fair and equitable standard in a particular case. Rather, bearing in mind the absence of any express reference to the standard by the majority, and the detailed application by the majority of the specific standards in the operative provisions of the FCN Treaty between the United States and Italy, and the Supple-mentary Agreement thereto, the better view is that the majority opinion in ELSI did not seek to apply the fair and equitable standard to the facts'.
390. Stone, *supra* n. 380, at 94, referring to a number of cases.
391. Newcombe & Paradell, *supra* n. 206, at 251, referring to the concept of 'substantive' arbitrariness concerning arbitrary conduct and using the expression 'procedural' arbitrariness in the context of due process and denial of justice.
392. UNCTAD, *supra* n. 11, at 78. *See: Alex Genin, Eastern Credit Limited, Inc. and A.S. Baltoil v. Estonia,* ICSID No. ARB/99/2, Award, (25 June 2001), para. 370; *Siemens A.G. v. Argentina,* ICSID No. ARB/02/8, (17 January 2007), para. 319.
393. *Enron Corporation and Ponderosa Assets, L.P. v. Argentina*, Award, (22 May 2007), para. 281.

used rationality[394] or legitimacy[395] as a yardstick to determine arbitrariness. They have defined arbitrary measures as those made 'on the basis of irrelevant considerations'[396] or those that are unjustified and unexplained by objective reasons.[397] Heiskanen proposed the following two-fold test:

> The decision-maker assesses the international legality of the governmental measure in question by focusing on the relationship between the measure and its underlying policy justification. Has any rationale or justification been put forward in support of the measure in the first place? In the affirmative, is such a rationale or justification related to a legitimate governmental policy? If the answer to the first question is in the negative, and if there is no conceivable rationale that could justify it, the measure can be classified as 'arbitrary'. This 'definition' of arbitrary is also largely in line with the standard definition of arbitrary in legal dictionaries - an arbitrary measure can indeed be defined as a measure taken without any justification, actual or conceivable. If the answer to the first question is yes - if a rationale or justification has in fact been put forward for the measure - then the relevant question is whether there is a reasonable relationship between such a purported justification and a legitimate governmental policy. If there is no such relationship (eg if the measure discriminates between investors based on their eye colour), then the measure in question can be considered 'unreasonable'.[398]

---

394. Newcombe & Paradell, *supra* n. 206, at 250-251; Weiler & Laird, *supra* n. 236, at 284-285 ('international law prohibits state officials from exercising their authority in an abusive, arbitrary, or discriminatory manner. The tell-tale sign of the kind of state conduct which attracts such liability is an apparently arbitrary, capricious, and/or overtly discriminatory governmental action which causes damage to a foreign investment. If state officials can demonstrate that the decision was actually made in an objective and rational (ie reasoned) manner, they will defeat any claim made under this standard. If they cannot, the arbitrary conduct must be remedied').

395. Schreuer, *supra* n. 66, at 8-9 ('The decisions dealing with arbitrary conduct indicate that measures are arbitrary if they inflict damage on the investor without serving any apparent legitimate purpose. In addition, a measure would be arbitrary if it is not based on legal standards but on discretion, prejudice or personal preference. Also, a measure would be arbitrary if it is taken for reasons that are different from those put forward by the decision maker, especially if a public purpose is merely a pretence for a different motive'). The definition was endorsed by the tribunal in: *EDF (Services) Limited v. Romania*, ICSID Case No. ARB/05/13, Award, (8 October 2009), para. 303.

396. Ian Laird, *MTD Equity Sdn. Bhd. and MTD Chile S.A. v. Republic of Chile - Recent Developments in the Fair and Equitable Treatment Standard*, 1(4) Transnational Disp. Mgmt. 6 (2004).

397. Lemaire, *supra* n. 306, at 39.

398. V. Heiskanen, *Arbitrary and Unreasonable Measures*, in *Standards of Investment Protection* 111, 104 (A. Reinisch ed., Oxford U. Press 2008). The same test is put forward by Diehl, *supra* n. 3, at 453. Hamrock, *supra* n. 380, at 852 ff., proposes the following test: 'Governmental action would be deemed arbitrary if: (1) the action taken was not authorized by law; (2) the action was taken for an improper purpose; (3) the action was taken because of irrelevant circumstances; or (4) the action was patently unreasonable. (...) First, governmental conduct must pass the legal-authority test. Under this test, the Court asks whether the government agency or official whose conduct is claimed to be arbitrary possesses the authority under domestic law to so act. In short, does the law authorize the actor to perform as it did? (...) Second, the governmental action would need to pass the proper-purpose test. [It] evaluates the motivations of the actor. It asks: "For what purpose did the actor exercise its discretionary power?" If that purpose is inconsistent with or irrelevant to the statutory authority, then the act fails the test and is an arbitrary exercise of power. Why is an improperly motivated action arbitrary? An improper motivation is irrelevant to the authorizing statute, and an actor essentially goes beyond the statute in deciding whether or not to act. By doing so, the actor exceeds its statutory framework and violates the legal authority test explained above. As a

While some writers have equated the concept of arbitrariness with that of non-discrimination,[399] others examine the two separately.[400] We will touch upon the concept of non-discrimination in a separate section below.[401]

A number of writers have also concluded that 'unreasonableness' is synonymous with the concept of arbitrariness.[402] However, Heiskanen (based on the two-fold test just mentioned) demonstrates that there is a difference between the notions of arbitrariness and unreasonableness.[403] For him, unreasonableness is in fact the second part of the two-fold test. Other writers[404] and tribunals[405] consider the concept of 'reasonableness' as identical to that of the FET standard. In a non-NAFTA context, a

---

result, the actor performs in an arbitrary manner. (...) The third test is the relevant-circumstances test. This test is similar to the proper-purpose test in that it probes the decision-making process of the governmental actor. The relevant-circumstances test asks: "What factors did the actor consider in reaching a decision to act?" The actor may fail the test in two ways. First, the actor can give weight to factors that are irrelevant to the actor's exercise of power as defined by the empowering statute. Second, the actor can fail to give weight to factors that are essential under the empowering statute. Either failure will produce arbitrary governmental conduct, because the failure represents a departure from statutory authority. (...) The fourth proposed test, the patent-reasonableness test, examines the questioned governmental conduct and the actor's justifications for the conduct. The test asks: "Does a rational connection exist between the statutory power and the action taken?" The test functions as a final check against arbitrary conduct by the actors and connect the first three proposed tests. (...) The fourth proposed test guarantees that any action taken that is not specifically approved by the statute but is taken in an effort to comply with the statute, is rationally related to the statutory power'.

399. Kläger, *supra* n. 13, at 187, 196 ('tribunals are not distinguishing between the notions of non-discrimination, non-arbitrariness and reasonableness. They therefore seem to derive from the broad principle of non-discrimination a general precept of non-arbitrariness which is mostly described as a duty to act reasonably without any precondition of a differential treatment'). *See also*: Diehl, *supra* n. 3, at 448.

400. Newcombe & Paradell, *supra* n. 206, at 249.

401. *See*, section §3.02[E].

402. Diehl, *supra* n. 3, at 448 ff; *Restatement of the Law Third: The Foreign Relations Law of the United States*, para. 712, fn 11 (American Law Institute Publ. 1987*)* (defining arbitrary conduct as 'unfair and unreasonable, and inflicts serious injury to established rights of foreign nationals, though falling short of an act that would constitute an expropriation'); *Lauder v. Czech Republic*, Final Award, (3 September 2002), para. 232 (an arbitrary act is 'not founded on reason or fact nor on the law').

403. Heiskanen, *supra* n. 398, at 104 ('The distinction between arbitrary and unreasonable governmental conduct boils down to this: a governmental measure can be considered 'arbitrary' if no justification or rationale at all has been provided for the measure (i.e. if there is no relationship at all, let alone a rational relationship, between the measure and a legitimate governmental policy); and it can be considered 'unreasonable' if a justification or a rationale has in fact been provided for the measure, but there is no reasonable (or rational) relationship between the purported justification and a legitimate governmental policy').

404. Newcombe & Paradell, *supra* n. 206, at 304. *See*, however, Kingsbury & Schill, *supra* n. 56, at 10, 16, identifying 'reasonableness and proportionality' as one of the 'five clusters of normative principles' which 'recur in the more detailed specification by arbitral tribunals of elements of fair and equitable treatment'.

405. *Saluka v. Czech Republic*, UNCITRAL, Partial Award, (17 March 2006), para. 460 ('[t]he standard of "reasonableness" has no different meaning in this context than in the context of the "fair and equitable treatment" standard with which it is associated [...]').

number of tribunals have examined reasonableness as a stand-alone obligation, an analysis which contrasts with that undertaken in NAFTA case law.[406]

In the NAFTA context, several claimants have argued that reasonableness is a stand-alone obligation.[407] NAFTA Parties have, on the contrary, consistently opined that an unreasonable action does not breach the FET standard.[408] For them, reasonableness is merely one factor that a tribunal can consider when deciding whether or not a State's conduct breaches other elements of the FET standard.[409] All NAFTA tribunals have agreed with this position thus far. They have rightly held that reasonableness is a general factor to be weighed when determining whether or not the host State has breached its due process obligation (*Pope & Talbot*[410]), committed an arbitrary conduct (*Glamis*[411]) or violated an investor's legitimate expectations (*Thunderbird*,[412] *ADF*[413]).

---

406. Tyler, *supra* n. 60, at 47-48 (Disclaimer: The present author was Mr. Tyler's supervisor for his Research Paper. He was also my research assistant in 2011 in examining the question of reasonableness in NAFTA case law).

407. *Ibid.*, at 49, referring to the following examples: *Pope & Talbot Inc. v. Canada*, Claimant's Memorial (Phase 2), (5 September 2005), para. 106; *ibid.*, Claimant's Post-Hearing Submissions, (14 December 2001), para. 2; *ADF v. United States*, Claimant's Post-Hearing Submission, (11 July 2002), paras. 47, 55, 62; *Metalclad v. Mexico*, Claimant's Memorial, (8 October 1997), at 37, 38; *ibid.*, Claimant's Reply Memorial, (21 August 1998), paras. 284, 379, 413; *Methanex v. United States*, Claimant's Counter-Memorial on Jurisdiction, (12 February 2001), at 13; *Merrill & Ring. v. Canada*, Investor's Reply, (15 December 2008), para. 343.

408. *Merrill & Ring v. Canada*, Canada's Rejoinder, (27 March 2009), para. 2. *See*, however, *Metalclad v. Mexico*, Mexico's Counter-Memorial, (11 February 1998), para. 841, referring to reasonableness as a duty prescribed by the FET standard along with good faith and the prohibitions on abusive, arbitrary and discriminatory conduct.

409. Tyler, *supra* n. 60, at 50, 68-69 (referring to: *S.D. Myers Inc. v. Canada*, Canada's Counter-Memorial, (5 October 1999), paras. 323, 328-329; *Robert Azinian, Kenneth Davitian, & Ellen Baca v. Mexico* [hereinafter *Azinian v. Mexico*], ICSID No. ARB (AF)/97/2; *ibid.*, Mexico's Counter Memorial, (1 April 1998), paras. 237, 239; *ibid.*, Mexico's Post-Hearing Brief, (16 July 1999), para. 52.

410. *Pope & Talbot Inc. v. Canada*, Award on the Merits (Phase 2), (10 April 2001), para. 181, concluding, *inter alia*, that Canada denied the investor's reasonable requests of information in breach of the due process obligation under Article 1105. This case is further discussed below at section §3.02[G][6]. *See*, however, Vandevelde, *supra* n. 27, at 63 (examining this case from the angle of 'reasonableness' as an autonomous FET element).

411. *Glamis v. United States*, Award, (8 June 2009), paras. 779, 786, 788, 803, 805, 807, 817, 824, 828, where the tribunal refers to 'lack of reasons' along with other elements of the FET standard. See, for instance, para. 779: 'our only task is to decide whether Claimant has adequately proven that the agency's review and conclusions exhibit a gross denial of justice, manifest arbitrariness, blatant unfairness, a complete lack of due process, evident discrimination, or a manifest lack of reasons so as to rise to the level of a breach of the customary international law standard embedded in Article 1105'. The tribunal, however, examined reasonableness only in the context of allegations of arbitrariness. This case is further discussed below at section §3.02[D][4].

412. *Thunderbird v. Mexico*, Award, (26 January 2006), para. 165. This case was examined above at section §3.02[B][2].

413. *ADF v. United States*, Award, (9 January 2003), para. 189 ('The second submission of the Investor is that the FHWA of the U.S. Department of Transportation refused to follow and apply pre-existing case-law in respect of ADF International in the Springfield Interchange Project, thus ignoring the Investor's legitimate expectations generated by that case-law. We do not believe that the refusal of the FHWA to follow prior rulings, judicial or administrative is, in

The *Merrill & Ring* tribunal seemed to interpret reasonableness as some sort of an all-encompassing governing principle of the FET standard.[414]

Allegations of arbitrariness have been raised by investors in several claims brought under Article 1105. In this section, it was decided not to examine cases where tribunals have not analyzed the notion of arbitrariness even though it had been argued by the parties in their pleadings.[415] Similarly, cases where the issue of arbitrariness was discussed by tribunals in the different context of expropriation allegations will not be examined in this section.[416] Cases where tribunals have examined allegations of arbitrariness when deciding whether or not a certain conduct constituted a denial of justice will also not be touched upon in this section.[417] The *S.D. Myers, ADF* and *Merrill & Ring* cases, which have all briefly referred to the concept of arbitrariness, will be examined in the conclusion section.[418]

[2]   Waste Management

The *Waste Management* case involved a dispute arising from the execution of a fifteen-year Concession Contract signed by the government of the State of Guerrero, the municipality of Acapulco, and Acaverde S.A. de C.V., the Mexican subsidiary of Waste Management Inc. (a US company). The contract granted the latter the exclusive rights to provide waste management services (clean the streets, collect and dispose of all solid waste) to the City of Acapulco. After the parties entered into the agreement, several engagements were not honored: Acapulco failed to honor the exclusivity terms of the contract, there was resistance by residents of the city with respect to private collection services, and the city failed to provide the investor with the promised landfill facilities for the disposal of the collected waste. The claimant alleged that Mexico breached Articles 1105 and 1110 for acts committed by the State of Guerrero, the City Counsel of

---

itself, in the circumstances of this case, grossly unfair or unreasonable'). This case was examined above at section §3.02[B][1].
414. *Merrill & Ring v. Canada*, Award, (31 March 2010), stating that the FET standard 'protects against all such acts or behaviour that might infringe on a sense of fairness, equity and reasonableness' (para. 210). The tribunal also states that Article 1105 'provides for the fair and equitable treatment of alien investors within the confines of reasonableness' (para. 236). The tribunal concluded that Canada's log export regime was not 'manifestly unreasonable' (para. 236).
415. This is, for instance, the case of *UPS v. Canada*, where the concept was discussed by Canada in its pleading (Canada's Counter-Memorial, (22 June 2005), paras. 45, 924, 928, 937-939, 988; Canada's Rejoinder, (6 October 2005), paras. 294, 316, 317). In *ADF v. United States*, Award, (9 January 2003), paras. 116, 118, 121, 118, 124, while the claimant had not specifically framed its argument based on allegations of arbitrary conduct, this did not prevent the parties from discussing the concept in their pleadings.
416. *Feldman v. Mexico*, Award, (16 December 2002), paras. 99, 143.
417. *Azinian v. Mexico*, Award, (1 November 1999), para. 103; *Mondev v. United States*, Award, (2 October 2011), para. 127; *Thunderbird v. Mexico*, Award, (26 January 2006), paras. 194, 197, 200.
418. *See*, at section §3.02[D][6] below.

the municipality of Acapulco, and the State-owned bank (Banobras).[419] One of claimant's two grounds of complaint under Article 1105 was that its investment has been 'subjected to arbitrary acts of the Mexican Governments, which ultimately rendered the investment valueless'.[420] More specifically, the investor argued that all three levels of the Mexican government and Banobras had breached Article 1105 by arbitrarily not respecting its obligation under the contract.[421] It is noteworthy that in its pleadings, Mexico seemed to agree that Article 1105 includes a prohibition against arbitrary conduct, but nevertheless denied that mere contractual breaches could be considered arbitrary in violation of that provision.[422]

At the outset, the tribunal mentioned that the 'minimum standard of treatment of fair and equitable treatment is infringed by conduct attributable to the State and harmful to the claimant if the conduct is arbitrary'.[423] This statement clearly indicates that arbitrary conduct is a stand-alone element of the FET standard under Article 1105.[424] Later in the award, the tribunal makes reference to 'wholly arbitrary'[425] conduct rather than 'arbitrary' conduct. The use of this term suggests the adoption of a higher threshold of liability for finding a violation of this provision.

---

419. Payments by the municipality of Acapulco were guaranteed by a State-owned bank, Banco Nacional de Obras y Servicios Públicos, S.N.C. ('Banobras'), and counter-guaranteed by the State of Guerrero under a separate line-of-credit arrangement.

420. *Waste Management v. Mexico*, Award, (30 April 2004), Claimant's Reply, (22 January 2003), para. 4.32. *See also*: Claimant's Memorial, (29 September 1999), para. 5.14 ('Where a State effectively revokes a concession by preventing profitable operations by the concessionaire, through measures that frustrate or undermine the purposes of the concession or that demonstrate bad faith constituting arbitrary conduct, responsibility under international law attaches'). The other ground of complaint under Article 1105 was denial of justice. This question is examined below at section §3.02[G][9].

421. *Ibid.*, Claimant's Reply, (22 January 2003), para. 4.34 ('Claimant in this case was arbitrarily deprived of the value of its Concession by concerted efforts of the Mexican Governments that were inconsistent with notions of due process of law. During Concession negotiations, all three levels of the Mexican Governments enticed Claimant to invest in the Acapulco Concession. But none of the three Mexican Governments felt bound by their word. For example, although the City and Federal Governments agreed to the terms and conditions of the Concession, neither saw any difficulty in not living up to its obligations. Although the City agreed to enforce Acaverde's exclusivity rights, it never did. Although Banobras agreed to guarantee the City's payment obligations, it refused to do so at the first instance of opposition from the City and the State. In short, the Mexican Governments made agreements with a foreign investor with which they had no intention of complying. By arbitrarily granting and denying their assurances to Claimant, the Mexican Governments failed to give Claimant's investment fair and equitable treatment in accordance with minimal standards of international law').

422. *Ibid.*, Mexico's Counter-Memorial, (6 December 2002), para. 243(h).

423. *Ibid.*, Award, (30 April 2004), para. 98.

424. Later in the award (at *Ibid.*, para. 130), the tribunal also refers to the relevance of arbitrary conduct to determine whether or not the actions of courts constitute a denial of justice: 'the Tribunal does not discern in the decisions of the federal courts any denial of justice as that concept has been explained by NAFTA tribunals, notably in the *Azinian, Mondev, ADF* and *Loewen* cases. The Mexican court decisions were not, either ex facie or on closer examination, evidently arbitrary, unjust or idiosyncratic. There is no trace of discrimination on account of the foreign ownership of Acaverde, and no evident failure of due process'. This question is examined below at section §3.02[G][9].

425. *Ibid.*, para. 115.

The tribunal concluded that the actions of Banobras and the State of Guerrero did not constitute a breach of Article 1105.[426] What is more interesting for the purpose of this book is the tribunal's reasoning to support its conclusion that the conduct of the City was not arbitrary. As per the contract, Acaverde undertook to build a waste landfill and the City agreed to provide a site and a free loan.[427] The City never made the land available for the landfill, nor did it ever abide by the free loan agreement.[428] The City also made only one full and two partial payments out of twenty-six invoices issued by Acaverde.[429] It also wrote a letter to Banobras, asking it to stop issuing payments to Acaverde through its line of credit, because Acaverde allegedly failed to perform its obligations.[430] The tribunal acknowledged that the City had 'failed in a number of respects to fulfil its contractual obligations to Claimant under the Concession Agreement (…) most obviously, with respect to the monthly payments, which immediately fell into arrears'.[431] However, the tribunal also recognized countervailing factors, which showed that the City had invoked the Concession Agreement in proceedings brought against it, that it had attempted to enforce it and also tried to find a site for the disposal of waste.[432] The tribunal also indicated that the Concession Agreement was 'unpopular with a significant proportion of the residents of the concession area'[433] and that Acaverde worsened the situation by issuing invoices to all residents. The tribunal reiterated that the 'financial plans of the City, and thus of the Claimant, were severely affected by the Mexican financial crisis, which lasted well into 1996 and severely affected the City's capacity to perform its obligations'.[434] Unable to pay Acaverde or Banobras, the City resorted to offering land holdings to both in lieu of payment, but they refused.[435] The tribunal added that it did not 'suggest that financial stringency or public resistance are, as such, excuses for breaches of contractual commitments on the part of a municipality'.[436] In any event, the tribunal was not required to take position

---

426. *Ibid.*, paras. 102, 105–107.
427. *Ibid.*, para. 45.
428. *Ibid.*, para. 55.
429. *Ibid.*, para. 58.
430. *Ibid.*, para. 61. The tribunal found (at para. 63) the City's letter accurate insofar as Acaverde had failed to keep the City clean.
431. *Ibid.*, para. 109.
432. *Ibid.*, para. 110 ('The City did make at least some attempts to enforce the 1995 Ordinance. It defended proceedings brought against it by local residents challenging the Concession Agreement and the 1995 Ordinance. It made at least some attempts to encourage local residents and business groups to contract with Acaverde. Contrary to the Claimant's allegations, it did bring at least some proceedings against the "pirates" and even against its own employees caught moonlighting in the concession area. It made at least some attempts, through the deployment of inspectors, to enforce the Cleaning Services Ordinance. And some steps were taken, in conjunction with Acaverde, to identify a location for the permanent waste disposal site and to obtain secure title over it. For example, the City brought non-contentious proceedings before an Agrarian Court in Guerrero to give an agreement made with the holders of customary title over the land the status of an order of the Court; on 8 April 1996 the Court granted the order accordingly').
433. *Ibid.*, para. 111.
434. *Ibid.*, para. 112.
435. *Ibid.*, para. 112.
436. *Ibid.*, para. 114.

on this contractual dispute since it only had to determine whether or not the allegation of breach of contract amounted to a violation of Article 1105.

Ultimately, the tribunal held that the City did not act 'in a wholly arbitrary way or in a way that was grossly unfair':

> [The City] performed part of its contractual obligations, but it was in a situation of genuine difficulty, for the reasons explained above. It sought alternative solutions to the problems both parties faced, without finding them. The most important default was its failure to pay (...). For present purposes it is sufficient to say that even the persistent non-payment of debts by a municipality is not to be equated with a violation of Article 1105, provided that it does not amount to an outright and unjustified repudiation of the transaction and provided that some remedy is open to the creditor to address the problem. In the present case the failure to pay can be explained, albeit not excused, by the financial crisis which meant that at key points the City could hardly pay its own payroll. There is no evidence that it was motivated by sectoral or local prejudice.[437]

The tribunal found that a mere contractual breach (such as payment failure) does not amount to an arbitrary act in violation of the FET standard under Article 1105. An additional requirement exists for a breach of that provision to occur: it must be shown that the government committed an 'outright and unjustified repudiation of the transaction'[438] and that it also prevented the creditor from having any recourse to remediate the situation. Arbitrariness would therefore occur if and when these two conditions are met.[439] The tribunal also suggests that arbitrary conduct would arise if failure to pay is 'motivated by sectoral or local prejudice'.[440]

[3] Gami

GAMI, an American company, acquired a stake in Grupo Azucarero Mexico (GAM), a company that was involved in processing sugar in Mexico. In 1997–1998, Mexico adopted a method for determining the national reference price for sugarcane, and measures intended to establish export quotas and production ceilings.[441] In 2001, Mexico expropriated five mills owned by GAM. GAMI alleged that Mexico had not carried out 'the Mexican Sugar Program in accordance with their terms'[442] and that such failure to implement and enforce its own laws was 'flagrant and arbitrary' in violation of Article 1105.[443] Thus, according to the claimant, Mexico 'arbitrarily and discriminatorily implemented certain aspects of the law and capriciously refused to

---

437. *Ibid.*, para. 115.
438. *Ibid.*
439. Vandevelde, *supra* n. 27, at 72.
440. *Waste Management, Inc. v. Mexico*, Award, (30 April 2004), para. 115.
441. GAMI alleged that Mexico had set unrealistically high reference prices for sugarcane, but failed to enforce export quotas and never set production ceilings, causing the price of sugarcane to rise and the price of blended sugar to fall.
442. *Gami v. Mexico*, Award, (15 November 2004), para. 86.
443. *Ibid.*, para. 88. *See:* Claimant's Memorial, (9 April 2002), para. 7 (referring to 'Mexico's arbitrary conduct with respect to implementation and application of Mexico's sugar regime and (...) its arbitrary and discriminatory expropriation of GAM's sugar mills').

implement and enforce others, thereby substantially destroying GAMI's invest-ment'.[444]

Interestingly enough, the investor acknowledged that 'a state's failure to comply with its own law or authority in a particular situation does not automatically constitute a violation of Article 1105 or international law'[445] and that (quoting the *ADF* award[446]) 'something more than simple illegality' is 'necessary to render an act or measure inconsistent with the customary international law requirements of Article 1105(1)'.[447] Mexico agreed with that proposition[448] and therefore did not deny that arbitrary conduct is one of the elements of the FET standard under this provision. According to the investor, it was Mexico's *arbitrary* failure to comply with its own law that violated Article 1105.[449] Mexico rejected the allegation by stating that GAMI had not established that its conduct 'r[ose] to the level of arbitrariness in violation of international law' established in the ICJ *ELSI* case.[450]

The tribunal first acknowledged that the Mexican Sugar Program was 'not carried out in accordance with their terms,'[451] by specifically referring to three instances of such 'failure of implementation and enforcement'.[452] However, the tribunal found that 'a government's failure to implement or abide by its own law in a manner adversely affecting a foreign investor may but will not necessarily lead to a violation of Article 1105' and that 'much depends on context'.[453] Thus, 'something more than simple illegality' needs to be shown 'to render an act or measure inconsistent with the customary international law requirements of Article 1105(1)'.[454] The tribunal explained that a government's failure to implement its own laws and regulations does not amount to an arbitrary act in violation of Article 1105. In accordance with the reasoning of the *Waste Management* tribunal, the *Gami* tribunal added that something more must be shown: a maladministration that amounts to an 'outright and unjustified repudiation' of these laws and regulations. The tribunal futher explained that:

> A claim of maladministration would likely violate Article 1105 if it amounted to an 'outright and unjustified repudiation' of the relevant regulations. There may be situations where even lesser failures would suffice to trigger Article 1105. It is the record as a whole — not dramatic incidents in isolation — which determines whether a breach of international law has occurred.[455]

---

444. *Ibid.*, Claimant's Memorial, (9 April 2002), para. 83.
445. *Ibid.*, para. 77.
446. *ADF v. United States*, Award, (9 January 2003), para. 190.
447. *Gami v. Mexico*, Claimant's Memorial, (9 April 2002), para. 77.
448. *Ibid.*, Mexico's Statement of Defense, (24 November 2003), para. 243.
449. *Ibid.*, Claimant's Memorial, (9 April 2002), para. 78 ('the arbitrariness of the violations may constitute that 'something more' that renders the conduct inconsistent with the minimum standard').
450. *Ibid.*, Mexico's Statement of Defense, (24 November 2003), para. 251.
451. *Ibid.*, Award, (15 November 2004), para. 86.
452. *Ibid.*, para. 87.
453. *Ibid.*, para. 91.
454. *Ibid.*, para. 98.
455. *Ibid.*, para. 103. *See also*, para. 101 (discussing the reasoning of the *Waste Management* tribunal).

The tribunal's reference to 'situations where even lesser failures' than outright and unjustified repudiation could breach Article 1105 is intriguing. Later, the tribunal asked rhetorically whether 'something less than repudiation', such as 'an egregious failure to regulate', would 'still be actionable under Article 1105'.[456] However, the tribunal did not provide any answer. Yet, an earlier passage of the award suggests that the tribunal had already answered the question positively. Thus, the tribunal explained that NAFTA Parties must 'accept liability if its officials fail to implement or implement regulations in a discriminatory or arbitrary fashion'.[457] This statement suggests that a State's failure to implement its own regulations *based on arbitrary grounds* could fulfil the requirement of that 'something more' necessary to demonstrate a breach of Article 1105.

The tribunal concluded that no such maladministration had occurred in the case at hand,[458] and that, in any event, no specific failure to implement regulation could be directly attributable to the Mexican government.[459]

[4]   Glamis

The facts of this case have already been examined above.[460] The claimant argued, *inter alia*, that the actions taken by the State of California and the U.S. federal government were arbitrary since they were designed to block the Imperial Project in violation of Article 1105.[461] It argued that the duty to accord an FET includes protection from arbitrariness,[462] and made some valuable effort towards defining this concept.[463] The United States argued, on the contrary, that Article 1105 does not impose any general obligation on States to refrain from 'arbitrary' conduct.[464] The United States also contended that the claimant was essentially requesting that the tribunal pass judgment on legislation perceived as imperfect or 'unwise'.[465] In any event, in the United States' view, even an illegal act under domestic law would not constitute a violation of

---

456. *Ibid.*, para. 105.
457. *Ibid.*, para. 94.
458. *Ibid.*, para. 103 ('GAMI has not been able to show anything approaching "outright and unjustified repudiation" of the relevant regulations. The Sugarcane Decree and its related measures certainly did not operate in accordance with their terms. But there is no evidence that Mexico set its face against implementation').
459. *Ibid.*, paras. 108, 110.
460. *See*, section §3.02[B][4].
461. *Glamis v. United States*, Award, (8 June 2009), para. 561.
462. *Ibid.*, para. 583.
463. *Ibid.*, paras. 585–587.
464. *Ibid.*, US Counter-Memorial, (19 September 2006), at 227 ('Glamis has also failed to present any evidence of relevant State practice to support its contention that Article 1105(1) imposes a general obligation on States to refrain from "arbitrary" conduct. Instead, it relies exclusively on judicial and arbitral decisions, that, when subject to scrutiny, do not support its contention. No Chapter Eleven tribunal has held that decision-making by an administrative or legislative body that appears "arbitrary" to some parties is sufficient to constitute a violation of Article 1105(1). To the contrary, NAFTA Chapter Eleven tribunals have consistently held that a high level of deference must be accorded to administrative decision-making').
465. *Ibid.*, Award, (8 June 2009), paras. 589, 591.

international law[466] since proof of 'manifest arbitrariness falling below international standards' is required.[467]

The tribunal rejected the investor's argument that customary international law had moved beyond the minimum standard of treatment of aliens as defined in *Neer*.[468] The tribunal mentioned the 'abundant and continued use of adjective modifiers throughout arbitral awards, as evidencing the existence of a strict standard'.[469] The tribunal clearly enumerated 'arbitrariness' as one of the elements contained within the FET standard: 'claimant has sufficiently substantiated its arguments that a duty to protect investors from arbitrary measures exists in the customary international law minimum standard of treatment of aliens'.[470] The tribunal also endorsed *Thunderbird's* terminology of 'manifest arbitrariness'.[471] It made reference to an 'obligation of each of the NAFTA State Parties inherent in the fair and equitable treatment standard of Article 1105 that they do not treat investors of another State in a *manifestly* arbitrary manner'.[472] The tribunal further explained that the modifier 'manifest' before the adjective 'arbitrariness' was proof of the standard of deference that NAFTA tribunals must exercise towards governmental decisions. As such, a breach of Article 1105 'requires something greater than mere arbitrariness, something that is surprising, shocking, or exhibits a manifest lack of reasoning'.[473]

The tribunal also agreed with the *ELSI* case's proposition that 'arbitrariness that contravenes *the* rule of law, rather than *a* rule of law, would occasion surprise not only from investors, but also from tribunals'.[474] It provided two examples of such a contravention to 'a' rule of law not amounting to a breach of Article 1105: 'a tribunal's determination that an agency acted in a way with which the tribunal disagrees or that a state passed legislation that the tribunal does not find curative of all of the ills presented'.[475] The tribunal referred to these situations as an 'appearance of arbitrariness'. On the contrary, arbitrariness that 'contravenes the rule of law' would reach the

---

466. *Ibid.*, para. 596, referring to US Rejoinder, (15 March 2007), at 206: 'A finding of the local courts that an act was unlawful may well be relevant to an argument that it was also arbitrary; but by itself, and without more, unlawfulness cannot be said to amount to arbitrariness. ... Nor does it follow from a finding by a municipal court that an act was unjustified, or unreasonable, or arbitrary, that that act is necessarily to be classed as arbitrary in international law, though the qualification given to the impugned act by a municipal authority may be a valuable indication'.
467. *Ibid.*, Award, (8 June 2009), para. 597, referring to US Counter-Memorial, (19 September 2006), at 227, 228 (itself quoting from *Thunderbird v. Mexico*, Award, (26 January 2006), para. 194).
468. *See*, the discussion at Chapter 2 section §2.03[B][2] above.
469. *Glamis v. United States*, Award, (8 June 2009), para. 614 (quoting from *Thunderbird v. Mexico*, Award, (26 January 2006), para. 194).
470. *Ibid.*, para. 626.
471. *Ibid.*, para. 616 ('to violate the customary international law minimum standard of treatment codified in Article 1105 of the NAFTA, an act must be sufficiently egregious and shocking—a gross denial of justice, manifest arbitrariness (...)'). *See also*, para. 627.
472. *Ibid.*, para. 626, emphasis added.
473. *Ibid.*, para. 617.
474. *Ibid.*, para. 625, emphasis in the original.
475. *Ibid.*

'level of arbitrariness' that amounts to a 'gross denial of justice or manifest arbitrariness falling below acceptable international standards'.[476] The tribunal also added that the mere illegality of a governmental measure would not reach the level of arbitrariness necessary to breach Article 1105:

> A finding of arbitrariness requires a determination of some act far beyond the measure's mere illegality, an act so manifestly arbitrary, so unjust and surprising as to be unacceptable from the international perspective.[477]

Having made these findings, the tribunal examined claimant's three allegations of arbitrariness related to the actions of the federal government.[478]

The first allegation was that a legal opinion (the 'M-Opinion') was an 'arbitrary contravention' to existing mining law which in turn 'violated Respondent's obligation to maintain a fair and transparent business environment on which an investor may base reasonable expectations' that its project would be approved.[479] This argument has already been discussed above in the section dealing with legitimate expectations.[480] While the tribunal recognized that the M-Opinion 'represented a significant change from settled practice',[481] it concluded that it was not arbitrary since it 'did not exhibit a manifest lack of reasons' nor did it involve any 'blatant unfairness or evident discrimination to this particular investor' because of its general applicability.[482] The tribunal added that while it was 'possible' that some aspects of the issuance of the 1999 M-Opinion 'could rise to the level of a violation of customary international law', what mattered in the end was the fact that any such deficiencies had been promptly remedied in a second (2001) legal opinion.[483]

The second allegation concerned the 'intentional and unreasonable'[484] delay of review of the Project which was said to be arbitrary.[485] On this point, the tribunal simply noted that the 'failure of a governmental body to diligently pursue administrative review while also defending an arbitration with respect to that same review' was not 'manifestly arbitrary'.[486]

Claimant's third allegation was that the denial of the Project by the government was discriminatory since 'numerous other projects with significant and similar cultural characteristics were approved, both before and after the denial of the Imperial Project,

---

476. *Ibid.*, quoting from *Thunderbird v. Mexico*, Award, (26 January 2006), para. 194.
477. *Ibid.*, para. 626.
478. *Ibid.*, para. 631.
479. *Ibid.*, para. 633.
480. *See*, section §3.02[B][4].
481. *Glamis v. United States*, Award, (8 June 2009), para. 759.
482. *Ibid.*, paras. 764, 765. *See also*, para. 763.
483. *Ibid.*, para. 771.
484. *Ibid.*, para. 631.
485. *Ibid.*, para. 631. One litigious aspect was the fact that the review process had continued after the claimant had filed its Notice of Intent in these arbitration proceedings. The review was, however, later discontinued by the government based on its belief that the claimant had in fact abandoned its claim.
486. *Ibid.*, para. 776.

without complete backfilling and despite severe impacts to their cultural resources'.[487] To the claimant's argument that the Project 'contained no cultural attributes that would differentiate it from other projects in the area',[488] the United States responded that, on the contrary, it was 'unique among its neighbors with respect to cultural significance'.[489] The tribunal did not take a stance on this issue and simply noted that the 'processes and the decisions' based upon which the United States had come to the conclusion that the Project was indeed 'culturally unique' were not 'manifestly arbitrary, completely lacking in due process, exhibiting evident discrimination, or manifestly lacking in reasons'.[490]

The tribunal then moved to examine claimant's allegations that Senate Bill 22 of the State of California and State Mining and Geology Board ('SMGB') regulations were 'specifically targeted'[491] at the Project and were therefore 'clearly discriminatory'.[492] It should be noted that the tribunal examined this discrimination argument as part of its analysis of arbitrariness.[493] In any event, the tribunal rejected the allegation that the Project had been specifically targeted by the Bill.[494] Thus, the Bill was of 'general application'[495] as it 'appears to apply to potentially several mines, if not yet at present, then in the future'.[496]

Claimant also argued that Senate Bill 22 requiring mandatory complete backfilling of open-pit metallic mines was arbitrary because it was 'not rationally related to its stated purpose of protecting cultural resources' and, in fact, could cause greater environmental degradation.[497] In its pleadings, the United States recognized that 'arbitrariness could be found in legislation bearing no rational relationship to the purported aims, but that this [was] not the case with the California measures'.[498] At the outset, the tribunal reiterated that the standard to be applied to resolve this allegation was whether or not Senate Bill 22 was 'manifestly arbitrary'.[499] It concluded that it was

---

487. *Ibid.*, para. 645. The claimant also referred (at para. 650) to a number of other features of the review which it considered as arbitrary.
488. *Ibid.*, para. 780.
489. *Ibid.*, para. 781.
490. *Ibid. See also*, at para. 788. Other allegations put forward by the claimant were also not considered by the tribunal as arbitrary (*see*, at paras. 782–787).
491. *Ibid.*, para. 681.
492. *Ibid.*, para. 677.
493. This is clear from this passage (at *Ibid.*, para. 542, footnote 1087): 'as part of the duty prescribed by Article 1105 to not act arbitrarily, there is a duty to not unfairly target a particular investor, whether based upon nationality or some other characteristic'.
494. *Ibid.*, para. 797. *See also*, para. 820.
495. *Ibid.*, para. 687. *See also*, at para. 820, where the tribunal explains that the 'likely characteristics of a law of general application' is that 'it is not strictly limited in time or geographic scope, and it is not crafted so as to exclude from its regulation all, or most, other similarly situated actors'.
496. *Ibid.*, paras. 793, 794. *See also*, para. 796.
497. *Ibid.*, para. 687. *See also*, para. 677.
498. *Ibid.*, para. 716, quoting from Counsel for Respondent, Tr. 1409:7-14.
499. *Ibid.*, para. 803 ('To begin its assessment of Claimant's argument that SB 22 is actionably arbitrary in that it does not protect cultural resources and may even cause environmental harm, the Tribunal notes the standard articulated above as to when an act is so manifestly arbitrary as to breach a State's obligations under Article 1105: this is not a mere appearance of arbitrariness—a tribunal's determination that an agency acted in way with which the tribunal disagrees or a State passed legislation that the tribunal does not find curative of all the ills

not the case here since the Bill 'was rationally related to its stated purpose and reasonably drafted to address its objectives'.[500] Finally, the tribunal addressed the claimant's allegation that the SMGB Regulations (also requiring complete backfilling of open-pit mines) were 'arbitrary in that they [were] not rationally related to their objectives'.[501] According to the claimant, the fact that the regulations excluded non-metallic mines was indicative of a lack of rationality.[502] The tribunal concluded that there was not a 'manifest lack of reasons' supporting the distinction between non-metallic and metallic mines[503] and that it was therefore not arbitrary.[504]

Ultimately, the tribunal concluded that none of the allegations raised by the claimant, considered individually[505] or as a whole,[506] were arbitrary in breach of Article 1105.

[5] Cargill

This case involves Cargill, Inc., a US corporation, which filed a notice of arbitration against Mexico on behalf of itself and its wholly-owned subsidiary, Cargill de Mexico S.A. de C.V. (a Mexican company). Along with two other NAFTA Chapter 11 disputes (*ADM*[507] and *Corn Products*[508]) and a closely intertwined trade dispute between the United States and Mexico,[509] the protection of the sugar industry in Mexico was at the

---

presented; rather, this is a level of arbitrariness that, as *International Thunderbird* put it, amounts to a "gross denial of justice or manifest arbitrariness falling below acceptable international standards." The act must, in other words, "exhibit a manifest lack of reasons"').
500. *Ibid. See also*, para. 807 ('Claimant has not satisfied the Tribunal that Senate Bill 22 is manifestly arbitrary, is evidently discriminatory, or exhibits a complete lack of reasons').
501. *Ibid.*, para. 816.
502. *Ibid.*
503. *Ibid.*, para. 817.
504. *Ibid.*
505. *Ibid.*, para. 824 ('The Tribunal holds that Claimant has not established that the individual measures taken by the federal and California state governments fall below the customary international law minimum standard of treatment and constitute a breach of Article 1105 in that they are not egregious and shocking—a gross denial of justice, manifest arbitrariness, blatant unfairness, a complete lack of due process, evident discrimination, or a manifest lack of reasons').
506. The tribunal mentioned (at para. 825) that 'for acts that do not individually violate Article 1105 to nonetheless breach that article when taken together, there must be some additional quality that exists only when the acts are viewed as a whole, as opposed to individually'. It added (at para. 826) that 'it cannot see that the conduct as a whole would be a violation of the fair and equitable treatment standard when the individual acts comprising that whole are not, without a finding of intent'. Thus, 'the intent of the federal and California state governments to work together to halt the Imperial Project would be a powerful element in the Tribunal's determination of a violation of Article 1105' (para. 826). The tribunal concluded (at para. 826) that the claimant had not established such intent.
507. *Archer Daniels Midland Company and Tate & Lyle Ingredients Americas, Inc. v. Mexico*, ICSID No. ARB (AF)/04/5, Award, (21 November 2007).
508. *Corn Products International, Inc. v. Mexico*, ICSID No. ARB (AF)/04/1, Decision on Responsibility, (15 January 2008).
509. *See, Cargill, Inc. v. Mexico*, Award, (18 September 2009), paras. 102, 103.

heart of this dispute.[510] In December 2001, Mexico made an amendment to a statute imposing an excise tax on certain goods and services, including a 20% tax on soft drinks that used sweeteners other than cane sugar.[511] As a result of this new tax, many soft drink producers in Mexico which used HFCS decided to switch back to sugar cane. The changes resulted in monetary losses for many HFCS producers and suppliers.[512] In December 2001, Mexico also published decrees imposing new tariff rates on the importation of HFCS as well as new import permit requirements for HFCS from the United States.[513] This measure was especially relevant to Cargill which did not produce HFCS in Mexico and therefore had to rely entirely on HFCS imports for its business. Mexico finally repealed the tax in 2007, some five years after its entry into force.[514]

Cargill asserted that Mexico's measures violated several NAFTA provisions, including Article 1105, and sought more than USD 100 million in damages. One of the allegations regarding breach of Article 1105 concerned arbitrariness.[515] The tribunal held that it only had jurisdiction over allegations related to the import permit requirements.[516] In this respect, Cargill's key allegations were the unavailability of import permits, the lack of published criteria or procedure to obtain them and the fact that each of its permit request had been rejected.[517]

The tribunal first examined some theoretical elements pertaining to the claimant's allegation of arbitrariness. Mexico did not deny that the FET standard prevents arbitrariness, but added that the concept had been narrowly defined by tribunals (referring to the *ELSI* case).[518] The tribunal essentially agreed with Mexico and endorsed the position adopted by the *ELSI* case to the effect that 'arbitrariness is not so much something opposed to a rule of law, as something opposed to the rule of law' and that an 'arbitrary action' is 'a wilful disregard of due process of law, an act which shocks, or at least surprises, a sense of juridical propriety'.[519] Mexico also contended that 'even poor administration of government programs' does not amount to a

---

510. Producers of soft drinks have traditionally used cane sugar as a sweetener. But cane sugar has gradually been replaced in certain markets (such as in the United States) by a competing product: high fructose corn syrup ('HFCS'). In Mexico, the soft drinks market is still dominated by cane sugar, but HFCS has an increasingly important market share.
511. *Cargill, Inc. v. Mexico,* Award, (18 September 2009), para. 105.
512. *Ibid.,* para. 107.
513. *Ibid.,* para. 117.
514. In the mean time, the United States challenged the tax before the WTO and in October 2005 a panel ruled that Mexico had violated its obligations under Article III of the GATT (*see, ibid.,* para. 113).
515. *Ibid.,* para. 255: 'Claimant next argues that Respondent's HFCS measures were arbitrary, ambiguous and inconsistent as illustrated by three alleged facts: (1) the IEPS Tax was imposed solely in response to domestic political and protectionist pressure, rather than an attempt to raise revenue; (2) the permit requirement was not reasonably related to any purpose other than excluding HFCS imported from the United States, as illustrated by Respondent's failure to announce criteria for obtaining the permits; and (3) the IEPS Tax was in reality a tax on HFCS, not soft drinks, as soft drinks sweetened solely by sugar cane were exempted'.
516. *Ibid.,* para. 297.
517. *Ibid.,* paras. 118, 120.
518. *Ibid.,* para. 257.
519. *Ibid.,* para. 291. The tribunal added that the *ELSI's* definition of arbitrariness had been accepted by at least two of the NAFTA Parties as the 'best expression' of arbitrariness (referring to

violation of the minimum standard of treatment under customary international law.[520] Again, the tribunal endorsed Mexico's point of view:

> an actionable finding of arbitrariness must not be based simply on a tribunal's determination that a domestic agency or legislature incorrectly weighed the various factors, made legitimate compromises between disputing constituencies, or applied social or economic reasoning in a manner that the tribunal criticizes.[521]

The tribunal further explained that the 'inconsistent or questionable' application of policy or procedure is not arbitrary under international law per se; additional elements are required. It must be shown that the action 'constitutes an unexpected and shocking repudiation' of the host State's policy's purpose and goals or that it 'grossly subverts a domestic law or policy for an ulterior motive'.[522]

The tribunal concluded that the import permit requirement put in place by Mexico had violated Article 1105. Yet, at first, it is not entirely clear which specific element(s) of the FET standard had been breached. A closer examination of the tribunal's reasoning nevertheless shows that its conclusion was based on an analysis of arbitrary conduct.[523]

At the outset, the tribunal stated that the import permit 'was put into effect by Mexico with the express intention of damaging Claimant's HFCS investment to the greatest extent possible' which 'surpass[ed] the standard of gross misconduct and [was] more akin to an action in bad faith'.[524] The tribunal also concluded that the

---

Canada's position as described in *ADF v. United States*, Award, (9 January 2003), para. 121, and to Mexico's position in *Ibid.*, Mexico's Second Article 1128 Submission, (22 July 2002), at 16–18).

520. *Cargill, Inc. v. Mexico,* Award, (18 September 2009), para. 258.
521. *Ibid.*, para. 292. *See also*: 'The Tribunal also agrees with the view expressed in *S.D. Myers* [at para. 261] that a tribunal, in assessing whether an action of a State is arbitrary, need recognize that governments "make many potentially controversial choices" and, in doing so, may "appear to have made mistakes, to have misjudged the facts, proceeded on the basis of a misguided economic or sociological theory, placed too much emphasis on some social values over others and adopted solutions that are ultimately ineffective or counterproductive"'.
522. *Ibid.*, para. 293 ('The Tribunal thus finds that arbitrariness may lead to a violation of a State's duties under Article 1105, but only when the State's actions move beyond a merely inconsistent or questionable application of administrative or legal policy or procedure to the point where the action constitutes an unexpected and shocking repudiation of a policy's very purpose and goals, or otherwise grossly subverts a domestic law or policy for an ulterior motive'). Later in the award, at para. 296, the tribunal reiterated that 'to determine whether an action fails to meet the requirement of fair and equitable treatment, a tribunal must carefully examine whether the complained of measures were (…) arbitrary beyond a merely inconsistent or questionable application of administrative or legal policy or procedure so as to constitute an unexpected and shocking repudiation of a policy's very purpose and goals, or to otherwise grossly subvert a domestic law or policy for an ulterior motive (…)'.
523. This is clear from the fact that earlier in the award the tribunal mentioned (*Ibid.*, paras. 243, 288) that the claimant argued that the FET standard included four distinct elements. The tribunal concluded that the minimum standard of treatment under customary international law did not include two of these four obligations (stable and predictable environment protecting the investor's reasonable expectations, and transparency). The tribunal also refused to examine a third element (discrimination). The tribunal's analysis concerning Article 1105 was therefore necessarily made from the angle of arbitrariness (i.e., the fourth element of the FET standard mentioned by the claimant).
524. *Ibid.*, para. 298.

permit's objective was to injure the United States' HFCS producers and that there was no 'relationship between the means and the end of this requirement' other than to persuade the US government to change its trade policy:[525]

> Reviewing closely the record of this case, the Tribunal finds ample support for the conclusion that the import permit was one of a series of measures expressly intended to injure United States HFCS producers and suppliers in Mexico in an effort to persuade the United States government to change its policy on sugar imports from Mexico. The Tribunal finds that the sole purpose of the import permit requirement was to change the trade policy of the United States; while the sole effect was to virtually remove Claimant from the Mexican HFCS market. There is no other relationship between the means and the end of this requirement. The Tribunal finds the institution of a permit requirement for a few foreign producers in an attempt to persuade another nation to alter its trade practices to be manifestly unjust.[526]

Mexico thus 'targeted the few suppliers of HFCS that originated in the United States' which were 'forced to bear the entire burden of Respondent's effort to act on what it views as the United States' failure to comply with international obligations'.[527] The tribunal found that 'this willful targeting, by its nature, [was] a manifest injustice'.[528] More specifically, the tribunal was critical of the complete lack of objective criteria for the issuance of permits:

> [T]he import permit requirement surpasses the standard of gross misconduct and is more akin to an action in bad faith is supported by the fact that there was a complete lack of objective criteria put forth by the Mexican government by which a company could obtain a permit. The Tribunal finds Respondent's explanation that 'the publication of the criteria for applying import permits will be established when 'the necessary conditions' exist' to be insufficient, given that the existence of such conditions depended entirely on the actions of an unrelated third party with respect to its trade policies.[529]

---

525. It should be recalled here that in the context of the negotiations which led to the NAFTA, a fifteen year transition period was agreed by the United States and Mexico which provided for a gradual elimination of barriers to trade for both sugar and HFCS (*Ibid.*, para. 68). In 1997, Mexico adopted anti-dumping measures against imports of HFCS from the United States. The duties were challenged by the United States in the WTO. Two WTO panels found in 2000 and in 2001 that the measures were inconsistent with Mexico's obligations under the Anti-Dumping Agreement (para. 102). Some US suppliers of HFCS also pursued NAFTA Chapter 19 proceedings against Mexico. Panels rendered decisions in 2001 and 2002 asking Mexico to revoke its anti-dumping duties (para. 103). Finally, Mexico requested the establishment of a panel under NAFTA Chapter 20 (State-State dispute settlement), but no panel was ever established to resolve this dispute.
526. *Ibid.*, para. 299.
527. *Ibid.*, para. 300.
528. *Ibid. See also*, para. 500 ('With respect to Article 1105, the Tribunal finds that Respondent, in an attempt to further its goals regarding United States trade policy, targeted a few suppliers of HFCS, all but annihilating a series of investments for the time that the permit requirement was in place. The Tribunal finds this willful targeting to breach the obligation to afford Claimant fair and equitable treatment').
529. *Ibid.*, para. 301.

Finally, the tribunal 'acknowledge[d] the dire and difficult circumstances that faced Mexico at the time of the measures in terms of the crisis gripping its sugar industry and the many citizens employed in that industry', but added that:

> The Tribunal does not assert that Mexico could not enact any laws and regulations to aid this industry and its populace. Rather, the Tribunal finds that the import permit requirement simultaneously breached the requirement to provide fair and equitable treatment under Article 1105(1). Mexico may seek to attain its objective by the regulation chosen, but it may not under Article 1105(1) leave the Claimant to bear the costs of this choice.[530]

Ultimately, the tribunal held that Mexico had breached NAFTA Articles 1102, 1105 and 1106. It ordered Mexico to pay to the claimant the sum of USD 77,329,240 in compensation. However, the tribunal did not explain which portion of that amount was specifically allocated as a compensation for the breach of Article 1105.

[6] Conclusion

Only one NAFTA Party (Mexico in *Cargill*) has been found responsible for arbitrary conduct in violation of Article 1105. Tribunals have made a number of important findings with respect to the scope of this concept. In the following paragraphs, seven observations will be made with regards to NAFTA case law.

First, a number of NAFTA tribunals have concluded that there exists a prohibition against arbitrary conduct under the minimum standard of treatment. Such was the finding of the *Glamis* tribunal which affirmed that 'a duty to protect investors from arbitrary measures exists in the customary international law minimum standard of treatment of aliens'.[531] The *Thunderbird*,[532] *Waste Management*[533] and *Mobil*[534] tribunals have also come to the same conclusion. The *Merrill & Ring* tribunal also implicitly endorsed this position.[535] A number of scholars also consider the prohibition of

---

530. *Ibid.*, para. 304.
531. *Glamis v. United States*, Award, (8 June 2009), para. 626.
532. *Thunderbird v. Mexico*, Award, (26 January 2006), para. 194: 'acts that would give rise to a breach of the minimum standard of treatment prescribed by the NAFTA and customary international law as those that, weighed against the given factual context, amount to a gross denial of justice or *manifest arbitrariness* falling below acceptable international standards', emphasis added.
533. *Waste Management v. Mexico*, Award, (30 April 2004), para. 98: the 'minimum standard of treatment of fair and equitable treatment is infringed by conduct attributable to the State and harmful to the claimant if the conduct is *arbitrary* (...)', emphasis added.
534. *Mobil v. Canada*, Decision on Liability and on Principles of Quantum, (22 May 2012), para. 152: 'the fair and equitable treatment standard in customary international law will be infringed by conduct (...) that is *arbitrary*', emphasis added.
535. *Merrill & Ring v. Canada*, Award, (31 March 2010), para. 187. Thus, while the tribunal did not openly affirm the existence of a prohibition against arbitrary conduct under the minimum standard of treatment, it nevertheless referred to the concept as a 'general principle of law' which is 'part of international law' and added that 'no tribunal today could be asked to ignore' such a 'basic obligation' under international law.

arbitrariness as an obligation under the minimum standard of treatment under custom.[536]

Second, it is noteworthy that while there is consensus amongst NAFTA tribunals on the customary nature of the prohibition against arbitrary conduct, none of these tribunals have actually gone through the exercise of examining State practice and opinio juris on the matter. In fact, NAFTA tribunals have based their support for this affirmation solely on previous findings of other tribunals.[537] Tribunals have typically referred to the reasoning of the ICJ in the *ELSI* case. Similarly, following its statement that 'previous [NAFTA] tribunals have indeed found a certain level of arbitrariness to violate the obligations of a State under the fair and equitable treatment standard',[538] the *Glamis* tribunal concluded that 'claimant has sufficiently substantiated its arguments that a duty to protect investors from arbitrary measures exists in the customary international law minimum standard of treatment of aliens'.[539] Yet, the *Glamis* tribunal did not examine State practice and opinio juris.

Third, NAFTA tribunals have considered arbitrary conduct as a stand-alone element of the FET standard under Article 1105 (*S.D. Myers*,[540] *Waste Management*,[541] *Gami*,[542] *Thunderbird*,[543] *Merrill & Ring*,[544] *Cargill*[545] and *Mobil*[546]). The most straight-forward affirmation to that effect is found in the *Glamis* award where the tribunal stated: 'there is an obligation of each of the NAFTA State Parties inherent in the fair and equitable treatment standard of Article 1105 that they do not treat investors of another State in a *manifestly* arbitrary manner'.[547] As mentioned above, it is true that a number of other tribunals have referred to the concept of arbitrariness in the context of their analysis of denial of justice (*Azinian*,[548] *Mondev*[549]). Still, these few tribunals

---

536. Newcombe & Paradell, *supra* n. 206, at 237, 249–250; Dolzer & Schreuer, *supra* n. 71, at 176; Todd Weiler, *Methanex Corp. v. U.S.A: Turning the Page on NAFTA Chapter Eleven?*, 6(6) J. World Invest. & Trade 917 (2005); Todd Weiler & Laird, *supra* n. 236, at 284–285. *Contra*: Heiskanen, *supra* n. 398, at 110 (for whom 'non-impairment standard [prohibiting arbitrary and unreasonable acts] imposes a standard of conduct on governments that is arguably substantially higher than that required by customary international law'); Paparinskis, *supra* n. 18, at 239; S. Montt, *State Liability in Investment Treaty Arbitration* (Hart Publ. 2009), at 295, 310.
537. For instance, the tribunal in *Thunderbird v. Mexico,* Award, (26 January 2006), refers in footnotes (at paras. 193–194) to several NAFTA awards (*S.D. Myers, Mondev, ADF, Azinian, Loewen*), one non-NAFTA award (*Genin*) and one ICJ case (*ELSI*). *See also*: *Waste Management v. Mexico*, Award, (30 April 2004), para. 98.
538. *Glamis v. United States*, Award, (8 June 2009), para. 625.
539. *Ibid.*, para. 626.
540. *S.D. Myers, Inc. v. Canada*, First Partial Award, (13 November 2000), para. 263.
541. *Waste Management v. Mexico*, Award, (30 April 2004), para. 98.
542. *Gami v. Mexico*, Award, (15 November 2004), paras. 98, 103.
543. *Thunderbird v. Mexico*, Award, (26 January 2006), para. 194. The tribunal, however, discussed arbitrariness in its analysis of the other FET element of due process.
544. *Merrill & Ring v. Canada*, Award, (31 March 2010), para. 208.
545. *Cargill, Inc. v. Mexico*, Award, (18 September 2009), paras. 292–293.
546. *Mobil v. Canada*, Decision on Liability and on Principles of Quantum, (22 May 2012), para. 152.
547. *Glamis v. United States*, Award, (8 June 2009), para. 626 (emphasis in the original).
548. *Azinian v. Mexico*, Award, (1 November 1999), para. 99.
549. *Mondev v. United States*, Award, (2 October 2011), para. 127.

have not rejected the proposition that the prohibition of arbitrariness is a stand-alone obligation under Article 1105.

Fourth, the main reason why NAFTA tribunals have been so keen on stating that arbitrary conduct is a stand-alone element of the FET standard is because Article 1105 does not contain any specific reference to the prohibition of arbitrary (or discriminatory) treatment.[550] Non-NAFTA tribunals that have interpreted similarly-drafted FET clauses (containing no express reference to arbitrariness) have also concluded that the prohibition of arbitrariness is one of the elements of the FET standard.[551] This is also the dominant opinion of authors.[552] It should be noted, however, that others have treated arbitrariness as a component of the denial of justice/due process category.[553]

This specific feature of NAFTA contrasts with that of a great number of BITs that include an FET clause containing additional substantive content, such as specific prohibition of arbitrary, unreasonable and discriminatory measures.[554] The present author's own survey of 365 BITs has shown that this is the case for 197 of them.[555] Parties include such language to be 'more precise about the content of the FET obligation and more predictable in its implementation and subsequent interpretation'.[556] The inclusion of the word 'arbitrary' in such a clause is largely perceived as redundant since the FET standard includes a prohibition of arbitrariness.[557] This is why some tribunals have applied these two standards together interchangeably.[558]

In addition to containing an FET clause, a number of BITs are comprised of *another distinct* stand-alone non-impairment clause explicitly prohibiting 'arbitrary', 'unjustified' 'unreasonable' or 'discriminatory' measures (sometimes in conjunction

---

550. Schreuer, *supra* n. 66, at 5; Diehl, *supra* n. 3, at 448; Yannaca-Small, *supra* n. 44, at 121. *See also*: Stone, *supra* n. 380, at 98 ('Because the term "arbitrary" is not found in any of the Chapter 11 provisions under which investors have based their claims, no tribunal has been required or at least felt compelled to inquire as to its plain or ordinary meaning').
551. Stone, *supra* n. 380, at 95, referring to a number of non-NAFTA cases.
552. *Ibid.*, at 91-92; Choudhury, *supra* n. 44, at 317; Salacuse, *supra* n. 11, at 238-241; Tudor, *supra* n. 3, at 179-180; Newcombe & Paradell, *supra* n. 206, at 249; Schill, *supra* n. 24, at 19-20; Lemaire, *supra* n. 306, at 39; Mayeda, *supra* n. 66, at 286-287; UNCTAD, *supra* n. 306, at 40; Vasciannie, *supra* n. 389, at 133.
553. OECD, *supra* n. 39, at 26 (indicating that one of the elements encompassed in the FET standard is 'due process including non denial of justice and lack of arbitrariness'), at 40 ('due diligence and due process including non-denial of justice and lack of arbitrariness are elements well grounded in international customary law'); OECD, *International Investment Law: A Changing Landscape: A Companion Volume to International Investment Perspectives* 73 (2005).
554. For instance, the Agreement between Mexico and the Federal Republic of Germany on the Promotion and Reciprocal Protection of Investments contains the following FET clause: 'Each Contracting State shall in any case accord investments of the other Contracting State fair and equitable treatment. Neither Contracting State shall in any way impair by arbitrary or discriminatory measures the operation, management, maintenance, use, enjoyment or disposal of such investments'.
555. P. Dumberry, *Rules of Customary International Law in the Field of International Investment Law*, SSHRC Research Project, (2012-2014).
556. UNCTAD, *supra* n. 11, at 29.
557. *Ibid.*, at 31 ('the notion of arbitrariness, unreasonableness and discrimination are intrinsic to the FET standard'); Newcombe & Paradell, *supra* n. 206, at 301.
558. Schreuer, *supra* n. 66, at 6, referring to a number of cases.

with one or the other ('and') and other times disjunctively ('or')[559].[560] Tribunals have
interpreted clauses of this nature inconsistently.[561] While a number of tribunals have
examined the FET standard clause and the arbitrary measure clause separately,[562]
others have applied these two standards in close conjunction.[563] The real impact of a
specific prohibition of arbitrary measures in a provision distinct from the FET clause is
also controversial amongst scholars. Several opine that there is essentially no substantive difference between the two clauses insofar as a measure violating a stand-alone
arbitrary clause would necessarily also violate the arbitrary element of an FET
clause.[564] Others consider that the fact that a BIT contains two distinct provisions is
evidence of the existence of different types of violations.[565] As such, while a violation
of the non-impairment standard would amount to a violation of the FET standard,[566]
'the finding that the non-impairment obligation has not been breached does not
necessarily mean that the FET standard has not been breached either'.[567] In any event,
this debate is not relevant in the context of NAFTA which does not contain any distinct
clause prohibiting arbitrary conduct.

Fifth, it is noteworthy that the position of NAFTA Parties has evolved over time
with respect to the issue of whether or not arbitrary conduct is a stand-alone element
of the FET standard under Article 1105. For instance, Canada's traditional position has
been to the effect that arbitrariness is not an independent source of obligation under
Article 1105; it is only relevant for the interpretation of other elements that are part of
the customary international minimum standard, such as denial of justice.[568] While

---

559. The question whether or not the use of these different words result in different meanings is
     examined in: Kläger, *supra* n. 13, at 289; Stone, *supra* n. 380, at 91; Heiskanen, *supra* n. 398,
     at 87; Schreuer, *supra* n. 66, at 4.
560. Dolzer & Schreuer, *supra* n. 71, at 173-174; Stone, *supra* n. 380, at 90-91; Newcombe &
     Paradell, *supra* n. 206, at 299.
561. Schreuer, *supra* n. 66, at 5 ff; Knahr, *supra* n. 236, at 510.
562. UNCTAD, *supra* n. 11, at 78. *See*, for instance: *LG&E v. Argentina*, Decision on Liability, (3
     October 2006), para. 162 ('characterizing the measures as not arbitrary does not mean that
     such measures are characterized as fair and equitable'); *Joseph C. Lemire v. Ukraine*, Decision
     on Jurisdiction and Liability, (21 January 2010), para. 259 ('The literal reading of Article II.3 of
     the BIT is more helpful. In accordance with the words used, Ukraine is assuming a positive and
     a negative obligation: the positive is to accord FET to the protected foreign investments, and the
     negative is to abstain from arbitrary or discriminatory measures affecting such investments.
     Any arbitrary or discriminatory measure, by definition, fails to be fair and equitable. Thus, any
     violation of subsection (b) seems *ipso iure* to also constitute a violation of subsection (a). The
     reverse is not true, though. An action or inaction of a State may fall short of fairness and equity
     without being discriminatory or arbitrary. The prohibition of arbitrary or discriminatory
     measures is thus an example of possible violations of the FET standard').
563. Schreuer, *supra* n. 66, at 5, referring to a number of cases.
564. Stone, *supra* n. 380, at 91; Knahr, *supra* n. 236, at 506-507; Vasciannie, *supra* n. 389, at 133;
     Heiskanen, *supra* n. 398, at 94.
565. Schreuer, *supra* n. 66, at 7; Dolzer & Schreuer, *supra* n. 71, at 175; Diehl, *supra* n. 3, at 449.
566. Tudor, *supra* n. 3, at 180 ('when it is found that a measure has clearly been arbitrary and
     discriminatory, the breach of the FET obligation is almost a natural conclusion').
567. Diehl, *supra* n. 3, at 452, *see also* at 450 ('a breach of the non-impairment standard will always
     be a breach of the FET standard, while the absence of discrimination will not have any impact
     on the findings concerning the breach of FET') and at 452.
568. *UPS v. Canada*, Canada's Counter-Memorial, (22 June 2005), paras. 924, 928.

Canada took the same stance (as a matter of principle) in *Merrill & Ring*,[569] it also put forward a fall-back position emphasizing the high threshold of liability for arbitrariness under the minimum standard of treatment.[570] The final stage of the evolution of Canada's view on this issue seems to have been completed in the recent cases of *Gallo*[571] and *Mobil*.[572] In these recent cases, Canada no longer denies that arbitrary conduct is an element of the FET standard under Article 1105, but instead emphasizes the requirement that such conduct be *manifestly* arbitrary.

The evolution of the United States' viewpoint on this issue is similar. In earlier cases, it systematically argued that there was no general obligation to refrain from 'arbitrary' conduct under Article 1105.[573] In recent cases, the United States has continued to maintain this basic argument,[574] but added that 'if there is an obligation for a State to not act arbitrarily',[575] a high threshold would nevertheless apply to consider arbitrariness as a violation of Article 1105.[576] In contrast, Mexico has consistently acknowledged that arbitrariness is one of the elements of the FET standard under Article 1105[577] and that the threshold to establish arbitrariness is high.[578]

Sixth, the threshold applied by NAFTA tribunals in order to establish a finding of arbitrariness has been consistently high. This restrictive interpretation results from tribunals adopting the standard set out by the ICJ in *ELSI* requiring, *inter alia*, that a

---

569. *Merrill & Ring v. Canada*, Canada's Counter-Memorial, (13 May 2008), paras. 492 (the 'so-called prohibition against arbitrary conduct is in fact not an independent source of legal obligation under NAFTA'), 494 ('no stand-alone obligation preventing arbitrariness exists at international law'). *See also*, at para. 498.
570. *Ibid.*, Canada's Rejoinder, (27 March 2009), para. 172. *See also*: Canada's Counter-Memorial, (13 May 2008), paras. 557, 559 ('the concept of arbitrariness has been discussed in several NAFTA cases which affirmed a high threshold for breach').
571. *Vito G. Gallo v. Canada*, Canada's Statement of Defence, (15 September 2008), para. 182. In the same document (paras. 196, 197) Canada also rejected claimant's allegation that Article 1105 includes a number of obligations (such as transparency, good faith and legitimate expectation), but did not enumerate arbitrariness in that list.
572. *Mobil v. Canada*, Canada's Counter-Memorial, (5 October 1999), para. 246. Canada also indicates (at para. 247) that the *Glamis v. United States*, Award, (8 June 2009), para. 627 (which refers to 'manifest arbitrariness'), had 'summarized the minimum standard of treatment as it currently exists under customary international law'.
573. *ADF v. United States*, Award, (9 January 2003), para. 116.
574. *Glamis v. United States*, US Counter-Memorial, (19 September 2006), at 227.
575. *Ibid.*, US Rejoinder, (15 March 2007), at 206, quoted in: Award, (8 June 2009), para. 596.
576. *Ibid.*, US Counter-Memorial, (19 September 2006), paras. 227, 228, 230. This is discussed in: Award, (8 June 2009), para. 597.
577. *Metalclad v. Mexico*, Mexico's Counter-Memorial, (11 February 1998), para. 841 ('The fair and equitable treatment standard requires the Respondent to act in good faith, reasonable, without abuse, *arbitrariness* or discrimination', emphasis added).
578. *ADF v. United States*, Mexico's Second Article 1128 Submission, (22 July 2002), at 14, 15; *Mondev v. United States*, Award, (2 October 2011), para. 108 (where the tribunal quoted Mexico to the effect that the ICJ *ELSI* case discussion on the notion of arbitrariness was 'instructive as to the standard of review that the international tribunal must employ when examining whether a State has violated the international minimum standard'). *See also*, Mexico's position in: *Waste Management v. Mexico*, Award, (30 April 2004), Mexico's Counter-Memorial, (undated), para. 243(h); *Gami v. Mexico*, Mexico's Statement of Defense, (24 November 2003), para. 243; *Cargill, Inc. v. Mexico*, Award, (18 September 2009), para. 257; *Thunderbird v. Mexico*, Mexico's Statement of Defense, (18 December 2003), para. 244; *ibid.*, Mexico's Rejoinder, (7 April 2004), paras. 149, 150.

finding of arbitrariness 'shocks, or at least surprises, a sense of juridical propriety'.[579] Similar wording has been used by earlier NAFTA tribunals, including *S.D. Myers* (referring to treatment that 'rises to the level that is unacceptable from the international perspective'[580]), *Waste Management* (speaking of '*wholly* arbitrary' conduct[581]) and *Thunderbird* (requiring proof of 'manifest arbitrariness falling below international standards'[582]). The *Thunderbird* award was the first one to set the threshold level at 'manifest arbitrariness' (although its reasoning was made in the different context of allegations of lack of due process[583]). Later, the *Glamis* tribunal reiterated that a breach of Article 1105 'requires something greater than mere arbitrariness, something that is surprising, shocking, or exhibits a manifest lack of reasoning'.[584] It also set the threshold of liability at 'manifest arbitrariness'.[585] Finally, the *Cargill* tribunal also imposed a high threshold of liability.[586]

On the contrary, after having examined case law pertaining to Article 1105, the *Mobil* tribunal 'summarized the applicable standard' under that provision as requiring 'arbitrary' conduct, without using any qualifying adjective.[587] This is surprising considering the fact that the tribunal referred to (and endorsed) the high threshold mentioned in the *Glamis* and *Thunderbird* awards.[588] Similarly, the *Merrill & Ring* tribunal stated that conduct which is, *inter alia*, 'arbitrary' 'has also been noted by NAFTA tribunals as constituting a breach of fair and equitable treatment'.[589] In that case, the tribunal's decision not to use the expression 'manifest arbitrariness' was clearly deliberate. Thus, the same expression ('arbitrary' without the modifier 'manifest') is used throughout the award.[590] The tribunal also adopted a much lower threshold of liability whereby Article 1105 'provides for the fair and equitable treatment of alien investors within the confines of reasonableness'.[591] The practical

---

579. Stone, *supra* n. 380, at 100 (indicating that '[o]f the ten tribunals that feature a threshold for determining arbitrariness, seven reference the *ELSI* standard either directly or indirectly'). *See*, for instance: *Mondev v. United States*, Award, (2 October 2011), para. 127; *Pope & Talbot Inc. v. Canada*, Award on the Merits (Phase 2), (10 April 2001), paras. 63, 64.
580. *S.D. Myers, Inc. v. Canada*, First Partial Award, (13 November 2000), para. 263.
581. *Waste Management v. Mexico*, Award, (30 April 2004), para. 115 (emphasis added).
582. *Thunderbird v. Mexico*, Award, (26 January 2006), para. 194.
583. *See*, section §3.02[G][10].
584. *Glamis v. United States*, Award, (8 June 2009), para. 617.
585. *Ibid.*, paras. 626–627.
586. *Cargill, Inc. v. Mexico*, Award, (18 September 2009), para. 293. *See also* para. 296 ('to determine whether an action fails to meet the requirement of fair and equitable treatment, a tribunal must carefully examine whether the complained of measures were (…) arbitrary beyond a merely inconsistent or questionable application of administrative or legal policy or procedure so as to constitute an unexpected and shocking repudiation of a policy's very purpose and goals, or to otherwise grossly subvert a domestic law or policy for an ulterior motive (…)').
587. *Mobil v. Canada*, Decision on Liability and on Principles of Quantum, (22 May 2012), para. 152.
588. *Ibid.*, paras. 143, 146.
589. *Merrill & Ring v. Canada*, Award, (31 March 2010), para. 208.
590. For instance, the tribunal refers (at para. 236) to Canada's policy which 'could not be fairly described in this context as meeting any of the adjectives that have been used over the years, such as egregious, outrageous, *arbitrary*, grossly unfair or manifestly unreasonable' (emphasis added). *See also*, at para. 239.
591. *Ibid.*, para. 123. Evidence of such a lower threshold is also clear from this other passage: 'What matters is that the [FET] standard protects against all such acts or behavior that might infringe a sense of fairness, equity and reasonableness' (para. 210).

consequence of adopting *Merrill & Ring*'s low threshold of mere 'reasonableness' would be to greatly facilitate future tribunals' findings of a breach of arbitrariness.[592] In the present author's view, this low threshold of liability should not be used by tribunals in the future.

Seventh, the application of this high threshold of liability by most NAFTA tribunals largely explains why they (for all except one, *Cargill*) have not found arbitrary conduct to amount to a breach of Article 1105. It should be noted that the *Cargill* case was a clear example of arbitrary conduct. The tribunal held that Mexico had deliberately and intentionally targeted the US investor in retaliation for a US trade policy. The high threshold of liability under NAFTA Article 1105 contrasts with the situation prevailing outside of NAFTA where a number of tribunals have found violations of arbitrariness based on a lower threshold.[593] Stone explains that the following measures have been found to be (or not to be) in violation of the prohibition of arbitrariness outside of NAFTA:

> Government measures that have been found to be arbitrary include threats and the blocking of payments to a foreign-owned water treatment company, the transfer of contractual rights of a foreign-owned media company to one that was domestically owned [*Lauder*] administrative decisions causing investor confusion regarding a country's tax regime, [*Occidental*] a breach of contract and eventual privatization of a state-owned hotel that had contracted with a foreign investor [*Alpha*], and the permanent suspension of a foreign investor's operations after substantial investment [*Siemens*]. Conversely, instances in which claims of arbitrariness were found wanting involved measures that were deemed arbitrary but did not substantially impair the investment [*CMS*] that had been the subject of negotiations with the investor; [*LG&E*] that were consistent with pre-investment measures, if not more onerous; [*AES*] that were justified by a period of economic transition in an emerging economy; [*Genin*] and that were made in response to an economic crisis [*Enron, Sempra*].[594]

In sum, there is consensus that 'arbitrariness' is a stand-alone obligation under Article 1105. In light of the case law examined above, a number of conclusions can be drawn about the contours of this prohibition of arbitrariness:

- A measure that is common in the 'internal legal systems or in the administrative practice of many states'[595] will generally not be considered as

---

592. It should be noted, however, that in this case the tribunal concluded that Canada's conduct was not arbitrary (*Ibid.*, paras. 235, 236).
593. Stone, *supra* n. 380, at 103 ('Where the two regimes begin to diverge is the level of arbitrariness that could lead to a successful claim. While both regimes typically use high thresholds (*ELSI*), [non-NAFTA] arbitral tribunals have been willing to entertain lower thresholds for finding arbitrariness than their NAFTA counterparts. This is likely tied to the attention afforded to the meaning of "arbitrariness" by [non-NAFTA] tribunals versus the lack of any discussion whatsoever on the topic by NAFTA tribunals. As a probable corollary to these differences in threshold, NAFTA tribunals have yet to find a single instance of arbitrary conduct that amounts to a breach of Article 1105, whereas [non-NAFTA] tribunals have found several breaches occasioned by arbitrariness'). It should be noted that Stone's article was published in 2009, before the *Cargill* award was rendered.
594. *Ibid.*, at 97.
595. *ADF v. United States*, Award, (9 January 2003), para. 188.

arbitrary in violation of the FET standard under Article 1105. The *ADF* tribunal thus concluded that a U.S. measure dealing with domestic content and performance requirements in governmental procurement was common to all NAFTA Parties (as well as many other States) and therefore could not 'be characterized as idiosyncratic or aberrant and arbitrary'.[596]

– A government's failure to implement or to abide by its own laws and regulations does not amount to an arbitrary act in violation of the FET standard under Article 1105 (*Gami*[597] endorsed by *Cargill*[598]), unless it can be shown that the government committed a maladministration that amounts to an 'outright and unjustified repudiation' of such laws and regulations (*Gami*[599]).[600]

– A government's 'inconsistent' or 'questionable' application of its own policy or procedure does not amount to an arbitrary act in violation of the FET standard (*Cargill*[601]). For a breach of Article 1105 to occur, it must be shown that the application 'constitutes an unexpected and shocking repudiation of a policy's very purpose and goals' or that it 'grossly subverts a domestic law or policy for an ulterior motive' (*Cargill*[602]). Similarly, the fact that a government makes a 'mistake' does not amount to an arbitrary act in violation of the FET standard under Article 1105 (*S.D. Myers*[603] endorsed by *Gami*[604]). Also, the mere fact that a government agency 'acted in a way with which the tribunal disagrees' or that it adopted policy 'that the tribunal does not find curative of all of the ills presented' does not amount to an arbitrary act (*Glamis*[605]).

---

596. *Ibid.*
597. *Gami v. Mexico*, Award, (15 November 2004), paras. 91, 103. The tribunal also mentioned that one of the four 'implications' of the *Waste Management* award was that 'the failure to fulfil the objective of administrative regulations without more does not necessarily rise to the breach of international law' (para. 97).
598. *Cargill, Inc. v. Mexico*, Award, (18 September 2009), para. 287.
599. *Gami v. Mexico*, Award, (15 November 2004), paras. 91, 103, 104. The reasoning of the tribunal (at para. 94) also suggests that a State's failure to implement its own regulations based on arbitrary grounds could breach Article 1105.
600. Schreuer, *supra* n. 66, at 22 ('It follows that a violation by the host State of its own law will not automatically amount to a breach of the FET standard. This would be the case only if the violations were systemic and were to affect the stability and transparency of the investment's legal environment').
601. *Cargill, Inc. v. Mexico*, Award, (18 September 2009), paras. 98, 293, 296. *See also*, at para. 292 ('an actionable finding of arbitrariness must not be based simply on a tribunal's determination that a domestic agency or legislature incorrectly weighed the various factors, made legitimate compromises between disputing constituencies, or applied social or economic reasoning in a manner that the tribunal criticizes').
602. *Ibid.*, paras. 293, 296.
603. *S.D. Myers, Inc. v. Canada*, First Partial Award, (13 November 2000), para. 261. The tribunal listed the following examples of such mistakes: 'to have misjudged the facts, proceeded on the basis of a misguided economic or sociological theory, placed too much emphasis on some social values over others and adopted solutions that are ultimately ineffective or counterproductive'.
604. *Gami v. Mexico*, Award, (15 November 2004), para. 93.
605. *Glamis v. United States*, Award, (8 June 2009), para. 625. *See also*, at para. 779 ('The Tribunal agrees with this statement. It is not the role of this Tribunal, or any international tribunal, to

- The fact that a governmental measure is illegal under domestic law does not necessarily make it arbitrary in violation of the FET standard under Article 1105 (*ADF*,[606] *Glamis*,[607] *Cargill*[608]).

- A government's legislation or regulation is arbitrary in violation of the FET standard when it can be shown that there is a 'manifest lack of reasons for the legislation' such as when the legislation bears no rational relationship to its stated purpose and when it is not 'reasonably drafted to address its objectives' (*Glamis*[609]).

- A government changing its past regulatory practice based on a legal opinion is not arbitrary unless this opinion 'exhibit[s] a manifest lack of reasons' (*Glamis*[610]) or unless these changes are specifically targeting an investor (*Glamis*[611]).

- A governmental measure (such as an import permit requirement) adopted with the express intention to injure and cause damage to an investor's investment is an arbitrary conduct in violation of Article 1105 (*Cargill*[612]). The *Waste Management* tribunal also mentioned that a 'deliberate conspiracy— that is to say, a conscious combination of various agencies of government without justification to defeat the purposes of an investment agreement' would breach Article 1105.[613] Similarly, a governmental measure that 'unfairly target[s] a particular investor, whether based upon nationality or some other

---

supplant its own judgment of underlying factual material and support for that of a qualified domestic agency. Indeed, our only task is to decide whether Claimant has adequately proven that the agency's review and conclusions exhibit a gross denial of justice, manifest arbitrariness, blatant unfairness, a complete lack of due process, evident discrimination, or a manifest lack of reasons so as to rise to the level of a breach of the customary international law standard embedded in Article 1105').

606. *ADF v. United States*, Award, (9 January 2003), para. 190 ('the Tribunal has no authority to review the legal validity and standing of the U.S. measures here in question under U.S. internal administrative law. We do not sit as a court with appellate jurisdiction with respect to US measures. Our jurisdiction is confined by NAFTA Article 1131(1) to assaying the consistency of the U.S. measures with relevant provisions of NAFTA Chapter 11 and applicable rules of international law. The Tribunal would emphasize, too, that even if the U.S. measures were somehow shown or admitted to be *ultra vires* under the internal law of the United States, that by itself does not necessarily render the measures grossly unfair or inequitable under the customary international law standard of treatment embodied in Article 1105(1). An unauthorized or *ultra vires* act of a governmental entity of course remains, in international law, the act of the State of which the acting entity is part, if that entity acted in its official capacity. But something more than simple illegality or lack of authority under the domestic law of a State is necessary to render an act or measure inconsistent with the customary international law requirements of Article 1105(1)').
607. *Glamis v. United States*, Award, (8 June 2009), para. 626.
608. *Cargill, Inc. v. Mexico*, Award, (18 September 2009), para. 303.
609. *Glamis v. United States*, Award, (8 June 2009), paras. 803, 817. *See also*: *Cargill, Inc. v. Mexico*, Award, (18 September 2009), para. 299.
610. *Glamis v. United States*, Award, (8 June 2009), para. 759.
611. *Ibid.*, paras. 542, 689, 763-765, 793-794.
612. *Cargill, Inc. v. Mexico*, Award, (18 September 2009), paras. 298, 301.
613. *Waste Management v. Mexico*, Award, (30 April 2004), para. 138, *see also*, at paras. 100, 137.

characteristic' also constitutes an arbitrary conduct in violation of Article 1105 (*Glamis*,[614] *Cargill*[615]).

- A governmental measure imposing a permit requirement involving a 'complete lack of objective criteria' as to how such a permit can be obtained is considered as an arbitrary conduct in violation of Article 1105 (*Cargill*[616]).

- A mere contractual breach (such as a failure of payment) does not amount to an arbitrary act in violation of the FET standard, unless it can be shown that the government committed an 'outright and unjustified repudiation of the transaction' (and prevented the creditor from having any remedy to address the problem), or unless it can be shown that the breach of contract was 'motivated by sectoral or local prejudice' (*Waste Management*[617]).[618]

[E]   Discriminatory Conduct

[1]   *Fair and Equitable Treatment Clauses Cover Discriminatory Measures other than Nationality-Based*

International law does not prohibit a State from providing for certain types of distinctions of treatment between nationals and foreigners in its legislation per se.[619] Thus, as mentioned by Thomas, '[a]t customary international law, a state has considerable freedom to discriminate in the treatment that it accords to other states, to restrict aliens' entry into its territory, and to prohibit them from working or conducting business there'.[620] Another example of discrimination that is permitted is the yielding of the right to vote exclusively to nationals.[621]

BITs typically contain two clauses (national treatment and Most-Favored-Nation ('MFN') clauses) which address the issue of nationality-based discrimination of foreign investors.[622] Under a national treatment clause, the host State 'extends to foreign

---

614. *Glamis v. United States*, Award, (8 June 2009), para. 542.
615. *Cargill, Inc. v. Mexico*, Award, (18 September 2009), paras. 300, 303, referring, for instance, to measures specifically targeting investors of one country for the sole purpose of persuading that country to change its policy as 'willful targeting' and 'a manifest injustice' contrary to Article 1105.
616. *Ibid.*, para. 301.
617. *Waste Management v. Mexico*, Award, (30 April 2004), para. 115.
618. The more general question of whether or not a contractual breach can be considered as a breach of the FET standard has already been discussed above at section §3.02[A].
619. *See*, the authorities referred to by the United States in these pleadings: *Grand River v. United States*, US Counter-Memorial, (22 December 2008), paras. 472, 473, 475; *Methanex v. United States*, US Amended Statement of Defense, (5 December 2003), para. 367.
620. J.C. Thomas, *Reflections on Article 1105 of NAFTA: History, State Practice and the Influence of Commentators*, 17(1) ICSID Rev. 24 (2002).
621. Newcombe & Paradell, *supra* n. 206, at 250.
622. National treatment and MFN protection are, however, generally not considered to be part of customary international law: MacLachlan et al., *supra* n. 37 at 17, 212-213, 251, 262-263; C. McLachlan, *Investment Treaties and General International Law*, 57 ICLQ 400 (2008); Barton Legum, *Dallas Workshop 2001: Commentary Scene III: ICSID Proceedings in the Absence of a Bilateral Investment Treaty*, 18(3) Arb. Int'l 306 (2002); Abdullah Al Faruque, *Creating*

investors treatment that is at least as favourable as the treatment that it accords to national investors in like circumstances'.[623]

A significant number of BITs also contain an FET clause which specifically and expressly prohibits 'discriminatory' (as well as arbitrary and unreasonable) measures. These clauses have already been examined above.[624] The real impact of adding this type of language to BITs is limited since it is generally considered that the FET standard prohibits some types of discriminatory treatment of foreign investors (and their investments).[625] A number of non-NAFTA tribunals have, indeed, held that the FET standard prohibits the discriminatory treatment of foreign investors and their investments.[626] A number of writers also believe that non-discrimination is one of the constitutive elements of the FET standard.[627]

It is generally recognized that a national treatment clause deals with a specific type of discrimination. Therefore, while such a clause covers discrimination based on the *foreign nationality* of an investor,[628] an FET clause (which expressly refers to the prohibition against discrimination) covers *other types* of discrimination against a foreign investor:

> While the national treatment and MFN standards deal with nationality-based discrimination, the non-discrimination requirement as part of the FET standard appears to prohibit discrimination in the sense of specific targeting of a foreign investor on other manifestly wrongful grounds such as gender, race or religious belief, or the types of conduct that amount to a 'deliberate conspiracy [...] to destroy or frustrate the investment' [quoting *Glamis v. United States*, Award, 8 June 2009, para. 542]. A measure is likely to be found to violate the FET standard

---

Customary International Law Through Bilateral Investment Treaties: A Critical Appraisal, 44 Indian JIL 304 (2004); Newcombe & Paradell, *supra* n. 206, at 149; N. Stephan Kinsella & Noah D. Rubins, *International Investment, Political Risk, and Dispute Resolution* 185 (Oceana 2005).

623. UNCTAD, *National Treatment* 1 (United Nations 1999).
624. *See*, section §3.02[D][6] on arbitrary conduct.
625. UNCTAD, *supra* n. 11, at 31; Newcombe & Paradell, *supra* n. 206, at 301.
626. *CME Czech Republic B.V. v. Czech Republic*, UNCITRAL, Partial Award and Separate Opinion, (13 September 2001), paras. 611, 612; *Eureko B.V. v. Poland*, UNCITRAL, Partial Award and Dissenting Opinion, (19 August 2005), para. 233. Some tribunals came to the same conclusion when faced with a BIT containing an FET clause as well as *another separate clause* prohibiting discriminatory measures: *CMS Gas Transmission Company v. Argentina*, Award, (12 May 2005), para. 290 ('any measure that might involve arbitrariness or discrimination is in itself contrary to fair and equitable treatment'); *Victor Pey Casado and President Allende Foundation v. Chile*, ICSID No. ARB/98/2, Award, (8 May 2008), paras. 671–674.
627. Newcombe & Paradell, *supra* n. 206, at 250, 288-289; Kläger, *supra* n. 13, at 187, 195; UNCTAD, *supra* n. 11, at 62; G. Schwarzenberger, *The Abs-Shawcross Draft Convention on Investments Abroad*, 14 C.L.P. 221 (1961); Vasciannie, *supra* n. 389, at 133 ('if there is discrimination on arbitrary grounds, or if the investment has been subject to arbitrary or capricious treatment by the host State, then the fair and equitable standard has been violated'); Choudhury, *supra* n. 44, at 311-314; S. Schill, *Revisiting a Landmark: Indirect Expropriation and Fair and Equitable Treatment in the ICSID Case Tecmed*, 3(2) Transnational Disp. Mgmt. 19 (2006); Diehl, *supra* n. 3, at 448; Tudor, *supra* n. 3, at 177-179, 182 ('A breach of [the non-discrimination] obligation triggers almost automatically a breach of FET since a discriminatory treatment could not possibly be fair and equitable'); Knahr, *supra* n. 236, at 506; Vandevelde, *supra* n. 27, at 65.
628. *See* Dolzer & Schreuer, *supra* n. 71, at 176; Frederico Ortino, *Non-Discriminatory Treatment in Investment Disputes*, in *Human Rights in International Investment Law and Arbitration* 348 ff (P.M. Dupuy, F. Francioni & E.U. Petersmann, eds., Oxford U. Press 2009).

if it evidently singles out (*de jure* or *de facto*) the claimant and there is no legitimate justification for the measure.[629]

Specific types of discrimination (other than nationality-based) prohibited under the FET standard include that based on race, sex and religion.[630] The *Universal Declaration of Human Rights* prohibits several types of discrimination.[631] The majority of the provisions contained within this instrument are generally considered to reflect customary international law.[632] Newcombe and Paradell refer to three other forms of discrimination that violate the FET standard: 'unjustifiable or arbitrary regulatory distinctions made between things that are like or treating unlike things in the same way', 'conduct targeted at specific persons or things motivated by bad faith or with an intent to injure or harass' and 'discrimination in the application of domestic law'.[633] This enumeration clearly highlights the overlap between the concepts of discrimination, 'arbitrariness',[634] and denial of justice. Scholars,[635] tribunals[636] and NAFTA Parties[637] alike attest that discrimination against a foreign litigant in court proceedings is one example of denial of justice. Generally, there is no ambiguity with respect to the FET standard

---

629. UNCTAD, *supra* n. 11, at 82.
630. Newcombe & Paradell, *supra* n. 206, at 149, 250, 288-289; L. Paradell, *The BIT Experience of the Fair and Equitable Treatment Standard*, in *Investment Treaty Law: Current Issues II* 129 (F. Ortino et al. eds., British IICL 2007).
631. United Nations, Universal Declaration of Human Rights, adopted on 10 December 1948 by G.A. Res. 271 A (III) UN Doc A/810. Article 2 provides that 'Everyone is entitled to all the rights and freedoms set forth in this Declaration, without distinction of any kind, such as race, colour, sex, language, religion, political or other opinion, national or social origin, property, birth or other status (…).' Article 7 further adds that 'All are equal before the law and are entitled without any discrimination to equal protection of the law. All are entitled to equal protection against any discrimination in violation of this Declaration and against any incitement to such discrimination'.
632. John H. Currie, Craig Forcese & Valerie Oosterveld, *International Law: Doctrine, Practice, and Theory* 558 (Irwin Law 2007); John Ruggie, *Current Developments. Business and Human Rights: The Evolving International Agenda*, 101 AJIL 833 (2007); Andrew Clapham, *Human Rights Obligations of Non State Actors* 86 (Oxford U. Press 2006); Javaid Rehman, *International Human Rights Law. A Practical Approach* 59-60 (Longman Pub. 2003).
633. Newcombe & Paradell, *supra* n. 206, at 288-289.
634. *Ibid.*, at 303. In fact, several authors (Kläger, *supra* n. 13, at 187, 196; Diehl, *supra* n. 3, at 448) analyze the concept of non-discrimination together with that of arbitrariness.
635. UNCTAD, *supra* n. 11, at 80; Newcombe & Paradell, *supra* n. 206, at 251 ('If domestic courts apply domestic law in a discriminatory manner (e.g., if a foreigner is denied the right to commence a claim in domestic courts based on the foreigner's nationality), the foreign investor will have grounds for claiming a breach of the customary minimum standard based on a denial of justice').
636. In *Loewen Group, Inc. and Raymond L. Loewen v. United States* [hereinafter *Loewen v. United States*], ICSID No. ARB(AF)/98/3, Award, (26 June 2003), the tribunal examined issues related to discrimination from the specific angle of denial of justice. This case is further discussed below at section §3.02[G][8].
637. *Grand River v. United States*, US Counter-Memorial, (22 December 2008), at 132 ('the minimum standard of treatment obligation requires governments to grant aliens access to their courts and judicial remedies on a non-discriminatory basis'); *Methanex v. United States*, US Amended Statement of Defense, (5 December 2003), para. 375.

not covering 'simple' *nationality*-based discrimination between national and foreign investors.[638] Yet, there may be some exceptions.[639]

The question further addressed below is whether an FET clause that *does not* contain any specific reference to discrimination, such as NAFTA Article 1105, implicitly prohibits discriminatory measures (not related to nationality).

Before examining NAFTA case law (in the next section), a few observations should be made on the requirements to prove discrimination (other than nationality-based) in violation of the FET standard. Discrimination requires more than a simple difference in treatment between national and foreign investors.[640] An investor must show that such a distinction is arbitrary, unreasonable and not 'based upon a rational foundation'.[641] There is no breach of the FET standard when there exists a 'reasonable justification' for such a distinction,[642] i.e., that it 'bears a reasonable relationship to rational policies not motivated by a preference for other investments over the foreign-owned investment'.[643] Tribunals have generally used an objective test which takes the consequences of a measure into account rather than the intent of the State.[644]

---

638. Newcombe & Paradell, *supra* n. 206, at 289 ('The argument against interpreting fair and equitable treatment as including nationality-based discrimination is that it would make national and MFN treatment provisions redundant, contrary to an effet utile interpretation. Second, the prevailing view is that national and MFN treatment are treaty-based obligations that do not arise under customary international law. If fair and equitable treatment is viewed as synonymous with the minimum standard of treatment, national treatment and MFN treatment would have become customary international law obligations. Third, national and MFN treatment obligations are often subject to a number of exceptions and reservations. These reservations typically do not apply to fair and equitable treatment. Since the overwhelming IIA treaty practice is to prohibit nationality-based discrimination through specific national and MFN treatment provisions, the intent to do so through general fair and equitable treatment provisions should not lightly be inferred without specific evidence of the parties' intentions. Accordingly, the better view is that a general fair and equitable treatment clause does not encompass relative standard of treatment guarantees'). *Contra*: Vandevelde, *supra* n. 27, at 65, 66 ('discriminatory conduct violates the fair and equitable treatment standard, but only when it lacks a reasonable justification. Nationality, of course, is not a reasonable basis for discrimination. Discrimination can be justified only by a legitimate, non discriminatory purpose').
639. Newcombe & Paradell, *supra* n. 206, at 306, explain that when a BIT does not contain separate national treatment and MFN provisions, a general reference to discrimination in the treaty should be interpreted as including nationality-based discrimination.
640. *Joseph Charles Lemire v. Ukraine*, ICSID No. ARB/06/18, Decision on Jurisdiction and Liability, (14 January 2010), para. 261.
641. Kläger, *supra* n. 13, at 193; Newcombe & Paradell, *supra* n. 206, at 290 ('Tribunals have confirmed that different treatment of similarly situated investments is discriminatory unless the state can establish a reasonable basis for the differential treatment'); Vandevelde, *supra* n. 27, at 63 ('The fair and equitable treatment standard, however, appears to prohibit only unreasonable discriminations'); Laird & Weiler, *supra* n. 236, at 287 ff.
642. *Saluka v. Czech Republic*, Partial Award, (17 March 2006), para. 313; *Joseph Charles Lemire v. Ukraine*, Decision on Jurisdiction and Liability, (14 January 2010), para. 261 ('To amount to discrimination, a case must be treated differently from similar cases without justification'); UNCTAD, *supra* n. 11, at 82 ('a measure is likely to be found to violate the FET standard if it evidently singles out (*de jure* or *de facto*) the claimant and there is no legitimate justification for the measure'); Kläger, *supra* n. 13, at 196.
643. *Saluka v. Czech Republic*, Partial Award, (17 March 2006), para. 307.
644. Dolzer & Schreuer, *supra* n. 71, at 177. *See*, for instance, *Siemens AG v. Argentina*, ICSID No. ARB/02/8, Award and Separate Opinion, (17 January 2007), para. 321 ('The Tribunal concurs that intent is not decisive or essential for a finding of discrimination, and that the impact of the

[2] The Reasons for Not Examining a Number of NAFTA Cases in this Section

The present author has decided not to examine cases where tribunals have discussed discrimination allegations in the different context of breach of the national treatment clause (Article 1102).[645] In some cases (not discussed here), tribunals have actually decided to examine such allegations under Article 1102 even though claimants had argued that the measures were in breach of the FET standard under Article 1105.[646] A number of other cases where tribunals have addressed discrimination allegations only in the context of denial of justice will not be elaborated upon. For instance, the *Loewen* tribunal held that 'a decision which is in breach of municipal law and is discriminatory against the foreign litigant amounts to manifest injustice according to international law'.[647] Similarly, while the *Waste Management* tribunal mentioned in its award that a conduct that is 'discriminatory and exposes the claimant to sectional or racial prejudice' would breach Article 1105,[648] it only examined discrimination allegations in the context of its enquiry as to whether or not any arbitrary conduct or denial of justice had been committed.[649] The *Gami* award is another example where the tribunal only addressed discrimination allegations in the context of a claim of arbitrariness.[650]

---

measure on the investment would be the determining factor to ascertain whether it had resulted in nondiscriminatory treatment'). A different position was adopted by the tribunal in *LG&E Energy Corp v. Argentina*, Decision on Liability, (3 October 2006), para. 146 ('a measure is considered discriminatory if the intent of the measure is to discriminate or if the measure has a discriminatory effect').

645. *See*, for instance: *Feldman v. Mexico*, Award, (16 December 2002), para. 184.
646. This is, for instance, the case in the *ADF* award where the investor argued that the Buy American program resulted in 'effective discrimination' in breach of Article 1105, but where the tribunal only examined the question under Article 1102 (*ADF v. United States*, Award, (9 January 2003), paras. 114, 157–158). Similarly, in *Merrill & Ring* the investor argued that certain aspects of the Log Export Regime were discriminatory against private log producers like him and that Article 1105 entailed, *inter alia*, an obligation 'not to act in an arbitrary or discriminatory manner'. On the contrary, Canada's position was that there was no obligation prohibiting discrimination under Article 1105. The tribunal only examined the issue of discrimination in the context of its analysis of Article 1102. *See*: *Merrill & Ring v. Canada*, Award, (31 March 2010), paras. 155, 166–167, 170; *ibid.*, Investor's Memorial, (13 February 2008), paras. 141, 200, Award, (31 March 2010), paras. 155, 167; *ibid.*, Canada's Counter-Memorial, (13 May 2008), paras. 501–506. Another example is the *Cargill* case where the claimant argued that the measures adopted by Mexico were discriminatory in violation of Article 1105. Based on the fact that in its pleadings the claimant simply replicated its arguments concerning a violation of Article 1102, the tribunal held that 'a discussion of whether a finding of discrimination will independently violate Article 1105 of the NAFTA is not called for at this time' (*Cargill, Inc. v. Mexico*, Award, (18 September 2009), para. 295).
647. *Loewen v. United States*, Award, (26 June 2003), para. 135. This case is examined below at section §3.02[G][8].
648. *Waste Management, Inc. v. Mexico*, Award, (30 April 2004), para. 98. This case is examined below at section §3.02[G][9].
649. *Ibid.*, paras. 87, 130, 132.
650. *Gami v. Mexico*, Award, (15 November 2004), paras. 24, 98; *ibid.*, Claimant's Notice of Arbitration, (9 April 2002), at 3, 4.

In the *S.D. Myers* case, the claimant alleged that measures taken by Canada were discriminatory in violation of, *inter alia*, Articles 1102 and 1105.[651] The majority of the tribunal decided not to examine the specific application of Article 1105 to the facts of the case, but to rely instead on its previous finding that a breach of Article 1102 had occurred. According to the majority of the tribunal, the breach of an international law provision designed to protect investments would 'tend to weigh heavily in favor' of the finding of a breach of Article 1105. The two arbitrators therefore concluded that the discriminatory treatment that the claimant had been subjected to in breach of Article 1102 'essentially establish[ed] a breach of Article 1105 as well'.[652] For this reason, the *S.D. Myers* award will not be analyzed in this section.

In *Glamis*, the claimant listed 'protection against arbitrariness and discrimination' as one of the duties imposed by Article 1105.[653] In the award, the tribunal nevertheless explained that the claimant was 'not arguing a duty of non-discrimination as a duty separate from those included in the requirement of fair and equitable treatment under Article 1105',[654] but within the broader element of arbitrariness.[655] For this reason, the tribunal examined the discrimination allegation from the angle of arbitrary conduct.[656] The analysis undertaken in some parts of the *Glamis* award is nevertheless relevant in the context of non-discrimination and will be discussed in the conclusion section.[657] Similarly, the *Grand River* tribunal's few pertinent observations on non-discrimination will also be examined in that section.

[3] Methanex

The dispute arose from the passage of an Executive Order, in March 1999, by the governor of the State of California prescribing for the removal of the gas additive MTBE from gasoline by no later than the end of 2002. The claimant (a Canadian company claiming for itself and on behalf and its US subsidiary) is a producer of methanol, a key ingredient in the production of MTBE. It argued, *inter alia*, that the measure was intended to discriminate against foreign investors and their investments, and that such 'intentional discrimination' was by definition unfair and contrary to Article 1105.[658]

---

651. *S.D. Myers Inc. v. Canada*, Claimant's Memorial on Merits, (20 July 1999), paras. 140, 141; *ibid.*, Claimant's Statement of Claim, (30 October 1998), para. 35; *ibid.*, Claimant's Reply to Mexico's Article 1128 Submission, (28 January 2000), paras. 25, 26.
652. *Ibid.*, First Partial Award, (13 November 2000), paras. 264, 266. On this point, arbitrator Edward C. Chiasson dissented and considered that a violation of Article 1105 must be based on a demonstrated failure of that clause and that the breach of another provision is not a foundation for such a conclusion.
653. *Glamis v. United States*, Award, (8 June 2009), para. 542.
654. *Ibid.*, para. 559, footnote 1128.
655. *Ibid. See also*, Claimant's Memorial, (5 May 2006), para. 521.
656. These allegations have already been examined above at section §3.02[D][4].
657. *See*, at section §3.02[E][4].
658. *Methanex v. United States*, Award, (3 August 2005), Part II, Ch. D, para. 27; *ibid.*, Claimant's Second Amended Statement of Claim, (5 November 2002), para. 313. The claimant also argued that the measures constituted a substantial interference having the effect of ending its business in breach of Article 1110.

The United States submitted several arguments to demonstrate that nationality-based discrimination was cabined exclusively under Article 1102, not Article 1105.[659] First, the minimum standard of treatment is an 'absolute' standard (i.e., that its content does not depend on how a State treats its own nationals) while the non-discrimination prohibition under Article 1102 is a 'relative' standard (i.e., an obligation based on how a Party treats its own investors/investments).[660] Second, to consider Article 1105 as incorporating a general obligation prohibiting discrimination would necessarily result in the infectiveness of NAFTA Article 1108 which contains several exceptions to the non-discrimination obligation under Article 1102.[661] Third, the claimant had failed to supply any 'legal support for its suggestion that discrimination is per se violative of customary international law's minimum standard'[662] for the simple reason that 'customary international law contains no general prohibition on economic discrimination against aliens'.[663]

The United States nevertheless acknowledged the existence of a prohibition of discrimination with regards to denial of justice under Article 1105:

> The principle of denial of justice includes the notion that aliens should not be discriminated against in terms of access to judicial remedies or treatment by the courts. The international minimum standard guarantees to aliens the right of free access to the courts on a non-discriminatory basis.[664]

It also made reference to another specific obligation under Article 1105 (al. 2) 'to compensate aliens and nationals on an equal basis for damages incurred during such times of violence, insurrection, conflict or strife'[665] in the broader context of a State's obligation to provide full protection and security to foreign investors.

---

659. *Ibid.*, US Amended Statement of Defense, (5 December 2003), para. 356.
660. *Ibid.*, paras. 358, 360 ('Methanex's attempt to read a general standard of non-discrimination – necessarily a relative standard – into Article 1105(1) thus cannot be squared with the ordinary meaning of its terms. Those terms clearly contemplate an absolute standard. Methanex's argument thus conflates the content of Article 1105(1) with that of Article 1102, when the two were clearly intended to be different').
661. *Ibid.*, paras. 361, 362 ('Thus, if Article 1105(1) incorporated a general obligation of non-discrimination, measures and activities permissible under the provisions of the NAFTA specifically addressing discrimination (notably Articles 1102 and 1103) would be rendered violations of the NAFTA under Article 1105(1). This would render ineffective the exceptions set forth in Article 1108 and scores of pages of annexes, contrary to the principle that treaties should be construed to render their provisions effective. Put another way, if the NAFTA Parties had contemplated that Article 1105(1) incorporated a general obligation of non-discrimination, they would have included exceptions in Article 1108 to exempt from Article 1105(1)'s ambit the discriminatory activities they considered permissible. The fact that the Parties did not address Article 1105(1) in Article 1108's exceptions shows that the Parties did not consider Article 1105(1) to encompass any general obligation of non-discrimination').
662. *Ibid.*, para. 366.
663. *Ibid.*, para. 367. *See also*, para. 368.
664. *Ibid.*, para. 375.
665. *Ibid.*, para. 376. The United States also acknowledged (at paras. 373–374) the existence of a prohibition of discrimination in the context of expropriation.

The tribunal first examined the claimant's allegations under Article 1102 and concluded that no discrimination had been proven.[666] The tribunal then moved to examine whether the FET standard under Article 1105 had been breached.

The tribunal stated that 'the plain and natural meaning of the text of Article 1105 does not support the contention that the minimum standard of treatment precludes governmental differentiations as between nationals and aliens' for the simple reason that 'Article 1105(1) does not mention discrimination'.[667] In the present author's view, from the mere fact that Article 1105 does not specifically mention discrimination, it cannot be deduced that it necessarily excludes it. By analogy, there is a general consensus that the FET standard under Article 1105 does prohibit arbitrary conduct and denial of justice even though these terms are not expressly mentioned in the provision. In fact, a number of writers believe that non-discrimination is one of the elements of the FET standard.[668] This is also the stance taken by some non-NAFTA tribunals faced with an FET clause that does not mention the word discrimination at all.[669] In any event, the *Methanex* tribunal's reflection on this point 'attributes excessive importance to the formulation of treaty rules in the determination of the content of customary law'.[670] The relevant question to be decided by the tribunal was indeed whether or not customary international law provides for a rule of non-discrimination.[671]

---

666. *Ibid.*, Award, (3 August 2005), Part IV, Ch. B, para. 22. For the tribunal, 'even assuming that Methanex, as a methanol producer, is deemed to be affected, as a legal and factual matter, under NAFTA and international law, by California's ban of MTBE, Methanex's claim under Article 1102 would fail because it did not receive treatment less favourable than United States investors in like circumstances'. Thus, 'the California MTBE ban did not differentiate between foreign and domestic MTBE producers' (para. 38).

667. *Ibid.*, Part IV, Ch. C, para. 14.

668. *See*, the writers mentioned above at *supra* n. 627.

669. The tribunal in *Parkerings-Compagniet AS v. Lithuania*, Award on Jurisdiction and Merits, Award, (11 September 2007), para. 287, had to interpret an FET clause not containing any specific reference to the prohibition of discriminatory measures and took the position that discriminatory action was a violation of the FET standard per se. The tribunal, however, concluded (at para. 290) that no discriminatory action had occurred in the case at hand since there was no other investor in a similar situation (in like circumstances) with which to compare the treatment given to the claimant. Another interesting example is *Victor Pey Casado and President Allende Foundation v. Chile*, ICSID No. ARB/98/2, Award, (8 May 2008). The tribunal had to interpret a BIT containing a *separate clause* prohibiting discriminatory measures and an FET clause, which *also* referred specifically to prohibition against discrimination. The tribunal concluded that discriminatory conduct would breach the FET clause even when a clause *does not* refer at all to the word discrimination: 'Il est constant dans la jurisprudence internationale et dans la doctrine qu'un traitement discriminatoire de la part d'autorités étatiques envers ses investisseurs étrangers constitue une violation de la garantie de traitement "juste et équitable" inclus dans des traités bilatéraux d'investissement. Un comportement discriminatoire sera couvert comme violation du traitement "juste et équitable" notamment dans les cas où le traité bilatéral en question ne contient pas de garantie expresse contre des actes arbitraires ou discriminatoires. Même dans les cas où le traité bilatéral contient une interdiction expresse de comportement arbitraire et discriminatoire, les tribunaux arbitraux ont décidé qu'un tel comportement violerait, en même temps, l'obligation de traiter ses investisseurs de manière "juste et équitable"' (paras. 670–672).

670. Paparinskis, *supra* n. 18, at 245.

671. *Ibid.*, at 245 ('if customary law provides a rule of non-discrimination, treaty parties have to either explicitly agree to remove it by a treaty rule or agree on an exhaustive rule of special customary law to prevent it from being brought into the treaty. Non-confirmation is insufficient

The tribunal continued its analysis by contrasting the language used at Article 1105 (al. 1), which does not mention discrimination, with that of Article 1105 (al. 2) which does prohibit discrimination between nationals and aliens with respect to measures relating to the losses suffered by investments due to armed conflict or civil strife. The tribunal opined that the fact that Article 1105 (al. 2) refers specifically to some prohibited discriminatory conducts while Article 1105 (al. 1) does not make it 'clear that discrimination is not included' as a component of Article 1105 (al. 1).[672] This reasoning is difficult to reconcile with the first words contained within Article 1105 (al. 2) which indicate that it is to be applied '[w]ithout prejudice to paragraph 1'. The more appropriate view is that Article 1105 (al. 2) establishes 'a specific obligation that does not limit the scope of paragraph 1'.[673] In other words, from the fact that paragraph 2 contains a specific type of prohibited discrimination it cannot be deduced that all other types of discrimination are excluded by paragraph 1. In any event, it is not at all clear why paragraph 2 was included in Article 1105 in the first place.[674]

The tribunal also stated that its conclusion that Article 1105 does not include any obligation of non-discrimination was further supported by the fact that '[e]lsewhere, when the NAFTA Parties wished to incorporate a norm of non-discrimination, they did so'.[675] The tribunal specifically referred to Article 1110(1)(b) which requires that a lawful expropriation be effected 'on a non-discriminatory basis'. The tribunal also referred to Article 1110(1)(c) which establishes that another requirement for a lawful expropriation is that it be effected 'in accordance with due process of law and Article 1105(1)'. The tribunal considered that the language of Article 1110(1)(c) 'makes [it] clear that the NAFTA Parties did not intend to include discrimination in Article 1105(1)'.[676] Thus, 'if Article 1105(1) had already included a non-discrimination

---

to preclude otherwise valid reference to customary law'). He argues (at 247) that the minimum standard of treatment under customary law prohibits discrimination.

672. *Methanex v. United States*, Award, (3 August 2005), Part IV, Ch. C, para. 14. The tribunal further explains that 'By prohibiting discrimination between nationals and aliens with respect to measures relating to losses suffered by investments owing to armed conflict or civil strife, the second paragraph imports that the preceding paragraph did not prohibit - in all other circumstances - differentiations between nationals and aliens that might otherwise be deemed legally discriminatory: *inclusio unius est exclusio alterius*. The textual meaning is reinforced by Article 1105(3), which makes clear that the exception in paragraph 2 is, indeed, an exception'.

673. M. Kinnear, A. Bjorklund & J.F.G. Hannaford, *Investment Disputes under NAFTA: An Annotated Guide to NAFTA Chapter 11* (Kluwer Law International, 2006), section on Article 1105, at 52. *See also*: Weiler, *supra* n. 536, at 916.

674. Kinnear et al. *supra* n. 673, at 52: 'It is unclear why the NAFTA Parties chose to include this non-discrimination obligation in the context of a provision addressing the objective minimum standard of treatment under international law. The negotiating texts cast little light on this question. It is possible that the Parties considered that this obligation would arise in such exceptional situations that it best belonged with paragraph 1, which prescribed the equally exceptional minimum standard. Canada has removed this aspect of the provision from the article concerning the minimum standard of treatment in its new Model FIPA and placed the relevant paragraphs under their own heading, "Compensation for Losses." The United States has likewise created in some of its agreements a freestanding obligation concerning "Treatment in Case of Strife," which is analogous to, but more detailed than, the last two paragraphs of Article 1105'.

675. *Methanex v. United States*, Award, (3 August 2005), Part IV, Ch. C, para. 15.

676. *Ibid.*, Part IV, Ch. C, para. 15.

requirement, there would be no need to insert that requirement in Article 1110(1)(b), for it would already have been included in the incorporation of Article 1105(1)'s due process requirement'.[677] The tribunal is certainly right on this point. It concluded its reasoning by stating that '[w]hen the NAFTA Parties did not incorporate a non-discrimination requirement in a provision in which they might have done so, it would be wrong for a tribunal to pretend that they had'.[678] As a result, 'even if Methanex had succeeded in establishing that it had suffered a discrimination for its claim under Article 1102, it would not be admissible for it, as a matter of textual interpretation, to establish a claim under Article 1105'.[679]

Finally, the tribunal also provided another reason to support its conclusion. It affirmed that the third paragraph of the FTC Note[680] 'confine[s] claims based on alleged discrimination to Article 1102, which offers full play for a principle of non-discrimination'.[681] It is difficult to see how the Note can be read as suggesting that all discrimination issues are only covered by Article 1102. The Note is not limited specifically to the relationship between Articles 1102 and 1105.

The tribunal finally turned to the question of differentiation under custom. It stated that international law was 'clear': 'In the absence of a contrary rule of international law binding on the States parties, whether of conventional or customary origin, a State may differentiate in its treatment of nationals and aliens'.[682] The tribunal then added that under customary international law, 'some differentiations are discriminatory'.[683] It should be recalled that the United States made reference in its pleadings to three types of discrimination prohibited under international law. In the award, the tribunal simply referred to one passage from the *Waste Management* ruling which states that a conduct that is 'discriminatory and exposes the claimant to sectional or racial prejudice' breaches Article 1105.[684] However, the *Methanex* tribunal did not take a stance on the soundness of such a statement.[685] In doing so, the tribunal therefore refused to address the controversial question of whether or not Article 1105 covers some type of discrimination other than nationality-based. In truth, the tribunal could hardly be criticized for failing to examine this issue. Thus, the tribunal had already come to the conclusion (when examining the claim of breach of Article 1102) that the California ban on MTBE was not discriminatory and did not expose the claimant to 'sectional or racial prejudice'.[686] In fact, the whole section on Article 1105 can be

---

677. *Ibid.*
678. *Ibid.*, Part IV, Ch. C, para. 16.
679. *Ibid.*
680. Providing as follows: 'A determination that there has been a breach of another provision of the NAFTA, or of a separate international agreement, does not establish that there has been a breach of Article 1105(1)'.
681. *Methanex v. United States*, Award, (3 August 2005), Part IV, Ch. C, para. 24.
682. *Ibid.*, Part IV, Ch. C, para. 25. In fact, for the tribunal 'the text of NAFTA indicates that the States parties explicitly excluded a rule of non-discrimination from Article 1105'.
683. *Ibid.*, para. 26.
684. *Waste Management, Inc. v. Mexico*, Award, (30 April 2004), para. 98.
685. *Methanex v. United States*, Award, (3 August 2005), Part IV, Ch. C, para. 26. This point is further examined in the next section.
686. *Ibid.*

considered as obiter dictum.[687] The tribunal concluded that the United States had committed no breach of Article 1105.[688]

[4]   Conclusion

In the following paragraphs, five observations will be made on NAFTA case law regarding the question whether or not Article 1105 includes any prohibition of discrimination.

First, the reasoning of some tribunals suggests that discrimination is one of the elements of the FET standard that is protected under Article 1105.[689] For instance, in one passage the *Merrill & Ring* tribunal stated that '[c]onduct which is unjust, arbitrary, unfair, *discriminatory* or in violation of due process has also been noted by NAFTA tribunals as constituting a breach of fair and equitable treatment, even in the absence of bad faith or malicious intention on the part of the state'.[690] Here, the tribunal clearly lists discrimination along-side other elements of the FET standard. Moreover, earlier in the award, the *Merrill & Ring* tribunal openly questioned the soundness of Canada's argument that discrimination was *not* a stand-alone obligation under Article 1105. The tribunal stated that the prohibition of discrimination was a 'general principle [...] of law' which was 'part of international law'.[691] It therefore seems that the *Merrill & Ring* tribunal considered the prohibition of discrimination as one of the constitutive elements of the FET standard.[692]

Similarly, there are several passages in the *Glamis* award that suggest that discrimination is a component of Article 1105 (and that the threshold of liability required is that such discrimination be 'evident').[693] This question will be further discussed at the end of this section. Finally, it should be added that the *S.D. Myers* tribunal's conclusion that discrimination under Article 1102 establishes a breach of Article 1105 suggests that the FET standard covers some type of discrimination. At

---

687. Weiler, *supra* n. 536, at 910-911, 917.
688. *Methanex v. United States*, Award, (3 August 2005), Part IV, Ch. C, para. 13.
689. Choudhury, *supra* n. 44, at 314.
690. *Merrill & Ring v. Canada*, Award, (31 March 2010), para. 208 (emphasis added).
691. *Ibid.*, para. 187 ('Even if the Tribunal were to accept Canada's argument to the effect that good faith, the prohibition of arbitrariness, discrimination and other questions raised in this case are not stand-alone obligations under Article 1105(1) or international law, and might not be a part of customary law either, these concepts are to a large extent the expression of general principles of law and hence also a part of international law').
692. The tribunal also does not make a distinction between nationality-based and other type of discrimination.
693. *Glamis v. United States*, Award, (8 June 2009), para. 22 ('to violate the customary international law minimum standard of treatment codified in Article 1105 of the NAFTA, an act must be sufficiently egregious and shocking—a gross denial of justice, manifest arbitrariness, blatant unfairness, a complete lack of due process, *evident discrimination*, or a manifest lack of reasons—so as to fall below accepted international standards and constitute a breach of Article 1105(1)', emphasis added). *See also*, paras. 22, 24, 627, 762, 765, 776, 779, 788, 824, 828, where the tribunal also refers to 'evident discrimination' along-side other elements of the FET standard.

least, this would be the case for discrimination treatments that 'rise to the level that is unacceptable from the international perspective'.[694]

In his separate opinion in *Thunderbird*, Wälde seems to have reached a *different* conclusion. He explains that in the context of Article 1105 'discriminatory elements have to play a role in the process of determining if problematic conduct has risen to the required threshold of intensity required under [that provision]'.[695] Reference to the 'role' to be played by discriminatory conduct in determining whether Article 1105 has been breached suggests that the prohibition of discrimination is *not* a stand-alone element of the FET standard.

Second, the (somewhat ambiguous) position adopted by these tribunals contrasts with that of the NAFTA Parties which have repeatedly affirmed that there is no stand-alone obligation prohibiting discrimination under Article 1105. To that effect, Canada affirmed that NAFTA already includes a comprehensive and specific legal regime (Articles 1102 to 1104) governing nationality-based discrimination.[696] Canada considers that its conclusion is also supported by the fact that Article 1102 is subject to a long list of reservations contained in annexes to the NAFTA, which 'do not apply to the minimum standard of treatment in respect of which no reservations were allowed because it is an absolute standard'.[697] In any event, Canada submitted that 'there exists no rule of customary international law that prohibits a State from differentiating between nationals and aliens'.[698]

As mentioned above in the context of the *Methanex* case, the United States argued that there is no general obligation of non-discrimination encompassed within Article 1105. The same objections were raised in *Grand River*.[699] Moreover, it affirmed that customary international law does not prohibit discrimination against foreign investors, but in fact allows for such discrimination.[700] The United States nevertheless admitted

---

694. *S.D. Myers Inc. v. Canada*, First Partial Award, (13 November 2000). The tribunal noted (at para. 263) that a breach of Article 1105 'occurs only when it is shown that an investor has been treated in such an unjust or arbitrary manner that the treatment rises to the level that is unacceptable from the international perspective'. *See also*: Kläger, *supra* n. 13, at 197, for whom the reasoning of the tribunal suggests that a distinction between foreign and national investors would violate the prohibition of discrimination under Article 1105 if it is 'borne by a clearly protectionist intent or the legitimate aim could be achieved by less intrusive means'.
695. *Thunderbird v. Mexico*, Separate Opinion of Thomas Wälde, (1 December 2005), para. 103.
696. *Merrill & Ring v. Canada*, Canada's Counter-Memorial, (13 May 2008), paras. 501–505; *S.D. Myers Inc. v. Canada*, Canada's Counter-Memorial on Merits, (5 October 1999), paras. 296–302, 334.
697. *Merrill & Ring v. Canada*, Canada's Counter-Memorial, (13 May 2008), paras. 501–505.
698. *Ibid.*
699. *Grand River v. United States*, US Counter-Memorial, (22 December 2008), at 126, 130.
700. *Ibid.*, Award, (12 January 2011), para. 199; *ibid.*, US Counter-Memorial, (22 December 2008), at 131, 132: 'In fact, "a degree of discrimination in the treatment of aliens as compared with nationals is, generally, permissible as a matter of customary international law". For example, States routinely limit or deny aliens the right to vote and the right to work without running afoul of international law. Furthermore, customary international law upholds the right of governments to limit the property rights of aliens within their territories. While States frequently agree to refrain from discriminating against aliens in economic matters by undertaking national treatment and most-favored-nation obligations in their international agreements, they are not required to do so by customary international law. In fact, as one scholar has explained, if the

(in both *Methanex*[701] and *Grand River*[702]) that Article 1105 prohibits discrimination in some specific contexts, including denial of justice, full protection and security and expropriation claims. However, in *Grand River*, the United States denied the existence of a custom rule specifically protecting indigenous investors[703] (one reason being that Article 1105 provides protection to investments, not investors).[704] In contrast, some passages extracted from Mexico's pleadings suggest that it views Article 1105 as prohibiting discrimination.[705]

Third, a number of tribunals have come to the conclusion that *nationality-based* discrimination is covered by Article 1102, not Article 1105. This is in fact *Methanex's* major contribution. The same conclusion was also reached by the *Glamis* tribunal (indicating that nationality-based discrimination 'falls under the purview of Article 1102').[706] The *Grand River* also concluded that:

> The language of Article 1105 does not state or suggest a blanket prohibition on discrimination against alien investors' investments, and one cannot assert such a rule under customary international law. States discriminate against foreign investments, often and in many ways, without being called to account for violating the customary minimum standard of protection.[707]

Fourth, both the *Methanex* and *Grand River* tribunals have also concluded that, under customary international law, there exists no general prohibition on discrimination against foreign investors. Moreover, the *Grand River* tribunal added that the minimum standard of treatment applies (by definition) to all investors and therefore denied the

---

principle of non-discrimination were reflected in customary international law, "most-favored-nation provisions in commercial and other treaties would be superfluous or, by sheer volume, merely declaratory by now", but that is decidedly not the case'.

701. *Methanex v. United States*, US Amended Statement of Defense, (5 December 2003), paras. 373–376.
702. *Grand River v. United States*, US Counter-Memorial, (22 December 2008), at 132: 'First, the minimum standard of treatment obligation requires governments to grant aliens access to their courts and judicial remedies on a non-discriminatory basis. Second, the minimum standard of treatment obligation requires governments to "[a]ccord to foreigners to whom damage has been caused by its armed forces or authorities in the suppression of an insurrection, riot or other disturbance the same indemnities as it accords to its own nationals in similar circumstances." Third, the minimum standard of treatment prohibits discrimination against aliens in the taking of property'.
703. *Ibid.*, at 134 ('the minimum standard of treatment cannot be construed to include particular protections for certain classes of aliens and not for others'). The United States also rejected the claimant's argument that customary international law imposes any obligation to consult indigenous investors and that, in any event, it was clearly not part of the minimum standard of treatment due to all aliens. *See: Ibid.*, Award, (12 January 2011), para. 200.
704. *Ibid.*, US Counter-Memorial, (22 December 2008), at 126.
705. *Metalclad v. Mexico*, Mexico's Counter-Memorial, (17 February 1998), para. 841 (the FET standard requires States 'to act in good faith, reasonably, without abuse, arbitrariness or discrimination').
706. *Glamis v. United States*, Award, (8 June 2009), para. 542, footnote 1087.
707. *Grand River v. United States*, Award, (12 January 2011), para. 208. *See also*, para. 209 ('neither Article 1105 nor the customary international law standard of protection generally prohibits discrimination against foreign investments').

existence of any custom rule imposing an obligation prohibiting discrimination specifically against indigenous peoples.[708] The tribunal also rejected the claimant's allegation of the existence of a 'principle of customary international law requiring governmental authorities to consult indigenous peoples on governmental policies or actions significantly affecting them'.[709]

Fifth, while it is clear that *nationality-based* discrimination is *not* covered by Article 1105, the reasoning of some NAFTA tribunals can be interpreted, to some extent, as suggesting that this provision may cover some *other* type of discrimination. This is, for instance, the case of the *Waste Management* award where the tribunal specifically indicated that a conduct that is 'discriminatory and exposes the claimant to sectional or racial prejudice'[710] would be in breach of the FET standard under Article 1105. This proposition was subsequently endorsed by the *Mobil* tribunal (which did not examine any discrimination allegations).[711]

The *Methanex* tribunal also examined the above-mentioned passage from the *Waste Management* award by emphasizing the word 'and' after the word discriminatory.[712] This suggests that the *Methanex* tribunal interpreted the *Waste Management dictum* to the effect that a violation of Article 1105 would not occur as a result of 'simple' discriminatory conduct, but would require 'sectional or racial prejudice'.[713] However, the *Methanex* tribunal expressly stated that it 'need not comment on the accuracy of the cumulative requirement' mentioned by the *Waste Management* tribunal.[714] The *Methanex* tribunal therefore refused to rule on the question of whether or not 'sectional or racial prejudice' (as referred to in *Waste Management*) can be considered as one of the few prohibited forms of discrimination under Article 1105.[715] The tribunal only went so far as to say that 'some differentiations are discriminatory' under customary international law.[716] The tribunal did not, however, specify whether this is in the context of Article 1105 or other provisions (such as Article 1110). The tribunal also did not indicate whether it agreed with the United States' assertion that under custom, some forms of discrimination are prohibited in the context of denial of justice and in the context of other protections offered under a BIT (expropriation, full protection and security). In the end, it is not clear at all whether the *Methanex* tribunal

---

708. *Ibid.*, para. 209.
709. *Ibid.*, para. 210. The tribunal first indicated that such principle may very well exist and noted that this was in fact the position of one of the arbitrators. In any event, even if such obligation were to exist it would apply to the indigenous peoples' community as a whole, and not to individual investors (para. 211). Moreover, an obligation to consult specific investors simply cannot be considered as a customary rule since '[t]he notion of specialized procedural rights protecting some investors, but not others, cannot readily be reconciled with the idea of a minimum customary standard of treatment due to all investments' (para. 213).
710. *Waste Management, Inc. v. Mexico*, Award, (30 April 2004), para. 98.
711. *Mobil v. Canada*, Decision on Liability and on Principles of Quantum, (22 May 2012), para. 152.
712. *Methanex v. United States*, Award, (3 August 2005), Part IV, Ch. C, para. 26.
713. Vandevelde, *supra* n. 27, at 65.
714. *Methanex v. United States*, Award, (3 August 2005), Part IV, Ch. C, para. 26.
715. *Ibid.*
716. *Ibid.*

believed that Article 1105 covers some type of discrimination other than nationality-based distinctions, such as sectional or racial prejudice. At most, it can be said that the *Methanex* tribunal did not openly and expressly reject this proposition.

In the *Glamis* award, the tribunal mentioned that 'discrimination that is founded on the targeting of a particular investor or investment' was clearly different from nationality-based discrimination (covered by Article 1102).[717] The tribunal indicated that, in the case at hand, the discrimination 'argument appears primarily in the discussion of Article 1110'.[718] It also explained (in a footnote) why the claimant had not put forward discrimination allegations under Article 1105.[719] In any event, the tribunal ultimately 'interpret[ed] Claimant's arguments made in its Memorial' regarding discrimination 'as an assertion that, as part of the duty prescribed by Article 1105 to not act arbitrarily, there is a duty to not unfairly target a particular investor, whether based upon nationality or some other characteristic'.[720] The tribunal therefore examined this discrimination-related allegation in the context of arbitrariness.[721] Yet, it is significant that throughout the award, the tribunal nevertheless referred some eleven times to the terms 'evident discrimination' alongside other elements of the FET standard such as denial of justice, arbitrariness and due process.[722] The consistent repetition of this expression strongly suggests that the *Glamis* tribunal was of the view that some types of 'discrimination' (other than nationality-based) are covered by Article 1105. The present author believes that this is indeed the case.

[F]   Good Faith

Good faith has been described by the ICJ as 'one of the basic principles governing the creation and performance of legal obligations' in international law.[723] It is also a central principle in the context of international investment law.[724] It has been argued by

---

717. *Glamis v. United States*, Award, (8 June 2009), para. 542, footnote 1087.
718. *Ibid.*
719. *Ibid.* ('Claimant does not argue the discriminatory nature of the California measures in its Article 1105 claim, explaining that *Waste Management* was criticized in *obiter dictum* by the *Methanex* tribunal to the extent that *Waste Management* implies a duty of non-discrimination in Article 1105(1) (...). Claimant asserts that *Waste Management* does so, however, only in circumstances where the claimant's allegations of discrimination were offered in regard to Article 1102 and only incidentally as regards a claim under Article 1105(1). Claimant continues to explain, however, that *Loewen Group v. United States* does state that discrimination can be unfair and inequitable in the context of Article 1105(1)'.
720. *Ibid. See also*, para. 559, footnote 1128.
721. *See*, at section §3.02[D][4].
722. *See*, for instance, *Glamis v. United States*, Award, (8 June 2009), para. 616 ('to violate the customary international law minimum standard of treatment codified in Article 1105 of the NAFTA, an act must be sufficiently egregious and shocking—a gross denial of justice, manifest arbitrariness, blatant unfairness, a complete lack of due process, evident discrimination, or a manifest lack of reasons—so as to fall below accepted international standards and constitute a breach of Article 1105(1)'). *See also*, at paras. 22, 24, 627, 762, 765, 776, 779, 788, 824, 828.
723. *Nuclear Tests (Australia v. France)*, Judgement, (20 December 1974) ICJ Rep. 1974, at 268, para. 46.
724. *See* the analysis of Diehl, *supra* n. 3, at 348 ff; Eric De Brabandere, *"Good Faith", "Abuse of Process" and the Initiation of Investment Treaty Claims*, 3(3) JIDS 609 (2012).

scholars[725] and tribunals[726] that the FET standard is in fact an expression of the principle of good faith. The principle of good faith is also considered by many as a 'guiding principle' to determine whether or not a breach of the FET standard has been committed by the host State.[727] What is clear is that good faith is not an autonomous stand-alone obligation under the FET standard (like arbitrariness or denial of justice).[728] The ICJ has also come to the conclusion that the principle of good faith is 'not in itself a source of obligation where none would otherwise exist'.[729]

In the context of NAFTA arbitration, some investors seem to argue that the principle of good faith should be considered as a stand-alone obligation under the FET standard.[730] NAFTA Parties have consistently opined that Article 1105 does not impose any free-standing, substantive obligation of good faith.[731] NAFTA tribunals have all concluded that the principle of good faith is not a stand-alone obligation under the FET standard, but rather a guiding principle relevant to determine whether a breach of Article 1105 has been committed. An illustration of this position can be found in the separate opinion of Wälde in the *Thunderbird* case where he speaks of good faith as a 'guiding principle' 'for applying' the FET standard under Article 1105.[732]

In *ADF*, the claimant maintained that the United States had 'violated its Article 1105(1) obligation by failing to perform its NAFTA obligations in good faith'[733] and that 'the principle of good faith performance has clearly attained the status of customary international law and is subsumed in the Article 1105(1) obligations undertaken by the

---

725. Newcombe & Paradell, *supra* n. 206, at 276; Kläger, *supra* n. 13, at 132; Dolzer & Schreuer, *supra* n. 71, at 145.
726. *Técnicas Medioambientales Tecmed, S.A. v. Mexico*, Award, (29 May 2003), para. 153; *Sempra Energy International v. Argentina*, ICSID No. ARB/02/16, Award, (28 September 2007), para. 298; *Siemens AG v. Argentina*, Award and Separate Opinion, (17 January 2007), para. 308.
727. *Técnicas Medioambientales Tecmed, S.A. v. Mexico*, Award, (29 May 2003), para. 154. *See also*: Kläger, *supra* n. 13, at 131; Diehl, *supra* n. 3, at 358; Laird, *supra* n. 96, at 272.
728. Kläger, *supra* n. 13, at 131; Diehl, *supra* n. 3, at 358; Tudor, *supra* n. 3, at 174; Vandevelde, *supra* n. 27, at 97; Choudhury, *supra* n. 44, at 316, 317; OECD, *supra* n. 39, at 40; Paparinskis, *supra* n. 18, at 243-245. *Contra*: T. Weiler, *supra* n. 344, at 725, for whom an investor is 'entitled to make a claim under Article 1105 for any way in which its investment has been treated that constitutes a breach of the general international law principle of good faith' since this principle is a general principle of international law within the meaning of Article 38(1) of the ICJ Statute. He adds, however, that as a result of the FTC Note, 'The NAFTA Parties thus effectively removed the argument, from each would-be claimant's quiver, that a breach of the principle of good faith, and of itself, constitutes a breach of NAFTA Article 1105(1)'.
729. *Concerning Border and Transborder Armed Actions (Nicaragua v. Honduras)*, Jurisdiction and Admissibility, Judgment, (20 December 1988), ICJ Rep. 1988, paras. 105, 106.
730. *See, Merrill & Ring v. Canada*, Claimant's Memorial, (13 February 2008), para. 198, arguing that: 'The obligation to act in good faith [under Article 1105] entails several specific obligations. For the purposes of this NAFTA claim, six obligations are particularly important: a) Obligation of fairness and good faith (...)'. Elsewhere, the investor adopted the more traditional view that 'The NAFTA parties' obligation to treat investors fairly and equitably is grounded in their obligation to act in good faith' (para. 193). *See also*: *Ibid.*, Award, (31 March 2010), para. 155.
731. *Grand River v. United States*, US Counter-Memorial, (22 December 2008), at 94; *Methanex v. United States*, US Rejoinder, (23 April 2004), at 25, 26; *Merrill & Ring v. Canada*, Canada's Rejoinder, (27 March 2009), paras. 186, 187; *UPS v. Canada*, Canada's Counter-Memorial, (22 June 2005), paras. 915, 921.
732. *Thunderbird v. Mexico*, Separate Opinion of Thomas Wälde, (1 December 2005), para. 25.
733. *ADF v. United States*, Claimant's 1st Post-Hearing Submission, (11 July 2002), para. 86.

U.S. in respect of investors and their investments'.[734] The tribunal was unconvinced and stated that '[a]n assertion of breach of a customary law duty of good faith adds only negligible assistance in the task of determining or giving content to a standard of fair and equitable treatment'.[735]

In *Waste Management*, the tribunal dealt with allegations of arbitrary conduct and denial of justice. The tribunal framed the denial of justice allegation as follows: 'Acaverde was subjected to a denial of justice at the hands of the City, Guerrero and Banobras, which conspired to obstruct its access to judicial and arbitral forums to resolve claims under the concession (...).'[736] The tribunal made the following comment regarding the allegation of conspiracy:

> The Tribunal has no doubt that a deliberate conspiracy—that is to say, a conscious combination of various agencies of government without justification to defeat the purposes of an investment agreement—would constitute a breach of Article 1105(1). A basic obligation of the State under Article 1105(1) is to act in good faith and form, and not deliberately to set out to destroy or frustrate the investment by improper means.[737]

The tribunal clearly does not refer to good faith as a stand-alone obligation under Article 1105. The award has nevertheless been interpreted by some as supporting the proposition that the 'obligation to act in good faith [is] a basic obligation under the FET standard as contained in Article 1105 of the NAFTA' and that 'in particular, a deliberate conspiracy by government authorities to defeat the investment would violate this principle'.[738]

The *Merrill & Ring* tribunal has seemingly taken a different approach. The tribunal was quite reluctant to accept Canada's argument that good faith was not a stand-alone element of the FET standard under Article 1105. In any event, it concluded that good faith was a 'general principle of law' and that 'no tribunal today could be asked to ignore th[is] basic obligation [...] of international law'.[739] The *S.D. Myers* tribunal also referred to good faith in a rather ambiguous way.[740]

Numerous tribunals[741] and scholars[742] have also generally recognized, on the one hand, that an investor does not have to show that the host State has acted in bad faith

---

734. *Ibid.*, para. 89.
735. *ADF v. United States*, Award, (9 January 2003), para. 191.
736. *Waste Management, Inc. v. Mexico*, Award, (30 April 2004), para. 87.
737. *Ibid.*, para. 138.
738. Dolzer & Schreuer, *supra* n. 71, at 145.
739. *Merrill & Ring v. Canada*, Award, (31 March 2010), para. 187.
740. *S.D. Myers Inc. v. Canada*, First Partial Award, (13 November 2000), para. 134 ('Article 1105 of the NAFTA requires the Parties to treat investors of another Party in accordance with international law, including fair and equitable treatment. Article 1105 imports into the NAFTA the international law requirements of due process, economic rights, obligations of good faith and natural justice').
741. *See, inter alia: Técnicas Medioambientales Tecmed, S.A. v. Mexico*, Award, (29 May 2003), para. 153; *Azurix Corp. v. Argentina*, ICSID No. ARB/01/12, Award, (14 July 2006), paras. 369, 372; *CMS Gas Transmission Company v. Argentina*, Award, (25 April 2005), para. 280.
742. UNCTAD, *supra* n. 11, at 58; M.A. Orellana, *International Law on Investment: The Minimum Standard of Treatment (MST)*, 3 Transnational Disp. Mgmt. 6 (2004); Paradell, *supra* n. 630, at

in order to prove the commission of a violation of the FET standard. Thus, a breach of the FET standard may occur even if the host State has acted in good faith. The same conclusion was reached by all NAFTA tribunals.[743] On the other hand, tribunals[744] and scholars[745] have recognized that the fact that the host State acted in bad faith is indicative of the existence of a breach of the FET standard. The *Glamis* tribunal also came to the same conclusion.[746]

[G]   Denial of Justice and Due Process

[1]   Interaction between Denial of Justice, the Fair and Equitable Treatment and the Minimum Standard of Treatment

As mentioned above,[747] under NAFTA Article 1105 the FET standard must be considered as one of the elements included in the umbrella concept of the minimum standard of treatment. This is clear from the fact that the text of the provision requires States to provide foreign investors with a treatment consistent with 'international law' (a reference to the minimum standard of treatment as reaffirmed by the FTC Note[748]), *including* FET. This is also the approach adopted by NAFTA tribunals, including *Waste Management*[749] and *Cargill*.[750] Where does the concept of 'denial of justice' fit in this

---

126; Schreuer, *supra* n. 2, at 384-385; Salacuse, *supra* n. 11, at 243; Vandevelde, *supra* n. 27, at 55; Dolzer & Schreuer, *supra* n. 71, at 146.

743. *Mondev v. United States*, Award, (2 October 2011), para. 116 ('a State may treat foreign investment unfairly and inequitably without necessarily acting in bad faith'); *Glamis v. United States*, Award, (8 June 2009), para. 616 ('The Tribunal notes that one aspect of evolution from *Neer* that is generally agreed upon is that bad faith is not required to find a violation of the fair and equitable treatment standard, but its presence is conclusive evidence of such. Thus, an act that is egregious or shocking may also evidence bad faith, but such bad faith is not necessary for the finding of a violation'), para. 560 ('most tribunals agree that a breach of Article 1105 does not require bad faith'); *Loewen v. United States*, Award (26 June 2003), para. 132 ('Neither State practice, the decisions of international tribunals nor the opinion of commentators support the view that bad faith or malicious intention is an essential element of unfair and inequitable treatment or denial of justice amounting to a breach of international justice. Manifest injustice in the sense of a lack of due process leading to an outcome which offends a sense of judicial propriety is enough, even if one applies the Interpretation according to its terms'); *Merrill & Ring v. Canada*, Award, (31 March 2010), para. 208 ('Conduct which is unjust, arbitrary, unfair, discriminatory or in violation of due process has also been noted by NAFTA tribunals as constituting a breach of fair and equitable treatment, even in the absence of bad faith or malicious intention'); *Waste Management, Inc. v. Mexico*, Award, (30 April 2004), para. 93.

744. *Alex Genin, Eastern Credit Limited, Inc. and A.S. Baltoil v. Estonia*, ICSID No. ARB/99/2, Award, (25 June 2001), para. 367.

745. UNCTAD, *supra* n. 11, at 58; Newcombe & Paradell, *supra* n. 206, at 293; Schreuer, *supra* n. 2, at 384; Tudor, *supra* n. 3, at 175; Dolzer & Schreuer, *supra* n. 71, at 145; Lemaire, *supra* n. 306, at 43.

746. *Glamis v. United States*, Award, (8 June 2009), paras. 22, 616.

747. *See*, Chapter 1 section §1.03[C].

748. *See*, Chapter 2 section §2.02[C][3].

749. *Waste Management v. Mexico*, Award, (30 April 2004), para. 98 (referring to the 'minimum standard of treatment of fair and equitable treatment').

750. *Cargill Inc. v. Mexico*, Award, (18 September 2009), para. 296 ('Tribunal finds that the obligations in Article 1105(1) of the NAFTA are to be understood by reference to the customary

picture? In the *specific context* of NAFTA Article 1105, the issue can be examined through two different perspectives.

First, the obligation not to deny justice can be considered as one of the many principles existing under the minimum standard of treatment under customary international law. The prohibition of denial of justice is indeed widely recognized by scholars,[751] the OECD,[752] and UNCTAD[753] as being part of custom. Under this scenario, the obligation not to deny justice would exist for States under the minimum standard of treatment alongside other principles such as the obligation to provide foreign investors with a FET as well as full protection and security. The first scenario can be illustrated by the following simple graph:

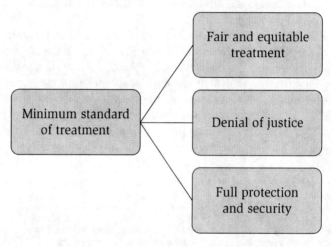

Second, the obligation not to deny justice can also be envisaged as one of the many elements comprising the obligation for States to provide foreign investors with the FET standard. There is a consensus amongst scholars to that effect that the obligation not to deny justice is certainly one of the elements of the FET standard.[754]

---

international law minimum standard of treatment of aliens. The requirement of fair and equitable treatment *is one aspect of this minimum standard'*, emphasis added).
751. Newcombe & Paradell, *supra* n. 206, at 236-238; Tudor, *supra* n. 3, at 62; J. Paulsson, *Denial of Justice in International Law* 7 (Cambridge U. Press 2006); Andrea Bjorklund, *Reconciling State Sovereignty and Investor Protection in Denial of Justice Claims*, 45 Va. J. Int'l L 837 (2005); Yannaca-Small, *supra* n. 44, at 119; F.V. García Amador, Louis B. Sohn & R.R. Baxter, *Recent Codification of the Law of State Responsibility for Injuries to Aliens* 180 (Oceana Publ. 1974); Sornarajah, *supra* n. 11, at 172; M. Sornarajah, *The International Law on Foreign Investment* 329 (2nd ed., Cambridge U. Press 2004); Paparinskis, *supra* n. 18, at 182, 229, 248.
752. OECD, *supra* n. 39, at 9; OECD, *supra* n. 553, at 108, 125.
753. UNCTAD, *supra* n. 11, at 44.
754. *Ibid.*, at 62, 80; Tudor, *supra* n. 3, at 157-163; Diehl, *supra* n. 3, at 455 ff; Kläger, *supra* n. 13, at 118, 217 ff; Lemaire, *supra* n. 306, at 40; Schreuer, *supra* n. 2, at 381; Salacuse, *supra* n. 11, at 241; Vandevelde, *supra* n. 27, at 50, 89 ff; Paparinskis, *supra* n. 18, at 181 ff. *Contra*: Sornarajah, *supra* n. 11, at 175-176.

Several NAFTA tribunals have concluded as such, including *Mobil*,[755] and *Waste Management*.[756] The inclusion of denial of justice as one of the elements of the FET standard is also clear from the 2004 US Model BIT,[757] as well as a number of recent of FTAs entered into by the United States.[758] Under this scenario, this obligation would exist under the FET standard alongside other elements (such as the prohibition of arbitrary conduct). This hypothesis can be illustrated as follows:

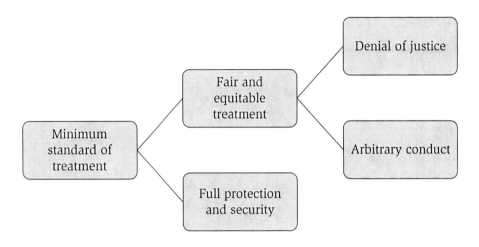

---

755. *Mobil v. Canada*, Decision on Liability and on Principles of Quantum, (22 May 2012), para. 152 ('the fair and equitable treatment standard in customary international law will be infringed by conduct attributable to a NAFTA Party and harmful to a claimant that is arbitrary, grossly unfair, unjust or idiosyncratic, or is discriminatory and exposes a claimant to sectional or racial prejudice, or involves a lack of due process leading to an outcome which offends judicial propriety').

756. *Waste Management v. Mexico*, Award, (30 April 2004), para. 98, where the tribunal stated that 'the minimum standard of treatment of fair and equitable treatment is infringed by conduct attributable to the State' if the conduct, *inter alia*, 'involves a lack of due process leading to an outcome which offends judicial propriety—as might be the case with a manifest failure of natural justice in judicial proceedings'.

757. 2004 US Model BIT, Article 5(2)a): the FET standard 'includes the obligation not to deny justice in criminal, civil or administrative adjudicatory proceedings in accordance with the principle of due process embodied in the principal legal systems of the world (...)'.

758. US-Chile Free Trade Agreement, signed on 6 June 2003, entered into force on 1 January 2004, (Article 10.4(2)(a)); US-Singapore Free Trade Agreement, signed on 6 May 2003, entered into force on 1 January 2004 (Article 15.5(2)(a)); US-Australia Free Trade Agreement, signed on 18 May 2004, entered into force on 1 January 2005 (Article 11.5); US-Morocco Free Trade Agreement, signed on 15 June 2004, entered into force on 1 January 2006 (Article 10.5); Dominican Republic-Central America-US Free Trade Agreement (CAFTA-DR), signed on 5 August 2004, entered into force between 2006 and 2009 (Article 10.5); US-Oman Free Trade Agreement, signed on 19 January 2006, entered into force on 1 January 2009 (Article 10.5); US-Peru Trade Promotion Agreement, signed on 12 April 2006, entered into force on 1 February 2009 (Article 10.5); US-Colombia Free Trade Agreement, signed on 22 November 2006, entered into force on 15 February 2012 (Article 10.5); US-Panama Trade Promotion Agreement, signed on 28 June 2007, entered into force on 31 October 2012, (Article 10.5); US-Korea Free Trade Agreement, signed on 30 June 2007, entered into force on 15 March 2012 (Article 11.5).

In truth, this theoretical question is of little practical importance due to the fact that the obligation not to deny justice exists under international law. All States therefore have an obligation to protect foreign investors from a denial of justice under custom. The obligation exists even in situations where no BIT governs the relationship between an investor and the State or where a BIT does not contain an FET clause. The limited practical relevance of this question is also clear in the specific context of Article 1105 where NAFTA tribunals have to apply the minimum standard of treatment under customary international law (which includes protection against denial of justice).

[2]   Defining Denial of Justice

The present section does not intend to provide a comprehensive analysis of the concept of denial of justice.[759] The objective is to highlight the most salient features of the concept before examining its concrete application by NAFTA tribunals. Defining what constitutes a denial of justice under international law is no easy task.[760] Under

---

759. See: C. Focarelli, Denial of Justice, in The Max Planck Encyclopedia of Public International Law (R. Wolfrum ed., Oxford U. Press 2009); C. Eagleton, Denial of Justice in International Law, 22 AJIL 538 (1928); J.W. Garner, International Responsibility of States for Judgments of Courts and Verdicts of Juries Amounting to a Denial of Justice, 10 British YIL 181 (1929); G.G. Fitzmaurice, The Meaning of the Term "Denial of Justice", 13 British YIL 93 (1932); C. De Visscher, Le deni de justice en droit international, 52 Rec Cours 367 (1936); A.V. Freeman, The International Responsibility of States for Denial of Justice (Longman, Green & Co. 1938); H.W. Spiegel, Origin and Development of Denial of Justice 32 AJIL 63 (1938); E. Borchard, The "Minimum Standard" of the Treatment of Aliens, 3 Mich LR 445 (1940); García-Amador et al., supra n. 751; Bjorklund, supra n. 751; Paulsson, supra n. 751; Roger P. Alford, Ancillary Discovery to Prove Denial of Justice, 53(1) Va.J.Int'l L 127 (2013); Rym Ben Khelifa, Le déni de justice en droit de l'investissement international: l'affaire Loewen c. les États-Unis d'Amérique, in: Où va le droit international de l'investissement?: Désordre normatif et recherche d'équilibre: actes du colloque organisé à Tunis les 3 et 4 mars 2006 239 (Pedone 2007); Louis-Christophe Delanoy & Tim Portwood, La responsabilité de l'Etat pour déni de justice dans l'arbitrage d'investissement, 3 Rev. arb. 603 (2005); Francesco Francioni, Access to Justice, Denial of Justice and International Investment Law, 20(3) EJIL 729 (2009); Jurgen Kurtz, Access to Justice, Denial of Justice and International Investment Law: A Reply to Francesco Francioni, 20(4) EJIL 1077 (2009); Susan L. Karamanian, Denial of Justice and the Foreign Investor: Lessons from North America, in: International Law: Issues and Challenges, vol. 2 16 (Hope India Publications 2009); Alexis Mourre & Alexandre Vagenheim, Some Comments on Denial of Justice in Public and Private International Law after Loewen and Saipem, in: Liber amicorum Bernardo Cremades 843 (La Ley 2010); Mavluda Sattorova, Denial of Justice Disguised? Investment Arbitration and the Protection of Foreign Investors From Judicial Misconduct, 61(1) ICLQ 223 (2012); D. Wallace, Fair and Equitable Treatment and Denial of Justice: Loewen v. US and Chattin v. Mexico, in International Investment Law and Arbitration: Leading Cases from the ICSID, NAFTA, Bilateral Treaties and Customary International Law 669 (T. Weiler ed., Cameron May 2005); Don Wallace, State Responsibility for Denial of Substantive and Procedural Justice under NAFTA Chapter Eleven, 23 Hastings Int'l & Comp.L.Rev. 393 (2000); A.O. Adede, A Fresh Look at the Meaning of the Doctrine of Denial of Justice under International Law, 14 Can YIL 73 (1976); Thomas W. Wälde, Denial of Justice: A Review Comment on Jan Paulsson, Denial of Justice in International Law, 21(2) ICSID Rev. 449 (2006); Stephen M. Schwebel, The United States 2004 Model Bilateral Investment Treaty and Denial of Justice in International Law, in: International Investment Law for the 21st Century: Essays in Honour of Christoph Schreuer 519-521 (Oxford U. Press 2009); Carlos Andrés Hécker Padilla, Denial of Justice to Foreign Investors, 3(1) Cuadernos de derecho transnacional, 296-301 (2011).
760. On this question, see Paulsson, supra n. 751, at 59 ff, indicating (at 98) that 'no enumerative approach to defining denial of justice has succeeded in the past, and there is no prospects that one will emerge in the future'. See also: Wallace, supra n. 759, at 672 ff.

international law, a State is responsible for the actions of its courts.[761] A denial of justice occurs in the context of the maladministration of the host State's judicial system toward an investor. Thus, Paulsson describes the concept as arising when 'a state incurs responsibility if it administers justice to aliens in a fundamentally unfair manner'.[762] Newcombe et al. speak of 'minimum standards of administration of justice' to which foreign investors are entitled.[763]

One important point to highlight is that only 'gross or manifest instances of injustice' will be considered a denial of justice.[764] Thus, 'a simple error, misinterpretation or misapplication of domestic law is not per se a denial of justice'.[765] There is indeed a threshold for denial of justice to occur.[766] Paulsson speaks of 'egregious' actions by the State and of 'fundamental violations' of international law.[767] This position has been endorsed by tribunals.[768] The existence of such a threshold of liability is significant as an international tribunal does not serve as a court of appeal reviewing decisions emanating from lower courts.

Before being given the option to claim any denial of justice on the international plane, it is paramount that the investor exhausts all available procedural remedies before local courts. This will allow higher courts to correct any maladministration committed earlier by lower courts. This preliminary requirement is essential since, as stated by one writer, 'denial of justice arises where a national legal *system* fails to provide justice – not where there is a single procedural irregularity or misapplication of the law at some level of the judicial system'.[769] In the words of Paulsson, 'international

---

761. Article 4(1), *Titles and Texts of the Draft Articles on Responsibility of States for Internationally Wrongful Acts Adopted by the Drafting Committee on Second Reading*, 26 July 2001, U.N. Doc. A/CN.4/L.602/Rev.1.ILC ('I.L.C. Articles on State Responsibility').
762. Paulsson, *supra* n. 751, at 4, *see also* at 62.
763. Newcombe & Paradell, *supra* n. 206, at 238. *See also*, at 240 ('customary international law requires states to maintain a judicial system that meets international minimum standards of due process in its treatment of foreigners'). *See also*: Paulsson, *supra* n. 751, at 7.
764. Newcombe & Paradell, *supra* n. 206, at 238; Diehl, *supra* n. 3, at 467.
765. UNCTAD, *supra* n. 11, at 80. *See also*: Newcombe & Paradell, *supra* n. 206, at 238; Kläger, *supra* n. 13, at 227; Paulsson, *supra* n. 751, at 73 ff, 87 ff; Diehl, *supra* n. 3, at 462, 503 (highlighting the fact that denial of justice has nothing to do with situations where domestic tribunals disregard or misapply international law). On this point, *see*: Paulsson, *supra* n. 751, at 84-87; Paparinskis, *supra* n. 18, at 186-187.
766. Diehl, *supra* n. 3, at 503, 456 ('under international law, the general notion of denial of justice leads to State liability whenever an uncorrected national judgment is vitiated by fundamental unfairness. In other words: There has to be discreditable legal outcome or one that offends judicial propriety and not merely an incorrect outcome').
767. Paulsson, *supra* n. 751, at 60.
768. *Chevron Corporation (USA) and Texaco Petroleum Company (USA) v. Ecuador*, UNCITRAL, PCA Case No. 34877, Partial Award on Merits, (30 March 2010), para. 244 ('The test for establishing a denial of justice sets, as the Respondent has argued, a high threshold. While the standard is objective and does not require an overt showing of bad faith, it nevertheless requires the demonstration of "a particularly serious shortcoming" and egregious conduct that "shocks, or at least surprises, a sense of judicial propriety"'); *Joseph Charles, Lemire v. Ukraine*, ICSID No. ARB/06/18, Decision on Jurisdiction and Liability, (14 January 2010), para. 249 (footnote 71) ('for claims based on denial of justice, aggravating circumstances like outrage, bad faith, willful neglect of duty or other egregious behavior are required').
769. Newcombe & Paradell, *supra* n. 206, at 240–241 (emphasis in the original). *See also*: Diehl, *supra* n. 2, at 503 ('If the courts of a State do not function in a proper manner and administer justice in a fundamentally unfair fashion, they commit a delict commonly referred to as "denial

law does not impose a duty on States to treat foreigners fairly at every step of the legal process'.[770] In fact, 'the duty is to create and maintain a system of justice which ensures that unfairness to foreigners either does not happen, *or is corrected'*.[771] In this context, it has been rightly suggested that the exhaustion of local remedies is 'an inherent material element of the delict'.[772] Thus, the requirement of the exhaustion of local remedies is considered as a 'substantive requirement of the cause of action of denial of justice'.[773] This requirement therefore applies despite any waiver contained within an international instrument.[774]

One earlier attempt to clarify the meaning of the principle of denial of justice was made in 1929 with the publication of *The Law of Responsibility of States for Damages Done in Their Territory to the Person or Property of Foreigners* by Harvard University.[775] Recently, UNCTAD listed the following instances of denial of justice:

(a) Denial of access to justice and the refusal of courts to decide.

(b) Unreasonable delay in proceedings.

(c) Lack of a court's independence from the legislative and the executive branches of the State.

(d) Failure to execute final judgments or arbitral awards.

(e) Corruption of a judge.

(f) Discrimination against the foreign litigant.

(g) Breach of fundamental due process guarantees, such as a failure to give notice of the proceedings and failure to provide an opportunity to be heard.[776]

---

of justice". While the focus of FET claims based on administrative conduct is not on a systemic failure but usually on individual and grave misconduct by administrative agencies or other executive actors whose actions are imputable to the State, denial of justice only occurs in the case of a fundamental breakdown in a judicial system, that is, if the system as such has been at fault').

770. Paulsson, *supra* n. 751, at 7.

771. *Ibid.*, at 7 (emphasis in the original), *see also*, at 100-130.

772. *Ibid.*, at 8, 102 ff.

773. Diehl, *supra* n. 3, at 503.

774. It should be noted that a number of authors have been critical of this position: McLachlan et al., *supra* n. 37, at 232-233; Bjorklund, *supra* n. 751, at 858.

775. *The Law of Responsibility of States for Damages Done in Their Territory to the Person or Property of Foreigners,* 23 AJIL Spec Supp 174 (1929), Article 9 ('Denial of justice exists where there is a denial, unwarranted delay or obstruction of access to courts, gross deficiency in the administration of judicial or remedial process, failure to provide those guaranties which are generally considered indispensable to the proper administration of justice or a manifestly unjust judgment. An error of a national court which does not produce manifest injustice is not a denial of justice'). The commentary to the document also provided a series of examples considered as a denial of justice: 'the failure to apprehend a criminal, denial of free access to the courts, failure to render a decision or undue delay in rendering judgment, corruption in the judicial proceedings, discrimination or ill-will against the alien as such, or as a national of a particular state, the refusal in bad faith to apply the local law, executive interference with the freedom or impartiality of the judicial process, failure to execute judgment, denial of an appeal where local law ordinarily permits it, negligently permitting a prisoner to escape, refusal to prosecute the guilty, or premature pardon of a convicted person, have all been deemed, under particular circumstances, instances of "denial of justice"'.

776. UNCTAD, *supra* n. 11, at 80.

Paulsson provides the following list of instances where tribunals have found a denial of justice:

> Some denials of justice may be readily recognised: refusal of access to court to defend legal rights, refusal to decide, unconscionable delay, manifest discrimination, corruption, or subservience to executive pressure. (...) No definitive list of instances could be presented, for it would soon be invalidated by new fact patterns, untested forms of organisation of systems of justice, and the boundless capacities of human invention. Recurring instances are unreasonable delay, politically dictated judgments, corruption, intimidation, fundamental breaches of due process, and decisions so outrageous as to be inexplicable otherwise than as expressions of arbitrariness or gross incompetence. A further basic postulate is that some acts or omissions by governmental authorities are sufficiently closely related to the administration of justice that they must also be deemed capable of generating international delinquency under the heading of denial of justice: failures of enforcement, the implementation of sanctions against persons or property without trial, failure of investigation or indictment, lengthy imprisonment without trail, arbitrarily lenient or harsh punishment.[777]

[3] Distinguishing Denial of Justice and Due Process

The concept of 'denial of justice' is closely interconnected with that of 'due process'. The requirement of due process is considered by many as an element of the FET standard.[778] According to many writers, States are required under custom to provide investors with due process in their administration of justice.[779] Under domestic law, the concept of the 'rule of law' is generally considered to encompass a 'procedural' dimension which is governed by the principle of 'due process'.[780] Thus, due process 'requires that one to whom the coercive power of the state is to be applied receive notice of the intended application and an opportunity to contest that application before an impartial tribunal'.[781] A denial of justice occurs when a breach of due process in the administration of justice is not corrected by the judicial system.[782] Paulsson puts it

---

777. Paulsson, *supra* n. 751, at 204-205, *see* at 176-206. *See also*, the comprehensive analysis of case law by Paparinskis, *supra* n. 18, at 189 ff.

778. Diehl, *supra* n. 3, at 432, 437; Choudhury, *supra* n. 44, at 316.

779. Newcombe & Paradell, *supra* n. 206, at 238, 241, 243-244; Vandevelde, *supra* n. 27, at 50. *See also*: *AAPL v. Sri Lanka*, ICSID Case No. ARB/87/3, Final Award, (June 27, 1990), dissenting opinion of Judge Asente ('the general obligation of the host state to exercise due diligence in protecting foreign investment in its territories, an obligation that derives from customary international law').

780. Vandevelde, *supra* n. 27, at 49.

781. *Ibid.*

782. *Ibid.*, at 50 ('Customary international law long has required that foreign investors be accorded due process before local courts or administrative agencies. Failure to do so constitutes a denial of justice. Denial of justice—that is, a failure of due process— constitutes a violation of the fair and equitable treatment standard. Thus, fair and equitable treatment requires conduct consistent with the procedural dimension of the rule of law'); Newcombe & Paradell, *supra* n. 206, at 243.

bluntly: 'in international law, denial of justice is about due process, nothing else – and that is plenty'.[783]

While the term denial of justice is sometimes used in a much broader way,[784] most scholars limit its scope to the maladministration of the host State's *judicial system*.[785] This includes the actions of *all agents* of the State in the maladministration of justice, and not only actions by judicial officials per se.[786] On the contrary, the concept of due process is *not* limited to the judicial system; it applies to all forms of governmental decision-making, including measures taken by the government (both the executive and legislative branches) and the administration.[787] For the purpose of this book, the term denial of justice will therefore only be used to refer to a State's maladministration of its judicial system, while due process will cover all other forms of governmental decision-making.

[4]   The Reasons for Not Examining a Number of NAFTA Cases in this Section

It was decided not to examine a number of cases in this section. For instance, in *Feldman* the tribunal held that there had been no denial of justice, but solely in the context of its analysis of allegations of expropriation under Article 1110.[788] In *Grand*

---

783. Paulsson, *supra* n. 751, at 7. He strongly rejects (at 81 ff) the distinction between 'procedural' and 'substantive' denial of justice and denies the existence of anything such as 'substantive' denial of justice under modern international law.
784. OECD, *supra* n. 553, at 108 ('In the broadest sense, [the concept of denial of justice] "seems to embrace the whole field of State responsibility, and has been applied to all types of wrongful conduct on the part of the State towards aliens", it includes therefore acts or omissions of the authorities of any of the three branches of government, i.e. executive, legislative or judiciary. In the narrowest sense, it is "limited to refusal of a State to grant an alien access to its courts or a failure of a court to pronounce a judgement". There is also an intermediary sense, in which it is "employed in connection with the improper administration of civil and criminal justice as regards an alien, including denial of access to courts, inadequate procedures, and unjust decisions". The majority of the cases examined approach fair and equitable treatment in the intermediate sense and many also address in their analysis the concept of arbitrariness').
785. Wallace, *supra* n. 759, at 672; Diehl, *supra* n. 3, at 455-457; Adede, *supra* n. 759, at 91.
786. Paulsson, *supra* n. 751, at 44 ff, 59; Schreuer, *supra* n. 2, at 381; Dolzer & Schreuer, *supra* n. 71, at 142. It should be noted that for a number of writers, denial of justice also covers executive conduct per se: Dirk Pulkowski, *The Final Award In Loewen v. United States*, in *The Reasons Requirement in International Investment Arbitration: Critical Case Studies* 315 (Guillermo Aguilar Alvarez & W. Michael Reisman eds., Nijhoff 2008).
787. Diehl, *supra* n. 3, at 431 ff.
788. *Feldman v. Mexico*, Award, (16 December 2002). The tribunal stated that 'Mexican courts and administrative procedures at all relevant times [had] been open to the Claimant' and because of the 'availability of court review' (para. 139) it concluded that 'there appears to have been no denial of due process or denial of justice there as would rise to the level of a violation of international law' (para. 140). The tribunal mentioned at the outset of the award (at para. 24) that the claimant alleged that Mexico's actions were not only tantamount to expropriation but also 'constitute[d] a denial of justice in violation of the rules and principles of international law and NAFTA Articles 1110 and 1105(1)'. Later in the award (at para. 89), however, the tribunal described the denial of justice allegation as only relevant in the context of its analysis of expropriation: 'The Claimant asserts that the "measures" he has complained about may also be characterized as a "denial of justice" (one aspect of denial of due process) under article 1110'. The tribunal therefore examined the question of due process solely from the angle of

River, the tribunal held that it did not have jurisdiction over the allegations of denial of justice raised by the claimants.[789]

It was also decided not to specifically examine the *Azinian* case.[790] The central question to be decided by the tribunal in this case was whether or not the annulment of a contract by the municipality of Naucalpan, Mexico, could be considered as an act of expropriation in violation of Article 1110. The tribunal therefore did not examine any allegation of breach of Article 1105.[791] The tribunal nevertheless made some important findings with respect to the interpretation of denial of justice under that provision. For instance, when examining the question regarding whether Mexican courts' decisions in favor of the validity of the annulment of the contract were in breach of NAFTA Chapter 11, the tribunal noted that an error of law committed by a court would not constitute a denial of justice:

> [E]ven if the claimants were to convince this Arbitral Tribunal that the Mexican courts were wrong with respect to the invalidity of the Concession Contract, this would not per se be conclusive as to a violation of NAFTA. More is required; the claimants must show either a denial of justice, or a pretence of form to achieve an internationally unlawful end'.[792]

The *Azinian* tribunal concluded that it was not necessary to further examine the question since the claimants had not raised any denial of justice allegations against Mexican courts.[793] In an obiter dictum, the tribunal nevertheless held that these court decisions were not in violation of NAFTA.[794] In this context, it identified the following four different types of denial of justice:

> A denial of justice could be pleaded if the relevant courts refuse to entertain a suit, if they subject it to undue delay, or if they administer justice in a seriously

---

expropriation. In any event, the tribunal held (at para. 141) that it simply had no jurisdiction to decide the question whether or not any violation of Article 1105 had been committed since 'Article 1105 is not available in tax cases'.

789. In *Grand River v. United States*, Award, (12 January 2011), one of the allegations raised by the claimants (the so-called 'fourth' Article 1105 claim) was that they had been denied due process in connection with multiple State legislatures' adoption of the Allocable Share Amendments (para. 182). Thus, the claimants did not argue that US courts had committed any denial of justice, but rather that State legislatures were responsible (paras. 193, 226). The tribunal also noted that the claimants had argued their case based on due process and denial of justice as existing under Canadian and US law rather than international law (para. 222). In any event, the tribunal held that it did not have jurisdiction over this claim based on its earlier Decision on Jurisdiction of July 2006 (para. 227).

790. *Azinian v. Mexico*, Award, (1 November 1999). The case involved Mr. Azinian and two other American nationals, who were shareholders of a Mexican corporation, Desechos Sólidos de Naucalpan S.A. de C.V. ('DESONA'). In 1993, a 15-year Concession Contract was entered into between DESONA and the City Counsel of the municipality of Naucalpan, Mexico, for the collection and disposal of solid waste. Soon after the signature of the Contract, the local administration complained about a number of irregularities in the implementation of the Contract and gave the claimants the opportunity to respond to those defects. The City Counsel finally nullified the Contract and three Mexican Courts later confirmed the legality of this annulment under Mexican law.

791. *Ibid.*, para. 92. The tribunal noted that the claimants' complaint under Article 1105 only 'figured very fleetingly in their later pleadings'.

792. *Ibid.*, para. 99.

793. *Ibid.*, paras. 100-101.

794. *Ibid.*, para. 101.

inadequate way. There is no evidence, or even argument, that any such defects can
be ascribed to the Mexican proceedings in this case.

There is a fourth type of denial of justice, namely the clear and malicious
misapplication of the law. This type of wrong doubtless overlaps with the notion
of "pretence of form" to mask a violation of international law. In the present case,
not only has no such wrong-doing been pleaded, but the Arbitral Tribunal wishes
to record that it views the evidence as sufficient to dispel any shadow over the
bona fides of the Mexican judgments. Their findings cannot possibly be said to
have been arbitrary, let alone malicious.[795]

The identification of these four types of denial of justice has subsequently been
endorsed by several tribunals and by NAFTA Parties. These findings are further
discussed in the concluding section of the present chapter.[796]

[5]   Metalclad

The facts of the *Metalclad* case have already been examined above.[797] As previously
mentioned,[798] while this case is generally analyzed from a lack of transparency
standpoint, the present author submits that the tribunal also found that Mexico had
breached its obligation of due process.[799] This position is supported by the fact that
toward the end of its analysis on the allegations pertaining to Article 1105, the tribunal
refers to 'procedural and substantive deficiencies' related to the permit denial which,
amongst other factors, led to its conclusion that the actions of the Municipality had
been 'improper'.[800] Breach of due process was therefore one of the factors that the
tribunal took into account when concluding that 'the totality of these circumstances
demonstrates a lack of orderly process' and that Mexico had failed to 'ensure a
transparent and predicable framework' in breach of Article 1105.[801]

The tribunal described the following circumstances under which the Municipality denied Metalclad's application for a construction permit: 'the permit was denied at
a meeting of the Municipal Town Council of which Metalclad received no notice, to
which it received no invitation, and at which it was given no opportunity to appear'.[802]
This is a clear reference to the due process obligation requiring States to provide foreign
investors with the opportunity to be heard and to present evidence at an administrative
hearing.[803] More specifically, this passage suggests that such obligation is breached

---

795. *Ibid.*, paras. 102-103.
796. *See*, at section §3.02[G][11].
797. *See*, at section §3.02[B][1].
798. *See*, at section §3.02[C][1].
799. This is also the position of these writers: Laird, *supra* n. 96, at 58; Weiler, *supra* n. 96, at 692;
Weiler, *supra* n. 344, at 716; Schill, *supra* n. 48, at 45; Dolzer & Schreuer, *supra* n. 71, at 143.
800. *Metalclad v. Mexico*, Award, (30 August 2000), para. 97. The full passage reads as follows: 'The
actions of the Municipality following its denial of the municipal construction permit, coupled
with the procedural and substantive deficiencies of the denial, support the Tribunal's finding,
for the reasons stated above, that the Municipality's insistence upon and denial of the
construction permit in this instance was improper'.
801. *Ibid.*, para. 99.
802. *Ibid.*, para. 91.
803. Choudhury, *supra* n. 44, at 306; Schreuer, *supra* n. 2, at 382.

whenever an investor is not informed and not invited to a hearing discussing a permit application and whenever it is not given any opportunity to appear and to present evidence before this administrative body.[804]

The tribunal also contested the reasons used by the authorities to justify the rejection of the permit. It concluded that the permit was 'denied without any consideration of, or specific reference to, construction aspects or flaw of the physical facility'.[805] In fact, the tribunal found that the Town Council had denied the permit to Metalclad due, *inter alia*, to the local population's opposition to the hazardous waste landfill site and because construction had already begun when the application was submitted.[806] The tribunal's (limited) reasoning on this point suggests that a breach of the obligation of due process occurs whenever an investor is denied a permit based on reasons that are unrelated to existing requirements for issuing that permit.[807]

[6]   Pope & Talbot

In 1999, the Oregon-based company Pope & Talbot Inc. filed a claim on behalf of its Canadian subsidiary located in British Columbia against the Canadian government seeking USD 507.5 million in compensation. The source of the dispute was Canada's implementation of the 1996 bilateral Canada–United States *Softwood Lumber Agreement* (the 'Agreement') dealing with the exports of Canadian softwood lumber to the United States. Under this Agreement, Canada committed itself to monitor and restrain the export of softwood lumber from four Canadian Provinces (the so-called 'Listed Provinces' which include British Columbia). A permit mechanism allocating quotas was put in place, whereby producers of softwood lumber from these four Provinces were required to obtain a permit and to pay a fee to export to the United States.[808] The Agreement established an annual 'fee-free' export quota limit of 14.7 billion board feet of softwood lumber for producers of the Listed Provinces and also imposed two different levels of permit fees for exports exceeding that quota (a lower and an upper fee base). The quota allocation mechanism for the right of a limited number of companies originating from the Listed Provinces to export 'fee-free' and at a lower rate was enacted by a Canadian regulation based on historical records of exports to the United States.[809] In addition, these quotas were subject to a reserve which allowed the Canadian Minister of Foreign Affairs and International Trade to use its discretion to allocate a percentage of the quota for companies qualifying as 'new entrants'.

---

804. Diehl, *supra* n. 3, at 437.
805. *Metalclad v. Mexico*, Award, (30 August 2000), para. 93.
806. *Ibid.*, para. 92.
807. Diehl, *supra* n. 3, at 437; Choudhury, *supra* n. 44, at 306.
808. Softwood lumber producers from the six other Canadian Provinces and the two Territories did not have to pay an export permit fee in order to export to the United States.
809. The allocation was made on a provincial basis, with each of the four Provinces receiving a certain percentage of the total and the individual producers receiving their share on a pro-rata basis within each provincial quota.

The claimant alleged that Canada's implementation of the Agreement breached four NAFTA provisions, including Article 1105. In its (second) award of April 2001,[810] the tribunal concluded that only one aspect of Canada's implementation of the softwood lumber quota allocation system breached Article 1105: the so-called 'verification review process'.[811] Canada's Softwood Lumber Division ('SLD') created this administrative review process after the claimant had filed its 'Notice of Intent to Submit a Claim to Arbitration'. The process was set up to determine whether the claimant had received the appropriate allocation of quotas. The tribunal noted that while the implementation of the Agreement was administrated 'in most instances, in an open and cooperative spirit',[812] the verification review process was an entirely different story:

> The relations between the SLD and the Investment during 1999 were more like combat than co-operative regulation, and the Tribunal finds that the SLD bears the overwhelming responsibility for this state of affairs. It is not for the Tribunal to discern the motivations behind the attitude of the SLD; however, the end result for the Investment was being subjected to threats, denied its reasonable requests for pertinent information, required to incur unnecessary expense and disruption in meeting SLD's requests for information, forced to expend legal fees and probably suffer a loss of reputation in government circles. While administration, like legislation, can be likened to sausage making, this episode goes well beyond the glitches and innocent mistakes that may typify the process. In its totality, the SLD's treatment of the Investment during 1999 in relation to the verification review process is nothing less than a denial of the fair treatment required by NAFTA Article 1105, and the Tribunal finds Canada liable to the Investor for the resultant damages.[813]

In sum, Canada had breached its obligation to provide due process to the investor.

The tribunal was, however, forced to revisit the issue in its subsequent Award on Damages of May 2002 as a result of the FTC's Note of Interpretation.[814] As mentioned above,[815] the tribunal rejected Canada's contention that proof of egregious conduct

---

810. The tribunal's first award (Interim Award on Merits - Phase One, 26 June 2000) dealt with allegations of breach of Articles 1110 (expropriation) and 1106 (performance requirement), while the second award (Interim Award on Merits - Phase Two, 10 April 2001) tackled allegations of breach of the national treatment clause (Article 1102) and Article 1105. The second (and the third) awards are examined in: P. Dumberry, *The Quest to Define "Fair and Equitable Treatment" for Investors under International Law: The Case of the NAFTA Chapter 11 Pope & Talbot Awards*, 3(4) J. World Invest. 657-691 (2002).

811. The tribunal determined that the creation of a 'super fee' in 1999 and the policy of allocating quotas to 'new entrants' based on the current capacity of the different companies instead of their historical records of production did not breach Article 1105. The fact that no internal appeal mechanism existed against decisions on the allocation of quotas was determined by the tribunal not to be relevant since any unsatisfied investor could seek judicial review before Canadian courts (*see, Pope & Talbot Inc. v. Canada*, Award on the Merits (Phase 2), (10 April 2001), paras. 182 ff). Other issues were determined by the tribunal to be not contrary to Article 1105, *see Ibid.*, paras. 122–128.

812. *Ibid.*, para. 180.

813. *Ibid.*, para. 181.

814. These aspects of the award have already been examined above, *see* at Chapter 2 sections §2.02[C][3][a] and §2.03[B][1].

815. *See*, at Chapter 2 section §2.03[B][1].

was necessary to breach the minimum standard of treatment under customary international law.[816] It nevertheless concluded that *'even applying Canada's proposed standard*, damages would be owing to the Investor as a result of the Verification Review Episode'.[817] This is because Canada's conduct had been 'egregious'.[818] The tribunal reiterated its strong criticism of the verification review process in these words:

> Briefly, the Tribunal found that when the Investor instituted the claim, in these proceedings, Canada's Softwood Lumber Division ("SLD") changed its previous relationship with the Investor and the Investment from one of cooperation in running the Softwood Lumber Regime to one of threats and misrepresentation. Figuring in this new attitude were assertions of non–existent policy reasons for forcing them to comply with very burdensome demands for documents, refusals to provide them with promised information, threats of reductions and even termination of the Investment's export quotas, serious misrepresentations of fact in memoranda to the Minister concerning the Investor's and the Investment's actions and even suggestions of criminal investigation of the Investment's conduct. The Tribunal also concluded that these actions were not caused by any behaviour of the Investor or the Investment, which remained cooperative until the overreaching of the SLD became too burdensome and confrontational.[819]

The final words of the tribunal were clear as to the egregious nature of the Canada's actions: '[o]ne would hope that these actions by the SLD would shock and outrage every reasonable citizen of Canada; they did shock and outrage the Tribunal'.[820] For the tribunal, SLD's conduct therefore breached Article 1105 'even using Canada's strict formulation of that requirement'.[821] The tribunal awarded the investor USD 461,566 in compensation. The reasoning of the tribunal suggests that in a number of circumstances, specific features of an administrative process constitute a breach of the due process requirement under Article 1105:

- Whenever an investor is 'subjected to threats' by an administrative body.[822]
- Whenever an administrative body asserts 'non-existent policy reasons' to force an investor to comply with 'very burdensome demands for documents' having for consequence that the investor is incurring 'unnecessary expense and disruption'.[823]
- Whenever an administrative body refuses to provide the investor with 'promised information'[824] and denies its 'reasonable requests for pertinent information'[825] on administrative matters.

816. *Pope & Talbot Inc. v. Canada*, Award in Respect of Damages, (31 May 2002), paras. 57–58.
817. *Ibid.*, para. 65, emphasis in the original.
818. *Ibid.*, para. 67.
819. *Ibid.*, para. 68.
820. *Ibid.*
821. *Ibid.*, para. 69.
822. *Ibid.*, Award on the Merits (Phase 2), (10 April 2001), para. 181.
823. *Ibid.*, Award in Respect of Damages, (31 May 2002), para. 68.
824. *Ibid.*, Award on the Merits (Phase 2), (10 April 2001), para. 181.
825. *Ibid.*, Award in Respect of Damages, (31 May 2002), para. 68.

[7]   Mondev

This case involves a Canadian company, Mondev International Ltd., commencing arbitration proceedings on its behalf and on behalf of its American subsidiary against the United States claiming USD 50 million in compensation.[826] At the heart of the dispute was a three-party contract between, on the one hand, claimant's American company (Lafayette Place Associates, 'LPA'), and, on the other hand, the City of Boston and its planning and development agency (Boston Redevelopment Authority, 'BRA'). Phase I of the contract consisted of building a shopping complex and a hotel in downtown Boston. It also included the exclusive right and option for LPA to buy an adjoining piece of property for Phase II of the project from the City. Phase I was completed in 1985. Shortly after its completion, LPA notified the City of its intent to acquire the parcel needed to begin Phase II. However, the City refused to sell the parcel at the price formula agreed upon in the contract for its acquisition.[827] The City then allegedly pressured LPA to accept a new deal, which was refused by LPA. In the end, the only option left for LPA was to negotiate a distress sale of its interest in the project to another Canadian Company, Campeau Corp. However, the City's agency refused to approve the transfer of ownership in the project and, as a result, LPA was only able to enter into a less valuable lease agreement with Campeau Corp. in 1988.[828]

In 1992, LPA filed suit before the Suffolk County Superior Court in Boston, Massachusetts, alleging breach of contract by the City and tortious interference by the City's planning agency (BRA) regarding the contract sale to Campeau Corp. In 1994, a jury returned a special verdict awarding LPA USD 9.6 million in tort against the City and USD 6.4 million against BRA. However, the trial judge dismissed the USD 6.4 million verdict against BRA on the grounds that it was subsumed within the verdict against the City and that BRA had immunity under the Massachusetts Tort Claims Act. On appeal, the Supreme Judicial Court of Massachusetts affirmed the trial court's ruling on the question of BRA's immunity. It also vacated the USD 9.6 million award against the City on the ground that LPA had failed to demonstrate that it was willing and able to perform its own contractual obligations. A petition to appeal to the Supreme Judicial Court and later a certiorari petition to the Supreme Court of the United States were both denied.

According to the claimant, the unprincipled and arbitrary decision rendered by the Supreme Judicial Court of Massachusetts, which denied it any compensation, amounted to both a substantive and a procedural denial of justice in violation of Article 1105. The claimant also contended that the Court did not act in accordance with the due process obligation when it reversed the jury's finding which it substituted with its

---

826. *Mondev v. United States*, Award, (2 October 2002).
827. As a consequence of the rise in property value in Boston in the 1980s, by 1985 the fair market value of the parcel far exceeded the price agreed in 1978.
828. The alleged interference from the City's agency resulted in Campeau Corp. never being able to buy the parcel from the City. Phase II of the project could therefore not be completed and the shopping complex ultimately failed and was foreclosed.

own interpretation without hearing the facts and observing the witnesses.[829] The claimant also alleged that the Court's decision with respect to BRA's immunity was a denial of justice.

The tribunal first noted that the only claim of breach of Article 1105 it had to examine was related to denial of justice.[830] It also made this controversial statement: 'under NAFTA it is not true that the denial of justice rule and the exhaustion of local remedies rule "are interlocking and inseparable"'.[831] This affirmation has been rightly criticized by scholars for suggesting that an investor claiming denial of justice does not have to exhaust local remedies in domestic courts before undertaking NAFTA arbitration proceedings.[832] As further discussed below, subsequent tribunals (*Loewen, Waste Management*) have, on the contrary, held that the exhaustion of local remedies is an essential requirement in the context of a denial of justice claim.

The tribunal affirmed that it was not the 'function of NAFTA tribunals to act as courts of appeal'.[833] It also endorsed the above-mentioned four different types of denial of justice as identified by the *Azinian* tribunal.[834] The tribunal then noted that the ICJ in the *ELSI* case had described an 'arbitrary conduct' as one which displays 'a wilful disregard of due process of law (...) which shocks, or at least surprises, a sense of judicial propriety'.[835] While the tribunal recognized that the ICJ dealt in that instance with administrative conduct rather than that of the judiciary branch, it nevertheless held that the criterion were 'useful also in the context of denial of justice'.[836] The tribunal then defined what would constitute a denial of justice in the form of the following 'test':

> The test is not whether a particular result is surprising, but whether the shock or surprise occasioned to an impartial tribunal leads, on reflection, to justified concerns as to the judicial propriety of the outcome, bearing in mind on the one hand that international tribunals are not courts of appeal, and on the other hand that Chapter 11 of NAFTA (like other treaties for the protection of investments) is intended to provide a real measure of protection. In the end the question is whether, at an international level and having regard to generally accepted standards of the administration of justice, a tribunal can conclude in the light of all the available facts that the impugned decision was clearly improper and discreditable, with the result that the investment has been subjected to unfair and inequitable treatment.[837]

---

829. The claimant accused the Court of having ignored established Massachusetts's case law that reserves issues of breach and performance of contract to a decision by a jury. Another allegation was that the Court's decision created new and retroactive rules requiring a higher standard of proof in cases involving breach of contract claims brought against a government respondent.
830. *Mondev v. United States*, Award, (2 October 2002), para. 96.
831. *Ibid.*, para. 96, quoting from: C. Eagleton, *The Responsibility of States in International Law* (New York U. Press 1928), at 113.
832. Paulsson, *supra* n. 751, at 111, stating that the tribunal was 'wrong'.
833. *Mondev v. United States*, Award, (2 October 2002), para. 126.
834. *Ibid.*, para. 126, referring to *Azinian v. Mexico*, Award, (1 November 1999), paras. 102–103.
835. *Ibid.*, para. 127, quoting from *ELSI*, at 76 (para. 128).
836. *Ibid.*
837. *Ibid.*

In other words, for a judicial decision to constitute a denial of justice, it must be 'clearly improper and discreditable' in the sense that it would 'shock or surprise' any impartial observer and raise 'justified concerns as to the judicial propriety of the outcome' of the case. The test set out in *Mondev* has been subsequently endorsed by the *Waste Management* and *Loewen* tribunals.

The tribunal then analyzed the decision of the Supreme Judicial Court of Massachusetts. It first examined the Court's dismissal of LPA's contract claim against the City. It rejected the claimant's argument that this decision involved a 'significant and serious departure' from its previous case law and that it had made 'new law'.[838] In any event, the tribunal opined that 'even if it had done so its decision would have fallen within the limits of common law adjudication'.[839] Thus, 'there is nothing here to shock or surprise even a delicate judicial sensibility'.[840] This statement suggests that a court decision which makes a 'significant and serious departure' from its previous case law would not amount to a denial of justice under international law. This proposition is in line with the *Azinian* award affirming that no denial of justice occurs in situation where a domestic court makes an error of law.[841]

The tribunal then moved to examine Mondev's argument that the Court 'should have remanded questions of fact to the jury, in particular the question whether Mondev was willing and able to perform or whether the City had constructively repudiated the contract'.[842] The tribunal stated that these were local procedural matters which were unlikely to violate Article 1105 ('except in extreme cases') and would, moreover, require NAFTA tribunals to act as courts of appeal.[843] In any event, the tribunal noted that, in the case at bar, there 'was no trace of a procedural denial of justice'.[844]

Finally, the tribunal examined the trial judge's decision (which was later confirmed by the Supreme Judicial Court of Massachusetts) to decline to enter the jury's verdict against BRA because it was entitled to immunity for intentional torts as a 'public employer' under the Massachusetts Tort Claims Act.[845] At the outset, the tribunal stated that 'circumstances can be envisaged where the conferral of a general

---

838. *Ibid.*, para. 133. On a related question, the tribunal also indicated that 'it is normally a matter for local courts to determine whether and in what circumstances to apply new decisional law retrospectively' (para. 137).
839. *Ibid.*, para. 133.
840. *Ibid.*
841. *Azinian v. Mexico*, Award, (1 November 1999), para. 99.
842. *Mondev v. United States*, Award, (2 October 2002), para. 135.
843. *Ibid.*, para. 136: 'Questions of fact-finding on appeal are quintessentially matters of local procedural practice. Except in extreme cases, the Tribunal does not understand how the application of local procedural rules about such matters as remand, or decisions as to the functions of juries vis-à-vis appellate courts, could violate the standards embodied in Article 1105(1). On the approach adopted by Mondev, NAFTA tribunals would turn into courts of appeal, which is not their role'.
844. *Ibid.*, para. 136.
845. *Ibid.*, para. 140. The tribunal summarised the claimant's argument as follows: 'In the present proceedings, Mondev did not challenge the correctness of this decision as a matter of Massachusetts law. Rather, it argued that for a NAFTA Party to confer on one of its public authorities immunity from suit in respect of wrongful conduct affecting an investment was in itself a failure to provide full protection and security to the investment, and contravened Article 1105(1)'.

immunity from suit for conduct of a public authority affecting a NAFTA investment could amount to a breach of Article 1105(1) of NAFTA'.[846] In fact, the tribunal referred to one such circumstance.[847] However, it declined to further discuss this issue since considering hypothetical situations was not within its mandate.[848] The tribunal also added that 'reasons can well be imagined why a legislature might decide to immunize a regulatory authority, mandated to deal with commercial redevelopment plans, from potential liability for tortious interference'.[849] Ultimately, the tribunal held that the fact that BRA benefited from immunity under Massachusetts law was a matter of domestic law and that it would not amount to a denial of justice:

> [T]he Tribunal is not persuaded that the extension to a statutory authority of a limited immunity from suit for interference with contractual relations amounts in this case to a breach of Article 1105(1). Of course such an immunity could not protect a NAFTA State Party from a claim for conduct which was substantively in breach of NAFTA standards – but for this NAFTA provides its own remedy, since it gives an investor the right to go directly to international arbitration in respect of conduct occurring after NAFTA's entry into force. In a Chapter 11 arbitration, no local statutory immunity would apply. On the other hand, within broad limits, the extent to which a State decides to immunize regulatory authorities from suit for interference with contractual relations is a matter for the competent organs of the State to decide.[850]

The tribunal therefore rejected the claimant's allegations of breach of Article 1105.

[8]   Loewen

Loewen Group Inc., a Canadian funeral services company, and its owner Raymond L. Loewen (hereinafter 'the claimants') filed a claim in 1998 against the United States alleging breaches of several NAFTA provisions and claimed USD 725 million in compensation. The facts of this case can be summarized as follows: Loewen Group Inc. (hereinafter 'Loewen') was the defendant before the Mississippi State Court in a

---

846. *Ibid.*, para. 151. *See*, the discussion in Paulsson, *supra* n. 751, at 138 ff.
847. *Ibid.*, para. 152: 'For example, the Massachusetts legislation immunizes public authorities from liability for assault and battery. An investor whose local staff had been assaulted by the police while at work could well claim that its investment was not accorded "treatment in accordance with international law, including... full protection and security" if the government were immune from suit for the assaults. In such a case, the availability of an action in tort against individual (possibly unidentifiable) officers might not be a sufficient basis to avoid the situation being characterised as a breach of Article 1105(1)'.
848. *Ibid.*, para. 153.
849. *Ibid.*
850. *Ibid.*, para. 154. For a critical assessment of the tribunal's finding on this point, *see* J. Cantegreil, *The Final Award in Mondev International v. United States of Amercia*, in *The Reasons Requirement in International Investment Arbitration: Critical Case Studies* 45–46 (Guillermo Aguilar Alvarez & W. Michael Reisman eds., Nijhoff 2008) ('this conclusion is not supported by reasons. Under this rationale the United States may perfectly avoid international responsibility by local enactments purporting to confer immunity on governmental bodies'). He also criticized the tribunal's decision for having failed to address the question whether or not some form of sovereign immunity can consist in a denial of justice. *See also*, the discussion in: Paulsson, *supra* n. 751, at 142–146.

lawsuit involving a commercial dispute with a local American businessman (Mr. O'Keefe), who was a competitor in the funeral home and insurance industry in Mississippi. Mr. O'Keefe sought less than USD 5 million in damages before the Mississippi Court. Loewen was ultimately found guilty. The jury returned a total verdict of USD 500 million, including USD 400 million in punitive damages. According to the claimants, they were later 'forced to settle the case under conditions of extreme duress' in an out of court settlement of USD 175 million for a commercial dispute involving transactions worth less than USD 5 million.[851]

The claimants alleged that the excessive jury verdict by the Mississippi court constituted a 'substantive denial of justice' in breach of Article 1105. The claimants also argued that by permitting racially motivated comments and 'anti-Canadian' testimony from counsel, which 'inflamed the passion of the jury, and produced the grossly excessive verdict and judgment',[852] the trial court had committed a 'procedural denial of justice'. The claimants also maintained that the arbitrary application of the appellate bond requirement by the Mississippi Supreme Court constituted another 'procedural denial of justice'.[853] The respondent argued that the claimants had not exhausted local remedies as one appeal avenue had not been used (i.e., the US Supreme Court).[854] Moreover, it stated that it had not found any international decision in which a denial of justice claim was permitted where the claimant had settled out of court.[855] In any event, for the United States the trial proceedings had been conducted in accordance with the minimum standard of justice and there was no evidence that the high monetary value of the verdict was influenced by any improper bias against the claimants.[856]

Although the *Loewen* case is certainly the most important NAFTA case involving allegations of denial of justice, it remains that the claim was ultimately rejected by the tribunal based on mere jurisdictional grounds entirely unrelated to the denial of justice

---

851. *Loewen v. United States*, Claimant's Notice of Claim, (30 October 1998), para. 6.
852. *Ibid.*, para. 139.
853. *Ibid.*, Award, (26 June 2003), para. 39, In its award, the tribunal summarized the position of the claimants as follows: '(1) the trial court, by admitting extensive anti-Canadian and pro-American testimony and prejudicial counsel comment, violated Article 1102 of NAFTA which bars discrimination against foreign investors and their investments; (2) the discrimination tainted the inexplicably large verdict; (3) the trial court, by the way in which it conducted the trial, in particular by its conduct of the voir dire and its irregular reformation of the initial jury verdict for $260,000,000, by permitting extensive nationality-based, racial and class-based testimony and counsel comments, violated Article 1105 of NAFTA which imposes a minimum standard of treatment for investments of foreign investors, including a duty of "full protection and security" and a right to "fair and equitable treatment" of foreign investors; (4) the excessive verdict and judgment (even apart from the discrimination) violated Article 1105; (5) the Mississippi courts' arbitrary application of the bonding requirement violated Article 1105; and (6) the discriminatory conduct, the excessive verdict, the denial of Loewen's right to appeal and the coerced settlement violated Article 1110 of NAFTA, which bars the uncompensated appropriation of investments of foreign investors'.
854. *Ibid.*, US Counter-Memorial on the Merits, (30 March 2001), at 4, 110; US Rejoinder-Memorial on the Merits, (27 August 2001), at 106, 110.
855. *Ibid.*, US Counter-Memorial on the Merits, (30 March 2001), at 74.
856. *Ibid.*, at 133, 175.

allegations. Thus, the tribunal held that it did not have jurisdiction over the claim because Loewen had not maintained a 'continuous' Canadian nationality as a result of a recent corporate reorganization of the company.[857] In this context, the tribunal stated that the international law rule of continuous nationality requires a person to maintain the same nationality until 'the date of the resolution of the claim'.[858] This position has been rejected by many scholars.[859] Another feature of the award that has attracted criticism is the tribunal's approach regarding Mr. Loewen in his personal capacity as an investor.[860] This issue was important since he had remained a Canadian national at all relevant times, including when the award was rendered. However, these issues are beyond the scope of this book. It is of importance to note that the rest of the tribunal's award on denial of justice is an obiter dictum.[861] This peculiar feature of the award has also been criticized by scholars.[862] The award nevertheless contains important findings regarding the concept of denial of justice.

In its award, the tribunal made it clear that the conduct of the trial by the Mississippi court constituted a manifest injustice: '[w]e have reached the firm conclusion that the conduct of the trial by the trial judge was so flawed that it constituted a miscarriage of justice amounting to a manifest injustice as that expression is understood in international law'.[863] Yet, whether or not such a manifest injustice amounted to a denial of justice in breach of Article 1105 constituted a different question altogether: '[w]hether this conclusion results in a violation of Article 1105 depends upon the resolution of Respondent's submissions still to be considered, in particular the submission that State responsibility arises only when final action is taken by the State's judicial system *as a whole*'.[864]

The tribunal explained that the trial was conducted from beginning to end based on the premise that Mr. O'Keefe was a war hero who 'epitomised local business

---

857. *Ibid.*, Award, (26 June 2003), para. 240.
858. *Ibid.*, para. 225.
859. Paulsson, *supra* n. 751, at 183-184; Diehl, *supra* n. 3, at 482-483; M.S. Duchesne, *The Continuous Nationality of Claims Principle: Its Historical Development and Current Relevance to Investor-State Investment Disputes*, 36 Geo. Wash. Int'lL.Rev. 801-802 (2004): P. Acconci, *The Requirement of Continuous Corporate Nationality and Customary International Rules on Foreign Investment: the Loewen Case*, 14 Italian Y.I.L 195-223 (2005); M. Mendelson, *The Runaway Train: The Continuous Nationality Rule from the Panevezys-Saldutiskis Railway Case to Loewen*, in *International Investment Law and Arbitration: Leading Cases from the ICSID, NAFTA, Bilateral Treaties and Customary International Law* 97-149 (T. Weiler ed., Cameron May 2005); F. Orrego Vicuña, *Changing Approaches to the Nationality of Claims in the Context of Diplomatic Protection and International Dispute Settlement*, in *Liber amicorum Ibrahim F.I. Shihata: International Finance and Development Law* 503-525 (S. Schlemmer-Schulte & K.-Y. Tung eds., Kluwer Law International 2001); R. Wisner, & N. Gallus, *Nationality Requirements in Investor-State Arbitration*, 5 J. World Invest. & Trade 927-945 (2004); N. Rubins, *Loewen v. United States: The Burial of an Investor-State Arbitration Claim*, 21 Arb. Int'l 23-36 (2005); J. Paulsson, *Continuous Nationality in Loewen*, 20 Arb. Int'l 213 (2004); Wallace, *supra* n. 759, at 669; Pulkowski, *supra* n. 786, at 300-309.
860. Diehl, *supra* n. 3, at 483; Rubins, *supra* n. 859, at 29; Pulkowski, *supra* n. 786, at 309-311.
861. Diehl, *supra* n. 3, at 481; Wallace, *supra* n. 759, at 689.
862. Pulkowski, *supra* n. 786, at 292.
863. *Loewen v. United States*, Award, (26 June 2003), Award, para. 54.
864. *Ibid.*, para. 55 (emphasis added).

interests' against a 'ruthless foreign (Canadian) corporate predator' (i.e., Loewen).[865]
As the tribunal noted, the constant reference to Loewen's Canadian nationality during
the trial by Mr. O'Keefe's counsel was a strategy 'calculated to appeal to the jury's
sympathy for local home-town interests as against the wealthy and powerful foreign
competitor'.[866] Counsel also 'played the race card' (apparently to appeal to the black
judge and the predominantly African-American jurors[867]) by suggesting that his client
'did business with black and white people alike whereas Loewen did business with
white people'.[868] Mr. O'Keefe's counsel also appealed to class-based prejudice by
portraying Loewen 'as a large, wealthy foreign corporation', an image he contrasted
with that he painted of his client as a 'small, local, family businessman'.[869]

The tribunal then moved to examine the argument submitted by the United States
that Loewen's counsel did not object to the opposing counsel's strategy to appeal to
nationality/racial/class based prejudice. The reason why the United States argued this
position was quite simple: 'If Loewen's counsel did not object, then, so the argument
runs, there was no error on the part of the trial judge in failing to intervene of his own
motion'.[870] This is an important point since for the United States to be held responsible
under international law for conduct of a Mississippi court, it must be established 'that
the trial judge permitted or failed to take steps (which he should have taken) to prevent
the alleged conduct of O'Keefe's counsel and witnesses'.[871] The tribunal explained that
while it was true that Loewen's counsel 'did not object to comments or evidence on
these matters when they could have done so', there were also a number of possible
explanations.[872] In any event, despite counsel's silence 'the trial judge was aware of the
problem and should have taken action himself'.[873]

On this point, the tribunal concluded that there was a 'gross failure on the part of
the trial judge to afford the due process due to Loewen in protecting it from the tactics
employed by O'Keefe and its counsel'.[874] The tribunal's reasoning suggests that a court
that permits or fails to take steps in order to prevent one party (or its counsel) from

---

865. *Ibid.*, para. 56.
866. *Ibid.*, para. 56. *See also*, para. 63.
867. *Ibid.*, para. 3.
868. *Ibid.*, para. 65.
869. *Ibid.*, para. 68. *See also*, at para. 70: 'It is artificial to split the O'Keefe strategy into three
     segments of nationality-based, race and class-based strategies. When the trial is viewed as a
     whole right through from the voir dire to counsel's closing address, it can be seen that the
     O'Keefe case was presented by counsel against an appeal to home-town sentiment, favouring
     the local party against an outsider. To that appeal was added the element of the powerful
     foreign multi-national corporation seeking to crush the small independent competitor who had
     fought for his country in World War II. Describing 'Loewen' as a Canadian was simply to
     identify Loewen as an outsider. The fact that an investor from another state, say New York,
     would or might receive the same treatment in a Mississippi court as Loewen received is no
     answer to a claim that the O'Keefe case as presented invited the jury to discriminate against
     Loewen as an outsider'.
870. *Ibid.*, para. 71.
871. *Ibid.*
872. *Ibid.*, paras. 72, 74. *See also*, at paras. 74–77.
873. *Ibid.*, para. 73.
874. *Ibid.*, para. 87.

appealing to nationality/racial/class based prejudice breaches its due process obligation. In other words, not only do courts have an obligation not to discriminate against
foreign investors themselves, but they also have an obligation to prevent others from
using discriminatory practice during a trial.

The tribunal then explained that Mississippi law requires bifurcation whereby the
jury has to determine liability and compensatory damages at a first stage of the
procedure while the question of punitive damages is only dealt with at a second stage.
Throughout the trial, Mr. O'Keefe's counsel consistently addressed these two distinct
issues interchangeably and the objections raised by Loewen's counsel on this point
were overruled by the trial judge.[875] Ultimately, the jury returned a verdict of USD 260
million in favor of Mr. O'Keefe which included some USD 160 million in punitive
damages. The tribunal held that 'the way in which the verdict was constructed,
including, as it did, compensatory and punitive damages, demonstrates that there was
a failure adequately to instruct the jury to limit their initial award to compensatory
damages'.[876] Moreover, the judge denied the motion filed by Loewen to the effect that
the verdict was 'biased, excessive and procedurally defective because it covered
punitive damages'.[877] Instead, the trial judge informed the jury that he 'did not accept'
the part of the award concerning punitive damages.[878] For the tribunal, 'the jury may
well have interpreted the rejection of this award as an indication that it was inadequate'.[879] The jury ultimately returned a second and final verdict of USD 400 million
in punitive damages. The trial judge also later rejected Loewen's submission that the
'jury's verdict exhibited bias, passion and prejudice against [it]'.[880]

The tribunal noted that this award of a total of USD 500 million 'was by far the
largest ever awarded in Mississippi'[881] and that the claimants 'had a very strong case'
for arguing that such damages 'were excessive, and that the amounts were so inflated
as to invite the inference that the jury was swayed by prejudice, passion or sympathy'.[882] Thus, the total award was 'grossly disproportionate to the damage suffered by
O'Keefe'[883] considering the value of the dispute at stake.[884] Later in the award, the
tribunal touched upon this issue yet again and stated that 'if a single instance of the
unfair treatment that was accorded Loewen at the trial level need be cited, it would be

---

875. *Ibid.*, paras. 90–91.
876. *Ibid.*, para. 95.
877. *Ibid.*, para. 96.
878. *Ibid.*
879. *Ibid.*
880. *Ibid.*, paras. 102–103.
881. *Ibid.*, para. 104.
882. *Ibid.*, para. 105. The tribunal rejected the United States' argument that the excessive verdict
     was somewhat caused by Loewen's flawed trial strategy. The tribunal acknowledged that
     Loewen's strategy may have been 'unwise' (para. 116) and that its business practices in the
     funeral services industry may have also been 'predatory and aggressive' (para. 118), but
     concluded that the 'magnitude of the verdict suggests that the verdict was influenced by bias,
     prejudice, passion or sympathy' (para. 115).
883. *Ibid.*, para. 113.
884. *Ibid.* The tribunal explains that 'the dispute involved three contracts valued at $980,000 and an
     exchange of two funeral homes worth approximately $2.5 million for a Loewen funeral
     insurance company valued at approximately $4 million'.

the manner in which the large and excessive verdict was constructed by the judge and the jury'.[885] The tribunal even added that 'the methods employed by the jury and countenanced by the judge were the antithesis of due process'.[886] In its final conclusions concerning the trial, the tribunal was quite blunt:

> By any standard of measurement, the trial involving O'Keefe and Loewen was a disgrace. By any standard of review, the tactics of O'Keefe's lawyers, particularly Mr Gary, were impermissible. By any standard of evaluation, the trial judge failed to afford Loewen the process that was due.[887]

Having set the table, the tribunal moved to examine the question of whether or not 'the whole trial, and its resultant verdict, satisfied minimum standards of international law' under Article 1105.[888] The tribunal first noted that the United States did not deny that customary international law imposes an obligation 'to maintain and make available to aliens, a fair and effective system of justice'.[889] The tribunal agreed that the due process obligation under international law requires a State to 'provide a fair trial of a case to which a foreign investor is a party',[890] and, specifically, to 'ensure that litigation is free from discrimination against a foreign litigant and that the foreign litigant should not become the victim of sectional or local prejudice'.[891]

The tribunal also explained that 'bad faith or malicious intention' is not necessary to prove the existence of a denial of justice.[892] It specified that 'manifest injustice in the sense of a lack of due process leading to an outcome which offends a sense of judicial propriety is enough' to demonstrate a denial of justice.[893] Furthermore, the tribunal cited and approved the definition given by the *Mondev* tribunal to the effect that a decision must be 'clearly improper and discreditable, with the result that the investment has been subjected to "unfair and inequitable treatment"'.[894] The tribunal also stated that a 'decision which is in breach of municipal law and is discriminatory against the foreign litigant amounts to manifest injustice according to international law'.[895] In the present case, the decision was discriminatory because the 'trial court permitted the jury to be influenced by persistent appeals to local favoritism as against a foreign litigant'.[896] The tribunal's conclusion was that 'the whole trial and its resultant verdict were clearly improper and discreditable and cannot be squared with minimum standards of international law and fair and equitable treatment'.[897]

---

885. *Ibid.*, para. 122.
886. *Ibid.*
887. *Ibid.*, para. 119.
888. *Ibid.*, para. 121. *See also*, at paras. 124–137.
889. *Ibid.*, para. 129.
890. *Ibid.*, para. 123.
891. *Ibid.*
892. *Ibid.*, para. 132.
893. *Ibid.*
894. *Ibid.*, para. 133.
895. *Ibid.*, para. 135.
896. *Ibid.*, para. 136.
897. *Ibid.*, para. 137. *See also*, at para. 142. Bjorklund, *supra* n. 751, at 870, rightly noted that this very general conclusion 'leaves the reader not knowing which particular parts of the trial failed

Following its in-depth examination of the trial, the tribunal then proceeded to analyze 'the rest of the process, and its availability to Loewen'.[898] This examination was necessary to establish any violation of Article 1105 because 'the trial court proceedings are only part of the judicial process that is available to the parties'.[899] The tribunal qualified the exhaustion of local remedies rule as a 'procedural' requirement rather than a substantive one,[900] in conformity with the prevailing view amongst writers.[901] Yet, the tribunal's reasoning suggests that in the context of a claim of denial of justice, the requirement to exhaust local remedies is *substantive*.[902] The tribunal's rationale is not at all clear with respect to this pivotal point.[903] It seems to highlight a distinction between the exhaustion of local remedies rule and some sort of a 'finality requirement'.[904] The existence of such distinction has been contested by many writers.[905] Some of these writers have nevertheless concurred with the tribunal's position that denial of justice claims must be treated differently than other types of violations of international law insofar as they always require that local remedies be exhausted.[906] Another related controversial feature of the award is the tribunal's failure to thoroughly address the nature and scope of the waiver contained at NAFTA Article

---

to comport with the international minimum standard, and fails to give guidance as to what acts in particular might be sufficient to trigger international liability'.
898. *Ibid.*, para. 137.
899. *Ibid.*
900. *Ibid.*, para. 149.
901. *See,* the analysis in: Diehl, *supra* n. 3, at 487.
902. *Loewen v. United States*, Award, (26 June 2003), paras. 142–157.
903. *See,* the detailed discussion in: Diehl, *supra* n. 3, at 485-488; Kläger, *supra* n. 13, at 221; Wallace, *supra* n. 759, at 691 ff.
904. The title of the award's section on this point refers to 'the necessity for finality of action on the part of the State's legal system'. *See,* B.K. Gathright, *A Step in the Wrong Direction: The Loewen Finality Requirement and the Local Remedies Rule in NAFTA Chapter Eleven,* 54 Emory L.J. 1116 (2005); Diehl, *supra* n. 3, at 485. Pulkowski, *supra* n. 786, at 312, explains the distinction as follows: 'The exhaustion of local remedies rule is defined as operating as a bar to jurisdiction' while the finality requirement 'operates as a special substantive bar to a finding of unlawfulness, applying exclusively to judicial acts'. For him, the tribunal therefore establishes a 'theory of two-tiered responsibility' whereby 'as far as original judicial wrongs are concerned, an unsuccessful attempt to remedy the wrong in domestic judicial proceedings is, in addition, a pre-condition for substantive responsibility'. *See also*: Diehl, *supra* n. 3, at 486.
905. Pulkowski, *supra* n. 786, at 312-314; Diehl, *supra* n. 3, at 486.
906. *See,* Paulsson, *supra* n. 751, at 103, 107, 104 ('There must be some defensible foundation for distinguishing claims of denial of justice; It is no answer to invent labels like "substantive" or "finality" and to declare arbitrarily that they define a higher threshold of admissibility'), at 108 ('In the particular case of denial of justice, however, claims will not succeed unless the victim has indeed exhausted municipal remedies, or unless there is an explicit waiver of a type yet to be invented. (...) This is neither a paradox nor an aberration, for it is in the very nature of the delict that a state is judged by the final product or at least a sufficiently final product - of its administration of justice. A denial of justice is not consummated by the decision of a court of first instance. Having sought to rely on national justice, the foreigner cannot complain that its operations have been delictual until he has given it scope to operate, including by the agency of its ordinary corrective functions'). It should be noted that a number of other scholars have rejected the tribunal's position on this point: McLachlan et al., *supra* n. 37, at 232-233; Gathright, *supra* n. 904; Pulkowski, *supra* n. 786, at 311 ff.

1121.[907] The tribunal stated that this provision 'involves no waiver of the duty to pursue local remedies in its application to a breach of international law constituted by a judicial act'.[908] This statement suggests that Article 1121 simply does not apply in the specific context of denial of justice claims.[909] The tribunal's reasoning on this point has been subjected to strong criticism.[910]

Less controversially, the tribunal then explained the purpose of the exhaustion of local remedies requirement as being to 'afford the State the opportunity of redressing through its legal system the inchoate breach of international law occasioned by the lower court decision'.[911] Concerning the actual scope of this requirement, the tribunal made reference to an 'obligation to exhaust remedies which are effective and adequate and are reasonably available to the complainant in the circumstances in which it is situated'.[912] It also added that the assessment of whether or not remedies are 'reasonable' must be made 'in light' of the investor's 'situation' and must also take its 'financial and economic circumstances' into account.[913] In other words, the tribunal seems to introduce a subjective test to determine the reasonability of the remedies available to the investor.[914] Ultimately, as further discussed below, the tribunal failed to apply this subjective test to the facts of the case.[915]

The tribunal then applied these theoretical findings to the facts of the case. As pointed out by one author, the issue in this instance was not really whether any appeal procedure existed (which was clearly the case), but rather whether such procedure was reasonably available.[916] Thus, under Mississippi law, unless the losing defendant wishing to pursue an appeal against a judgment posts a (security) bond for which the amount is equal to 125% of the verdict, that judgment remains enforceable by the

---

907. Under this provision, investors are required to 'waive their right to initiate or continue before any administrative tribunal or court under the law of any Party ... any proceedings with respect to the measure of the disputing Party that is alleged to be a breach' of NAFTA.
908. *Loewen v. United States*, Award, (26 June 2003), para. 164. This aspect of the award has been criticized by Diehl, *supra* n. 3, at 484-486.
909. Paulsson, *supra* n. 751, at 104.
910. *See, ibid.*, at 103-106; Diehl, *supra* n. 3, at 484-484; Wallace, *supra* n. 759, at 691, 697-699; Pulkowski, *supra* n. 786, at 313-315; Paparinskis, *supra* n. 18, at 206.
911. *Loewen v. United States*, Award, (26 June 2003), para. 156. The tribunal added (at para. 154) that '[n]o instance has been drawn to our attention in which an international tribunal has held a State responsible for a breach of international law constituted by a lower court decision when there was available an effective and adequate appeal within the State's legal system'.
912. *Ibid.*, paras. 168–170.
913. *Ibid.*: 'Availability is not a standard to be determined or applied in the abstract. It means reasonably available to the complainant in the light of its situation, including its financial and economic circumstances as a foreign investor, as they are affected by any conditions relating to the exercise of any local remedy. If a State attaches conditions to a right of appeal which render exercise of the right impractical, the exercise of the right is neither available nor effective nor adequate. Likewise, if a State burdens the exercise of the right directly or indirectly so as to expose the complainant to severe financial consequences, it may well be that the State has by its own actions disabled the complainant from affording the State the opportunity of redressing the matter of complaint. The scope of the need to exhaust local remedies must be considered in the light of these considerations'.
914. Diehl, *supra* n. 3, at 489.
915. Pulkowski, *supra* n. 786, at 318.
916. Paulsson, *supra* n. 751, at 120.

winning party. In other words, while Loewen could have pursued an appeal proceeding, it clearly ran the risk that its assets would be subject to enforcement procedure if it did not post a bond of USD 625 million. The claimants' requests to stay enforcement of part of the judgment or to reduce the bond requirement were rejected by both the trial judge and (subsequently) the Mississippi Supreme Court. While it is technically true that such a 'refusal to relax the bonding requirement was not a denial of the appeal',[917] it undoubtedly resulted in rendering such proceedings very unlikely. More controversially, the tribunal concluded that these decisions by the trial judge and the Mississippi Supreme Court did not constitute a violation of Article 1105.[918]

The tribunal recognized, however, that the risk of the immediate execution of the judgment by Mr. O'Keefe was real.[919] According to the tribunal, 'if exercising the right of appeal, at the risk of immediate execution on Loewen's Mississippi assets, was the only alternative available to Loewen, it would not have been, "a reasonably available remedy" to Loewen'.[920] In other words, had there been no other alternatives for Loewen but to pursue an appeal in these circumstances, the tribunal would have recognized the unavailability of reasonable remedies. The tribunal did, however, conclude that other alternatives were indeed available to Loewen.[921]

One option available to Loewen was to file a petition for certiorari and to seek a stay of execution in the US Supreme Court by arguing that the bond requirement violated due process. The tribunal considered this remedy reasonably available and adequate.[922] This conclusion is surprising considering the fact that the evidence presented by the expert witnesses from both parties was contradictory on this point. In fact, the evidence was so conflicting that the tribunal held that it was 'not in a position to decide' which of the two opinions was 'to be preferred'.[923] Yet, in the same paragraph, the tribunal seems to have endorsed the view of the respondent's expert to the effect that there was a 'reasonable prospect or possibility' that this relief would be granted.[924] Many writers have concluded, on the contrary, that Loewen had in fact exhausted local remedies because of the limited prospects of a successful appeal to the US Supreme Court.[925] Moreover, it was later revealed in the context of a request filed by the United States to the tribunal for a 'supplemental decision' that Loewen had in fact put forward significant expert evidence showing that any recourse to the Supreme

---

917. *Loewen v. United States*, Award, (26 June 2003), para. 188.
918. *Ibid.*, paras. 189, 197. The tribunal added (at para. 189) that the decision of the trial judge was 'at worst an erroneous or mistaken decision'. *See*, the critical analysis of Paulsson, *supra* n. 751, at 123.
919. *Loewen v. United States*, Award, (26 June 2003), para. 208: 'Without posting the bond, Loewen's right of appeal could be exercised only at the risk of sustaining immediate execution on Loewen's assets in Mississippi, to be followed by execution against Loewen's assets in other States, with the inevitable consequence that Loewen's share price would collapse'.
920. *Ibid.*, para. 208.
921. One such alternative briefly discussed by the tribunal (at *Ibid.*, para. 209) was filing for bankruptcy under US law.
922. *Ibid.*, paras. 214–217.
923. *Ibid.*, para. 211.
924. *Ibid.*
925. Newcombe & Paradell, *supra* n. 206, at 242; Wallace, *supra* n. 759, at 692-693; Rubins, *supra* n. 859, at 17-23; Francioni, *supra* n. 759, at 733-735.

Court had almost no chance of success.[926] One writer opined that the tribunal 'ignored, or possibly simply forgot and overlooked' several affidavits from Loewen's adviser on that specific point which made its findings 'disingenuously removed from reality, and also inaccurate'.[927]

The tribunal ruled that Loewen ultimately 'failed to present evidence disclosing its reasons for entering into the settlement agreement in preference to pursuing other options'.[928] This view is debatable.[929] In fact, Loewen had presented strong and undisputed evidence as to why it had decided to enter into the settlement agreement.[930] Moreover, the tribunal held that 'although entry into the settlement agreement may well have been a reasonable course for Loewen to take', it remains that it was not the 'only course which Loewen could reasonably be expected to take'.[931] The tribunal's reasoning on this point has also been criticized by writers.[932] The tribunal's position is indeed difficult to reconcile with its earlier statement that any assessment of whether or not remedies are 'reasonable' must be made in light of an investor's financial and economic circumstances.[933] The tribunal should have considered the fact that Loewen had been convincingly told by its own legal experts that the settlement was in fact the only reasonable course of action available in view of the fact that chances of success of an appeal to the Supreme Court were close to nil. Ultimately, the general impression one gets from reading the award is that the tribunal was simply not interested in any argument regarding the reasonability of the settlement.

The tribunal's conclusion (which is, as mentioned above, an obiter dictum) was therefore that Loewen had failed to exhaust local remedies because it did not apply to the US Supreme Court to review the Mississippi proceedings.[934] As a result, no denial of justice had been committed by the United States.

The award has been the object of a torrent of criticism by writers.[935] Clearly, the tribunal was simply looking for any possible excuse to find the United States not responsible for this denial of justice.[936] The first pretext was its controversial decision

---

926. *Loewen v. United States*, Claimants' Article 58 Submissions as to Raymond L. Loewen's Article 1116 Claim, (19 September 2003), para. 5 (quoting from Claimants' Submission Concerning the Jurisdictional Objections of the United States, (26 May 2000), para. 62). *See also*: Paulsson, *supra* n. 751, at 124.
927. Wallace, *supra* n. 759, at 692.
928. *Loewen v. United States*, Award, (26 June 2003), para. 215.
929. Rubins, *supra* n. 859, at 22. The tribunal's reliance on burden of proof to solve the issue at stake has also been contested by writers: Diehl, *supra* n. 3, at 491; Rubins, *supra* n. 859, at 20; Pulkowski, *supra* n. 786, at 318-320.
930. *Loewen v. United States*, Claimants' Article 58 Submissions as to Raymond L. Loewen's Article 1116 Claim, (19 September 2003), paras. 5–6.
931. *Ibid.*, Award, (26 June 2003), para. 216. In its subsequent Decision on Request for Reconsideration, (13 September 2004), para. 22, the tribunal simply stated that it was not 'satisfied' by the evidence presented during the proceedings by the claimants that the settlement agreement was the only course for Loewen to take.
932. Paulsson, *supra* n. 751, at 123.
933. *Loewen v. United States*, Award, (26 June 2003), paras. 169–170.
934. *Ibid.*, para. 217.
935. *See*, for instance: Wallace, *supra* n. 759; Rubins, *supra* n. 859; Pulkowski, *supra* n. 786, at 291.
936. Rubins, *supra* n. 859, at 1 ('many wondered how a complaint that the arbitrators themselves recognised was substantively well founded, arising out of government measures that are clearly egregious, could be wholly dismissed. *Prima facie*, it seemed to some unlikely that the

that it lacked jurisdiction over the claim based on its peculiar (and widely contested) application of the international law rules of continuous nationality. The second pretext was to conclude that Loewen had not exhausted all local remedies before US courts.[937] The interesting question is, of course, why the tribunal was so disinclined to award damages against the United States. The answer may be found in the few paragraphs which were added by the tribunal after the order. The tribunal noted that '[t]oo great a readiness to step from outside into the domestic arena, attributing the shape of an international wrong to what is really a local error (however serious), will damage both the integrity of the domestic judicial system and the viability of NAFTA itself'.[938] This comment suggests that the arbitrators may have contemplated the strong negative reactions by some actors on the political scene in the United States (especially US Congress) which would have resulted from a condemnation to pay damages to a foreign investor.[939] The tribunal would have us believe that by failing to act when faced with such a clear case of denial of justice, they have somewhat 'saved' NAFTA Chapter 11.

More generally, however, one cannot deny the importance of the tribunal's reasoning (albeit in obiter) on the scope and content of the concept of denial of justice.[940] This is a conclusion that is not unanimous; some have even qualified the award as itself 'a miscarriage and denial of justice'.[941] Yet, what matters more (at least in the specific context of this book) is what the tribunal *said* about what constitutes a denial of justice rather than how it actually *failed to apply* these principles to the facts of the case. As further examined below, the reasoning of the *Loewen* tribunal with regards to denial of justice was largely endorsed by other NAFTA tribunals.

---

outcome of the case would have been the same had Mexico or Congo been the respondent rather than the United States. From this perception arose the question: if the United States managed to escape liability under an applicable investment treaty even in so extreme a case as Loewen, do arbitral tribunals hold capital exporting states to the same standards of investment protection as they do developing countries? (...) It would be ludicrous to suggest that such eminent arbitrators as Sir Anthony Mason and Lord Mustill are somehow dependent on the United States; they obviously made their decision in complete independence from the US government's influence. But there can also be little doubt that in part because the arbitration was against the world's most important capital exporter, the arbitrators had broader concerns in mind than the resolution of the dispute before them. These concerns appear to have contributed to conclusions that are difficult to justify in light of the facts of the Loewen case').

937. Wallace, *supra* n. 759, at 691 ff.
938. *Loewen v. United States*, Award, (26 June 2003), para. 242.
939. Rubins, *supra* n. 759, at 32; Wallace, *supra* n. 759, at 699-700.
940. Paulsson, *supra* n. 751, at 192.
941. Wallace, *supra* n. 759, at 696-697. *See also*, at 700 ('with respect to the doctrine of denial of justice concerning judicial acts, it seems clear that the Loewen case does not shed much useful light, although it does succeed in bringing to the surface much of the terminology of the already muddled doctrine. Nor does it shed light on whether denial of justice has become a constituent part of the emerging, jurisprudence and doctrine of fair and equitable treatment'); Diehl, *supra* n. 3, at 492 ('one cannot help but concluding that the Loewen award is only a leading award in so far as it leads one in different directions without giving a clear guidance as to the proper way').

[9]   *Waste Management*

The facts of this case have already been examined above.[942] One of the claimant's grounds for complaint was that it had been 'subjected to a denial of justice at the hands of the Mexican Governments, which conspired with one another to obstruct Acaverde's access to judicial and arbitral forums to resolve its claims under the Concession'.[943]

The tribunal first noted that the FET standard would be infringed by State conduct that, *inter alia*, 'involves a lack of due process leading to an outcome which offends judicial propriety—as might be the case with a manifest failure of natural justice in judicial proceedings or a complete lack of transparency and candour in an administrative process'.[944] Previously in the award, the tribunal had also explicitly endorsed the test put forward by the *Mondev* tribunal to the effect that a denial of justice occurs when a decision by a domestic court is 'clearly improper and discreditable' in the sense that it would 'shock or surprise' any impartial observer and would raise 'justified concerns as to the judicial propriety of the outcome' of the case.[945] The tribunal also approved the definition of denial of justice given by the *Loewen* tribunal,[946] and its conclusion that 'discriminatory violations of municipal law' constitute a denial of justice.[947] It also endorsed *Loewen's* position that in the context of a denial of justice claim, it is the system of justice as a whole which must be assessed (the 'system must be tried and have failed')[948] and 'not any individual decision in the course of proceedings'.[949] As a result, in the context of denial of justice claims, 'the notion of exhaustion of local remedies is incorporated into the substantive standard and is not only a procedural prerequisite to an international claim'.[950] The tribunal therefore adopted the position of the *Loewen* tribunal and rejected an earlier statement that had been made by the *Mondev* tribunal.[951]

The tribunal then moved to the examination of the facts of the case. The tribunal had already rejected the allegations against the State of Guerrero and the State-owned bank (Banobras) and concluded that the City Counsel of the municipality of Acapulco had not 'acted in a wholly arbitrary way or in a way that was grossly unfair'.[952] The tribunal then examined the question of 'the availability of local remedies to an investor faced with contractual breaches' to determine whether or not Article 1105 had been

---

942. *See,* section §3.02[D][2].
943. *Waste Management v. Mexico,* Claimant's Reply, (22 January 2003), para. 4.32. *See also:* Award, (30 April 2004), para. 87.
944. *Ibid.,* Award, (30 April 2004), para. 98.
945. *Ibid.,* para. 95 (quoting from *Mondev v. United States,* Award, (2 October 2002), para. 127).
946. *Ibid.,* para. 97 (quoting from *Loewen v. United States,* Award, (26 June 2003), para. 132), defining denial of justice as 'manifest injustice in the sense of a lack of due process leading to an outcome which offends a sense of judicial propriety'.
947. *Ibid.,* para. 97 (quoting from *Loewen v. United States,* Award, (26 June 2003), para. 135).
948. *Ibid.*
949. *Ibid.*
950. *Ibid.*
951. *See,* at section §3.02[G][7].
952. *Waste Management v. Mexico,* Award, (30 April 2004), para. 115.

breached.[953] Thus, 'even if the conduct of the City or Banobras in itself did not violate the Article 1105 standard, the question remains whether the situation presented by their conduct was adequately responded to by the Mexican courts'.[954]

The tribunal first examined the claimant's local arbitration proceedings in Mexico against the City. It concluded that CANACO had 'behaved in a proper and impartial way'[955] and that there was no 'evidence of collusion between CANACO and the City with respect to the conduct of the arbitration or of discrimination against Acaverde on account of its foreign ownership'.[956] The tribunal then analyzed the claimant's two separate proceedings against Banobras before the federal courts of Mexico City for unpaid invoices. These courts rendered unfavorable decisions which were both unsuccessfully appealed by the claimant. The tribunal observed that it could not act as a court of appeal with respect to decisions rendered by Mexican courts.[957] In any event, it concluded that there was no trace of any denial of justice in these decisions:

> [T]he Tribunal does not discern in the decisions of the federal courts any denial of justice as that concept has been explained by NAFTA tribunals, notably in the Azinian, Mondev, ADF and Loewen cases. The Mexican court decisions were not, either *ex facie* or on closer examination, evidently arbitrary, unjust or idiosyncratic. There is no trace of discrimination on account of the foreign ownership of Acaverde, and no evident failure of due process. The decisions were reasoned and were promptly arrived at. Acaverde won on key procedural points, and the dismissal in the second proceedings, in particular, was without prejudice to Acaverde's rights in the appropriate forum.[958]

Finally, the tribunal addressed the claimant's argument that the litigation strategy adopted by the City itself amounted to a denial of justice in breach of Article 1105. On this point, the tribunal held that 'a *litigant* cannot commit a denial of justice unless its improper strategies are endorsed and acted on by the court, or unless the law gives it some extraordinary privilege which leads to a lack of due process'.[959] There was no such evidence in the instant case: 'the decisions themselves nor other evidence before the Tribunal suggest that these proceedings involved discrimination, bias on grounds of sectional or local prejudice, or a clear failure of due process'.[960] The tribunal therefore rejected the claim of denial of justice.

[10]   *Thunderbird*

The facts of this case have already been examined above.[961] The claimant submitted that Mexico had failed to provide due process (an 'administrative' denial of justice) and

---

953. *Ibid.*, para. 116.
954. *Ibid.*, para. 118.
955. *Ibid.*, para. 123. The proceedings were started before the Permanent Commission of Commercial Arbitration of the National Chamber of Commerce ('CANACO').
956. *Ibid.*
957. *Ibid.*, para. 129.
958. *Ibid.*, para. 130.
959. *Ibid.*, para. 131 (emphasis in the original).
960. *Ibid.*, para. 132.
961. *See*, section §3.02[B][2].

committed 'manifest arbitrariness' in the administration of the proceedings before Mexican authorities in charge of gambling regulation (SEGOB).[962] Specifically, these allegations were related to an administrative hearing (which was allegedly 'shockingly arbitrary') that took place after the closing down of one of the investor's facilities.[963] Certain allegations were also related to the 'Resolución Administrativa' issued by SEGOB which declared that the EDM machines were prohibited gambling equipment and ordered the official closure of other facilities.[964] On the contrary, Mexico argued that the SEGOB administrative proceedings were not illegal, arbitrary or unfair.[965]

The tribunal described 'acts that would give rise to a breach of the minimum standard of treatment prescribed by the NAFTA and customary international law as those that, weighed against the given factual context, amount to a gross denial of justice or manifest arbitrariness falling below acceptable international standards'.[966] It is noteworthy that while the tribunal clearly enumerates denial of justice as one of the elements of the FET standard under Article 1105, it also establishes the high threshold of 'gross' denial of justice 'falling below acceptable international standards' for a breach of this provision to occur.[967] Later in the award, the tribunal also speaks of a 'minimum level of gravity' required under Article 1105.[968]

When the tribunal applied this high threshold of liability to the facts of the case, it concluded that it was 'not convinced that Thunderbird ha[d] demonstrated that Mexico's conduct violated the minimum standard of treatment'.[969] The tribunal stated that it could not find 'sufficient evidence on the record establishing that the SEGOB proceedings were arbitrary or unfair, let alone so manifestly arbitrary or unfair as to violate the minimum standard of treatment'.[970] Thus, the investor had been given a 'full opportunity to be heard and to present evidence' at the administrative hearing.[971] The tribunal also could 'not find anything reproachable about the Administrative Order'. The tribunal described the order as being 'adequately detailed and reasoned; it review[ed] the evidence presented by Thunderbird at the hearing; and discusses at

---

962. *Thunderbird v. Mexico,* Award, (26 January 2006), para. 186.
963. *Ibid.,* Claimant's Reply, (9 February 2004) at 62. Thus, 'rather than procuring any evidence to demonstrate that Thunderbird was failing to comply with the terms of the solicitud, Vargas [the president of the hearing] rejected all of Thunderbird's evidence on the most facile of grounds'.
964. *Ibid.,* Award, (26 January 2006), paras. 73 ff.
965. *Ibid.,* para. 191. *See also*: Mexico's Rejoinder, (7 April 2004) para. 6: 'Were the administrative proceedings in which EDM's machines were found to be illegal arbitrary or unfair so as to violate any standard of international law, when the decision itself indicates that EDM's evidence was taken into account even when not in strict accordance with the applicable domestic legal requirements, and when the decision sets out a reasoned basis for its conclusions? Can the administrative proceedings carried out by Gobernacion be considered arbitrary or unfair so as to violate any applicable standard of international law, when the procedure was transparent and in compliance with Mexican laws, validated by EDM's lawyers who were experts in Mexican law, and given that had there been a violation during these proceedings, there were appropriate judicial remedies available to challenge it?'.
966. *Ibid.,* Award, (26 January 2006), para. 194.
967. The tribunal's reasoning on 'manifest arbitrariness' has already been examined above, at section §3.02[D][6].
968. *Thunderbird v. Mexico,* Award, (26 January 2006), para. 200.
969. *Ibid.,* para. 195.
970. *Ibid.,* para. 197.
971. *Ibid.,* para. 198.

length the legal grounds on which SEGOB based its determination that the EDM machines were prohibited gambling equipment'.[972] The tribunal also added that the proceedings were subject to judicial review by Mexican courts.[973]

Finally, the tribunal noted that it did 'not exclude that the SEGOB proceedings may have been affected by certain irregularities', but added that this was not the question to be decided when assessing allegations of breach of Article 1105.[974] The relevant test was whether or not any of these irregularities 'were grave enough to shock a sense of judicial propriety' to give rise to a breach of the minimum standard of treatment.[975] The tribunal answered in the negative. Finally, the tribunal made this intriguing statement:

> As acknowledged by Thunderbird, the SEGOB proceedings should be tested against the standards of due process and procedural fairness applicable to administrative officials. The administrative due process requirement is lower than that of a judicial process.[976]

The tribunal did not, however, explain why the level of due process required in the administration is necessarily 'lower' than the one for judicial process.[977] The tribunal therefore rejected the claim of denial of justice.

[11] Conclusion

One of the most important aspects of NAFTA case law is that all Parties (Canada,[978] the United States,[979] and Mexico[980]) have recognized not only that Article 1105 imposes an obligation not to deny justice, but also the customary nature of such obligation under the minimum standard of treatment. Not surprisingly, all NAFTA awards discussed in this section have also held that there exists an obligation not to deny justice and to respect due process under Article 1105. This conclusion has also been reached by a number of other tribunals that did not examine denial of justice and due process

---

972. *Ibid.*
973. *Ibid.*, para. 201.
974. *Ibid.*, para. 200.
975. *Ibid.*
976. *Ibid.*
977. Diehl, *supra* n. 3, at 439 ('unfortunately, the Thunderbird tribunal did not give any reasons for its proposition. The tribunal could have argued, for example, that the adversarial nature of judicial proceedings makes it necessary to impose a higher standard').
978. *Merrill & Ring v. Canada*, Canada's Rejoinder, (27 March 2009), para. 172 ('denial of justice is clearly part of the minimum standard of treatment under custom'); *Mobil v. Canada*, Canada's Counter-Memorial, (1 December 2009), paras. 247–248 (endorsing the definition of the FET standard given by the tribunal in *Glamis v. United States*, Award, (8 June 2009), para. 627).
979. *Grand River v. United States*, Award, (12 January 2011), para. 197 ('In the Respondent's view, the customary law minimum standard includes obligations to prevent denial of justice as the concept is understood in customary international law'); *ibid.*, US Counter-Memorial, (22 December 2008), at 90, 141, 143-144; *ibid.*, US Rejoinder, (22 December 2008), at 89-90; *Loewen v. United States*, US Rejoinder, (28 August 2001), at 106-107; *ibid.*, US's Counter-Memorial, (30 March 2001), at 131; *ADF v. United States*, US Post Hearing Submission, (27 June 2002) at 2-4; *Mondev v. United States*, US Counter-Memorial, (1 June 2001), at 44.
980. *Loewen v. United States*, Mexico's Article 1128 Submission, (9 November 2001), at 15-16.

allegations (*Methanex*,[981] *S.D. Myers*,[982] and *Mobil*[983]). Ultimately, only two tribunals (*Metalclad* and *Pope & Talbot*) have come to the conclusion that a State had breached its obligation to provide due process to a foreign investor.

NAFTA tribunals have made some important findings which have defined the content and the scope of the prohibition of denial of justice under Article 1105. In the following paragraphs, five observations will be made on NAFTA case law regarding denial of justice (the due process obligation will be examined later in this section).

First, a foreign investor must have exhausted all remedies in domestic courts before a complaint of a denial of justice can be filed before a NAFTA tribunal. This proposition, which had been (somewhat ambiguously) stated by the *Loewen* tribunal,[984] was affirmed by the *Waste Management* tribunal.[985] These two tribunals therefore rejected an earlier statement made by the *Mondev* tribunal to the effect that denial of justice and exhaustion of local remedies were not interlocked and inseparable.[986]

Second, the obligation to exhaust all remedies in domestic courts is, however, limited to those remedies that are 'effective and adequate and are reasonably available to the complainant'.[987] Each time, a tribunal must conduct a subjective analysis of the 'reasonableness' of the remedies in place 'in the light of [the] situation' of the investor and taking into account its 'financial and economic circumstances'.[988]

Third, a tribunal must assess the system of justice of the host State as a whole rather than focusing on individual domestic court decisions. This proposition was put forward by the *Loewen* tribunal,[989] and later endorsed by the *Waste Management* tribunal.[990]

Fourth, all NAFTA awards examined in this section have reiterated the obvious point that allegations of denial of justice before a NAFTA Chapter 11 tribunal cannot serve as an appeal mechanism to contest domestic court decisions. This is indeed the conclusion reached by the *Loewen* tribunal:

---

981. *Methanex v. United States*, Award, (3 August 2005), Part IV, Chapter C, Page 8, para. 15, referring to 'Article 1105(1)'s due process requirement'.
982. *S.D. Myers Inc. v. Canada*, First Partial Award, (13 November 2000), para. 134 ('Article 1105 imports into the NAFTA the international law requirements of due process, economic rights, obligations of good faith and natural justice'). The tribunal explained (at para. 134) that one of the grounds of complaint under Article 1105 was the allegation that the export ban 'was done in a discriminatory and unfair manner that constituted a denial of justice and a violation of good faith under international law'. But the tribunal did not further examined this allegation of denial of justice since it concluded that the breach of Article 1102 which had already been identified 'essentially establishe[d] a breach of Article 1105 as well' (para. 266).
983. *Mobil v. Canada*, Decision on Liability and on Principles of Quantum, (22 May 2012), para. 152, using the exact same words as in *Waste Management v. Mexico*, Award, (30 April 2004), para. 98 (a breach of Article 1105 occurs when State conduct 'involves a lack of due process leading to an outcome which offends judicial propriety').
984. *Loewen v. United States*, Award, (26 June 2003), paras. 142–157. *See*, the discussion at section §3.02[G][8].
985. *Waste Management v. Mexico*, Award, (30 April 2004), para. 97.
986. *Mondev v. United States*, Award, (2 October 2002), para. 96.
987. *Loewen v. United States*, Award, (26 June 2003), para. 168.
988. *Ibid.*, para. 169.
989. *Ibid.*, para. 54.
990. *Waste Management v. Mexico*, Award, (30 April 2004), para. 97.

> Whether the conduct of the trial amounted to a breach of municipal law as well as international law is not for us to determine. A NAFTA claim cannot be converted into an appeal against the decisions of municipal courts.[991]

Fifth, two NAFTA tribunals have put forward a general 'test' to determine when a denial of justice occurs. The *Mondev* tribunal considered that a denial of justice occurs whenever a decision by a domestic court is 'clearly improper and discreditable' in the sense that it would 'shock or surprise' any impartial observer and would raise 'justified concerns as to the judicial propriety of the outcome' of the case.[992] The *Loewen* tribunal also adopted a very similar test referring to 'manifest injustice' such as a lack of due process that leads to an outcome which 'offends a sense of judicial propriety'.[993] These two similar tests were subsequently endorsed by the *Waste Management* tribunal.[994] These statements suggest a high threshold of severity for the finding of a denial of justice; only the gravest cases will be considered in breach of Article 1105. Yet, an investor does not have to demonstrate the domestic court's 'bad faith or malicious intention' to establish a denial of justice.[995]

NAFTA tribunals have also provided several examples of what concretely constitutes a denial of justice under Article 1105. In the following paragraphs, four observations will be made on NAFTA case law.

First, a clear situation of denial of justice arises when the host State does not provide the investor with a 'fair trial'.[996] Thus, the *Azinian* tribunal held that a denial of justice occurs when a domestic court 'refuses to entertain a suit', when it subjects a suit to 'undue delay', or, more generally, when a court 'administer[s] justice in a seriously inadequate way'.[997] This important finding was later approved by the *Mondev* tribunal.[998]

Second, one important aspect of the obligation to provide a fair trial is related to discrimination against foreign investors. One NAFTA case (*Loewen*) has shown in vivid terms that a fair trial requires the State to provide investors with discrimination-free litigation where it is not the victim of 'sectional or local prejudice'.[999] In fact, the tribunal's reasoning suggests a much broader obligation for host States: a denial of justice would occur whenever a court permits or fails to take steps in order to prevent one party (or its counsel) from resorting to a nationality/racial/class based prejudice strategy.[1000] Similarly, the *Waste Management* tribunal speaks of 'improper strategies' utilized by one party that are 'endorsed and acted on by the court'.[1001] Courts therefore not only have an obligation not to discriminate against foreign investors themselves,

---

991. *Loewen v. United States*, Award, (26 June 2003), para. 134.
992. *Mondev v. United States*, Award, (2 October 2002), para. 127.
993. *Loewen v. United States*, Award, (26 June 2003), para. 132.
994. *Waste Management v. Mexico*, Award, (30 April 2004), paras. 95, 97.
995. *Loewen v. United States*, Award, (26 June 2003), para. 132.
996. *Ibid.*, para. 123.
997. *Azinian v. Mexico*, Award, (1 November 1999), paras. 102–103.
998. *Mondev v. United States*, Award, (2 October 2002), para. 126.
999. *Loewen v. United States*, Award, (26 June 2003), para. 123. *See also: Waste Management v. Mexico*, Award, (30 April 2004), para. 132.
1000. *Loewen v. United States*, Award, (26 June 2003), para. 87. *See also*, at paras. 136–137.
1001. *Waste Management v. Mexico*, Award, (30 April 2004), para. 131.

but also to prevent others from using discriminatory tactics during a trial. The *Loewen* award also suggests that a denial of justice would arise in a situation where a judge fails to redress a 'large and excessive verdict'[1002] where the amount of compensation awarded by a jury is inflated by bias and prejudice.[1003]

Third, tribunals have concluded that a decision in breach of municipal law does not constitute a denial of justice per se unless it is also discriminatory against a foreign investor (*Loewen*,[1004] endorsed by *Waste Management*[1005]). Another situation where a wrong decision with regards to a matter of domestic law would constitute a denial of justice is an instance where a 'clear and malicious misapplication of the law' by the court can be demonstrated (*Azinian*,[1006] approved by *Mondev*[1007]).

Fourth, NAFTA tribunals have also made a number of findings as to what should not be considered as a denial of justice under Article 1105. These are some of the circumstances *not* amounting to a denial of justice that have been mentioned by tribunals:

- An error of law made by a domestic court (*Azinian*[1008]).
- A court decision involving a 'significant and serious departure' from its previous case law (*Mondev*[1009]).
- A court decision on matters of local procedural practice (except in 'extreme cases') (*Mondev*[1010]).

NAFTA tribunals have also made important observations related to the scope of the host State's obligation to provide due process under Article 1105. In the following paragraphs, four observations will be made on NAFTA case law regarding due process.

First, tribunals have examined what constitutes proper State conduct in the context of administrative hearings. Case law suggests that a State breaches its obligation of due process whenever an investor is not given the 'full opportunity to be heard and to present evidence' at an administrative hearing.[1011] This requirement includes informing an investor of any administrative hearing involving matters relevant to its business and also inviting it to appear and present evidence at that hearing.[1012] One passage from the *Glamis* award (in the context of arbitrariness allegations) suggests, however, that no breach of Article 1105 would occur when any such procedural error is 'corrected quickly and effectively through domestic channels'.[1013]

1002. *Loewen v. United States*, Award, (26 June 2003), para. 122.
1003. *Ibid.*, para. 105. *See also*, at para. 137.
1004. *Ibid.*, para. 135.
1005. *Waste Management v. Mexico*, Award, (30 April 2004), para. 97.
1006. *Azinian v. Mexico*, Award, (1 November 1999), paras. 102–103.
1007. *Mondev v. United States*, Award, (2 October 2002), para. 126.
1008. *Azinian v. Mexico*, Award, (1 November 1999), para. 99.
1009. *Mondev v. United States*, Award, (2 October 2002), para. 133.
1010. *Ibid.*, para. 136.
1011. *Thunderbird v. Mexico*, Award, (26 January 2006), para. 198.
1012. *Metalclad v. Mexico*, Award, (30 August 2000), para. 91.
1013. *Glamis v. United States*, Award, (8 June 2009), para. 771 ('It is possible that the issuance of the 1999 M-Opinion without the promulgation of regulations and the opportunity for notice and

Second, NAFTA tribunals have also examined in some details the scope of the obligations existing for States in the specific context of permit approval/renewal. These findings apply more generally to any matters involving administrative bodies. Case law suggests that a State does not breach its obligation of due process when mere administrative 'irregularities' are committed, unless such irregularities are 'grave enough to shock a sense of judicial propriety' (*Thunderbird*[1014]). The difficult question is, of course, to actually distinguish the two.

Third, as a matter of principle, the 'administrative due process requirement is lower than that of a judicial process'.[1015] In other words, international law is less stringent in terms of the standard of behaviors required of the administration than that required of domestic courts. Yet, NAFTA case law shows that tribunals have in fact been quite demanding regarding the level of conduct required by the host State in order for it to respect its due process obligation. A reading of the following circumstances where tribunals have held that an administration had breached its obligation of due process is clear to that effect:

- When an investor is not informed and not invited to a hearing discussing a permit application and whenever it is not given any opportunity to appear and present evidence before this administrative body (*Metlaclad*[1016]).
- When an investor is denied a permit based on reasons that are unrelated to specific existing requirements for issuing that permit (*Metlaclad*[1017]).
- When an investor is 'subjected to threats' from an administrative body (*Pope & Talbot*[1018]).
- When an administrative body asserts 'non-existent policy reasons' to force an investor to comply with 'very burdensome demands for documents' having for consequence that the investor is incurring 'unnecessary expense and disruption' (*Pope & Talbot*[1019]).
- When an administrative body refuses to provide the investor with 'promised information'[1020] and denies its 'reasonable requests for pertinent information'[1021] on administrative matters (*Pope & Talbot*).
- When an administrative order is not 'adequately detailed and reasoned', such as, for instance, in cases where an order does not review the evidence

---

comment by interested parties could rise to the level of a violation of customary international law. It is also possible that Claimant could prove that the process was so unusual and non-transparent as to be manifestly arbitrary and completely lacking in due process. Perhaps, if the 1999 M-Opinion had stood, these hypotheticals might be questions for the Tribunal. However, as any deficiency in the 1999 M-Opinion was remedied so quickly by the 2001 M-Opinion, there is no outstanding issue for this Tribunal. If there was a procedural error, it was corrected quickly and effectively through domestic channels, a process that does not evince "a complete lack of due process"').

1014. *Thunderbird v. Mexico*, Award, (26 January 2006), para. 200.
1015. *Ibid.*
1016. *Metlclad v. Mexico*, Award, (30 August 2000), para. 91.
1017. *Ibid.*, para. 93.
1018. *Pope & Talbot Inc. v. Canada*, Award on the Merits (Phase 2), (10 April 2001), para. 181.
1019. *Ibid.*, Award in Respect of Damages, (31 May 2002), para. 68.
1020. *Ibid.*, Award on the Merits (Phase 2), (10 April 2001), para. 181.
1021. *Ibid.*, Award in Respect of Damages, (31 May 2002), para. 68.

presented by a party at a hearing or where the order does not discuss the legal grounds on which that administrative body has based its decision (*Thunderbird*[1022]).

Finally, while all NAFTA tribunals have recognized the well-established fact that States have an obligation to provide due process and not to deny justice under the MST, it is noteworthy that some tribunals seem to have adopted a high threshold of liability. One example is the *Thunderbird* tribunal which indicated that Article 1105 requires a 'gross denial of justice' that 'fall[s] below acceptable international standards'.[1023] Likewise, in the *Glamis* award, the tribunal refers to a 'gross' denial of justice and a 'complete' lack of due process on several occasions throughout the award.[1024] The *Glamis* tribunal held that it is precisely because NAFTA tribunals have consistently used modifiers such as, *inter alia*, 'gross' in front of the term denial of justice that it concluded that customary international law had not moved beyond the minimum standard of treatment of aliens as defined in the *Neer* case.[1025] The *Cargill* tribunal also stated that in order for a measure to be considered in breach of the FET, it must, *inter alia*, 'involve an utter lack of due process so as to offend judicial propriety'.[1026] In the present author's view, a claimant does *not* need to show the existence of a 'gross' denial of justice in order to convince a NAFTA tribunal that a breach of Article 1105 has occurred. Customary international law prohibits 'simple' denial of justice by States.

[H]   General Conclusion on NAFTA Case Law

This chapter aimed to examine NAFTA case law and to determine what falls within the 'box' of the concept of the FET standard under Article 1105. In other words, the objective was to determine which 'elements' (or 'principles') have been recognized by NAFTA tribunals to be encompassed within the FET standard under Article 1105.

Four NAFTA tribunals have made general attempts at defining the concept of the FET standard under Article 1105 thus far:

–   *Waste Management* (2004):
    Taken together, the S.D. Myers, Mondev, ADF and Loewen cases suggest that the minimum standard of treatment of fair and equitable treatment is infringed by conduct attributable to the State and harmful to the claimant if the conduct is arbitrary, grossly unfair, unjust or idiosyncratic, is discriminatory and exposes the claimant to sectional or racial prejudice, or involves a lack of due process leading to an outcome which offends judicial propriety –as might be the case with a manifest failure of natural justice in judicial proceedings or a complete lack of transparency and candour in an administrative process. In applying the standard it is relevant that the treatment is in

---

1022. *Thunderbird v. Mexico*, Award, (26 January 2006), para. 198.
1023. *Ibid.*, para. 194.
1024. *Glamis v. United States*, Award, (8 June 2009), paras. 22, 24, 614, 616, 625, 627.
1025. *Ibid.*, para. 614.
1026. *Cargill Inc. v. Mexico*, Award, (18 September 2009), para. 296.

breach of representations made by the host State which were reasonably relied on by the claimant.[1027]

– *Glamis* (2009):

The Tribunal therefore holds that a violation of the customary international law minimum standard of treatment, as codified in Article 1105 of the NAFTA, requires an act that is sufficiently egregious and shocking—a gross denial of justice, manifest arbitrariness, blatant unfairness, a complete lack of due process, evident discrimination, or a manifest lack of reasons—so as to fall below accepted international standards and constitute a breach of Article 1105. Such a breach may be exhibited by a 'gross denial of justice or manifest arbitrariness falling below acceptable international standards;' or the creation by the State of objective expectations *in order to induce* investment and the subsequent repudiation of those expectations. The Tribunal emphasizes that, although bad faith may often be present in such a determination and its presence certainly will be determinative of a violation, a finding of bad faith is not a requirement for a breach of Article 1105(1).[1028]

– *Cargill* (2009):

In summation, the Tribunal finds that the obligations in Article 1105(1) of the NAFTA are to be understood by reference to the customary international law minimum standard of treatment of aliens. The requirement of fair and equitable treatment is one aspect of this minimum standard. To determine whether an action fails to meet the requirement of fair and equitable treatment, a tribunal must carefully examine whether the complained of measures were grossly unfair, unjust or idiosyncratic; arbitrary beyond a merely inconsistent or questionable application of administrative or legal policy or procedure so as to constitute an unexpected and shocking repudiation of a policy's very purpose and goals, or to otherwise grossly subvert a domestic law or policy for an ulterior motive; or involve an utter lack of due process so as to offend judicial propriety. The Tribunal observes that other NAFTA tribunals have expressed the view that the standard of fair and equitable treatment is not so strict as to require 'bad faith' or 'willful neglect of duty'. The Tribunal agrees. However, the Tribunal emphasizes that although bad faith or willful neglect of duty is not required, the presence of such circumstances will certainly suffice.[1029]

– *Mobil* (2012):

(1) the minimum standard of treatment guaranteed by Article 1105 is that which is reflected in customary international law on the treatment of aliens;

(2) the fair and equitable treatment standard in customary international law will be infringed by conduct attributable to a NAFTA Party and harmful

---

1027. *Waste Management v. Mexico*, Award, (30 April 2004), para. 98.
1028. *Glamis v. United States*, Award, (8 June 2009), para. 627 (emphasis in the original).
1029. *Cargill Inc. v. Mexico*, Award, (18 September 2009), para. 296.

to a claimant that is arbitrary, grossly unfair, unjust or idiosyncratic, or is discriminatory and exposes a claimant to sectional or racial prejudice, or involves a lack of due process leading to an outcome which offends judicial propriety.

(3) In determining whether that standard has been violated it will be a relevant factor if the treatment is made against the background of

    (i) clear and explicit representations made by or attributable to the NAFTA host State in order to induce the investment, and

    (ii) were, by reference to an objective standard, reasonably relied on by the investor, and

    (iii) were subsequently repudiated by the NAFTA host State.[1030]

From the reading of these four descriptions of the FET standard and, more specifically, the analysis of NAFTA case law undertaken in this chapter, it is submitted that two general conclusions emerge:

– On the one hand, tribunals have recognized that the FET standard under Article 1105 contains a limited number of specific elements of protection which must be accorded to investors (section §3.02[H][1]); and

– On the other hand, tribunals have also emphasized that a high threshold of severity and gravity is required in order to conclude that the host State has breached any of the elements contained within the FET standard under Article 1105 (section §3.02[H][2]).

These two general conclusions will now be discussed.

[1]   *A Shopping List Containing a Limited Number of Elements*

The first conclusion is related to the specific elements which have been accepted by tribunals as components of the obligation for host States to provide foreign investors with a FET. Three observations will be made.

First, tribunals have generally adopted the 'shopping list' approach used by a number of writers whereby the FET standard is described as comprised of a number of 'elements'. NAFTA tribunals have not endorsed any of the comprehensive theories put forward by writers which have equated the FET standard with the rule of law under domestic law[1031] or, more generally, the idea of justice.[1032]

Second, one reason which may explain why NAFTA tribunals have not endorsed any grand theories on the FET standard is the fact that they are required, under Article 1105, to apply the minimum standard. This standard involves a *higher* threshold of

---

1030. *Mobil v. Canada*, Decision on Liability and on Principles of Quantum, (22 May 2012), para. 152.

1031. This is the position defended by, *inter alia*: Schill, *supra* n. 48, at 34, 40-41, 79-80; Diehl, *supra* n. 3, at 330-337; Vandevelde, *supra* n. 27, at 52, 106.

1032. Kläger, *supra* n. 13, at 129 ff.

liability than an unqualified FET clause. In other words, the FET standard under Article 1105 is meant to solely address (to paraphrase the *Glamis* tribunal's view on the matter) acts that are 'sufficiently egregious and shocking—a gross denial of justice, manifest arbitrariness, blatant unfairness, a complete lack of due process, evident discrimination, or a manifest lack of reasons—so as to fall below accepted international standards and constitute a breach of Article 1105'.[1033] These are the kinds of acts that warrant international arbitration. As opposed to the *Merrill & Ring* tribunal's view, the objective of the FET standard under Article 1105 is clearly *not* to protect investors 'against all such acts or behaviour that might infringe on a sense of fairness, equity and reasonableness'.[1034]

As pointed out by UNCTAD, such a high threshold of liability 'provides assurance to host States that they will not be exposed to international responsibility for minor malfunctioning of their agencies and that only manifest and flagrant acts of maladmin- istration will be punished'.[1035] Thus, while 'simple' (or 'mere') arbitrariness may violate the rule of law under domestic law, NAFTA tribunals have consistently affirmed that such conduct was *not* severe enough to constitute a breach of the FET standard under Article 1105. Tribunals have set the necessary threshold much higher in requiring proof of '*manifest*' arbitrariness to constitute a breach of Article 1105. In sum, the theory that equates the FET standard with the rule of law may ultimately simply not be *necessary* in the context of NAFTA Chapter 11 which involves three democracies applying the rule of law. That theory is probably better suited for interpreting FET clauses contained in BITs involving States (or at least one State) where the domestic law does *not* offer the basic rule of law protection.

As mentioned above,[1036] a number of writers have emphasized the need for tribunals to apply a three-step proportionality test ((1) suitability, (2) necessity and (3) comparative-balancing) when assessing allegations of breach of the FET standard. Writers have referred to a number of NAFTA cases where tribunals have apparently used this test in the context of Article 1105.[1037] It is true that a number of passages from the *Pope & Talbot* award suggest that the tribunal has indeed implicitly applied some elements of the proportionality test when referring to the reasonableness of the conduct of the administrative agency to conclude that no breach of Article 1105 had oc- curred.[1038] Yet, it should be noted that the *Pope & Talbot* tribunal's decision was rendered in the pre-FTC Note era; as such, this tribunal interpreted the FET standard as an autonomous standard not linked to the minimum standard of treatment.

In the present author's view, the use of a proportionality test is *less useful* in the specific context of Article 1105 where the FET standard is a reference to the MST under

---

1033. *Glamis v. United States,* Award, (8 June 2009), para. 627.
1034. *Merrill & Ring v. Canada,* Award, (31 March 2010), para. 210.
1035. UNCTAD, *supra* n. 11, at 88. *See also*: Picherack, *supra* n. 66, at 267-270.
1036. *See*, at section §3.01[B].
1037. *See*, for instance, Diehl, *supra* n. 3, at 235 (referring to *Pope & Talbot Inc. v. Canada,* Award on the Merits (Phase 2)); Kläger, *supra* n. 13, at 240 (referring to *S.D. Myers Inc. v. Canada,* First Partial Award, para. 255).
1038. *Pope & Talbot Inc. v. Canada,* Award on the Merits (Phase 2), (10 April 2001), paras. 123, 125, 128, 155. It should be mentioned that the tribunal did, however, find that Canada had breached Article 1105 regarding another aspect: the verification review process.

custom and where tribunals have applied a high threshold of severity. This is because the proportionality test presupposes that the objective behind a contested measure taken by a State is *legitimate*. The 'suitability for a legitimate government purpose' is indeed the first question to be examined by a tribunal when applying the proportionality test.[1039] It is difficult to conceive how a measure considered as 'sufficiently egregious and shocking'[1040] could ever be deemed by a tribunal as serving a legitimate governmental purpose. In other words, because under Article 1105 the threshold of severity is so high, it is submitted that the contested measure will *never satisfy* the first step of the proportionality test. When faced with an egregious and shocking measure, a NAFTA tribunal need not apply the proportionality test. This is indeed what happened in the *Cargill* case where the tribunal concluded that the import permit imposed by Mexico 'was one of a series of measures expressly intended to injure United States HFCS producers and suppliers in Mexico' and that there was no 'relationship between the means and the end of this requirement' other than to persuade the US government to change its trade policy.[1041] In other words, it is precisely because the measures were undoubtedly egregious that they were not considered to have been adopted by Mexico for any legitimate purpose. As a consequence, the *Cargill* tribunal did not have to carry out the three-step analysis of the proportionality test.

Third, at first glance, the reading of the above-mentioned passages extracted from the four awards (*Waste Management, Glamis, Cargill* and *Mobil*) suggests that a great number of elements have been recognized constituents of the definition of the FET standard under Article 1105. A closer examination of NAFTA case law in fact shows that NAFTA tribunals have been much more restrained. Out of the large number of elements that are typically enumerated by writers as components of the FET standard, NAFTA tribunals have found that only a few of them are actually covered by Article 1105.[1042] In this respect, NAFTA case law sharply contrasts with the position adopted by non-NAFTA tribunals. Thus, non-NAFTA tribunals have been increasingly willing to recognize new requirements as components of the ever-enlarged concept of the FET.[1043] Prime examples of such new 'requirements' recognized by these tribunals are the obligation to provide a stable and predictable business environment and transparency as well as the obligation to protect an investor's legitimate expectations.

The next paragraphs will summarize this chapter's findings regarding the six principles which were specifically examined.

Legitimate expectations. Thus far, no NAFTA tribunal has found that a host State stood in violation of an investor's legitimate expectations under Article 1105. The

---

1039. Schill & Kingsbury, *supra* n. 61, at 86 ('the first step in proportionality reasoning is the analysis of whether the measure adopted by the state or government agency serves a legitimate government purpose and is generally suitable to achieve this purpose. The task the decision maker has to achieve is thus two-fold (...). The first element of the task is to ascertain whether the measure adopted aims at a legitimate purpose. Consequently, illegitimate purposes can be filtered out at this early stage').
1040. *Glamis v. United States*, Award, (8 June 2009), para. 627.
1041. *Cargill Inc. v. Mexico*, Award, (18 September 2009), para. 299.
1042. *See*, the elements listed by writers referred to at *supra* n. 44.
1043. Picherack, *supra* n. 66, at 271.

Glamis award[1044] (and to some extent the *Thunderbird* award[1045]) are the only ones that support the view that the concept of legitimate expectations constitutes a stand-alone element of the FET standard under Article 1105. Yet, these tribunals have not actually demonstrated the customary nature of the concept of legitimate expectations.

In the present author's view, the *Mobil* tribunal (as well as the *Waste Management*[1046] and *Cargill*[1047] tribunals) adopted a more convincing approach. They have held that the host State's failure to respect an investor's legitimate expectations does not constitute a breach of the FET standard, but is rather a 'factor' to be taken into account when assessing whether or not *other well-established* elements of the standard have been breached.[1048] These tribunals have thus endorsed the NAFTA Parties' position to the effect that the so-called 'obligation' to protect an investor's legitimate expectations is not a component of the customary international law minimum standard of treatment. In the present author's view, there is indeed little evidence to support the assertion that there exists under custom an obligation for host States to protect investors' legitimate expectations. Scholars have also interpreted the concept of legitimate expectations as a general principle of law based on its recognition in many domestic legal systems. This argument is of limited relevance in the specific context of Article 1105. This is because the binding FTC Note is clear to the effect that NAFTA tribunals should look *solely* to custom as a source of international law in their interpretation of Article 1105, and not at general principles of law. The position adopted by the majority of NAFTA tribunals contrasts with that of many tribunals outside NAFTA that have recognized that the FET standard encompasses an obligation to protect an investor's legitimate expectations.

Moreover, NAFTA tribunals have repeatedly narrowly qualified the concept of legitimate expectations in order to significantly reduce its scope of protection.

For instance, unlike non-NAFTA tribunals, NAFTA tribunals (with the possible exception of *Merrill & Ring*[1049]) have not pinpointed an obligation to maintain a stable legal and business framework under Article 1105. All NAFTA tribunals that have examined the concept have endorsed the four-elements definition of legitimate expectations adopted by the *Thunderbird* tribunal: (1) conduct or representations have been made by the host State; (2) the claimant has relied on such conduct or representations to make its investment; (3) such reliance by the claimant on these representations was

---

1044. *Glamis v. United States,* Award, (8 June 2009), para. 627.
1045. *Thunderbird v. Mexico,* Award, (26 January 2006), para. 147. *See also,* the separate opinion of Wälde stating that the legitimate expectations principle is a 'self-standing subcategory and independent basis for a claim under the "fair and equitable standard" as under Art. 1105 of the NAFTA' (para. 37).
1046. *Waste Management v. Mexico,* Award, (30 April 2004), para. 98.
1047. *Cargill Inc. v. Mexico,* Award, (18 September 2009), para. 296, where the tribunal does not list the concept of legitimate expectations amongst the elements of the FET standard under Article 1105.
1048. *Mobil v. Canada,* Decision on Liability and on Principles of Quantum, (22 May 2012), para. 152.
1049. *Merrill & Ring v. Canada,* Award, (31 March 2010), para. 233. The tribunal mentioned that while 'a requirement for transparency may not at present be proven to be part of the customary law standard', it also added that such requirement was 'nonetheless approaching that stage' (para. 231, *see also* at para. 187).

'reasonable'; and (4) the host State subsequently repudiated these representations therefore causing damage to the investor. Another manifestation of a much narrower approach favored by NAFTA tribunals is the fact that they have continued to further restrictively *qualify* these four requirements in subsequent awards. Thus, the *Glamis* award (subsequently endorsed by other tribunals: *Cargill*,[1050] *Mobil*,[1051] and *Grand River*[1052]) required that an investor's expectations be *objective* and be based on 'definitive, unambiguous and repeated'[1053] specific 'commitments'[1054] (or 'assurances'[1055]) made by the host State to have 'purposely and specifically induced the investment'[1056] by the investor.

Similarly, no NAFTA tribunal has held that legitimate expectations can be protected without any *specific* representations made by the host State. NAFTA tribunals have also concluded that legitimate expectations *cannot* simply be based on the host State's existing domestic legislation on foreign investments at the time when the investor makes its investment. For instance, the *Glamis* award emphasized the threshold requirement of a *quasi-contractual* relationship between the investor and the host State. This situation contrasts with that of non-NAFTA tribunals that have held that legitimate expectations can be protected *without any specific* representations made by the host State. The *Mobil* tribunal clearly stated that no violation of Article 1105 occurs as a result of the host State changing its regulation (even drastically) upon which the investor may have based its expectations when it made its investment. The *Glamis* award also confirmed that an investor's expectation is not violated by the mere fact that the host State has breached a contract.

Transparency. All NAFTA tribunals that have examined the concept of transparency (*Glamis*,[1057] *Merrill & Ring*,[1058] and *Cargill*[1059]) have come to the conclusion that it is *not* a stand-alone element of the FET standard and that it does not impose any obligation on host States under Article 1105. The only exception is the *Metalclad* award[1060] which was, however, set aside in judicial review before a B.C. Court precisely with regards to this point.[1061] The concept of transparency is relevant to aid tribunals in assessing whether or not *other established* elements of the FET standard (such as due process[1062]) have been breached by a State. On the contrary, a number of non-NAFTA tribunals have found that the stability and predictability of the legal

1050. *Cargill Inc. v. Mexico*, Award, (18 September 2009), para. 290.
1051. *Mobil v. Canada*, Decision on Liability and on Principles of Quantum, (22 May 2012), paras. 152, 170.
1052. *Grand River v. United States*, Award, (12 January 2011), para. 141.
1053. *Glamis v. United States*, Award, (8 June 2009), para. 802.
1054. *Ibid.*, para. 767.
1055. *Ibid.*, paras. 800–801.
1056. *Ibid.*, para. 766. *See also*: para. 767.
1057. *Ibid.*, para. 561.
1058. *Merrill & Ring v. Canada*, Award, (31 March 2010), para. 231.
1059. *Cargill Inc. v. Mexico*, Award, (18 September 2009), para. 294.
1060. *Metalclad v. Mexico*, Award, (30 August 2000), paras. 70, 76, 88, 99.
1061. *Mexico v. Metalclad*, Supreme Court of British Columbia, Judgment and Reasons for Decision (2 May 2001), paras. 68, 72.
1062. *Waste Management v. Mexico*, Award, (30 April 2004), para. 98.

framework, including an obligation of transparency, is an essential element of the FET standard.

Arbitrary conduct. Several tribunals (*Thunderbird*,[1063] *Waste Management*,[1064] *Mobil*,[1065] *Merrill & Ring*[1066]) have come to the conclusion that there exists an obligation for host States prohibiting arbitrary conduct under the minimum standard of treatment under custom. Yet, none of these tribunals have undertaken an examination of State practice and opinio juris on the matter. All NAFTA tribunals have listed the prohibition of arbitrary conduct as a stand-alone element of the FET standard under Article 1105.[1067] It is noteworthy that the NAFTA Parties' position has evolved over time. They no longer deny that arbitrary conduct is an element of the FET standard under Article 1105, but instead emphasize the requirement that such conduct be *manifestly* arbitrary.

The threshold of severity applied by NAFTA tribunals has been consistently high. Tribunals have thus referred to treatment that 'rises to the level that is unacceptable from the international perspective',[1068] to '*wholly* arbitrary' conduct,[1069] and to 'manifest arbitrariness falling below international standards'.[1070] For instance, the *Glamis* tribunal stated that Article 1105 'requires something greater than mere arbitrariness, something that is surprising, shocking, or exhibits a manifest lack of reasoning'[1071] and sets the threshold of liability at 'manifest arbitrariness'.[1072] The application of such a high threshold of liability by most NAFTA tribunals[1073] largely explains why they (except for *Cargill*) have not found arbitrary conduct to amount to a breach of Article 1105. Non-NAFTA tribunals have, on the contrary, often found violations of arbitrariness based on a lower threshold of liability.

In light of case law, a number of conclusions can be reached concerning the contours of this prohibition of arbitrary conduct. A government's failure to implement or to abide by its own laws and regulations does not amount to an arbitrary act unless it can be shown that the government committed a maladministration that amounts to an 'outright and unjustified repudiation' of such laws and regulations.[1074] Similarly, a

---

1063. *Thunderbird v. Mexico,* Award, (26 January 2006), para. 194.
1064. *Waste Management v. Mexico,* Award, (30 April 2004), para. 98.
1065. *Mobil v. Canada,* Decision on Liability and on Principles of Quantum, (22 May 2012), para. 152.
1066. *Merrill & Ring v. Canada,* Award, (31 March 2010), para. 187.
1067. *S.D. Myers Inc. v. Canada,* First Partial Award, (13 November 2000), para. 263; *Waste Management v. Mexico,* Award, (30 April 2004), para. 98; *Gami v. Mexico,* Award, (15 November 2004), paras. 98, 103; *Thunderbird v. Mexico,* Award, (26 January 2006), para. 194; *Merrill & Ring v. Canada,* Award, (31 March 2010), para. 208; *Cargill Inc. v. Mexico,* Award, (18 September 2009), paras. 292–293; *Mobil v. Canada,* Decision on Liability and on Principles of Quantum, (22 May 2012), para. 152; *Glamis v. United States,* Award, (8 June 2009), para. 626.
1068. *S.D. Myers Inc. v. Canada,* First Partial Award, (13 November 2000), para. 263.
1069. *Waste Management v. Mexico,* Award, (30 April 2004), para. 115 (emphasis added).
1070. *Thunderbird v. Mexico,* Award, (26 January 2006), para. 194.
1071. *Glamis v. United States,* Award, (8 June 2009), para. 617.
1072. *Ibid.,* paras. 626–627. *See also*: *Cargill Inc. v. Mexico,* Award, (18 September 2009), para. 296.
1073. Only two awards have referred to 'arbitrary' conduct without using any qualifying adjective such as 'manifest': *Mobil v. Canada,* Decision on Liability and on Principles of Quantum, (22 May 2012), para. 152; *Merrill & Ring v. Canada,* Award, (31 March 2010), para. 208.
1074. *Gami v. Mexico,* Award, (15 November 2004), paras. 91, 103, 104.

mere contractual breach does not amount to an arbitrary act, unless it can be shown that the government committed an 'outright and unjustified repudiation of the trans-action' or that the breach was 'motivated by sectoral or local prejudice'.[1075] A government's 'inconsistent' or 'questionable' application of its own policy or proce-dure (or the fact that it made a mistake in its application) does not amount to an arbitrary act.[1076] The fact that a governmental measure is illegal under domestic law does not necessarily make it arbitrary in violation of the FET standard under Article 1105. A violation of this provision occurs when there is a 'manifest lack of reasons for the legislation' such as when the legislation bears no rational relationship with its stated purpose, when it is not 'reasonably drafted to address its objectives,'[1077] or when a governmental measure is adopted with the express intention to injure and cause damage to an investor's investment.

Discriminatory conduct. With the exception of *Merrill & Ring*,[1078] other NAFTA tribunals (*Methanex*,[1079] *Grand River*,[1080] *Glamis*[1081]) have come to the conclusion that nationality-based discrimination is not covered by Article 1105 and that customary international law contains no general prohibition of discrimination against foreign investors. Moreover, the *Grand River* tribunal added that the minimum standard of treatment applies to *all investors* (by definition) and therefore denied the existence of any custom rule prohibiting discrimination specifically against indigenous peoples. The reasoning of some NAFTA tribunals (*Waste Management*,[1082] *Glamis*,[1083] and to a lesser extent that of *Methanex*) can be interpreted as suggesting that Article 1105 covers some types of specific 'discrimination' (*other* than nationality-based), such as 'sec-tional or racial prejudice'.[1084] Case law is unsettled on this point.

Good faith. NAFTA tribunals have all concluded that the principle of good faith is not a stand-alone obligation under the FET standard, but rather a guiding principle that is relevant to the determination of whether or not a breach of Article 1105 has occurred.[1085] They have also concluded that an investor does not have to show that the

---

1075. *Waste Management v. Mexico*, Award, (30 April 2004), para. 115.
1076. *Cargill Inc. v. Mexico*, Award, (18 September 2009), paras. 98, 293.
1077. *Glamis v. United States*, Award, (8 June 2009), paras. 803, 817. *See also: Cargill Inc. v. Mexico*, Award, (18 September 2009), para. 299.
1078. *Merrill & Ring v. Canada*, Award, (31 March 2010), para. 208.
1079. *Methanex v. United States*, Award, (3 August 2005), Part IV, Chapter C, Page 7, paras. 14–27.
1080. *Grand River v. United States*, Award, (12 January 2011), para. 208. *See also*, at para. 209.
1081. *Glamis v. United States*, Award, (8 June 2009), para. 542, footnote 1087.
1082. *Waste Management v. Mexico*, Award, (30 April 2004), para. 98, endorsed by *Mobil v. Canada*, Decision on Liability and on Principles of Quantum, (22 May 2012), para. 152.
1083. While the tribunal examined discrimination-related allegations in the context of arbitrariness (*Glamis v. United States*, Award, (8 June 2009), para. 542, footnote 1087; para. 559, footnote 1128), it nevertheless referred some 11 times to the terms 'evident discrimination' alongside other elements of the FET standard such as denial of justice, arbitrariness and due process (*see* at paras. 22, 24, 616, 627, 762, 765, 776, 779, 788, 824, 828).
1084. It is unclear whether this is also the position adopted by the *Methanex* tribunal (*Methanex v. United States*, Award, (3 August 2005), Part IV, Chapter C, Page 11, para. 26).
1085. *Thunderbird v. Mexico*, Award, (26 January 2006), Separate Opinion of Thomas Wälde, para. 25; *ADF v. United States*, Award, (9 January 2003), para. 191. *See*, however, the more ambiguous position taken by the tribunals in: *Waste Management v. Mexico*, Award, (30 April 2004), para. 138; *Merrill & Ring v. Canada*, Award, (31 March 2010), para. 187.

host State has acted in bad faith to prove a violation of the FET standard.[1086] Yet, proof of bad faith would be conducive to a finding of a breach of the FET standard.[1087]

Denial of justice and due process. All NAFTA tribunals have held that there exists an obligation not to deny justice and to respect due process under Article 1105.[1088] In light of case law, a number of conclusions can be reached with respect to the parameters under which this prohibition of denial of justice and the obligation to respect due process operate. A foreign investor must have exhausted all remedies made available by domestic courts before a complaint of a denial of justice can be filed before a NAFTA tribunal. Case law shows that this obligation is, however, limited to those remedies that are 'effective and adequate and are reasonably available to the complainant'.[1089] A tribunal must assess the *system* of justice of the host State *as a whole* rather than focusing on individual domestic court decisions. The *Mondev* tribunal (endorsed by other tribunals, including *Loewen*) has put forward a general 'test': a denial of justice occurs whenever a decision by a domestic court is 'clearly improper and discreditable' in the sense that it would 'shock or surprise' any impartial observer and would raise 'justified concerns as to the judicial propriety of the outcome' of the case.[1090] These findings suggest a high threshold of severity for finding a denial of justice; only the most severe cases will be considered in breach of Article 1105. This conclusion is also supported by other tribunals' references to 'gross denial of justice' that is 'falling below acceptable international standards'.[1091]

Case law has shown that a denial of justice arises when the host State does not provide the investor with a fair trial, such as when a domestic court 'refuses to entertain a suit', when it subjects a suit to 'undue delay', or, more generally, when a court 'administer[s] justice in a seriously inadequate way'.[1092] A fair trial also requires that States provide investors with discrimination-free litigation. Also, a court decision in breach of municipal law does not constitute a denial of justice per se unless it is also

---

1086. *Mondev v. United States*, Award, (2 October 2002), para. 116; *Glamis v. United States,* Award, (8 June 2009), para. 616; *Loewen v. United States*, Award, (26 June 2003), para. 132; *Merrill & Ring v. Canada*, Award, (31 March 2010), para. 208; *Waste Management v. Mexico*, Award, (30 April 2004), para. 93.

1087. *Glamis v. United States*, Award, (8 June 2009), paras. 22, 616.

1088. *Azinian v. Mexico*, Award, (1 November 1999), paras. 102–103; *Metalclad v. Mexico*, Award, (30 August 2000), paras. 91, 93; *Pope & Talbot Inc. v. Canada*, Award on the Merits (Phase 2), (10 April 2001), para. 181; *ibid.*, Award in Respect of Damages, (31 May 2002), para. 68; *Mondev v. United States*, Award, (2 October 2002), paras. 96, 126-127; *Loewen v. United States*, Award, (26 June 2003), paras. 54–55, 87, 119, 122, 124-137; *Waste Management v. Mexico*, Award, (30 April 2004), paras. 95, 97, 98; *Thunderbird v. Mexico*, Award, (26 January 2006), para. 194; *Methanex v. United States*, Award, (3 August 2005), Part IV, Chapter C, Page 8, para. 15; *S.D. Myers Inc. v. Canada*, First Partial Award, (13 November 2000), para. 134; *Mobil v. Canada*, Decision on Liability and on Principles of Quantum, (22 May 2012), para. 152.

1089. *Loewen v. United States*, Award, (26 June 2003), para. 168.

1090. *Mondev v. United States*, Award, (2 October 2002), para. 127.

1091. *Thunderbird v. Mexico*, Award, (26 January 2006), para. 194. In *Glamis*, the tribunal refers on many occasions in the award to 'gross' denial of justice and a 'complete' lack of due process (*Glamis v. United States*, Award, (8 June 2009), paras. 22, 24, 614, 616, 625, 627). *See also*: *Cargill Inc. v. Mexico*, Award, (18 September 2009), para. 296.

1092. *Azinian v. Mexico*, Award, (1 November 1999), paras. 102–103.

discriminatory against a foreign investor or unless a 'clear and malicious misapplication of the law' by the court can be demonstrated.[1093] On the contrary, an error of law made by a domestic court or a decision deviating from previous case law would not amount to a denial of justice. Overall, NAFTA case law illustrates that tribunals have been quite demanding in terms of the level of conduct required by host States for them to respect their due process obligation.

In sum, NAFTA case law suggests that only the prohibition of arbitrary conduct, denial of justice and the obligation of due process are unambiguously stand-alone elements of the FET obligation under Article 1105. Other terms that are often used by tribunals, such as 'grossly unfair, unjust or idiosyncratic',[1094] are better viewed as encompassed within these three elements. Such a finding shows that NAFTA Article 1105 is significantly different from other FET clauses found in BITs (those containing unqualified FET clauses where no reference to international law is found). Thus, the present analysis of Article 1105 case law does not support the more general conclusion reached by UNCTAD in its 2012 report that 'a *de facto* convergence has been taking place between the qualified and unqualified FET standards as far as the main substantive elements of the standard are concerned'.[1095] The report indicates that the content of the FET standard (for both qualified and unqualified FET clauses) 'include[s] the limited protection of investors' legitimate expectations, a prohibition of arbitrary and discriminatory treatment, denial of justice and abusive conduct towards investors'.[1096] As mentioned above, our analysis of Article 1105 case law does *not* support the view that the protection of investors' legitimate expectations and nationality-based discrimination are elements of the FET standard. On the other hand, our analysis of Article 1105 case law *does* support the UNCTAD report's other conclusion that 'transparency, consistency, legality and stability of regulatory framework' are not part of custom.[1097] Thus, the concepts of transparency and legitimate expectations are considered by the majority of NAFTA tribunals as 'factors' to be taken into account when assessing whether or not other well-established elements of the FET standard have been breached. Similarly, the principle of good faith is considered as a guiding principle relevant to the determination of whether a breach of Article 1105 has occurred.

The present author's findings also highlight the specific nature of Article 1105. As mentioned above, supporters of the theory which equates the FET standard and the rule of law believe that the '[d]ifferences in the contexts in which the [FET] standard appears have made little difference to tribunals interpreting the standard' and that 'awards have yielded a single coherent theory of the standard, although perhaps not

---

1093. *Ibid.*
1094. *Waste Management v. Mexico*, Award, (30 April 2004), para. 98; *Cargill Inc. v. Mexico*, Award, (18 September 2009), para. 296.
1095. UNCTAD, *supra* n. 11, at 90.
1096. *Ibid.*
1097. *Ibid.*

consciously so'.[1098] While this conclusion may, as a matter of principle, be perfectly valid for *unqualified* FET clauses not linked to international law, it is not accurate in the specific context of NAFTA Article 1105. Thus, case law shows that Article 1105 only covers a handful of the many elements that these writers typically list as being part of the FET standard.[1099]

[2] A Necessary High Threshold of Severity

The second conclusion of this chapter is related to the high threshold of severity and gravity which tribunals have consistently required in order to conclude that the host State has breached any of the few elements contained within the FET standard under Article 1105. The *Glamis*,[1100] *Cargill*,[1101] *Waste Management*,[1102] *ADF*,[1103] and *Thunderbird*[1104] tribunals have all set a very high threshold of liability. As pointed out by the *Glamis* and the *Cargill* tribunals, the existence of such a high threshold is clear given NAFTA tribunals' consistent use of qualifiers such as 'manifest', 'gross', 'evident', 'blatant', and 'complete'.[1105] In fact, the existence of this high threshold of severity is probably the predominant characteristic of NAFTA case law.[1106] It is, indeed, one aspect that clearly differentiates it from awards rendered by non-NAFTA tribunals

---

1098. Vandevelde, *supra* n. 27, at 47. *See also*: Schill, *supra* n. 48, at 33 ('it is questionable whether substantial differences result from the different framing of the standard with a view to the actual practice of investment tribunals').

1099. *See*, for instance, Schill, *supra* n. 48, at 70: 'The survey of investment decision shows that the concept underlying fair and equitable treatment is functionally equivalent to the understanding of the requirements deduced from the rule of law under domestic legal systems and other international law regimes. Investment tribunals have thus interpreted fair and equitable treatment so as to encompass sub-elements the rule of law is associated with in various domestic legal systems. In this respect, the jurisprudence of arbitral tribunals concerning fair and equitable treatment can be analyzed as including (1) the requirement of stability and predictability of the legal framework and consistency in the host state's decision-making, (2) the principle of legality, (3) the protection of investor confidence or legitimate expectations, (4) procedural due process and denial of justice, (5) protection against discrimination and arbitrariness, (6) the requirement of transparency and (7) the concept of reasonableness and proportionality'. *See also*: Vandevelde, *supra* n. 27, at 104 ('Tribunals have interpreted fair and equitable treatment to embrace five principles that are elements of the procedural and substantive dimensions of the rule of law: reasonableness, consistency, nondiscrimination, transparency, and due process').

1100. *Glamis v. United States*, Award, (8 June 2009), para. 627.

1101. *Cargill Inc. v. Mexico*, Award, (18 September 2009), paras. 285, 296.

1102. *Waste Management v. Mexico*, Award, (30 April 2004), para. 115.

1103. *ADF v. United States*, Award, (9 January 2003), para. 190.

1104. *Thunderbird v. Mexico*, Award, (26 January 2006), para. 194.

1105. *Cargill Inc. v. Mexico*, Award, (18 September 2009), para. 285 ('As outlined in the Waste Management II award quote above, the violation may arise in many forms. It may relate to a lack of due process, discrimination, a lack of transparency, a denial of justice, or an unfair outcome. But in all of these various forms, the "lack" or "denial" of a quality or right is sufficiently at the margin of acceptable conduct and thus we find (...) that the lack or denial must be "gross", "manifest", "complete", or such as to "offend judicial propriety"'); *Glamis v. United States*, Award, (8 June 2009), para. 616.

1106. UNCTAD, *supra* n. 11, at 56 ('The above review of different [NAFTA] awards suggests, *inter alia*, that a simple illegality at the domestic level is insufficient to establish a breach of the standard; "something more" is required. Indeed, claimants must satisfy a rather high

which have often used a lower threshold of liability when applying an unqualified FET clause.[1107]

Only two NAFTA awards have taken a different stance. In its 2001 award, the *Pope & Talbot* tribunal ruled that 'compliance with the fairness elements must be ascertained free of any threshold that might be applicable to the evaluation of measures under the minimum standard of international law'.[1108] However, this award was made before the FTC Note was issued and the tribunal subsequently abandoned this position in its 2002 award.

As is often the case, the *Merrill & Ring* award is the 'odd man out' among NAFTA awards. It is the only one to have adopted a much lower threshold of liability. In its award, the tribunal first acknowledged that 'in the NAFTA context, a number of tribunals have adopted th[e] demanding standard' set out in the older *Neer* and *ELSI* cases.[1109] The tribunal even recognized that it was 'quite evident that NAFTA jurisprudence ha[d] stiffened since the FTC Interpretation'[1110] and explicitly referred to the consistent use of qualifiers (such as 'manifest', 'gross', 'evident', 'blatant', 'complete') by these tribunals.[1111] Yet, in its summary of case law, the tribunal simply stated: '[c]onduct which is unjust, arbitrary, unfair, discriminatory or in violation of due process has also been noted by NAFTA tribunals as constituting a breach of fair and equitable treatment'.[1112] The striking feature of this short sentence is, of course, the absence of any of the different qualifiers that have consistently been used by all other NAFTA tribunals. Ultimately, the tribunal adopted an even lower threshold of severity. It held that the FET standard provides protection 'against all such acts or behaviour that might infringe on a sense of fairness, equity and reasonableness'[1113] and that it

---

evidential burden to show that the State conduct is notably arbitrary or grossly unfair and that the measure in question relates to an area effectively regulated by customary international law').

1107. Picherack, *supra* n. 66, at 268-269 ('The trend that emerges regarding the interpretation of the minimum standard of treatment in the context of fair and equitable treatment analysis by NAFTA Tribunals is one of a continuing high threshold necessary to establish a breach'), at 270 ('In contrast to the conservative ruling of the NAFTA and other tribunals discussed in the previous section, the decisions of a number of recent arbitral tribunals outside of the NAFTA context have arguably pushed the bounds of the minimum standard and the fair and equitable treatment standard to well past their previous contours. Underlying many of these recent decisions is a re-conceptualization of the standard away from a traditional interpretation that imposes obligations on States not to treat investors unfairly or inequitably understood in accordance with the minimum standard as traditionally applied, and towards a belief that the standard imposes additional and stricter obligations on States to act proactively in favour of the investor in order to promote, stimulate and ensure the investor's investment'). *See also*: UNCTAD, *supra* n. 11, at 87, 90 ('The difference between the two expressions of the standard is that the liability threshold under an unqualified FET standard will be somewhat lower than under the qualified one').
1108. *Pope & Talbot Inc. v. Canada*, Award on the Merits (Phase 2), (10 April 2001), para. 111. *See also*, at para. 118.
1109. *Merrill & Ring v. Canada*, Award, (31 March 2010), para. 198.
1110. *Ibid.*, para. 199.
1111. *Ibid.*, paras. 198–200.
1112. *Ibid.*, para. 208.
1113. *Ibid.*, para. 210.

'provides for the fair and equitable treatment of alien investors within the confines of reasonableness'.[1114]

Despite having set the threshold at such a low level, the tribunal nevertheless bizarrely decided to examine the facts of the case based on two different 'scenarios':[1115]

> The Tribunal has considered a possible breach of the protections provided by Article 1105(1) under two different scenarios. The first is based on the Investor's view that the protection provided by Article 1105(1) is significant and that the threshold to be applied to establish breach is a comparatively low one, and thus the log export regime's interference with its business could readily result in a breach of Article 1105(1). The second scenario, while not relying on the Neer or some other similarly high threshold, is based on the view that for there to be an 1105(1) breach, a state's wrongful conduct or behavior must be sufficiently serious as to be readily distinguishable from an ordinary effect of otherwise acceptable regulatory measures.[1116]

The tribunal decided to consider these two scenarios because the arbitrators could not agree amongst themselves as to what the threshold of severity should be.[1117] The tribunal then examined the claimant's allegations of breach of Article 1105 based on these two different threshold scenarios. This open disagreement amongst arbitrators undermines the award as a solid precedent to be followed by other tribunals in the future regarding the question of the threshold of severity.[1118]

In (yet) another rather peculiar twist, the tribunal ultimately determined that it did not have to choose which of the two scenarios it should hold in its decision with respect to the allegations of breach of the FET standard:

> Before determining which of the two above scenarios should guide the conclusions of the Tribunal and whether, under either such scenario, Canada may be said to have breached its Article 1105(1) obligations, matters on which there were different opinions, the Tribunal considers it advisable first to determine whether the Investor has proven it was damaged by Canada's alleged breaches.[1119]

The tribunal had thus already concluded that the investor had failed to prove any breaches of NAFTA Articles 1102, 1106 and 1110. The only claim left to be decided upon was the one regarding Article 1105. However, the arbitrators could not agree on which of the two scenarios to use in its examination of these allegations. The tribunal thus found a way not to have to make a decision.[1120] It simply examined whether the investor had proven any damages because, as the tribunal explained, 'a finding of liability without a finding of damage would be difficult to explain in the context of investment law arbitration and would indeed be contrary to some of its fundamental

---

1114. *Ibid.*, para. 213.
1115. *See*, C. Lévesque, *Chronique de Droit international économique en 2010-2011 – Investissement*, 49 Can YIL 366-367 (2011).
1116. *Merrill & Ring v. Canada*, Award, (31 March 2010), para. 219.
1117. *Ibid.*, para. 266 ('the Tribunal held different views in respect of both the applicable threshold and possible breach thereof').
1118. *See*, Lévesque, *supra* n. 1115, at 366-370.
1119. *Merrill & Ring v. Canada*, Award, (31 March 2010), para. 243.
1120. *See*, Lévesque, *supra* n. 1115, at 366-367.

tenets'.[1121] The tribunal concluded that no damage had been proven and therefore dismissed the Article 1105 claim.[1122]

The concrete consequence of the consistent application of this high threshold of liability by NAFTA tribunals (with the notable exception of *Merrill & Ring*) is that very few tribunals have come to the conclusion that the host State has violated Article 1105. Only one tribunal (*Cargill*) concluded that Mexico had committed an arbitrary conduct. This was a clear case of arbitrariness. The tribunal held that Mexico had deliberately and intentionally targeted the US investor in retaliation for a US trade policy. Two other tribunals (*Metalclad* and *Pope & Talbot*) held that the host States (Mexico and Canada, respectively) had breached their obligation to provide due process to a foreign investor. The *S.D. Myers* award does not explain which element(s) of the FET standard was (or were) breached by Canada.

UNCTAD has recently noted a significant statistical difference between the lower success rates of FET claims under NAFTA when compared to the much higher one under BITs. By October 2010, tribunals addressed the merits of FET claims in eighty-four treaty-based disputes. Of this overall number, the FET claim was successful in forty-five cases and rejected in thirty-nine cases. In NAFTA cases, only 22% of those claims were successful (four out of eighteen), while in BIT cases, 62% were accepted by tribunals (forty-one out of sixty-six).[1123]

1121. *Merrill & Ring v. Canada*, Award, (31 March 2010), para. 245.
1122. *Ibid.*, para. 266 ('Even if the scenario most favorable to the Investor were to be adopted, and breach of the Article 1105(1) obligation assumed, damages have not been proven to the satisfaction of the Tribunal').
1123. UNCTAD, *supra* n. 11, at 61. The report explains that these numbers exclude cases dismissed on jurisdictional grounds and awards where the merits of the FET claim were not addressed by tribunals due to a finding of expropriation.

CHAPTER 4

The Relationship between Article 1105 and Other NAFTA Provisions

This chapter examines the interaction between Article 1105 and different clauses typically found in BITs, such as national treatment, Most-Favored-Nation ('MFN'), expropriation and full protection and security. As noted by UNCTAD, these different protections seem to come in a 'packaged deal' where the FET standard is generally accorded (although most often in a separate provision) with both national treatment and MFN treatment.[1]

§4.01 THE FAIR AND EQUITABLE TREATMENT, AN OVERRIDING OBLIGATION?

One controversial question in the field of international investment law pertains to whether or not the FET standard should be analyzed as an 'overriding obligation'.[2] In other words, does the FET 'set out the general rule while the other standards amount to specific applications of the general rule'?[3] This is, indeed, the position adopted by Mann,[4] although in the specific context of UK BITs (which are generally considered as imposing such an 'overriding obligation').[5] In a number of BITs,[6] the World Bank

---

1. UNCTAD, *Fair and Equitable Treatment*, UNCTAD Series on Issues in International Investment Agreements, 16 (1999).
2. *Ibid.*, at 34 ff.
3. *Ibid.*, at 34. *See also*: Andrew Newcombe & Luis Paradell, *Law and Practice of Investment Treaties: Standards of Treatment*, 259 (Kluwer 2009), providing examples of national treatment and MFN clauses being subsumed within the FET.
4. F.A. Mann, *British Treaties for the Promotion and Protection of Investments*, in *Further Studies in International Law* (F.A. Mann ed., Clarendon Press 1990), at 238 ('it may well be that other provisions of the Agreements affording substantive protection are no more than examples or specific instances of this overriding duty').
5. UNCTAD, *supra* n. 1, at 34.

Guidelines,[7] as well as the Energy Charter Treaty ('ECT'),[8] the FET is considered as such an overriding obligation. This is also the position adopted by a few tribunals.[9]

One of the practical consequences of considering the FET standard as an 'overriding obligation' would be to impose an obligation to respect the national treatment or the MFN treatment even when the BIT does not expressly include these two clauses. Moreover, a breach of these two clauses would necessarily amount to a violation of the FET standard.[10] For these reasons, the FET clause is treated, in the vast majority of BITs, as an 'autonomous standard' of protection independent from the MFN treatment and the national treatment clauses.[11] As explained by Kläger, 'the idea of an overriding obligation carries an inherent danger that, even though a particular obligation has been deliberately omitted in an agreement, this obligation may be introduced into an agreement through the back door of fair and equitable treatment' which would 'hardly comply with the original intentions of the parties to the agreement'.[12] It is therefore generally agreed that 'where a treaty makes provision for fair and equitable treatment, but does not expressly incorporate the national treatment standard, it cannot be assumed that the treaty automatically includes the national treatment standard'.[13] In any event, the structure and the language of NAFTA Chapter 11 clearly do not support the conception of the FET standard as an 'overriding obligation'.[14]

---

6. Several examples are found in: Stephen Vasciannie, *The Fair and Equitable Treatment Standard in International Investment Law and Practice*, 70 British YIL 130-133 (1999); UNCTAD, *supra* n. 1, at 36; L. Paradell, *The BIT Experience of the Fair and Equitable Treatment Standard*, in *Investment Treaty Law: Current Issues II* 1277 (F. Ortino et al. eds., British IICL 2007).
7. Article III(2) of the World Bank Guidelines recommends this clause: 'Each state will extend to investments established in its territory by nationals of any other state fair and equitable treatment according to the standards recommended in these guideline'.
8. Under Article 10 of the ECT, the FET standard of FET is embedded in a provision that also refers to a number of other obligations, such as full protection and security, a prohibition against unreasonable or discriminatory measures and, finally, an umbrella clause imposing an obligation to provide treatment required by international law and to observe obligations entered into by the State. In *Petrobart v. Kyrgyz Republic*, SCC Case No. 126/2003, Award, (29 March 2005), the tribunal seems to have interpreted this clause as imposing an overriding FET obligation.
9. C. Schreuer, *Fair and Equitable Standard (FET): Interaction with Other Standards*, 4(5) Transnational Disp. Mgmt. 1 (2007), referring to *Noble Ventures, Inc. v. Romania*, ICSID No. ARB/01/11, Award, (12 October 2005), para. 182. ('Considering the place of the fair and equitable treatment standard at the very beginning of Art. II(2), one can consider this to be a more general standard which finds its specific application in *inter alia* the duty to provide full protection and security, the prohibition of arbitrary and discriminatory measures and the obligation to observe contractual obligations towards the investor').
10. UNCTAD, *supra* n. 1, at 36.
11. *Ibid.*, at 37; Ioana Tudor, *The Fair and Equitable Treatment Standard in International Foreign Investment Law* 183 (Oxford U. Press 2008); R. Dolzer & C. Schreuer, *Principles of International Investment Law* 123 (Oxford U. Press 2008); Schreuer, *supra* n. 9, at 2; Roland Kläger, *Fair and Equitable Treatment in International Investment Law* 308-310 (Cambridge U. Press 2011); Rudolf Dolzer, *Fair and Equitable Treatment* 39 Int'l Law 91 (2005); Vasciannie, *supra* n. 6, at 133.
12. Kläger, *supra* n. 11, at 309-310. *See also*: Alexandra Diehl, *The Core Standard of International Investment Protection: Fair and Equitable Treatment* 9-10, 37 (Wolters Kluwer 2012).
13. UNCTAD, *supra* n. 1, at 37.
14. *Ibid.*, at 33 ('If FET is understood as part of the minimum standard of treatment under customary international law, it becomes clear that a violation of a treaty obligation does not necessarily amount to a violation of a customary norm. The purpose of this provision is to

The fact that the FET standard is an autonomous standard of protection does not mean that it operates in isolation from other clauses.[15] The following sections examine the interaction between the FET standard and other elements of protection offered to investors: MFN treatment, national treatment, expropriation and full protection and security.[16]

§4.02   A FINDING OF A BREACH OF ANOTHER PROVISION DOES NOT ESTABLISH A VIOLATION OF ARTICLE 1105

As mentioned above, in *S.D. Myers* the claimant argued that an export ban imposed by Canada was arbitrary and discriminatory in violation of Article 1105. The majority of the tribunal decided not to examine the specific application of this provision to the facts of the case, but to rely instead on its previous finding regarding a breach of Article 1102. According to the majority, the breach of an international law provision designed to protect investments would 'tend to weigh heavily in favor' of finding a breach of Article 1105.[17] It also concluded that in the instant case, the discrimination suffered by the claimant in breach of the national treatment provision 'essentially establish[es] a breach of Article 1105 as well'.[18] On this point, arbitrator Chiasson dissented and considered that a violation of Article 1105 must be based on a demonstrated failure of that clause and that a breach of another provision is not a foundation for such a conclusion.[19]

Soon after the *S.D. Myers* award was rendered in 2000, the United States filed an Article 1128 submission in the context of the on-going *Pope & Talbot* case. It argued in unequivocal terms that 'the panel majority incorrectly define[d] the scope of Article 1105(1) and incorrectly link[ed] Article 1102 to Article 1105(1)'.[20] It noted that while Article 1105 refers to the minimum standard of treatment under custom, the national treatment and MFN clauses were not customary international law obligations, but only treaty-based obligations. As a result, 'concluding that Article 1102 has been breached does not establish a breach of Article 1105(1)'.[21] The United States also criticized the panel majority's reliance on the writing of Mann considering that under Article 1105, the FET is clearly 'a subset of customary international law, not an overarching duty that

---

prevent tribunals from automatically finding a breach of the FET standard when another provision in the IIA [international investment agreements] has been breached').
15. Schreuer, *supra* n. 9, at 2.
16. The interaction between the FET and separate clauses specifically prohibiting discriminatory and arbitrary measures has already been discussed above (*see*, Chapter 3 section §3.02[D][6]).
17. *S.D. Myers Inc. v. Canada*, UNCITRAL, First Partial Award, (13 November 2000), para. 265 (referring to the writing of F.A. Mann, *British Treaties for the Promotion and Protection of Investments*, 52 British YBIL 241, 243 (1981)).
18. *Ibid.*, paras. 264, 266. The tribunal nevertheless indicated that it 'does not rule out the possibility that there could be circumstances in which a denial of the national treatment provision of the NAFTA would not necessarily offend the minimum standard provision'.
19. *Ibid.*, para. 267.
20. *Pope & Talbot Inc. v. Canada*, UNCITRAL, US Fifth Submission, (1 December 2000), para. 3.
21. *Ibid.*, paras. 4–7.

subsumes all other instances of substantive protection'.[22] Both Mexico and Canada also filed Article 1128 submissions which rejected the majority's position in *S.D. Myers*.[23] Canada, for instance, argued that Articles 1102 and 1105 put forward distinct obligations that require a separate legal analysis because the former 'is a comparative provision that necessitates an assessment of the treatment of foreign investments relative to that of domestic investments', while the latter 'is an absolute standard that necessitates the assessment of the treatment accorded the foreign-owned investment, independent of the treatment accorded domestic investments'.[24]

As mentioned above,[25] the third paragraph of the FTC Note of Interpretation aimed to overrule the reasoning in the *S.D. Myers* award. The Note makes it clear that the finding of a breach of a separate provision does not establish a breach of Article 1105. NAFTA tribunals have since then endorsed this conclusion.[26] Since the 2001 Note, NAFTA Parties have integrated this clarification into their Model BITs[27] as well as into their respective BITs[28] and some recent FTAs.[29]

The fact that a finding of a breach of Article 1102 does not establish a breach of Article 1105 does not mean that a violation of the national treatment clause is altogether irrelevant to the analysis of the FET. Thus, the finding of a violation of the

---

22. *Ibid.*
23. *Ibid.*, Mexico's Article 1128 Post-Hearing Submission on the Second Phase Merits Issues, (1 December 2000), at 3-5; *ibid.*, Canada's Response to Phase Two Post-Hearing Submissions of Mexico and the United States, (15 December 2000), paras. 3–6.
24. *Ibid.*, Canada's Response to Phase Two Post-Hearing Submissions of Mexico and the United States, (15 December 2000, paras. 3–6.
25. *See*, Chapter 2 section §2.02[C][3][a].
26. *Methanex Corporation v. United States* [hereinafter *Methanex v. United States*], UNCITRAL, Award, (3 August 2005), Part IV, Ch. C, paras. 16, 17; *Grand River Enterprises Six Nations, Ltd., et al. v. United States*, UNCITRAL, Award, (12 January 2011), paras. 180–181.
27. Canada Model FIPA (2004), Article 5(3); US Model BIT (2012), Article 5(3).
28. *See*, for instance, the Mexico-Singapore BIT (2009), Article 4(3). *See also*, the following BITs entered into by Canada: Agreement between Canada and the Slovak Republic for the Promotion and Protection of Investments, signed at Bratislava, on 20 July 2010, entered into force on 14 March 2012, Article III(1)c); Agreement between Canada and Romania for the Promotion and Reciprocal Protection of Investments, signed at Bucharest on 8 May 2009, entered into force on 23 November 2011, Article II(2)c); Agreement between Canada and the Republic of Latvia for the Promotion and Protection of Investments, signed at Riga on 5 May 2009, entered into force on 24 November 2011, Article II(2)c); Agreement between Canada and the Hashemite Kingdom of Jordan for the Promotion and Protection of Investments, signed at Amman on 28 June 2009, entered into force on 14 December 2009, Article 5(3): Agreement between Canada and the Czech Republic for the Promotion and Protection of Investments, signed at Prague on 6 May 2009, entered into force on 22 January 2012, Article III(1)c); Agreement between Canada and the People's Republic of China for the Promotion and Reciprocal Protection of Investments, signed on 9 September 2012, Article 4(3) (not yet entered into force). *See also*, the following BITs entered into by the United States: Treaty between the United States and Rwanda Concerning the Encouragement and Reciprocal Protection of Investment, signed at Kigali on 19 February 2008, entered into force on 1 January 2012, Article 5(3); Treaty between the United States and Uruguay Concerning the Encouragement and Reciprocal Protection of Investment, with Annexes and Protocol, signed on 4 November 2005, entered into force on 1 November 2006, Article 5(3).
29. *See, inter alia*: United States-Australia Free Trade Agreement, signed at Washington on 18 May 2004, entered into force on 1 January 2005, Chapter, 11, Article 11.5 (al. 3); United States-Chile Free Trade Agreement, signed at Miami on 6 June 2003, entered into force on 1 January 2004, Article 10.4(3).

national treatment clause may evidence a treatment that is also unfair and inequitable.[30]

§4.03 ARTICLE 1105 AND EXPROPRIATION

The FET standard and the prohibition of expropriation are different legal concepts. Some BITs contain a provision pertaining to expropriation that explicitly refers to the FET.[31] NAFTA Article 1110 on expropriation is one such clause. It requires that a legal expropriation be, *inter alia*, in accordance with due process of law and the FET standard under Article 1105.[32] *A contrario*, an expropriation that does not respect the FET standard will be considered an unlawful expropriation under international law. It is not entirely clear, however, whether a tribunal must undertake a complete analysis of Article 1105 in the context of an allegation of a breach of Article 1110(1).[33]

NAFTA case law has shown that the express reference to the FET standard at Article 1110(1)(c) is especially relevant in the context of tax measures.[34] This is because, under NAFTA Article 2103, tax measures are not subject to Article 1105. However, Article 2103(6) also indicates that the exclusion of tax measures is not absolute and that Article 1110 is applicable to such measures (with some limitations). As pointed out by the *Feldman* tribunal, this means that while no tribunal has jurisdiction to examine whether a tax measure breaches Article 1105 per se, it will nevertheless be allowed to conduct such an analysis via Article 1110(1)(c) whenever a claimant alleges that an expropriation took place.[35]

NAFTA case law has also highlighted the fact that allegations of non-respect of an investor's legitimate expectations are relevant to both claims of a violation of Articles 1105 and 1110.[36] This has been confirmed by the *Methanex*[37] and the *Thunderbird*

---

30. Charles H. Brower II, *Structure, Legitimacy, and NAFTA's Investment Chapter 11*, 36 Vand. J. Transnat'l L. 78-79 (2003); Barnali Choudhury, *Evolution or Devolution? Defining Fair and Equitable Treatment in International Investment Law*, 6(2) J. World Invest. & Trade 314 (2005).
31. Schreuer, *supra* n. 9, at 23.
32. Article 1110(1) reads in relevant part as follows: '1. No Party may directly or indirectly nationalize or expropriate an investment of an investor of another Party in its territory or take a measure tantamount to nationalization or expropriation of such an investment "expropriation",'), except: (a) for a public purpose; (b) on a non-discriminatory basis; (c) in accordance with due process of law and Article 1105(1); and d) on payment of compensation in accordance with paragraphs 2 through 6'.
33. M. Kinnear, A. Bjorklund & J.F.G. Hannaford, *Investment Disputes under NAFTA: An Annotated Guide to NAFTA Chapter 11* section on Article 1110, at 35-36 (Kluwer Law International 2006).
34. Non-NAFTA cases are discussed in: Schreuer, *supra* n. 9, at 24-25.
35. *Marvin Roy Feldman Karpa v. Mexico*, ICSID No. ARB (AF)/99/1, Award, (16 December 2002), para. 141. ('While there may be an argument for a violation of Article 1105 under the facts of this case (a denial of fair and equitable treatment), this Tribunal has no jurisdiction to decide that issue directly. As noted earlier, Article 1105 is not available in tax cases, but may be relevant in the cross-reference of Article 1110(1)(c).') *See also*, para. 109, footnote 9.
36. Stephen Fietta, *Expropriation and the 'Fair and Equitable' Standard: The Developing Role of Investor 'Expectations' in International Investment Arbitration*, 23(5) J. Int'l Arb. 385 (2006).
37. *Methanex v. United States*, Award, (3 August 2005), Part IV, Ch. D, paras. 7, 10: 'as a matter of general international law, a non-discriminatory regulation for a public purpose, which is enacted in accordance with due process and, which affects, *inter alios*, a foreign investor or investment is not deemed expropriatory and compensable *unless specific commitments* had been given by

tribunals.[38] Yet, it remains that the focus of the analysis will differ. On the one hand, in the context of a claim of breach of Article 1105, the tribunal will focus its analysis on whether specific commitments have been made by the responsible authorities to the claimant. On the other hand, for allegations related to a breach of Article 1110, the tribunal will examine the level of interference by the State with the investment.[39] In the words of Diehl, in the context of expropriation allegations, 'the focus is not so much on what the investor expected but on what the State did and what effect its measures had' and, as a result, 'the motivations of the State are more important than the motivations of the investor'.[40] Moreover, a different threshold of liability will apply depending on whether the non-respect of an investor's legitimate expectations is alleged to be in violation of Article 1105 or Article 1110. It has thus been argued that it is probably easier for an investor to demonstrate that a State's failure to respect its legitimate expectations is in breach of Article 1105 than in violation of Article 1110.[41] For this reason, it has been pointed out by writers that tribunals are increasingly examining the issue of legitimate expectations in the context of the FET standard instead of expropriation.[42] This point is highlighted by Wälde in his separate opinion in *Thunderbird*.[43]

More generally, the burden of proof to demonstrate an expropriation is higher than to establish a violation of the FET.[44] As explained by the *PSEG* tribunal, the fact that allegations of breach of the FET standard may somehow be easier to demonstrate than expropriation allegations can partially explain the increased popularity of FET claims before BIT tribunals in recent decades.[45] In other words, it has been suggested that tribunals 'may be using FET to hold a State accountable of conduct that does not

---

the regulating government to the then putative foreign investor contemplating investment that the government *would refrain from such regulation*' (emphasis added).

38. *International Thunderbird Gaming Corporation v. The United Mexican States* [hereinafter *Thunderbird v. Mexico*], UNCITRAL, Award, (26 January 2006), para. 137, where the tribunal examined the issue of legitimate expectations on its own, i.e. before evaluating specifically whether any breaches of Articles 1105 and 1110 had occurred. The award has been criticized by writers precisely for this reason: Fietta, *supra* n. 36, at 395, 397.

39. Fietta, *supra* n. 36, at 391.

40. Diehl, *supra* n. 12, at 528.

41. Fietta, *supra* n. 36, at 398.

42. *Ibid.*, at 399; Schreuer, *supra* n. 9, at 23.

43. *Thunderbird v. Mexico*, Separate Opinion of Thomas Wälde, (1 December 2005), para. 37 (the legitimate expectations principle in the context of FET 'provides a more supple way of providing a remedy appropriate to the particular situation as compared to the more drastic determination and remedy inherent in [the] concept of regulatory expropriation. It is probably partly for these reasons that "legitimate expectation" has become for tribunals a preferred way of providing protection to claimants in situations where the tests for a "regulatory taking" appear too difficult, complex and too easily assailable for reliance on a measure of subjective judgment').

44. Schreuer, *supra* n. 9, at 23 ('In an investment dispute the burden of proof for an investor to demonstrate a violation of FET is usually lighter than to establish an expropriation'); Kläger, *supra* n. 11, at 298; Diehl, *supra* n. 12, at 9; Fietta, *supra* n. 36, at 398.

45. *PSEG Global, Inc., The North American Coal Corporation, and Konya Ingin Electrik Üretim ve Ticaret Limited Sirketi v. Turkey*, ICSID No. ARB/02/5, Award, (19 January 2007), para. 238 ('The standard of fair and equitable treatment has acquired prominence in investment arbitration as a consequence of the fact that other standards traditionally provided by international law might not in the circumstances of each case be entirely appropriate. This is particularly the case when the facts of the dispute do not clearly support the claim for direct expropriation, but when

meet the high threshold of substantial deprivation required to prove expropriation yet nonetheless injures the investor and deserves to be remedied'.[46] The *Sempra* tribunal openly endorsed this position by indicating that the FET standard 'ensures that even where there is no clear justification for making a finding of expropriation, as in the present case, there is still a standard which serves the purpose of justice and can of itself redress damage that is unlawful and that would otherwise pass unattended'.[47]

As a result of this different threshold, the *Feldman* tribunal rightly observed that when an investor demonstrates a violation of Article 1105, 'this alone does not establish the existence of an illegal expropriation under Article 1110'.[48] Thus, 'it may be appropriate for a NAFTA tribunal to find a violation of Article 1105 and at the same time decline to find a violation of Article 1110(1)(c)'.[49] On the other hand, proof of an illegal expropriation may support, in some circumstances, an unfair treatment in breach of Article 1105.[50]

§4.04   ARTICLE 1105 AND THE MFN CLAUSE

[A]   The Potential Use of the MFN Clause in Relation with the Fair and Equitable Treatment Clause

The MFN clause is a typical feature of BITs along with the FET and the national treatment clauses. The FET and the MFN clauses are usually *separate* provisions in a BIT.[51] An MFN clause ensures that an investor from State A must be treated by the

---

there are notwithstanding events that need to be assessed under a different standard to provide redress in the event that the rights of the investor have been breached'). *See also*: Kläger, *supra* n. 11, at 298.

46. Meg Kinnear, *The Continuing Development of the FET Standard*, in *Investment Treaty Law: Current Issues III* 36 (paper version) (Andrea K. Bjorklund, Ian A. Laird & Sergey Ripinsky eds., British IICL, 2009). *See also*: Katia Yannaca-Small, *Fair and Equitable Treatment Standard: Recent Developments*, in *Standards of Investment Protection* 112, 129 (A. Reinisch ed., Oxford U. Press 2008); Christina Knahr, *Fair and Equitable Treatment and its Relationship with other Treatment Standards*, in *Austrian Arb. Yb 2009*, 493 (Christian Klausegger et al. eds., C.H. Beck, Stämpfli & Manz 2009); Fietta, *supra* n. 36, at 398.

47. *Sempra Energy International v. Argentina*, ICSID No. ARB/02/16, Award, (28 September 2007), paras. 300, 301. The tribunal added: 'It must also be kept in mind that on occasion the line separating the breach of the fair and equitable treatment standard from an indirect expropriation can be very thin, particularly if the breach of the former standard is massive and long-lasting. In case of doubt, however, judicial prudence and deference to State functions are better served by opting for a determination in the light of the fair and equitable treatment standard. This also explains why the compensation granted to redress the wrong done might not be too different on either side of the line'.

48. *Marvin Roy Feldman Karpa v. Mexico*, Award, (16 December 2002), para. 141.

49. *Ibid.*, para. 141. *See also*: Schreuer, *supra* n. 9, at 23 ('[a] look at decisions rendered over the last couple of years shows clearly that Tribunals frequently find a violation of the FET standard but at the same time deny that there has been an expropriation').

50. Schreuer, *supra* n. 9, at 23 ('it is difficult to envisage an uncompensated expropriation that would not also involve a violation of the FET standard').

51. Only in a limited number of BITs, is the FET standard actually set by reference to the MFN treatment. In *MTD Equity Sdn. Bhd. and MTD Chile S.A. v. Chile*, ICSID No. ARB/01/7, Award, (25 May 2004), the tribunal had to interpret the Chile-Malaysia BIT which includes a traditional FET clause (Article 2(2)) as well as another clause (Article 3(1)) which reads as follows

other party to the treaty (State B) (and *vice versa*) 'no less favorably' with respect to a given subject-matter than an investor from any third country with which State B has entered into a BIT. The practical effect of the clause comes in full force whenever the BIT between States B and C contains a clause which provides for 'better treatment' than the one existing under the BIT between A and B (the so-called 'basic treaty'). In such a case, the investor from State A may invoke the MFN clause contained within the 'basic treaty' (between A and B) and claim the benefit of the better treatment prevailing under the BIT between B and C. In other words, via the MFN clause contained within one treaty, an investor will be able to claim a better standard of treatment contained in *another* treaty.

The MFN argument can be used by an investor regarding the treatment of its investment, i.e., the substantive rights or material aspects of the treatment granted to investors. Whether or not the MFN clause also covers procedural rights and dispute settlement clauses is a controversial matter and case law seems to be divided on this point.[52] Nevertheless, it is generally recognized that in the event where a BIT does not confer *jurisdiction* to a tribunal over FET claims, the MFN clause contained within that treaty cannot be used to import a broader dispute resolution clause contained in another BIT that provides for arbitration of FET claims.[53]

A number of possibilities can be envisaged as to how the MFN clause may be used in the context of an FET clause that confers substantial rights to foreign investors.

The first scenario involves a BIT between States A and B containing no FET clause at all. In this context, an investor from State A could invoke the MFN clause (contained within the BIT between States A and B) to claim the benefit of an FET clause (contained within a BIT between States B and C).[54] In such a case, the BIT between States B and C containing an FET clause certainly offers a better treatment and a more extensive protection for investors from Party A than a BIT (such as the one between States A and B) that is comprised of no such clause.[55] The use of the MFN clause in this context is the object of controversy. In practical terms, it would mean that States that have deliberately refused to include an FET clause in their BITs may be obliged to provide such a standard of protection to all investors.[56] As stated by UNCTAD, '[t]reaty practice suggests that countries that have not included an FET obligation or a reference to it into their treaty have done so purposefully to avoid being exposed to this standard of protection'.[57] For this reason, UNCTAD is of the view that 'any introduction of an FET

'Investments made by investors of either Contracting Party in the territory of the other Contracting Party shall receive treatment which is fair and equitable, and not less favourable than that accorded to investments made by investors of any third State'. This type of clauses is examined in: Tudor, *supra* n. 11, at 190; Diehl, *supra* n. 12, at 535-537.

52. *See*, the discussion in: Dolzer & Schreuer, *supra* n. 11, at 253-257; Diehl, *supra* n. 12, at 71-79; S. Schill, *The Multilateralization of International Investment Law* (Cambridge U. Press 2009), at 151 ff.
53. Case law is examined in: Diehl, *supra* n. 12, at 92; Schill, *supra* n. 52, at 163 ff.
54. Diehl, *supra* n. 12, at 534.
55. Vasciannie, *supra* n. 6, at 149.
56. Kläger, *supra* n. 11, at 265.
57. UNCTAD, *Fair and Equitable Treatment* 20 (UNCTAD Series on Issues in International Investment Agreements II, United Nations 2012).

clause from another IIA [international investment agreement] through the MFN clause should be done with care and take into account the clear intention of the parties'.[58] At any rate, this scenario will scarcely apply. The present author's own survey of some 365 BITs has shown that only 28 of them did not contain an FET clause.[59]

There is also a second scenario that can be envisaged where the BIT between States A and B *does* contain an FET clause. The question then arises as to whether or not an investor can invoke the MFN clause (contained within the BIT between A and B) in order to claim the benefit of a 'better' FET clause found in another BIT (between States B and C)? At the heart of this question is the difficult task of determining precisely what would constitute a 'better' FET clause.

As mentioned above, while the vast majority of BITs do include an FET clause, there exist several different formulations of these clauses.[60] The most important drafting distinction lies between the following two groups of provisions: clauses explicitly linking the FET to the standard existing under international law, and clauses containing an unqualified formulation of the FET obligation.[61] As highlighted above,[62] drafting variations in FET clauses have been interpreted by tribunals as entailing different content as well as different thresholds of liability.[63] The vast majority of tribunals have interpreted an unqualified FET standard as providing a higher level of treatment than its counterpart that is linked to the MST.[64] It would therefore seem that an unqualified FET clause provides (at least in theory) a 'better' legal protection for a foreign investor than an FET clause linked to the MST.[65]

This is precisely where the MFN clause comes fully into play. As shown by recent non-NAFTA case law,[66] an investor faced with a 'less-advantageous' FET clause (i.e.,

58. *Ibid.* A slightly different situation arose in the context of *Bayindir Insaat Turizm Ticaret ve Sanayi AŞ v. Pakistan*, ICSID No. ARB/03/29, Decision on Jurisdiction, (14 November 2005), paras. 227–235, involving the Pakistan-Turkey BIT, which did not include an FET standard in the main text of the treaty, but where reference to the FET standard was found in the preamble. The tribunal held that such reference to the FET standard in the preamble of the BIT allowed the use of the MFN clause in that treaty to import an FET standard found in another BIT that had been entered into by Pakistan with another State. *See,* the discussion in: Tudor, *supra* n. 11, at 191 ff.
59. P. Dumberry, *Rules of Customary International Law in the Field of International Investment Law*, SSHRC Research Project, (2012-2014).
60. *See,* Chapter 1 section §1.02[C].
61. UNCTAD, *supra* n. 57, at 17.
62. *See,* Chapter 1 section §1.03[B].
63. UNCTAD, *supra* n. 57, at 8.
64. *Ibid.*, at 22, 13 ('[A] reference in an FET clause to the minimum standard of treatment of aliens conveys a clear message that only the very serious acts of maladministration can be seen as violating the treaty. In contrast, arbitral tribunals applying unqualified FET clauses have not limited themselves to the most serious breaches and have found violations of the FET standard where they considered the State's conduct in question to be simply unfair towards the claimant').
65. This conclusion is, of course, contested by those writers who support the 'convergence theory' (*see,* Chapter 2 section §2.03[B][2][c]) whereby as a result of the alleged rapid evolution of customary international law the level of legal guarantees existing under the MST is said to be the same as those offered under an unqualified FET clause. This is, for instance, the position of Kläger, *supra* n. 11, at 288, 85 ff.
66. *MTD Equity Sdn Bhd and MTD Chile SA v. Chile,* Award, (25 May 2004), para. 104; *Rumeli Telekom A.S. and Telsim Mobil Telekomunikasyon Hizmetleri A.S. v. Kazakhstan*, ICSID No. ARB/05/16, Award, (29 July 2008), para. 575.

one where the FET is linked to the MST) can invoke the MFN clause in a BIT to obtain the 'better' protection offered by an unqualified FET clause contained within another BIT. More globally, the practical effect of such an application of the MFN clause in the context of the FET standard would be, as noted by one writer, that 'any potential difference between the different formulations of the fair and equitable treatment will likely be moot'.[67] The next section examines how NAFTA tribunals have reacted to the use of the MFN argument in the context of Article 1105.

[B]   NAFTA Case Law on the MFN Clause and Article 1105

The question examined in this section pertains to whether or not NAFTA tribunals have allowed investors to invoke NAFTA's MFN clause (Article 1103) in order to seek a 'better' FET protection contained within other BITs entered into by NAFTA Parties. This is important since NAFTA States have all entered into a great number of BITs with non-NAFTA States. These BITs generally contain FET clauses within which the language is similar to that of NAFTA Article 1105.[68] The only exceptions are some BITs entered into by Mexico,[69] and one of Canada's BITs.[70]

One potential difference between NAFTA Article 1105 and FET clauses contained in other treaties has been put forward by investors. It has been argued that FET clauses contained within these BITs have not been 'affected' by the 'limitation' imposed on Article 1105 as a result of the 2001 FTC's Note of Interpretation. In other words, an FET clause that refers to treatment in accordance with 'international law' would mean something *different* than in the context of Article 1105 with respect to which the expression 'international law' is considered as a reference to the MST under custom. Thus, as a result of the 'restrictive' interpretation now being given to the FET under Article 1105, non-NAFTA foreign investors (i.e., those originating from States that are parties to BITs with NAFTA Parties) are being offered a more favorable FET protection than the one actually accorded to foreign investors from NAFTA countries. It has been argued by several writers that foreign investors from NAFTA countries should consequently be allowed to use Article 1103 to claim the benefit of these 'better' FET clauses found in BITs entered into by NAFTA Parties.[71] The next two sections examine whether NAFTA tribunals have accepted this argument.

---

67. Newcombe & Paradell, *supra* n. 3, at 260, *see also*, at 270-271.
68. Earlier treaty practice of NAFTA Parties before the entry into force of NAFTA (1994) has already been examined above, see Chapter 2 section §2.01[A].
69. Gabriel Cavazos Villanueva, *The Fair and Equitable Treatment Standard,* 89 (VDM Verlag 2008), indicating that BITs entered into by Mexico offer a greater variety: 'some of the Mexican BITs make reference to the FET standard with respect to international law, some of them do not make such a reference, and some others do not even consider the standard'.
70. *See*, Article III (1) of the Agreement between Canada and Hungary for the Promotion and Reciprocal Protection of Investments, signed on 3 October 1991, entered into force on 21 November 1993, referring to the FET standard without any mention of 'international law'.
71. Diehl, *supra* n. 12, at 130; Charles Brower II, *Investor-State Disputes Under NAFTA: The Empire Strikes Back*, 40 Colum J. Transnat'l L. 56, ft. 71 (2001-2002); Todd Weiler, *NAFTA Investment Law in 2001: As the Legal Order Starts to Settle, the Bureaucrats Strike Back*, 36 Int'l Law 347 (2002); Todd Weiler, *NAFTA Investment Arbitration and the Growth of International Economic Law*, 2 Bus. L. Int'l 158 at 185, 187 (2002).

[1]   The Pope & Talbot Awards

In its 2001 award, the *Pope & Talbot* tribunal controversially held that, under Article 1105, investors from NAFTA countries are entitled to the protection of the minimum standard of treatment in international law *plus* the so-called 'fairness elements'.[72] The different arguments put forward by the tribunal to arrive at this conclusion have already been examined above.[73] One such argument was the 'basic unlikelihood' that NAFTA Parties intended for Article 1105 to provide each other's investors (and investments) with a more limited protection than the one actually granted in BITs to foreign investors of other countries with whom they do not share a relationship as close as the one prevailing amongst NAFTA Members.[74] The tribunal opined that it was also 'doubtful that the NAFTA Parties would want to present to potential investors and investments from other NAFTA countries the possibility that they would have no recourse to protection against anything but egregiously unfair conduct'.[75] Finally, the tribunal mentioned the following 'practical reason' for its interpretation of Article 1105:

> As noted, the contrary view of that provision would provide to NAFTA investors a more limited right to object to laws, regulation and administration than accorded to host country investors and investments as well as to those from countries that have concluded BITs with a NAFTA party. This state of affairs would surely run afoul of Articles 1102 and 1103, which give every NAFTA investor and investment the right to national and most favoured nation treatment. NAFTA investors and investments that would be denied access to the fairness elements untrammeled by the "egregious" conduct threshold that Canada would graft onto Article 1105 would simply turn to Articles 1102 and 1103 for relief.[76]

In other words, the tribunal considered that if it were to interpret Article 1105 as providing for the MST, an investor from the United States could simply turn to Article 1103 to claim the benefit of a better FET clause (one where investors receive the MST protection *plus* the 'fairness elements') found in any of the BITs entered into by Canada with other States. However, the tribunal did not have to apply its reasoning to the facts of the case for the simple reason that the claimant had withdrawn its claim under Article 1103. The tribunal's analysis on this point has been supported by some scholars.[77]

Soon after the Note was issued in July 2001, the tribunal sent a first letter to the parties to the proceedings enquiring, *inter alia*, on 'what would be the implication of Article 1103 on the Tribunal's ruling'.[78] A few months later, the tribunal sent a second letter specifically asking the NAFTA Parties the following question: 'was the Commission advised of possible conflict between the interpretation it was asked to adopt (or

---

72. *Pope & Talbot Inc. v. Canada*, Award on the Merits of Phase II, (10 April 2001), para. 110.
73. *See*, at Chapter 2 section §2.03[B][1].
74. *Pope & Talbot Inc. v. Canada*, Award on the Merits of Phase II, (10 April 2001), para. 115.
75. *Ibid.*, para. 116.
76. *Ibid.*, para. 117.
77. Tudor, *supra* n. 11, at 192; Schill, *supra* n. 52, at 142.
78. *Pope & Talbot Inc. v. Canada*, Tribunal's Response to Canada's Letter Re: NAFTA FTC Statement, (14 August 2001).

proposed to adopt) and Article 1103?'[79] In that letter, the tribunal explained its own position on the matter in unambiguous terms: '[t]he [Free Trade] Commission's interpretation would, because of Article 1103 (in the words of Article 32 of the Vienna Convention) produce the absurd result of relief denied under Article 1105 but restored under Article 1103'.[80] In other words, the 'absurdity' would consist of, on the one hand, adopting the FTC's interpretation linking the FET standard to the MST under custom, and of, on the other hand, applying the unqualified FET standard contained in other BITs entered into by Canada (through the MFN clause at NAFTA Article 1103). Canada first responded that the question asked by the tribunal was 'irrelevant and beyond its jurisdiction'[81] since no submission with respect to an Article 1103 claim was made (the investor had abandoned that claim earlier during the proceedings). In any event, Canada argued that the FTC Interpretation was binding on tribunals and that 'NAFTA cannot operate so as to create a conflict between Article 1103 and the interpretation'.[82] Mexico and the United States openly supported Canada's view on this point.[83]

In its subsequent award rendered in 2002,[84] the tribunal did not further discuss the effect of Article 1103 on the FET standard under Article 1105; it simply reiterated the position that it had earlier taken in its previous award.[85]

[2]   Awards Rendered after the FTC's Note

Soon after the FTC issued its Note, several investors started to invoke Article 1103 to benefit from the 'better' FET protection found in BITs entered into by the United States and Canada with other States. Thus, in ADF, the Canadian claimant sought relief under Article 1103 by turning to US BITs entered into with Albania and Estonia.[86] A similar argument was also advanced by the Canadian claimant in the Methanex case. It argued

---

79. *Ibid.*, Tribunal's Second Response Re: NAFTA FTC Statement, (17 September 2001), at 2.
80. *Ibid.*
81. *Pope & Talbot Inc. v. Canada*, Canada's Second Submission Re: the NAFTA FTC Statement, (1 October 2001), at 3.
82. *Ibid.*, Canada's Letter (1 October 2001), at 3. Canada also added that 'it would be absurd' 'for a tribunal to ignore or question a binding interpretation of the Commission through reference to another provision of the NAFTA, or such provisions' supposed "practical" effects'.
83. *Ibid.*, Mexico's Letter, (5 October 2001); US Sixth Submission, (2 October 2001).
84. The award is examined at Chapter 2 section §2.03[B][1].
85. *Pope & Talbot Inc. v. Canada*, Award in Respect of Damages, (31 May 2002), para. 9: 'Briefly, the Tribunal determined that, notwithstanding the language of Article 1105, which admittedly suggests otherwise, the requirement to accord NAFTA investors fair and equitable treatment was independent of, not subsumed by the requirement to accord them treatment required by international law. The Tribunal believed that this interpretation was compelled for three reasons: (...) Since investors from countries signatory to those treaties [i.e. BITs concluded by NAFTA Parties with other States] were thus entitled to fair and equitable treatment without regard to any limitations that might be inherent in international law, NAFTA investors could claim the same rights under the most favoured nation provisions of Article 1103. Consequently, the Tribunal concluded that it would make no sense to deny those rights under Article 1105, only to find them revived pursuant to Article 1103 (...)'.
86. *ADF Group Inc. v. United States*, ICSID No. ARB (AF)/00/1, Investor's Reply to the US Counter-Memorial on Competence and Liability, (28 January 2002), paras. 219, 221 ff.

that it was entitled to the same FET protection as the more favorable one accorded to investors under US BITs entered into with Argentina and Tunisia.[87]

The controversial effect of Article 1103 on the FET standard was first examined by the *UPS* tribunal. The US investor argued that it was entitled to the 'higher' standard of protection found in BITs entered into by Canada which refers to the FET in accordance with 'international law' rather than the 'lower' standard of protection under Article 1105.[88] Canada argued that the investor had failed to demonstrate that these other BITs included a more favorable FET protection than Article 1105.[89] In fact, according to Canada, the treaties provided for the exact same treatment as NAFTA.[90] The tribunal simply rejected the Article 1103 claim on the ground that the investor had not specifically argued this head of damages during the proceedings.[91]

In *ADF*, the Canadian investor also tried to expand Article 1105's scope by relying on Article 1103.[92] Specifically, the investor alluded to the US-Albania and US-Estonia BITs and argued that both treaties provided a higher standard of protection to which NAFTA investors were entitled.[93] The United States responded that the tribunal lacked jurisdiction to hear an Article 1103 claim.[94] It also argued that the FET standard under these BITs was the same as the one under Article 1105.[95] The tribunal first reiterated its earlier conclusion that the '[i]nvestor ha[d] not been able persuasively to document the existence of such autonomous [FET] standards' distinct from customary international law.[96] It therefore rejected the claimant's argument that these BITs provide a better treatment compared to the one contained within NAFTA Article 1105.[97] The tribunal ultimately denied the investor's Article 1103 claim based on technical grounds: NAFTA

---

87. *Methanex v. United States*, Letter by the Claimant to the Tribunal, (18 September 2001), at 21, 22; Investor's First Submissions on FTC Notes, (18 September 2001), at 3, 21, 22.
88. *United Parcel Service of America Inc. v. Canada* [hereinafter *UPS v. Canada*], UNCITRAL, Investor's Memorial (Merits), (23 March 2005), paras. 682, 707.
89. *Ibid.*, Canada's Counter-Memorial (Merits), (22 June 2005), paras. 998, 1008, 1015–1016.
90. *Ibid.*, paras. 1009, 1011–1014.
91. *Ibid.*, Award on Jurisdiction, (24 May 2007), para. 184. Thus, after having summarized the Parties' respective position on Article 1103, the tribunal stated that 'At the hearing counsel for UPS gave very limited attention to the claimed breaches of the most favored nation obligation to this argument' focusing instead on egregious nature of claimed breaches of Article 1105. The tribunal simply noted that 'in the absence of any further specification of the claimed breaches of article 1103 (and 1104) this claim must fail'.
92. *ADF Group Inc. v. United States*, Investor's Reply to the US Counter-Memorial on Competence and Liability, (28 January 2002), para. 221.
93. *Ibid.*, paras. 222–223, 238–239.
94. *Ibid.*, US Rejoinder, (29 March 2002), at 4, 38.
95. *Ibid.*, at 40-44. To support its argument, the United States referred to the US Department of State's statements in submitting these treaties to the United States Senate for advice and consent, which clearly indicated that the FET standard contained in both BITs 'sets out a minimum standard of treatment based on standards found in customary international law'.
96. *Ibid.*, Award, (9 January 2003), para. 194.
97. *Ibid.* This conclusion is also supported by the tone used by the tribunal in the award (para. 196): 'Assuming, once more, for purposes of argument merely, that the U.S.-Albania and U.S.-Estonia treaties do provide for better treatment for Albanian and Estonian investors and their invest-ments in the United States'. In any event, the tribunal further stated that 'the Investor has not shown that the U.S. measures are reasonably characterized as in breach of such standards'.

Article 1108(7)(a) excludes the application of Article 1103 in a case involving governmental procurement by a Party (such as in the instant case).[98] This case shows the limited effectiveness of an MFN clause that contains explicit restrictions to its application.[99]

The US investor in *Chemtura* argued that 'if the Tribunal holds that the standard under Article 1105 is less favorable than the independent FET standard provided in third party BITs to which Canada is a party, the claimant is entitled to receive the more favorable treatment by virtue of NAFTA Article 1103 combined with a third party BIT'.[100] In other words, the claimant argued that it should be entitled to the 'higher' FET standard found in Canada's BITs through Article 1103.[101] In fact, the investor referred specifically to 16 post-1994 BITs signed by Canada which provide for the FET in accordance with 'international law' or the 'principles of international law'.[102] In response, Canada argued, *inter alia*, that its post-NAFTA investment agreements offer no more favorable treatment to investors than Article 1105 since they all point to the application of the FET in accordance with the minimum standard of treatment.[103] In any event, Canada also argued that the claimant had failed to establish any of the legal elements necessary to demonstrate a breach of Article 1103.[104] Mexico and the United States agreed with Canada's position that Article 1103 does not alter the substantive content of the FET obligation under Article 1105.[105]

The *Chemtura* tribunal first noted that there was simply no proof supporting the claimant's allegation that its investment had been the object of any discrimination by Canada. It concluded that its claim was therefore 'deprived of legal foundation'.[106] The tribunal also held that even if it were possible to import a higher FET protection through Article 1103, this standard was not breached given the evidence presented by the claimant:

> [T]he Tribunal turns to the alternative claim that the Claimant's investment was
> treated in breach of a more favorable FET clause applicable through Article 1103 of

---

98. *Ibid.*, paras. 197, 198.
99. Schill, *supra* n. 52, at 142-143.
100. *Chemtura Corporation v. Canada*, UNCITRAL, Award, (2 August 2010), para. 226.
101. *Ibid.*, Investor's Memorial, (2 June 2008), paras. 489–494; Investor's Reply, (15 May 2009), at 143-179.
102. *Ibid.*, Award, (2 August 2010), para. 226, referring to Investor's Memorial, (2 June 2008), para. 489-490. According to the investor, these BITs 'stand in contrast to the NAFTA and to a limited number of bilateral treaties in which fair and equitable treatment is specifically tied to the minimum standard of treatment provided for in customary international law'.
103. *Ibid.*, Canada's Counter Memorial, (20 October 2008), paras. 875, 887, 889, 896; *ibid.*, Canada's Rejoinder, (10 July 2009), paras. 235, 245; *ibid.*, Award, (2 August 2010), para. 228.
104. *Ibid.*, Award, (2 August 2010), para. 229: 'More specifically, the Respondent argues that the Claimant has failed to establish any of the legal elements necessary for a breach of Article 1103. In particular, it fails to establish (i) that a "treatment" was accorded; (ii) that such treatment was "with respect to the establishment, acquisition, expansion, management, conduct, operation, and sale or other disposition of investments"; (iii) that such treatment was accorded "in like circumstances"; and (iv) that it was "less favourable" than the treatment accorded to investors or investments of a non-Party.'
105. *Ibid.*, US Article 1128 Submission, (31 July 2009); Mexico's Article 1128 Submission, (31 July 2009).
106. *Ibid.*, Award, (2 August 2010), para. 234.

NAFTA. The Respondent as well as the United States and Mexico in their Article 1128 interventions (US Submission, 31 July 2009; Mexico's Submission, 31 July 2009) firmly oppose of the possibility of importing a FET clause from a BIT concluded by Canada. The Tribunal can dispense with resolving this issue as a matter of principle. Indeed, even if it were admissible to import a BIT FET clause, the conclusions reached by the Tribunal on the basis of the facts would remain unchanged.[107]

In the next paragraph, the tribunal further explained that it had found 'no facts in the conduct of the Respondent that would even come close to the type of treatment required for a breach of the FET standard'.[108] In any event, the tribunal mentioned that the investor did not prove that the FET standard under a BIT provides a higher level of protection than that accorded by NAFTA: 'the Claimant has not established that the FET clause of any of the treaties to which it indistinctly refers grants any additional measure of protection not afforded by Article 1105 of NAFTA'.[109] The claimant had 'not established that the Respondent's conduct was in breach of such hypothetical additional measure of protection allegedly afforded by an imported FET clause'.[110]

It is submitted that both the *ADF* and the *Chemtura* tribunals were correct in their assessment (and that the *Pope & Talbot* tribunal was incorrect). FET clauses in BITs and Article 1105 basically provide for the *same level* of protection: the MST under customary international law. This has been the intent of the NAFTA Parties all along. The FTC's Note does not in any way 'restrict' the scope of the FET standard under Article 1105. For this reason, it is submitted that there is simply no reason for investors to invoke Article 1103 in the specific context of Article 1105.[111]

§4.05 ARTICLE 1105 AND NATIONAL TREATMENT

Under a national treatment clause, the host country must provide foreign investors with a treatment that is at least as favorable as the treatment that it accords to its own national investors in like circumstances.[112] In BITs, the national treatment and the FET standard are found in separate clauses because of their different nature.[113] The national

---

107. *Ibid.*, para. 235.
108. *Ibid.*, para. 236. The tribunal added that 'Quite to the contrary, the record shows that the Respondent treated the Claimant and its investment in good faith and on an equal footing with other registrants of lindane-based products'.
109. *Ibid.*
110. *Ibid.*
111. It should be added that Canada's Model BIT (2004) explicitly prevents investors from invoking the MFN clause to get any better treatment under other BITs entered into by Canada, *see* Annex III entitled 'Exceptions from Most-Favoured-Nation Treatment', Article 1: 'Article 4 [the MFN clause] shall not apply to treatment accorded under all bilateral or multilateral international agreements in force or signed prior to the date of entry into of this Agreement'.
112. UNCTAD, *National Treatment*, 1 (UNCTAD Series on Issues in International Investment Agreements, United Nations, 1999).
113. *UPS v. Canada*, Award on Jurisdiction, (22 November 2002), para. 80 ('The other two protections are very common in international treaty practice. They require national treatment under article 1102 and most favoured nation treatment under article 1103 (with the better treatment of the two being accorded under article 1104). Those obligations are relative. They depend simply and solely on the specifics of the treatment the Party accords to its own investors

treatment clause sets out a 'relative' standard that is defined according to the treatment granted to the host State's own investors. The FET is an 'absolute' and 'objective' standard of protection. It applies to 'investments in a given situation without reference to how other investments or entities are treated by the host State' and, accordingly, the host State is 'unable to resist a claim under this standard by saying that the treatment is no different from that experienced by their own nationals or other foreign investors operating in their economy'.[114] As explained by the *ADF* tribunal, 'where the treatment accorded by a State under its domestic law to its own nationals falls below the minimum standard of treatment required under customary international law, non-nationals become entitled to better treatment than that which the State accords under its domestic law'.[115] The MST is also an 'objective' standard of protection.[116]

. The fact that the national treatment and the FET standard offer different types of legal protection to foreign investors has some practical consequences. On the one hand, the host State's compliance with the national treatment standard can neverthe-less be considered as breaching the obligation to provide foreign investors with an FET.[117] This is in fact the conclusion reached by the *Pope & Talbot* tribunal.[118]

On the other hand, the finding of a discriminatory act in violation of Article 1102 is not automatically conducive to a breach of Article 1105.[119] As mentioned above,[120] the FTC Note overruled the reasoning of the *S.D. Myers* award[121] and made it clear that

---

or investors of third States. Article 1105, by contrast, states a generally applicable, minimum standard which, depending on the circumstances, may require more than the relative obliga-tions of articles 1102 and 1103').

114. UNCTAD, *supra* n. 57, at 6.

115. *ADF Group Inc. v. United States*, Award, (9 January 2003), para. 178.

116. *S.D. Myers Inc. v. Canada*, First Partial Award, (13 November 2000), para. 259: 'The inclusion of a 'minimum standard' provision is necessary to avoid what might otherwise be a gap. A government might treat an investor in a harsh, injurious and unjust manner, but do so in a way that is no different than the treatment inflicted on its own nationals. The 'minimum standard' is a floor below which treatment of foreign investors must not fall, even if a government were not acting in a discriminatory manner'. *See also: Glamis Gold, Ltd. v. United States*, UNCITRAL, Award, (8 June 2009), para. 615: 'The customary international law minimum standard of treatment is just that, a minimum standard. It is meant to serve as a floor, an absolute bottom, below which conduct is not accepted by the international community. Although the circum-stances of the case are of course relevant, the standard is not meant to vary from state to state or investor to investor. The protection afforded by Article 1105 must be distinguished from that provided for in Article 1102 on National Treatment. (...) The treatment of investors under Article 1102 is compared to the treatment the State's own investors receive and thus can vary greatly depending on each State and its practices. The fair and equitable treatment promised by Article 1105 is not dynamic; it cannot vary between nations as thus the protection afforded would have no minimum' (*see also*, para. 619).

117. Kläger, *supra* n. 11, at 285; Diehl, *supra* n. 12, at 534.

118. *Pope & Talbot Inc. v. Canada*, Award on the Merits of Phase II, (10 April 2001), paras. 104, 181. The tribunal concluded that the measure adopted by Canada did not breach Article 1102, but that one aspect of the program (the so-called 'verification review process') was in violation of Article 1105.

119. Kläger, *supra* n. 11, at 285.

120. *See*, Chapter 2 section §2.02[C][3][a].

121. *S.D. Myers Inc. v. Canada*, First Partial Award, (13 November 2000), paras. 264–266.

the finding of a breach of one provision does not establish a breach of Article 1105.[122] This is because, as mentioned above,[123] both provisions deal with different types of discrimination: Article 1102 covers discrimination based on the foreign nationality of an investor, and Article 1105 covers other types of discrimination against a foreign investor (such as specific targeting and discrimination based on race, sex and religion[124]). The fact that the FET standard protects investors from some types of (non-nationality based) discrimination is largely supported by scholars.[125] Yet, as mentioned above,[126] NAFTA case law on this last point is still unsettled. At the most, it can be said that the reasoning of some NAFTA tribunals can be interpreted, to some extent, as suggesting that Article 1105 may cover some type of discrimination (other than nationality-based).[127]

§4.06   ARTICLE 1105 AND FULL PROTECTION AND SECURITY

The host State's obligations to provide full protection and security ('FPS') and the FET are closely linked. In fact, they are often part of the same treaty provision. This is, indeed, the case with NAFTA Article 1105.[128]

Yet, the two obligations are nonetheless distinct.[129] The main difference lies in the fact that FPS imposes a due diligence obligation to respect the physical protection of investors against acts of violence and harassment.[130] Earlier ICSID cases interpreting this clause (such as *AAPL v. Sri Lanka*,[131] *AMT v. Zaire*[132] and *Wena v. Egypt*[133]) involved acts of violence and destruction to persons and property during armed conflict and riots.[134] It is generally recognized that the standard imposes a 'general obligation

---

122. *See also, ibid.*, para. 266, where the tribunal mentioned that it did 'not rule out the possibility that there could be circumstances in which a denial of the national treatment provision of the NAFTA would not necessarily offend the minimum standard provision'.
123. *See,* Chapter 3 section §3.02[E][1].
124. UNCTAD, *supra* n. 57, at 82.
125. *See,* Chapter 3 section §3.02[E][1] for reference to several writers.
126. *See,* Chapter 3 section §3.02[E][4].
127. *Waste Management, Inc. v. Mexico ("Number 2")*, ICSID No. ARB(AF)/00/3, Award, (30 April 2004), para. 98; *Methanex v. United States*, Award, (3 August 2005), Part IV, Ch. C, para. 26; *Glamis Gold, Ltd. v. United States*, Award, (8 June 2009), paras. 616, 22, 24, 627, 762, 765, 776, 779, 788, 824, 828.
128. Article 1105: 'Each Party shall accord to investments of investors of another Party treatment in accordance with international law, including fair and equitable treatment *and full protection and security*' (emphasis added).
129. Christoph Schreuer, *Full Protection and Security*, 1(2) JIDS 13 (2010) ('The view that the two standards are to be seen as different obligations appears to be the better one. As a matter of interpretation, it appears unconvincing to assume that two standards listed separately in the same document have the same meaning. An interpretation that deprives a treaty provision of meaning is implausible'); Diehl, *supra* n. 12, at 534.
130. Tudor, *supra* n. 11, at 185; Kläger, *supra* n. 11, at 295; Dolzer & Schreuer, *supra* n. 11, at 149; Diehl, *supra* n. 12, at 529.
131. *AAPL v. Sri Lanka*, ICSID No. ARB/87/3, Award, (27 June 1990).
132. *AMT Inc. v. Zaire*, ICSID No. ARB/93/1, Award, (10 February 1997).
133. *Wena Hotels Ltd. v. Egypt*, ICSID No. ARB/98/4, Award, (8 December 2000).
134. UNCTAD, *Investor–State Dispute Settlement and Impact on Investment Rulemaking*, 46 (United Nations 2007).

for the host State to exercise due diligence' in the protection of foreign investment, but not 'strict liability'.[135] The threshold for finding a breach of the FPS obligation remains high.

The difference with the FET standard is clear. Thus, while FPS is concerned with 'failures by the State to protect the investor's property from actual damage caused by either miscreant State officials, or by the actions of others, where the State has failed to exercise due diligence', the FET deals with 'the process of decision-making by the organs of the State' and 'the exercise of police power'.[136] The FET and the FPS standards are therefore complementary: 'one cover[s] the physical protection of the investments and investors, [while] the other one cover[s], the treatment of investments and investors as a whole'.[137] Also, one standard (FPS) imposes an active obligation to do something on States while the other (FET) simply prevents States from doing something.[138]

Recent case law has, however, blurred this apparent clear-cut distinction between the two standards. Thus, some awards have examined these standards (contained within separate clauses) together, without making any distinction between the two.[139] Moreover, a number of other tribunals have interpreted the FPS obligation to cover not only physical protection but also a much broader obligation for States to guarantee 'stability in a secure environment, both physical, commercial and legal'.[140] Such is the case of the *Azurix* tribunal which, while considering both concepts as

---

135. R. Dolzer & M. Stevens, *Bilateral Investment Treaties* (Martinus Nijhoff 1995), at 149, 150; Schreuer, *supra* n. 129, at 14; Dolzer & Schreuer, *supra* n. 11, at 149, 150; Diehl, *supra* n. 12, at 530 ('the obligation to provide full protection and security is discharged if the State has taken some measures of vigilance that do not seem unreasonable. Due diligence thus amounts to the taking of reasonable measures of prevention which a well-administered government could be expected to implement under similar circumstances').
136. C. McLachlan, L. Shore & M. Weiniger, *International Investment Arbitration: Substantive Principles*, 226-247 (Oxford U. Press 2007). *See also*: Diehl, *supra* n. 12, at 531; Schreuer, *supra* n. 129, at 14.
137. Diehl, *supra* n. 12, at 531. *See also*: Tudor, *supra* n. 11, at 185.
138. Schreuer, *supra* n. 9, at 4 ('As a matter of substance, the content of the two standards is distinguishable. The fair and equitable treatment standard consists mainly of an obligation on the host State's part to desist from a certain course of action. By contrast, by promising full protection and security the host State assumes an obligation to actively create a framework that grants security').
139. *See*, cases examined in: Giuditta Cordero Moss, *Full Protection and Security*, in *Standards of Investment Protection* 146-149 (August Reinisch ed., Oxford U. Press 2008).
140. *Biwater Gauff (Tanzania) Ltd. v. Tanzania*, ICSID No. ARB/05/22, (24 July 2008), para. 729 ('The Arbitral Tribunal adheres to the Azurix holding that when the terms "protection" and "security" are qualified by "full," the content of the standard may extend to matters other than physical security. It implies a State's guarantee of stability in a secure environment, both physical, commercial and legal. It would in the Arbitral Tribunal's view be unduly artificial to confine the notion of "full security" only to one aspect of security, particularly in light of the use of this term in a BIT, directed at the protection of commercial and financial investments'). *See also*: *CME Czech Republic B.V. v. Czech Republic*, UNCITRAL, Award, (14 March 2003), para. 613; *Siemens A.G. v. Argentina*, ICSID No. ARB/02/8, Award, (17 January 2007), paras. 286, 303, 308; *Compañiá de Aguas del Aconquija S.A. and Vivendi Universal S.A. v. Argentina*, ICSID No. ARB/97/3, (20 August 2007) paras. 7.4.12, 7.4.15, 7.4.17; *Frontier Petroleum Services Ltd. v. Czech Republic*, UNCITRAL, Final Award, (12 November 2010), para. 263; *National Grid plc v. Argentina*, UNCITRAL, Award, (3 November 2008), para. 189.

consisting of separate obligations,[141] nonetheless concluded that the obligation to accord FPS extended further than physical security and included the 'stability afforded by a secure investment environment'.[142] The tribunal based its position on the use of the word 'full' before 'protection and security'.[143] A number of writers support the view that FPS covers legal security.[144] The consequence of extending the scope of FPS is that a treatment contrary to the FET 'automatically entails an absence of full protection and security'.[145] This consequence has led a number of other tribunals to continue distinguishing the two concepts. They have adopted the traditional interpretation which limits FPS solely to physical protection.[146] This distinction is also supported by writers.[147]

In sum, arbitral practice has not been uniform with regards to the actual scope of the obligation to provide FPS to investors.[148] However, these uncertainties will only have a limited practical impact since most BITs include provisions granting both FET and the FPS protections.[149] The present author's own survey of 365 BITs has shown that some 91 of them did not contain any reference to FPS.[150] In such cases, there is no doubt that an FET clause (contained within an overwhelming majority of BITs[151]) would cover physical protection of investors against acts of violence and harassment traditionally associated with the FPS clause. This has led some writers to argue that 'a guarantee of full protection and security seems to add little to a fair and equitable treatment clause in an investment agreement'.[152]

No NAFTA tribunal has addressed the interaction between the FET and the FPS obligations. In their pleadings, NAFTA Parties have, however, drawn a distinction

---

141. *Azurix Corp. v. Argentina*, ICSID No. ARB/01/12, Award, (14 July 2006), para. 407.
142. *Ibid.*, para. 408.
143. *Ibid.* ('when the terms "protection and security" are qualified by "full" and no other adjective or explanation, they extend, in their ordinary meaning, the content of this standard beyond physical security').
144. Newcombe & Paradell, *supra* n. 3, at 313; Dolzer & Schreuer, *supra* n. 11, at 149, 151; T.W. Wälde, *Energy Charter Treaty-based Investment Arbitration*, 5 J. World Invest. & Trade 390-391 (2004).
145. *Occidental Exploration and Production Company v. Ecuador*, LCIA No. 3467, Award, (1 July 2004), para. 187. *See also*: *PSEG Global, Inc., The North American Coal Corporation, and Konya Ingin Electrik Üretim ve Ticaret Limited Sirketi v. Turkey*, Award, (19 January 2007), paras. 257–259.
146. *Enron Corporation and Ponderosa Assets, L.P. v. Argentina*, ICSID No. ARB/01/3, Award, (22 May 2007), para. 286; *PSEG Global Inc. and Konya Elektrik Uretim ve Ticaret Limited Sirketi v. Turkey*, Award, (17 January 2007), paras. 257, 258, 259; *Saluka Investments B.V. v. Czech Republic*, UNCITRAL Partial Award, (17 March 2006), paras. 483, 484; *BG Group Plc. v. Argentina*, UNCITRAL, Award, (24 December 2007), para. 324; *Rumeli Telekom A.S. and Telsim Mobil Telekomunikasyon Hizmetleri A.S. v. Kazakhstan*, Award, (29 July 2008), para. 668; *Eastern Sugar B.V. (Netherlands) v. Czech Republic*, SCC No. 088/2004, Award, (12 April 2007), para. 203.
147. Dolzer & Schreuer, *supra* n. 11, at 149; Schreuer, *supra* n. 129, at 34; Diehl, *supra* n. 12, at 531.
148. Dolzer & Schreuer, *supra* n. 11, at 149; Kläger, *supra* n. 11, at 294; Newcombe & Paradell, *supra* n. 3, at 312.
149. Newcombe & Paradell, *supra* n. 3, at 313.
150. Dumberry, *supra* n. 59.
151. *Ibid.*, of the 365 BITs examined, only 28 of them did not contain a reference to the FET standard.
152. Kläger, *supra* n. 11, at 295; Tudor, *supra* n. 11, at 186.

between the two different types of protection.[153] As a result of the wider interpretation given by some (non-NAFTA) tribunals to the FPS obligation, the US Model BIT now expressly states that the FPS obligation requires 'each party to provide the level of police protection required under customary international law'.[154] As have a number of non-NAFTA tribunals,[155] NAFTA Parties have long recognized that the MST under customary international law includes an obligation for host States to provide FPS. This is clear from the heading of Article 1105 (which refers to MST) and the FTC Note.[156]

---

153. *Merrill & Ring Forestry L.P. v. Canada*, UNCITRAL, Canada's Counter Memorial, (13 May 2008), para. 541.
154. US Model BIT (2012), Article 5(2)(b).
155. *AAPL v. Sri Lanka*, Award, (27 June 1990), paras. 85–86; *Amco Asia Corporation and Others v. Indonesia*, ICSID No. ARB/81/1, Award, (20 November 1984), para. 172; *Noble Ventures, Inc. v. Romania*, Award, (12 October 2005), para. 164.
156. The Note indicates that both the FPS and the FET 'do not require treatment in addition to or beyond that which is required by the customary international law minimum standard of treatment of aliens'.

CHAPTER 5

Assessment of Damages

BITs generally include specific provisions on compensation concerning expropriation without alluding to non-expropriatory breaches. Thus, NAFTA Articles 1105, 1102 and 1103 do not give any indication concerning the assessment of compensation in the case of a breach. This section examines how NAFTA tribunals have assessed damages in cases of breach of the FET standard.[1] However, before undertaking such an analysis, we must first examine the basic rules of international law regarding reparation (section §5.01) as well as some of the applicable principles in the specific context of breach of the FET standard (section §5.02).

§5.01 BASIC RULES ON REPARATION UNDER INTERNATIONAL LAW

Article 31 of the I.L.C.'s Articles on State Responsibility provides that a State must make 'full reparation' for any 'injury' caused to another State by an internationally

---

1. K. Hobér, *Compensation: A Closer Look at Cases Awarding Compensation for Violation of the Fair and Equitable Treatment Standard*, in *Arbitration under International Investment Agreements: A Guide to the Key Issues* (Katia Yannaca-Small ed., Oxford U. Press 2010); M. Weiniger, *The Standard of Compensation for Violation of the Fair and Equitable Treatment Standard*, in *Investment Treaty Law, Current Issues II* (F. Ortino ed., 2007); K. Hobér, *Fair and Equitable Treatment: Determining Compensation*, 6 Transnational Disp. Mgmt. (2007): B.C. Kaczmarek, *Compensation for Non-Expropriatory Treaty Violations: An Analytical Framework*, 3 Transnational Disp. Mgmt. (2006); Kathryn Khamsi, *Compensation for Non-Expropriatory Investment Treaty Breaches in the Argentine Gas Sector Cases: Issues and Implications*, in *The Backlash Against Investment Arbitration: Perceptions and Reality* (Michael Waibel et al., eds., Kluwer Law 2010); Jorge E. Viñuales & Pierre-Yves Tschanz, *Compensation for Non-Expropriatory Breaches of International Investment Law-The Contribution of the Argentine Awards*, 26 J. Int. Arb. 729–743 (2009); Sergey Ripinsky & Kevin Williams, *Damages in International Investment Law* (British IICL 2008); Irmgard Marboe, *Calculation of Compensation and Damages in International Investment Law* (Oxford U. Press 2009).

wrongful act.[2] The same provision also states that the concept of 'injury' includes 'any damage, whether material or moral, caused by the internationally wrongful act of a State'.[3] Article 34 of the I.L.C. Articles indicates that there are three different methods of reparation: restitution, compensation and satisfaction. The general rule under Article 35 is that a 'State responsible for an internationally wrongful act is under an obligation to make restitution', i.e., 'to re-establish the situation which existed before the wrongful act was committed'. Compensation is considered the appropriate reparatory measure whenever restitution *in integrum* is not possible. I.L.C. Article 36 reads as follows:

1. The State responsible for an internationally wrongful act is under an obligation to compensate for the damage caused thereby, insofar as such damage is not made good by restitution.
2. The compensation shall cover any financially assessable damage including loss of profits insofar as it is established.

Thus, according to the I.L.C., 'material and moral damage resulting from an internationally wrongful act will normally be financially assessable and hence covered by the remedy of compensation'.[4] The only limitation to compensation as the appropriate reparatory measure is that the damage must be 'financially assessable'.[5]

The I.L.C. Articles include a third type of reparation: 'satisfaction'. Under Article 37(1), '[t]he State responsible for an internationally wrongful act is under an obligation to give satisfaction for the injury caused by that act insofar as it cannot be made good by restitution or compensation'.[6] The I.L.C. Commentaries suggest that satisfaction is an exceptional form of reparation for injury.[7] In fact, NAFTA Article 1135 limits the remedies to monetary damages or restitution of property.

---

2. Article 31, *Titles and Texts of the Draft Articles on Responsibility of States for Internationally Wrongful Acts Adopted by the Drafting Committee on Second Reading*, 26 July 2001, U.N. Doc. A/CN.4/L.602/Rev.1.ILC (hereinafter 'I.L.C. Articles on State Responsibility').
3. Article 31(2).
4. *Commentaries to the Draft Articles on Responsibility of States for Internationally Wrongful Acts Adopted by the International Law Commission at its Fifty-Third Session (2001)*, November 2001, Report of the I.L.C. on the work of its Fifty-Third Session, Official Records of the General Assembly, Fifty-Sixth Session, Supplement No. 10 (A/56/10), chp.IV.E.2) (hereinafter 'I.L.C. Commentaries'), at 264.
5. According to the I.L.C. Commentaries, *ibid.*, at 264, 'material and *moral damage* resulting from an internationally wrongful act will *normally* be financially assessable and hence covered by the remedy of compensation' (emphasis added).
6. Articles 37(2), 37(3), I.L.C. Articles on State Responsibility, *supra* n. 2, read as follows: '2. Satisfaction may consist in an acknowledgement of the breach, an expression of regret, a formal apology or another appropriate modality; 3. Satisfaction shall not be out of proportion to the injury and may not take a form humiliating to the responsible State'.
7. I.L.C. Commentaries, *supra* n. 4, at 263 ('[i]t is only in those cases where those two forms [i.e. restitution and compensation] have not provided full reparation the satisfaction may be required').

§5.02 REPARATION FOR BREACH OF THE FAIR AND EQUITABLE TREATMENT STANDARD

Restitution in kind is rarely ordered by BIT tribunals.[8] The same is true for satisfaction due to the fact that this method has been considered by many international courts and tribunals as the proper means of reparation for non-material injury caused *directly to a State*.[9] Since investment tribunals (almost always) deal with claims submitted by *investors* (not States), the issue of satisfaction (almost) never arises.[10] The *dictum* of two recent awards[11] has, however, raised the issue of whether a tribunal established under a BIT can remediate *moral damages* suffered by a foreign investor with satisfaction in the form of a declaration of wrongfulness.[12]

The usual form of reparation in investor-State arbitration is monetary compensation.[13] It should be noted that there is some debate in academia surrounding the determination of whether the term 'damages' should be used for non-expropriatory breaches (such as the FET) instead of the word 'compensation'.[14] In any event, scholars recognize a basic distinction between two situations of a breach of the FET standard which call for different evaluation methods:

- Cases where a violation of the FET standard leads to a *total loss* or deprivation of the investment (section §5.02[A]).

---

8. C. Schreuer & R. Dolzer, *Principles of International Investment Law* 270 (Oxford U. Press 2008). The issue is examined in: Christoph Schreuer, *Non-Pecuniary Remedies in ICSID Arbitration*, 20(4) Arb. Int. 325-332 (2004); Abby Cohen Smutny, *Some Observations on the Principles Relating to Compensation in the Investment Treaty Context*, 22(1) ICSID Rev. 4-5 (2007); T.W. Wälde & B. Sabahi, *Compensation, Damages, and Valuation*, in *The Oxford Handbook of International Investment Law* 1058-1059 (Peter Muchlinski, Federico Ortino & Christoph Schreuer eds., Oxford U. Press 2008).

9. *Second Report on State Responsibility*, by Mr. Gaetano Arangio-Ruiz, Special Rapporteur, in *Yearbook ILC*, vol. II, Part one (1989) (A/CN.4/425), at 1-59, at para. 136.

10. It should be added that two recent cases (*Europe Cement Investment & Trade S.A. v. Turkey*, ICSID No. ARB(AF)/07/2, Award, (13 August 2009); *Cementownia 'Nowa Huta' S.A. v. Turkey*, ICSID No. ARB(AF)/06/2, Award, (17 September 2009)) have raised the unprecedented issue of the proper remedy for moral damages suffered by a *State* in international investment law. In both related cases, Turkey sought an award of monetary compensation for moral damages it allegedly suffered with regards to its 'reputation and international standing' as a result of baseless claims filed by the investors. This unusual request by a respondent State raises the question whether satisfaction is the appropriate remedy to redress any moral damages suffered *by a State* in the context of international investment law. The question is examined in: P. Dumberry, *Satisfaction as a Form of Reparation for Moral Damages Suffered by Investors and Respondent States in Investor-State Arbitration Disputes*, 3(1) JIDS 205-242 (2012).

11. *Victor Pey Casado and President Allende Foundation v. Chile*, ICSID No. ARB/98/2, Award, (8 May 2008); *Joseph Charles Lemire v. Ukraine*, ICSID No. ARB/06/18, Award, (28 March 2011).

12. *See*, Dumberry, *supra* n. 10.

13. Dolzer & Schreuer, *supra* n. 8, at 271.

14. Some scholars (and some tribunals, *see*: *LG&E Energy Corp., LG&E Capital Corp., and LG&E International, Inc v. Argentina* [hereinafter *LG&E v. Argentina*], ICSID No. ARB/02/1, Award, (25 July 2007), para. 38) distinguish the concept of 'compensation' (resulting from a *lawful* expropriation) from that of 'damages' (which is limited to *unlawful* expropriation or *non-expropriatory* breaches). These distinctions are discussed in: Marboe, *supra* n. 1, para. 2.03 ff. Most authors, however, use the term compensation to cover all situations.

- Cases where a violation of the FET standard only results in a *decrease* in the value of the investment (section §5.02[B]).

[A]   Situations where a Breach of the Fair and Equitable Treatment Standard Leads to a Total Loss of the Investment

There are instances where a violation of the FET standard leads to a *total loss* or deprivation of the investment. Since such cases are akin to expropriation, the same valuation method (i.e., 'fair market value'[15]) is used.[16]

For instance, in *Metalclad* the tribunal came to the conclusion that Mexico had committed both a violation of Article 1105 and an expropriation. Since the claimant had lost its investment in its entirety, the tribunal held that the valuation method existing for expropriation should be used:

> In this instance, the damages arising under NAFTA, Article 1105 and the compensation due under NAFTA, Article 1110 would be the same since both situations involve the complete frustration of the operation of the landfill and negate the possibility of any meaningful return on Metalclad's investment. In other words, Metalclad has completely lost its investment.[17]

The *Metalclad* tribunal then referred to NAFTA Article 1110(2) which 'specifically requires compensation to be equivalent to the fair market value of the expropriated investment immediately before the expropriation took place'.[18] The tribunal also explained that '[n]ormally, the fair market value of a going concern which has a history of profitable operation may be based on an estimate of future profits subject to a discounted cash flow analysis'.[19] It also added that 'where the enterprise has not operated for a sufficiently long time to establish a performance record or where it has failed to make a profit, future profits cannot be used to determine going concern or fair market value'.[20] In this context, any award based on future profits would be wholly

---

15. The tribunal in *Enron Corporation and Ponderosa Assets, LP v. Argentina*, ICSID No. ARB/01/3, Award, (22 May 2007), para. 361, described the fair market value method as follows: 'the price at which property would change hands between a hypothetical willing and able buyer and an hypothetical willing and able seller, absent compulsion to buy or sell, and having the parties reasonable knowledge of the facts, all of it in an open and unrestricted market'. Another similar definition is given by the tribunal in *Sempra Energy International v. Argentina*, ICSID No. ARB/02/16, Award, (28 September 2007), para. 405 ('the price, expressed in terms of cash equivalents, at which property would change hands between a hypothetical willing and able buyer and hypothetical and able seller, acting at arm's length in an open and unrestricted market, when neither is under compulsion to buy or sell and when both have reasonable knowledge of the relevant facts').
16. C. McLachlan, L. Shore & M. Weiniger, *International Investment Arbitration: Substantive Principles* 334 (Oxford U. Press 2007); Weiniger, *supra* n. 1, at 199; Ripinsky & Williams, *supra* n. 1, at 92; Christopher Dugan, Noah D. Rubins, Don Wallace & Borzu Sabahi, *Investor-State Arbitration* 579 (Oxford U. Press 2008) (including in this category cases where the violation of the FET standard led to significant losses causing a near-total deprivation of the investment).
17. *Metalclad Corporation v. Mexico*, ICSID No. ARB(AF)/97/1, Award, (30 August 2000), para. 113.
18. *Ibid.*, para. 118.
19. *Ibid.*, para. 119.
20. *Ibid.*, para. 120.

speculative since in the instant case the landfill had never been operative.[21] The tribunal therefore decided to award Metalclad compensation based on its 'actual investment in the project'.[22]

This approach adopted by the *Metalclad* tribunal is favored by Heiskanen arguing that whenever a tribunal is faced with allegations of breaches of different BIT clauses, it should always, based on the principle of judicial economy, first examine whether an expropriation took place.[23] Whenever this is the case, a tribunal should provide compensation solely based on that breach. It should therefore not be required to further examine any compensation issue related to other alleged BIT breaches.[24] Thus, there would be no point in conducting such an analysis since the investor would have already been fully compensated through a finding of expropriation.

[B] Situations where a Breach of the Fair and Equitable Treatment Standard Leads to a Decrease in the Value of the Investment

There are other instances where a violation of the FET standard will not lead to a total loss of the investment, but only to a *decrease* in the value of the investment. In such circumstances, the valuation method used for expropriation is not appropriate since the investment still exists.[25] Tribunals have adopted divergent approaches as to how damages should be evaluated in this context.[26] In the following paragraphs, six observations will be made on case law.

First, an investor must have suffered a loss or a damage as a result of a breach of Article 1105 committed by the host State.[27] The burden is on the investor to prove the actual quantum of the losses for which it claims compensation in relation to a breach of the FET standard.[28] Thus, in *Gami*, the tribunal dismissed the investor's FET claim on the ground that the complaint was 'not connected with a demonstration of specific and quantifiable prejudice'.[29] In its award on damages, the *S.D. Myers* tribunal added that the quantum 'must be neither speculative nor too remote'.[30] Yet, the tribunal also mentioned that 'fairness to the claimant requires that the court or tribunal should approach the task both realistically and rationally'.[31] This comment suggests that the burden of proof for establishing the quantum should not be applied too strictly.

---

21. *Ibid.*, para. 121.
22. *Ibid.*, para. 122.
23. V. Heiskanen, *Arbitrary and Unreasonable Measures*, in *Standards of Investment Protection* 91 (A. Reinisch ed., Oxford U. Press 2008). He refers to case law where the approach was adopted.
24. *Ibid.*, at 91.
25. McLachlan, *supra* n. 16, at 334; Weiniger, *supra* n. 1, at 199; Dugan et al., *supra* n. 16, at 579; Ripinsky & Williams, *supra* n. 1, at 93, 97.
26. Hobér, *supra* n. 1, at 596 ff.
27. Ioana Tudor, *The Fair and Equitable Treatment Standard in International Foreign Investment Law* 137 (Oxford U. Press 2008).
28. *S.D. Myers, Inc. v. Canada*, UNCITRAL, First Partial Award, (13 November 2000), para. 316.
29. *Gami Investments, Inc. v. Mexico*, UNCITRAL, Final Award, (15 November 2004), para. 83, *see also*, paras. 84–85.
30. *S.D. Myers Inc. v. Canada*, Second Partial Award, (21 October 2002), para. 173.
31. *Ibid.*

The *Pope & Talbot* award is the only case where a NAFTA tribunal has quantified the amount of damages resulting *solely* from a breach of Article 1105 (the *S.D. Myers* tribunal quantified the damages for *both* violations of Articles 1102 and 1105 and the *Cargill* tribunal examined compensation for breaches of Articles 1102, 1105 and 1106 *conjointly*). As mentioned above, the *Pope* tribunal concluded that the so-called 'verification review episode' breached Article 1105. The tribunal rejected two heads of damages submitted by the investor.[32] It accepted to compensate the investor for two others:

> The heads of damages claimed that the Tribunal finds to be recoverable are (1) out of pocket expenses relating to the Verification Review Episode, including the applicable accountants' and legal fees, as well as the fees and expenses incurred by the Investor in lobbying efforts to counter the actions of the SLD and the consequent possibility of reductions in the Investment's export quotas, and (2) out of pocket expenses directly incurred by the Investor with respect to the Interim Hearing held in January 2000.[33]

The tribunal did not explain what these out of pocket expenses connected to the interim hearing were nor did it quantify them. The tribunal awarded the investor USD 461,566 in compensation.

Second, tribunals have highlighted the importance of causation.[34] The *Feldman* tribunal concluded that Mexico had breached Article 1102, but had not committed any expropriation. The tribunal noted that 'what is owed by the responding Party is the amount of loss or damage that is adequately connected to the breach'.[35] The same conclusion was also reached by the *S.D. Myers* tribunal. In its first award, the tribunal explained that 'compensation is payable only in respect of harm that is proved to have a sufficient causal link with the specific NAFTA provision that has been breached'.[36] In its second award, the tribunal specified, with regards to the issue of causation, that 'compensation should be awarded for the overall economic losses sustained by SDMI that are a proximate result of Canada's measure'.[37] NAFTA Parties have approved these findings.[38]

---

32. *Pope & Talbot Inc. v. Canada*, UNCITRAL, Award on Damages, (31 May 2002), paras. 81–84. The value of management time devoted to the claim was rejected because it was a fixed cost and no additional costs in salaries were incurred as a direct result of the verification review episode. The tribunal also examined alleged losses flowing from a seven day shutdown of Pope's three British Columbia mills which were linked to the verification review episode. The tribunal rejected the claim based on the ground that the investor had suffered no loss of profits from the shutdown.
33. *Ibid.*, para. 85.
34. *Joseph Charles Lemire v. Ukraine*, Award, (28 March 2011), para. 252; *LG&E v. Argentina*, Award, (25 July 2007), paras. 45, 58.
35. *Marvin Roy Feldman Karpa v. Mexico* [hereinafter *Feldman v. Mexico*], ICSID No. ARB(AF)/99/1, Award, (16 December 2002), para. 194.
36. *S.D. Myers Inc. v. Canada*, First Partial Award, (13 November 2000), para. 316. *See also Ibid.*, Second Partial Award, (21 October 2002), paras. 159, 160.
37. *Ibid.*, Second Partial Award, (21 October 2002), para. 122.
38. *See*, for instance: *Merrill & Ring Forestry L.P. v. Canada*, UNCITRAL, Canada's Counter Memorial, (13 May 2008), para. 795; *International Thunderbird Gaming Corporation v. Mexico* [hereinafter *Thunderbird v. Mexico*], UNCITRAL, Mexico's Escrito de Contestación, (18 December 2003), para. 324; *Cargill, Inc. v. Mexico*, ICSID no. ARB(AF)/05/02, Award, (18 September 2009), paras. 436, 437.

Third, tribunals have interpreted the lack of any specific guidance in BITs with respect to the assessment of damages in the context of FET violations as implicitly providing for a certain level of discretion.[39] The conclusion reached by the *S.D. Myers* tribunal is consistent with this analysis:

> By not identifying any particular methodology for the assessment of compensation in cases not involving expropriation, the Tribunal considers that the drafters of the NAFTA intended to leave it open to tribunals to determine a measure of compensation appropriate to the specific circumstances of the case, taking into account the principles of both international law and the provisions of the NAFTA.[40]

The *Feldman* tribunal also alluded to the 'considerable discretion' that tribunals exercise when assessing damages:

> It is obvious that in both of these earlier cases (Pope and SD Myers), which as here involved non-expropriation violations of Chapter 11, the tribunals exercised considerable discretion in fashioning what they believed to be reasonable approaches to damages consistent with the requirements of NAFTA.[41]

In this context, tribunals have generally turned to customary international law to fill the gap and to determine appropriate compensation in cases not involving expropriation.[42] The starting point of their analysis is typically a reference to the *Chorzow Factory* case[43] and the relevant provisions of the I.L.C. Articles on State Responsibility.[44] NAFTA Parties have acknowledged that tribunals have some discretion in assessing non-expropiatory breaches and that they should rely on these basic international law principles.[45]

Fourth, by hinging on the PCIJ's famous *dictum* in the *Chorzow Factory* case, tribunals have often used the 'differential method' to calculate damages for non-expropriatory acts.[46] As succinctly putted by the *Lemire* tribunal, 'the purpose of the

39. *LG&E v. Argentina*, Award, (25 July 2007), para. 40; *CMS Gas Transmission Company v. Argentina*, ICSID No. ARB/01/8, Award, (12 May 2005), para. 409.
40. See, *S.D. Myers, Inc. v. Canada*, First Partial Award, (13 November 2000), para. 309.
41. *Feldman v. Mexico*, Award, (16 December 2002), para. 197.
42. *S.D. Myers Inc. v. Canada*, First Partial Award, (13 November 2000), para. 310. See also, *LG&E v. Argentina*, Award, (25 July 2007), para. 30; *Siemens AG v. Argentina*, ICSID No. ARB/02/8, Award and Separate Opinion, (17 January 2007), para. 249.
43. *Case Concerning the Factory at Chorzów (Indemnity)*, P.C.I.J. Ser. A. No. 17, at 47 (13 September 1928), indicating that reparation must be sufficient to wipe out all the consequences of the illegal act and to 're-establish the situation which would, in all probability, have existed if that act had not been committed'.
44. See cases examined in: K. Hobér, *Fair and Equitable Treatment: Determining Compensation, Comment*, in *The International Convention on the Settlement of Investment Disputes (ICSID), Taking Stock after 40 Years* 81 ff. (Rainer Hofmann, Christian J. Tams eds., Nomos 2007).
45. See, for instance, *Chemtura Corporation v. Canada*, Canada's Counter Memorial, (20 October 2008), paras. 952, 953; *Merrill & Ring Forestry L.P. v. Canada*, Canada's Counter Memorial, (13 May 2008), para. 801; *Grand River Enterprises Six Nations, Ltd., et al. v. United States* [hereinafter *Grand River v. United States*], UNCITRAL, US Counter-Memorial, (22 December 2008), at 163-165.
46. Marboe, *supra* n. 1, paras. 2.105, 3.136, 3.151 ('It can be concluded that a number of different international courts and tribunals have correctly applied the principle of full reparation as formulated by the PCIJ in *Factory at Chorzów* in cases of State responsibility. They calculated the amount of damages by way of the differential method, namely as the difference between the

compensation must be to place the investor in the same pecuniary position in which it would have been if respondent had not violated the BIT'.[47] This differential method consists of examining the investor's *actual* financial situation and comparing it with 'the one that would have prevailed had the act not been committed'.[48] In other words, the comparison is made with the situation which would have hypothetically prevailed using a 'but for' scenario.[49] One recent example where the 'differential method' was endorsed is that of the *Cargill* award. The tribunal concluded that the appropriate approach to assess damages for violations of NAFTA Articles 1102, 1105 and 1106 was to determine the 'present value of net lost cash flows' that the investor would have garnered 'but for' the Mexican illegal conduct.[50]

Tribunals that have adopted the 'differential method' have also highlighted the importance of according 'full compensation' for the *actual* loss suffered by the investor.[51] Yet, tribunals have often used different *methods* to calculate full reparation. Some tribunals have based their calculation on the amount of out-of-pocket investment actually made by the investor, while others have taken the lost profit valuation of the investment into account.[52] The *PSEG* tribunal rejected the use of the loss of profit approach because the claim involved an infant industry and an unperformed work.[53] Tribunals also seem to be divided with respect to the question whether or not the 'fair market value' method (typically used for expropriation) can also be applied in the context of a violation of the FET standard (this question will be elaborated upon in the following paragraphs).

Fifth, many tribunals have *rejected* the use of the 'fair market value' method in the context of assessment of damages for a violation of the FET standard.[54]

---

actual and the hypothetical financial situation of the injured person. This usually implies a subjective and concrete valuation approach because the valuation is based on the comparison of the concrete financial situation of the affected individual with and without the unlawful act').

47. *Joseph Charles, Lemire v. Ukraine*, Award, (28 March 2011), para. 149. *See also*: *LG&E v. Argentina*, Award, (25 July 2007), para. 58.
48. Dolzer & Schreuer, *supra* n. 8, at 272.
49. *Joseph Charles, Lemire v. Ukraine*, Award, (28 March 2011), paras. 244, 253.
50. *Cargill, Inc. v. Mexico*, ICSID no. ARB(AF)/05/02, Award, (18 September 2009), paras. 432, 444, 447.
51. *MTD Equity Sdn Bhd and MTD Chile SA v. Chile*, ICSID No. ARB/01/7, Award, (25 May 2004), para. 238; *LG&E v. Argentina*, Award, (25 July 2007), paras. 31, 58; *Enron Corporation and Ponderosa Assets, LP v. Argentina*, Award, (22 May 2007), para. 359. *See also*: Ripinsky & Williams, *supra* n. 1, at 88-90; Hobér, *supra* n. 1, at 598.
52. Hobér, *supra* n. 44, at 101 ('when it comes to the *method* of establishing and calculating "full reparation", customary international law does not provide much guidance. The cases discussed above illustrate that the method chosen depends on, and varies with, the circumstances of each individual case, including, *inter alia*, the nature of the violation of the fair and equitable treatment standard and the kind and nature of the investment in question. Sometimes the starting point might be the amount actually invested, in other cases it might be more appropriate to focus on lost future profits as established by using the DCF method').
53. *PSEG Global, Inc., The North American Coal Corporation, and Konya Ingin Electrik Üretim ve Ticaret Limited Sirketi v. Turkey*, ICSID No. ARB/02/5, Award, (19 January 2007), paras. 313-315. *See also LG&E v. Argentina*, Award, (25 July 2007), paras. 88, 96.
54. *PSEG Global, Inc., The North American Coal Corporation, and Konya Ingin Electrik Üretim ve Ticaret Limited Sirketi v. Turkey*, Award, (19 January 2007), para. 308.

This was indeed the conclusion reached by *S.D. Myers* tribunal.[55] The tribunal openly doubted that the fair market value method referred to at Article 1110 was the appropriate standard to use in evaluating non-expropriatory damages.[56] The tribunal acknowledged that 'in some non-expropriation cases a tribunal might think it appropriate to adopt the "fair market value" standard' but added that 'in other cases it might not'.[57] In the instant case, however, the tribunal considered that 'the application of the fair market value standard is not a logical, appropriate or practicable measure of the compensation to be awarded'.[58] This is because no expropriation had taken place against the claimant's investment. The tribunal opined that 'fixing the fair market value of an asset that is diminished in value may not fairly address the harm done to the investor'.[59] Having rejected the fair market value method, the tribunal then 'turn[ed] for guidance to international law'[60] and referred to the *Chorzow Factory* case.[61]

There is substantial support for the *S.D. Myers* tribunal's finding that the use of the fair market value method is not appropriate in situations where a breach of the FET standard does not result in a total loss of the investment. Other (non-NAFTA) tribunals have also adopted this position,[62] as have NAFTA Parties.[63] The *Feldman* tribunal also stated that the fair market value method 'necessarily applies only to situations that fall

---

55. As mentioned above, the tribunal held that the measures taken by Canada were in breach of Articles 1102 and 1105, but did not constitute an expropriation.
56. *S.D. Myers Inc. v. Canada*, First Partial Award, (13 November 2000), para. 306. Thus, the drafters of the NAFTA 'did not state that the 'fair market value of the asset' formula applies to all breaches of Chapter 11' and 'they expressly attached [that method] to expropriations' (para. 307).
57. *Ibid.*, para. 309.
58. *Ibid.*
59. *Ibid.*, para. 308.
60. *Ibid.*, para. 310.
61. *Ibid.*, para. 315. The *S.D. Myers* tribunal mentioned that the parties would have the opportunity in a second stage of the proceedings to make submissions on the question of the precise methodology to be used, but added that it was paramount that the approach taken 'should reflect the general principle of international law that compensation should undo the material harm inflicted by a breach of an international obligation' (para. 315). The tribunal also briefly addressed the question of 'double recovery' of damages in cases where a measure breaches more than one BIT provision (para. 318). But in the present case, the tribunal concluded that 'the damages to which SDMI is entitled arising out of Canada's breach of Article 1102 are neither increased not diminished by its breach of Article 1105' (para. 319). The tribunal ultimately decided in a subsequent award (*S.D. Myers Inc. v. Canada*, Second Partial Award, (21 October 2002), paras. 174, 222, 228) that the appropriate primary measure of compensation for lost profits was the value of the claimant's lost net income stream. The tribunal awarded some CAD 6 million in damages to the investor.
62. *See*, for instance, *Nykomb Synergetics Technology Holding AB v. Latvia*, SCC, Award, (16 December 2003), at 53.
63. *See*, for instance, *Chemtura Corporation v. Canada*, Canada's Counter Memorial, (20 October 2008), para. 955; *Vito G. Gallo v. Canada*, UNCITRAL, Canada's Counter-Memorial, (29 June 2010), para. 515; *Merrill & Ring Forestry L.P. v. Canada*, Canada's Counter Memorial, (13 May 2008), para. 802; *Grand River v. United States*, US Counter-Memorial, (22 December 2008), at 164, 165; *Thunderbird v. Mexico*, Mexico's Escrito de Contestación, (18 December 2003), paras. 235, 238.

within that Article 1110'.[64] It added that a tribunal should award damages to compensate an investor for its *actual loss* resulting from a non-expropriatory violation.[65]

In contrast with the NAFTA cases of *S.D. Myers* and *Feldman*, non-NAFTA tribunals have often applied the fair market value method in the context of breach of FET.[66] In most cases, the claimants had themselves referred to the fair market value method and this solution had not been contested by the respondents. These tribunals therefore simply applied the valuation method based on the parties' choice.[67] A different situation arose in the *CMS* case where the tribunal held that even though no expropriation had been committed, the 'cumulative nature of the breaches' would be 'best dealt with by resorting to the standard of fair market value'.[68] The tribunal considered that even if 'this standard figures prominently in respect of expropriation', it 'might also be appropriate for breaches different from expropriation if their effect results in important long-term losses'.[69] Other tribunals that have found a violation of the FET standard and that an expropriation had taken place have simply used the fair market value method for the calculation of damages.[70]

Sixth, tribunals have the power to take the investor's behavior into account when assessing compensation to be awarded.[71] Relevant factors would include any illegal actions committed by the investor, any contributory negligence or its failure to mitigate

---

64. *Feldman v. Mexico*, Award, (16 December 2002), para. 194.
65. *Ibid.*
66. Marboe, *supra* n. 1, para. 3.154. *See*, for instance, *Enron Corporation and Ponderosa Assets, LP v. Argentina*, Award, (22 May 2007), para. 363 ('On occasions, the line separating indirect expropriation from the breach of fair and equitable treatment can be rather thin and in those circumstances the standard of compensation can also be similar on one or the other side of the line. Given the cumulative nature of the breaches that have resulted in a finding of liability, the Tribunal believes that in this case it is appropriate to apply the fair market value to the determination of compensation'); *Sempra Energy International v. Argentina*, Award, (28 September 2007), para. 403 (where the tribunal stated that in cases where a non-expropriatory breach caused 'significant disruption to the investment made', it 'might be very difficult to distinguish the breach of fair and equitable treatment from indirect expropriation or other forms of taking and it is thus reasonable that the standard of reparation might be the same'); *Azurix Corp. v. Argentina*, ICSID No. ARB/01/12, Award, (14 July 2006), para. 424.
67. Marboe, *supra* n. 1, para. 3.165.
68. *CMS Gas Transmissions Company v. Argentina*, Award, (12 May 2005), para. 410.
69. *Ibid.*
70. *Wena Hotels Ltd. v. Arab Republic of Egypt*, ICSID No. ARB/98/4, Award, (8 December 2000), para. 118; *Técnicas Medioambientales Tecmed, S.A. v. Mexico*, ICSID No. ARB (AF)/00/2, Award, (29 May 2003), paras. 151, 174, 187, 188. These findings have been contested in doctrine on the ground that 'if tribunals apply the same rules for the assessment of compensation for a breach of fair and equitable treatment as would be applied to an expropriation, then the difference between these two substantive obligations becomes academic' (Zachary Douglas, *The International Law of Investment Claims* 104 (Cambridge U. Press 2009).
71. Dolzer & Schreuer, *supra* n. 8, at 273; N. Gallus, *The Fair and Equitable Standard of Treatment and the Circumstances of the Host State*, in *Evolution in Investment Treaty Law and Arbitration* 243 (C. Brown & K. Miles eds., Cambridge U. Press 2011) ('Several investment treaty tribunals have found that, regardless of the actual damage to the claimant, they can adjust the compensation to ensure that it is equitable'); Andrew Newcombe & Luis Paradell, *Law and Practice of Investment Treaties: Standards of Treatment* 189 (Kluwer 2009).

its damages.[72] Tudor argues that 'considering the Investors' conduct when calculating the compensation due for breach of FET is justified in the light of the meaning of fairness and equitableness'.[73] She refers to the following types of investors' conduct that should have an impact on calculating compensation: 'corrupt practices; misrepresentation as to competence; bad business judgement; absence of due diligence, risk assessment, and realistic expectations; bad faith; lack of awareness of or compliance with the regulatory environment; and breach of human rights'.[74] A number of writers, including myself,[75] have recently argued that allegations of human rights violations committed by an investor should have, *inter alia*, an impact on a tribunal's assessment of compensation for damages claimed by that investor. Thus, compensation should be reduced 'proportionally to the investor's violation' of human rights obligations.[76] Moreover, the present author has argued elsewhere that, based on the doctrine of 'clean hands', a tribunal should also be mindful of any human rights violations committed by an investor when deciding a claim's admissibility.[77]

Some arbitral awards have indeed reduced compensation based on the investor's behavior.[78] In *MTD*, the tribunal evaluated at USD 21.5 million the amount for the

---

72. Article 39, I.L.C. Articles on State Responsibility, *supra* n. 2: 'In the determination of reparation, account shall be taken of the contribution to the injury by wilful or negligent action or omission of the injured State or any person or entity in relation to whom reparation is sought'.
73. Tudor, *supra* n. 27, at 222, *see also*, at 212-213, 217 ('Therefore, even though the liability of the State is established objectively, the compensation to be paid to the Investor is tailored in such a way as to give each party what it deserves in order to achieve an equitable result').
74. *Ibid.*, at 218. *See also*, Gabriel Cavazos Villanueva, *The Fair and Equitable Treatment Standard* 89, 189 (VDM Verlag 2008).
75. Patrick Dumberry & Gabrielle Dumas-Aubin, *How to Impose Human Rights Obligations on Corporations under Investment Treaties?*, 4 Yb Int'l Invest. L. & Pol. 585, 592 (2011-2012).
76. Ioana Knoll-Tudor, *The Fair and Equitable treatment Standard and Human Rights Norms*, in *Human Rights in International Investment Law and Arbitration* 342 (P.M. Dupuy, F. Francioni & E.U. Petersmann eds., Oxford U. Press 2009).
77. Dumberry & Dumas-Aubin, *supra* n. 75, at 593. Thus, while a tribunal would have jurisdiction over the investor's claim, it should nevertheless refuse to hear it based on the investor's breach of human rights obligations. To the extent that recent tribunals have denied admissibility of claims based on bribery or misrepresentations made by the claimant (*see, inter alia, Gustav FW Hamester GmbH & Co KG v. Ghana*, ICSID No. ARB/07/24, Award, (10 June 2010), at 123), it is submitted that they should do the same when faced with human rights violations. In other words, the solution that prevailed so far for bribery, should, *a fortiori*, apply when a tribunal finds fundamental human rights abuses by the claimant. In the present author's view, these are precisely the kind of investments not worthy of protection under a BIT. In any event, there is no doubt that a tribunal should find inadmissible a claim submitted by an investor having committed *jus cogens* violations (*Phoenix Action, Ltd. v. Czech Republic*, ICSID No. ARB/06/5, Award, (15 April 2009), para. 78). *See also* P. Dumberry & G. Dumas-Aubin, *When and How Allegations of Human Rights Violations Can Be Raised in Investor-State Arbitration*, 13(3) J. World Invest. & Trade 349-372 (2012); P. Dumberry & G. Dumas-Aubin, *The Doctrine of "Clean Hands" and the Inadmissibility of Claims by Investors Breaching International Human Rights Law*, 10(1) Transnational Disp. Mgmt. Special Issue: Aligning Human Rights and Investment Protection (2013). More generally, on the question of an investor's conduct in the context of claims for breach of the fair and equitable treatment, *see* Peter Muchlinski, *'Caveat Investor'? The Relevance of the Conduct of the Investor under the Fair and Equitable Treatment Standard*, 55(3) ICLQ 527-557 (2006).
78. *Iurii Bogdanov v. Moldova*, Ad hoc-SCC Arbitration Rules, Award, (22 September 2005), para. 84; *Occidental Petroleum Corporation and Occidental Exploration and Production Company v. Ecuador*, ICSID No. ARB/06/11, Award, (15 October 2012), paras. 681, 687.

expenditures that could have been avoided by the investor had there been no breach of the FET. However, it also held that Chile could not be held responsible for the consequences of unwise business decisions made by the investor or for its lack of diligence. The tribunal accordingly decided to reduce the amount eligible for compensation by 50%.[79] It has been argued that such a reduction of the amount of compensation may be the result of the tribunal's belief that the investor had failed to establish a causal link for some of the expenditures claimed or that it factored the investor's contributory negligence into its reasoning.[80]

Finally, tribunals also have the power to take into account the circumstances of the host State when awarding damages for breach of the FET.[81]

---

79. *MTD Equity Sdn Bhd and MTD Chile SA v. Chile*, Award, (25 May 2004), paras. 241–243.
80. Hobér, *supra* n. 44, at 86.
81. Gallus, *supra* n. 71, at 243; Tudor, *supra* n. 27, at 208 ('Elements that may excuse, justify, or that may have contributed to the behavior of the State may be taken into account only in the last phase of the proceedings, namely the calculation of compensation').

Summary of Findings

The most significant findings of this book can be summarized through the following sixty-six observations.

I   **THE NATURE OF THE FET STANDARD UNDER ARTICLE 1105**

1. In the specific context of NAFTA, the long-standing debate as to whether or not the 'minimum standard of treatment' exists under custom is moot. The title of Article 1105 refers expressly to the 'minimum standard of treatment'. Moreover, NAFTA Parties have explicitly referred to the minimum standard of treatment as being a composing element of customary international law. NAFTA tribunals (including *ADF* and *Mondev*) have endorsed this position.

2. If there is no doubt that there exists a minimum standard of treatment, its actual content is subject to some controversy. The minimum standard is an umbrella concept, which in and of itself incorporates different elements. While the standard is often described as highly indeterminate and vague, there is a large consensus to the effect that it encompasses (at the very least) an obligation for host States to prevent denial of justice, to prevent arbitrary conduct, to provide investors with 'full protection and security', and not to expropriate a foreign investor's investment (unless the taking is for a public purpose, as provided by law, conducted in a non-discriminatory manner and with compensation in return).[1]

3. One of the most controversial questions discussed in scholarship in recent years pertains to the rationale supporting States' inclusion of the term 'fair and equitable treatment' ('FET') in their BITs throughout the 1960s and 1970s. Different narratives

---

1. The question whether or not in the specific context of NAFTA Article 1105 the fair and equitable treatment standard is one of the elements encompassed within the minimum standard of treatment is discussed below.

have been put forward by writers. According to one view, Western States have started to incorporate the FET concept to reflect the minimum standard of treatment that existed under international law. In other words, FET was simply used as shorthand for the minimum standard of treatment. Yet, this interpretation overlooks the fact that at the time, developing States rejected the very existence of such a minimum standard. It has been convincingly argued that Western States began to refer to FET in their BITs precisely to counter the assertion made by developing States about the inexistence of the minimum standard. Logically, the term FET should therefore be considered as a reference to something other than the minimum standard of treatment (this is certainly the case when the FET clause does not contain any reference to international law).

4. While the vast majority of BITs include an FET clause, there nevertheless remains a considerable degree of variation of their actual content. The most important drafting distinction lies between two groups of provisions: clauses explicitly linking the FET standard to the standard existing under international law and clauses containing an 'unqualified' formulation of the FET obligation (i.e., a stand-alone obligation to provide that treatment without any reference to international law).

5. Case law shows that drafting variations in FET clauses have been interpreted as indicative of different content as well as different thresholds of liability. Thus, the vast majority of non-NAFTA tribunals have interpreted an 'unqualified' FET clause as having a distinct and separate meaning from the minimum standard of treatment. From this perspective, the level of treatment required by the host State would be more extensive than that existing under custom. Foreign investors would therefore be given more rights. Tribunals (outside NAFTA) have been more divided with respect to the proper interpretation to be given to an FET clause containing an explicit reference to 'international law'. A significant number of them have held that this is a reference to the minimum standard under custom. From this viewpoint, the FET standard would not provide treatment protections above and beyond the minimum standard of treatment.

6. In the present author's view, the historical developments highlighted above generally support the theory that the FET is an independent treaty standard with an autonomous meaning from that of the minimum standard of treatment. This is certainly the case when an FET clause is unqualified and contains no reference whatsoever to international law.

7. Yet, this approach is not convincing in cases (such as in that of NAFTA Article 1105) where the treaty explicitly links the FET standard to 'international law'. Moreover, the interpretation mentioned above is simply not sustainable in situations where the parties to a treaty have expressly stated their intention that the FET standard be considered as a reference to the minimum standard of treatment under custom. This is clearly the case under NAFTA Article 1105 (as further examined below).

8. The debate as to whether the FET is an autonomous standard or linked to the minimum standard of treatment under international law is not relevant in the context of NAFTA Article 1105. Under that provision, the FET is linked to the minimum

standard of treatment. In fact, the FET must be considered as one of the elements included in the umbrella concept of the minimum standard of treatment. The adequacy of this view is evident given the fact that the provision requires NAFTA Parties to provide foreign investors treatment in accordance with 'international law' (a reference to the minimum standard of treatment as clarified by the FTC Notes of Interpretation ('FTC Note')), *including* fair and equitable treatment.

9. In sum, the FET standard at Article 1105 must be analyzed under very specific parameters that do not exist under most BITs containing an unqualified FET clause not at all linked to international law. The specific features of Article 1105 also mean, in turn, that many of the findings related to this provision are not easily transferable and applicable to tribunals interpreting unqualified FET clauses. Yet, the conclusions drawn from NAFTA case law do apply to FET clauses containing language similar to that of Article 1105.

II   THE MEANING OF THE FET STANDARD UNDER ARTICLE 1105

10. The earlier practices of Canada (except for one treaty) and the United States regarding FET clauses show that all BITs signed by them before 1994 explicitly linked the FET standard to 'international law'. But none of these BITs contained the same language as Article 1105. As opposed to this provision's final text, references to treatment 'in accordance with international law' in these BITs appeared after the mention of FET. The same language was also found in the first drafts of Article 1105. The NAFTA's available negotiation documents do not provide any explanation as to why the Parties ultimately changed the order of the wording when adopting the final version of the text of Article 1105. It is also noteworthy that the phrase 'customary international law' is not mentioned in any of the different drafts. As further discussed below, evidence suggests that at the time (i.e., 1994), the use of the term 'international law' in FET clauses contained in these BITs was meant, for both Canada and the United States, to be a reference to the minimum standard of treatment under custom. In sum, the history of Article 1105 does not provide much guidance as to the meaning of the FET standard under this clause.

[A]   General Rules of Treaty Interpretation

11. According to NAFTA Article 1131(1), a tribunal set up to resolve a dispute between an investor and a NAFTA Party under Chapter 11 must 'decide the issues in dispute in accordance with this Agreement and applicable rules of international law'. One source that has consistently been applied by tribunals to interpret NAFTA provisions are the rules of treaty interpretation codified in Articles 31 and 32 of the *Vienna Convention on the Law of Treaties*. Under Article 31(1), Article 1105 must be interpreted according to the ordinary meaning given to the terms used in the provision while taking into account the context, object, and purpose of the NAFTA.

309

12. Article 1105 provides for an 'absolute' and 'objective' standard of treatment that offers protection to 'investments of investors' and not to investors themselves. The FET standard comports a single obligation that has a specific content of its own. What constitutes the actual content of that standard is, of course, a controversial question. An examination of the ordinary meaning of the words 'fair' and 'equitable' does not provide much guidance as to the scope of the provision since it leads to equally vague terms (such as 'just', 'unbiased', etc.). Under Article 1105, 'international law' is the 'controlling element' in applying the concept of FET and determining its content. Yet, the determination of the actual meaning of the term 'international law' has proven to be a very contentious issue. The debate amongst tribunals and scholars has opposed those according to whom the concept refers only to the minimum standard of treatment under custom to others supporting an interpretation based on all sources of international law.

13. NAFTA Article 102(2) indicates that the Parties shall interpret and apply NAFTA provisions 'in the light of [NAFTA's] objectives set out in [Article 201(1)]'. However, case law shows that examining the object and purpose of the NAFTA provides limited insight into the actual meaning of Article 1105. The purpose of the NAFTA (like all international investment treaties) is the protection and promotion of foreign investments and the deepening of mutual economic relations between the contracting States. These are very general objectives that are not particularly helpful in determining the meaning of FET.

14. The heading of Article 1105 ('Minimum Standard of Treatment') clearly suggests that the words 'international law' refer to the minimum standard of treatment under custom. Other contextual elements are examined in the following paragraphs.

[B]   Subsequent Practice between the Parties on the Interpretation of Article 1105

15. Article 31(3) of the *Vienna Convention* indicates that the context of a provision includes any 'subsequent agreement' between the parties regarding the interpretation of a provision and any 'subsequent practice' in the application of the treaty which establishes the agreement of the parties regarding its interpretation. The present book has highlighted several examples of subsequent practice by the Parties that were indicative of the proper interpretation to be given to Article 1105.

16. NAFTA Article 1128 allows non-disputing Parties (i.e., those not acting as respondents) to intervene in arbitration proceedings by filing written submissions concerning questions pertaining to treaty interpretation with a tribunal. NAFTA Parties have made frequent use of such submissions in the context of arbitration proceedings related to Article 1105. One tribunal (*Canadian Cattleman*) rightly concluded that these Article 1128 submissions can be considered as subsequent practice since they are 'concordant, common, and consistent' in supporting the same interpretation (i.e., that the FET under Article 1105 is a reference to the minimum standard of treatment under custom).

17. The Model BITs adopted by the Unites States (in 2004 and 2012) and Canada (in 2004) also make it clear that treatment in accordance with 'international law' refers to the minimum standard of treatment under custom. Model BITs have adopted such language to refute the expanding interpretation applied by some NAFTA tribunals, most notably the *Pope & Talbot* tribunal, and to incorporate the clarification made in the FTC Note of July 2001. The Model BITs should not be considered as 'subsequent practice' since they were not drafted 'in the application' of the NAFTA, but conceived as models for the drafting of future BITs. Yet, it remains that significant weight should be given to these instruments with regards to the interpretation of Article 1105.

18. Unilateral official statements were made by both Canada and the United States when NAFTA was being implemented. They were subsequently endorsed by Mexico. These statements consist of Canada's 1994 'Statement on Implementation' as well as numerous US State Department's transmittal statements made in 1993–1994 onward (in the context of BITs containing language similar to that of NAFTA Article 1105). These statements do not qualify as 'subsequent' practice for the purposes of Article 31(3)(b) of the *Vienna Convention* because they were issued before or simultaneously with the entry into force of the NAFTA. Yet, this timing is precisely the reason why significant weight should be given to these statements. Their importance is further confirmed by the fact that they are 'concordant, common, and consistent' with respect to the proper meaning to be given to Article 1105; they unanimously state that the FET to be accorded under 'international law' is a reference to the minimum standard of treatment under custom.

19. Most importantly, this common interpretation is also confirmed by a 'subsequent agreement between the parties' regarding the meaning of Article 1105, namely the FTC Note issued in July 2001.

[C]   **A Subsequent Agreement between the Parties on the Interpretation of Article 1105: The FTC Note**

20. The Note was issued by the FTC in reaction to the controversial rulings rendered by three tribunals in 2000–2001: *Metalclad*, *S.D. Myers* and *Pope & Talbot*. The Note aimed to 'correct' three 'mistakes' that had been made by these tribunals. The first two paragraphs of the Note overruled *Pope & Talbot*'s holding that the FET standard of protection should be considered in *addition* to the minimum standard of treatment existing under international law. The Note is clear to the effect that FET is a reference to the minimum standard of treatment existing under customary international law and that it does not require treatment in addition to or beyond that standard. These two paragraphs were also intended to address the *Metalclad* tribunal's expanding interpretation that the FET standard included an obligation of transparency. The third paragraph of the Note overruled the *S.D. Myers* award's reasoning that a breach of one provision of Chapter 11 (or a breach of a separate international agreement) could establish a breach of another provision.

311

21. The Note's issuance in July 2001 was made in great part due to timing. NAFTA Parties were concerned that the controversial findings of these three awards would set a trend that would be followed by future tribunals. At the time, several other high profile NAFTA arbitration cases were pending.

22. The Note has been criticized for being an opportunistic method put in place by the Parties in order to avoid liability in on-going arbitration cases and an instance where they acted as both party and judge in these proceedings. There are good reasons to believe that some aspects of the procedure were indeed contrary to due process.

23. Yet, under NAFTA Article 1131(2) the Note is binding on NAFTA tribunals. One tribunal (*Methanex*) has held that the Note is in fact a subsequent agreement (pursuant to Article 31(3)a) of the *Vienna Convention*) which indicates the definitive meaning of Article 1105. Tribunals have generally agreed with the NAFTA Parties that the FTC interpretation does not change the meaning of Article 1105, but only clarifies the meaning that the provision has always had. While two tribunals (*Pope & Talbot, Merrill & Ring*) have made comments suggesting that the FTC Note is more akin to an amendment than a simple interpretation, the majority of tribunals have rightly held that they did not have the power to address this issue for themselves. In any event, all tribunals have ultimately recognized the limited practical consequences of this question as a result of the binding nature of the Note under Article 1131(2).

24. Article 32 of the *Vienna Convention* makes reference to 'supplementary means of interpretation', which includes the treaty's preparatory work (*travaux préparatoires*). One tribunal (*Methanex*) has rightly held that the use of such material would be of limited help in the specific context of Article 1105 where there exists a subsequent agreement and some subsequent practice between the Parties with regards to the proper interpretation of Article 1105.

25. In sum, all evidence (including a subsequent agreement and substantial subsequent practice between the Parties) supports the interpretation to the effect that the terms 'international law' at Article 1105 is a reference to the minimum standard of treatment under customary international law.

[D]   Tribunals' Divergent Application of the FTC Note

26. Not surprisingly, all tribunals (following the FTC Note of 2001) have concluded that Article 1105 provides for FET protection in accordance with the minimum standard of treatment under custom and that the clause does not require treatment in addition to that which exists under custom. While tribunals have all agreed on this fundamental issue, a limited number of peripheral questions related to the concrete application of the concept of customary international law have been controversial.

27. All tribunals (except perhaps for *ADF*) have concluded that arbitral awards do not constitute State practice and thus cannot create customary international law, but can

serve (in some circumstances) as illustrations of such custom. There is also now a consensus amongst tribunals to the effect that awards rendered by non-NAFTA tribunals interpreting 'unqualified' FET clauses are not relevant for the analysis of Article 1105 which belongs to a different species of FET clauses.[2] While some tribunals' reasoning (*ADF, Merrill & Ring*) suggests that when interpreting Article 1105, they are permitted to look beyond customary international law at other sources of international law, it remains that the predominant view (held by the majority of tribunals) is that they should turn solely to custom.

28. A more troubling issue pertains to the fact that some tribunals have challenged the letter and the spirit of the FTC Note and thereby undermined its real effectiveness. These tribunals have basically used two distinct (yet closely related) sets of arguments.

29. First, some tribunals have interpreted customary international law as an evolving and flexible concept. While there is a general agreement between NAFTA Parties that, as a matter of principle, customary international law is not static and can evolve over time, one of the most contentious issues remains whether or not any such evolution has actually taken place in the context of international investment law. Tribunals have so far provided conflicting answers.

30. Faced with the binding FTC Note that restricts the extent of investors' rights, a number of tribunals (*Pope & Talbot, Mondev, ADF* and others) have interpreted customary international law broadly by emphasizing its evolutionary character. Under this interpretation, the level of protection offered to foreign investors under Article 1105 is (at least theoretically) superior to the treatment under the minimum standard. However, these tribunals have not demonstrated that an evolution of the minimum standard has actually taken place. In doing so, these awards have (at least implicitly) challenged the FTC Note. Yet, it should be noted that the adoption of this 'evolutionary' approach by tribunals has had no practical impact on the outcome of these cases in terms of liability; these tribunals (except for *Pope & Talbot*) did not find the respondent States responsible for any breaches of Article 1105, even under this approach.

31. The *Merrill & Ring* tribunal later took this 'evolutionary' approach to the extreme by adopting the so-called theory of 'convergence'. According to this theory, the long-standing debate on the difference between the protection offered to investors under the minimum standard of treatment and an autonomous unqualified FET standard is no longer relevant. This is because the level of treatment to be accorded to foreign investors under the minimum standard of treatment has apparently evolved so rapidly in recent years that it is now said to be the same as that existing under BITs containing an unqualified FET clause. Thus, the *Merrill & Ring* tribunal held that the minimum standard had evolved to the point where it now protects all foreigners 'against all such

---

2. *A contrario*, NAFTA tribunals can be guided by non-NAFTA arbitral awards where tribunals have interpreted FET clauses similar to Article 1105 (where the standard is expressly linked to international law).

acts or behaviour that might infringe on a sense of fairness, equity and reasonable-ness'.[3] This approach is flawed for many reasons, including the failure to actually demonstrate the alleged rapid evolution of the minimum standard under custom. In any event, the adoption of this theory by the *Merrill & Ring* tribunal is a direct challenge to the FTC Note. It refutes the clear intention of the NAFTA Parties when they issued the Note to limit the level of protection to the one existing under custom. If one now considers that the level of treatment under the minimum standard has increased to the level under an unqualified FET clause, this means that, in practical terms, the FTC Note no longer has any purpose.

32. On the contrary, other tribunals (*Glamis, Cargill*) have concluded that no evidence had been presented to establish that current customary international law had moved beyond the minimum standard of treatment of aliens. Thus, to prove a violation of the minimum standard, an investor must show that the conduct was 'egregious' and 'shocking'.

33. Yet, the *Glamis* tribunal added that what is considered today as 'egregious' and 'shocking' has changed since the 1920s. Thus, while the 'test' may not have changed ('egregious' and 'shocking'), it nevertheless remains that the meaning of these words has evolved over time. The type of State conduct that would have certainly not been considered a breach of the minimum standard of treatment back then, may (depending on each tribunal) be deemed a violation of the standard today. In the present author's view, this is a sign of an evolution. The practical differences between the reasoning adopted by the *Glamis* tribunal, on the one hand, and that of the *Mondev* and *ADF* tribunals, on the other hand, may therefore in the end be more apparent than real. Whether or not this is the case will ultimately depend on how each tribunal evaluates changes in mentality with respect to what is to be considered 'egregious' and 'shocking'.

34. A second line of argumentation has also been used by some tribunals (*Pope & Talbot, Merrill & Ring*) to undermine the effectiveness of the Note. They have taken the position that the FET standard has become a rule of customary international law in and of itself. There are solid reasons to support the contrary. Moreover, investors (and writers) who advocate this approach do so in order to increase the standard of protection offered to investors in comparison to the lower level of protection existing under the minimum standard. This approach disregards the undeniable intention of the NAFTA Parties when they issued the Note to limit the scope of the FET protection to the level of treatment existing under custom.

---

3. *Merrill & Ring Forestry L.P. v. Canada* [hereinafter *Merrill & Ring v. Canada*], UNCITRAL, Award, (31 March 2010), para. 210.

III   THE SUBSTANTIVE CONTENT OF THE FET STANDARD UNDER ARTICLE 1105

[A]   The General Approach Adopted by NAFTA Tribunals

35. The concept of FET has a distinct meaning of its own. Since the FET is a 'standard', its application is flexible and will depend on the circumstances of each case. Such inherent flexibility leaves tribunals with a certain margin of discretion (but not an unlimited one) when interpreting an FET clause. Scholars have argued that tribunals have a creative role in determining the substantive content of the FET standard rather than merely interpreting and applying the law created by States. It should be noted that NAFTA tribunals' discretion is, however, limited by the fact that they must apply the minimum standard of treatment existing under custom.

36. More often than not, tribunals have simply looked at what other tribunals have done in the past to determine the content of the FET standard. Writers have criticized the constant reliance on precedents by tribunals and their general failure to provide any comprehensive assessment of the normative content of the FET standard. This situation has led a number of scholars to develop different theories on the nature and scope of the standard. Some writers have thus equated the FET standard with the rule of law under domestic law or, more generally, the idea of justice.

37. NAFTA tribunals have not endorsed any of these comprehensive theories developed by scholars. They have generally adopted the 'shopping list' approach favored by many writers. Tribunals have thus (based on their reviews of relevant case law) recognized that the FET standard under Article 1105 contains several specific elements of protection which must be accorded to investors.

38. One reason which may explain why NAFTA tribunals have not endorsed any grand theories on the FET standard is the fact that they are required, under Article 1105, to apply the minimum standard. This standard involves a higher threshold of liability than an unqualified FET clause. The FET standard under Article 1105 is meant to solely address (to paraphrase the *Glamis* tribunal) acts that are 'sufficiently egregious and shocking—a gross denial of justice, manifest arbitrariness, blatant unfairness, a complete lack of due process, evident discrimination, or a manifest lack of reasons—so as to fall below accepted international standards'.[4] As opposed to the *Merrill & Ring* tribunal's view, the objective of the FET standard under Article 1105 is clearly not to protect investors 'against all such acts or behaviour that might infringe on a sense of fairness, equity and reasonableness'.[5] Ultimately, tribunals simply do not need to resort to the theory that equates the FET and the rule of law in the context of NAFTA Chapter 11 which involves three democracies applying the rule of law. Similarly, the 'proportionality test' put forward by many scholars is less useful for tribunals in the

---

4. *Glamis Gold, Ltd. v. United States* [hereinafter *Glamis v. United States*], UNCITRAL, Award, (8 June 2009), para. 627.
5. *Merrill & Ring v. Canada*, Award, (31 March 2010), para. 210.

specific context of Article 1105 where they have applied a high threshold of severity for finding a breach of that provision.

[B]   The Elements of the FET Standard Covered by Article 1105

[1]   Legitimate Expectations

39. To date, no NAFTA tribunal has come to the conclusion that a host State stood in violation of an investor's legitimate expectations under Article 1105. The *Glamis* award (and to some extent the *Thunderbird* award) are the only ones that support the view that the concept of legitimate expectations constitutes a stand-alone element of the FET standard under Article 1105.

40. In the present author's view, the *Mobil* tribunal (as well as the *Waste Management* and *Cargill* tribunals) adopted a more convincing approach. They have held that the host State's failure to respect an investor's legitimate expectations does not in and of itself constitute a breach of the FET standard, but is rather a 'factor' to be taken into account when assessing whether or not other well-established elements of the standard have been breached. These tribunals have thus endorsed the position of the NAFTA Parties which have consistently argued that the so-called 'obligation' to protect an investor's legitimate expectations is not part of the customary international law minimum standard of treatment of aliens. The stance taken by the majority of NAFTA tribunals contrasts with that adopted by many tribunals outside NAFTA which have recognized that the FET standard encompasses an obligation to protect an investor's legitimate expectations.

41. Supporters of the inclusion of the concept of legitimate expectations as one of the elements of the FET standard have never carried out the exercise of establishing that the concept has been recognized as a rule of customary international law. Scholars have also interpreted the concept of legitimate expectations as a general principle of law on the grounds that it is said to be a recognized rule in many domestic legal systems. This argument is of limited relevance in the specific context of Article 1105 because the binding FTC Note makes it clear that NAFTA tribunals should look solely to custom as a source of international law in their interpretation of Article 1105, not at general principles of law.

42. Moreover, NAFTA tribunals have repeatedly narrowly qualified the concept of legitimate expectations in order to significantly reduce its scope of protection. For instance, unlike non-NAFTA tribunals, NAFTA tribunals (with the possible exception of *Merrill & Ring*) have not pinpointed an obligation to maintain a stable legal and business framework under Article 1105.

43. All NAFTA tribunals that have examined the concept have endorsed the four-elements definition of legitimate expectations adopted by the *Thunderbird* tribunal: (1) conduct or representations have been made by the host State; (2) the claimant has relied on such conduct or representations to make its investment; (3) such reliance by

the claimant on these representations was 'reasonable'; and (4) the host State subsequently repudiated these representations therefore causing damages to the investor. In subsequent awards, NAFTA tribunals have continued to further restric-tively qualify these four requirements. Thus, the *Glamis* award (subsequently endorsed by other tribunals: *Cargill, Mobil, Grand River*) required that an investor's expectations be objective and be based on 'definitive, unambiguous and repeated'[6] specific 'com-mitments'[7] (or 'assurances'[8]) made by the host State to have 'purposely and specifi-cally induced the investment'[9] by the investor.

44. NAFTA tribunals have also concluded that legitimate expectations cannot simply be based on the host State's existing domestic legislation on foreign investments at the time when the investor makes its investment. This is clear from the *Glamis* award's emphasis on a threshold requirement of a quasi-contractual relationship between the investor and the host State. The situation contrasts with that of non-NAFTA tribunals that have held that legitimate expectations can be protected without any specific representations made by the host State. The *Mobil* tribunal clearly stated that no violation of Article 1105 occurs as a result of the host State changing its regulation (even drastically) upon which the investor may have based its expectations when it made its investment. Finally, the *Glamis* award confirmed that under Article 1105, an investor's expectation is not violated by the mere fact that the host State has breached a contract.

[2] *Transparency*

45. All NAFTA tribunals that have examined the concept of transparency have come to the conclusion that it is not a stand-alone element of the FET standard and that it does not impose any obligation on host States under Article 1105. The only exception is the *Metalclad* award which was, however, set aside in judicial review before a B.C. Court precisely with regards to this point. The concept of transparency is nevertheless relevant to aid tribunals in assessing whether or not other established elements of the FET standard have been breached by a State. These findings contrast with that of non-NAFTA tribunals that have concluded that the stability and predictability of the legal framework, including an obligation of transparency, is an essential element of the FET standard.

[3] *Arbitrary Conduct*

46. Several tribunals (*Thunderbird, Waste Management, Mobil, Merrill & Ring*) have come to the conclusion that there exists a prohibition of arbitrary conduct under the

6. *Glamis v. United States*, Award, (8 June 2009), para. 802.
7. *Ibid.*, para. 767.
8. *Ibid.*, paras. 800–801.
9. *Ibid.*, paras. 766, 767.

minimum standard of treatment. Yet, none of these tribunals have actually undertaken the task of examining State practice and opinio juris on the matter; they have based their support for this affirmation solely on previous findings of other tribunals. NAFTA tribunals have typically referred to the reasoning of the ICJ in the *ELSI* case. All NAFTA tribunals have listed the prohibition of arbitrary conduct as a stand-alone element of the FET standard under Article 1105. It is noteworthy that the position of NAFTA Parties has evolved over time on the matter. They no longer deny that arbitrary conduct is an element of the FET standard under Article 1105, but instead emphasize the requirement that such conduct be manifestly arbitrary.

47. The threshold of gravity applied by NAFTA tribunals has been consistently high. They have thus referred to treatment that 'rises to the level that is unacceptable from the international perspective',[10] to 'wholly arbitrary' conduct,[11] and to 'manifest arbitrariness falling below international standards'.[12] For instance, the *Glamis* tribunal stated that Article 1105 'requires something greater than mere arbitrariness, something that is surprising, shocking, or exhibits a manifest lack of reasoning'[13] and sets the threshold of liability at 'manifest arbitrariness'.[14] The application of such a high threshold of liability by NAFTA tribunals (except for *Merrill & Ring*) largely explains why they (except for *Cargill*) have not found arbitrary conduct to amount to a breach of Article 1105. Non-NAFTA tribunals have, on the contrary, often found violations of arbitrariness based on a lower threshold of liability.

48. In light of NAFTA case law, a number of conclusions can be reached about the contours of this prohibition of arbitrary conduct. A government's failure to implement or to abide by its own laws and regulations does not amount to an arbitrary act unless it can be shown that the government committed a maladministration that amounts to an 'outright and unjustified repudiation' of such laws and regulations.[15] Similarly, a mere contractual breach does not amount to an arbitrary act, unless it can be shown that the government committed an 'outright and unjustified repudiation of the transaction' or that the breach was 'motivated by sectoral or local prejudice'.[16] A government's 'inconsistent' or 'questionable' application of its own policy or procedure (or the fact that it makes a mistake in its application) does not amount to an arbitrary act.[17] The fact that a governmental measure is illegal under domestic law does not necessarily make it arbitrary in violation of the FET standard under Article 1105. A violation of this provision occurs when there is a 'manifest lack of reasons for the legislation' such as when the legislation bears no rational relationship with its stated purpose, when it

---

10. *S.D. Myers Inc. v. Canada*, UNCITRAL, First Partial Award, (13 November 2000), para. 263.
11. *Waste Management, Inc. v. Mexico ("Number 2")* [hereinafter *Waste Management v. Mexico*], ICSID No. ARB(AF)/00/3, Award, (30 April 2004), para. 115.
12. *International Thunderbird Gaming Corporation v. Mexico* [hereinafter *Thunderbird v. Mexico*], UNCITRAL, Award, (26 January 2006), para. 194.
13. *Glamis v. United States*, Award, (8 June 2009), para. 617.
14. *Ibid.*, paras. 626–627. *See also*: *Cargill Inc. v. Mexico*, ICSID Case no. ARB(AF)/05/2, Award, (18 September 2009), para. 296.
15. *Gami Investments, Inc. v. Mexico*, UNCITRAL, Award, (15 November 2004), paras. 91, 103, 104.
16. *Waste Management, Inc. v. Mexico*, Award, (30 April 2004), para. 115.
17. *Cargill Inc. v. Mexico*, Award, (18 September 2009), paras. 98, 293.

is not 'reasonably drafted to address its objectives',[18] or when a governmental measure is adopted with the express intention to injure and cause damage to an investor's investment.

[4]   Non-discrimination

49. NAFTA tribunals (*Methanex, Grand River, Glamis*) have come to the conclusion that nationality-based discrimination is not covered by Article 1105 and that customary international law contains no general prohibition on discrimination against foreign investors. Moreover, the *Grand River* tribunal added that the minimum standard of treatment applies to all investors (by definition) and therefore denied the existence of any custom rule prohibiting discrimination specifically against indigenous peoples. Some NAFTA tribunals' reasoning (*Waste Management, Glamis,* and to a lesser extent that of *Methanex*) can be interpreted as suggesting that Article 1105 covers some types of specific 'discrimination' (other than nationality-based), such as 'sectional or racial prejudice'. Case law remains unsettled on this point.

[5]   Good Faith

50. NAFTA tribunals have all concluded that the principle of good faith is not a stand-alone obligation under the FET standard, but rather a guiding principle that is relevant to the determination of whether or not a breach of Article 1105 has been committed. Tribunals have also concluded that an investor does not have to show that the host State has acted in bad faith to prove a violation of the FET standard. Yet, proof of bad faith would be conducive to a finding of a breach of Article 1105.

[6]   Denial of Justice and Due Process

51. All NAFTA tribunals have held that there exists an obligation not to deny justice and to respect due process under Article 1105. In light of case law, a number of conclusions can be reached about the contours of this prohibition of denial of justice and the obligation to respect due process. A foreign investor must have exhausted all remedies made available by domestic courts before a complaint of a denial of justice can be made before a NAFTA tribunal. Case law shows that this obligation is, however, limited to those remedies that are 'effective and adequate and are reasonably available to the complainant'.[19] A tribunal must assess the system of justice of the host State as a whole rather than focusing on individual domestic court decisions. Also, allegations of denial of justice before a tribunal cannot serve as an appeal mechanism for

---

18. *Glamis v. United States*, Award, (8 June 2009), paras. 803, 817. *See also*: *Cargill Inc. v. Mexico*, Award, (18 September 2009), para. 299.
19. *Loewen Group, Inc. and Raymond L. Loewen v. United States*, ICSID No. ARB(AF)/98/3, Award on Merits, (26 June 2003), para. 168.

contesting domestic court decisions. The *Mondev* tribunal (endorsed by other tribunals, including *Loewen*) has put forward a general 'test': a denial of justice occurs
whenever a decision by a domestic court is 'clearly improper and discreditable' in the
sense that it would 'shock or surprise' any impartial observer and would raise 'justified
concerns as to the judicial propriety of the outcome' of the case.[20] These findings
suggest a high threshold of severity for finding a denial of justice; only the most severe
cases will be considered in breach of Article 1105. This conclusion is also supported by
other tribunals' references to 'gross denial of justice' that 'fall[s] below acceptable
international standards'.[21]

52. Case law has shown that denial of justice arises when the host State does not
provide the investor with a fair trial, such as when a domestic court 'refuses to
entertain a suit', when it subjects a suit to 'undue delay', or, more generally, when a
court 'administer[s] justice in a seriously inadequate way'.[22] A fair trial also requires
that States provide investors with discrimination-free litigation. Also, a court decision
in breach of municipal law does not constitute a denial of justice per se unless it is also
discriminatory against a foreign investor or unless a 'clear and malicious misapplication of the law' by the court can be demonstrated.[23] On the contrary, an error of law
made by a domestic court or a decision involving a change from its previous case law
would not amount to a denial of justice. A State breaches its obligation of due process
whenever an investor is not given the full opportunity to be heard and to present
evidence at an administrative hearing. There is, however, no such breach when a State
commits mere administrative 'irregularities'.

[7]   Conclusion

53. NAFTA case law therefore suggests that only the prohibition of arbitrary conduct,
denial of justice and the obligation of due process are unambiguously stand-alone
elements of the FET obligation under Article 1105. Other terms that are often used by
tribunals, such as 'grossly unfair, unjust or idiosyncratic',[24] are better viewed as
encompassed within these three elements. These findings confirm that NAFTA Article
1105 is significantly different from unqualified FET clauses found in most BITs. Thus,
non-NAFTA tribunals have been increasingly willing to recognize new requirements as
components of the ever-enlarged concept of FET. Prime examples of such new
'requirements' recognized by these tribunals are the obligation to provide a stable and

---

20. *Mondev International Ltd. v. United States*, ICSID No. ARB(AF)/99/2, Award, (2 October 2011),
    para. 127.
21. *Thunderbird v. Mexico*, Award, (26 January 2006), para. 194; *Glamis v. United States*, Award,
    (8 June 2009), paras. 22, 24, 614, 616, 625, 627; *Cargill Inc. v. Mexico*, Award, (18 September
    2009), para. 296.
22. *Robert Azinian, Kenneth Davitian, & Ellen Baca v. Mexico* [hereinafter *Azinian v. Mexico*], ICSID
    No. ARB (AF)/97/2, Award, (1 November 1999), paras. 102–103.
23. *Ibid.*
24. *Waste Management v. Mexico*, Award, (30 April 2004), para. 98; *Cargill Inc. v. Mexico*, Award,
    (18 September 2009), para. 296.

predictable business environment and transparency as well as the obligation to protect an investor's legitimate expectations. NAFTA tribunals have adopted a much more narrow interpretation of the FET standard. The concepts of transparency and legitimate expectations are considered by the majority of NAFTA tribunals as 'factors' to be taken into account when assessing whether or not other well-established elements of the FET standard have been breached. Similarly, the principle of good faith is considered as a guiding principle that is relevant to the determination of whether a breach of Article 1105 has occurred.

[C]   The High Threshold of Severity Required under Article 1105

54. The majority of NAFTA tribunals (*Glamis, Cargill, Waste Management, ADF, Thunderbird*) have also emphasized that a high threshold of severity and gravity is required in order to conclude that the host State has breached any of the elements contained within the FET standard under Article 1105. As pointed out by the *Glamis* and *Cargill* tribunals, the existence of such a high threshold is clear given NAFTA tribunals' consistent use of qualifiers such as 'manifest', 'gross', 'evident', 'blatant', and 'complete'.[25] The *Merrill & Ring* tribunal is the only one to have adopted a much lower threshold whereby the FET standard 'protects against all such acts or behavior that might infringe on a sense of fairness, equity and reasonableness'[26] and 'provides for the fair and equitable treatment of alien investors within the confines of reasonableness'.[27] Yet, for reasons explained above in chapter 3, the *Merrill & Ring* award is clearly not a solid precedent to be followed by other tribunals in the future regarding the question of the threshold of severity.

55. In fact, the existence of this high threshold of severity is a predominant characteristic of NAFTA case law. It is, indeed, one aspect that clearly differentiates it from awards rendered by non-NAFTA tribunals which have often used a lower threshold of liability. This is certainly the case of non-NAFTA tribunals when interpreting an unqualified FET clause.

56. The concrete consequence of the consistent application of this high threshold of liability by NAFTA tribunals (with the notable exception of *Merrill & Ring*) is that very few tribunals have come to the conclusion that the host State has violated Article 1105. One tribunal (*Cargill*) concluded that Mexico has committed an arbitrary conduct. This was, indeed, a clear case of arbitrary conduct. The tribunal held that Mexico had deliberately and intentionally targeted the US investor in retaliation for a US trade policy. Two other tribunals (*Metalclad* and *Pope & Talbot*) held that the host States (Mexico and Canada, respectively) had breached their obligation to provide due process to a foreign investor. The *S.D. Myers* award does not explain which element(s)

---

25. *Cargill Inc. v. Mexico*, Award, (18 September 2009), para. 285; *Glamis. v. United States*, Award, (8 June 2009), para. 616.
26. *Merrill & Ring v. Canada*, Award, (31 March 2010), para. 210.
27. *Ibid.*, para. 213.

of the FET standard was (or were) breached by Canada. UNCTAD has recently noted a significant statistical difference between the lower success rates of FET claims under NAFTA when compared to the much higher one under BITs.[28]

57. In sum, the fact that tribunals have found that only a limited number of elements are unequivocally part of the FET obligation under Article 1105, combined with their recognition that a high threshold of severity and gravity is required in order to conclude that the host State has breached any one of these elements, illustrate the specific parameters relevant to an analysis of Article 1105.

IV   THE RELATIONSHIP BETWEEN ARTICLE 1105 AND OTHER NAFTA PROVISIONS

58. The structure and language of NAFTA Chapter 11 clearly show that the FET standard is not an 'overriding obligation' which sets out the general rule while other standards are seen as specific applications of that rule. The FET clause at Article 1105 is a standard of protection that is independent from the Most-Favored-Nation (MFN) (Article 1103) and the national treatment (Article 1102) clauses.

59. As mentioned above, the third paragraph of the FTC Note was aimed at overruling the reasoning of the *S.D. Myers* award and makes it clear that the finding of a breach of a separate provision does not establish a breach of Article 1105. NAFTA tribunals have since then endorsed this conclusion. NAFTA Parties have also integrated this clarification in their Model BITs as well as in their respective BITs and some recent FTAs.

60. NAFTA case law illustrates that allegations of non-respect of an investor's legitimate expectations are relevant to both claims of violation of Articles 1105 and 1110. Yet, it remains that the focus of the analysis will be different. More generally, the fact that allegations of breach of the FET standard may somehow be easier to demonstrate than expropriation allegations can partially explain the increased popularity of FET claims before BIT tribunals in recent decades.

61. NAFTA tribunals (with the notable exception of *Pope & Talbot*) have not allowed investors to invoke NAFTA's MFN clause (Article 1103) to seek the allegedly 'better' FET protection contained within other BITs entered into by NAFTA Parties with non-NAFTA States. The *ADF* and *Chemtura* tribunals have refused to endorse the position submitted by claimant investors to the effect that FET clauses contained within these BITs (referring to treatment in accordance with 'international law') convey a different meaning than Article 1105, where the expression 'international law' is considered as a reference to the minimum standard of treatment under custom. In other words, non-NAFTA foreign investors are not being offered a more favorable FET protection under these BITs than the one actually accorded to foreign investors from

---

28. UNCTAD, *Fair and Equitable Treatment*, (UNCTAD Series on Issues in International Investment Agreements II, United Nations 2012), at 61.

NAFTA countries. All investors are treated in accordance with the minimum standard of treatment under custom.

62. Article 1105 is of a different nature than that of the national treatment clause (Article 1102) which sets out a 'relative' standard that is defined by reference to the treatment accorded to the host State's own investors. This means that a host State's compliance with the national treatment standard can nevertheless be considered as breaching the obligation to provide foreign investors with an FET. Yet, the finding of a discriminatory act in violation of Article 1102 is not automatically conducive to a breach of Article 1105. Both provisions deal with different types of discrimination: Article 1102 covers discrimination based on the foreign nationality of an investor, and Article 1105 covers other types of discrimination against a foreign investor (such as specific targeting, discrimination based on race, sex and religion, etc.). NAFTA case law on this last point is still unsettled.

63. While Article 1105 provides for both an obligation for the host State to provide full protection and security and the FET, these obligations are to be distinguished. It is generally considered that full protection and security imposes on States a due diligence obligation to respect the physical protection of investors against acts of violence and harassment. Some tribunals (outside NAFTA) have however recently interpreted this obligation to cover not only physical protection but also, more broadly, to provide a guarantee of 'legal' stability. In any event, no NAFTA tribunal has addressed the interaction between FET and the full protection and security obligation.

V   ASSESSMENT OF DAMAGES

64. Situations where a violation of the FET standard leads to a total loss or deprivation of the investment are similar to cases of expropriation and therefore the same valuation method (i.e., 'fair market value') is generally used. In other instances where a violation of the FET standard does not lead to a total loss of the investment, but only to a decrease in value of the investment, tribunals have adopted divergent evaluation methods.

65. NAFTA tribunals have held that the burden is on the investor to prove the actual quantum of the losses for which it claims compensation in relation to a breach of the FET standard. They have also highlighted the importance of causation. They have also interpreted the treaty's lack of any specific guidance on damages assessment for FET violation as leaving them with a certain level of discretion. Tribunals have often used the 'differential method' to calculate damages for non-expropriatory acts. NAFTA tribunals (S.D. Myers, Feldman) have rejected the use of the 'fair market value' method in the context of assessing damages for violation of Article 1105. This situation contrasts with how other tribunals (outside of NAFTA) have dealt with the fair market value method in this context.

66. The *Pope & Talbot* award is the only one that has actually quantified the amount of damages (USD 461,566) resulting solely from a breach of Article 1105. The *S.D. Myers* tribunal quantified the damages (CAD 6 million[29]) for both violations of Articles 1102 and 1105 and the *Cargill* tribunal examined compensation for breaches of Articles 1102, 1105 and 1106 conjointly (USD 77.329 million).

---

29. CAD 6,050,000 represented around USD 3.8 million in 2002.

Bibliography

BOOKS

Alvarez, José E. *The Public International Law Regime Governing International Investment*. The Hague Academy of International Law, 2011.

Alvarez, Guillermo Aguilar & Reisman, W. Michael (eds). *The Reasons Requirement in International Investment Arbitration: Critical Case Studies*. Nijhoff, 2008.

Blackaby, et al. *Redfern and Hunter on International Arbitration*. Oxford University Press, 2009.

Borchard, Edwin. *The Diplomatic Protection of Citizen Abroad*. Bank Law Publishing Co., 1915.

Brierly, J.L. *The Law of Nations*. Clarendon Press, 1963.

Brownlie, Ian. *Principles of Public International Law*. Oxford University Press, 1998.

Carreau, Dominique & Julliard, Patrick. *Droit international économique*. L.G.D.J., 1998.

Clapham, Andrew. *Human Rights Obligations of Non State Actors*. Oxford University Press, 2006.

Currie, John H., Forcese, Craig & Oosterveld, Valerie. *International Law: Doctrine, Practice, and Theory*. Irwin Law, 2007.

Diehl, Alexandra. *The Core Standard of International Investment Protection: Fair and Equitable Treatment*. Wolters Kluwer, 2012.

Dolzer, Rudolf & Stevens, Margrete. *Bilateral Investment Treaties*. Martinus Nijhoff Publisher, 1995.

Douglas, Zachary. *The International Law of Investment Claims*. Cambridge University Press, 2009.

Dugan, Christopher F., Wallace, Don, Rubins, Noah Jr., & Sabahi, Borzu. *Investor-State Arbitration*. Oxford University Press, 2008.

Eagleton, Clyde. *The Responsibility of States in International Law*. New York University Press, 1928.

Fatouros, A.A. *Government Guarantees to Foreign Investors*. Columbia University Press, 1962.

Freeman, A.V. *The International Responsibility of States for Denial of Justice*. Longman, Green & Co., 1938.

Gallagher, Norah & Shan, Wenhua. *Chinese Investment Treaties*. Oxford University Press, 2009.

García Amador, F.V., Sohn, Louis B. & Baxter, R.R. *Recent Codification of the Law of State Responsibility for Injuries to Aliens*. Oceana Publisher, 1974.

Gardiner, Richard K. *Treaty Interpretation*. Oxford University Press, 2008.

Hackworth, Green H. *Digest of International Law*. vol. 3, Department of State Publication, United States Department of State, 1942.

Jenning, Sir Robert & Watts, Sir Arthur. *Oppenheim's International Law*. Longman, 1996.

Kinnear, M., Bjorklund, A. & Hannaford, J.F.G. *Investment Disputes under NAFTA: An Annotated Guide to NAFTA Chapter 11*. Kluwer Law International, 2006.

Kinsella, Stephan & Rubins, Noah D. *International Investment, Political Risk, and Dispute Resolution*. Oceana, 2005.

Kiss, A. *L'abus de droit en droit international*. L.G.D.J., 1952.

Kläger, Roland. *Fair and Equitable Treatment in International Investment Law*. Cambridge University Press, 2011.

Laviec, Jean-Pierre. *Protection et promotion des investissements, étude de droit international économique*. P.U.F., 1985.

Mann, F.A. *The Legal Aspect of Money: with Special Reference to Comparative Private and Public International Law*. Clarendon Press, 1992.

Marboe, Irmgard. *Calculation of Compensation and Damages in International Investment Law*. Oxford University Press, 2009.

McLachlan, C., Shore, L. & Weiniger, W. *International Investment Arbitration: Substantive Principles*. Oxford University Press, 2007.

Montt, S. *State Liability in Investment Treaty Arbitration*. Hart Publisher, 2009.

Muchlinski, Peter. *Multinational Enterprises and the Law*. Oxford University Press, 1995.

Newcombe, Andrew & Paradell, Luis. *Law and Practice of Investment Treaties: Standards of Treatment*. Kluwer Publisher, 2009.

Paparinskis, Martins. *The International Minimum Standard and Fair and Equitable Treatment*. Oxford University Press, 2013.

Paulsson, J. *Denial of Justice in International Law*. Cambridge University Press, 2006.

Reed, L., Paulsson, J. & Blackaby. N. *A Guide to ICSID Arbitration*. Kluwer Law, 2004.

Rehman, Javaid. *International Human Rights Law. A Practical Approach*. Longman Publisher, 2003.

Ripinsky, Sergey & Williams, Kevin. *Damages in International Investment Law*. British IICL, 2008.

Roth, Andreas Hans. *The Minimum Standard of International Law Applied to Aliens*. A.W. Sijthoff, 1949.

Salacuse, Jeswald W. *The Law of Investment Treaties*. Oxford University Press, 2010.

Schill, Stephen. *The Multilateralization of International Investment Law*. Cambridge University Press, 2009.

Schreuer, C. & Dolzer, R. *Principles of International Investment Law*. Oxford University Press, 2008.

Schwartzenberger, G. *International Law as Applied by International Courts and Tribunals*. Stevens & Sons, 1949.

Schønberg, S. *Legitimate Expectations in Administrative Law*. Oxford University Press, 2000.

Shaw, M.N. *International Law*. Cambridge University Press, 2008.

Sinclair, Ian. *The Vienna Convention on the Law of Treaties*. Manchester University Press, 1984.

Sornarajah, M. *The International Law on Foreign Investment*. Cambridge University Press, 2004.

Tudor, Ionna. *The Fair and Equitable Treatment Standard in International Foreign Investment Law*. Oxford University Press, 2008.

Van Harten, Gus. *International Treaty Arbitration and Public law*. Oxford University Press, 2007.

Vandeveld, Kenneth J. *Bilateral Investment Treaties: History, Policy and Interpretation*. Oxford University Press, 2010.

Vandevelde, Kenneth J. *United States Investment Treaties: Policy and Practice*. Kluwer Law, 1992.

Villanueva, Gabriel Cavazos. *The Fair and Equitable Treatment Standard*: *The Mexican Experience*. VDM Verlag, 2008.

Villiger, Mark. *Commentary on the 1969 Vienna Convention on The Law of Treaties*. Martinus Nijhoff Publisher, 2009.

Wang, Dong. *China's Unequal Treaties: Narrating National History*. Rowman & Littlefield, 2008.

Weiler, Todd. *The Interpretation of International Investment Law: Equality, Discrimination and Minimum Standards of Treatment in Historical Context*. Martinus Nijhoff, 2013.

Weeramantry, Romesh. *Treaty Interpretation in Investment Arbitration*. Oxford University Press, 2012.

ARTICLES/CONTRIBUTION

Abi-Saab, Georges, *The Newly Independent States and the Rules of International Law: An Outline*, 8 Howard Law Journal 95 (1962).

Abs, Hermann & Shawcross, Hartley, *The Proposed Convention to Protect Private Foreign Investment: A Round Table: Comment on the Draft Convention by its Authors*, 9 Journal of Public Law 115 (1960).

Acconci, P., *The Requirement of Continuous Corporate Nationality and Customary International Rules on Foreign Investment: the Loewen Case*, 14 Italian Yearbook of International Law 195 (2005).

Adede, A.O., *A Fresh Look at the Meaning of the Doctrine of Denial of Justice under International Law*, 14 Canadian Yearbook of International Law 73 (1976).

Afilalo, Ari, *Meaning, Ambiguity and Legitimacy: Judicial (Re)Construction of NAFTA Chapter 11*, 25 Northwestern Journal of International Law & Business 279 (2004-2005).

Al Faruque, Abdullah, *Creating Customary International Law Through Bilateral Investment Treaties: A Critical Appraisal*, 44 Indian Journal of International Law 292 (2004).

Alford, Roger P., *Ancillary Discovery to Prove Denial of Justice*, 53(1) Virginia Journal of International Law 127 (2013).

Alvarez, Guillermo Aguilar & Park, William W., *The New Face of Investment Arbitration: NAFTA Chapter 11*, 28 Yale Journal of International Law 365 (2003).

Alvarez, H.C., *Setting Aside Additional Facility Awards: the Metalclad Case*, in: Gaillard, E. & Banifatemi, Y. (eds.), *Annulment of ICSID Awards*, Juris Publisher, 2004.

Arato, Julian, *Subsequent Practice and Evolutive Interpretation: Techniques of Treaty Interpretation over Time and Their Diverse Consequences*, 9 Law and Practice of International Courts and Tribunals 443 (2010).

Bjorklund, Andrea, *Reconciling State Sovereignty and Investor Protection in Denial of Justice Claims*, 45 Virginia Journal of International Law 809 (2005).

Borchard, Edwin M., *The Law of Responsibility of States for Damages Done in Their Territory to the Person or Property of Foreigners*, 23 American Journal of International law Spec. Supp. 140 (1929).

Borchard, Edwin M., *The "Minimum Standard" of the Treatment of Aliens*, 33 American Society of International Law Proceedings 51 (1939).

Bronfman, Marcela Klein, *Fair and Equitable Treatment: An Evolving Standard*, 10 Max Planck Yearbook of United Nations Law 609 (2006).

Brower II, Charles H., *Beware the Jabberwock: A Reply to Mr. Thomas*, 40 Columbia Journal of Transnational Law 465 (2002).

Brower II, Charles H., *Fair and Equitable Treatment under NAFTA's Investment Chapter; Remarks*, 96 American Society of International Law Proceedings 9 (2002).

Brower II, Charles H., *Hard Reset vs Soft Reset: Recalibration of Investment Disciplines Under Free Trade Agreements*, Kluwer Arbitration Blog (16 December 2009), online: http://kluwerarbitrationblog.com/blog.

Brower II, Charles H., *Investor-State Disputes Under NAFTA: A Tale of Fear and Equilibrium*, 29 Pepperdine Law Review 43 (2001-2002).

Brower II, Charles H., *Investor-State Disputes Under NAFTA: The Empire Strikes Back*, 40 Columbia Journal of Transnational Law 43 (2001-2002).

Brower II, Charles H., *Structure, Legitimacy, and NAFTA's Investment Chapter*, 36 Vanderbilt Journal of Transnational Law 37 (2003).

Brower II, Charles H., *Why the FTC Notes of Interpretation Constitute a Partial Amendment of NAFTA Article 1105*, 46 Virginia Journal of International Law 347 (2006).

Brower, Charles N., *NAFTA's Investment Chapter: Dynamic Laboratory, Failed Experiments and Lessons for the FTAA: Concerns of the NAFTA Parties and Civil Society*, 97 American Society of International Law Proceedings 251 (2003).

Caflisch, L., *La pratique suisse en matière de droit international public*, 36 Annuaire suisse de droit international 181 (1980).

Cantegreil, J., *The Final Award in Mondev International v. United States of Amercia*, in: Alvarez, Guillermo Aguilar & Reisman, W. Michael (eds.), *The Reasons Requirement in International Investment Arbitration: Critical Case Studies*, Nijhoff, 2008.

Carreau, D., 'investissements', in: *Répertoire de droit international*, Dalloz, 1998.

Cazala, Julien, *La protection des attentes légitimes de l'investisseur dans l'arbitrage international*, 23 Revue internationale de droit économique 5 (2009).

Choudhury, Barnali, *Evolution or Devolution? Defining Fair and Equitable Treatment in International Investment Law*, 6(2) Journal of World Investment & Trade 297 (2005).

Clodfelter, Mark, *U.S. State Department Participation in international Economic Dispute Resolution*, 42 South Texas Law Review 1273 (2001).

Coe, Jack J., Jr., *Fair And Equitable Treatment Under NAFTA's Investment Chapter*, 96 American Society of International Law Proceedings 9 (2002).

Coe, Jack J., Jr., *Taking Stock of NAFTA Chapter 11 in Its Tenth Year: An Interim Sketch of Selected Themes, Issues and Methods*, 36 Vanderbilt Journal of Transnational Law 1381 (2003).

Congyan, Cai, *International Investment Treaties and the Formation, Application and Transformation of Customary International Law Rules*, 7(3) Chinese Journal of International Law 659 (1998).

D'Aspremont, Jean, *International Customary Investment Law: Story of a Paradox*, in: De Brabandere, E. & Gazzini, T. (eds.), *International Investment Law: The Sources of Rights and Obligations*, Martinus Nijhoff, 2012.

Delanoy, Louis-Christophe & Portwood, Tim, *La responsabilité de l'Etat pour déni de justice dans l'arbitrage d'investissement*, 3 Revue de l'Arbitrage 603 (2005).

Dodge, W.S., *International Decisions: Metalclad Corporation v. Mexico; Mexico v. Metalclad Corporation*, 95 American Journal ot International law 916 (2001).

Dolzer, Rudolf, *Fair and Equitable Treatment, A Key Standard in Investment Treaties*, 39 Journal of International Arbitration (2005).

Dolzer, Rudolf, *Fair And Equitable Treatment International Law, Remarks*, 100 American Society of International Law Proceedings 69 (2006).

Dolzer, Rudolf & Von Walter, A., *Fair and Equitable Treatment - Lines of Jurisprudence on Customary Law*, in: Ortino, F. (ed.), *Investment Treaty Law, Current Issues II*, British Institute of International and Comparative Law, 2007.

Douglas, Zachary, *The Hybrid Foundations of Investment Treaty Arbitration*, 74(1) British Yearbook of International Law 151 (2003).

Duchesne, M.S., *The Continuous Nationality of Claims Principle: Its Historical Development and Current Relevance to Investor-State Investment Disputes*, 36 George Washington International Law Review 783 (2004).

Dumberry, P., *Are BITs Representing the "New" Customary International Law in International Investment Law?*, 28(4) Penn State International Law Review 675 (2010).

Dumberry, P., *Incoherent and Ineffective: The Concept of Persistent Objector Revisited*, 59 International and Comparative Law Quarterly 779 (2010).

Dumberry, P., *L'entreprise, sujet de droit international? Retour sur la question à la lumière des développements récents du droit international des investissements*, 108(1) Revue générale de droit international public 103 (2004).

Dumberry, P., *Satisfaction as a Form of Reparation for Moral Damages suffered by Investors and Respondent States in Investor-State Arbitration Disputes*, 3(1) Journal of International Dispute Settlement 205 (2012).

Dumberry, P., *The Last Citadel! Can a State Claim the Status of 'Persistent Objector' to Prevent the Application of a Rule of Customary International Law in Investor-State Arbitration?*, 23(2) Leiden Journal of International Law 379 (2010).

Dumberry, P., *The NAFTA Investment Dispute Settlement Mechanism: A Review of the Latest Case Law*, 2(1) Journal of World Investment 151 (2001).

Dumberry, P., *The Quest to Define 'Fair and Equitable Treatment' for Investors under International Law: The Case of the NAFTA Chapter 11 Pope & Talbot Awards*, 3(4) Journal of World Investment 657 (2002).

Dumberry, P. & Dumas-Aubin, G., *How to Impose Human Rights Obligations on Corporations under Investment Treaties?*, 4 Yearbook on International Investment of Law and Policy 585 (2011-2012).

Dumberry, P. & Dumas-Aubin, G, *The Doctrine of "Clean Hands" and the Inadmissibility of Claims by Investors Breaching International Human Rights Law*, 10(1) Transnational Dispute Management Special Issue: Aligning Human Rights and Investment Protection (2013).

Dumberry, P. & Dumas-Aubin, G., *When and How Allegations of Human Rights Violations can be Raised in Investor-State Arbitration*, 13(3) Journal of World Investment & Trade 349 (2012).

Eagleton, C., *Denial of Justice in International Law*, 22 American Journal of International law 538 (1928).

Eastman, Z.M., *NAFTA's Chapter 11: For Whose Benefit?*, 16(3) Journal of International Arbitration 105 (1999).

Falsafi, Alireza, *The International Minimum Standard of Treatment of Foreign Investors' Property: A Contingent Standard*, 30 Suffolk Transnational Law Review 317 (2006-2007).

Fietta, Stephen, *Expropriation and the 'Fair and Equitable' Standard: The Developing Role of Investor 'Expectations' in International Investment Arbitration*, 23(5) Journal of International Arbitration 375 (2006).

Fietta, Stephen, *International Thunderbird Gaming Corporation v. Mexico: An Indication of the Limits of "Legitimate Expectation" Basis of Claim under Article 1105 of NAFTA*, 3(2) Transnational Dispute Management (2006).

Fitzmaurice, G.G., *The Meaning of the Term "Denial of Justice"*, 13 British Yearbook of International Law 93 (1932).

Fitzmaurice, M. & Merkouris, P., *Canons of Treaty Interpretation: Selected Case Studies from the World Trade Organization and the North American Free Trade Agreement*, in: Fitzmaurice, M., Elias, O. & Merkouris, P. (eds.), *Treaty Interpretation and the Vienna Convention on the Law of Treaties: 30 Years on*, Martinus Nijhoff Publishers, 2010.

Focarelli, C., *Denial of Justice*, in: Wolfrum, R. (ed.), *The Max Planck Encyclopedia of Public International Law*, Oxford University Press, 2009.

Foy, Patrick G., *Effectiveness of NAFTA's Chapter 11 Investor-State Arbitration Procedures*, 18 ICSID Review—Foreign Investment Law Journal 44 (2003).

Foy, Patrick G. & Deane, Robert J.C., *Foreign Investment Protection under Investment Treaties: Recent Developments under Chapter 11 of the North American Free Trade Agreement*, 16 ICSID Review—Foreign Investment Law Journal 299 (2001).

Francioni, Francesco, *Access to Justice, Denial of Justice and International Investment Law*, 20(3) European Journal of International Law 729 (2009).

Gagné, Gilbert & Morin, Jean-Frédéric, *The Evolving American Policy on Investment Protection: Evidence from Recent FTAs and the 2004 Model BIT*, 9 Journal of International Economic Law 357 (2006).

Gaillard, Emmanuel, *C.I.R.D.I., Chronique des sentences arbitrales*, 130 Journal du Droit International (Clunet) 161 (2003).

Gallus, N., *The Fair and Equitable Standard of Treatment and the Circumstances of the Host State*, in: Brown, C. & Miles, K. (eds.), *Evolution in Investment Treaty Law and Arbitration*, Cambridge University Press, 2011.

Gantz, David A., *International Decision: Pope & Talbot*, 97 American Journal of International law 937 (2003).

Gantz, David A., *The Evolution of FTA Investment Provisions: From NAFTA to the United States - Chile Free Trade Agreement*, 19(4) American University Law Review 724 (2003).

Garner, J.W., *International Responsibility of States for Judgments of Courts and Verdicts of Juries Amounting to a Denial of Justice*, 10 British Yearbook of International Law 181 (1929).

Gathright, B.K., *A Step in the Wrong Direction: The Loewen Finality Requirement and the Local Remedies Rule in NAFTA Chapter Eleven*, 54 Emory Law Journal 1093 (2005).

Gazzini, T., *The Role of Customary International Law in the Protection of Foreign Investment*, 8(5) Journal of World Investment & Trade 691 (2007).

Guha-Roy, S., *Is the Law of Responsibility of States for Injuries to Aliens A Part of Universal International Law?*, 55 American Journal of International law 562 (1969).

Guzman, Andrew T., *Why LDCs Sign Treaties That Hurt Them: Explaining the Popularity of Bilateral Investment Treaties*, 38(4) Virginia Journal of International Law 639 (1998)

Haeri, Hussein, *A Tale of Two Standards: 'Fair and Equitable Treatment' and the Minimum Standard in International Law*, 27 Arbitration International 27 (2011).

Hamrock, K.J., *The ELSI Case: Toward an International Definition of 'Arbitrary Conduct'*, 27(3) Texas International Law Journal 837 (1992).

Hanna, John, Jr, *Is Transparency of Governmental Administration Customary International Law in Investor-Sovereign Arbitrations? Courts and Arbitrators May Differ*, 21(2) Arbitration International 187 (2005).

Hécker Padilla, Carlos Andrés, *Denial of Justice to Foreign Investors*, 3(1) Cuadernos de derecho transnacional 296 (2011).

Heiskanen, V., *Arbitrary and Unreasonable Measures*, in: Reinisch, A. (ed.), *Standards of Investment Protection*, Oxford University Press, 2008.

Hindelang, Steffen, *Bilateral Investment Treaties, Custom and a Healthy Investment Climate: the Question of Whether BITs Influence Customary International Law Revisited*, 5 Journal of World Investment & Trade 789 (2004).

Hober, K., *Compensation: a Closer Look at Cases Awarding Compensation for Violation of the Fair and Equitable Treatment Standard*, in: Yannaca-Small, Katia (ed.),

Arbitration under International Investment Agreements: a Guide to the Key Issues, Oxford University Press, 2010.

Hobér, K., *Fair and Equitable Treatment: Determining Compensation,* 6 Transnational Dispute Management (2007).

Hobér, K., *Fair and Equitable Treatment: Determining Compensation, Comment,* in: Hofmann, Rainer & Tams, Christian J. (eds.), *The International Convention on the Settlement of Investment Disputes (ICSID), Taking Stock after 40 Years,* Nomos, 2007.

Jennings, R., *General Course on Principles of International Law,* 121 Collected Courses of the Hague Academy of International Law 323 (1967-II).

Juillard, P., *L'évolution des sources du droit des investissements,* 250 Collected Courses of the Hague Academy of International Law 9 (1994).

Jurgen, Kurtz, *Access to Justice, Denial of Justice and International Investment Law: A Reply to Francesco Francioni,* 20(4) European Journal of International Law 1077 (2009).

Kaczmarek, B.C., *Compensation for Non-Expropriatory Treaty Violations: An Analytical Framework,* 3 Transnational Dispute Management (2006).

Kahn, Jordan C., *Striking NAFTA Gold: Glamis Advances Investor-State Arbitration,* 33 Fordham International Law Journal 101 (2009-2010).

Karamanian, Susan L., *Denial of Justice and the Foreign Investor: Lessons from North America,* in: *International Law: Issues and Challenges, vol. 2,* Hope, India Publications, 2009.

Kaufmann-Kohler, Gabrielle, *Interpretive Powers of the NAFTA Free Trade Commission – Necessary Safety Valve or Infringement of the Rule of Law?,* in: Bachand, Frédéric (ed.), *Fifteen Years of NAFTA Chapter 11 Arbitration,* JurisNet, 2011.

Khalil, M., *Treatment of Foreign investment in BITs,* 8 ICSID Review—Foreign Investment Law Journal 339 (1992).

Khamsi, Kathryn, *Compensation for Non-Expropriatory Investment Treaty Breaches in the Argentine Gas Sector Cases: Issues and Implications,* in: Waibel, Michael *et al.* (eds.), *The Backlash Against Investment Arbitration: Perceptions and Reality,* Kluwer Law, 2010.

Khelifa, Rym Ben, *Le déni de justice en droit de l'investissement international: l'affaire Loewen c. les États-Unis d'Amérique,* in: *Où va le droit international de l'investissement?: Désordre normatif et recherche d'équilibre: actes du colloque organisé à Tunis les 3 et 4 mars 2006,* Pedone, 2007.

Kill, Theodore, *Don't Cross the Streams: Past and Present Overstatement of Customary International Law in Connection with Conventional Fair and Equitable Treatment Obligations,* 106 Michigan Law Review 678 (2008).

Kingsbury, Benedict & Schill, Stephan W., *Investor-State Arbitration as Governance: Fair and Equitable Treatment, Proportionality and the Emerging Global Administrative Law,* New York Univ. Public Law & Legal Theory Research Paper Series Working Paper No. 09-46.

Kinnear, Meg, *The Continuing Development of the FET Standard,* in: Bjorklund, Andrea K, Laird, Ian A. & Ripinsky, Sergey (eds.), *Investment Treaty Law: Current Issues III,* British Institute of International and Comparative Law, 2009.

Kirkman, Courtney C., *Fair and Equitable Treatment: Methanex v. United States and the Narrowing Scope of NAFTA Article 1105*, 34 Law and Policy in International Business 343 (2002-2003).

Kishoiyian, Bernard, *The Utility of Bilateral Investment Treaties in the Formulation of Customary International Law*, 14(2) Northwestern Journal of International Law 327 (1994).

Knahr, Christina, *Fair and Equitable Treatment and its Relationship with other Treatment Standards*, in: Klausegger, Christian *et al.* (eds.), *Austrian Arbitration Yearbook*, C.H. Beck, Stämpfli & Manz, 2009.

Knoll-Tudor, Ioana, *The Fair and Equitable treatment Standard and Human Rights Norms*, in: Dupuy, P.M., Francioni, F. & Petersmann, E.U. (eds.), *Human Rights in International Investment Law and Arbitration*, Oxford University Press, 2009.

Kotera, Akira, *Regulatory Transparency*, in: Muchlinski, Peter, Ortino, Federico & Schreuer, Christoph (eds.), *The Oxford Handbook of International Investment Law*, Oxford University Press, 2008.

Kraft, Matthias-Charles, *Les accords bilatéraux sur la protection des investissements conclus par la Suisse*, in: Dicke, D.C. (ed.) *Foreign Investment in the Present and New International Economic Order*, University Press Fribourg, 1987.

Kreindler, R.H., *Fair and Equitable Treatment – A Comparative International Law Approach*, 3(3) Transnational Dispute Management (2006).

Laird, Ian A., *A Community of Destiny - The Barcelona Traction Case and the Development of Shareholder Rights to Bring Investment Claims*, in: Weiler, Todd (ed.) *International Investment Law and Arbitration: Leading Cases from the ICSID, NAFTA, Bilateral Treaties and Customary International Law*, Cameron, 2005.

Laird, Ian A., *Betrayal, Shock and Outrage - Recent Developments in NAFTA Article 1105*, in: Weiler, Todd. (ed.), *NAFTA Investment Law and Arbitration: The Early Years*, Transnational Publisher, 2004.

Laird, Ian A., *MTD Equity Sdn. Bhd. and MTD Chile S.A. v. Republic of Chile - Recent Developments*, 1(4) Transnational Disp. Mgmt. 6 (2004).

Leben, Charles, *L'évolution du Droit International des Investissements*, in: Société Française pour le Droit International, *Un accord multilatéral sur l'investissement: d'un forum de négociation à l'autre?*, 1999.

Legum, Barton, *Dallas Workshop 2001: Commentary Scene III: ICSID Proceedings in the Absence of a Bilateral Investment Treaty*, 18(3) Arbitration International 303 (2002).

Legum, Barton, *The Innovation of Investor-State Arbitration Under NAFTA*, 43 Harvard International Law Journal 531 (2002).

Lemaire, A., *Le nouveau visage de l'arbitrage entre État et investisseur étranger: Le chapitre 11 de l'ALENA*, Revue de l'arbitrage 43 (2001).

Lemaire, A., *Traitement juste et equitable*, 124 Gazette du palais, Cahiers de l'arbitrage 43 (2004).

Lévesque, Céline, *Chronique de Droit international économique en 2010-2011 – Investissement*, 45 Canadian Yearbook of International Law 353 (2007).

Lévesque, Céline, *Influences on the Canadian Model FIPA and US Model BIT: NAFTA Chapter 11 and Beyond*, 44 Canadian Yearbook of International Law 249 (2006).

Lévesque, Céline & Newcombe, Andrew, *Commentary on the Canadian Model Foreign Promotion and Protection Agreement,* in: Brown, Chester (ed.), *Commentaries on Selected Model International Investment Agreements,* Oxford University Press, 2013.

Liebeskind, Jean-Christophe, *The Legal Framework of Swiss International Trade and Investments,* 7(3) Journal of World Investment & Trade 331 (2006).

Lowe, V., *Fair and Equitable Treatment under NAFTA's Investment Chapter; Remarks,* 100 American Society of International Law Proceedings 69 (2006).

Lowenfeld, Andreas F., *Investment Agreements and International Law,* 42 Columbia Journal of Transnational Law 123 (2003).

Mann, F.A., *British Treaties for the Promotion and Protection of Investments,* 52 British Yearbook of International Law 241(1981).

Matiation, Stefan, *Arbitration with Two Twists: Loewen v. United States and Free Trade Commission Intervention in NAFTA Chapter 11 Disputes,* 24 University of Pennsylvania Journal of International Economic Law 451 (2003).

Mayeda, Graham, *Playing Fair: The Meaning of Fair and Equitable Treatment in Bilateral Investment Treaties,* 41(2) Journal of World Trade 273 (2007).

McLachlan, C., *Investment Treaties and General International Law,* 57(2) International and Comparative Law Quarterly 361 (2008).

Mendelson, M., *The Runaway Train: the Continuous Nationality Rule from the Panevezys-Saldutiskis Railway Case to Loewen,* in: Weiler, Todd (ed.) *International Investment Law and Arbitration: Leading Cases from the ICSID, NAFTA, Bilateral Treaties and Customary International Law,* Cameron May, 2005.

Montt, Santiago, *The Award in Thunderbird v. Mexico,* in: Alvarez, Guillermo Aguilar & Reisman, W. Michael (eds.), *The Reasons Requirement in International Investment Arbitration: Critical Case Studies,* Nijhoff, 2008.

Moss, Giuditta Cordero, *Full Protection and Security,* in: Reinisch, August (ed.), *Standards of Investment Protection,* Oxford University Press, 2008.

Mourre, Alexis & Vagenheim, Alexandre, *Some Comments on Denial of Justice in Public and Private International Law after Loewen and Saipem,* in: *Liber amicorum Bernardo Cremades,* La Ley, 2010.

Muchlinski, Peter, *'Caveat Investor'? The Relevance of the Conduct of the Investor under the Fair and Equitable Treatment Standard',* 55(3) International and Comparative Law Quarterly 527 (2006).

Murphy, Sean D., *The ELSI Case: An Investment Dispute at the International Court of Justice,* 16 Yale Journal of International Law 391 (1991).

Mutis Téllez, Felipe, *Conditions and Criteria for the Protection of Legitimate Expectations Under International Investment Law,* 27(2) ICSID Review—Foreign Investment Law Journal 432 (2012).

Newcombe, Andrew, *The Boundaries of Regulatory Expropriation in International Law,* 4 Transnational Dispute Management (2007).

Nguyen, Huu-Tru, *Le réseau suisse d'accords bilatéraux d'encouragement et de protection des investissements,* 92 Revue générale de droit international public 577 (1988).

Orakhelashvili, Alexander, *The Normative Basis of "Fair and Equitable Treatment": General International Law on Foreign Investment?,* 1 Archive des Völkerrechts 74 (2008).

Orellana, M.A., *International Law on Investment: The Minimum Standard of Treatment (MST)*, 3 Transnational Dispute Management (2004).

Orrego Vicuña, F., *Changing Approaches to the Nationality of Claims in the Context of Diplomatic Protection and International Dispute Settlement*, in: Schlemmer-Schulte, S. & Tung, K.-Y. (eds.), *Liber amicorum Ibrahim F.I. Shihata: International Finance and Development Law*, Kluwer Law International, 2001.

Ortino, Frederico, *Non-Discriminatory Treatment in Investment Disputes*, in: Dupuy, P.M., Francioni, F. & Petersmann, E.U. (eds.), *Human Rights in International Investment Law and Arbitration*, Oxford University Press, 2009.

Paradell, L., *The BIT Experience of The Fair And Equitable Treatment Standard*, in: Ortino, Federico *et al.* (eds.), *Investment Treaty Law, Current Issues II*, British Institute of International and Comparative Law, 2007.

Paulsson, J., *Continuous Nationality in Loewen*, 20 Arbitration International 213 (2004).

Paulsson, J. & Petrochilos, G., *Neer-ly Misled?*, 22(2) ICSID Review—Foreign Investment Law Journal 242 (2007).

Picherack, J. Roman, *The Expanding Scope of the Fair and Equitable Treatment Standard: Have Recent Tribunals Gone Too Far?*, 9(4) Journal of World Investment & Trade 255 (2008).

Porterfield, Matthew C., *A Distinction Without a Difference? The Interpretation of Fair and Equitable Treatment Under Customary International Law by Investment Tribunals*, 3(3) Investment Treaty News 3 (2013).

Porterfield, Matthew C., *An International Common Law of Investor Rights?*, 27 University of Pennsylvania Journal of International Economic Law 79 (2006).

Preiswerk, Roy, *New Developments in Bilateral Investment Protection - With Special Reference to Belgian Practice*, 3 Revue belge de droit international 173 (1967).

Roberts, A., *Power and Persuasion in Investment Treaty Interpretation: The Dual Role of States*, 104 American Journal of International law 179 (2010).

Robin, Patricia M., *The BIT Won't Bite: The American Bilateral Investment Treaty Program*, 33 American University Law Review 931 (1984).

Romero Jiménez, Maximo, *Considerations of NAFTA Chapter 11*, 2 Chicago Journal of International Law 243 (2001).

Root, Elihu, *The Basis of Protection to Citizens Residing Abroad*, 4 American Journal of International law 517 (1910).

Rubins N., *Loewen v. United States: the Burial of an Investor-State Arbitration Claim*, 21 Arbitration International 1 (2005).

Ruggie, John, *Current Developments. Business and Human Rights: The Evolving International Agenda*, 101 American Journal of International law 819 (2007).

Ryan, Margaret Clare, *Glamis Gold, Ltd. v. The United States and the Fair and Equitable Treatment Standard*, 56(4) McGill Law Journal 919 (2011).

Salacuse, J.W., *The Treatification of International Investment Law: a Victory of Form Over Life? A Crossroads Crossed?*, 3(3) Transnational Dispute Management (2006).

Salacuse, J.W., *Towards a Global Treaty On Foreign Investment: The Search for a Grand Bargain*, in: Horn, N. & Kröll, S. (eds.), *Arbitrating Foreign Investment Disputes. Procedural and Substantive Legal Aspects*, 2004.

Salacuse, J.W. & Sullivan, N.P., *Do BITs Really Work? An Evaluation of Bilateral Investment Treaties and Their Grand Bargain*, 46 Harvard International Law Journal 67 (2005).

Sattorova, Mavluda, *Denial of Justice Disguised? Investment Arbitration and the Protection of Foreign Investors From Judicial Misconduct*, 61(1) International and Comparative Law Quarterly 223 (2012).

Schill, Stephan W., *Fair and Equitable Treatment as an Embodiment of the Rule of Law*, in: Hofmann, R. & Tams, C. (eds.), *The International Convention on the Settlement of Investment Disputes (ICSID): Taking Stock after 40 Years*, Nomos, 2007.

Schill, Stephan W., *Revisiting a Landmark: Indirect Expropriation and Fair and Equitable Treatment in the ICSID Case Tecmed*, 3(2) Transnational Dispute Management (2006).

Schill, Stephan W., *The Fair and Equitable Treatment Standard in International Foreign Investment Law* (Book Review of Ionna Tudor), in: 20 European Journal of International Law (2009).

Schill, Stephan W. & Kingsbury, Benedict, *Public Law Concepts to Balance Investors' Rights with State Regulatory Actions in the Public Interest - The Concept of Proportionality*, in: Schill, Stephan (ed.), *International Investment Law and Comparative Public Law*, Oxford University Press, 2010.

Schreuer, Christoph, *Decisions Ex Aequo et Bono Under the ICSID Convention*, 11 ICSID Review—Foreign Investment Law Journal 3 (1996).

Schreuer, Christoph, *Fair and Equitable Standard (FET): Interaction with Other Standards*, 4(5) Transnational Dispute Management (2007).

Schreuer, Christoph, *Fair and Equitable Treatment in Arbitral Practice*, 6(3) Journal of World Investment & Trade 357 (2005).

Schreuer, Christoph, *Full Protection and Security*, 1(2) Journal of International Dispute Settlement 353 (2010).

Schreuer, Christoph, *Non-Pecuniary Remedies in ICSID Arbitration*, (4) Arbitration International 325 (2004).

Schreuer, Christoph, *Protection against Arbitrary or Discriminatory Measures*, in: Alford, R.P. & Rogers, C.A. (eds.), *The Future of Investment Arbitration*, Oxford University Press, 2009.

Schwarzenberger, G., *The Abs-Shawcross Draft Convention on Investments Abroad*, 14 Current Legal Problems 147 (1961).

Schwebel, Stephen M., *Investor-State Disputes and the Development of International Law: the Influence of Bilateral Investment Treaties on Customary International Law*, 98 American Society of International Law Proceedings 27 (2004).

Schwebel, Stephen M., *Is Neer far from Fair and Equitable?*, 27(4) Arbitration International 555 (2011).

Schwebel, Stephen M., *The United States 2004 Model Bilateral Investment Treaty: an Exercise in the Regressive Development of International Law*, in: *Global Reflections on International Law, Commerce and Dispute Resolution, Liber Amicorum in honour of Robert Briner*, ICC Publisher No. 693, 2005.

Schwebel, Stephen M., *The United States 2004 Model Bilateral Investment Treaty and Denial of Justice in International Law*, in: *International Investment Law for the 21st Century: Essays in Honour of Christoph Schreuer*, Oxford University Press, 2009.

Seymour, Courtney N., *The NAFTA Metalclad Appeal- Subsequent Impact or Inconsequential Error? Only Time Will Tell*, 34 University of Miami Inter-American Law Review 189 (2002).

Smutny, Abby Cohen, *Some Observations on the Principles Relating to Compensation in the Investment Treaty Context*, 22(1) ICSID Review—Foreign Investment Law Journal 1 (2007).

Snodgrass, E., *Protecting Investors' Legitimate Expectations and Recognizing and Delimiting a General Principle*, 21 ICSID Review—Foreign Investment Law Journal 1 (2006).

Spiegel, H.W., *Origin and Development of Denial of Justice*, 32 American Journal of International law 63 (1938).

Soloway, J.A., *NAFTA's Chapter 11: The Challenge of Private Party Participation*, 16(2) Journal of International Arbitration 1 (1999).

Sornarajah, M., *Power and Justice in Foreign Investment Arbitration*, 14(3) Journal of International Arbitration 103 (1997).

Sornarajah, M., *The Fair and Equitable Standard of Treatment: Whose Fairness? Whose Equity?*, in: Federico Ortino *et al.* (eds.), *Investment Treaty Law: Current Issues II*, British Institute of International and Comparative Law, 2007.

Stone, Jacob, *Arbitrariness, The Fair and Equitable Treatment Standard and the International Law of Investment*, 25(1) Leiden Journal of International Law 77 (2012).

Thomas, J.C., *A Reply to Professor Brower*, 40 Columbia Journal of Transnational Law 433 (2001-2002).

Thomas, J.C., *Fair and Equitable Treatment under NAFTA's Investment Chapter; Remarks*, 96 American Society of International Law Proceedings 9 (2002).

Thomas, J.C., *Reflections on Article 1105 of NAFTA: History, State Practice and the Influence of Commentators*, 17(1) ICSID Review—Foreign Investment Law Journal 21 (2002).

Tollefson, C., *Metalclad vs. United Mexican States Revisited: Judicial Oversight of Nafta's Chapter Eleven Investor-State Claim Process*, 11 Minnesota Journal of Global Trade 183 (2001-2002).

Tuck, Andrew P., *The "Fair And Equitable Treatment" Standard Pursuant to the Investment Provisions of the U.S. Free Trade Agreements with Peru, Colombia and Panama*, 16 Law and Business Review of the Americas 385 (2010).

Vandevelde, Kenneth J., *A Comparison of the 2004 and 1994 US Model BITs*, 1 Yearbook on International Investment of Law and Policy 283 (2008-2009).

Vandevelde, Kenneth J., *A Unified Theory of Fair and Equitable Treatment*, 43(1) New York University Journal of International Law & Politics 43 (2010).

Vandevelde, Kenneth J., *The Bilateral Treaty Program of the United States*, 21 Cornell International Law Journal 201 (1988).

Vandevelde, Kenneth J., *The Political Economy of a Bilateral Investment Treaty*, 92 American Journal of International law 621 (1998).

Vasciannie, Stephen, *The Fair and Equitable Treatment Standard in International Investment Law and Practice*, 70 British Yearbook of International Law 99 (1999).

Viñuales, Jorge E. & Tschanz, Pierre-Yves, *Compensation for Non-Expropriatory Breaches of International Investment Law-The Contribution of the Argentine Awards*, 26 Journal of International Arbitration 729 (2009).

Wälde, Thomas W., *Denial of Justice: A Review Comment on Jan Paulsson, Denial of Justice in International Law*, 21(2) ICSID Review—Foreign Investment Law Journal 449 (2006).

Wälde, Thomas W., *Energy Charter Treaty-based Investment Arbitration*, 5 Journal of World Investment & Trade 373 (2004).

Wälde, Thomas W. & Sabahi, B., *Compensation, Damages, and Valuation*, in: Muchlinski, Peter, Ortino, Federico & Schreuer, Christoph (eds.), *The Oxford Handbook of International Investment Law*, Oxford University Press, 2008.

Wallace, Don, *Fair and Equitable Treatment and Denial of Justice: Loewen v. US and Chattin v. Mexico*, in: Weiler, Todd (ed.), *International Investment Law and Arbitration: Leading Cases from the ICSID, NAFTA, Bilateral Treaties and Customary International Law*, Cameron May, 2005.

Wallace, Don, *State Responsibility for Denial of Substantive and Procedural Justice under NAFTA Chapter Eleven*, 23 Hastings International and Comparative Law Review 393 (2000).

Weiler, Todd, *An Historical Analysis of the Function of the Minimum Standard of Treatment in International Investment Law*, in: Weiler, Todd & Baetens, Freya (eds.), *New Directions in International Economic Law: In Memoriam Thomas Wälde*, Martinus Nijhoff, 2011.

Weiler, Todd, *Good Faith and Regulatory Transparency: The Story of Metalclad v. Mexico*, in: Weiler, Todd (ed.) *International Investment Law and Arbitration: Leading Cases from the ICSID, NAFTA, Bilateral Treaties and Customary International Law*, Cameron, 2005.

Weiler, Todd, *Metalclad v. Mexico: A Play in Three Parts*, 2 Journal of World Investment 685 (2001).

Weiler, Todd, *Methanex Corp. v. U.S.A: Turning the Page on NAFTA Chapter Eleven?*, 6(6) Journal of World Investment & Trade 903 (2005).

Weiler, Todd, *NAFTA Article 1105 and the Free Trade Commission; Just Sour Grapes, or Something more Serious?*, 29(11) International Business Lawyer 491 (2001).

Weiler, Todd, *NAFTA Chapter 11 Jurisprudence: Coming Along Nicely*, 9 Southwestern Journal of Law and Trade in the Americas 101 (2002-2003).

Weiler, Todd, *NAFTA Investment Arbitration and the Growth of International Economic Law*, 2 Business Law International 158 (2002).

Weiler, Todd, *NAFTA Investment Law in 2001: As the Legal Order Starts to Settle, the Bureaucrats Strike Back*, 36 International Business Lawyer 345 (2002).

Weiler, Todd & Laird, Ian A., *Standards of Treatment*, in: Muchlinski, Peter, Ortino, Federico & Schreuer, Christoph (eds.), *The Oxford Handbook of International Investment Law*, Oxford University Press, 2008.

Weiniger, M., *The Standard of Compensation for Violation of the Fair and Equitable Treatment Standard*, in: Ortino, Federico (ed.), *Investment Treaty Law, Current Issues II*, British Institute of International and Comparative Law, 2007.

Westcott, Thomas J., *Recent Practice on Fair and Equitable Treatment*, 8(3) Journal of World Investment & Trade 409 (2007).

Villanueva, Gabriel Cavazos & Martinez Serna, Luis F., *Private Parties in the NAFTA Dispute Settlement Mechanism: The Mexican Experience*, 77 Tulane Law Review 1017 (2003).

Williams, David, *Challenging Investment Treaty Arbitration Awards: Issues Concerning the Forum Arising from the Metatclad Case*, Business Law International 156 (2003).

Wisner, R., & Gallus, N., *Nationality Requirements in Investor-State Arbitration*, 5 Journal of World Investment & Trade 927 (2004).

De Visscher, C., *Le Deni de Justice en Droit International*, 52 Collected Courses of the Hague Academy of International Law 365 (1936).

Yannaca-Small, Katia, *Fair and Equitable Treatment Standard: Recent Developments*, in: Reinisch, A. (ed.), *Standards of Investment Protection*, Oxford University Press, 2008.

Zedalis, R.J., *Claims by Individuals in International Economic Law: NAFTA Developments*, 7(2) American Review of International Arbitration 115 (1996).

Zeyl, Trevor, *Charting the Wrong Course: the Doctrine of Legitimate Expectations in Investment Treaty Law*, 49(1) Alberta Law Review 203 (2011).

Zoellner, Carl-Sebastian, *Transparency an Analysis of an Evolving Fundamental Principle in International Economic Law*, 27 Michigan Journal of International Law 579 (2006).

THESIS/STUDIES/REPORTS

Dumberry, P., *Rules of Customary International Law in the Field of International Investment Law*, SSHRC Research Project, 2012-2014.

Fouret, J., *The Notion of Fair and Equitable Treatment of Foreign Direct Investment*, McGill University, LL.M. Thesis, 2003.

International Law Association (ILA), *Statement of Principles Applicable to the Formation of General Customary International Law*, Final Report of the Committee, London Conference, 2000.

International Law Commission, *Commentaries to the Draft Articles on Responsibility of States for Internationally Wrongful Acts Adopted by the International Law Commission at its Fifty-Third Session (2001)*, November 2001, Report of the I.L.C. on the work of its Fifty-third Session, Official Records of the General Assembly, Fifty-sixth Session, Supplement No. 10 (A/56/10), chp.IV.E.2).

International Law Commission, *Second Report on State Responsibility*, by Mr. Gaetano Arangio-Ruiz, Special Rapporteur, in: *Yearbook ILC*, vol. II, Part one, 1989 (A/CN.4/425).

OECD, *Committee on International Investment and Multinational Enterprise, Inter-Governmental Agreements Relating to Investment in Developing Countries*, Doc. No. 84/14, 27 May 1984.

OECD, *Draft Convention on the Protection of Foreign Property*, adopted on 12 October 1967, 7 I.L.M. 117, 1967.

OECD, *Fair and Equitable Treatment Standard in International Investment Law*, Working Papers on International Investment, Paper No. 2004/3, 2004.

OECD, *International Investment Law: A Changing Landscape: A Companion Volume to International Investment Perspectives*, 2005.

Restatement of the Law Third: The Foreign Relations Law of the United States, American Law Institute Publisher, 1987.

Tyler, Drew, *Fair, Equitable and Reasonable Treatment: the Concept of Reasonableness within the Fair and Equitable Treatment Standard*, LL.M Research Paper, University of Ottawa, 2011.

U.N. Centre on Transnational Corporation, *Key Concepts in International Investment Arrangements and Their Relevance to Negotiations on International Transactions in Services*, 1990.

U.N. Centre on Transnational Corporation, *The United Nations Code of Conduct on Transnational Corporations*, Current Studies, Series A (United Nations 1986) UN Doc. ST/CTC/SER.

U.N. Conference on Trade & Employment, Final Act and Related Documents 8–9, U.N. Doc. E/Conf. 2/78, U.N. Sales No. 1948.II.D.4, 1948.

UNCTAD, *Fair and Equitable Treatment*, UNCTAD Series on Issues in International Investment Agreements, 1999.

UNCTAD, *Fair and Equitable Treatment*, UNCTAD Series on Issues in International Investment Agreements II, United Nations, 2012.

UNCTAD, *International Investment Agreements: Key Issues*, 2004.

UNCTAD, *Investor–State Dispute Settlement and Impact on Investment Rulemaking*, United Nations, 2007.

UNCTAD, *Recent Developments in International Investment Agreements 3 (2007–June 2008)*, IIA Monitor No. 2, 2008.

UNCTAD, *National Treatment*, United Nations, 1999.

CONFERENCE

Lévesque, Céline, *The Risk of Inconsistency Inherent to International Investment Law: The Example of the Mexican Sweetener Trio of Cases under NAFTA*, ESIEL Conference, July 2010.

Vanduzer, Anthony, *NAFTA Chapter 11 to Date : The Progress of a Work in Progress*, at 13, NAFTA Chapter 11 Conference, Carleton University, 18 January 2002.

DICTIONARY

Black's Law Dictionary, 8th ed., West Group, 2004.

Oxford English Dictionary, 2nd ed., Clarendon Press, 1989.

The Concise Oxford Dictionary of Current English, 8th ed., Clarendon Press, 1990.

OTHERS

Canadian Press, *Canada Seeks Review of NAFTA's Chapter 11*, (13 December 2000).

Table of Cases

NAFTA Arbitration Pleading Documents

Non-NAFTA Arbitral Awards

ICJ and PCIJ Cases

Others Cases

Tables of Treaties and Conventions

Multilateral Treaties

ASEAN Comprehensive Investment Agreement, (2009), 44
ASEAN Treaty for the Promotion and Protection of Investments, (1987), 35
Colonia Protocol on Reciprocal Promotion and Protection of Investments, (1994), 35
COMESA Free Trade Area, (2007), 35, 44
Convention Establishing the Multilateral Investment Guarantee Agency, (1985), 35
Energy Charter Treaty (1995), 35
Free Trade Agreement between United States of America and Dominican Republic-Central America (CAFTA-DR), signed at Washington on 5 August 2004, entered into force between 2006 and 2009, 227
Havana Charter for an International Trade Organization, (1948), 29
Economic Agreement of Bogotá, (1948), 30, 33
Statute of the I.C.J., reprinted in International Court of Justice, Charter of the United Nations, Statute and Rules of Court and other Documents 61 (No. 4 1978), 57–59, 75, 77, 90–92, 96, 97, 121, 160, 161, 223
North American Free Trade Agreement, signed on 17 December 1992 and came into force on 1 January 1994, 1
Vienna Convention on the Law of Treaties, (1969), 53, 55, 59, 62–65, 74, 79–82, 85–88, 94, 102, 103, 130, 158, 286, 309–312
Legal Framework for the Treatment of Foreign Investment, World Bank, (1992), 7, 31

Bilateral Treaties

Agreement between the Government of Canada and the Government of the Czech Republic for the Promotion and Protection of Investments, signed at Prague on 6 May 2009, entered into force on 22 January 2012, 278
Agreement between the Government of Canada and the Government of the Czech and Slovak Federal Republic for the Promotion and Protection of Investments, signed on 15 November 1990, entered into force on 22 January 2012, 51
Agreement between the Government of Canada and the Government of the People's Republic of China for the Promotion and Reciprocal Protection of Investments, signed on 9 September 2012, 85, 91, 278

Others

Index